Reports of the Research Committee
of the
Society of Antiquaries of London
No. XXXIII

Excavations at Portchester Castle

Volume II : Saxon

By
Barry Cunliffe, M.A., Ph.D., F.S.A.

with sections by
K. E. Barber, Ph.D., A. Eastham, B.A., J. Fletcher, Ph.D., A. Grant, B.A.,
D. B. Harden, C.B.E., M.A., Ph.D., F.S.A., D. Hinton, B.A., R. Hodges, B.A., B. Hooper,
J. N. L. Myres, C.B.E., M.A., LL.D., D.Litt., D.Lit., F.B.A., Hon.V.-P.S.A.,
H. E. Pagan, B.A., D. Peacock, Ph.D., F.S.A., J. Startin, M. Welch, B.A.

Published by
The Society of Antiquaries of London
Distributed by
Thames and Hudson Ltd
1976

ISBN 0 500 99023 9

PRINTED IN ENGLAND BY
ADLARD AND SON LTD
BARTHOLOMEW PRESS, DORKING

CONTENTS

LIST OF FIGURES

LIST OF PLATES *(at end)*

PREFACE

IN the preface to the first volume I was able to pay tribute to the large number of people who made possible the twelve seasons of excavation at Portchester Castle from 1961–72. Their efforts, co-operation and good-will should be remembered equally in relation to this second volume.

The preparation of this present work for publication owes much to the small team who helped with the first volume. Mrs Judi Startin served as a general co-ordinator, organizing with great efficiency the excavated material and the field records, as well as conserving the small objects. Her carefully ordered work helped to make the preparation of this report a comparatively easy task. The pottery drawing was shared by Miss Jane Holdsworth, Mr Mike Rouillard and the present writer, while Mr Rouillard was wholly responsible for the fine series of finds drawings: he also laboured long to turn my plans and sections into presentable works suitable for the block-maker. The photographs of the small objects and the human skeletons were the work of Mr Bob Wilkins of the Institute of Archaeology, Oxford, who also produced publication prints of the excavations from the site negatives. The translation of the hand-written manuscript into a clean typescript was accomplished with customary capability by Miss Angela Blanch, while Mr Tim Ambrose gave valuable help at all stages during the production of this report.

Work on the preparation of the material for publication was greatly aided by generous grants from the Gulbenkian Trust and the Ancient Monuments Board of the Department of the Environment. The Pilgrim Trust financed part of the conservation work.

Finally I would like to record my thanks to the contributors whose reports are published below. Without their ready co-operation this volume would not have been possible.

Barry Cunliffe

Institute of Archaeology, Oxford
27 March 1974

I. INTRODUCTORY SECTIONS

GENERAL INTRODUCTION

THE first series of excavations which took place at Portchester Castle, Hants, from 1961 to 1972, exposed evidence of Saxon occupation spanning the period from the fifth to the eleventh century (for interim accounts see Cunliffe, 1963, 1966, 1969, 1970, 1971, 1972). A detailed consideration of the structures and material of this period form the content of the present volume, the second in the series of Portchester Excavation Reports.

The first volume has dealt with the general location of the site and the Roman occupation, and has shown that by the beginning of the fifth century there existed a massively defended enclosure of some 8·5 acres (3·4 hectares) protected by a masonry wall 10 ft. (3·05 m.) wide at the base and 20 ft. (6·10 m.) high, strengthened at regular intervals by forward projecting bastions. In the centres of the east and west walls were the two main gates, while smaller postern openings occupied the centres of the north and south walls. Internal structures consisted of cobbled roads and other areas of cobbling, together with light timber structures. The existence of a masonry-built bath house is suspected but unproven. It was within this environment that the Saxon occupation took place.

Saxon activity had comparatively little effect upon the general form of the site, apart from the construction of a new series of internal buildings, usually of timber. The supposed Roman bath house seems to have been gutted, and its tiles re-used in Saxon contexts, while the two main gates underwent some reconstruction. It is probable that the ditches outside the fort wall were allowed to silt up. Even by the mid-eleventh century the site is unlikely to have looked very different from its appearance at the beginning of the fifth century.

The division of the excavation report into separate volumes dealing with individual periods necessarily calls for some repetition and occasionally the need to refer back to the earlier volume. To have required the reader to refer constantly to the published sections in Vol. I would have been tiresome. For this reason the main section illustrations bearing on the interpretation of the Saxon features are repeated here, supported by a brief commentary on the relevant layers. Similarly, a number of the general plans are common to both reports. The present work can therefore be regarded as self-contained.

HISTORICAL EVIDENCE

The historical evidence directly relating to the Saxon occupation of Portchester is slight. Four texts, however, throw some light on the period and may be summarized before the purely archaeological data is assembled.

(a) *The Anglo-Saxon Chronicle* records for the year 501:

In this year Port and his two sons Bieda and Maegla came to Britain with two ships at the place which is called Portsmouth; and there they killed a [young] British man of very high rank (A. S. Chron. ed. Whitelock, 1961).

(b) A land transaction dated to 904 records that Edward, king of the west Saxons, granted to Denewulf, bishop of Winchester, and his cathedral clergy, in exchange for 40 "*cassati*" at *Porceastra* (Portchester) 38 "*manentes*" in *Waltham* (Bishops Waltham) (B.M. Add. MS. 15350, ff. 65^{v}–66 (s. xii)).

(c) *The Burghal Hidage*, written *c.* 920:

Then belong to Portchester 500 hides (Group B text, Hill, 1969a).

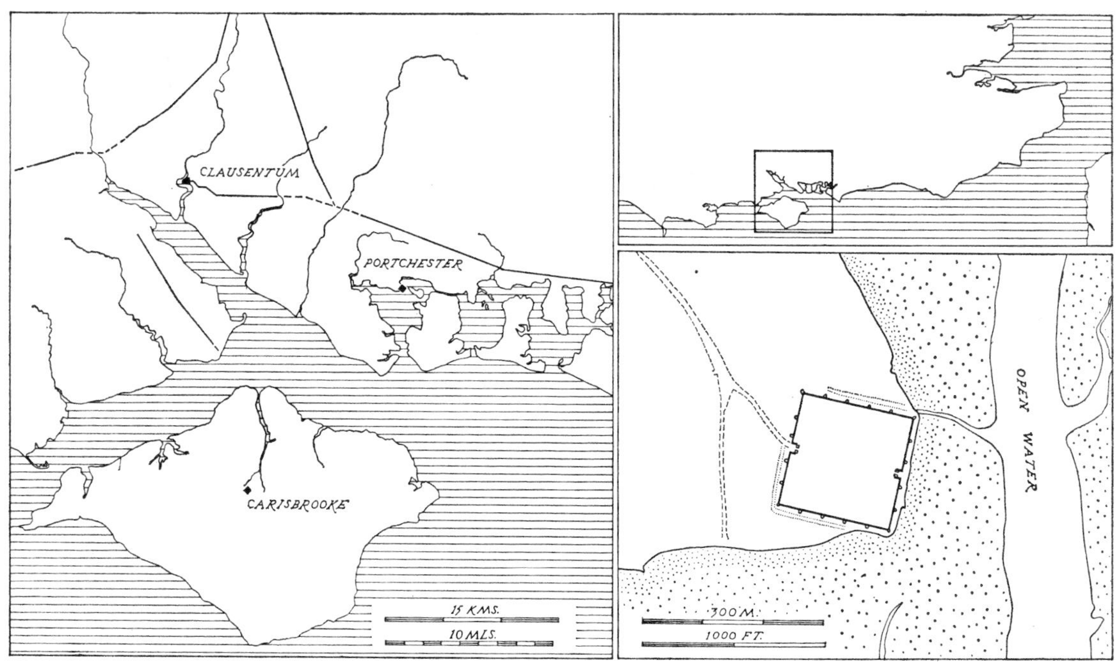

Fig. 1. The location of Portchester

(d) *The Domesday Survey*, of 1086, records that Portchester was held by William Mauduit. Before the conquest, it had belonged to the king, under whom it was divided into three manors:

3 freemen held it as 3 manors of King Edward. It then paid geld for 5 hides, now for 2½ hides, and it is one manor.

The reference to the exploits of Bieda and Maegla implies at the very least a conflict of late fifth- or early sixth-century date fought somewhere in the region of Portsmouth Harbour between newcomers and those already in residence. Portsmouth itself is unlikely to have been occupied, but the abundant evidence from Portchester, at the head of Portsmouth Harbour, shows that it was settled at this time. It is therefore possible that the old Roman walls of

Portchester might have offered protection to the local sub-Roman community who were under attack.

The next time that Portchester is specifically referred to is in the land deed dated to 904. The exchange was one of several instigated by Edward the Elder to enable him to acquire key sites for his programme of defence against threat of Danish attack. The fact that Portchester had previously been held by the Bishops of Winchester is unlikely to be of particular relevance, but Rigold (1965, 4) has suggested that this might imply the existence of an early church founded within the Roman defences.

Soon after Edward gained control of Portchester, the old fort was utilized as a *burh*, one of a chain of fortified sites which ringed the kingdom of Wessex. The *Burghal Hidage*, written in *c.* 920, records that Portchester was assessed at 500 hides. Given that each hide sent one man, and that each pole of defence was defended by four men, the length of defences allowed at Portchester was 2062 ft. In actual fact the total length of the Roman wall is 2440 ft. The discrepancy could however be explained by supposing that part of the seaward defences was theoretically unmanned (Hill, 1969b).

From the Domesday Survey we learn that Portchester was still held by the King, as three separate manors, until 1066, at which time it passed to William Mauduit. The Survey mentions the presence of a hall (*halla*) but there is no compelling reason to suppose that it lay within the Roman walls. Portchester remained in the hands of the Mauduit family until 1120, when its growing military significance led once more to its acquisition by the crown.

THE NATURE OF THE ARCHAEOLOGICAL EVIDENCE

Most of the data discussed below were derived from an area excavation of approximately 40,600 sq. ft. (3772 sq. m.) situated in the south-west quarter of the fort (fig. 2). Occupation began in the Roman period and continued until the early decades of the nineteenth century, after which this part of the site reverted to grass. Throughout the period the area was used in two ways, for occupation and for agriculture. Sometimes these activities appeared side by side, sometimes one replaced the other. At each stage there was necessarily destruction of earlier levels.

The site has been divided into three areas, A, B and C (figs. 101–103); between each the survival of Saxon material differs. Area C, closest to the centre of the fort, had been the most heavily disturbed. No Saxon occupation levels survived intact, since medieval and later activities had churned up the soil cover to the level of the natural brickearth. All that remained were pits, together with a large number of postholes, which could not be closely dated or assigned to recognizable structures; many of them are likely to have been medieval.

In Area B preservation was better. Distinct buildings could be isolated and some occupation levels survived, although there is clear evidence that ploughing took place on at least one occasion during the Saxon period, and must have disturbed the earlier levels.

Area A, against the south wall of the fort, contained by far the best evidence for sequence. Here, tips of occupation rubbish were piled up against the wall and remained largely undisturbed after early Saxon ploughing had ceased. Floor surfaces of buildings survived intact, together with the layers of occupation soil which sealed them. The structural and

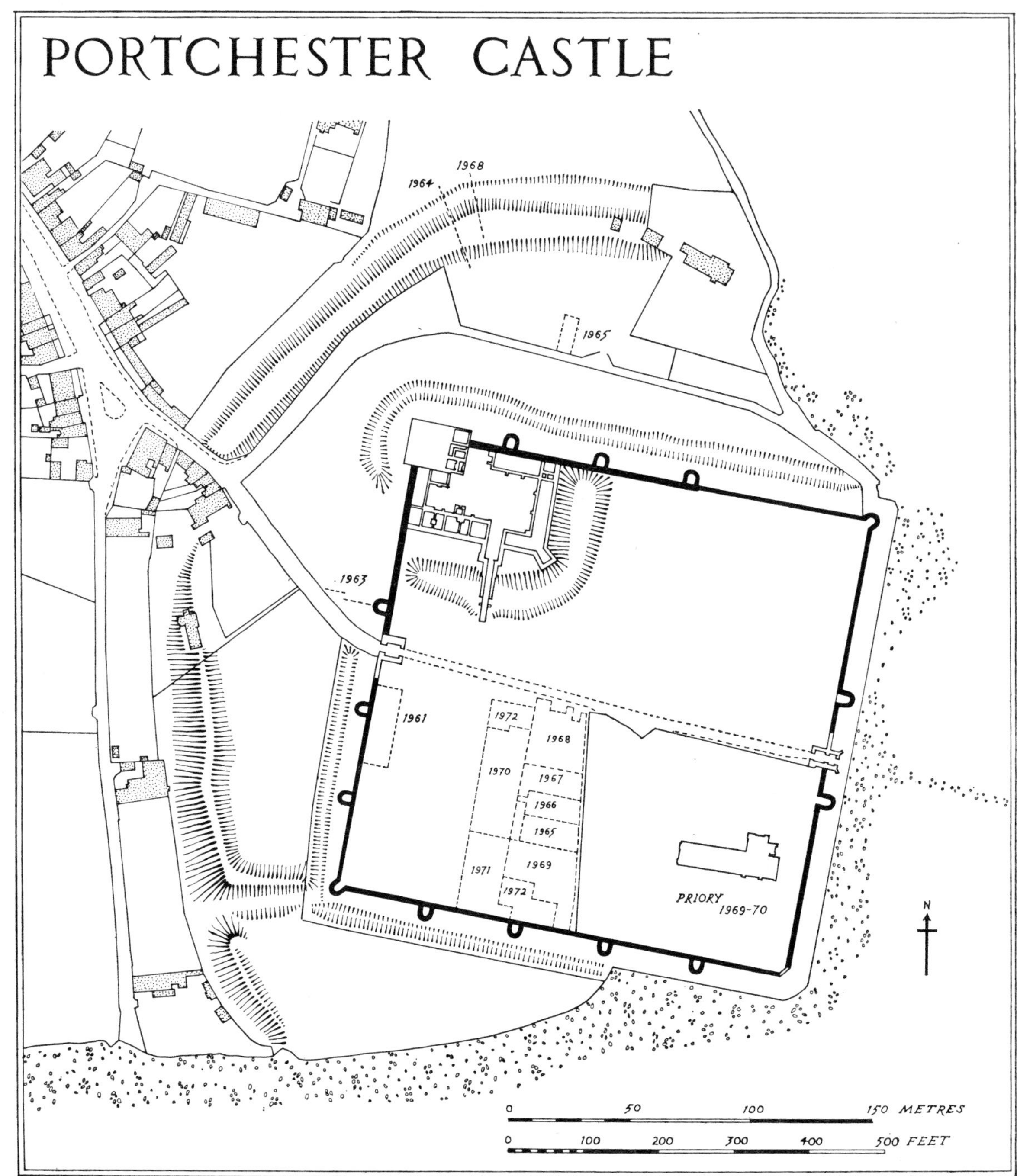

FIG. 2. General plan of the Castle and its surroundings

chronological relationships here provide excellent evidence for the establishment of sequences. Taken together with the data derived from the well (pit) 135, which produced a complex of stratified levels spanning the entire period of Saxon occupation, it is possible to reconstruct a complete ceramic sequence relevant to Portchester in particular and the region in general. Such a sequence enables the broad collation of otherwise isolated structures to be undertaken. Thus the raw material derived from the area excavation consists of timber structures, pits and wells related partly by direct stratigraphy and partly by reference to established sequences of pottery calibrated by means of associated datable artefacts.

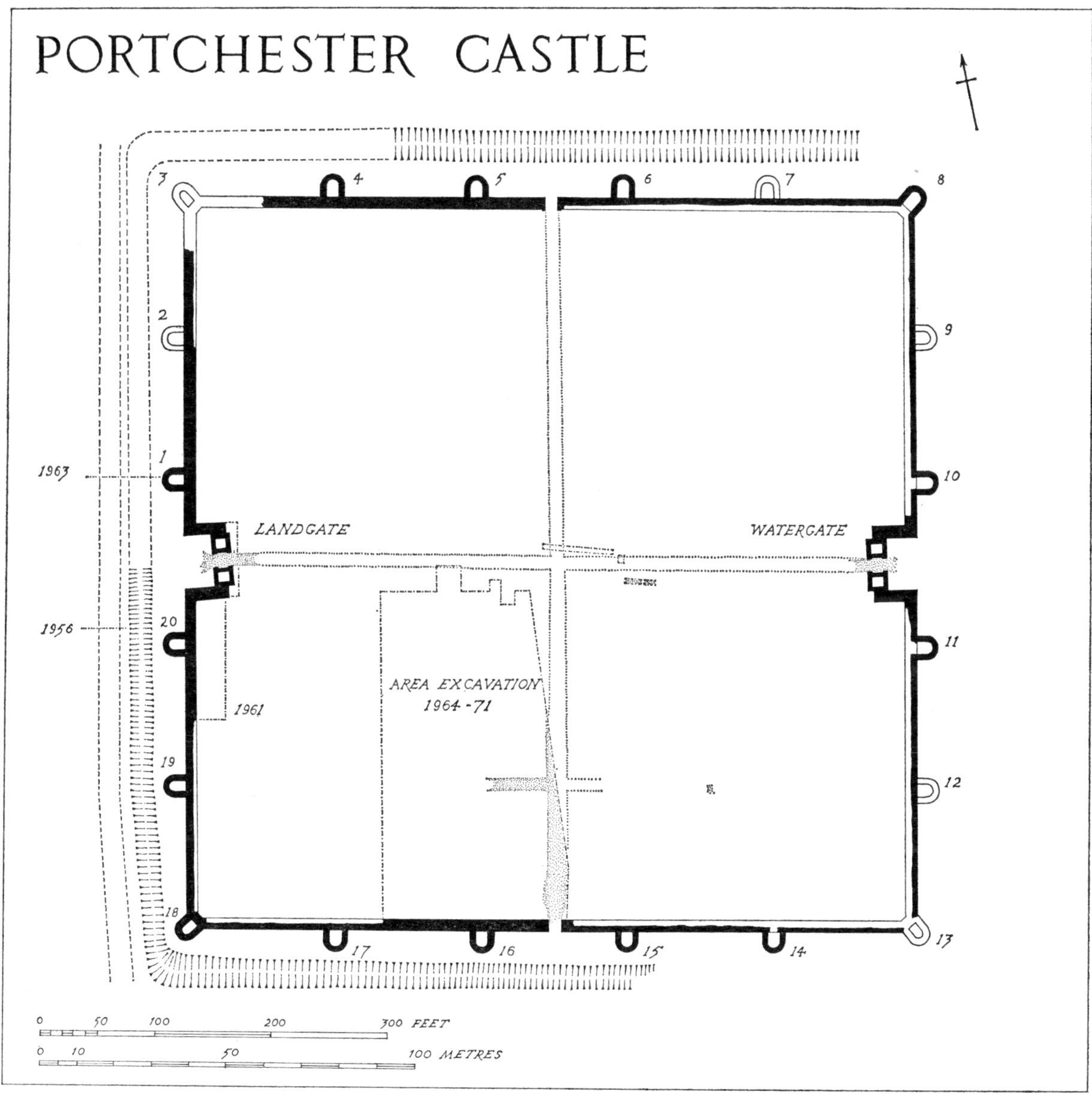

FIG. 3. The Roman defences showing areas excavated

Excavations elsewhere in the fort concentrated upon the two main gates, the landgate and the watergate. Saxon phases could be distinguished at both. A description is also given of the Saxon pit and related occupation material found in the excavation of 1961 against the west wall of the fort. No attempt has been made to describe the very limited evidence of Saxon activity found in the south-east corner of the fort during the excavation of the medieval priory, or in the north-west quarter, whilst the castle was being excavated. Details will be incorporated in subsequent volumes concerned specifically with these areas.

BIBLIOGRAPHY

CUNLIFFE, B. W. 1963. 'Excavations at Portchester Castle, Hants, 1961–3. First Interim Report.' *Antiq. J.* xliii, 218–27.

CUNLIFFE, B. W. 1966. 'Excavations at Portchester Castle, Hants, 1963–5. Second Interim Report.' *Antiq. J.* xlvi, 39–40.

CUNLIFFE, B. W. 1969. 'Excavations at Portchester Castle, Hants, 1966–8. Third Interim Report.' *Antiq. J.* xlix, 62–74.

CUNLIFFE, B. W. 1970. 'The Saxon culture-sequence at Portchester Castle.' *Antiq. J.* l, 67–85.

CUNLIFFE, B. W. 1971. 'The Tudor Store-House at Portchester Castle, Hants.' *Post-Med. Arch.* v, 188–90.

CUNLIFFE, B. W. 1972. 'Excavations at Portchester Castle, Hants, 1969–71. Fourth Interim Report.' *Antiq. J.* lii, 70–83.

HILL, D. 1969a. 'The Burghal Hidage: the establishment of a text.' *Med. Arch.* xiii (1969), 84–92.

HILL, D. 1969b. 'The Burghal Hidage: Southampton.' *Proc. Hants. F.C.* xxiv (1967), 59–61.

RIGOLD, S. E. 1965. *Portchester Castle, Hampshire.* H.M.S.O.

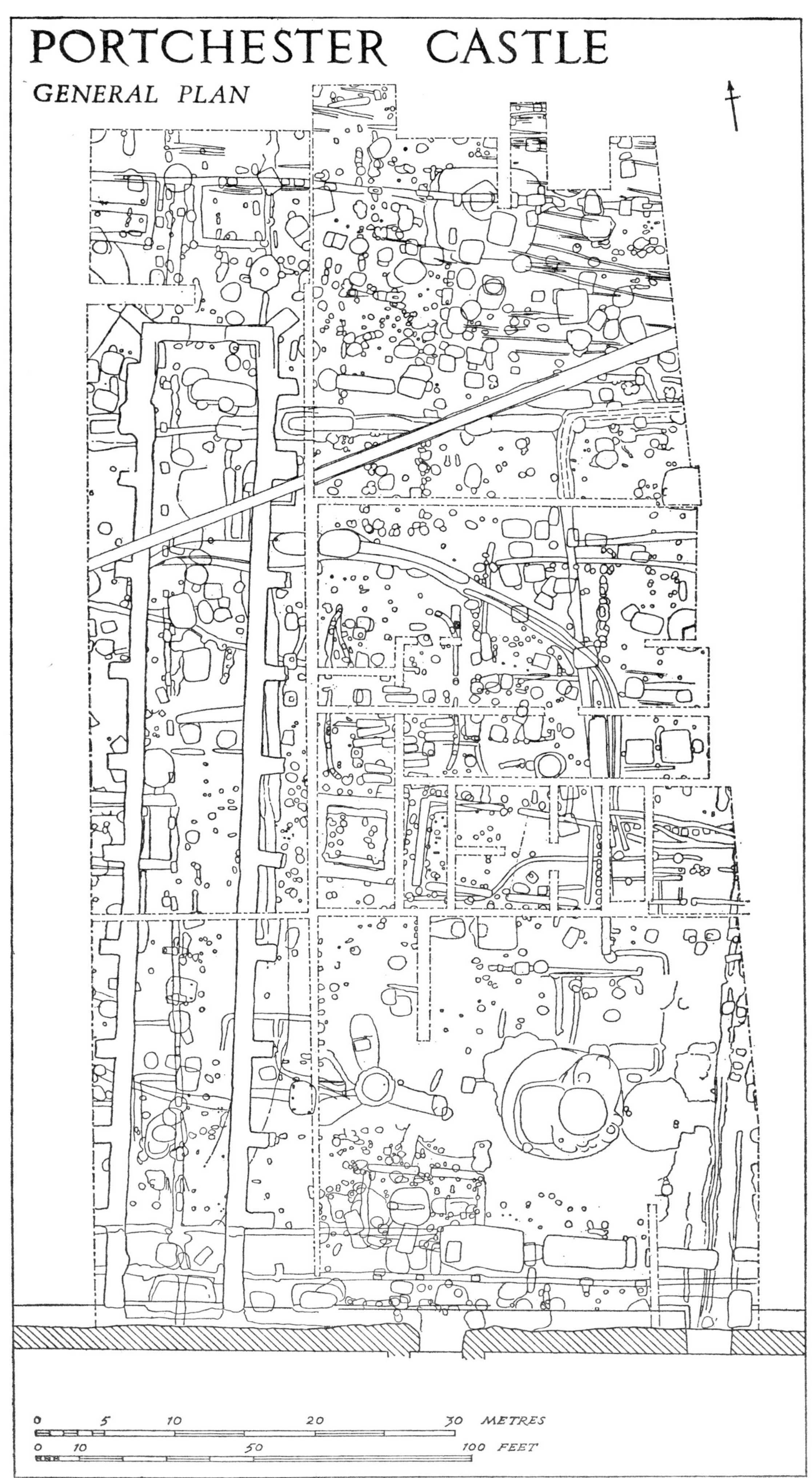

FIG. 4. General plan of the area excavated, showing all features of all dates

II. THE DESCRIPTION OF THE FEATURES AND STRUCTURES

THE WALLS AND THE GATES

AT the beginning of the Saxon period the Roman walls and gates of Portchester were standing to full height. Such was their stability that except for the rebuilding of the two main gates it is unlikely that the general appearance and form of the site changed much throughout the Saxon period. While it is possible that patching and localized rebuilding of the walls took place where necessary, direct evidence for this has not been recovered. Patching was so extensive in medieval and recent times that more ancient repairs will have been obscured or will have passed unnoticed.

THE LANDGATE AND ADJACENT AREA

(figs. 5, 6 and pl. III)

A detailed description of the Roman landgate has already been given in Vol. I (pp. 29–34) to which reference should be made. By the beginning of the fifth century the gate was probably intact although the pointing of the wall faces was already eroding, the washed out mortar and some fragments of building material accumulating in the corners of the forecourt and against the inner face of the gate-tower (section 3, layers 16 and 25).

At some stage in the Saxon period, three events took place which, though not proven to be contemporary, may well have been part of a single process of reconstruction. First of all, much of the superstructure of the guard chambers was robbed to foundation level with the exception of the front wall. At this time or very soon after, the south jamb of the Roman gate was rebuilt, using the original greensand blocks which were reset in clay (pl. III*b*). (The north jamb is now under the main through road and cannot be examined.) The implication of these observed changes is considerable, since it must be assumed that the entire Roman gate tower was removed except for the stumps of its front walls which still served to close the gap across the inner side of the gate courtyard. The rebuilding of the door jamb is an indication that the archway no longer survived in its original position, its place perhaps being taken by a lintel. Whether the drastic programme of rebuilding was occasioned by the instability of the Roman structure or the need for building stone is not immediately clear, but the lack of re-used greensand blocks in the Saxon levels of the excavated area, except incidentally as packing rubble, might suggest that the demolition of the gate was necessitated by considerations of safety. Stratigraphically the reconstruction phase can be shown to lie between the early fifth and early twelfth centuries, the only associated artefact being a single sherd of chaff-tempered pottery: greater precision in dating is impossible.

In front of the surviving gate-tower wall a timber fore-building was erected in a series of postholes (pl. III*a*), the details of which are recorded below. Only one side was available

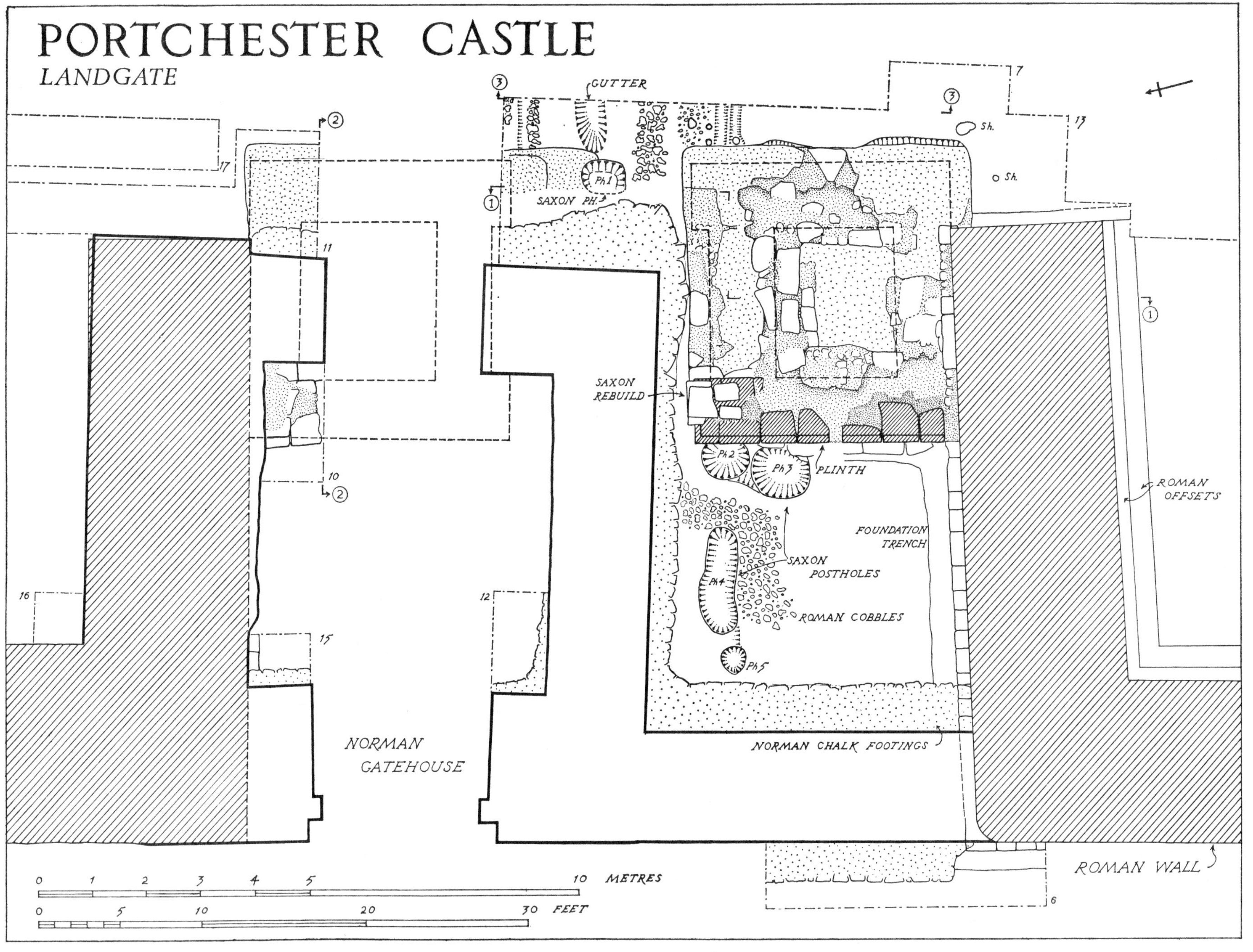

FIG. 5. Plan of the landgate excavations (section numbers are shown in circles)

for excavation, but if a similar construction existed on the opposite side of the original road, now beneath the present road, some kind of timber gatehouse would clearly be indicated. Such a structure would have certain similarities to the sixth-century gate found at South Cadbury, Somerset (Alcock, 1971, 3). No stratigraphical relationship survives between the reconstruction of the door jamb and the timber fore-gate, but it is reasonable to suggest that they may have been contemporary. A single massively bedded post (ph. 1) was found, cut through the Roman layers in the centre of the road. Since it pre-dates the early medieval gatehouse it must belong to the Saxon period. Functionally it can only have served to deflect traffic to right or left, though why this should have been necessary is difficult to understand.

The reconstructed gate may well have remained in use throughout the latter part of the Saxon period. No further changes could be detected until the medieval gatehouse was constructed in the early twelfth century.

Saxon Postholes (fig. 5)

ph 1. Sub-rectangular, 36 by 30 in. (0·91 × 0·76 m.), 56 + in. (1·42 m.) deep; packed with flints and clay.

ph 2. Circular, 36 by 25 in. (0·91 × 0·63 m.), 11 in. (0·28 m.) deep below contemporary surface. Filled with black soil and some flints.

ph 3. Circular, 43 by 36 in. (1·09 × 0·91 m.), 25 in. (0·63 m.) deep below contemporary surface. Filled with black soil and flints.

ph 4. Elongated trench 38 by 12 in. (0·97 × 0·31 m.), 38 in. (0·97 m.) deep. No traces of individual posts, uniform filling of black soil and redeposited brickearth.

ph 5. Circular, 8 in. (0·20 × 0·38 m.), 15 in. (0·38 m.) deep. Filled with black soil.

All postholes were cut through the uppermost Roman soil accumulations and were sealed by building levels contemporary with the construction of the early medieval landgate.

The 1961 Excavation to the South of the Landgate

The area examined in 1961 against the inner face of the fort wall immediately to the south of the landgate (Vol. I, pp. 180–4), produced little evidence of Saxon occupation, with the exception of a single pit (pit 24) and a scatter of sixth-century potsherds concentrated around the pit in trench 5 (layer 3). The implication would seem to be that the entire area remained unoccupied throughout the Saxon period apart from a brief phase of activity in the sixth century, traces of which spread into the south-east corner of the excavation.

The details of pit 24 are given on pp. 62–3; the Saxon pottery from layer 3 is illustrated with the early Saxon pottery, figs. 112, 114, 115, 116.

THE WATERGATE

(figs. 7, 8 and pls. I, II)

The Roman gatehouse in the centre of the east wall was of closely similar type to the Roman landgate (Vol. I, pp. 34–7). How long the superstructure remained standing it is impossible to say, but at some stage during the Saxon period the stone blocks of which the

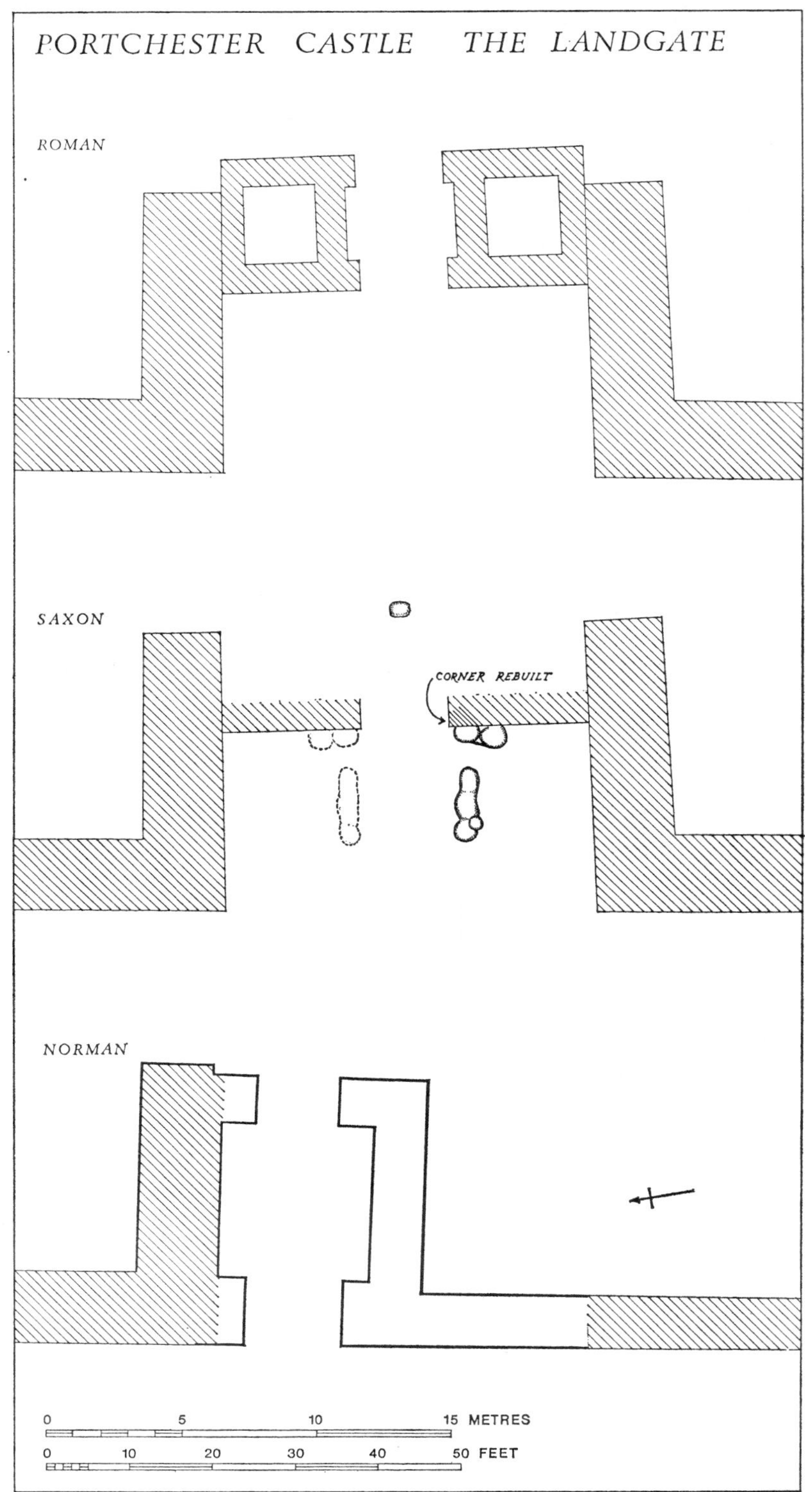

Fig. 6. The development of the landgate

gatehouse was built were removed to foundation level and some of the robber trenches filled with mortary rubble from the demolition (e.g. trench 32, layer 9 and trench 34, layer 13). Although the demolition was the act of a single period it seems that the robber trenches of the south guard chamber were left open, long enough for a thin turf line to form (trench 34, layers 12 and 30). After a while the old trenches were filled in (trench 34, layer 29) as part of a general levelling process in preparation for the erection of a new gatehouse.

The plan of the new structure (fig. 7) was in the form of a hollow square measuring 25 by 19 ft. (7·62 × 5·79 m.) externally, and 13½ ft. square (4·11 m.) internally. It was pierced by single arched openings in the east and west faces, the outer measuring 9 ft. (2·74 m.) wide, the inner 8 ft. (2·44 m.). It will be evident from the plan that the gatehouse was built over the southern half of the Roman gate-courtyard, its southern wall making use of the south Roman inturned wall (pl. II*b*), while its northern wall was firmly based on the Roman road surface. The space between the new gatehouse and the north Roman inturned wall was filled by a new length of curtain wall 5 ft. (1·52 m.) thick, which served to continue the line of the Roman curtain wall up to the face of the gatehouse (pl. II*a*). In the space between the north wall of the gate, the inner face of the new curtain wall and the northern inturned wall of the Roman gate, which was still standing above ground at this time, a thick layer of pinkish gritty mortar, mixed in places with rubble, represented the droppings from the building process. The layer (e.g. trench 34, layer 28) could be shown to abut the new walls just above their foundation levels.

Much of the first storey of the gatehouse still survives (fig. 8, pl. I). The original work is distinguishable from the medieval heightenings by virtue of the stone used. The original gatehouse incorporated large blocks of upper greensand and a ferruginous sandstone of lower greensand origin, while the later medieval construction made use of smaller blocks of fossiliferous limestone from either Bembridge or Purbeck. The junction between the two periods is very clearly shown at the north-west corner of the gatehouse (marked by the arrow on fig. 8). A further difference, in the infill material, is that the early gatehouse relied largely on flints, broken greensand and ironstone blocks, whereas the later work was less regular and contained a higher percentage of limestone and greensand slabs. Using these criteria it will be apparent that the inner (west) arch, with its alternating voussoirs of greensand and ironstone, is part of the original construction, together with the adjacent structure standing to *c.* 6 ft. (1·8 m.) above the present day ground surface. The two large limestone blocks on either side of the arch, cut partly into the voussoirs, were inserted in the early nineteenth century to hold a gate. Of the outer (east) arch only the basal blocks of ironstone survive. The structure was mostly rebuilt in the fourteenth century, when an outer gatehouse was erected, and has since largely collapsed. Another alteration made in the medieval period was the thickening of the wall at the south-west corner to accommodate a spiral staircase which led to an upper floor. It seems unlikely that the gate was more than one storey high in its original form.

The date of the early gatehouse is difficult to ascertain with any precision. Dr Butler, following Sir Mortimer Wheeler, proposed a Roman origin (Butler, 1955). He pointed to certain similarities in style to the porch of Titchfield church, thought to date to the tenth century, and suggested that the Titchfield arch had once stood as the Roman landgate of Portchester, but had subsequently been removed to Titchfield by sea and was there re-

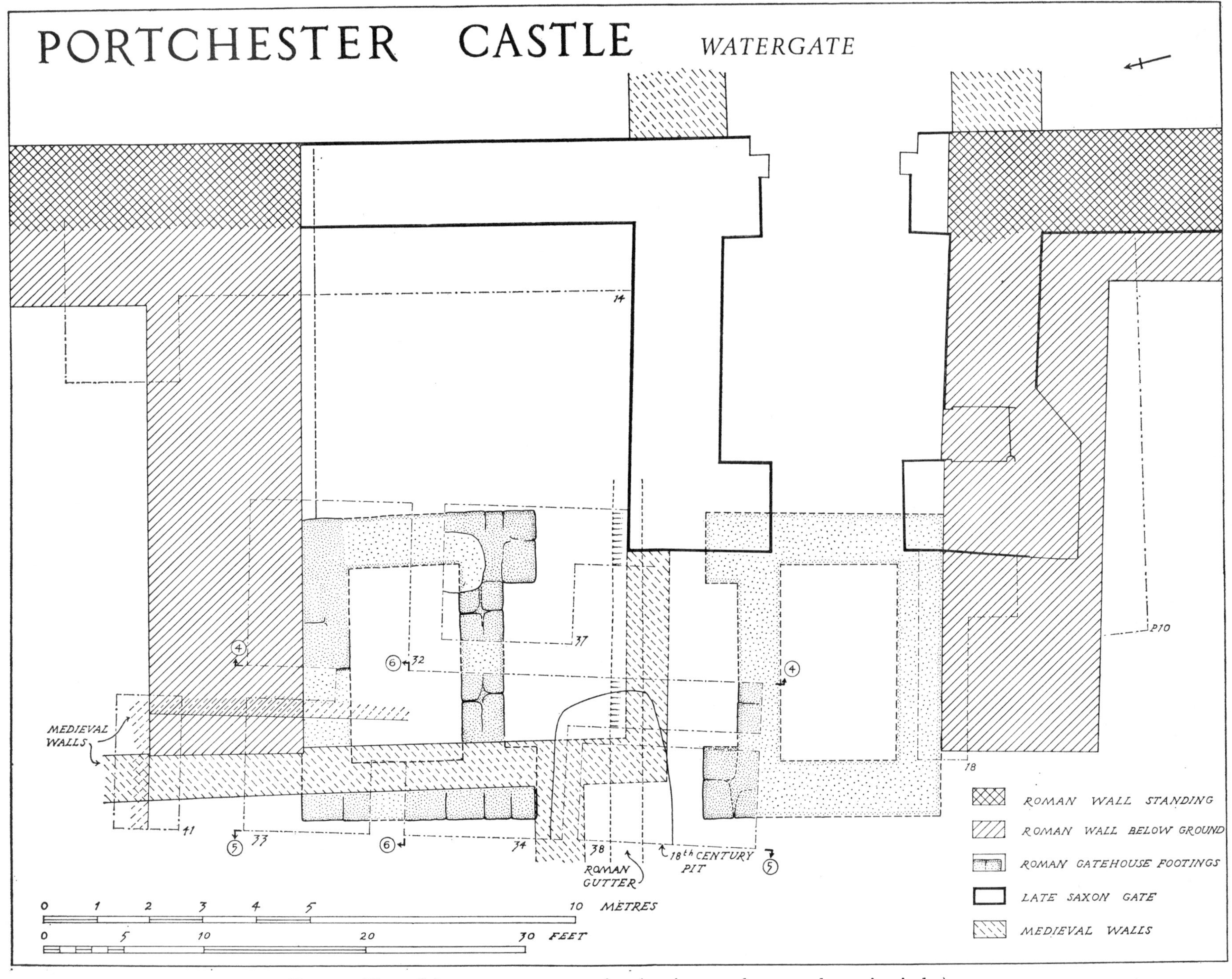

FIG. 7. Plan of the watergate excavation (section numbers are shown in circles)

constructed. Jope (1958) added his support by pointing out that ironstone was otherwise virtually unknown in Saxon structures. The excavations in 1961–3, however, demonstrated the existence of a totally separate Roman gate of different plan which pre-dated the present structure. Nevertheless the ironstone and greensand blocks were in all probability derived from this Roman predecessor since both materials are known to have been used elsewhere in

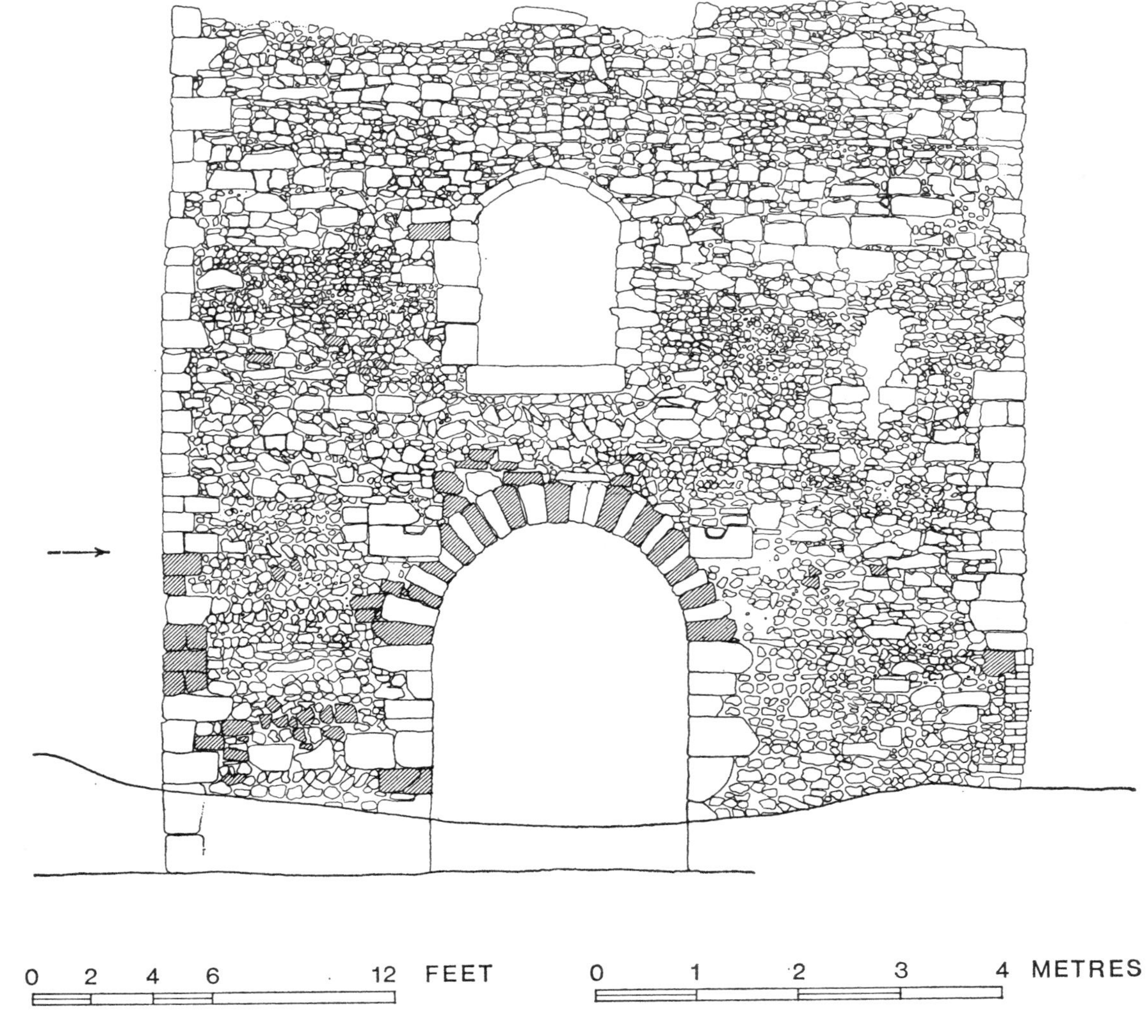

Fig. 8. Elevation of the west face of the watergate

the Roman structure (Vol. I, p. 31). Thus the argument about the origin of the Titchfield stones could indeed be true. It remains then to decide when the Portchester gate was erected.

Structural similarities to the Titchfield porch strongly suggest a broad contemporaneity which would therefore imply a late Saxon date for Portchester, a suggestion which is further supported by the dissimilarity of the gatehouse to the rest of the medieval work at the castle, dating to the early twelfth century and later. We are presented with three likely possibilities: either the gate was built in the late Saxon period, perhaps at the time that the fort was used as a burh in the early tenth century; or it was put up when the fort was being used as a residence in the late tenth to early eleventh century, or else it was constructed at the very beginning of the Norman period before the main phase of castle building had begun. Whichever explanation proves to be correct, the fact remains that the Portchester gatehouse is a rare example of secular masonry building of the tenth or eleventh century.

THE BUILDINGS

Altogether 18 recognizable buildings were discovered belonging to the period from the fifth to the eleventh century. As the simplified plan will show (fig. 9) the structures are well spaced out, there being only three cases in which building plans overlap, two of which probably represent reconstruction within a short space of time. Without the dating evidence afforded by associated pottery and stratigraphy, such an apparently simple plan might have given the impression that the settlement represented a village in which most of the buildings were in contemporary use. It will soon however be shown that, on the contrary, the overall plan represents virtually continuous use and rebuilding spanning six centuries and at no time were more than three or four houses in use together. Clearly, to be able to analyse the settlement plan in this way adds an important dimension which is seldom available on sites lacking comparable stratigraphy and associations.

Although buildings, fences, pits, wells and a cemetery can be distinguished, there remains a bewildering mass of postholes of which all that can be said is that they are post-Roman and pre-sixteenth century. From these can be extracted a small number which contained medieval pottery or belonged to medieval structures; of the rest most are probably Saxon, with the exception of many of those in the northern part of the excavated area flanking the east–west road, where the density of medieval material implies extensive medieval occupation to which a percentage of the undated posts probably belong.[1] The fact that much of the Saxon soil accumulation had been subjected to medieval ploughing, removing contemporary ground surfaces and truncating the tops of the posts, combined with the disturbance caused by the medieval gullies and sixteenth-century foundations, renders interpretation of these surviving posts difficult. The policy adopted here is to show on figs. 101–103 all features definitely and possibly Saxon and on the larger scale plans of individual buildings to include all the possibly Saxon postholes, together with their feature numbers. Measurements of the extraneous postholes will be found in appendix B. In three cases the ?Saxon postholes were so dense or regular as to suggest that they may have belonged to structures. These three areas are briefly described as posthole complexes A, B and C (pp. 52–5). A comparison of the areas covered in detail by figs. 10–33 with the overall distribution of posts (figs. 101–103) will show that, while a few remain outside the sphere of detailed discussion, they are scattered and unlikely to be of discoverable significance.

[1] The two large post pits shown on fig. 103 in the north ends of trenches 77 and 78 are similar to those of the aisled buildings. Since no dating evidence was available they will be considered with the other posts in this area in Volume III. The possibility remains, however, that they are part of the south row of aisle timbers of a late Saxon building.

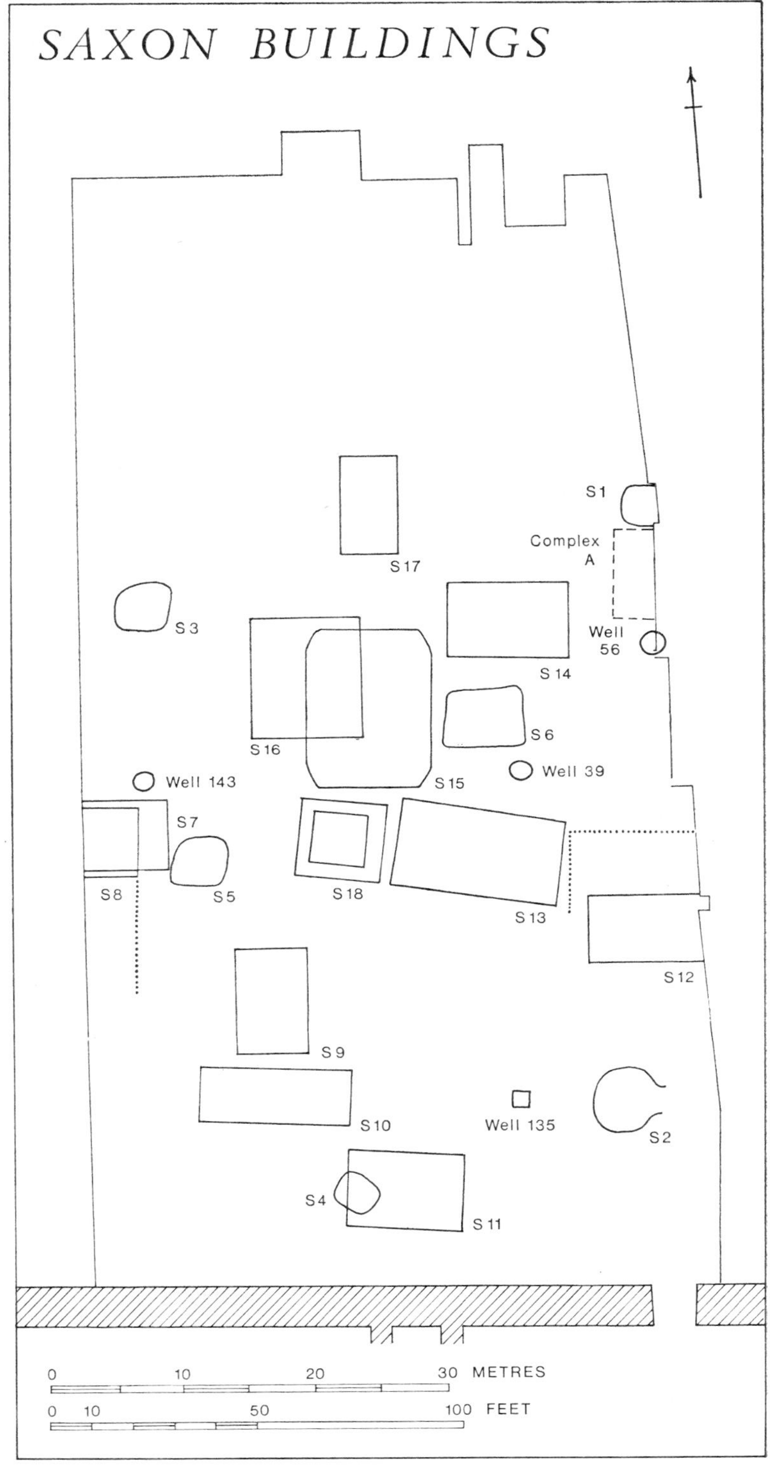

Fig. 9. Diagrammatic plan showing the positions of all Saxon buildings and wells

In the sections to follow, each building is described and illustrated and its dating evidence given. Then follows a discussion of the building types. The history of the development of the site as a whole is reserved for a separate section (pp. 121–7).

Small finds and pottery found in close association with the buildings are briefly described here with full references to the later sections in which the material is discussed in more detail.

Grubenhaus *S1*

(fig. 10 and pl. IV*a*)

(PC 67, trench 68, layer 18; PC 68, trench 76, layers 29 and 30)

Sub-rectangular, measuring 10 ft. 3 in. by approximately 11 ft. (3·12 × 3·35 m.) cut to a depth of 8 in. (0·20 m.) below the surface of the natural clay. The stratigraphy above had been disturbed in the medieval period down to the level of the natural surface, but the

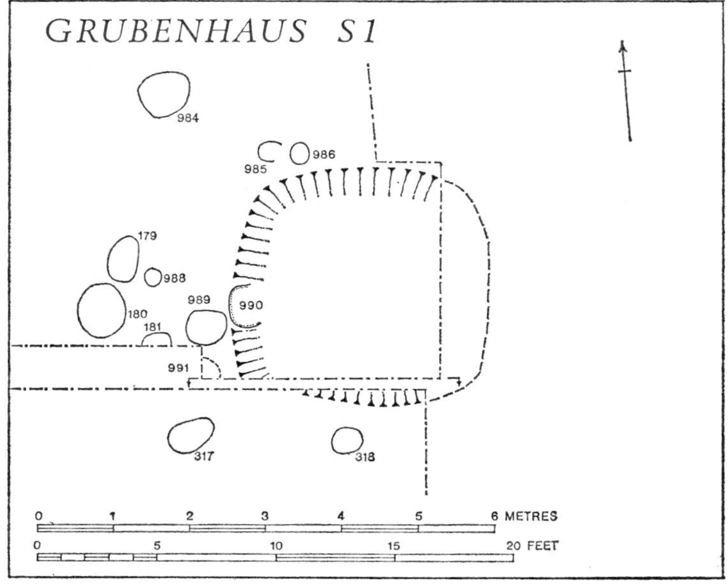

Fig. 10

filling of the *Grubenhaus* remained intact. The socket for one contemporary post (no. 990) survived in the centre of the west side: it was 1 ft. 10 in. (0·56 m.) in diameter and 11 in. (0·28 m.) deep. A posthole on the opposite side would have been destroyed by the churchyard wall. Details of nearby posts of unknown date are listed below (Appendix B). The floor of the *Grubenhaus* was featureless; the sides sloped up gradually to the natural surface.

Two layers of filling were distinguished: the lowest (trench 76, layer 30) consisted of black soil mixed with occupation rubbish and patches of redeposited natural brickearth. This gradually merged with layer 29 which contained more flint nodules and less brickearth. Layer 30 gave the appearance of having accumulated in position while layer 29 could represent a deliberate fill.

Small finds

From layer 29:

Gilded bronze disc brooch	(588): fig. 136, no. 45.
Circular loomweight	(—): fig. 141, no. 79.
Quernstone	(832): fragment, not illustrated.
Bone point	(820): not illustrated.

From layer 30:

Whetstone	(840): fig. 142, no. 89.
Worked bone	(599): fragment: not illustrated.

Pottery: early Saxon (fig. 111)

All from layer 30 except 139 which comes from layer 29.

136 S76 Jar represented by 1 rim and 7 body sherds in a black sandy ware with occasional large grits and pieces of chaff. The surface is well burnished and fired red.

137 S82 Jar represented by 2 rims and 3 large body sherds in dark grey sandy ware with occasional large flint grits and some chaff. The surface is smoothed.

138 S78 Bowl. Hard black sandy ware burnished inside and out.

139 S77 Shoulder of a bowl in hard black sandy ware with well smoothed surface.

140 S81 Rim of bowl in a black sandy ware tempered with some flint grits and fragments of chaff. The surface is well burnished.

141 S79 Rim of bowl in fine hard black sandy ware with a well sealed black burnished surface.

Not illustrated: 18 body sherds, 5 sherds from probably one vessel in coarse grey sandy ware with copious chaff tempering, and 13 sherds in grey sandy wares comparable to those illustrated.

Grubenhaus *S2*

(fig. 11)

(PC 69, trench 87, layer 40)

Sub-rectangular, measuring approximately 16 ft. (4·88 m.) across with an entrance passage 6 ft. (1·83 m.) wide leading down from the level of the Roman road cobbling. The floor had been dug to a depth of 1 ft. (0·31 m.) below the surviving top of the adjacent Roman surface. The sides sloped steeply to the floor, which was featureless except for the four postholes. The posts appeared to represent two pairs, one replacing the other: the first pair, nos. 645 and 704, were respectively 10 and 8 in. (0·25 and 0·20 m.) deep; the second pair, nos. 646 and 703, were both 17 in. (0·43 m.) deep. Post 703 was demonstrably later than 704, but the relationship between 645 and 646 could not be determined.

The lower filling (87, layer 40) consisted of dark stony soil containing much occupation rubbish and some wads of brickearth towards the west side, becoming more stony towards the top. It gave the appearance of having been a deliberate filling deposited at one time. The west side of the filling was cut by the erosion cone of the well (pit) 135.

No pottery or objects were found other than residual Roman material.

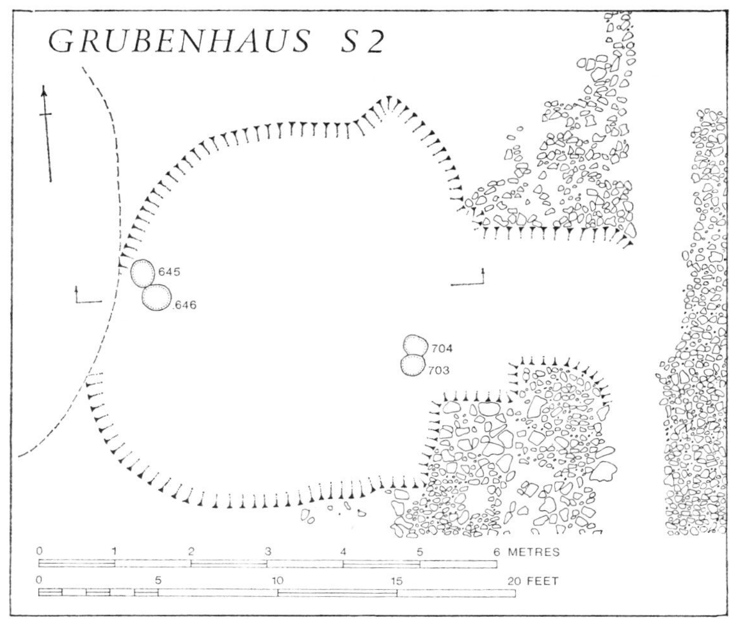
GRUBENHAUS S2
645
646
704
703
0
1
2
3
4
5
6 METRES
0
5
10
15
20 FEET

FIG. 11

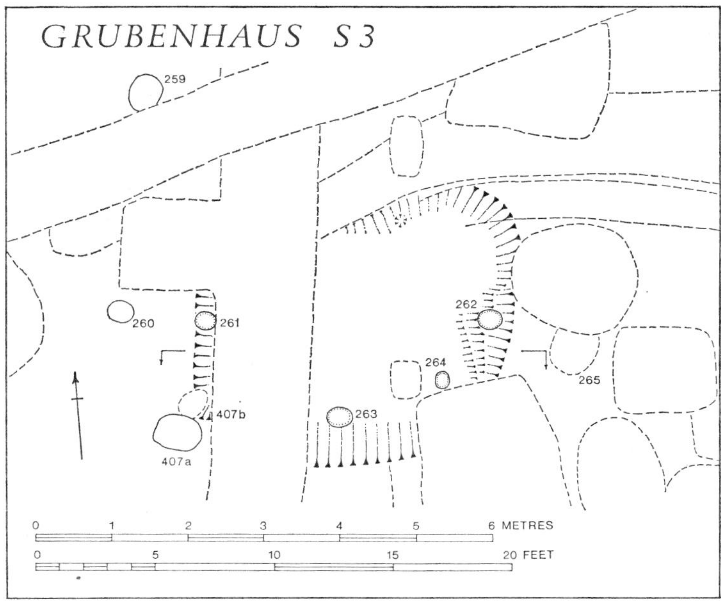
GRUBENHAUS S3
259
260
261
262
263
264
265
407b
407a
0
1
2
3
4
5
6 METRES
0
5
10
15
20 FEET

FIG. 12

Grubenhaus *S3*
(fig. 12)
(PC 70, trench 97, layers 29 and 48)

Sub-rectangular, measuring 12 by 14 ft. (3·66 × 4·27 m.), cut to a depth of 3 ft. (0·91 m.) below the surface of the natural brickearth, above which medieval ploughing had disturbed the sealing stratigraphy. The north and south sides sloped regularly to the floor, while the east and probably the west sides were stepped. The floor was flat and featureless. Substantial parts of the structure had been cut away by later features.

The two main postholes survived, nos. 261 and 262. Both were about 10 in. (0·25 m.) in diameter, no. 261 was 12 in. (0·31 m.) deep, no. 262, 33 in. (0·84 m.). Another posthole of similar character, no. 264, lay within the structure; it measured 8 in. (0·20 m.) across and 30 in. (0·76 m.) in depth. No. 263 may also have been contemporary; it was 9–11 in. (0·23–0·28 m.) across but only 2 in. (0·05 m.) deep.

The filling was uniform and apparently of one period, consisting of grey-brown clayey soil with wads of redeposited brickearth and marl, some flints and blocks of limestone. The chaff-tempered pottery came from immediately above the floor.

Pottery

Not illustrated: 3 body sherds in black sandy wares with chaff tempering.

Grubenhaus *S4*
(fig. 13)
(PC 72, trench 108, layer 93)

Irregular hollow measuring a maximum of 12 ft. (3·66 m.) across and cut to a maximum

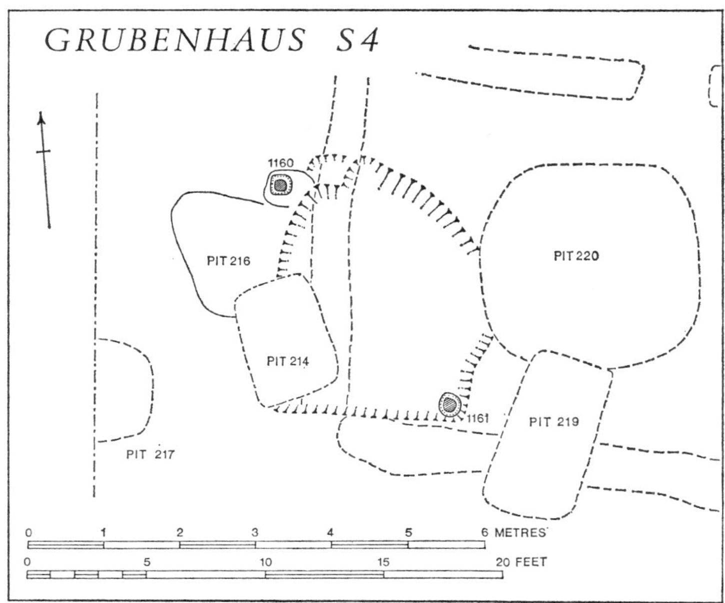

FIG. 13

depth of 11 in. (0·28 m.) below the surface of the Roman clay bank. Although identification as a sunken hut is debatable, the existence of the two posts (nos. 1160, 1161), one at either end of the sunken floor, is suggestive. Both posts were 5 in. (0·13 m.) in diameter and were set in postholes 11–12 in. (*c.* 0·3 m.) across.

GRUBENHAUS S1

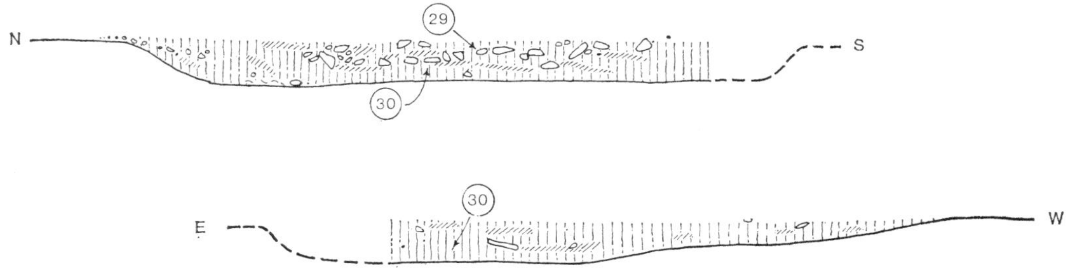

GRUBENHAUS S2

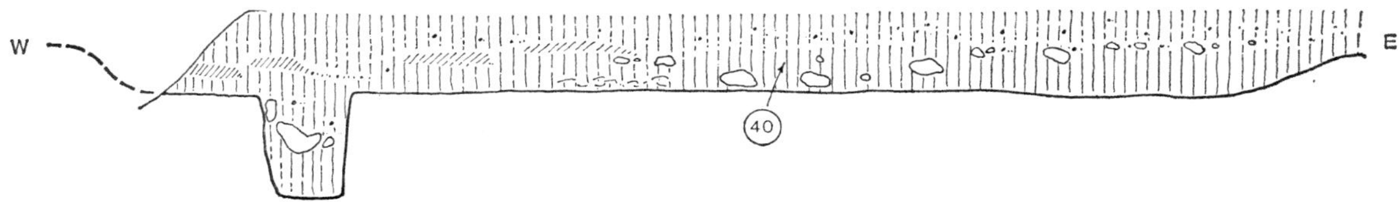

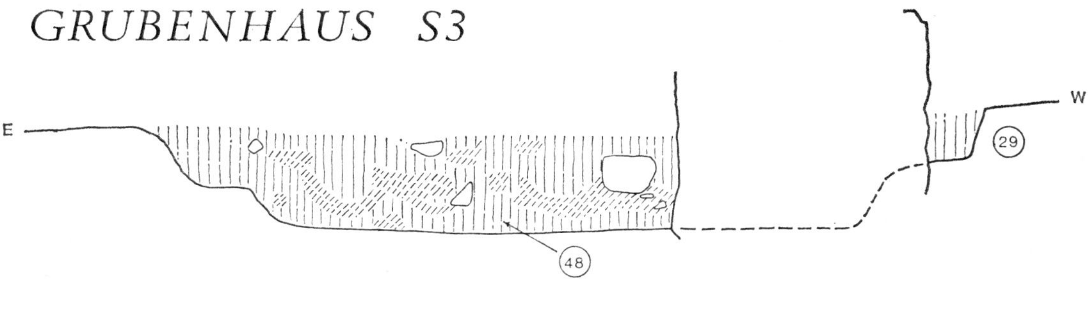

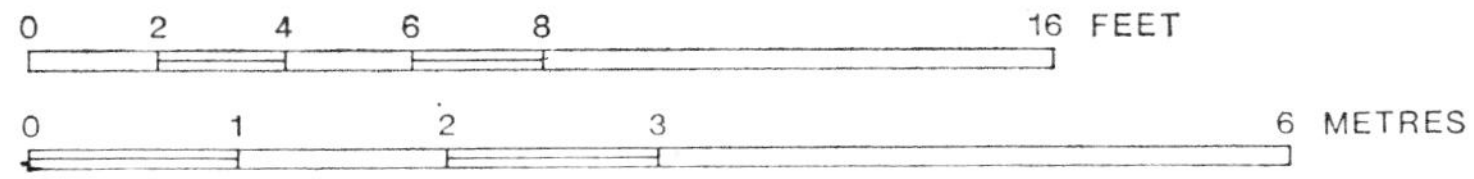

FIG. 14. Sections of the *Grubenhäuser*

The filling consisted of grey stony soil containing a high percentage of clay derived from the Roman clay bank, implying a deliberate filling.

The structure was cut by the Saxon pits 216 and 220, the wall slots for building S11, and medieval pit 214.

Dating depends on the single sherd of Saxon pottery, and the fact that the hut was cut by pit 220 dating to the eighth century.

Pottery: early–mid Saxon (fig. 111)

148 S342 Rim in grey sandy ware with crushed flint grits.

Building S5

(fig. 15)

Sub-rectangular building measuring approximately 13 ft. (3·96 m.) across. It was first recognized at the level of the top of the Roman occupation layer as a band of flint nodules,

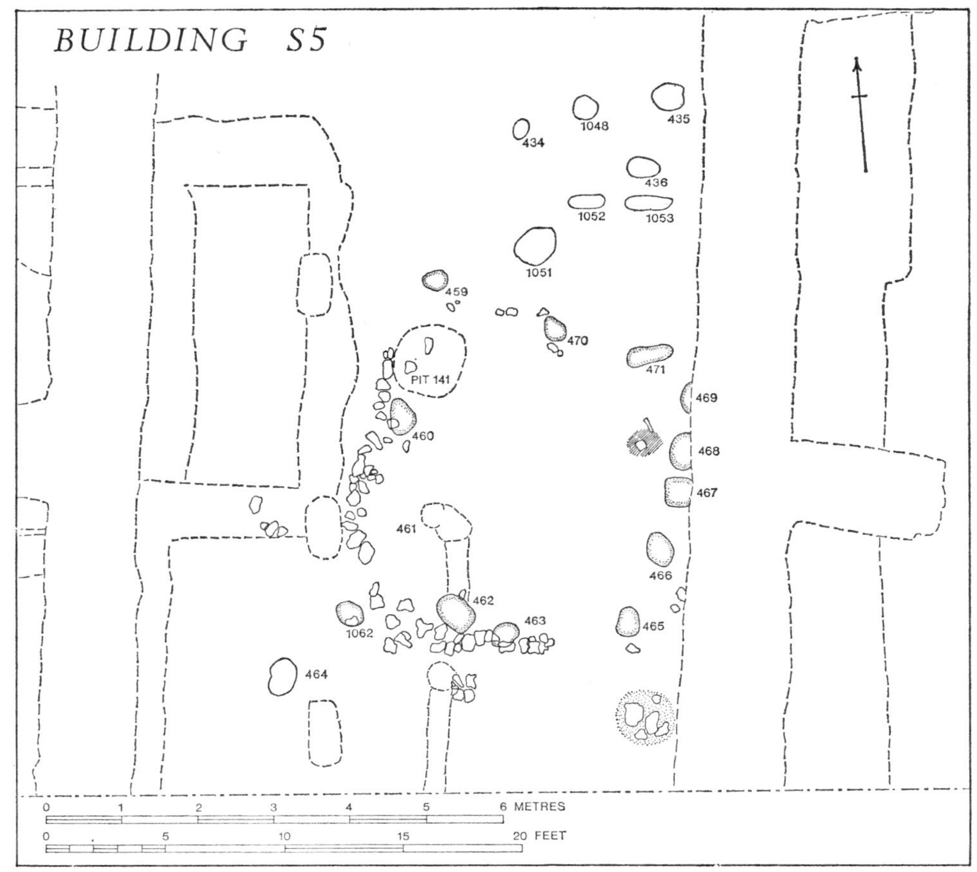

FIG. 15

packing a wall trench cut through the Roman layer. The flints were planned and removed. When excavation reached the Roman surface 6 in. (0·15 m.) below, the positions of a number of postholes became apparent. Although it was impossible to be sure that they had been dug through the Roman material from the level at which the flints first appeared, it seems reasonable to suppose that they were, and that the posts formed the weight-supporting uprights of a structure, the walls of which were bedded in a slot packed in places with large flints. No distinct floor surface survived the medieval ploughing, but a small patch of burnt soil may represent the position of a hearth since removed. The line of the wall was cut by pit 141 which contained chaff-tempered pottery.

The plan (fig. 15) shows the flint packing and all postholes which are likely to be post-Roman, and pre-eleventh century. Those considered to belong to the structure are described here; for the others see Appendix B.

No independent dating evidence was obtained from the postholes but, since the wall line was cut by pit 141 which contained chaff-tempered pottery, an early–mid Saxon date is indicated.

Description of postholes of the building

Postholes	Trench/layer	Diameter (in.)	Depth (in.)
460	94/119	*c.* 18	4
462	94/126	15–20	12
463	94/128	11–15	4
465	94/129	11–15	3
466	94/125	13–18	6
467	94/124	15	5
468	94/123	19	5
469	94/122	16	6
470	94/131	10–14	3
471	94/130	9–23	4
1062	94, ph 2	12–14	5

Building S6

(fig. 16)

Rectangular building measuring 24 by 16 ft. (7·32 × 4·88 m.) represented entirely by postholes and short sections of wall slots which were first recognized at the level of the natural clay. Close dating is difficult but several of the posts of the south wall were demonstrably later than the filling of Roman pits of the fourth century, while part of the north wall had been destroyed by pits of the eleventh century. A Saxon date is therefore reasonably established. The contemporary ground surface had been entirely removed by medieval ploughing.

Isolated postholes which are not demonstrably Roman or post-Saxon are shown on the plan (fig. 16) and are listed in Appendix B; postholes considered to belong to the structure are listed here:

Postholes	Trench/layer	Diameter (in.)	Depth (in.)
375	65, ph 8	15	9
381	65, ph 9	13	5
382	65, ph 20	15	3
385	65/6	14–21	8
386	65/10	18	10
387	65, ph 21	11–14	5
917	63, ph 11	14	9
920	63, ph 14	7–9	2
921	63, ph 15	10	10
922	63, ph 16	10	8
923	63, ph 17	11	4
924	63, ph 18	12	2
926	63, ph 20	8	4
927	63, ph 21	10	12
928	63, ph 22	12–15	11
929	63, ph 23	15	12
930	63, ph 24	13	5
931	63, ph 25	10	5
932	63, ph 26	11–15	9
1162	65–	13–20	5

The slots were between 2 and 5 in. deep.

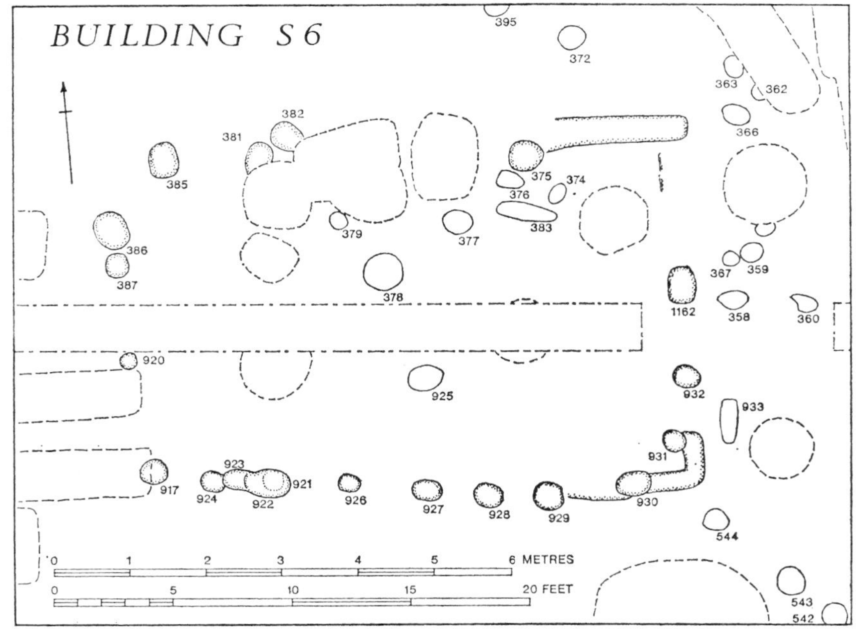

FIG. 16

Building S7
(fig. 17)

The east end of a rectangular building 18 ft. (5·49 m.) wide and more than 20 ft. (6·10 m.) long.

The building was defined by three bedding trenches, those for the north and south walls measuring 2 ft. 6 in.–2 ft. 9 in. (0·76–0·84 m.) wide, while the trench for the east wall was only 2 ft. (0·61 m.) wide at the most. The north trench was on average 8 in. (0·20 m.) deep, the east 3 in. (0·08 m.), the south 6 in. (0·15 m.), all measurements being from the surface of the natural clay.

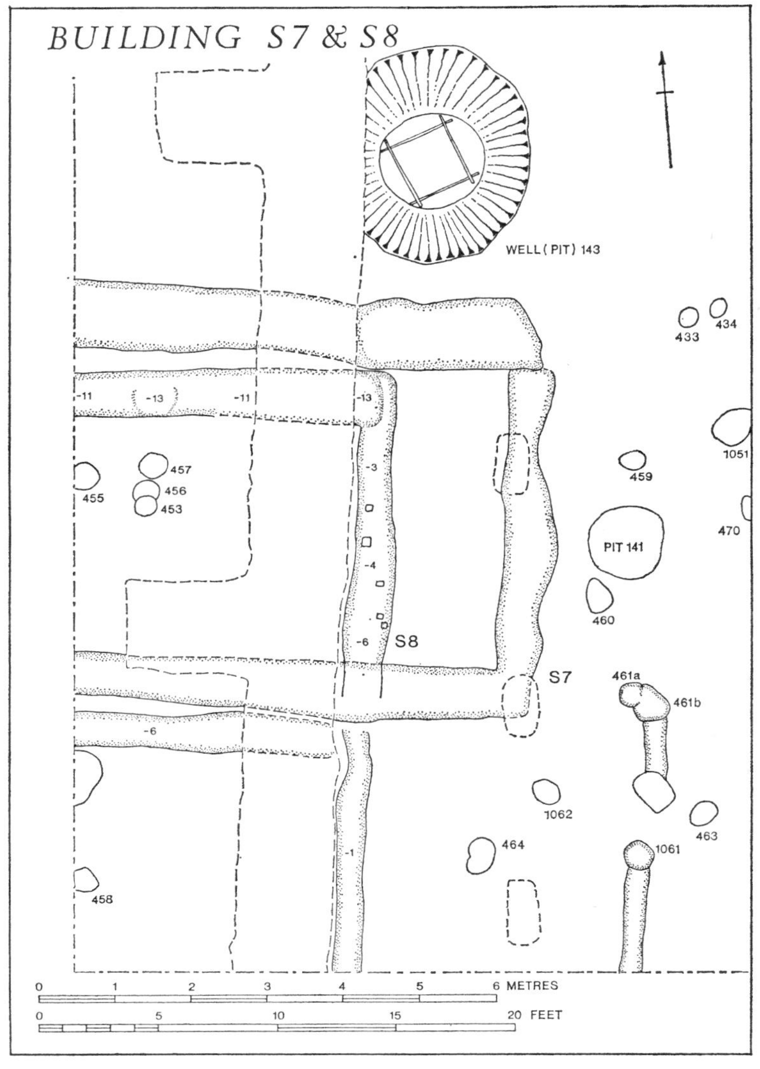

Fig. 17

All three trenches were filled with black stony soil and wads of redeposited clay. In spite of an extremely careful search, the positions for vertical timbers could not be discovered. While it is therefore a possibility that the slots served as trenches for horizontal sill beams, the exact nature of the structure must remain undecided.

All trace of the contemporary ground surface had been removed with the exception of a layer of clay to the east of the building (section 25, layer 75). Dating depends upon the facts that the building post-dated the filling of pit 137, the north slot contained two sherds of chaff-tempered pottery, and the structure was sealed by layers containing Portchester ware. The relationship of buildings 7 and 8 could not be demonstrated with absolute certainty, but it would appear that building 7 preceded building 8. The slots of building 8 produced sherds of Portchester ware and therefore presumably represent rebuilding at a later date.

Details of the layers

North slot: trench 95, layers 86 and 80.
East slot: trench 94, layer 117.
South slot: trench 94, layers 95 and 114.

Pottery

From trench 95, layer 86.
Not illustrated: 2 chaff-tempered body sherds.

Building S8

(fig. 17)

Rectangular building 17 ft. (5·18 m.) wide and of undefined length, but exceeding 14 ft. (4·27 m.). The building is represented by three foundation trenches cut to a depth of between 5 and 13 in. (0·12 and 0·33 m.) below the surface of natural clay. The north and south foundation trenches were the more substantial, and presumably supported the main wall timbers, the basal impressions for two of which could be traced in the northern trench. No comparable features were found in the southern trench, but for half of its exposed length it was cut through the top of pit 137 in which area its bottom was difficult to define precisely. The position of the east wall was represented by a slighter trench, a maximum of 6 in. (0·15 m.) deep, in the bottom of which the positions of five stakes of square cross-section could be traced, each impressed to a depth of between 1 and 2 in. (0·03 and 0·05 m.) below the bottom of the trench. The fillings of all three slots consisted of mixed black soil with wads of natural brickearth, presumably the material which had been dug from the trenches and repacked. No clear trace of vertical timbers could be seen in the filling.

The contemporary floor levels had been removed by medieval ploughing, and at least half of the exposed area destroyed by the sixteenth-century footings: thus no evidence of internal structures could be recognized. A few fragments of burnt daub showing wattle marks were found in adjacent plough soil accumulations.

The eastern slot appears to cut through the south slot of building S7, implying that building S8 was the later. This is supported by the evidence from the associated finds:

whereas the latest material from the slots of building S7 was two sherds of chaff-tempered pottery, the slots of building S8 produced one rilled sherd of Portchester ware and two gritty sherds of *c.* ninth- to tenth-century date. It is therefore reasonable to suppose that building S8 replaced building S7; both buildings were of almost exactly the same width and may well have been of the same length.

From the south-east corner of the building another trench was found running south. It was slight and showed no trace of vertical timbers. Together with a further trench, 56 ft. (17·07 m.) to the south, and broadly contemporary (i.e. post-Roman and pre-eleventh century), it may have defined a yard attached to the building. Beyond this 'fence' to the east were two short lengths of trench associated with postholes 461b and 1061. The trenches were between 4 and 7 in. (0·10 and 0·18 m.) deep and were filled with black soil. Their function is uncertain but they may have been part of an enclosure attached either to building S7 or S8.

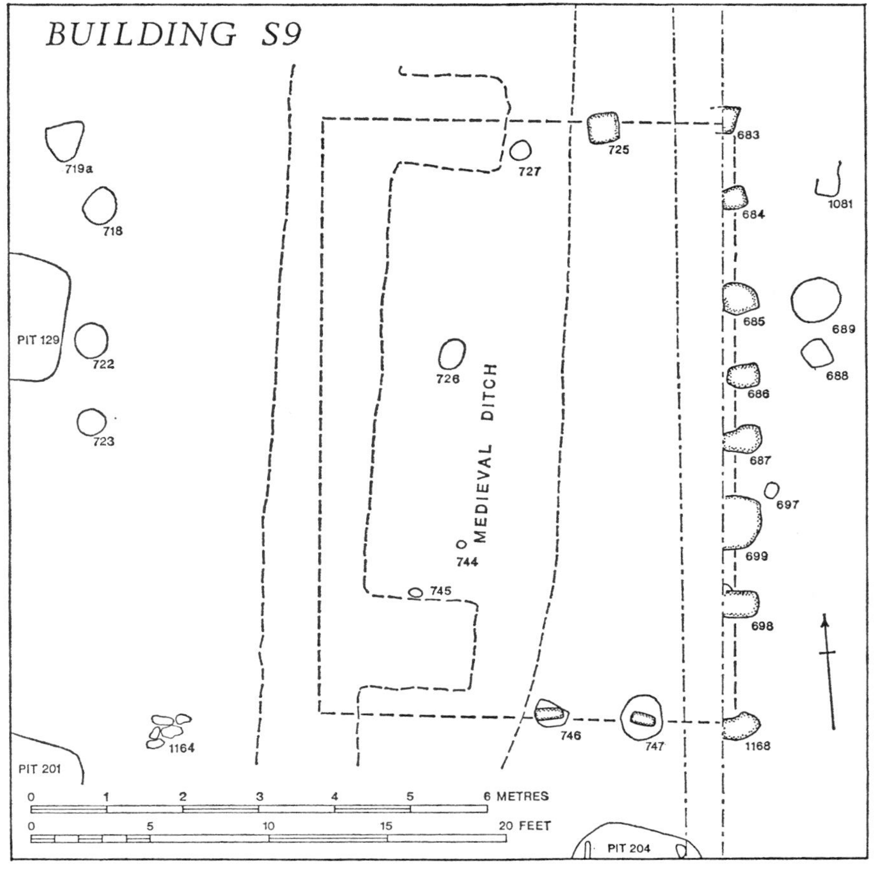

Fig. 18

Details of layers

North wall trench:	trench 94, layer 134.
East wall trench:	trench 94, layer 107a.
South wall trench:	trench 94, layer 94.
'Fence' west:	trench 94, layer 107.
'Fence' east:	trench 94, layers 126, 118.

Postholes	Trench/layer	Diameter (in.)	Depth (in.)
461b	94/115	17	10
1061	94, ph 1	14	11

Building S9
(fig. 18)

Rectangular building measuring 26 ft. by approximately 18 ft. (7·92 × 5·49 m.). Only the eastern part of the building survives, the rest including the entire west wall having been destroyed by sixteenth-century wall footings and a medieval ditch.

The individual timbers of which the structure was composed were evenly spaced and appeared to have been roughly rectangular: those of the east wall were set with their long axis at right angles to the line of the wall while those of the south wall were aligned with it.

Apart from the extreme south end of the building the contemporary ground surface had been destroyed by medieval ploughing. All postholes had been cut through the Roman occupation material and into natural or redeposited clay. Postholes 746 and 747 were clearly recognizable from the surviving Saxon ground surface as larger holes which narrowed towards the base. Their associated ground surface relates to the level from which pit 204 was cut, thus establishing contemporaneity and showing that building 9 pre-dates building 10.

No pottery other than Roman sherds was recovered from the postholes.

Description of the postholes

Postholes	Trench/layer	Diameter (in.)	Depth (in.)
683	90/46	14 × ?	10
684	90/47	12 × ?	11
685	90/48	18	8
686	90/49	17 × 12	8
687	90/51	14 × ?	9
698	90/76	14	10
699	90/82	28	7
725	100/109	16 × 16	3+
746	101/125	15 × 6	12
747	101/119	12 × 6	12
1168	90	12 × 18+	8

Building S10
(fig. 19 and pl. VII)

Rectangular building constructed of posts set in individual postholes. The building measures 14 ft. by 36 ft. (4·27 × 10·97 m.). The plan is incomplete, since parts of the north and south sides were cut away by the sixteenth-century footings, while much of the east end had been destroyed by a medieval lime kiln. Among the surviving posts, a certain regularity existed, both in spacing and in size, the individual posts being on average 3 ft. 9 in. (1·14 m.) apart and roughly rectangular in shape. At the three surviving corners the end posts of each wall were so arranged as to end short of the line of the adjacent wall, a feature also apparent in the trench-built structures, buildings S1, 7 and 11. Only two posts, nos. 751a/b and 773/4 showed signs of having been replaced.

Over the eastern half of the building areas of the original ground surface survived, while the western part was more deeply disturbed in medieval times. Even so, all the postholes of

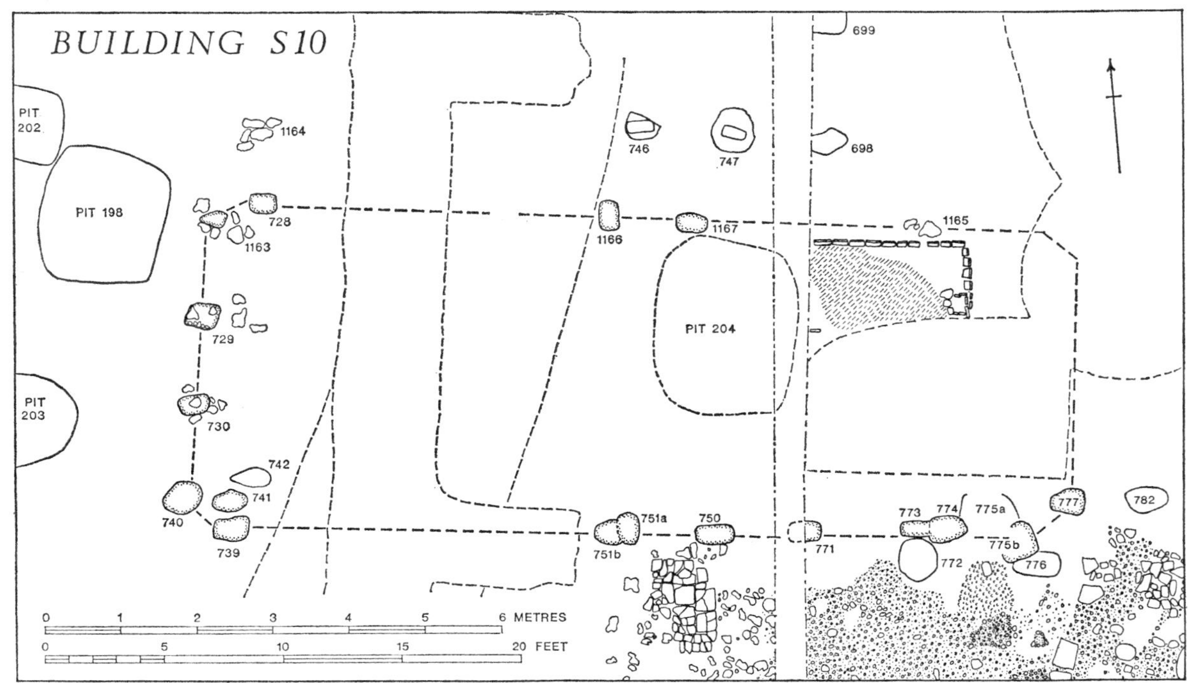

FIG. 19

the west wall were recognized first as soil discolorations with some flint packing, cut through the pre-building soil. All but no. 1163 were cut sufficiently deeply to penetrate the Roman clay bank. Along the north wall nos. 1166 and 1167 were recognized only as soil discolorations, while 1165 appeared as a flint-packed hole: none of these three penetrated the natural or redeposited clay. The postholes of the south wall were seen at the contemporary ground surface cut into the Roman redeposited clay.

Within the north-east corner of the building an area of burnt clay 2 in. (0·05 m.) thick survived, edged with fragments of Roman tegulae so laid that their flanges formed a straight outer edge (pl. VII*a*). A tile-lined socket was provided at one side, probably to retain the base of an upright timber. The function of the feature is difficult to determine, but it could have served as a simple hearth or for an industrial function. A discontinuous scatter of burnt material extended to the west of the burnt clay, defining the floor surface of the building which here could be shown to seal pit 204 and to be contemporary with the level from which postholes 1166 and 1167 were cut.

Outside the building to the south was a pathway some 6 ft. (1·83 m.) wide running between buildings S10 and S11. Its surface was formed by a thin spread of gravel, not exceeding 4 in. (0·10 m.) thick, with patches of flint nodules, chalk and Roman tiles. At the western extremity of the spread a large area of Roman tiles had been laid possibly to consolidate the ground in front of a central doorway framed by posts 751 and 750 (pl. VII*b*). A further observation which may be thought to support the idea of a door at this point is that the long axis of post 751a was set at right angles to the line of the wall as was its opposite number, post 1166 in the north wall, special treatment possibly associated with the hanging of a door. The pathway would therefore have run between the doors of the two contemporary buildings, S10 and S11 (see p. 31).

No independent evidence for dating was obtained for the building except that its construction post-dated pit 204 and pre-dated the appearance of 'Portchester ware' which was found in the level sealing it. A single sherd of ninth-century gritty ware was found in posthole 739.

Details of the postholes

Posthole	Trench/layer	Diameter (in.)	Depth below contemporary ground surface (in.)
729	101/73	17 × 14	14
730	101/74	17 × 11	12
739	101/110	18 × 13	14
740	101/112	22 × 18	14
741	101/127	18 × 10	12
751a	103/55	17	8
751b	103/55	14	8
750	103/54	19 × 10	10
771	108/125	12 × ?	11
773	108/114	14 × 8	7
774	108/113	14 × 20	17
775b	108/153	10	9
777	108/167	16 × 18	12
1165	90	*c.* 15 × 12	8
1166	103/90	15 × 11	9
1167	103/89	16 × 10	10

Building S11

(fig. 20 and pl. IX)

Rectangular building measuring externally 19 ft. by 28 ft. (5·79 × 8·53 m.). The main features of the building were extremely well preserved in spite of areas of destruction caused by the digging of later pits and postholes. The building structure was based on six separate lengths of foundation trench dug to an average depth of 8 in. (0·20 m.) below the contemporary surface: the trenches varied in width from 1 ft. 6 in. to 2 ft. (0·46–0·61 m.). The long sides of the structure were each provided with centrally placed doorways but no special provision for hanging the door is now evident. At the corners the trenches were so arranged as to stop short approximately on line with the inner face of the adjacent wall at right angles; there were no corner posts.

A careful examination in plan of the fillings of the foundation trenches revealed the positions of many of the original vertical wall timbers which, in almost every case, measured 12 in. (0·31 m.) by 6 to 9 in. (0·15–0·23 m.). They seem to have been arranged with their front faces aligned with the inner face of the wall. This was achieved by placing them close against the inner sides of their bedding trenches. The positions of the posts were recognized along the south wall as pockets of black soil clearly distinguishable from the flint packing

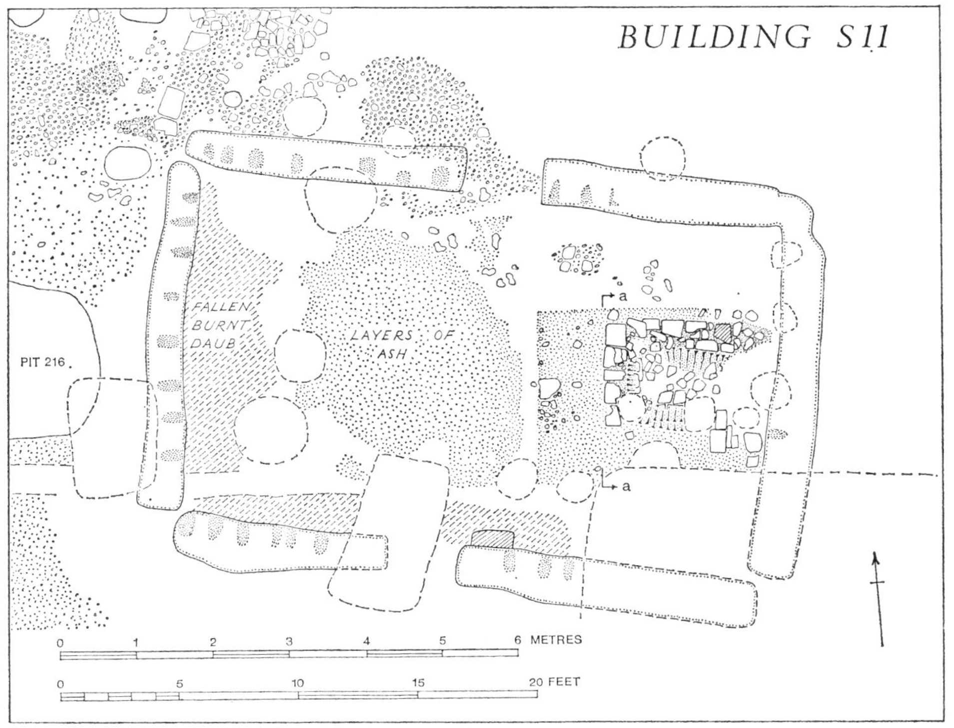

FIG. 20

between. The timbers of the east and south walls also appeared as soil-filled voids against a mixed packing of redeposited clay and soil. In the north-east corner disturbance of the upper levels and the presence of later postholes rendered the discovery of individual post positions impossible. The superstructure of the walls was no longer recoverable but a quantity of smooth sandy daub showing the marks of wattles *c.* $\frac{3}{4}$ in. in diameter was found within the building.

Centrally placed against the east wall of the building was an oven built largely of re-used Roman tiles and some lumps of limestone set in clay (pl. IX*b*). Although much of the south and east sides of the structure had been destroyed, sufficient survived to show that the walls were *c.* 15 in. (0·38 m.) thick and that the floors of the stoking chamber had worn considerably in use. The detailed structure of the oven is best appreciated by reference to figs. 20 and 23 and pl. IX*b*. After the oven had been removed traces of a lower oven were revealed consisting of a shallow scoop *c.* 3 ft. by 5 ft. (0·91 × 1·52 m.) and 9 in. (0·23 m.) deep showing signs of intensive burning. The hollow had been levelled with fragments of hard baked clay from the superstructure of its destroyed dome before the more substantial upper oven was built.

The area around the oven and in the centre of the building had been surfaced with a thin discontinuous layer of mortary daub, stony in patches. In the centre there had been considerable subsidence into pit 220 requiring levelling with ash and daub and some resurfacing. The only other internal feature to survive was a block of upper greensand just inside the south door set against the inner face of the wall.

Much of the contemporary ground surface beyond the building survived intact. To the west a spread of finely crushed chalk had been laid, seldom more than 1 in. (0·03 m.) thick. To the north the space between the building and building S10 had been consolidated with gravel and tiles to form a pathway leading between the doors of the two buildings. The metalling actually extended across the threshold of building S11 and over the bedding trench practically to the line of the wall face.

The chronological position of the building in relation to the well preserved stratigraphy of this part of the site can be summarized:

Pre-building	Pit 220.
Building; construction	Wall slots 108, layers 60, 66, 67, 89.
	Primary oven, 108, layers 193, 236.
	Secondary oven, 108, layer 192.
	Cobbles, 108, layer 46.
Building; occupation	In hollow over pit: 108, layers 53, 55.
	In secondary oven: 108, layer 58.
	Under fallen wall: 108, layer 78.
Destruction	
Occupation layer sealing destroyed building	108, layers 42, 44, 22, 30.
Clay spread sealing late occupation	108, layer 3.

Pottery

The pottery from pit 220 dates to the eighth century, thus providing a convenient *terminus post quem* for the construction of the building. From the wall slots the following sherds were recovered:

Layer 60: sherd of the decorated jar no. 171 (S94).

Layer 66: 149 (S344). Rim in smooth grey-red ware with grass tempering. The surface is black and burnished (same vessel as 116 (S318) from pit 198).

Not illustrated: 12 body sherds, 3 in grass-tempered fabrics, 3 in black sandy ware, 5 in grey ware with crushed flint grit tempering, 1 in fine hard grey sandy ware with a black slip, probably an import.

Layer 67: 150 (S345). Decorated sherd, red sandy ware with flint grit tempering, decorated with impressed circles.

Not illustrated: body sherd in grey ware with flint grit tempering.

Layer 89: Not illustrated: 3 body sherds in coarse grey sandy ware tempered with crushed flint grits.

Not illustrated: 4 body sherds of a coarse jar in grey sandy ware tempered with crushed flint grits.

The gritty sherds belong to the assemblage typified by the rubbish tip in the well (pit) 135 in which coarse flint-gritted wares were seen to replace sandy and chaff-tempered fabrics. The fragment of the imported vessel is consistent with the general character of this group. Together the evidence suggests a construction date in the ninth–tenth century.

The pottery from the occupation layers includes the following:

Layer 53: Not illustrated (S346). Rim in dark grey sandy ware with flint grit tempering, 5 body sherds in coarse grey ware, some fired red-brown, tempered with crushed flint grits.

Layer 58: Not illustrated: 2 body sherds, one in black ware with chaff tempering, the other in black sandy ware with some flint grits.

Layer 78: 151 (S347). Rim, hard black sandy ware, smoothed surface.

Not illustrated: 2 body sherds in coarse grey ware tempered with crushed flint grit.

This group lies in the same ninth- to tenth-century bracket as does the pottery from the construction levels. The destruction level of the building was sealed by a soil accumulation containing a predominance of Portchester ware types.

Building S12

(fig. 21)

The identification of the postholes and trenches shown in fig. 21 as a building must be regarded as open to some doubt. In the area concerned the stratigraphy was very shallow and the presence of a large medieval timber building had removed all Saxon and a substantial part of the Roman layers. All that remained were the bases of those features deep enough to penetrate the subsoil or the earliest Roman levels.

The surviving features can be divided into two groups, lengths of trenches, possibly the bedding trenches for a rectangular building, and two rows of postholes which might be interpreted as a fenced enclosure.

The trenches would have defined a building 17 ft. (5·18 m.) wide and in excess of 33 ft. (10·06 m.) long. The northern side was the best preserved: it was defined by a trench up to 2 ft. (0·61 m.) wide and varying from 8 to 12 in. (0·20–0·31 m.) deep. The positions of three posts were recognizable as impressions in the trench bottom, but no trace of vertical timbers could be seen in the loose flint packing filling the trench. It is possible that the gap in the north trench represented the position of a central doorway; if so the overall length of the building would have been about 37 ft. (11·28 m.). The southern wall trench was represented by a shallow straight-sided depression 2 in. (0·05 m.) deep cut into the Roman occupation levels and filled with black soil and some flints. As the plan will show, only parts of it could be traced together with one side of the supposed west wall. The bases of two posts, nos. 1172 and 1173, possibly relate to the building.

Although the surviving fragments of evidence are slight, similarities in size and structure to buildings S7, S11 and S13 tend to support the view that these scattered features do actually constitute a single structure.

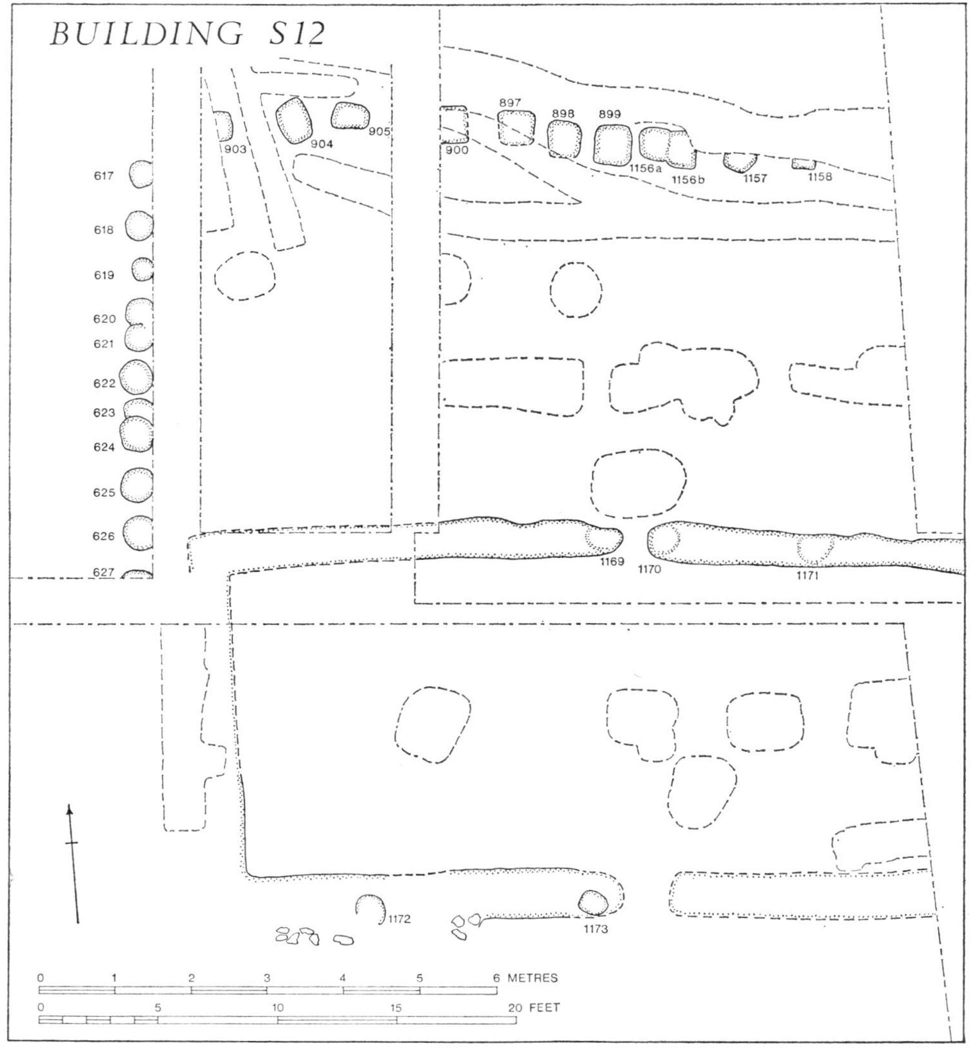

FIG. 21

The postholes to the north of the building would appear to have defined an enclosure. The western row lay parallel to the end of building S13 and was originally interpreted as buttress posts for the end of that structure, but it could well be argued that while buttressing was desirable along the sides a gable end would not have required such support. An alternative explanation is that building S13 was erected against an already existing fence. The destruction of the contemporary ground surface had removed any stratigraphical relationship (see further discussion, p. 36).

No pottery other than Roman sherds was recovered from the postholes and slots.

Description of the postholes

Posthole	Trench/layer	Diameter (in.)	Depth below natural surface (in.)
617	54, ph 3	14	2
618	54, ph 4	14	4
619	54, ph 5	11	1
620	54, ph 6	14	1
621	54, ph 7	14	1
622	54, ph 8	18	4
623	54, ph 9	14	4
624	54, ph 10	18	6
625	54, ph 11	17	5
626	54, ph 12	18	2
627	54, ph 13		3
897	57, ph 4	18	4
898	57, ph 5	18	3
899	57, ph 6	20	6
900	57, ph 7	12	6
903	45, ph 1	15	3
904	45, ph 2	16–20	3
905	45, ph 3	13–18	3
1156a	85/27	13–15	4
1156b	85/27	14–19	4
1157	85/12	14	7
1158	85/11	11	7

Building S13
(figs. 22, 23 and pl. VIII)

Rectangular building measuring 22 by 41 ft. (6·71 × 12·50 m.). It was represented by a series of discontinuous foundation trenches dug to varying depths below the surface of the natural clay. The trenches first became apparent as bands of loosely packed flints clearly distinguishable from the pre-building soil accumulation. A careful examination and dissection of the filling failed to demonstrate the positions of any of the upright timbers, but depressions made by the bases of some of the verticals of the south wall could be traced in the bottom of the bedding trench, thus giving the size and average spacing of the verticals, while at the same time proving that horizontal sole-plates had not been employed. A considerable quantity of hard, white, chalky daub with the marks of $\frac{1}{2}$ in. diameter wattles was found in the vicinity of the slots, and in one place along the south wall the wattle and daub facing appeared to have been taken down to below floor level since fragments *in situ* were found embedded in the packing of the wall trenches.

The entire north-west corner of the building had been rebuilt during use, the new wall trench, shallower than its predecessor, taking a slightly different alignment to the original but converging on the position of the north door and joining with the south wall at the south-west corner. It is possible that the rebuilding avoided as far as possible the ground disturbed by the line of the previous wall trench.

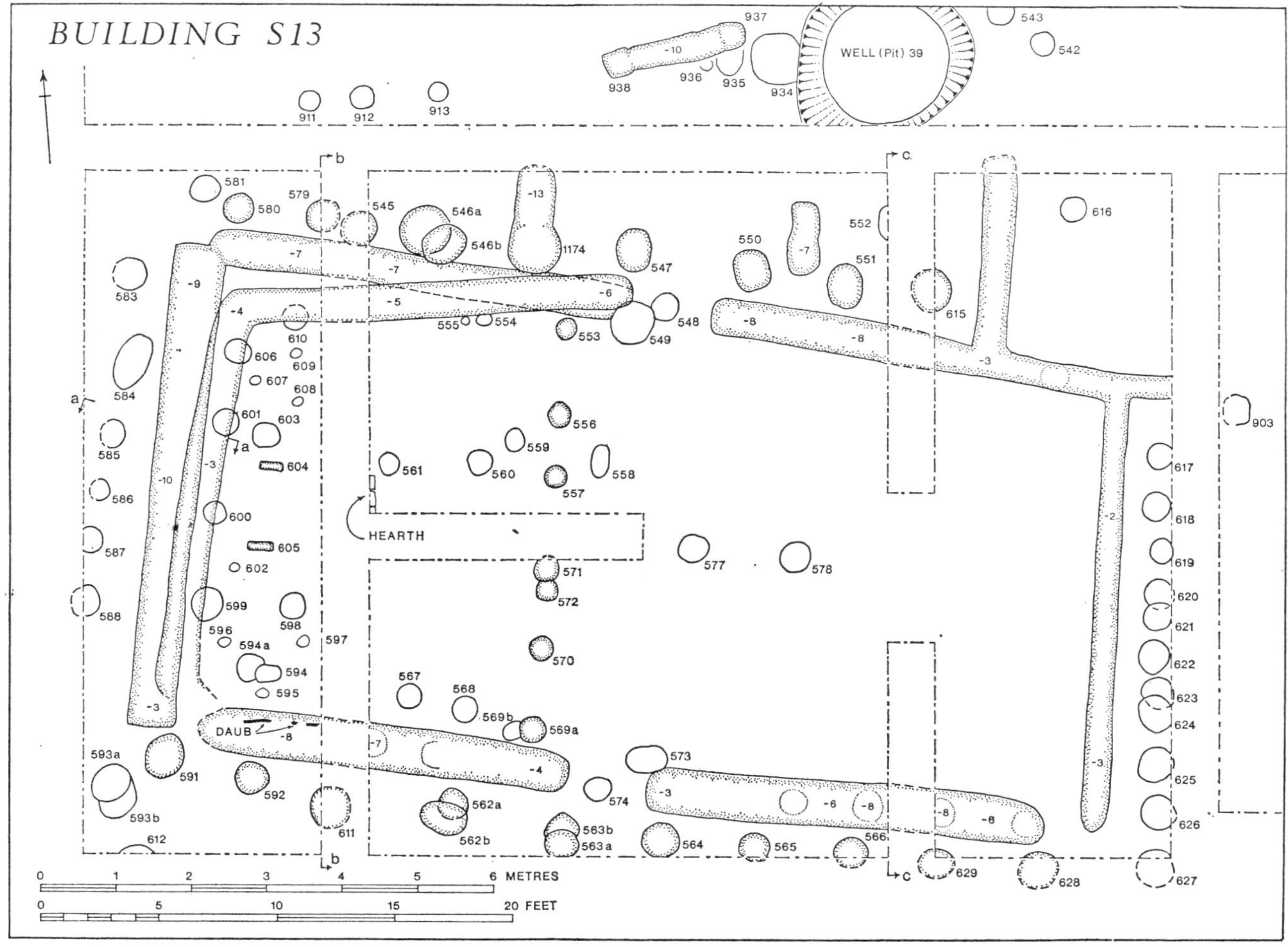

FIG. 22

It will be apparent from fig. 22 that outside the walls of the building were a number of postholes which might be thought to be related to the main structure. It has been suggested above (pp. 33–4) that the posts parallel to the east wall are best interpreted as a pre-existing fence against which the building was erected. Those outside the west wall may likewise be part of a separate complex to the west (p. 52), but the posts parallel to the north and south walls are altogether more regularly spaced, their arrangement being suggestive of buttress posts leaning towards the building and adding support to the beam taking the ends of the rafters. Such arrangements are well known elsewhere at this period. In support of this interpretation is the fact that the bases of postholes 562b, 563a, and 564 sloped inwards towards the building (fig. 23) in a manner strongly suggestive of their having taken leaning timbers. A further observation relevant to the relationship between the building and the external posts is that along the north wall the timbers stopped at the point where a wall slot joined the main wall at right angles, implying that buttress posts respected an attached structure of uncertain function.

Two of the buttress posts on the south wall were replaced during the life of the building, and it is possible that posts 545 and 546b were also replacements erected after the rebuilding of the north-west corner. Post 546b could be shown to post-date both the original wall trench and post 546a.

The gaps in the centres of the north and south walls represent the positions of doorways. It is possible that posts 549 and 573 supported a hinged door. Posts 574 and 548 might also have been related to the door structure, perhaps serving as door stops. The north door was provided with a wide porch constructed of timbers placed in two short lengths of bedding trenches set at right angles to the wall. In front of this and possibly related to it was a further length of wall trench, terminating in two postholes, 937 and 938, which had supported a wattle and daub screen. Fragments of daub were plentiful in the area. The relationship of these porch features to the well (pit) 39 is suggestive and it could be argued that the porch formed a well house to enable water to be drawn by the occupants of the building while still under cover. The way in which the side walls of the porch relate in plan to the buttress posts gives the impression that they are not a part of the original plan but were added later, possibly at the time of the rebuilding.

Inside the building are a number of postholes which may have been contemporary with the occupation of the house, but some, including nos. 599, 600, 601, 606 and 610, were partly obliterated by the rebuilding of the north-west corner. One row, however, nos. 553, 556, 557, 569a, 570, 571 and 572, gives the impression of having been part of a screen flanking the passage-way between the two doors, thus dividing off an inner chamber from the rest of the house. Within this room was a small hearth built of re-used Roman tiles. Between the hearth and the wall two deep rectangular postholes were found (nos. 604, 605) which supported a contemporary structure, perhaps a ladder leading to a loft.

The relationship of building S13 to neighbouring structures is reasonably well defined. It post-dates the filling of pits 34 and 35 and was probably erected after the fenced enclosure attached to building S12. In its later phase it was contemporary with the use of the well (pit) 39 and it can be clearly shown (fig. 23, p. 51) to have been out of use by the time of the rebuilding of the masonry tower.

Pottery evidence from pits 34 and 35 shows that the building must post-date the eighth century. From the wall trenches the following sherds were recovered:

56, layer 7	Portchester ware sherds: 1 rilled, 1 undercut rim and 2 plain body sherds.
56, layer 8	Portchester ware: 2 body sherds. Earlier Saxon material includes 1 chaff-tempered body sherd and the illustrated rims 142, 143, 144, 145, 197, all in grey sandy wares.
58, layer 7	Rim, no. 146, in grey sandy ware.

The sherds of Portchester ware are indicative of a construction date in the late tenth or

BUILDING S11

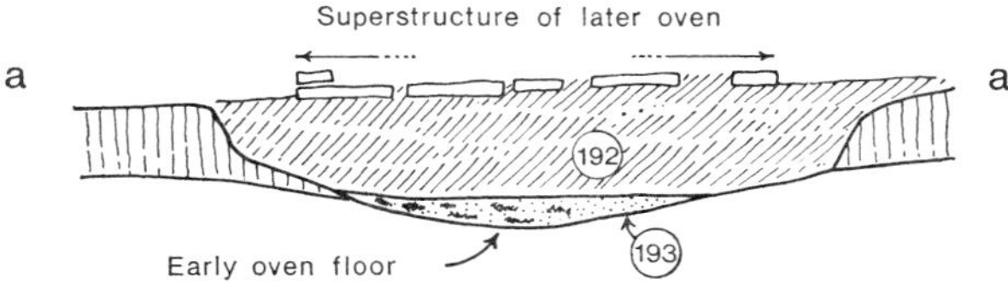

BUILDING S13

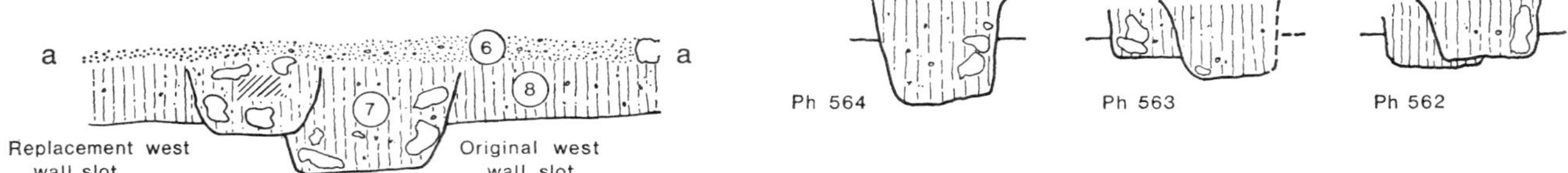

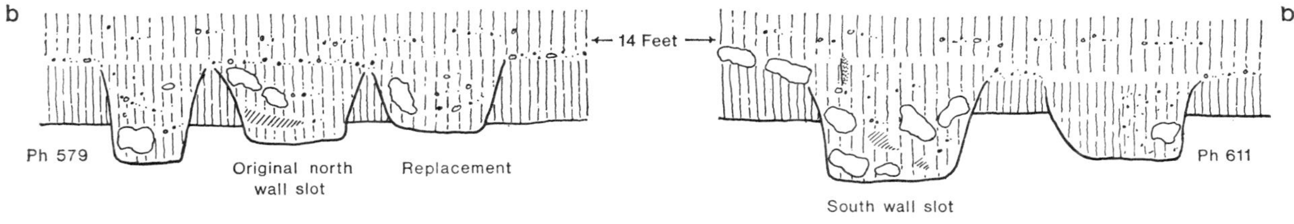

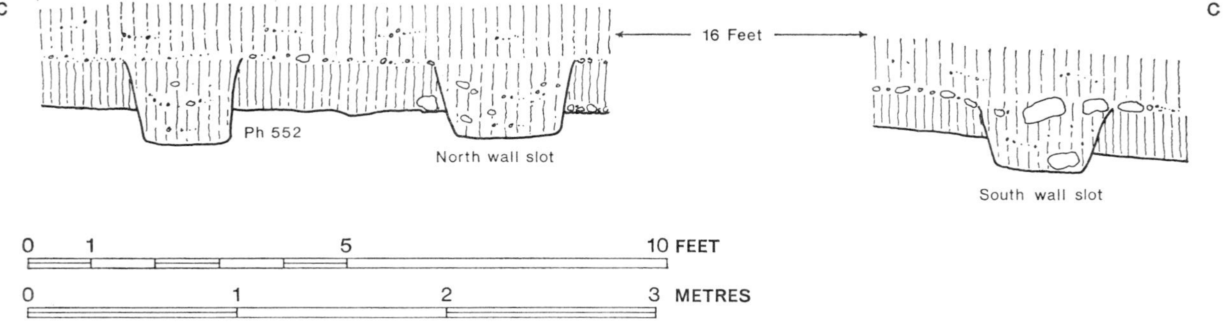

FIG. 23. Sections of buildings S11 and S13

early eleventh century, which corresponds to the time when the well (pit) 39 was in use. The soil accumulation broadly contemporary with the use of the building contained quantities of Portchester ware.

Description of the postholes (all depths are given below the level of the natural clay surface; the contemporary ground surface was approximately 8 in. above this)

Posthole	Trench/layer	Diameter (in.)	Depth (in.)
545	55/14	18	5
546a	55/13	26	12
546b	55/13	22–3	5
547	55/11	18–23	8
550	55/10	18–23	9
551	55/8	18–23	4
562a	56, ph 1	16	5
562b	56, ph 1	15–24	4
563a	56, ph 2	10	6
563b	56, ph 2	15	2
564	56, ph 3	18	10
565	56, ph 4	15	3
566	56, ph 5	16	3
579	58, ph 1	15	6
580	58, ph 2	13–16	7
591	58, ph 13	19–23	6
592	58, ph 14	17	6
553	55/25	12	5
556	55/24	12–13	3
557	55/23	12	2
569a	56, ph 8	12–13	5
570	56, ph 9	12	5
571	56, ph 10	12	5
572	56, ph 11	11	3
604	58, ph 26	3 × 12	7
605	58, ph 27	4 × 12	7
611	58, ph 33	20	8
615	54, ph 1	20	6
628	54, ph 14	16	—
629	54, ph 15	—	—
937	63, ph 31	14	10
938	63, ph 32	13	10
1174	55, ph 7	26	15

The wall slots

First phase: 54, layers 5 and 12.
55, layer 7.
56, layer 8.
58, layers 7, 10, 12.

Porch: west side, 55, layer 17.
east side, 55, layer 9.
north side, 63, layer 6.

Building S14
(fig. 24 and pl. IV*b*)

Rectangular building measuring 19 by 30 ft. (5·79 × 9·14 m.) constructed of vertical posts set in individual postholes. The north and south walls were built of posts up to 12 in. (0·31 m.) in diameter spaced at intervals averaging 2 ft. 6 in. (0·76 m.) while the east and

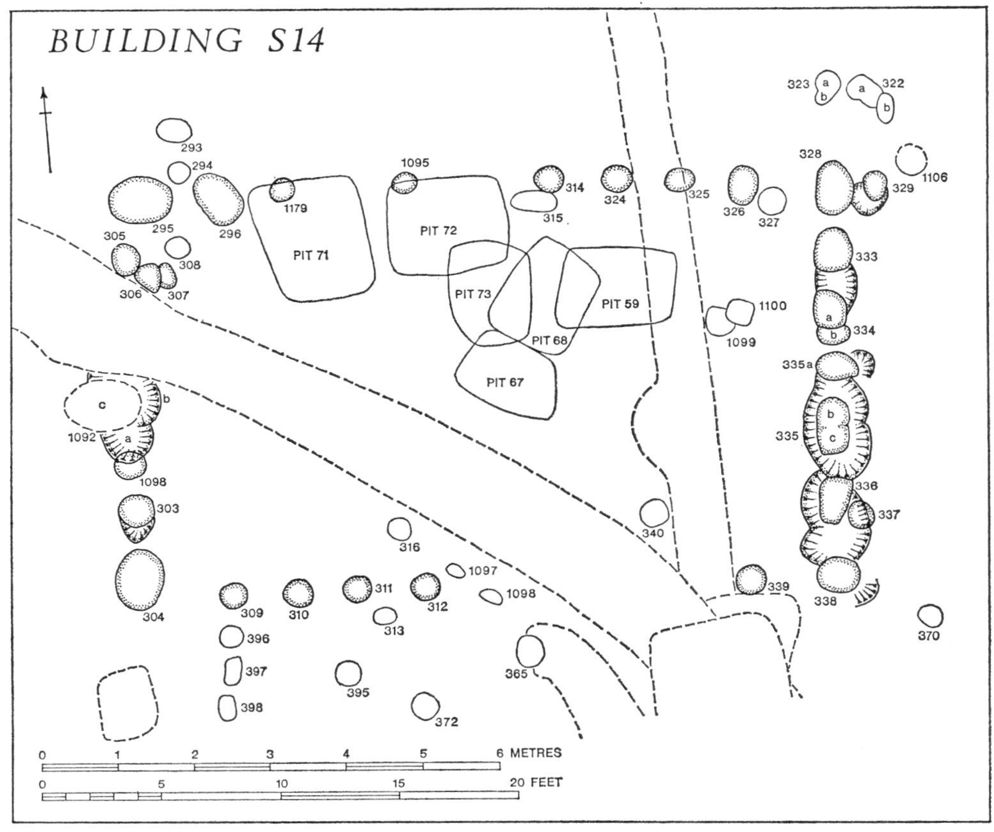

FIG. 24

west walls were built of rather more massive timbers replaced on at least one occasion. The erosion cones which formed around the tops of postholes 303, 1092a, b, 334, 335, 337, suggest that the timbers were uprooted and the voids left open to fill with material eroding from their upper edges. Along the east wall posts 337 and 329 can be shown to pre-date the last phase of the wall: 334a replaced 334b while 335a, b, c would appear to have been contemporary. The only posthole on the line of the west wall which can be shown to be earlier than the latest phase is no. 1098. Post 1092c is later than the eroded posts 1092a, b, and therefore presumably belonged to a period post-dating the use of the building (see p. 56). Fragments of burnt daub were recovered from postholes 333, 334 and 338.

Of the group of late Saxon pits which lie within the line of the walls (pits 59, 67, 68, 71, 72, 73), pits 71 and 72 can be shown to pre-date the building since postholes 1095 and 1179 were cut into the pit fillings.

Independent dating evidence is restricted to potsherds from the following postholes:

333: 1 Saxon sherd in sandy fabric.
335: Portchester ware, 3 body sherds, 1 rim.
337: 1 chaff-tempered sherd.
338: 1 Portchester ware sherd.
339: body sherd of cooking pot.

The building cannot therefore be earlier than the tenth century but is otherwise undated except that it had disappeared by the twelfth century when drainage gullies were cut across its site.

Details of the postholes

Posthole	Trench/layer	Diameter (in.)	Depth (in.)
295	70/38	32–24	10
296	70/13	29–20	5
303	69/25	25–18	7
304	69/18	32–24	12
305	69/38	16–14	6
306	69/35	16	5
307	69/37	15	3
309	69/50	14–13	5
310	69/51	14	5
311	69/45	14–13	6
312	69/46	14	5
314	70/39	14–13	9
324	68/19	15	7
325	68/28	14–12	8
326	68/29	17–15	7
327	68/30	15	9
328	68/17	29–19	10-flint packing
329	68/31	16–11	12
333	67/16	22–19	9
334a	67/17	19–15	8
334b	67/17	17–11	6
335a	67/18	20–14	5
335b	67/18	16	5
335c	67/18	10	8
336	67/19	24–14	10
337	67/20	14–13	6
338	67/21	20–18	7

Posthole	Trench/layer	Diameter (in.)	Depth (in.)
339	67/45	15	6
1092a	69, ph 1	38–27	15
1092b	69, ph 2	15	9
1095	69, ph 4	12	7
1098	69, ph 7	11–6	?
1179	69 (unnumbered)	11	5

Building S15

(fig. 25)

Rectangular building with rounded corners, measuring 42 by 31 ft. (12·80 × 9·45 m.). The main weight of the roof was supported on three pairs of piers, the walls being relatively insubstantial. Of the six piers, the foundation pits and postholes of four remained intact, another had been partially destroyed, while the sixth had been substantially cut away at the top. The detailed characteristics of each are summarized below and on figs. 25 and 27. All six consisted of rectangular post-pits averaging 2 ft. 6 in. (0·76 m.) square cut to a depth of between 20 and 30 in. (0·51 to 0·76 m.) below the contemporary surface. In each had been placed a post of circular section 12–15 in. (0·31–0·38 m.) in diameter packed in position with the redeposited soil and clay derived from the digging of the foundation pit. Four of the posts were placed in the corners of their individual pits, presumably to give greater stability. The other two were more centrally placed. A careful observation of the sections through posts showed a typical 'hour glass' profile of the kind which would have been caused by rocking the post to loosen it before removal. The fact that the post 'voids' were filled from the bottoms with daub, presumably derived from the destroyed walls, lends support to the suggestion that the building was deliberately demolished and useful timbers removed.

Since the six timber piers would have taken much of the weight of the roof, the side and end walls needed to be far less substantially built than those of the other types of house described above. The side walls were here represented by narrow foundation trenches 12–15 in. (0·31–0·38 m.) wide dug to a depth of 1–4 in. (0·03–0·10 m.) below the surface of natural clay, that is on average 10–12 in. (0·25–0·31 m.) below the contemporary ground surface. Within these trenches timbers of circular section had been placed. A few of them seem to have been more deeply bedded than their neighbours and are now represented by individual postholes. The question immediately posed by this observation is, were these the only main uprights, the intervening space being filled with material of lighter construction, or were the walls composed entirely of close-spaced verticals only, some of which were deeply bedded? Although a decisive answer cannot be given, there does appear to be some system in the spacing of the posts as if they were intended to strengthen the curved corners and at least one side of the centrally placed doorways. The fact that quantities of daub with wattle marks were recovered from the vicinity of the slots and from within the building gives added support to the view that there were lighter partition walls between the main uprights. The treatment of the ends of the building seems to have been much the same as the side walls with widely spaced verticals presumably infilled with wattle and daub screen work. Much of the area of the south wall had, however, been destroyed by later grave digging.

The curving of the side walls at the corners is a somewhat curious feature but is clearly implied by the plan of the bedding trenches. It remains a possibility, however, that the walls were originally straight, the ends of the west wall being taken on posts 273 and 507, the south end of the east wall terminating on post 912, while the line of the north end of the wall was represented by the shallow bedding trench shown on fig. 25. The trench was only 1 in.

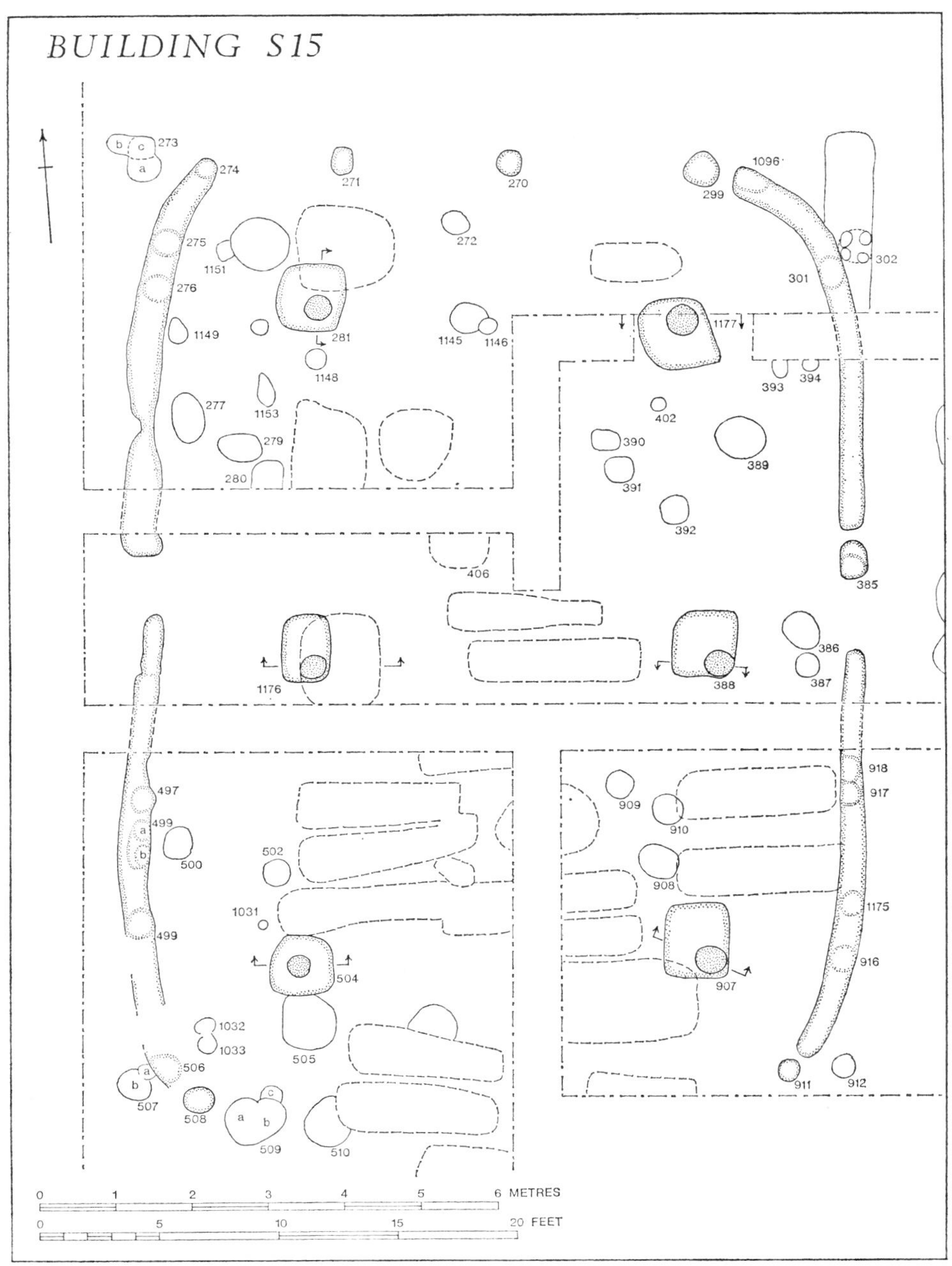

FIG. 25

(0·03 m.) deep below natural and its filling clearly pre-dated the filling of the curved slot. An interesting feature preserved within it was a group of four deep holes arranged in a manner suggestive of stakes driven into the ground to hold the base of an upright timber in position. While proof of a rebuilding is impossible to obtain, the points mentioned here are suggestive.

The chronological position of the building is well established by reference to the cemetery (pp. 60–1) which post-dates its demolition, and the aisle timbers of building S16, the pits for two of which can be shown to cut through the post-pits of building S15.

The pottery evidence relating to the structure may be summarized as follows:

Post 281	(packing):	2 sherds of Portchester ware, 1 rilled; 1 small sherd of white fabric with red paint.
Post 388	(packing):	2 sherds of Portchester ware.
	(void):	3 sherds of ?Portchester ware, 1 hand-made rim.
Post 504	(packing):	1 rilled Portchester ware sherd.
Post 907	(packing):	1 sherd ?Portchester ware.
	(void):	2 Portchester ware sherds, 1 of which is rilled.
Post 1176	(packing):	rim ? late Saxon–early medieval.
Post 1177	(packing):	8 Portchester ware sherds, 3 of which were rims, 1 rilled body sherd.
Wall slot, west:		1 chaff-tempered sherd, 4 Portchester ware sherds, 1 of which is rilled.
Wall slot, east:		7 Portchester ware sherds, of which 1 is a rim, 1 rilled and 1 rouletted.

Constructional details:

The main posts

Post	Trench	Post packing	Post void	Size of pit (in.)	Depth (in.)	Diameter of post (in.)
281	71	layer 25	layer 26	35 × 35	30	12
388	65	layer 20	layer 19	35 × 31	26	13
504	72	layer 57	layer 58	32 × 32	22	11
907	63	layer 16	layer 17	38 × 33	26	14
1176	66	layer 11	layer 10	24 × 36	17	12
1177	69	layer 12	layer 29	38 × 36	24	14

Wall slots

West: general fill: trench 71, layers 11, 27, 28; trench 72, layers 11, 20, 21, 22.
East: general fill: trench 69, layers 16; 65, layer 6; 63, layer 12. Early continuation?: trench 69, layer 21.

Postholes		Trench/layer	Diameter (in.)	Depth (in.)
West:	274	71/29	10	6
	275	71/28	16	7
	276	71/27	15	5
	497	72/20	12–14	6
	499a	72/21	10	6
	499b	72/21	8–10	8

Postholes		Trench/layer	Diameter (in.)	Depth (in.)
	499	72/22	14–15	6
	506	72/27	13–15	3
	508	72/28	15	5
East:	301	69/20	12–18	10
	385	65/6	14–21	8
	916	63, ph 10	12	10
	917	63, ph 13	10	9
	918	63, ph 12	10	9
	1096	69, ph 5	11–18	4
	1175	63–	12	4
North:	270	71/15	13	5
	271	71/13	11–15	4
	299	69/14	16–18	8
South:	508	72/28	15	5

Building S16

(fig. 26)

Rectangular aisled building of which only the aisle posts and one length of wall now survive. If the walls were originally placed in the same relationship to the central supports as in building S15, building S16 would have measured approximately 33 by 30 ft. (10·06 × 9·14 m.).

The six main verticals were placed in rectangular pits averaging 4 by 3 ft. (1·22 × 0·91 m.) and dug to a depth of about 2 ft. (0·61 m.). Where the ghosts of the actual timbers could be recognized they appear to have been squared, some 12 in. (0·31 m.) across and centrally placed in their pits.

The only surviving stretch of wall was discovered on the south side. It was represented by a shallow foundation trench cut to a depth of 8 in. (0·20 m.) below the contemporary surface. In the bottom the holes for a number of wattles were discovered, each wattle having been rammed through the floor of the trench to a depth of about 2 in. (0·05 m.). In spite of a careful search no further trace of walling survived. It is however clear that the entire west wall would have been destroyed by the sixteenth-century foundations, while the south-east corner was much disturbed by later graves. Elsewhere it is possible that some of the postholes shown on fig. 26 belonged to the structure, but proof is lacking. It must be admitted that if the north and east walls were constructed of wattle work and the wattles did not penetrate the natural subsoil, surviving traces may well have been missed.

The main posts show no trace of having been removed deliberately; all evidence points to the stumps having rotted in position, allowing the voids to fill gradually as the result of erosion from the sides. For this reason the positions of the posts were more difficult to recognize than those of building S15.

Two of the post-pits, 55 and 74, cut the fillings of the post-pits of building S15, but the south wall was partly destroyed by one of the graves. No floor surfaces or occupation levels survived the medieval ploughing.

Fig. 26

Pottery from the construction period consists of the following:

Pit 74 (packing): Portchester ware, 7 body sherds, 1 undercut rim.

Pit 76 (packing): Portchester ware, 3 body sherds.

Pit 148 (packing): 1 chaff-tempered sherd and 5 Portchester ware sherds and 3 in flint-gritted ware.
(void): 1 gritty sherd, late Saxon–early medieval.

Pit 153 (packing): 1 green glazed pre-Conquest pitcher sherd, 1 chaff-tempered sherd and 2 Portchester ware sherds, 1 of which is a rim.

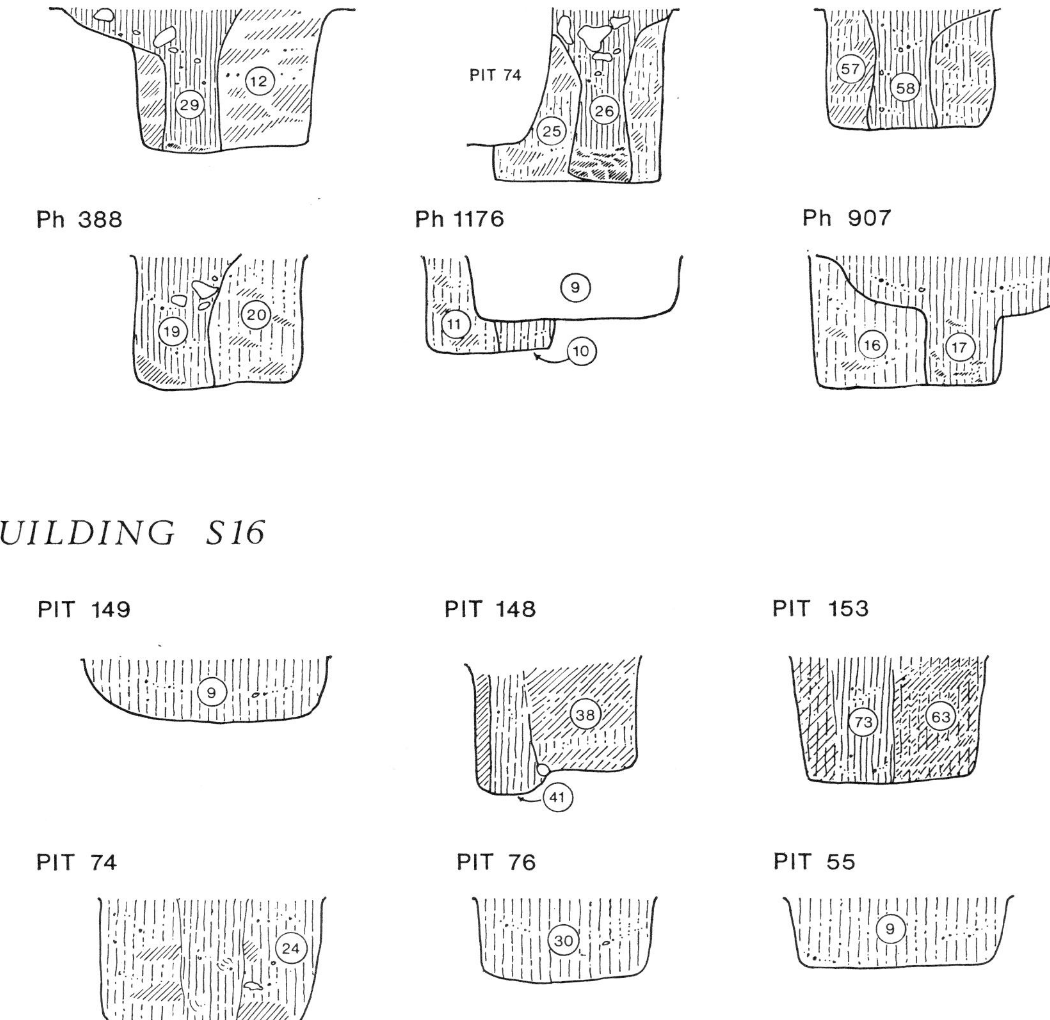

FIG. 27. Sections of the main posts of buildings S15 and S16

Constructional details

(The post-pits of the building were all given pit numbers as well as layer numbers.)

Post	Trench	Post packing	Post void	Size of pit (in.)	Depth (in.)	Diameter of post (in.)
Pit 55	66	layer 9	not differentiated	48 × 39	12	—
Pit 74	71	layer 24	not differentiated	42	21	12
Pit 76	71	layer 30	not differentiated	48 × 36	9	—
Pit 148	96	layer 38	layer 41	48 × 36	24	10
Pit 149	96	layer 39	not differentiated	48 × 34	12	—
Pit 153	96	layer 63	layer 73	42 × 36	23	12

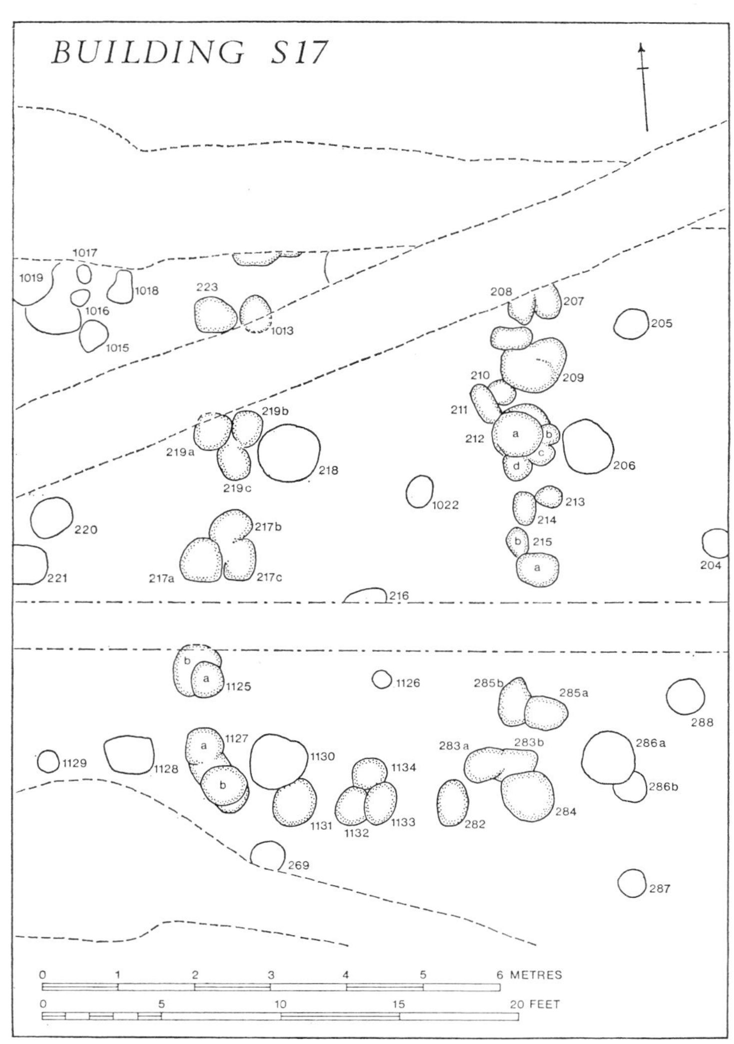

FIG. 28

Building S17

(fig. 28 and pl. VI*b*)

Rectangular building measuring approximately 16 by 26 ft. (4·88 × 7·92 m.). Much of the northern part of the building had been destroyed by a sixteenth-century ditch and an eighteenth-century brick sewer.

The posts of which the building was constructed were replaced on several occasions, the groups 217, 219, 283 and 1132–4 suggesting two phases of replacement subsequent to the initial building, but the northern part of the east wall may well have been rebuilt more often.

Four postholes, nos. 218, 206, 1130 and 286a, may belong to a separate 4-post structure but the point is incapable of proof. Post 1130 is later than post 1131.

No contemporary surface survived the medieval ploughing, nor can the building in any way be related to other Saxon structures.

Pottery from the postholes includes two sherds of Portchester ware from posthole 283 and one sherd from 1130.

Description of the postholes

Posthole	Trench/layer	Diameter (in.)	Depth (in.)
207	74/7	14–18	5
208	74/9	12–14	4
209a	74/8	31–26	6
209b	74/8	21–12	6
210	74/11	8	3
211	74/10	22–10	6-flint packing
212a	74/12	24	17-flint packing
212b	74/12	10	8
212c	74/12	12	10
212d	74/12	14	7
213	74/14	14–10	4
214	74/15	17–11	5-flint packing
215a	74/20	21–17	10-flint packing
215b	74/20	16–10	6
217a	73/27	23–20	12-flint packing
217b	73/27	22–15	8-flint packing
217c	73/27	21–26	6
219a	73/28	18	7
219b	73/28	15	5
219c	73/28	14	4
223	73/15	21–18	7
282	70/17	28–16	7-tile packing
283a	70/15	23–16	3-flint packing
283b	70/15	10	5
284	70/16	27–25	5
285a	70/5	22–18	8
285b	70/5	27–12	3
1013	73, ph 6	16	5

Posthole	Trench/layer	Diameter (in.)	Depth (in.)
1125a	71, ph 1	19–17	8
1125b	71, ph 1	26	7
1127a	71, ph 3	18	4
1127b	71, ph 3	22	10
1131	71, ph 7	22	7
1132	71, ph 8	21	4
1133	71, ph 9	22–15	6
1134	71, ph 10	18	3

Building S18

(fig. 29 and pl. X)

Rectangular masonry structure showing two periods of construction in the second of which the overall measurements were 20 by 19 ft. (6·10 × 5·79 m.).

The first period was represented by two trench-built walls 2 ft. (0·61 m.) wide and 6 in. (0·15 m.) deep, built of flints set in a white chalky mortar. In the second period the early walls were enclosed within more massively constructed masonry, consisting of trench-built footings, averaging 3 ft. (0·91 m.) wide composed of flints set in clay. Upon this foundation a superstructure of flint masonry bonded by a yellow mortar had been erected. Both the inner and outer faces had been rendered with mortar brought to a smooth surface. The overall thickness of the upstanding wall averaged 2 ft. 6 in. (0·76 m.): it survived to a maximum height of two courses on the north side. The south-east corner incorporated a block of tooled upper greensand, possibly removed from a Roman structure.

The position of the doorway has not been defined but the survival of faced superstructure on the west side precludes an entrance here. The western end of the north wall, the centre of the south and the centre of the east are all possibilities. The most likely is the south side, where the surviving mortar wall renderings on either side of the supposed entrance are ill-aligned.

The relationship between the period 1 and period 2 structures is well defined. In the north-west corner the period 1 wall was overlaid by period 2 mortar. In the south-west corner the period 1 wall ended raggedly where it had been cut by the foundation trench for the later footings but the foundation trench narrowed at this point, the earlier footings projecting into it. In the south-east and north-east corners the yellow mortar of period 2 overlay the white period 1 mortar and some lumps of early mortar and flints with early mortar attached were incorporated in the later masonry. The evidence of sequence is therefore clear enough. The ragged ends of the period 1 walls and the re-used early material in the later walls further implies that some of the early structure was destroyed, the possibility being that it originally possessed east and west walls which were totally removed by the east and west walls of the later building.

The floor of the period 1 building survived, consisting of a spread of very chalky mortar (layer 39) up to 1 in. (0·03 m.) thick, continuous except for a strip along the north wall where it had been removed by a medieval gully, and those places where later postholes had

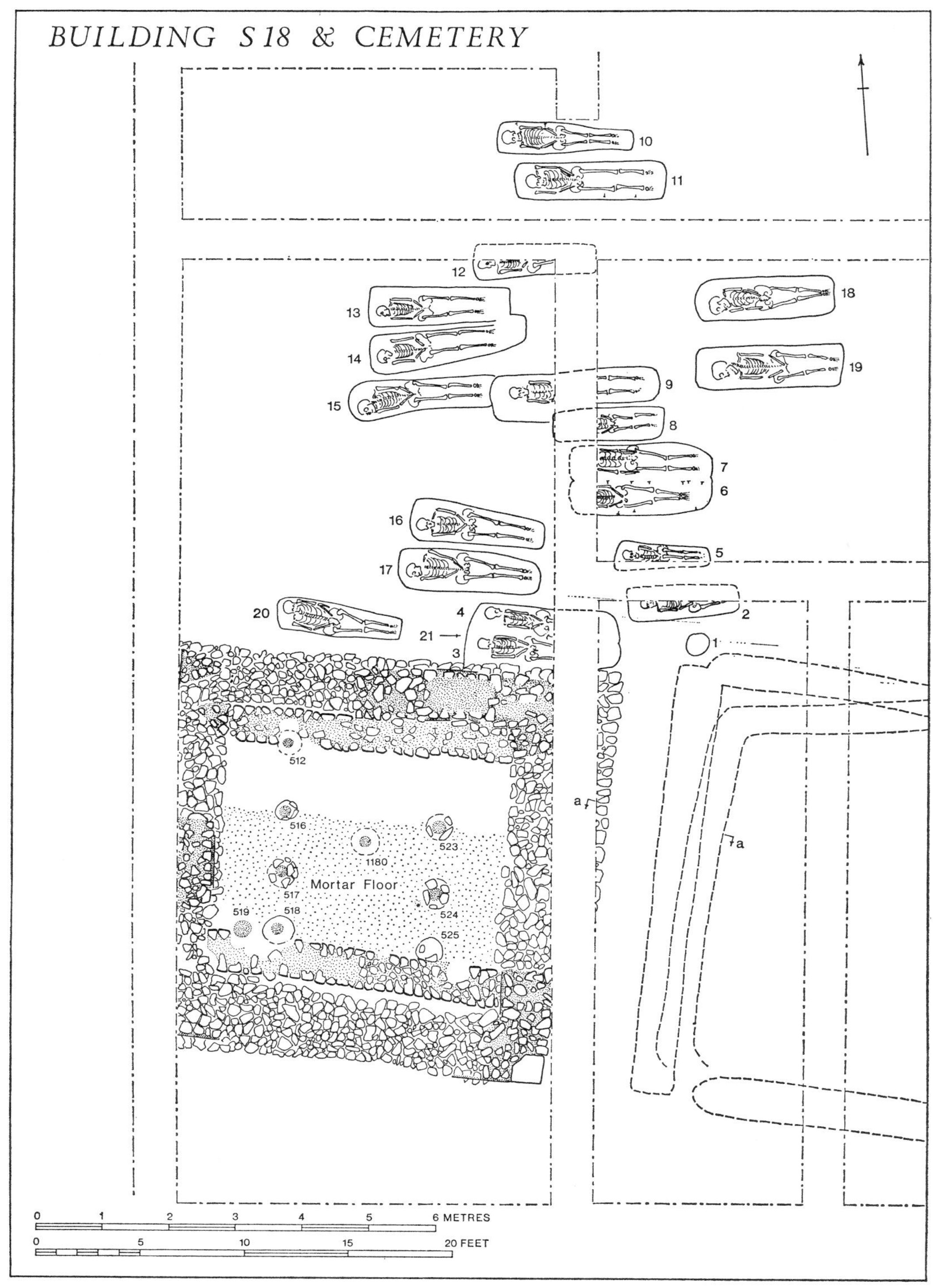
BUILDING S 18 & CEMETERY
10
11
12
13
14
15
9
8
7
6
16
17
5
18
19
20
4
21
3
2
1
512
516
1180
523
Mortar Floor
517
518
519
524
525
a
a
0 1 2 3 4 5 6 METRES
0 5 10 15 20 FEET

FIG. 29

cut through it. Parts of it had been scorched to a reddish colour, particularly along the west side and in the centre. The floor was laid up to the southern period 1 wall, which stood to a height of several inches above it.

The period 2 floor, if one ever existed, had been removed, possibly by contemporary wear. That it is likely to have been higher than the early floor and to have sealed the early walls is suggested by the fact that in the south-east corner the period 2 wall face had been plastered from a level above the remaining stump of the period 1 wall; moreover the top of the foundations of the later wall corresponded to this general level. Thus the combined evidence suggests that the period 1 walls were reduced to their present height at the time of the rebuilding, and that the floor level of the period 2 wall lay above the early footings at a level corresponding now to the top of the late footings and the bottom of the internal plaster rendering.

The only material to survive between the period 1 floor level and the material derived from the destruction of the period 2 building was a layer (layer 34) of grey stony soil some 6 in. (0·15 m.) thick. Through this had been cut nine postholes of which the details are given below. Nos. 512, 516, 517, 518 represent a single row parallel to the west wall, while 523, 524, 525 define a row parallel to the east wall; the possibility remains that a fourth post equivalent to 512 may have been dug to the top of the early wall but not through it, all other trace having been removed by the medieval gully. The centre was occupied by post 1180. No. 519 lay isolated towards one corner. Since the posts had cut the period 1 floor and walls but were sealed by the destruction layer of the period 2 building, they are likely to have belonged to the second period structure. With the exception of no. 519 all were quite small, the posts measuring 6 in. (0·15 m.) in diameter set in flint-packed holes about 12 in. (0·31 m.) across. In each case the void once occupied by the post itself had become filled with yellow mortary rubble.

Various functional explanations are possible for these posts. They could have served as temporary scaffolding during construction, only to be removed when the building was complete: alternatively they might represent internal fittings such as benches, supports for a raised timber floor, side galleries or partitions. On balance, complex internal scaffolding would seem unlikely and it could be argued that so many posts would have been unnecessary for a simple raised floor when all that would have been required were a few joists laid between the destroyed period 1 walls. Thus, supports for side galleries, partitions or for the floor of an upper storey would seem to be the more likely explanations.

The function and nature of the superstructure of the building will be discussed below (p. 60); here it is sufficient to say that no building material other than flints and mortar was recovered, nor is it possible to estimate the original height of the walls, since the structure was robbed in the early medieval period.

The relationship of the period 2 building to building S13 is clearly demonstrated by the section (fig. 23a–a) which shows the building spread belonging to the masonry structure (layer 6) sealing the wall slot of the timber building after the vertical timbers had disappeared. The building can also be shown to be later than grave 3 which it disturbed, but earlier than grave 20 which was cut through the building spread but sealed by the collapsed rubble from the destruction. Since the graves post-date building S15 the masonry structure must also post-date it. The relationship of the period 1 building to the adjacent structures cannot be demonstrated, but it is tempting to think that the graveyard developed while this building was standing.

The disuse of the period 2 structure was followed by the robbing of the walls, in some places down to the level of the footings. All usable flints were removed, the mortar rubbish being thrown back to give rise to layer 33. Later, in the medieval period, a gully was cut through the rubble (layer 40).

Pottery from the layers relating to the structure may be summarized as follows:

From construction layers for the period 2 masonry building: 2 plain cooking pot rims, eleventh-century type.
Soil accumulated on floor after disuse: cooking pot sherds of twelfth-century type.
Robber trench for north wall: glazed pitchers and cooking pots of thirteenth-century type.
Gully cut through robbed building: 2 sherds of thirteenth- to fourteenth-century type.

Description of the postholes

Posthole	Trench/layer	Diameter (in.)	Depth (in.)	Diameter of post (in.)
512	72/54	13	6	7
516	72/49	12	9	6
517	72/50	16	12	7
518	72/51	13	12	6
519	72/55	9+	6	9
523	72/44	15	9	8
524	72/45	19	7	6
525	72/46	15	5	—
1180	72/—	16	6	8

Posthole Complex A
(fig. 30)

Immediately to the north of well (pit) 56 were discovered a number of postholes of similar dimensions which appeared to have a certain regularity in their arrangement. It is possible that they constituted part of a Saxon timber building served by the well, but convincing reconstruction is impossible, with only part of the plan of the supposed building to argue from. The details of the individual postholes are given in Appendix B.

Posthole Complex B
(fig. 31)

A dense scatter of postholes was discovered in the vicinity of the masonry tower, building S18, in layers definitely or probably pre-dating the building. They presumably relate to a structure or structures which occupied the site between the fifth and tenth or eleventh century, but with so much of the plan destroyed by the foundations of the tower, the wall of the sixteenth-century store building and the medieval ditch, it is impossible to offer a convincing interpretation of the remains. Details of the individual postholes are given in Appendix B.

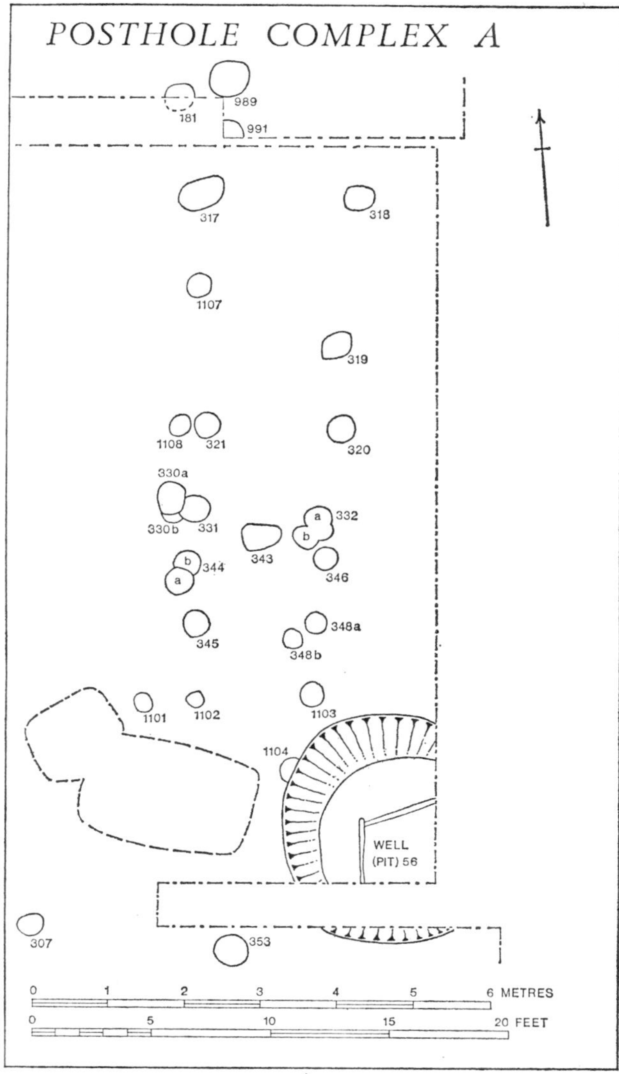

FIG. 30

Posthole Complex C

(fig. 32)

Building S11 lies in the middle of an area dense in postholes (see fig. 103). Since the building itself and its associated spreads of mortar and gravel form a well-defined stratigraphical horizon, it is possible to divide the posts into three groups, those pre-dating the building, those contemporary with it, and those which post-date it. The earliest group is shown in fig. 32A, together with building S4 and pit 220, which both pre-date the tenth-century construction level. The earliest phase of the oven belonging to the house is also indicated since it may have destroyed earlier posts. Of their date all that can be safely said

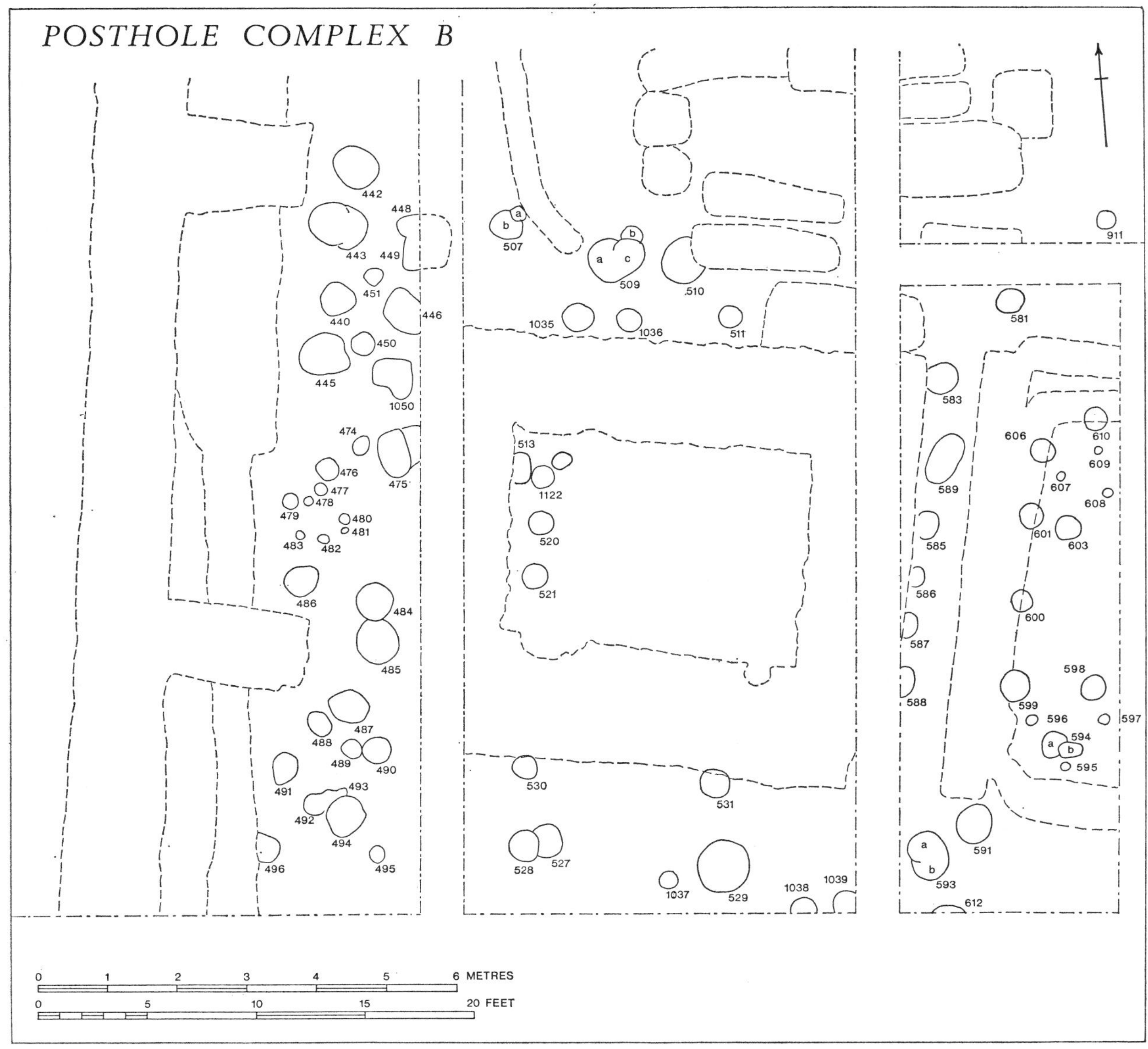

FIG. 31

is that they post-date the late Roman clay layer and pre-date the ninth- to tenth-century building. That some are of Roman origin is likely. It is impossible to isolate any convincing Saxon structures from the scatter.

The postholes shown on fig. 32B post-date the tenth-century building, but pre-date the early medieval level, thus belonging to a restricted period. A certain regularity in the plan suggests that most of them belong to a small building or shed. Details of the postholes shown on fig. 32 will be found in Appendix B.

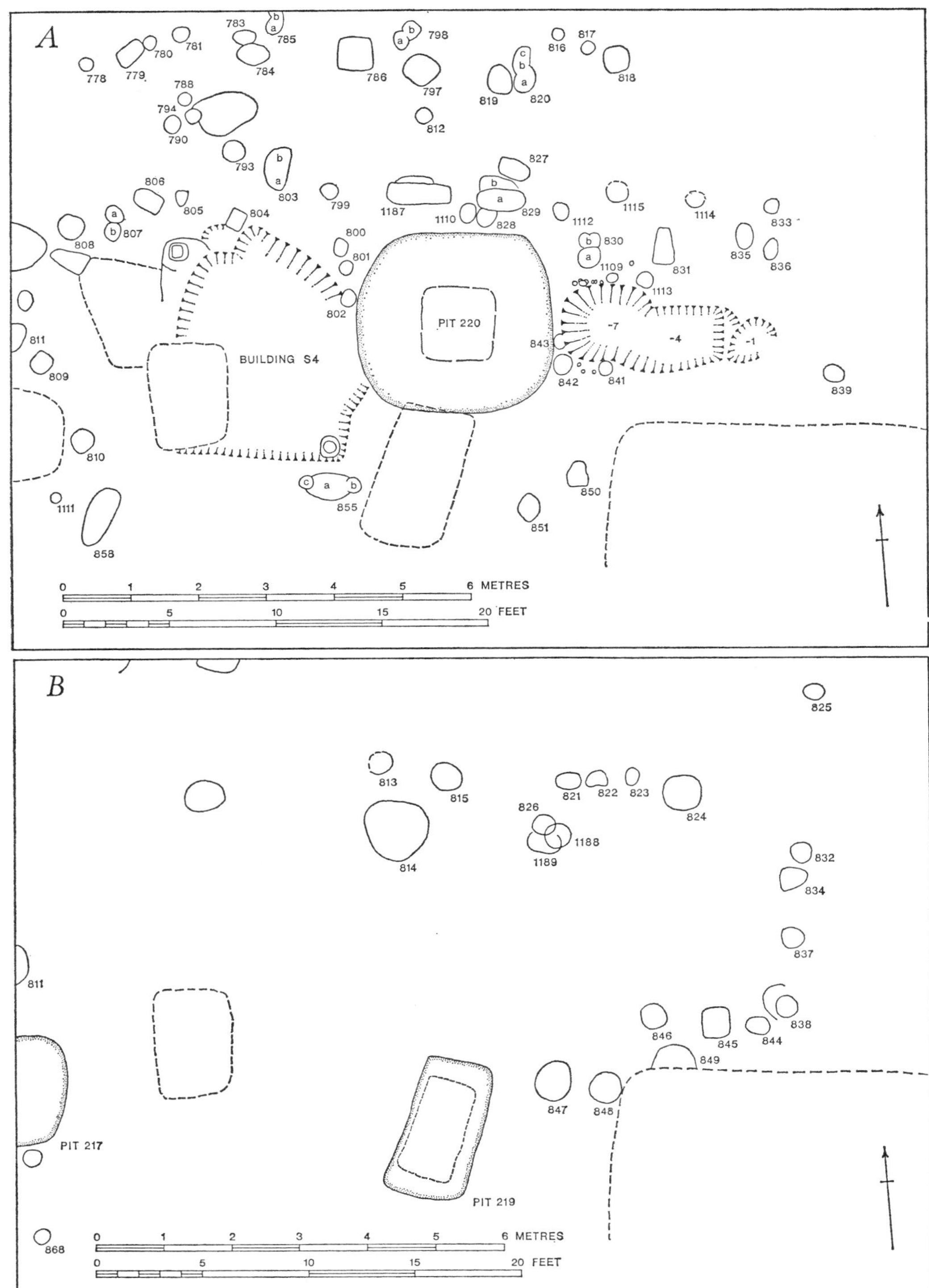

FIG. 32. Posthole complex C: A, below building S11; B, above building S11

Postholes in the Courtyard between Buildings S13, 14 and 15

(fig. 33)

Fig. 33 shows all the postholes discovered in the courtyard enclosed by buildings S13, 14 and 15, with the buildings themselves shaded. If the posts belonging to the early Saxon structure S6 are removed, it will be apparent that some nine large circular holes remain to be explained. Of these, postholes 1181, 384, 1183, 1184 lie in a row contiguous with the corner of building S14: all were packed with redeposited material and presumably once supported posts, but in only one, 384, could the position of the post be recognized: 1182 is similar in size and filling. The remainder, nos. 343, 403, 404, 1182 and 1185, were generally smaller, shallower and with more uniform soil fillings.

The postholes constituting the row do not appear to belong to an undefined building, nor is it necessary to interpret them as buttress posts for building S15. Two explanations are possible: either they represent a fence running between buildings S13 and S14, or, together with posts 1092 and 546a, they form an eastern boundary for the cemetery. This latter explanation, though unproven, is preferred.

Details of the postholes

Posthole	Trench/layer	Diameter (in.)	Depth (in.)	Filling
343	67/43	34	11	Grey stony soil.
384	65/8	34	16	Grey soil and redeposited brick-earth packing a post, the void of which was visible.
403	65, ph 4	30	12	Grey stony soil.
404	65, ph 35	28	11	Dark grey stony soil.
1181	65/7	26×36	14	Black soil mixed with redeposited brickearth.
1182	65/12	40×32	16	Black soil with redeposited brick-earth.
1183	63	36	22	Grey soil with large flints.
1184	63/11	32	17	Packed with grey soil, large flints and redeposited brickearth.
1185	60/17	32	11	Mixed grey soil with some large flints.

TYPES OF BUILDINGS: SUMMARY AND DISCUSSION

(fig. 34)

The 18 buildings described above divide into five types:

(a) Sunken-floor huts	S1, 2, 3, 4
(b) Post-built structures:	
(i) irregular	S5, 6
(ii) regular	S9, 10, 14, 17
(c) Foundation-trench structures	S7, 8, 11, 12, 13
(d) Aisled structures	S15, 16
(e) Masonry tower	S18

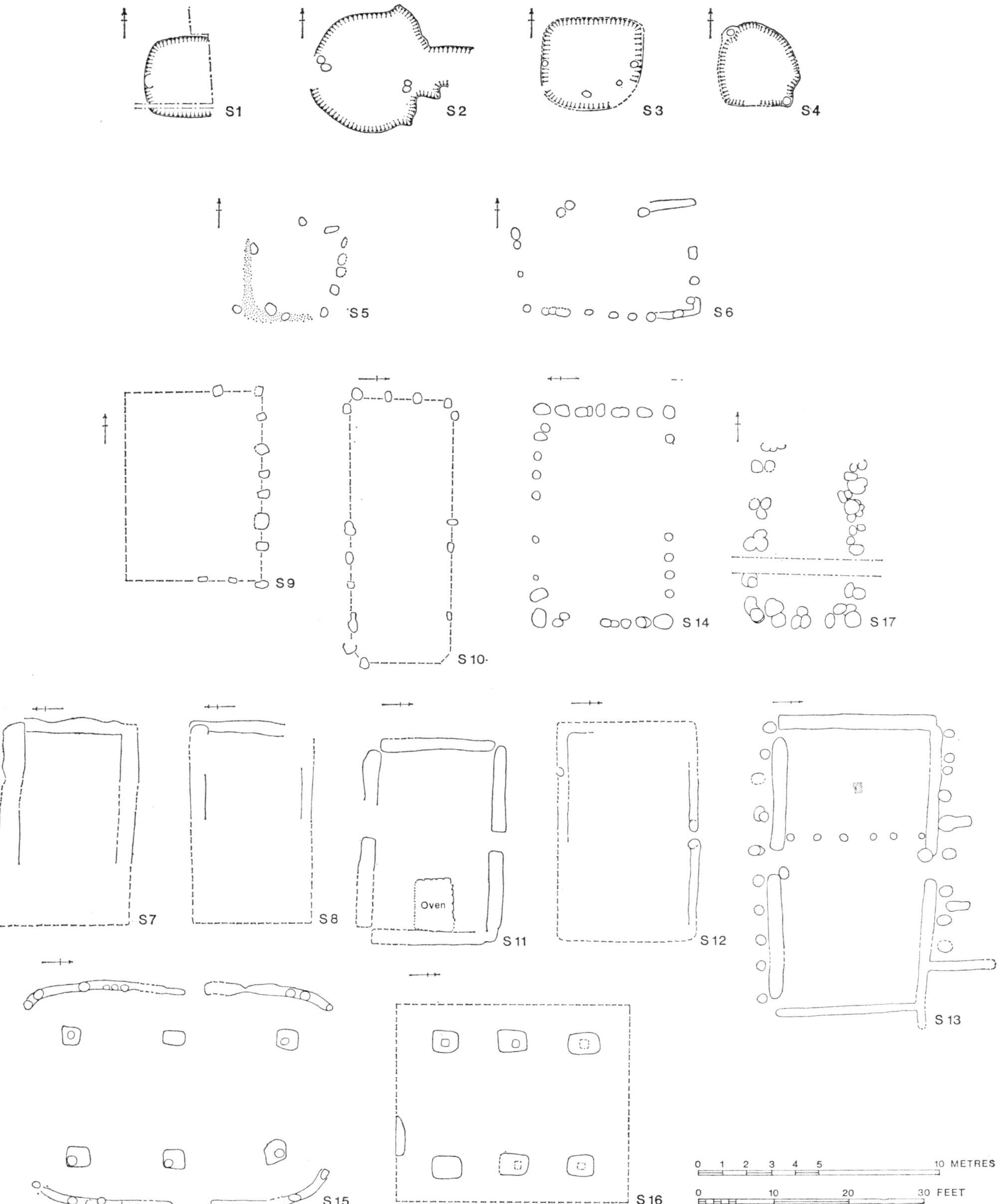

FIG. 34. Comparative plans of all the Saxon timber buildings

(d) *Aisled Structures*

Two aisled buildings were recovered at Portchester, S15 and S16, the one replacing the other, both dating to the period from the mid-tenth to mid-eleventh century. Although the basic structural technique was well known and widely practised in the Roman period (Smith, 1964) and recurs again as a common style from the twelfth century onwards, Saxon examples are unknown except at Portchester. Two explanations are possible; either the constructional technique survived from the Roman period, early and mid-Saxon examples remaining to be discovered, or it died out in Britain in the early fifth century and was re-introduced in late Saxon times. In the present state of knowledge it is necessary to leave the question open.

(e) *Stone-built Tower*

The foundations of the flint-built tower-like structure present difficulties of interpretation. The salient facts may first be summarized: (a) two periods of construction are represented, the second of which is demonstrably later than the last phase of the nearby timber building S13; (b) both phases are associated with the use of the adjacent cemetery; (c) the foundation of the later structure is substantial enough to have supported a considerable superstructure; (d) no trace of contemporary adjacent buildings could be discovered. The reasonable conclusion would seem to be that the second phase structure represented a tall, free-standing building, measuring externally almost exactly 20 ft. square (6·1 m.^{2}), to which certain religious connotations were attached. The contemporaneity of part of the cemetery with the slighter first phase building would imply that it too may have had a religious significance.

The closest parallel to the Portchester structure is with the somewhat larger tower found in the excavations at Sulgrave, Northants (Davison, 1969), for which a pre-Conquest date has been established. Only 20 miles away at Earls Barton, Northants., the well-known church tower appears to have originated as a free-standing structure of late Saxon date, to which the rest of the church was subsequently added. It is probably within this context, of the secular or 'church-and-dwelling' towers of a free-standing type, that the Portchester structure should be placed. The possible social implications of this will be returned to below (p. 303).

THE CEMETERY

(fig. 29 and pl. XI)

A complete cemetery containing 21 burials was discovered immediately to the north of the masonry building S18. The graves were arranged in a compact group extending over an area measuring 27 ft. by 24 ft. (8·23 × 7·32 m.). In general there was little overlapping, with the exception of grave 9, which cut into the end of grave 15 without disturbing the body. Grave 21 however lay above graves 3 and 4, but the skeleton was incomplete and possibly represents the reburial of a partly decomposed body disturbed during the rebuilding of the masonry structure: another collection of bones was reburied in a small hole referred to here as grave 1. With these two exceptions all the burials were extended inhumations, buried supine with heads to the west and with hands to the side or crossed on the pelvis.

No traces of coffins were found but coffin nails were recovered from graves 6, 10, 11 and 20. Grave 10 poses an interesting problem, for the grave, while 18 in. (0·46 m.) wide at the head end, was reduced to only 12 in. (0·31 m.) wide at the feet. If the two nails recovered represent a coffin it must have been extremely narrow. The only general point to be made about the plan of the cemetery is that most of the graves appear to be paired, e.g. graves 10 and 11, 13 and 14, 18 and 19, 8 and 9, 6 and 7, 16 and 17, 3 and 4, and 2 and 5. It is not impossible that a family relationship existed between the individuals in each pair.

The relationship of the cemetery to the late Saxon structures is well established. Grave 7 cut the packing of one of the aisle posts of building S15; grave 13 cut what appears to be the south wall of building S16, while the foundations for the second period of the masonry building S18 cut through the edge of grave 3, possibly, as we have seen, disturbing two bodies later reburied nearby. Only grave 20 can be shown to have been dug after the second period of building S18 and before it was demolished. Thus the cemetery post-dates buildings S15 and 16, but is largely contemporary with the first phase of the masonry building. It continued to be used during the building's second phase. The only direct dating evidence consisted of a few sherds of Portchester ware from graves. All graves contained Roman residual material. In addition to this, graves 12, 14, 15 and 16 produced body sherds of sandy and gritty fabrics of early-mid Saxon type. Sherds of rilled Portchester ware came from graves 3/4, 6 and 17. Nothing later than the early eleventh century was found in any grave.

A detailed account of the skeletal evidence is given below (pp. 235–61).

PLOUGHING

(figs. 101, 102 and pl. XIII*a*)

Traces of ploughing were visible in both areas A and B. In area B, trench 62, plough ruts were found to score through the latest areas of Roman cobbling and a Roman hearth, but were cut by drainage gullies dating to the thirteenth century. Since ploughing would not have begun until some soil had formed over the Roman cobble spread, the activity is unlikely to have commenced much before the middle of the fifth century, but there is no further evidence in this particular trench to demand a Saxon as opposed to an early medieval date.

In area A, plough ruts were found to score the top of the Roman clay bank where exposed in trenches 102 and 103. Here, however, the ploughsoil (section 9, trench 103, layer 23; section 10, layers 44, 46, 47, 48; section 13, layer 33a) could in several places be shown to be sealed by construction and occupation layers dating to the ninth to tenth centuries. Thus ploughing at this point must belong to the early or middle Saxon period.

Although only two areas of plough marks have been distinguished it seems probable that agricultural activity was more extensive. The superficial Roman layers have everywhere been broken up and mixed as might be expected if they had been ploughed: nowhere had a stone-free turf-line formed between Roman and Saxon layers, but only where the plough cut deep were distinguishable marks made on the underlying levels. Over most of the northern part of the site, where some trace might have been expected to have remained, medieval and later activities have destroyed almost all of the earlier stratigraphy. It is therefore impossible to trace the extent of Saxon soil disturbance further north than the presumed Saxon plough ruts in trench 62.

The plan of the individual plough scorings is shown on figs. 101 and 102. Where sectioned the grooves were V-shaped and upright, i.e. showing no sign that the plough had been tilted or the share set at an angle. Marks in one direction only were recorded while the fact that no overlapping occurred might hint at only a limited period of cultivation.

THE PITS AND THE WELLS

In the following section four wells and 57 pits are described. The style of description adopted is much the same as that used for the Roman pits in Vol. I. Each is illustrated with a section and a plan, the salient points of which are briefly described: then follows a list of the pottery, small finds and animal bones[1] suitably cross referenced to the more detailed specialist reports which follow. The pottery from the early and middle Saxon pits is described in some detail here, repeating the descriptions given in the pottery report, while the later Saxon material, which is far more standardized in fabric and form, is more summarily treated.

Of the four wells one, well (pit) 39, was only partially excavated. The remaining three, wells (pits) 56, 135 and 143, were totally examined, all producing evidence of their original timber box-linings, preserved beneath the water level. Well (pit) 39 was in use in the tenth–eleventh century, but the other three were abandoned in the late ninth or early tenth centuries. Well (pit) 135 is of particular importance both for its fine timber work and for the closely stratified sequence of material recovered from it.

There is little that needs to be said in general about the pits. Their characteristics were much the same, with the exception of nos. 192 and 204, which were once lined with planks and may have served as storage pits, while pits 191 and 207 were cesspits of considerable proportions, dug down behind the Roman wall and extending under its footings, possibly so as to improve drainage. As might be expected, pits dug for rubbish disposal or as cesspits tended to occur in groups in areas set aside for the purpose. This is particularly clearly demonstrated by the group later overlaid by building S14, and by the cluster lying to the north of the late Saxon hall complex.

Pit 24 (PC 61, trench 5, pit D)

Circular pit 4 ft. 6 in. (1·37 m.) in diameter dug to a depth of 2 ft. 10 in. (0·86 m.) from the contemporary ground surface, i.e. 1 ft. 8 in. (0·56 m.) below the surface of natural. The sides were vertical and the bottom flat.

The filling consisted of a uniform deposit of black soil mixed with flints, bones and mussel shells. Cut through the mixed Roman and Saxon occupation level, layer 3, but sealed by layer 3a.

[1] In the bone summaries the number following the name of the species is the percentage of the total number of fragments identified, excluding ribs and skull fragments (but including upper jaws with teeth and horn cores). Percentages are corrected to the nearest whole number; where no percentages are given for a pit, too few bones were recovered to make a percentage analysis meaningful. Where no percentage is given for an individual species, that species formed less than 0·5% of the total number of bones recovered for that pit.

The order of species listed for each pit is the order of importance in that pit.

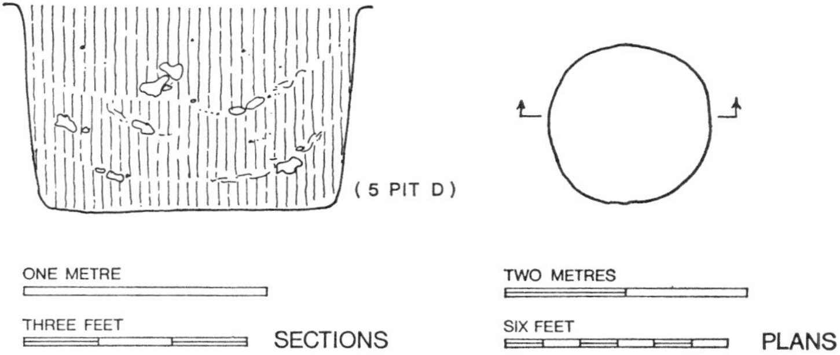

Fig. 35. Pit 24

Pottery. Early–mid Saxon (fig. 104)

1. S12. Rim sherd belonging to an open bowl. Rough surface burnishing on upper part of body with vertical wiping below. Dark grey-brown sandy ware with iron-stained sand grains: fired black.

Human Bone

Distal end of right humerus bearing a sword or knife mark.

Pit 34 (PC 65, trench 54, layer 7a–d)

Rectangular pit approximately 4 ft. (1·22 m.) across, dug to a depth of 4 ft. 9 in. (1·45 m.) below the contemporary surface: the bottom was rounded.

The lowest filling layer (layer 7d) consisted of a deposit of crumbly brown cesspit fill. This was overlaid by successive tips of oyster shells intermixed with some soil. The lowest levels contained quantities of winkles while towards the top was a lens of charcoal and soil (layer 7b).

The top filling of the pit was cut by a construction trench belonging to building S13.

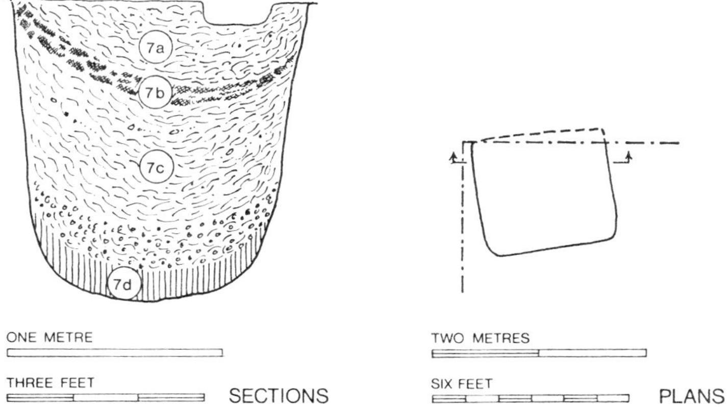

Fig. 36. Pit 34

Small Finds

Flint arrow head (219): late neolithic, see Vol. I, p. 8.

Glass

Rim sherd from a vessel, p. 234, fig. 145, no. 9.

Pottery. Mid Saxon (fig. 104)

2. S29. Jar with an everted rim of which substantial parts survive. Soft grey ware tempered with copious chopped chaff. The surface is burnished and fired to a red-brown colour.

Animal Bones

151 fragments identified (including 26 ribs and 6 skull fragments).
Species represented: sheep, 42; pig, 23; cattle, 19; bird, 10; fish, 4; red deer, 1; fallow deer, 1.

Pit 35 (PC 65, trench 54, layers 8, 13, 14)

Rectangular pit measuring *c.* 5 ft. (1·52 m.) across at the top. The bottom lay at 7 ft. 2 in. (2·18 m.) below the contemporary surface: it was flat and oval in plan measuring 2 by 3 ft.

The lowest layer (layer 14) consisted of crumbly brown soil derived from decomposed cesspit filling. Originally it would have filled the pit but it had compacted to a thickness of 2 ft. 6 in. (0·76 m.). This material was sealed by a layer of marly clay (layer 13) which had slumped considerably in the centre. Above the clay seal, and filling the central hollow caused by the compaction, was a layer of occupation rubbish consisting of black soil and oyster shells (layer 8).

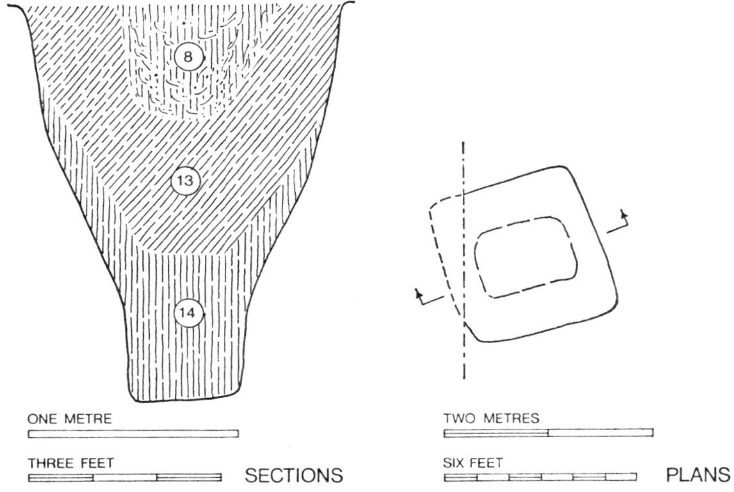

FIG. 37. Pit 35

Small Finds

From layer 14:

Flint flake	(87):	late Neolithic, not illustrated.
Roman bronze coin	(86):	Beata Tranquillitas (A.D. 322–4).
Lead, coiled strip	(95):	not illustrated.
Iron bar	(97):	fig. 134, no. 35.

Pottery. Early–mid Saxon (fig. 104)

From layer 14:

3. S20. Jar with smoothed surface in black sandy ware.

Animal Bones

65 fragments identified (including 11 ribs and 1 skull fragment).
Species represented: cattle, 38; bird, 23; sheep, 21; pig, 19.

Pit 37 (PC 66, trench 60, layers 10, 11, 12, 13)

Rectangular pit measuring 8 by 7 ft. (2·44 × 2·13 m.) cut to a depth of 3 ft. 4 in. (1·01 m.) below the top of natural.

The lowest layer (layer 13) was derived from the weathering of the pit sides giving rise to a mixture of leached chalk and soil. Above was a layer of decomposed cesspit filling of crumbly brown soil mixed with lenses of bone, oyster shells and pottery (layer 12). This was sealed by grey clayey soil containing large flints (layer 11). The upper part of the pit was filled with grey soil and occupation rubbish (layer 10).

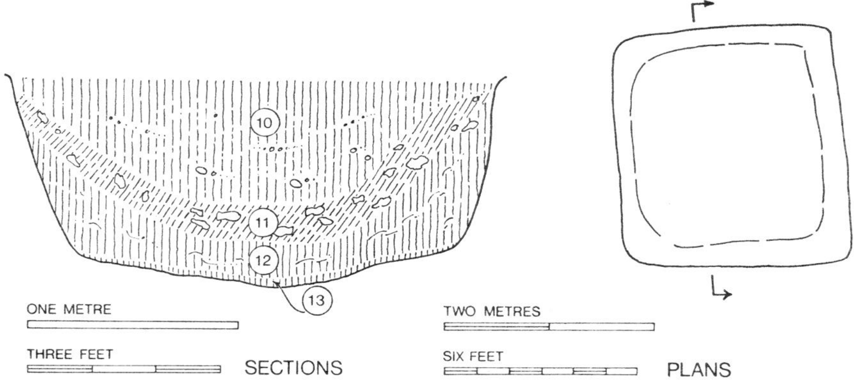

Fig. 38. Pit 37

Small Finds

From layer 10:

Roman bronze coin	(110):	Constantine I (A.D. 317–24).
Roman bronze coin	(111):	Constantine I (A.D. 317–20).
Bronze strap-end	(112):	fig. 136, no. 51.

From layer 12:

Roman bronze coin	(117):	totally illegible, probably Roman.
Iron knife	(113):	fig. 133, no. 21.

Pottery. Late Saxon (figs. 118–9)

Portchester ware and associated types, nos. 316–340.
Not illustrated: 62 body sherds; 34 in fabrics with flint and chalk tempering, 28 in Portchester ware of which 10 are rilled.

Animal Bones

144 fragments identified (including 14 ribs and 4 skull fragments).
Species represented: bird, 39; sheep, 29; cattle, 18; pig, 13; fallow deer, 1.
This pit contained a high percentage of bird bones.

Pit 38 (PC 66, trench 60, layers 9a and 9b)

Rectangular pit 6 ft. by 6 ft. 8 in. (1·83 × 2·03 m.) with a flat bottom, cut to a depth of 2 ft. 2 in. (0·66 m.) below the level of natural.

The lower filling (layer 9b) was typical grey-brown crumbly decomposed cesspit filling. It was sealed by tips of occupation rubbish composed of grey stony soil mixed with flints, oyster shells and several pieces of iron slag.

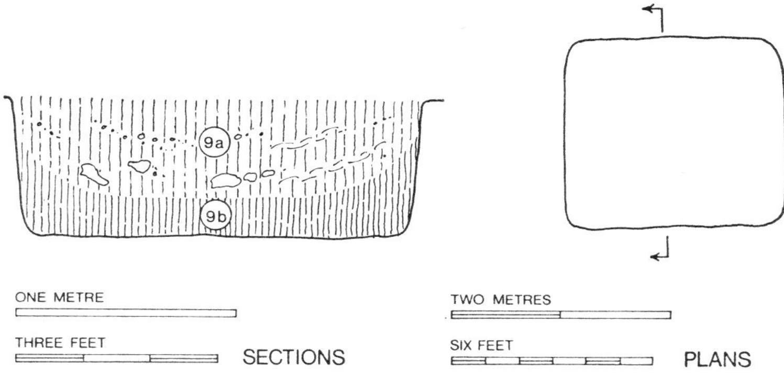

Fig. 39. Pit 38

Small Finds

From layer 9a:

Roman bronze coin	(205):	Victorinus (A.D. 268–90).
	(206):	Gloria Exercitus (A.D. 335–41).
Iron knife	(121):	fig. 133, no. 26.
Bone comb fragment with iron rivet	(207):	fig. 140, no. 73.
Shale spindle whorl	(114):	fig. 141, no. 81.

Pottery. Early–mid Saxon (fig. 104)

4. S51. Jar with everted rim slightly hollowed inside. Coarse black sandy ware with chaff tempering. The surface is unsmoothed.
5. S52. Upright rim. Fine black sandy ware, smoothed surface.
6. S56. Sherd near rim. Fine black sandy ware, burnished surface.
7. S55. Jar rim. Dark grey sandy ware fired red-brown on the surface. Burnished.
8. S54. Rim. Black sandy ware with flakes of mica. Smoothed surface.
9. S53. Rim. Black sandy ware, smoothed surface.

10. S50. Body sherd in a light grey sandy ware containing large flakes of mica. The surface has been decorated using a plain square stamp shallowly impressed.
11. S57. Body sherd, smooth black sandy ware tempered with chaff. The surface has been burnished and decorated with horizontal grooves.

Not illustrated: 13 body sherds: 4 chaff-tempered, 6 in sandy ware, 3 gritted.

Animal Bones

95 fragments identified (including 27 ribs and 4 skull fragments).
Species represented: sheep, 44; cattle, 34; pig, 17; bird, 3; fish, 2.

Pit (Well) 39 (PC 66, trench 60, layer 18; trench 63, layers 10, 10b)

Large well with the top eroded into a wide funnel 8 ft. (2·44 m.) in diameter: the circular shaft was originally 5 ft. 9 in. (1·76 m.) in diameter.

The bottom of the well was not reached at the limit of excavation 12 ft. (3·66 m.) below the surface of the natural clay. In excavation a distinction was made between the lower level

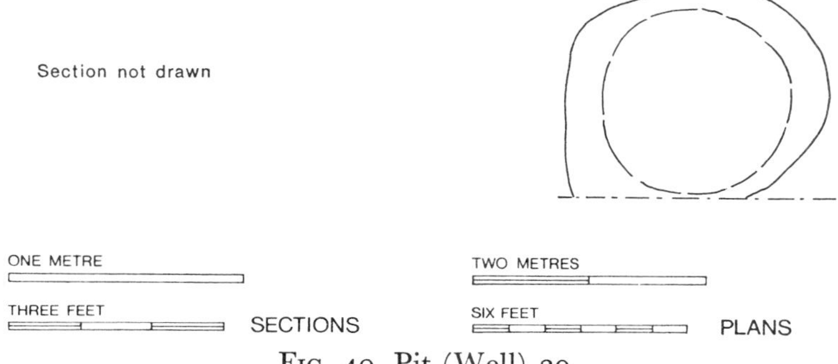

FIG. 40. Pit (Well) 39.

(layer 10b), from 12 ft. to 9 ft. 6 in. (3·66 to 2·90 m.) which was entirely waterlogged, and the upper fill (60, layer 18 and 63, layer 10) from 9 ft. 6 in. (2·90 m.) to the surface. The filling, however, was entirely uniform, consisting of grey stony soil mixed with flints, Roman tiles, lumps of stone and some fragments of daub showing wattle marks. There was no evident stratification, except for a more stony layer at 9 ft. (2·74 m.) and a thick lens of winkle shells in the top. It would appear that the entire shaft had been deliberately filled with rubbish in a short space of time.

Small Finds

From layer 10:

Roman bronze coin	(169):	Aurelian (*c.* A.D. 300).
Iron hook	(218):	fig. 130, no. 7.

From layer 10b:

Decorated bone strip	(220):	fig. 140, no. 67.

Pottery. Late Saxon (fig. 120)

Portchester ware and associated types, nos. 341–361.

Animal Bones

243 fragments identified (including 52 ribs and 5 skull fragments).
Species represented: cattle, 53; sheep, 22; pig, 15; red deer, 4; bird, 3; roe deer, 2; hare, 1.

Pit 42 (PC 66, trench 62, layer 13)

Small circular pit 3 ft. 6 in. (1·07 m.) in diameter and cut to a depth of 6 in. (0·15 m.) below the top of the natural surface.

Filled with black soil mixed with some clay. The pit cut pit 43.

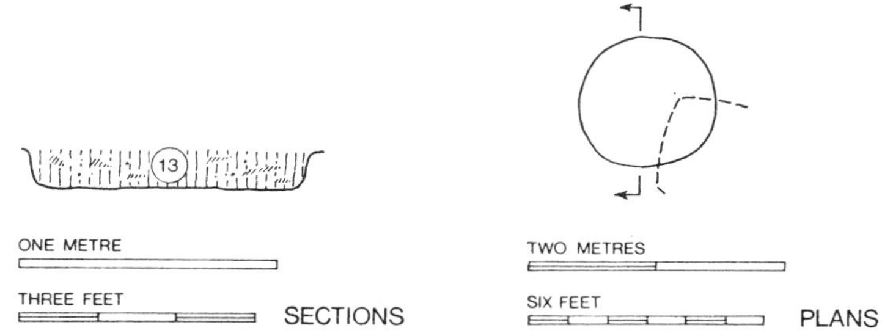

FIG. 41. Pit 42

Pottery. Late Saxon

Not illustrated: 4 Portchester ware body sherds.

Animal Bones

8 fragments identified (including 2 ribs).
Species represented: cattle, sheep, pig.

Pit (*Well*) *56* (PC 67, trench 67, layers 7, 28, 38, 39, 40, 41)

Circular well shaft *c.* 4 ft. 9 in. (1·45 m.) in diameter at the base, but with an erosion cone *c.* 9 ft. (2·74 m.) across. The shaft was dug to a depth of 14 ft. 6 in. (4·42 m.). The well lining was composed of 2 in. (0·05 m.) thick planks placed on edge (pl. XIV*a*), butted up to each other, and held in place by vertical poles driven into the bottom of the well at the corners. Only the lowest frame survived below the water table, those above having rotted. The space between the timber lining and the side of the well pit had been packed with chalky marl which had gradually eroded into the shaft as the planking rotted.

The lowest layer (layer 41), consisting of a deposit of black silty soil mixed with animal bones, represented the primary silting before erosion began. Thereafter (layers 39 and 40), came a considerable thickness of eroded clay and marl, derived from the weathering of the pit sides, mixed with tips of occupation rubbish and eventually sealed by a layer of flints (layer 38). The filling of the upper part of the shaft represented a more gradual accumulation of soil, stones and occupation rubbish (layer 28). The remaining hollow was filled eventually with flints and soil (layer 7).

Small Finds

From layer 28:

Roman bronze coin	(237):	Constantine (copy) (A.D. 330–45).
Gilded bronze binding strip	(235):	fig. 139, no. 62.
Gilded bronze binding strip	(236):	fig. 139, no. 63.
Iron rod	(286):	fig. 134, no. 34.
Bone pin beater	(238):	fig. 140, no. 65.

Pottery. Lower layers early–mid Saxon, upper layers late Saxon (fig. 104)

From layers 38–41:

12. S354. Rim, hard black sandy ware containing flecks of mica. Burnished surface.
Not illustrated: 2 body sherds of grey-black sandy ware tempered with chaff.

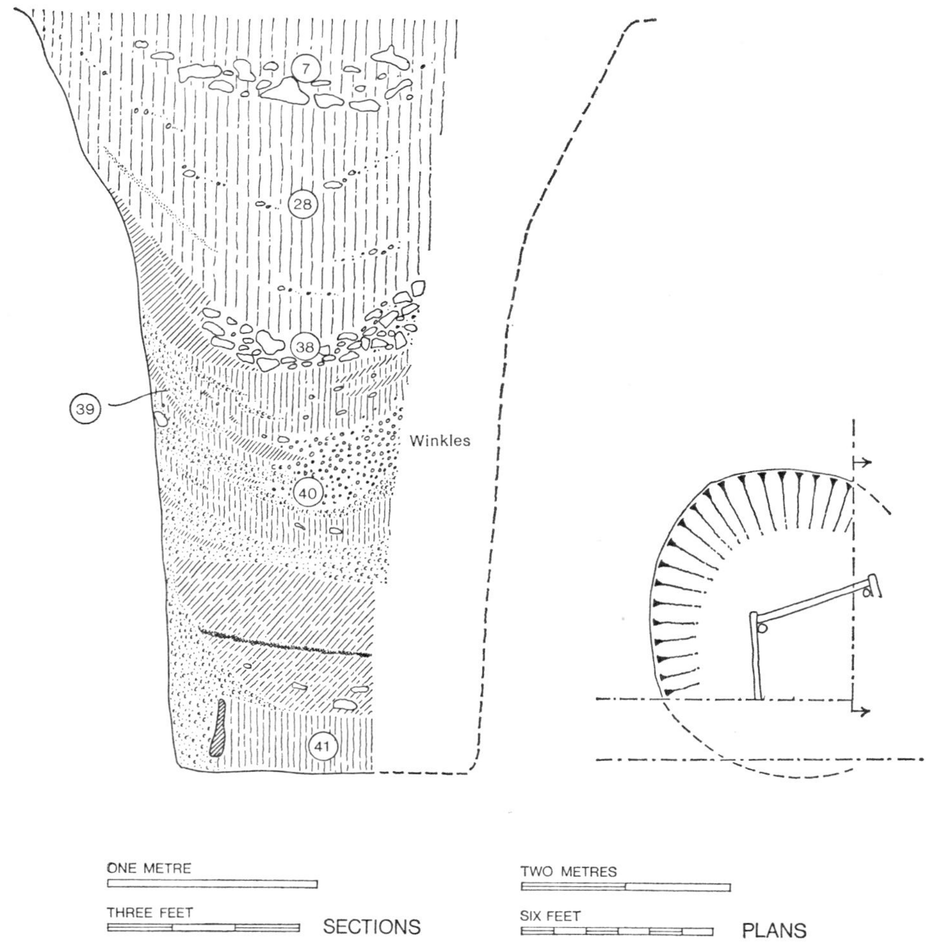

Fig. 42. Pit (Well) 56

From layer 28:

Not illustrated: 28 sherds: Portchester ware, 1 hollowed rim with rilled body and 5 body sherds; flint and chalk tempered wares, 8 rims and 24 body sherds.

From layer 7:

Not illustrated: a few body sherds including early medieval.

Animal Bones

From layers 34–41:

131 fragments identified (including 49 ribs and 15 skull fragments).

Species represented: sheep, 34; bird, 25; pig, 18; cattle, 13; horse, 7; roe deer, 2.

The remains of a neo-natal pig and sheep were found in this pit.

From layer 28:

263 fragments identified (including 69 ribs and 19 skull fragments).

Species represented: ox, 35; sheep, 28; pig, 18; bird, 9; horse, 4; red deer, 2; roe deer, 1; cat, 1; dog, 1; hare, 1; vole, 1.

Pit 58 (PC 67, trench 67, layer 10)

Small rectangular pit *c.* 3 by 4 ft. (0·91 × 1·22 m.) cut to a depth of 1 ft. 3 in. (0·38 m.) below the level of natural.

Filled with a uniform deposit of grey crumbly soil with few stones.

Pit 58 was cut by pit 57.

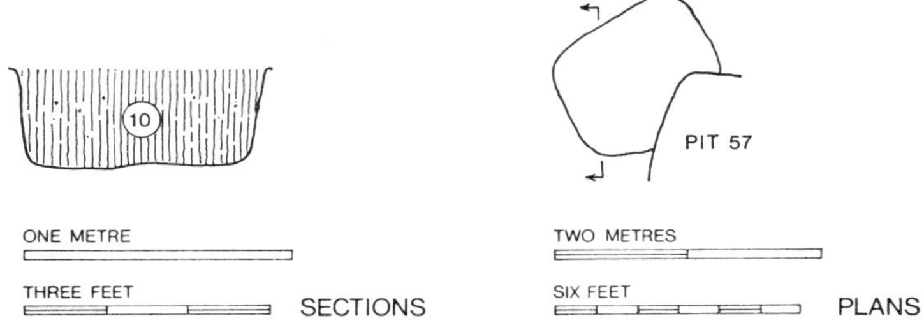

Fig. 43. Pit 58

Pottery. Late Saxon (fig. 121)

Portchester ware types: no. 362.

Not illustrated: 5 body sherds; Portchester ware, 2 rilled and 1 base; flint and chalk-tempered ware, 2 sherds.

Animal Bones

33 fragments identified (including 5 ribs and 2 skull fragments).

Species represented: sheep, cattle, pig, bird.

Pit 59 (PC 67, trench 67, layer 23)

Rectangular pit 5 ft. by 3 ft. 6 in. (1·55 × 1·06 m.) cut to a depth of 1 ft. 9 in. (0·53 m.) below the level of the natural surface.

Filled with a uniform crumbly brown soil.

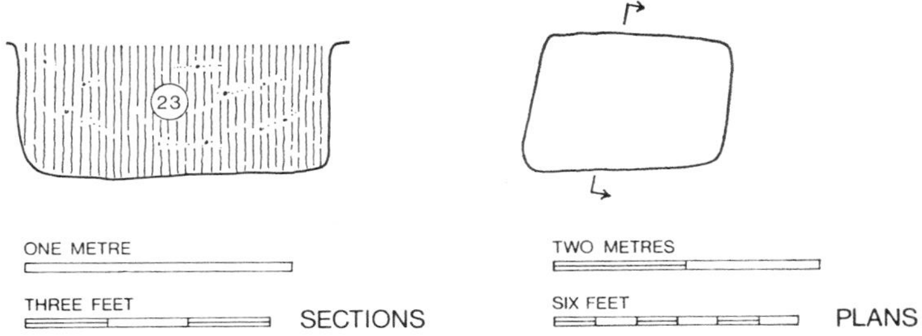

FIG. 44. Pit 59

Pottery. Late Saxon (fig. 121)

Portchester wares and associated types, nos. 363, 364.

Not illustrated: 28 body sherds; Portchester wares, 12 sherds of which 3 are rilled; coarse ware cooking pots, 16 sherds.

Animal Bones

33 fragments identified (including 9 ribs and 2 skull fragments).

Species represented: sheep, cattle, pig, bird, dog.

Pit 67 (PC 67, trench 69, layer 30)

Sub-rectangular pit 4 ft. 6 in. by 3 ft. (1·37 × 0·91 m.) cut to a depth of 1 ft. 2 in. (0·35 m.) below the natural surface.

Filled with a uniform mixture of black soil with some wads of redeposited natural brickearth.

Pit 67 cut into pit 68.

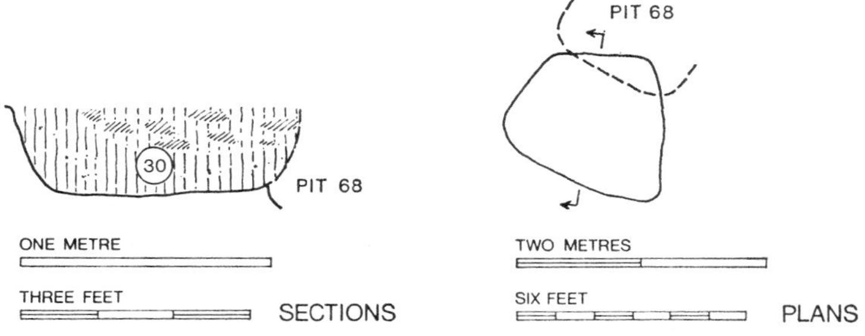

FIG. 45. Pit 67

Pottery. Late Saxon (fig. 121)

Portchester ware and associated types, nos. 366, 367.

Not illustrated: 8 body sherds, all in grey-brown ware with crushed flint and chalk tempering.

Animal Bones

119 fragments identified (including 35 ribs and 10 skull fragments).

Species represented: cat, 27; pig, 22; bird, 20; cattle, 16; sheep, 15.

The high percentage of cat bones in this pit is caused by the presence of the skeleton of a young cat.

Pit 68 (PC 67, trench 69, layer 31)

Sub-rectangular pit 4 ft. 6 in. by 3 ft. 6 in. (1·37 × 1·06 m.) cut to a depth of 1 ft. 4 in. (0·40 m.) below the level of the natural clay.

Filled with a uniform mixture of soil with some flints and wads of redeposited clayey marl.

Pit 68 was cut by pits 67 and 73: its relationship to pit 59 was not defined.

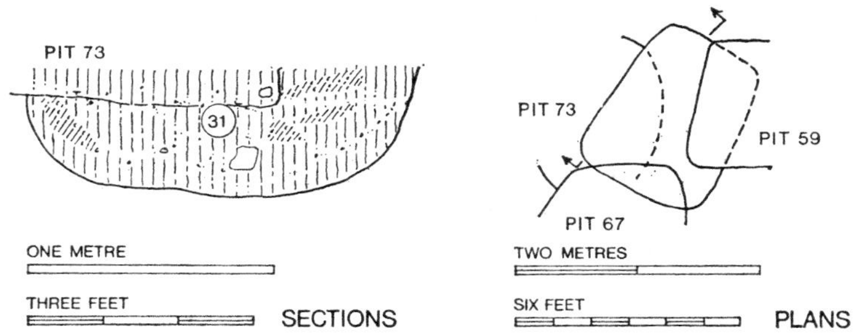

Fig. 46. Pit 68

Small Finds

Iron hooked bar	(356):	fig. 131, no. 14.
Iron strip	(317):	fig. 134, no. 29.

Pottery. Late Saxon (fig. 121)

Portchester wares and associated types, no. 365.

Not illustrated: 16 body sherds; Portchester ware, 8 sherds of which 3 are rilled; coarse cooking pots, 8 sherds.

Animal Bones

120 fragments identified (including 31 ribs and 7 skull fragments).

Species represented: bird, 38; sheep, 28; pig, 19; cattle, 9; frog, 4; red deer, 1; fox, 1.

Pit 71 (PC 67, trench 69, layers 32, 43, 42)

Sub-rectangular pit 5 ft. 6 in. by 4 ft. 6 in. (1·70 × 1·37 m.) dug to a depth of 2 ft. 3 in. (0·69 m.) below the level of natural clay.

The lowest filling (layer 42) consisted of green-grey crumbly cesspit fill. It was sealed by a layer of redeposited brickearth (layer 43) above which the filling was of grey soil and occupation debris (layer 32).

Small Finds

From layer 32:

Roman bronze coin	(360):	Constantine I (A.D. 308–13).
Iron bar	(328):	fig. 135, no. 39.
Iron fragment	(329):	not illustrated.

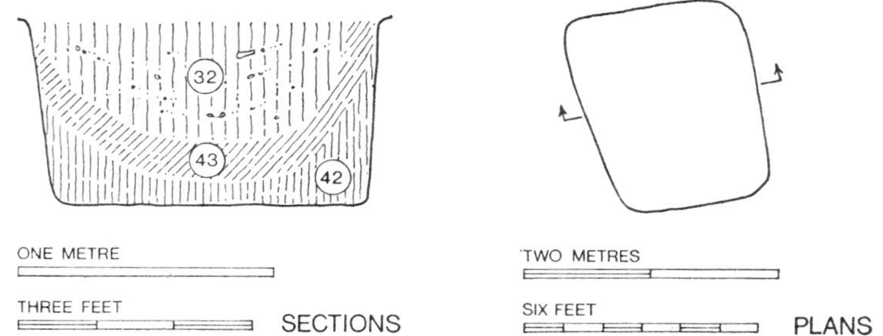

FIG. 47. Pit 71

Pottery. Late Saxon (fig. 121)

From layer 32:

Portchester ware and associated types, nos. 369–372.

Not illustrated: 18 sherds; Portchester ware, 10 body sherds of which 3 are rilled; coarse cooking pots, 8 body sherds.

From layer 42:

Portchester ware and associated types, nos. 368, 373.

Not illustrated: 11 body sherds; Portchester ware, 3; coarse cooking pots, 8.

Animal Bones

89 fragments identified (including 6 ribs and 3 skull fragments).

Species represented: bird, 39; sheep, 23; cattle, 20; pig, 10; fish, 6; red deer, 1; horse, 1.

This pit contained a high percentage of bird bones.

Pit 72 (PC 67, trench 69, layers 39, 40, 41)

Sub-rectangular pit 5 ft. by 4 ft. (1·52 × 1·22 m.) cut to a depth of 2 ft. (0·61 m.) below the level of natural clay.

The lower filling (layer 41) consisted of grey crumbly cesspit filling sealed by a layer of clayey marl (layer 40). Above this came a mixture of grey soil and occupation rubbish with some redeposited clay towards the top (layer 39).

Pit 72 was cut by pit 73.

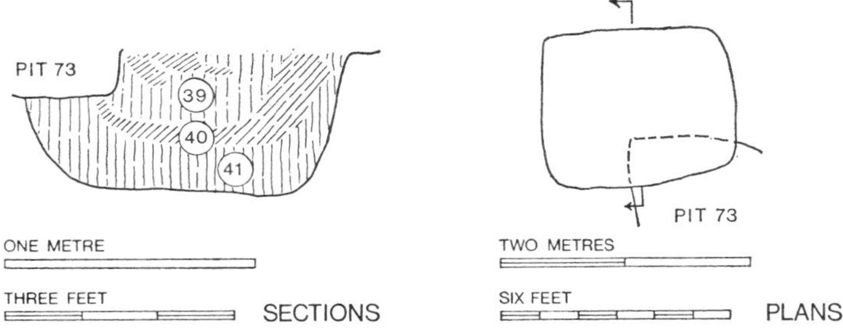

FIG. 48. Pit 72

Small Finds

From layer 39:

Iron disc	(330):	fig. 130, no. 6.
Iron horse shoe	(332):	fig. 131, no. 9.
Iron fragment	(331):	fig. 135, no. 38.
Iron fragment	(333):	fig. 134, no. 31.

Pottery. Late Saxon

From layer 39:

Not illustrated: 8 body sherds: Portchester ware, 7, of which 1 is rilled; coarse cooking pots, 1.

From layer 40:

Not illustrated: 2 Portchester ware body sherds.

Pit 73 (PC 67, trench 69, layer 34)

Irregular pit averaging 4 ft. (1·22 m.) across, cut to a depth of 6 in. (0·15 m.) below the level of the natural clay.

Filled with greenish-grey soil mixed with flints.

Pit 73 cut into the tops of pit 72, 67 and 68.

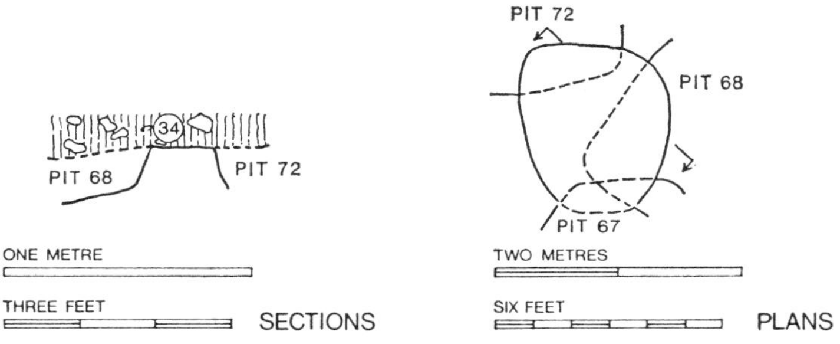

FIG. 49. Pit 73

Pottery. Late Saxon (fig. 121)

Portchester wares and associated types, nos. 374, 375.

Not illustrated: 17 body sherds; Portchester ware, 11 sherds, one of which is rilled; coarse cooking pots, 6 sherds.

Pit 80 (PC 68, trench 73, layer 39)

Irregular pit *c.* 3 ft. 6 in. (1·07 m.) in diameter, dug to a depth of 1 ft. 10 in. (0·56 m.) below the level of natural clay.

The filling (layer 39) consisted of black soil mixed with wads of redeposited natural brickearth. The upper part contained large flints.

Pottery. Late Saxon

Not illustrated: 8 sherds; Portchester ware, 6, of which 2 are rilled and 1 rouletted; coarse cooking pots, 1 rim, 1 sherd.

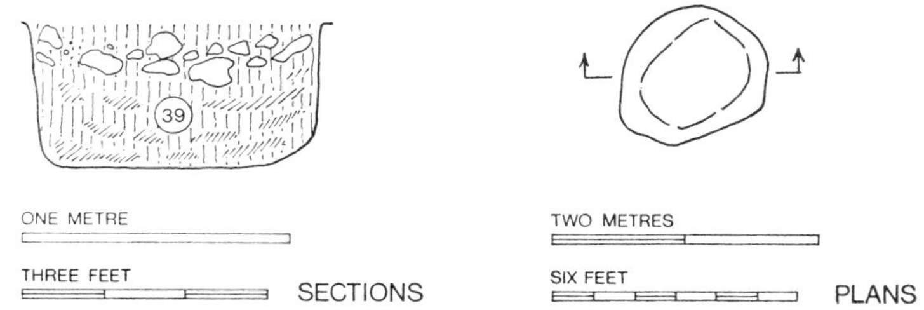

FIG. 50. Pit 80

Animal Bones

5 fragments identified.
Species represented: cattle, sheep, pig.

Pit 89 (PC 68, trench 74, layers 30, 49 and 50)

Rectangular pit measuring 6 ft. by 2 ft. 3 in. (1·83 × 0·69 m.) cut to a depth of 3 ft. (0·91 m.) with a roughly rectangular annex, only 1 ft. 6 in. (0·46 m.) deep on the north side.

The lower filling (layer 50) consisted of black soil mixed with lenses of stones, occupation rubbish and clay. This was sealed by a layer of brickearth containing flints towards the base (layer 49). The upper filling (layer 30) was of black soil, chalk and flint.

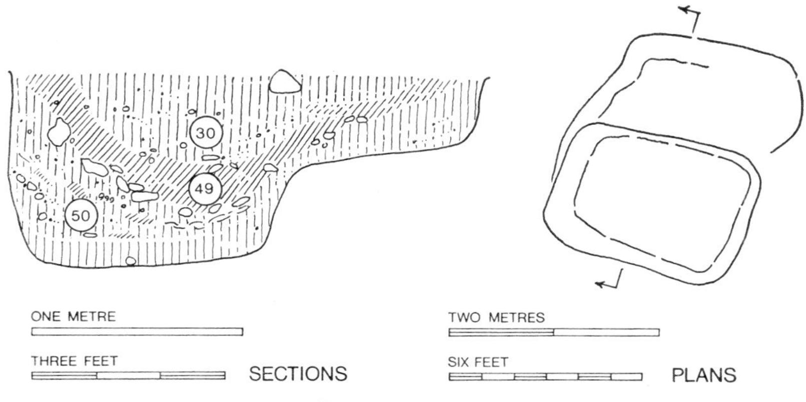

FIG. 51. Pit 89

Small Finds

From layer 50:
Roman bronze coin (810): Constantine I (A.D. 308–17).

Pottery. Late Saxon (fig. 122)

Portchester ware and associated types nos. 376–384.
Not illustrated: 133 sherds: Portchester ware, 10 hollow and undercut rims, 41 rilled sherds and 68 body sherds; coarse cooking pots, 3 rims and 11 body sherds.

Pit 91 (PC 68, trench 74, layers 29, 66, 67)

Circular pit 5 ft. (1·52 m.) in diameter, cut to a maximum depth of 3 ft. (0·91 m.) below the surface of natural clay.

The lower filling (layer 67) consisted of fine grey-black soil, possibly decomposed cesspit fill, streaked with flecks of charcoal. It was sealed by a thin lens of redeposited brickearth (layer 66) above which was a thickness of grey-brown soil mixed with flints and occupation debris.

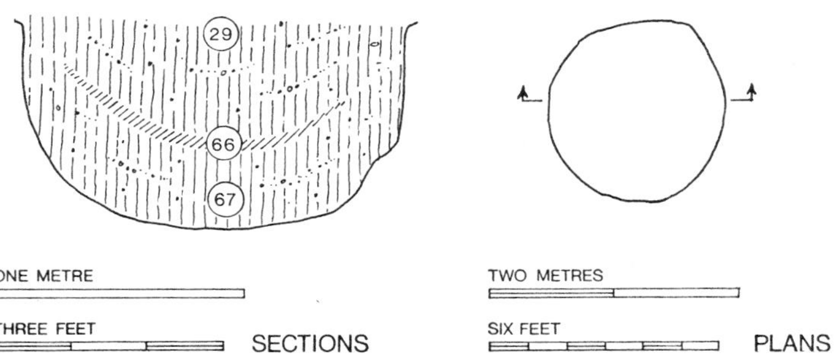

Fig. 52. Pit 91

Pottery. Late Saxon (fig. 122)

Portchester ware and associated types, nos. 385, 386.

Not illustrated: 6 sherds; 2 in coarse sandy wares, 1 rilled Portchester ware sherd; 3 coarse cooking pots of which 2 are rim fragments.

Animal Bones

70 fragments identified (including 22 ribs and 4 skull fragments).

Species represented: cattle, 57; sheep, 16; pig, 11; bird, 9; horse, 5; roe deer, 2.

Pit 93 (PC 68, trench 75, layer 15)

Oval shaped pit 5 ft. 6 in. by 4 ft. (1·68 × 1·22 m.) cut to a depth of 1 ft. 6 in. (0·46 m.) below the surface of natural clay.

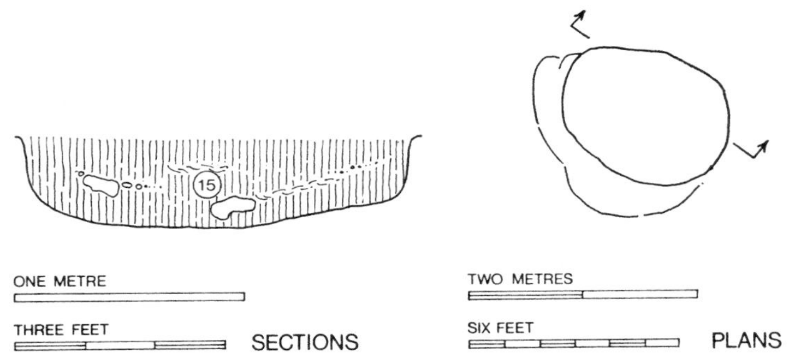

Fig. 53. Pit 93

The filling (layer 15) was uniform consisting of dark green-grey cesspit fill interspersed with lenses of occupation debris and occasional flints.

Pottery. Late Saxon

Not illustrated: 7 body sherds; 3 in Portchester ware fabrics, 4 in coarse cooking pot fabrics.

Pit 97 (PC 68, trench 76, layers 9, 33, 34, 36)

Oval pit 3 ft. 6 in. by 5 ft. (1·07 × 1·52 m.) cut to a depth of 2 ft. 4 in. (0·71 m.) below the surface of natural clay.

The lowest filling (layer 36) consisted of a fine brown crumbly soil, derived from decomposed cesspit filling, interspersed with some occupation material, including fragments of daub showing wattle marks. It was sealed with redeposited brickearth (layer 34), topped with redeposited chalk (layer 33). The uppermost fill (layer 9) was of grey soil and occupation debris.

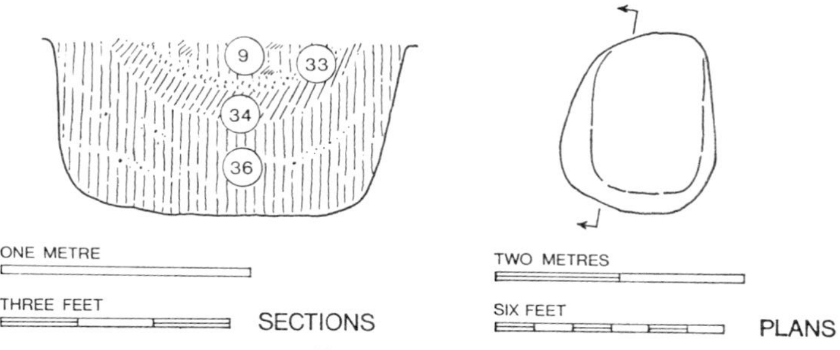

Fig. 54. Pit 97

Pottery. Late Saxon (fig. 122)

From layer 9:

Portchester ware and associated types, nos. 388.

Not illustrated: 2 sherds, 1 base of a Portchester ware vessel, and 1 body sherd in coarse cooking pot fabric.

From layer 36:

Portchester ware and associated types, no. 387.

Not illustrated: 8 body sherds, 7 in Portchester ware fabrics, 1 in coarse cooking pot fabric.

Animal Bones

40 fragments identified (including 4 ribs).

Species represented: sheep, cattle, pig, horse, bird.

Pit 101 (PC 68, trench 78, layers 6, 8, 11)

Irregular pit 4 ft. by 5 ft. 6 in. (1·22 × 1·68 m.) dug to a depth of 4 ft. 3 in. (1·30 m.) below the surface of the natural clay.

The lower filling (layer 11) consisted of black crumbly soil with some small pieces of chalk and a streak of charcoal. This was sealed by a thick layer of redeposited orange brickearth (layer 8). The upper hollow was filled with black occupation rubbish (layer 6).

Pit 101 was cut by pit 99.

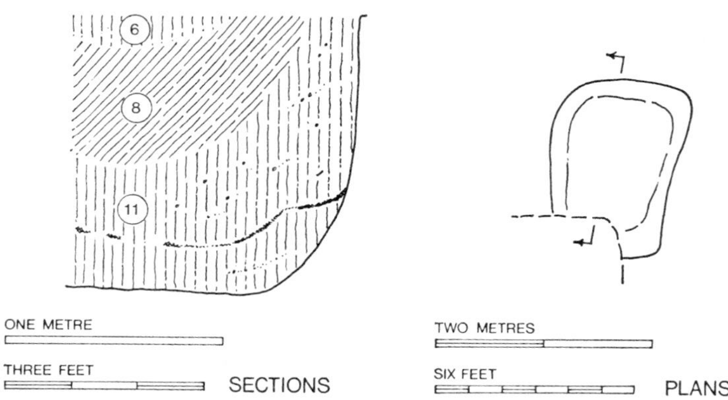

Fig. 55. Pit 101

Pottery. Late Saxon (fig. 123)

From layer 6:

Portchester ware and associated types, no. 390.

Not illustrated: 5 body sherds, 3 in Portchester ware, 2 in coarse cooking pot fabrics.

From layer 11:

Portchester ware and associated types, no. 389.

Not illustrated: 12 body sherds, 2 in sandy ware, 5 in Portchester ware and 5 in coarse cooking pot fabrics.

Animal Bones

89 fragments identified (including 21 ribs and 3 skull fragments).

Species represented: sheep, 32; cattle, 25; cat, 17; bird, 11; pig, 8; red deer, 6; horse, 1.

Pit 104 (PC 68, trench 78, layers 37, 38, 39, 40, 41, 42, 43)

Square pit about 6 ft. (1·83 m.) across, dug to a depth of 5 ft. 9 in. (1·76 m.) below the surface of the natural clay.

The lowest level (layer 43) consisted of greenish-grey cesspit filling containing some bones and pottery together with marl eroded in from the sides and sealed by a thick lens of charcoal (layer 42). Above this (layers 40 and 41) was a thick layer of black soil intermixed with lenses of redeposited brickearth, shells and animals bones. Towards the sides the redeposited clayey marl became thicker and at the top a heap of oyster shells had been thrown in (layer 39). Above these the filling continued as black soil and occupation rubbish (layer 38) interleaved with a thick lens of loosely packed shells, principally oysters, winkles and limpets, but with some animal bone.

Pottery. Late Saxon (fig. 123)

From layer 37:

Not illustrated: 23 sherds; Portchester ware, 20 body sherds, of which 6 are rilled, and 3 undercut rims.

From layer 38:

Portchester ware and associated types, nos. 392, 394, 397.

Not illustrated: 22 body sherds; Portchester ware, 20, of which 11 are rilled, and 2 in coarse cooking pot fabrics.

From layer 41:

Portchester ware and associated types nos. 391, 393, 395, 396, 398, 399.

Not illustrated: 28 body sherds; Portchester ware 27, of which 17 are rilled; 1 in coarse cooking pot fabric.

From layer 43:

Not illustrated: 7 Portchester ware sherds of which 5 are rilled; 1 coarse cooking pot rim.

Animal Bones

146 fragments identified (including 36 ribs and 2 skull fragments).

Species represented: cattle, 31; sheep, 27; bird, 25; pig, 12; horse, 5.

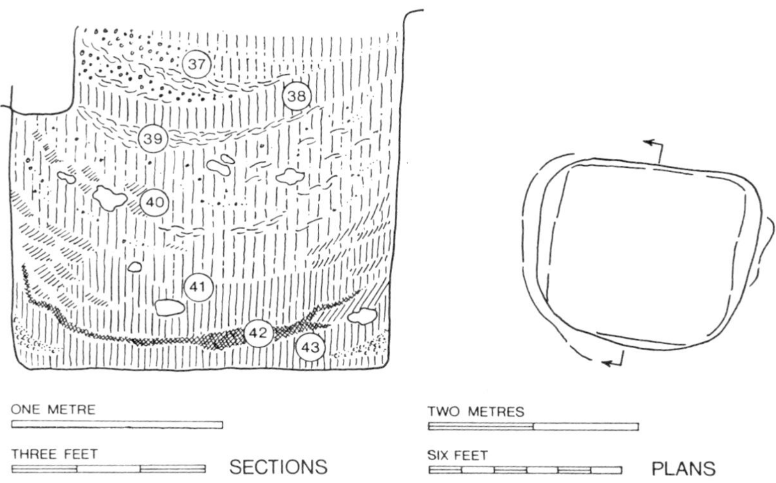

FIG. 56. Pit 104

Pit 106 (PC 68, trench 79, layer 26)

Oval pit 6 ft. by 7 ft. 6 in. (1·83 × 2·29 m.), dug to a maximum depth of 2 ft. 8 in. (0·81 m.) below the surface of the natural clay.

The filling was uniform consisting of brown soil mixed with redeposited natural clay and large flints towards the bottom. There was no evidence to suggest gradual silting — the appearance was of a single deliberate fill.

Pottery. Late Saxon (fig. 123)

Portchester ware and associated types, nos. 400, 401.

Not illustrated: 16 sherds: Portchester ware, 1 undercut rim, 6 rilled sherds and 7 plain sherds; coarse cooking pot fabrics, 1 rim and 1 body sherd.

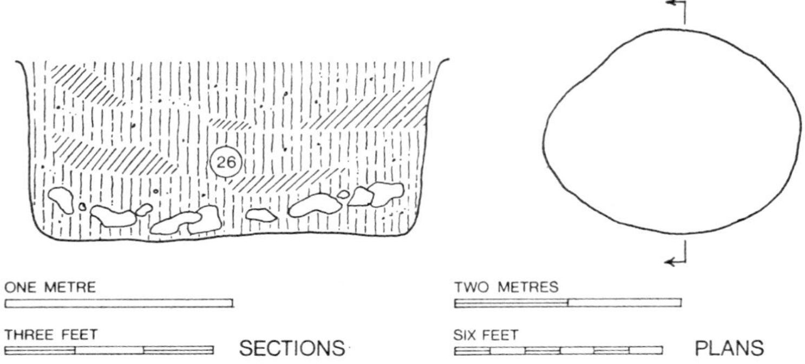

FIG. 57. Pit 106

Animal Bones

8 fragments identified (including 1 rib).
Species represented: cattle, pig.

Pit 107 (PC 68, trench 79, layer 23)

Rectangular pit 5 ft. 6 in. by 4 ft. (1·68 × 1·22 m.) dug to a depth of 2 ft. (0·61 m.) below the surface of natural clay.

The filling consisted of black soil mixed with occupation rubbish with a lens of stones towards the middle.

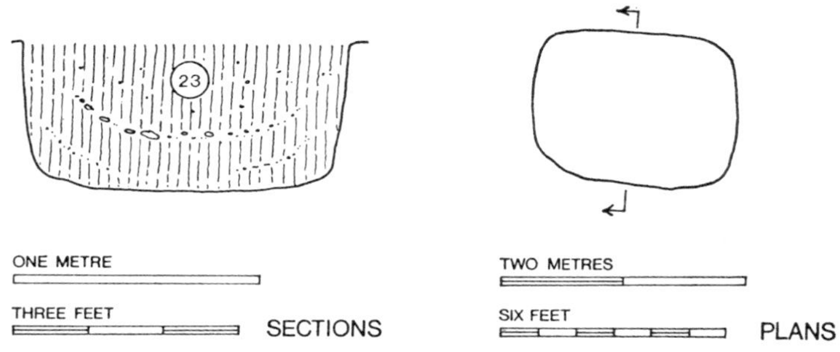

FIG. 58. Pit 107

Pottery. Late Saxon (fig. 123)

Portchester ware and associated types, nos. 402–407.
Not illustrated: 39 body sherds; Portchester ware, 13 rilled sherds, 20 plain; coarse cooking pots, 6 sherds.

Animal Bones

101 fragments identified (including 17 ribs and 9 skull fragments).
Species represented: bird, 43; sheep, 24; cattle, 20; pig, 12; fallow deer, 1.
This pit contained a high percentage of bird bones.

Pit 109 (PC 67, trench 76, layers 32, 35)

Rectangular pit 3 ft. by 4 ft. 9 in. (0·91 × 1·45 m.) dug to a depth of 1 ft. 3 in. (0·38 m.) below the surface of natural clay.

The principal fill consisted of mixed black occupation material (layer 35) which was sealed by a layer of redeposited brickearth (layer 32).

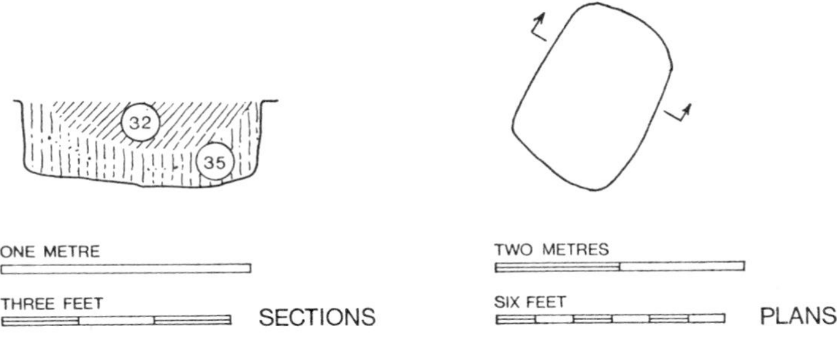

FIG. 59. Pit 109

Pottery. Late Saxon

Not illustrated: Portchester ware, 1 undercut rim, and 1 body sherd.

Animal Bones

10 fragments identified (including 3 ribs).
Species represented: cattle, sheep, horse, bird.

Pit 111 (PC 68, trench 79, layer 32)

Roughly oval pit 6 ft. by 8 ft. (1·83 × 2·44 m.) cut to a depth of 1 ft. 10 in. (0·56 m.) below the surface of the natural clay.

The filling was uniform, consisting of black charcoal and soil with occupation material and discontinuous layers of pebbles and marl.

Small Finds

Gold finger ring (839): fig. 139, no. 59.

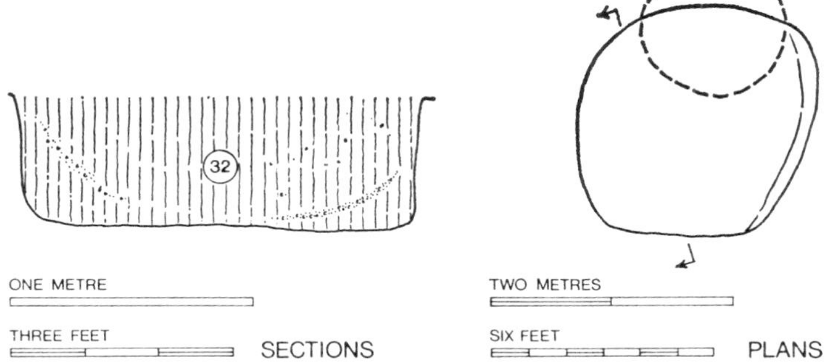

FIG. 60. Pit 111

Pottery. Late Saxon (fig. 124)

Portchester ware and associated types, nos. 408–425.
Not illustrated: 68 body sherds; Portchester ware, 13 rilled and 54 plain; coarse cooking pots, 1 sherd.

Animal Bones

61 fragments identified (including 11 ribs and 3 skull fragments).
Species represented: sheep, 32; cattle, 30; pig, 25; bird, 11; red deer, 2.

Pit 113 (PC 68, trench 79, layers 47, 51, 52)

Rectangular pit 6 ft. by 8 ft. (1·83 × 2·44 m.) cut to a depth of 2 ft. 6 in. (0·76 m.) below the surface of the natural clay.

The lowest filling (layer 52) consisted of mixed black soil, containing flints, occupation rubbish and clay washed in from the sides. This was sealed by a lens of redeposited brick-earth (layer 51), above which was more black soil and occupation rubbish (layer 47).

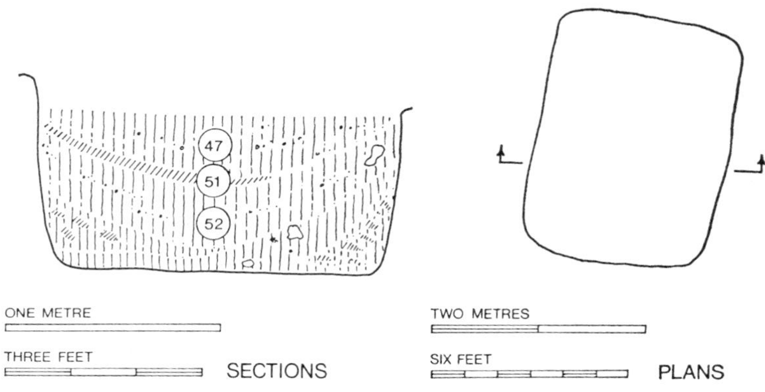

Fig. 61. Pit 113

Small Finds

From layer 47:

Iron spur	(944):	Roman type: not illustrated.
Bone spindlewhorl	(943):	fig. 140, no. 76.

Pottery. Late Saxon (fig. 124)

Portchester wares and associated types nos. 426–436.
Not illustrated: 50 body sherds: Portchester ware, 20 rilled sherds and 24 plain, 1 undercut rim; coarse cooking pots, 3; sandy chaff-tempered ware, 2 body sherds.

Animal Bones

96 fragments identified (including 32 ribs and 3 skull fragments).
Species represented: cattle, 46; pig, 25; sheep, 21; dog, 3; bird, 3; horse, 2.

Pit 115 (PC 68, trench 80, layers 28, 53, 54)

Rectangular pit 5 ft. by 3 ft. 6 in. (1·52 × 1·07 m.). The bottom slopes from 2 ft. 10 in. (0·86 m.) at the west to 3 ft. 4 in. (1·01 m.) at the east, both measurements taken from the surface of the natural clay.

The lower filling (layer 54) was typical of fine brown cesspit fill. It was sealed by a lens of brickearth with marl towards the bottom (layer 53). Above this was a filling of black soil mixed with occupation rubbish.

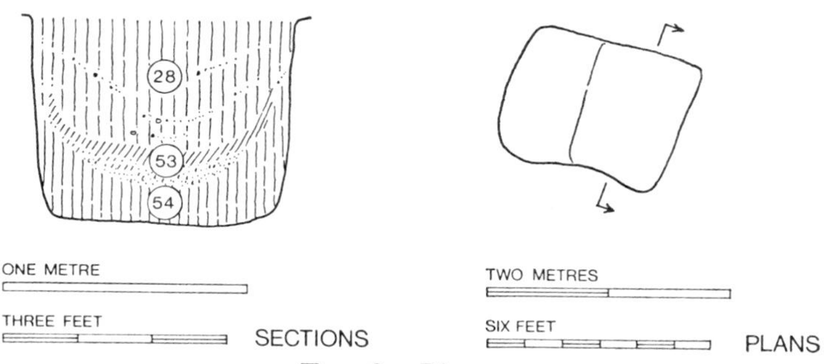

FIG. 62. Pit 115

Pottery. Late Saxon (fig. 124)

From layer 28:

Portchester wares and associated types nos. 437, 438, 440–443.

Not illustrated: 97 sherds: Portchester ware, 85 body sherds, of which 10 are rilled, and 1 is rouletted, 3 rims; coarse cooking pots, 5 rims and 7 body sherds.

From layer 53:

Portchester ware and associated types, no. 439.

Not illustrated: 8 Portchester ware body sherds.

From layer 54:

Not illustrated: 10 Portchester ware body sherds including 1 rim.

Animal Bones

78 fragments identified (including 20 ribs and 4 skull fragments).

Species represented: cattle, 44; sheep, 24; pig, 22; bird, 6; horse, 2; roe deer, 2.

Pit (Well) 135 (figs. 63–66 and pls. XIV*b*–XVII)

The complexity and significance of the feature, pit 135, requires a somewhat more extended treatment than has been given to the other pits and wells described in this section. Four distinct phases can be defined:

Phase 1: original Roman(?) well-shaft.
Phase 2: the creation of an irregular water-hole.
Phase 3: the construction of a timber-boarded well.
Phase 4: disuse and rubbish tipping.

The sequence spans the period from the beginning of the fifth to the middle of the eleventh century.

Phase 1

The original well-shaft was circular, measuring 5 ft. 3 in. (1·60 m.) in diameter, and was dug to a depth of 20 ft. (6·10 m.) below the surface of natural brickearth. Only the lower 5 ft. (1·52 m.) survived in its original form. No lining material remained and since the shaft was permanently water-logged it is improbable that any existed. The filling consisted of thick black silty sediment containing close-packed bands of flint nodules (layer 104).

The only dating material consisted of a few sherds of Roman pottery and, towards the top, an iron purse mount/strike-a-light (no. 1) for which an early fifth-century date is indicated. Whether the shaft was dug in the late fourth or early fifth century is impossible to decide. It conforms in general to well-shafts found elsewhere on the site, dating to the late Roman period, except that it is somewhat larger. If late Roman, the relatively thin deposit of silt would imply that it had remained in use into the fifth century.

Phase 2

During phase 2 the upper sides of the well were eroded back by spring sapping to create an irregularly shaped water-hole. As erosion took place, so the hole silted up with dark grey organic mud containing quantities of large flint nodules and saplings, which seem to have been rammed down the sides of the pit, possibly in an attempt to prevent further erosion. In all 7 ft. (2·13 m.) of silt accumulated. By the end of phase 2 (subdivided here as phase 2b) a turf line had formed (layers 33 and 86) which contained sherds of sixth-century stamped pottery. At this stage the water-hole consisted of a dished hollow some 25 ft. (7·62 m.) across and about 9 ft. 6 in. (2·90 m.) in depth below the contemporary surface. If the water table then was at its present level, the bottom of the hole would have contained permanent standing water.

Phase 3

Phase 3 was represented by the construction of a timber-lined well set in a rectangular well-pit 8 ft. (2·44 m.) square dug to a depth of about 14 ft. (4·27 m.) from the contemporary surface, i.e. some 4 ft. 6 in. (1·37 m.) below the bottom of the silted up water-hole. Within this pit a rectangular well was constructed measuring in plan exactly 3 ft. 6 in. by 4 ft. (1·07 × 1·22 m.) internally (pls. XV–XVII). Its structure can best be appreciated by reference to the detailed section drawings (figs. 63, 65) and the axonometric reconstruction (fig. 64). Originally it would have been composed of at least two and probably three tiers of vertical planking, the lower ends of one tier slotted behind the upper ends of the tier below, the whole structure braced by four internal frames, one at the bottom, one at the top and two between at the points of overlap of the vertical planking. What survives today is the complete lower tier of timbering together with its two sets of internal braces, and the ends of the planks belonging to the second tier. These relationships can best be understood from the plan and section (fig. 65) which show all the surviving timbers in position.

The strength and rigidity of the structure was created by the careful halving of the bracing timbers both in relation to themselves and to the adjacent corner planks. In theory such a structure would have required no pegging, but for ease of assembly the lowest bracing timbers were pegged at each end to the outer planks. Presumably this was done on the

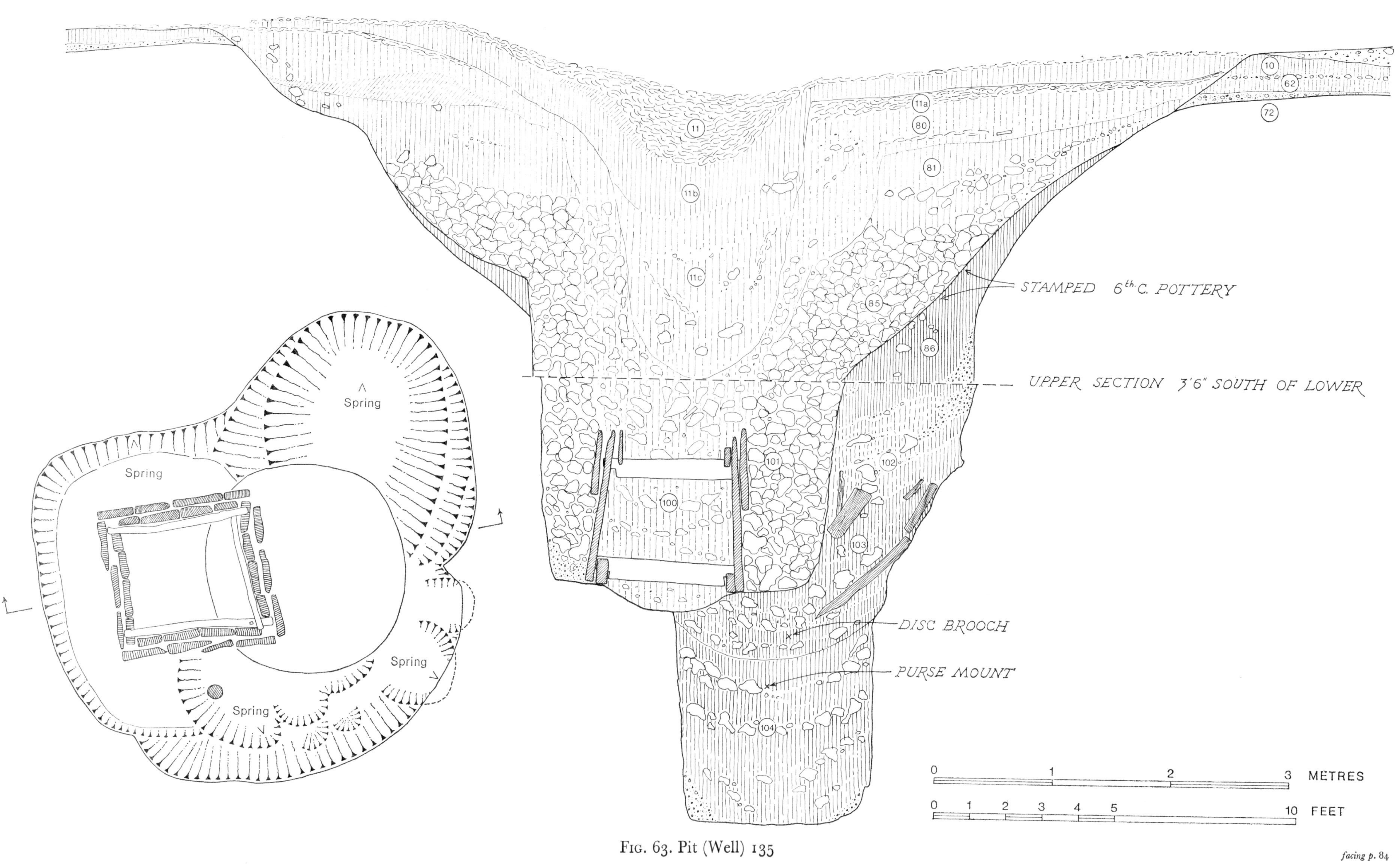

FIG. 63. Pit (Well) 135

facing p. 84

ground above, the four skeleton structures then being lowered into the pit. Next they would be slotted together at the bottom and held rigid at the top by the second frame of bracers, while flints were packed around the outside to prevent the timbers from falling outwards. When this stage had been achieved, all that was required was for the intermediate timber planks to be slotted into position to complete the lower tier. The second tier would have been

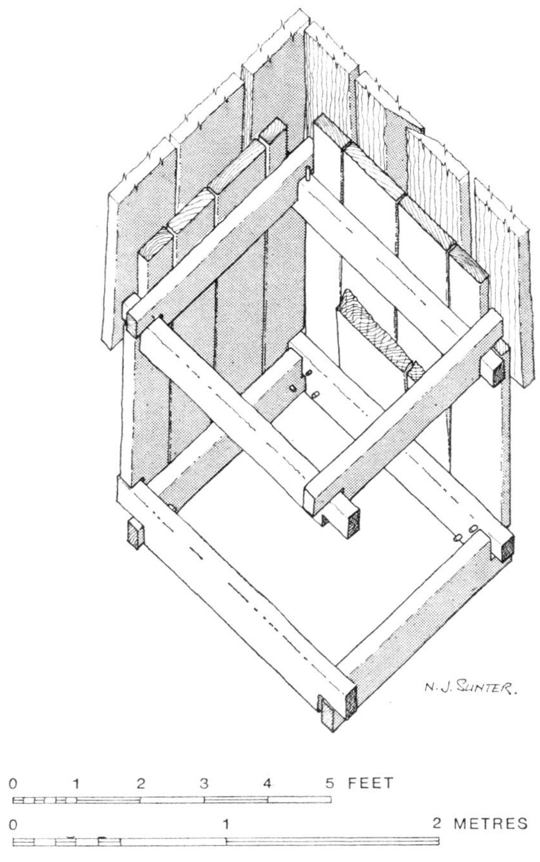

FIG. 64. Diagram to show the arrangement of the timber lining of the Saxon well in pit 135

begun by wedging timber planks behind those of the lower tier and presumably bracing them at the top in the usual way. The well is clearly a very fine piece of structural carpentry.

The vertical timbers consisted of planks 2–3 in. (0·05–0·08 m.) thick, averaging 12 in. (0·31 m.) wide. The bracers varied in size from 3 by 6 in. (0·08 × 0·15 m.) to 4 by 8 in. (0·10 × 0·20 m.) in cross section. Pegs were $\frac{1}{2}$–$\frac{3}{4}$ in. (0·01–0·02 m.) in diameter. All the wood was oak, its plain surfaces being carefully adzed. One repair was apparent (fig. 65, elevation bb); here the intermediate planks had been partly replaced by slotting new timbers behind the stumps of the old. This observation is of considerable interest in view of the dendrochronological evidence (pp. 299–300).

The space between the timber structure and the edge of the well-pit was packed with large flint nodules (layers 85 and 101) to a height of 10 ft. (3·05 m.) above the bottom of the well-pit. While the well was in use soil (layer 81) accumulated in the saucer-like depression around the top of the structure, presumably compensating for the hollow created by the packing down of the flints. The continued use of the well wore a hollow in its floor.

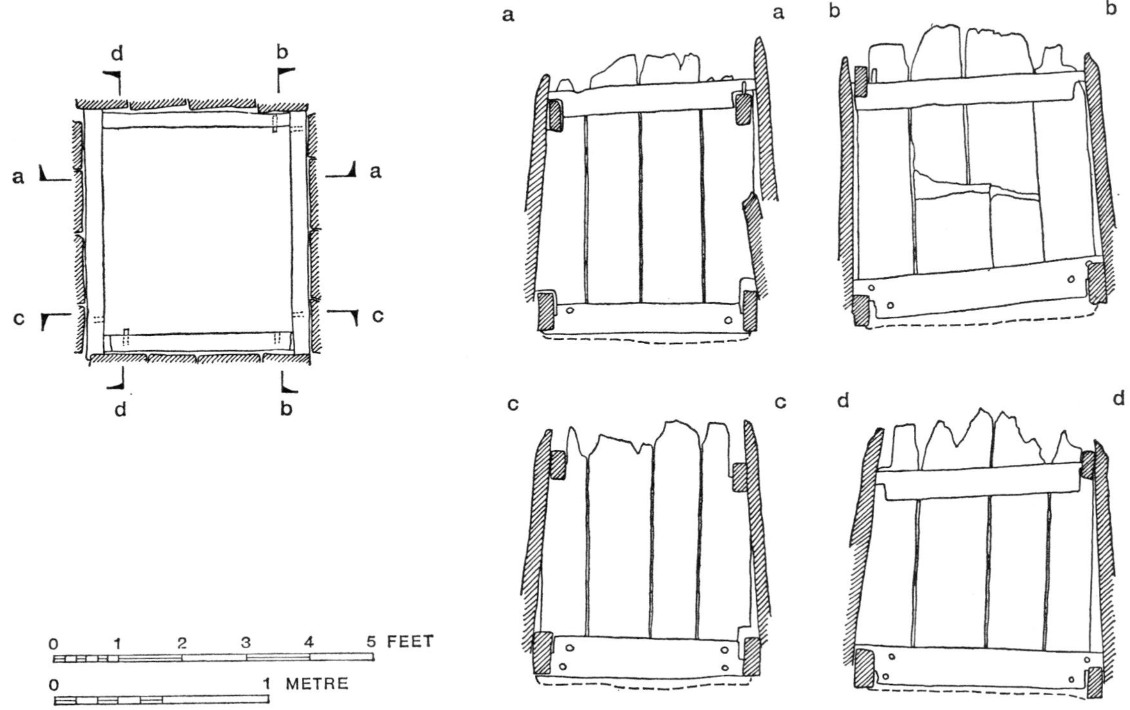

Fig. 65. Details of the timber lining of the Saxon well in pit 135

Phase 4

After the well had ceased to be maintained, silt and rubble was allowed to accumulate (layer 100). It contained a number of objects, including parts of buckets and cores from wood turning. Something of the immediate environment is indicated by the bracket fungi (*Dædalia quercina*) which grew on the timbers, while conditions in the surrounding area are shown by the pollen spectrum preserved in the lowermost silt (pp. 297–9).

After a while the upper timbers rotted and gave way, allowing the flint packing to slump into the void. Layers of rubbish which had accumulated around the edge (layers 80 and 11a) washed in to be mixed with additional tips (layer 11c). Eventually soil formed (layer 11b) but subsidence over the old well shaft continued, the hollow being filled with tips of oyster shells (layer 11).

The date of the construction of the well depends upon the fact that it was cut through a soil layer (layer 86) which contained stamped pottery of the sixth century. In a layer of clay which was probably derived from the digging of the well-shaft, and spread out on the surface to the west (trench 89, layer 26), a substantial part of a stamped urn was found (no. 171) to which a sixth-century date is also assigned (p. 184). Thus a construction date in the middle or later sixth century is indicated on archaeological grounds. Further

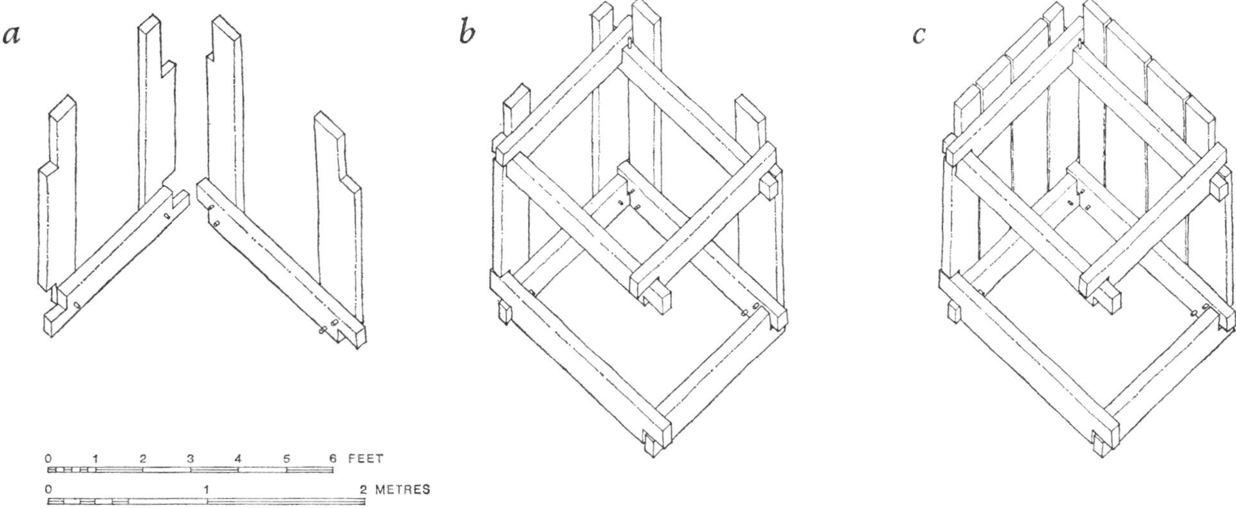

FIG. 66. Diagram to show the stages in the construction of the timber framing of the Saxon well in pit 135

dendrochronological work may well offer a more precise estimate. No closely datable material survives from the primary filling in the well-shaft, but from the soil and flint deposit around the top of the well (layer 31), representing a late phase in consolidation of the ground surface while the well was in use, was recovered a collection of pottery belonging to the intermediate phase between the chaff-tempered and gritty fabric stages which, it will be argued (p. 191), belongs to the middle of the eighth century. The well was probably still functioning at the end of the eighth century. Thereafter the tips of soil and rubbish containing predominantly gritty fabrics of the ninth to tenth centuries were thrown into the shaft and spread on the surrounding surface. The entire area was sealed by a soil accumulation (layer 9) which produced Portchester ware fabrics of the tenth to eleventh century.

A correlation of the layers may now be offered:

Phase	*Structure*	*Trench* 88	*Trench* 89	*Date*
1	Primary shaft: silting	104		Early fifth
2a	Water-hole: silting	82, 84, 103, 102		Later fifth
b	top silting and disuse	33, 86		Early sixth
3a	Timber well: construction	85, 101		Mid sixth ↓
b	use of	31, 81	89	Late eighth
c	disuse of, silting	100		Ninth
4a	Collapse and filling	80, 11c		↓
b		49, 11a	22	
c		52, 11b	28	
			29	
d		50, 12, 11	30	Late ninth
e		9		Tenth to eleventh

Small Finds

Phase 1

88, layer 104:

Iron purse mount	(1864):	fig. 129, no. 1.
Iron hook	(1869):	fig. 130, no. 4.
Iron bucket handle	(1865):	fragment: not illustrated.
Iron bucket filling	(1849):	not illustrated.
Bone object	(1946):	fig. 140, no. 69.

Phase 2a

88, layer 103:

Bronze disc brooch	(1811):	fig. 136, no. 44.
Iron stylus?	(1788):	fig. 135, no. 42.
Roman bronze coin	(1756):	Constantine I (A.D. 313–7).

Phase 2b

88, layer 86:

Bronze bracelet frag.	(1424):	Roman, not illustrated.

88, layer 33:

Roman bronze coin	(1112):	House of Constantine (A.D. 330–45).
	(1403):	Licinius I (A.D. 313–7).
	(1404):	Gratian (A.D. 375–8).
	(1405):	illeg. fourth century.
	(1406):	Constantinopolis (A.D. 330–45).
Bronze ring	(1407):	fig. 139, no. 58.
Bronze fragment	(1412):	Roman, not illustrated.
Bronze object	(1408):	fig. 139, no. 61.
Bronze bracelet	(1409):	Roman, not illustrated.
Glass bead	(1410):	Roman, not illustrated.
Whetstone	(1411):	p. 224, no. 88.
Sawn antler	(1417) (1418) (1422):	(nos. 96–98).

Phase 3a

88, layer 101:

Whetstone	(1691):	p. 221, no. 85.

88, layer 85:

Roman bronze coin	(1397):	Constantine I (A.D. 320–4).
Sawn antler	(1392):	not illustrated.
Bronze coin	(1391):	illeg. fourth century.

Phase 3b

88, layer 31:

Bronze bracelet	(1394):	Roman, not illustrated.
Bronze coin	(1395):	Constans (A.D. 335–7).
Bronze sheet	(1396):	fig. 139, no. 64.
Iron link	(1046):	fragment, not illustrated.
Whetstone	(1393):	p. 221, no. 84.

89, layer 89:

Roman bronze coin	(1325):	Constantinopolis (A.D. 330–5).

Phase 3c

88, layer 100:

Iron latch lifter	(1546):	fig. 130, no. 8.
Iron knife	(1567):	fig. 133, no. 23.
Iron knife	(1587):	fig. 133, no. 25.
Iron knife	(1611):	fig. 133, no. 24.
Iron binding	(1586):	corroded strips: not illustrated.
Iron bucket handle	(1612):	fig. 132, no. 17.
Iron bucket handle	(1614):	fig. 132, no. 16.
Iron fitting	(1610):	fig. 131, no. 15.
Withy binding	(1613):	not illustrated.
Wooden object	(1565):	fig. 143, no. 91.
	(1563):	fig. 143, no. 90.
Wooden cores	(1562) (1566) (1574) (1575): pl. XX*a* (nos. 92–95).	
Bracket fungus	(1576) (1586): *Dædalia quercina.*	

Phase 4c

88, layer 52:

Iron knife	(1063):	fig. 132, no. 19.

Phase 4d

88, layer 12:

Iron object	(1039):	fragment, not illustrated.

88, layer 11:

Bronze tag-end	(1400):	fig. 139, no. 57.
Iron awl	(1399):	fig. 130, no. 3.
Iron knife	(1082):	fig. 133, no. 27.
Iron fragment	(1059):	not illustrated.
Iron object	(1122):	fig. 134, no. 32.

Bone pin	(1060):	fig. 140, no. 66.
Carved bone handle	(1830):	fig. 140, no. 70.
89, layer 30:		
Iron object	(1190):	fig. 134, no. 33.
Iron nail	(1633):	not illustrated.
89, layer 28:		
Roman bronze coin	(1181):	Constantine I (A.D. 330–5).
89, layer 22:		
Iron object	(1164):	fig. 135, no. 41.
Whetstone	(1197):	p. 221, no. 87.

Pottery (figs. 105–108)

Phase 2a (trench 88, layers 82, 84, 102, 103)

88, layer 103: 13 S250: Base in fine grey sandy ware with smoothed surface (?Roman).

Not illustrated: 6 body sherds: 1 gritty, 2 sandy and 3 chaff-tempered. One of the chaff-tempered sherds is from a very large vessel.

layer 102: Not illustrated: 2 sandy sherds.

Phase 2b (trench 88, layers 33, 86)

88, layer 33:

14 S249: Decorated sherds in dark grey sandy ware with large quartz grits: the surface is smoothed, fired black and decorated with circular stamps in horizontal rows divided by horizontal shallow tooled lines (4 sherds).

15 S248: Rim, dark grey sandy ware with some chaff tempering, burnished surface with impressed decoration.

16 S129: Rim, fine sandy ware with chaff tempering, burnished surface fired black.

17 S244: Rim, grey sandy ware, burnished exterior.

18 S260: Rim, coarse black sandy ware.

19 S246: Rim, grey sandy ware.

20 S245: Rim, grey sandy ware with chaff tempering, smoothed surface.

21 S263: Body sherd, coarse grey sandy ware with crushed flint grits.

22 S261: Body sherd, fine light brown sandy ware, surface fired grey and burnished (?Roman).

23 S247: Decorated sherd, coarse grey sandy ware.

Not illustrated: 43 body sherds, 21 in chaff-tempered fabrics, 15 in coarse sandy ware, and 7 in fabrics tempered with sporadic flint grits.

88, layer 86: Not illustrated: 6 body sherds, 4 in chaff-tempered fabrics, 1 in coarse sandy ware, and 1 tempered with copious crushed flint grits.

Phase 3a (trench 88, layers 85 and 101)

88, layer 85: Not illustrated: 21 body sherds; 12 in chaff-tempered fabrics, some from very large jars with wall over 1 cm. thick; 4 in coarse sandy fabrics, 5 in grey sandy wares with crushed flint grits.

Phase 3b (trench 88, layers 31, 81; trench 89, layer 89)

88, layer 31: 24 S236: Rim, coarse grey sandy ware with quartz and mica grits, roughly smoothed surface.

25 S252: Decorated body sherd, part of vessel 171.
26 S251: Decorated body sherd in fine red-brown sandy ware fired dark grey on the surface, stamped.
27 S235: Rim, coarse black sandy ware, roughly smoothed surface.
28 S208: Rim, coarse grey sandy ware, roughly burnished surface.
29 S210, S211: Rim, grey sandy ware with chaff tempering (2 sherds).
30 S209: Rim, grey ware with copious chaff tempering.
31 S253: Rim, coarse grey sandy ware tempered with crushed flint grits.
32 S234: Rim, coarse grey sandy ware with sporadic large flint grits (2 sherds).
33 S212: Rim, grey sandy ware with chaff tempering.
34 S262: Rim, coarse grey ware tempered with crushed flint grits.

88, layer 81: Not illustrated: 4 body sherds in grey sandy ware with chaff tempering; 1 is very thick, 2 others have a highly burnished surface.

89, layer 89: Not illustrated: 3 body sherds, 2 in coarse grey sandy ware, 1 in a red ware containing inclusions of crushed flint and chalk.

Phase 4a (trench 88, layers 80 and 11c)

88, layer 80: Not illustrated: small sherd belonging to S249: 10 body sherds of grey chaff-tempered wares and 1 rim fragment in similar fabric; 8 body sherds of coarse sandy fabrics; 8 body sherds in grey fabrics tempered with crushed flint grit, 2 rims in similar fabrics; 1 sherd of hard light grey sandy ware, roughly corrugated. ? import.

Phase 4c (trench 88, layers 52 and 11b)

88, layer 52: 35 S111: Jar, coarse grey sandy ware with crushed flint grit tempering.
36 S115: Jar in coarse grey sandy ware with crushed flint and chalk tempering.

Not illustrated: 2 sherds of sandy ware, one of which is a small rim fragment; 14 sherds of coarse grey ware tempered with crushed flint grits, 1 of which is a small fragment of rim.

Phase 4d (trench 88, layers 11, 12, 50; trench 89, layers 22, 28, 29, 30)

89, layer 22: 37 S113: Jar, coarse grey sandy ware with crushed flint grit tempering.
38 S116: Jar, coarse grey sandy ware with some finely crushed flint and chalk tempering.
39 S114: Handle, grey sandy ware with crushed flint tempering.

Not illustrated: 2 body sherds in grey wares tempered with chaff; 17 body sherds in coarse grey-black wares tempered with crushed flint and chalk grit.

89, layer 28: 40 S110: Jar, red-grey ware tempered with crushed flint grits.
41 S117: Jar, coarse grey sandy ware with some crushed flint tempering.

Not illustrated: 2 body sherds in grey chaff-tempered ware; 6 in coarse grey sandy ware; 18 in coarse grey-brown wares tempered with crushed flint and chalk grits, two of which were rim fragments.

89, layer 30: Not illustrated: 1 body sherd in grey sandy ware and 2 in coarse grey sandy wares with grit and chaff tempering.

88, layer 12: 47 S128: Rilled Portchester ware sherd.
42 S125: Jar, grey sandy ware with finely crushed chalk and shell tempering.

43 S104: Jar in grey sandy ware with finely crushed flint tempering.

45 S126: Jar in coarse grey sandy ware, some flint grits.

46 S127: Jar in grey sandy ware with crushed flint grit tempering.

Not illustrated: 34 body sherds in coarse grey wares, mainly sandy and with a tempering of crushed chalk and flint grits in various sizes and quantities; 10 rim fragments in a similar range of ware; 9 body sherds of rilled Portchester ware; 1 small rim fragment in similar ware; 1 glazed sherd.

88, layer 50: 44 S112: Jar, grey ware tempered with chaff, burnished surface.

88, layer 11: 48–84 S95–107, 213–233, 237: Coarse jars with everted rims. The fabrics are all grey and sandy and all contain tempering of crushed flint, sometimes mixed with crushed chalk. The degree of fineness of the crushing varies. The surfaces are smoothed and occasionally roughly burnished. All vessels show irregularities demonstrating their hand-made origins (total of 49 sherds).

86 S108: Decorated jar in grey sandy ware tempered with flint and chalk grits. The chalk has leached out inside giving the fabric a vesicular appearance. The surface is smooth and decorated with panels of stamping and incision.

85 S109: Handle in hard light grey sandy ware. Imported vessel.

64 S241: Jar in hard grey sandy ware, smoothed surface.

80 S242: Jar in hard grey sandy ware, burnished surface.

79 S243: Jar in black sandy ware with chaff tempering, smoothed surface.

Not illustrated: 284 body sherds; 273 in the same range of gritty fabrics represented by the coarse jars described above; 8 in chaff-tempered ware; 3 in coarse sandy wares.

Phase 4e (trench 88, layer 9)

88, layer 9: 88 S239: Rim, coarse sandy grey ware, smoothed surface.

87 S240: Rim, grey ware heavily tempered with crushed flint and chalk grits.

89 S238: Rim, grey ware tempered with crushed flint and chalk grits, smoothed surface.

90–96 S118–S124: Wheel-made Portchester ware fabrics, hard grey sandy ware with finely crushed flint and chalk tempering. S124 is a dish, the others are from cooking pots with rilled and rouletted surfaces.

Not illustrated: 143 sherds: coarse gritty jars represented by 18 body sherds and 7 rim sherds; Portchester ware vessels by 63 plain body sherds, 8 base sherds, 27 rilled body sherds, 5 under-cut rims and 11 plain rims; 4 sherds of a dish.

Sealing layer above phase 4e layers (trench 88, layer 5)

97–100 S256–S259: Jars in Portchester ware, hard sandy fabric with finely crushed flint grits, wheel-turned.

101 S254: Jar in grey ware with copious crushed flint grits.

102 S255: Jar in grey ware with crushed flint grits.

Not illustrated: 36 sherds: coarse gritty jars represented by 3 body sherds, Portchester ware vessels by 2 base sherds, 8 rilled body sherds, 12 rim sherds and 11 body sherds.

Animal Bones

Phase 1

3 fragments identified.
Species represented: red deer. Three large red deer antlers were found.

Phase 2a

84 fragments identified (including 7 ribs and 4 skull fragments).
Species represented: cattle, 51; pig, 9; red deer, 7; sheep, 6.

Phase 2b

328 fragments identified (including 21 ribs and 8 skull fragments).
Species represented: cattle, 73; sheep, 11; pig, 11; horse, 4; red deer, 1; bird, roe deer.

Phase 3a

142 fragments identified (including 19 ribs and 4 skull fragments).
Species represented: cattle, 68; sheep, 10; pig, 10; horse, 6; red deer, 3; bird, 2; roe deer, 1.

Phase 3b

178 fragments identified (including 28 ribs and 3 skull fragments).
Species represented: cattle, 68; sheep, 16; pig, 10; bird, 5; red deer, 1; horse, 1.

Phase 3c

155 fragments identified (including 43 ribs and 6 skull fragments).
Species represented: cattle, 33; sheep, 26; pig, 22; bird, 8; roe deer, 5; red deer, 4; horse, 2.

Phase 4a

98 fragments identified (including 9 ribs and 9 skull fragments).
Species represented: cattle, 39; sheep, 31; pig, 12; red deer, 6; bird, 4; horse, 4; hare, 3; dog, 1.

Phase 4b

778 fragments identified (including 106 ribs and 104 skull fragments).
Species represented: cattle, 61; sheep, 18; pig, 13; red deer, 3; roe deer, 2; bird, 2; horse, badger.

Phase 4c

285 fragments identified (including 49 ribs and 14 skull fragments).
Species represented: cattle, 55; sheep, 21; pig, 19; bird, 2; red deer, 1; roe deer, horse.

Phase 4d

5704 fragments identified (including 1031 ribs and 524 skull fragments).
Species represented: cattle, 54; sheep, 21; pig, 15; red deer, 4; roe deer, 2; bird, 2; horse, 1; fallow deer, cat, dog, hare.

Phase 4e

824 fragments identified (including 102 ribs and 46 skull fragments).
Species represented: cattle, 53; sheep, 19; pig, 16; red deer, 7; horse, 3; roe deer, 1; bird, 1; cat, dog.

Summary

Phases 1 to 3c (incl.), Early to Middle

890 fragments identified (including 118 ribs and 25 skull fragments).
Species represented: cattle, 65; sheep, 14; pig, 12; horse, 3; bird, 3; red deer, 3; roe deer, 1.

Phases 4a to 4d (incl.), Middle to Late

6865 fragments identified (including 1195 ribs and 651 skull fragments).
Species represented: cattle, 54; sheep, 21; pig, 15; red deer, 4; bird, 2; roe deer, 1; horse, 1; fallow deer, hare, cat, dog, badger.

Phase 4d, Late (see above).

Total (all phases)

8579 fragments identified (including 1415 ribs and 722 skull fragments).
Species represented: cattle, 55; sheep, 20; pig, 15; red deer, 4; bird, 2; roe deer, 1; horse, 1; fallow deer, dog, hare, cat, badger.

Pit 137 (PC 70, trench 94, layers 89, 90, 110, 111, 112, 113)

Irregularly dug pit of sub-rectangular form measuring approximately 11 by 5 ft. (3·35 × 1·52 m.) dug to a depth of 3 ft. (0·91 m.) below the surface of natural clay.

The lowest layer (layer 113) consisted of washed-in clay and soil mixed together and sealed by a layer of black occupation material (layer 112). Above this was a sealing layer of redeposited orange brickearth (layer 111) separated by a lens of charcoal from a layer of redeposited chalky marl (layer 110). This was covered by an accumulation of soil (layer 90), the final hollow being deliberately filled with a mass of clay, flints and soil (layer 89).

The pit was cut by the construction trenches for buildings S7 and S8.

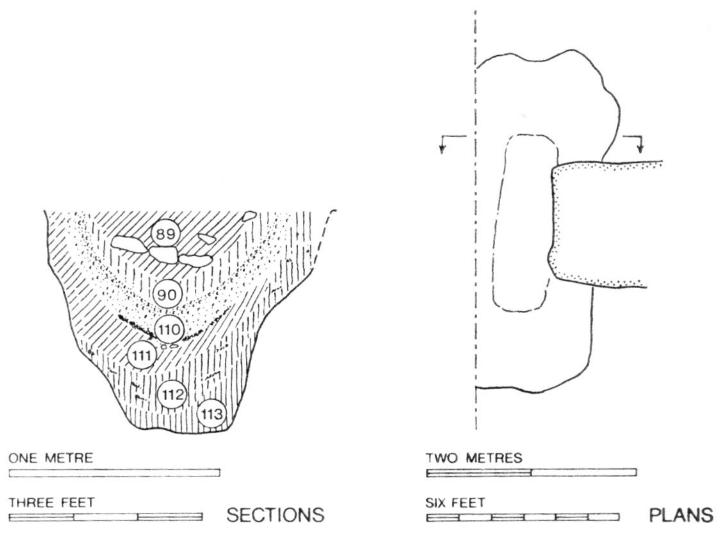

Fig. 67. Pit 137

Pottery. Early–mid Saxon (fig. 109)

From layer 111:

103. S355. Body sherd in fine black sandy ware. The surface is burnished and decorated with vertical grooves.

Not illustrated: one body sherd in grey sandy ware tempered with chaff and a body sherd in fine grey-brown sandy ware.

Animal Bones

33 fragments identified (including 11 ribs).
Species represented: sheep, cattle, pig.

Pit 139 (PC 70, trench 95, layer 77)

Small rectangular pit measuring 4 ft. (1·22 m.) across and dug to a depth of 1 ft. 2 in. (0·36 m.), below the level of the natural surface. Part of the pit had been dug away by the sixteenth-century footings.

The filling was uniform, consisting of dark grey soil with lenses of chalky marl eroded in from the sides.

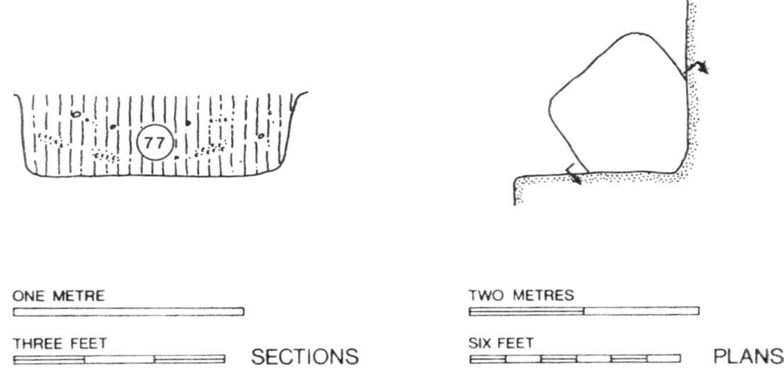

Fig. 68. Pit 139

Pottery. Late Saxon

Not illustrated: 3 Portchester ware body sherds.

Pit 141 (PC 70, trench 94, layer 106)

Small circular pit 3 ft. (0·91 m.) in diameter and 1 ft. 6 in. (0·46 m.) deep.

The filling was uniform consisting of brown soil, occupation rubbish, flints and a block of limestone. A few fragments of sandy daub with wattle marks were also recovered.

Pottery. Early–mid Saxon (fig. 109)

107. S339. Rim in grey-brown sandy fabric tempered with chaff. The surface is smoothed.

Not illustrated: 5 body sherds, 1 in coarse brown ware tempered with chaff and some flint grits; 4 in grey wares with crushed flint grits.

Animal Bones

14 fragments identified (including 5 ribs and 1 skull fragment).
Species represented, cattle, sheep.

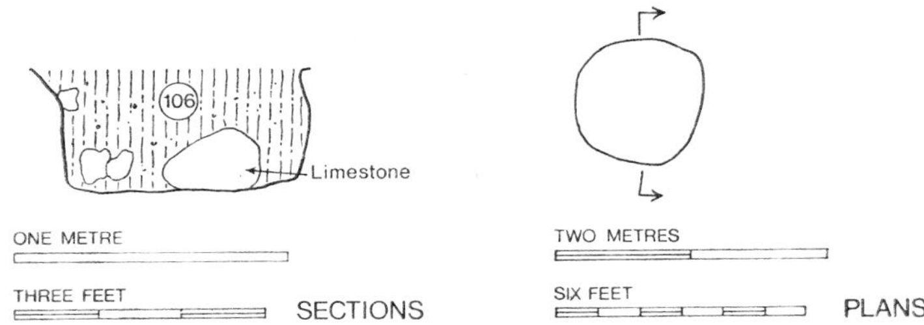

Fig. 69. Pit 141

Pit (Well) 143 (PC 70, trench 95, layers 82, 110–112, 121–133, 135, 143, 147, 149)

Circular well-shaft 4 ft. (1·22 m.) in diameter at the bottom expanding to 8 ft. (2·44 m.) at the top as the result of erosion. The overall depth from the surface of the natural clay was 14 ft. (4·27 m.).

The lowest frame of the timber lining survived in position. It consisted of four planks 1½–2 in. (0·03–0·05 m.) thick and 9 in. (0·23 m.) wide halved into each other, defining an enclosed square of 2 ft. 5½ in. (0·75 m.). The space between the timbers and the side of the well-pit had been packed with redeposited natural clay. The lower 5 ft. (1·52 m.) of the shaft was filled with layers of clay (layers 149, 147, 143, 133) which had eroded in as the result of natural weathering, presumably while the timber lining was still in position. Above these was a layer of redeposited chalky marl (layer 135), also the result of the weathering of the pit sides.

The next 4 ft. (1·22 m.) of the filling consisted of soil and occupation rubbish interleaved with material derived from the continuously eroding shaft (layers 124, 125, 126, 127, 128, 129, 130, 131, 132). This was followed by a deliberate packing of flints and soil (layer 123), the final hollow gradually accumulating tips of soil and occupation rubble with occasional lenses of redeposited clay (layers 122, 121, 110, 82).

Small Finds

From layer 82:
Roman bronze bracelet (1706): frag. not illustrated.
From layer 110:
Roman bronze coin (1721): Gratian (A.D. 375–8).
From layer 125:
Roman bronze coin (1717): Valentinian I (A.D. 364–75).

Pottery. Mid–late Saxon (figs. 109, 125)

The lower layers (130, 131, 133, 135) contained sherds of sandy and gritty wares of ninth- to tenth-century date, while the upper filling (layers 82, 110, 111, 123) produced Portchester wares.

From layer 135:

Not illustrated: body sherd in coarse grey gritty ware.

From layer 133:

Not illustrated: 1 sherd in an even grey ware with finely crushed chalk tempering, and another from a slightly angled base in red-brown sandy ware with crushed flint tempering.

From layer 131:

104. M401. Rim in coarse black ware tempered with crushed flint grits.
105. M402. Rim in coarse grey-brown ware tempered with coarse grits of quartz and mica.
106. M403. Rim in dark grey sandy ware.

Not illustrated: 3 body sherds in coarse grey-brown wares tempered with coarse flint grits, and 3 sherds of an angled sagging base in similar fabric.

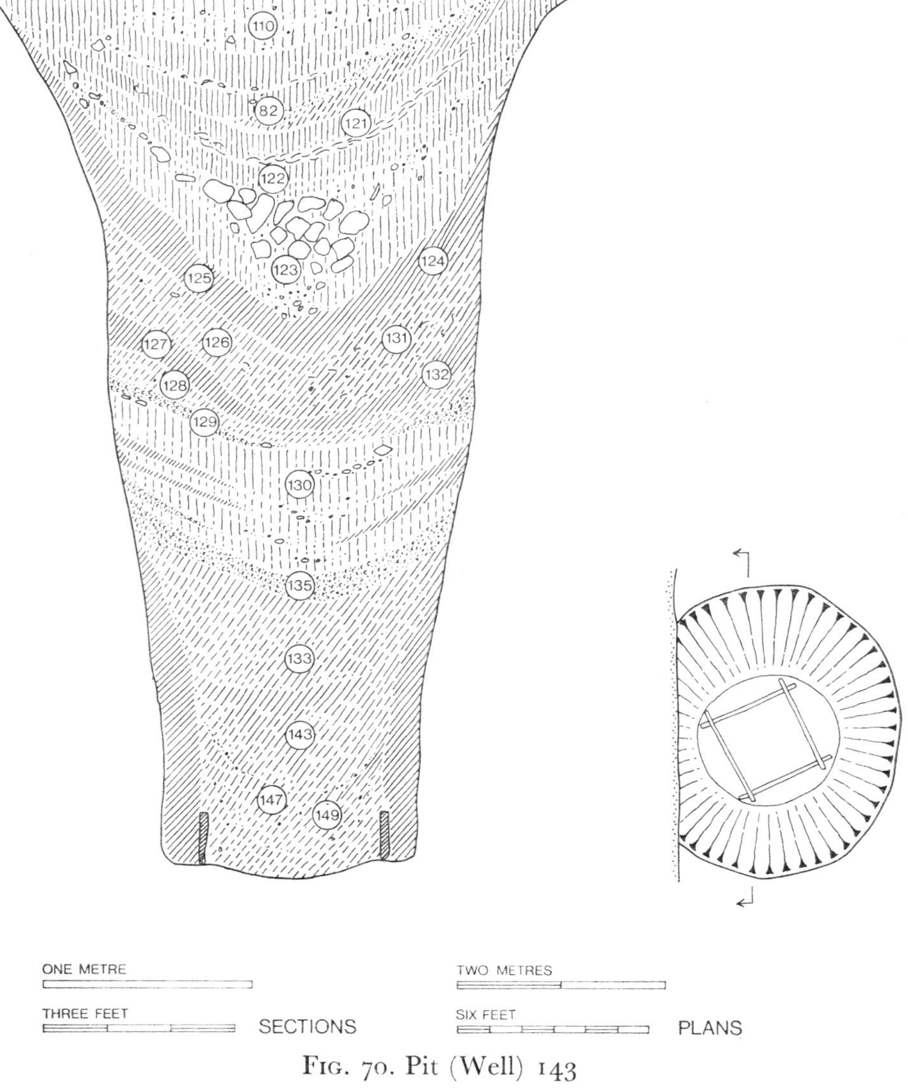

FIG. 70. Pit (Well) 143

From layer 130:
Not illustrated: body sherd of coarse grey sandy ware.
From layer 111:
Portchester ware and associated types no. 444.
Not illustrated: 8 sherds, 2 rims and 3 body sherds of coarse cooking pot fabrics; 1 sandy sherd, 2 in Portchester ware.
From layer 110:
Portchester ware and associated types, nos. 446–450.
Not illustrated: 54 sherds; Portchester ware, 1 undercut rim, 28 plain body sherds, 1 rilled sherd; coarse cooking pot fabrics, 3 rims and 21 body sherds.
From layer 82:
Portchester ware and associated types nos. 445, 451–458.
Not illustrated: 53 sherds; Portchester wares, 8 rilled, 19 body sherds; cooking pot fabrics, 26 sherds.

Animal Bones

Mid–late Saxon (layers 130–135):
21 fragments identified (including 7 ribs).
Species represented: cattle, pig, sheep.
Late Saxon (layers 82, 110, 111, 123):
285 fragments identified (including 95 ribs and 40 skull fragments).
Species represented: sheep, 34; cattle, 23; dog, 18; pig, 15; bird, 5; horse, 3; red deer, 1; cat, 1. The high percentage of dog bones in this pit is caused by the presence of an almost complete dog skeleton.

Pit 151 (PC 70, trench 96, layers 49, 50, 51)

Sub-rectangular pit 8 by 6 ft. (2·44 × 1·83 m.) cut to a depth of 4 ft. (1·22 m.) below the surface of the natural brickearth.

The lowest layer (layer 51) was of green-brown soil typical of decomposed cesspit filling. It was sealed by a layer of chalky marl (layer 50) which must originally have been laid horizontally across the filled pit, later to slump as the lower filling compacted. The hollow created above it was filled with grey soil mixed with occupation debris.

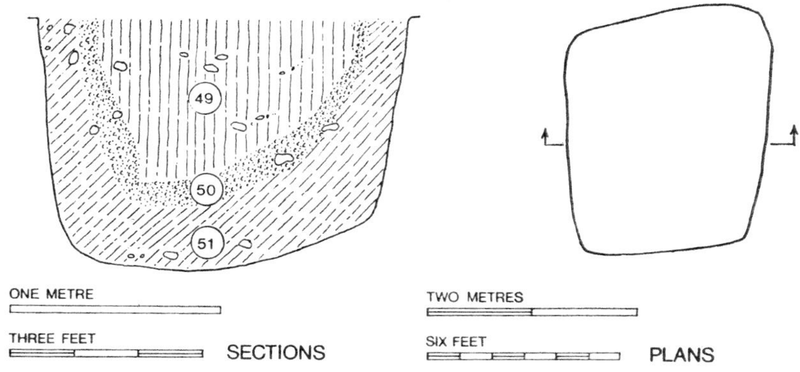

FIG. 71. Pit 151

Small Finds

From layer 51:

Roman bronze coin	(1755):	Carausius (A.D. 286–93).
Iron fragments	(1820):	not illustrated.
Iron fragments	(1823):	fig. 134, nos. 36, 37.

Pottery. Late Saxon (figs. 120–121)

From layer 51:
Portchester wares and associated types, no. 461.
Not illustrated: 2 cooking pot sherds.

From layer 49:
Portchester wares and associated types, nos. 459, 460, 462.
Not illustrated: 6 body sherds in Portchester ware, 1 of which is rilled.

Pit 154 (PC 70, trench 96, layer 35)

Small rectangular pit 3 ft. 9 in. by 2 ft. 3 in. (1·14 × 0·69 m.) cut to a depth of 1 ft. 2 in. (0·36 m.) below the surface of natural brickearth.

The filling was uniform consisting of black soil mixed with occupation debris.

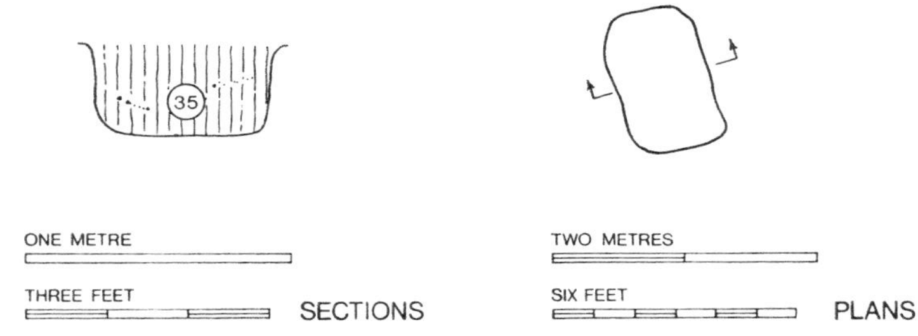

FIG. 72. Pit 154

Pottery. Late Saxon (fig. 125)

Portchester wares and associated types, nos. 463–467.
Not illustrated: 18 body sherds in Portchester ware of which 4 are rilled.

Animal Bones

16 fragments identified (including 4 ribs).
Species represented: sheep, cattle, pig.

Pit 156 (PC 70, trench 96, layers 58, 64, 65)

Large sub-rectangular pit $8\frac{1}{2}$ by 6 ft. (2·59 × 1·83 m.) cut to a depth of $4\frac{1}{2}$ ft. (1·37 m.) below the surface of the natural clay.

The lowest layer (layer 65) consisted of washed-in brickearth discoloured to a greenish colour. Above this was a mass of brown soil with flints and some occupation debris (layer 64) gradually merging with layer 58, which contained rather more occupation debris.

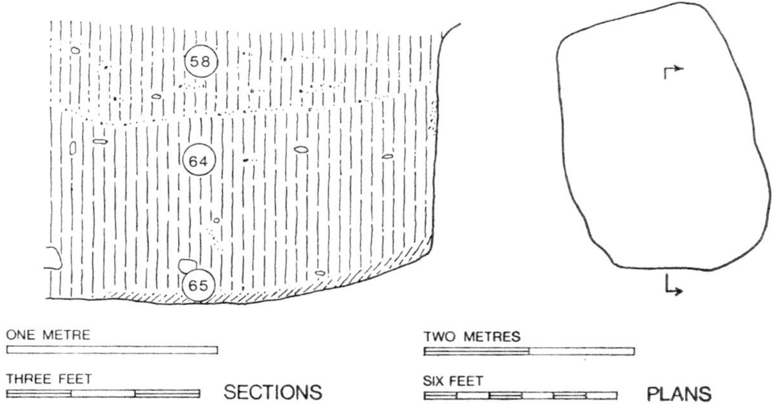

FIG. 73. Pit 156

Small Finds

From layer 58:

Iron rod	(1817):	fig. 135, no. 40.
Chalk spindle whorl	(1828):	fig. 141, no. 82.

From layer 65:

Roman bronze coin	(1905):	corroded, third to fourth century.

Pottery. Late Saxon (fig. 126)

From layer 58:

Portchester ware and associated types nos. 468–472.

Not illustrated: 58 sherds; Portchester ware, 18 rilled and 33 plain sherds; cooking pot fabrics, 7 sherds.

Animal Bones

15 fragments identified (including 5 ribs).

Species represented: cattle, bird.

Pit 158 (PC 70, trench 96, layers 59a, 59b)

Oval-shaped pit 5 ft. 9 in. by 3 ft. 9 in. (1·75 × 1·14 m.) dug to a maximum depth of 1 ft. 5 in. (0·43 m.) below the surface of natural clay.

The filling consisted of brown soil containing flints and fragments of brick, interleaved with discontinuous lenses of chalky marl.

Pottery. Late Saxon (fig. 126)

Portchester ware and associated types, nos. 473–474.

Not illustrated: 7 body sherds, 3 in Portchester ware fabrics, 4 in coarse cooking pot fabrics.

Animal Bones

34 fragments identified (including 9 ribs and 12 skull fragments).

Species represented: cattle, pig, bird, horse, dog.

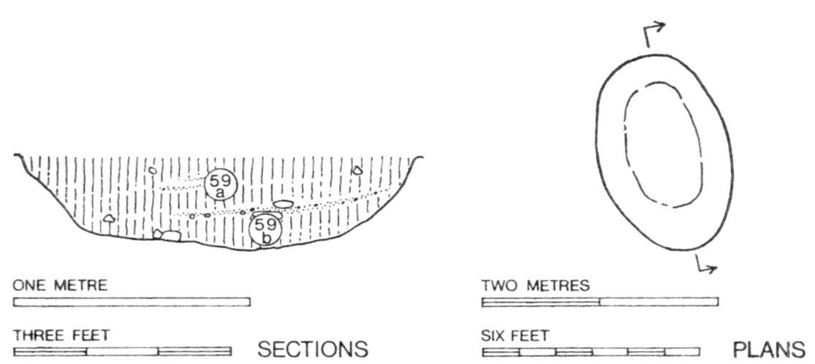

FIG. 74. Pit 158

Pit 159 (PC 70, trench 96, layer 66)

Roughly oval-shaped pit 4 by 3 ft. (1·22 × 0·91 m.) dug to a maximum depth of 1 ft. 3 in. (0·38 m.) below the surface of natural clay.

The filling was uniform consisting of soil with wads of redeposited clay. An area of darker soil in the centre gave the appearance of a filled post void but the evidence was indecisive.

Pottery. Late Saxon (fig. 126)

Portchester ware and associated types, nos. 475.
Not illustrated: 9 body sherds; Portchester ware, 1 body sherd; cooking pot fabrics, 7 body sherds, 1 rim fragment.

Animal Bones

18 fragments identified (including 9 ribs and 1 skull fragment).
Species represented: cattle, sheep, horse.

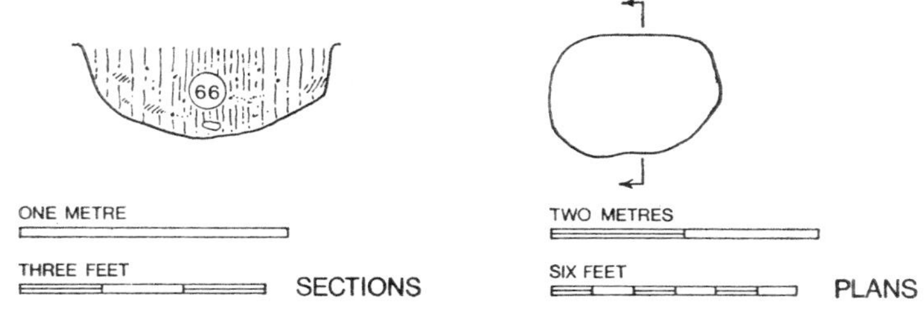

FIG. 75. Pit 159

Pit 167b (PC 70, trench 97, layers 59, 62, 63, 64, 65, 66)

Rectangular pit, 5 ft. by 6 ft. 3 in. (1·52 × 1·90 m.) partly cut away by a nineteenth-century brick sewer. The pit was cut to a maximum depth of 4 ft. (1·22 m.) below the surface of the natural clay.

The lowest layer (layer 66) was typical of decomposed cesspit filling, consisting of greenish-brown crumbly soil. It was covered by a mixed layer (layer 65) of grey soil and occupation debris containing lenses of brickearth, charcoal and oyster shells. The pit was then sealed with a thick deposit of redeposited brickearth (layer 64) above which was a further layer of brown soil mixed with occupation rubbish (layer 63). This was in turn sealed by a capping of redeposited chalky marl (layer 62), in the hollow above which was a further accumulation of soil (layer 59).

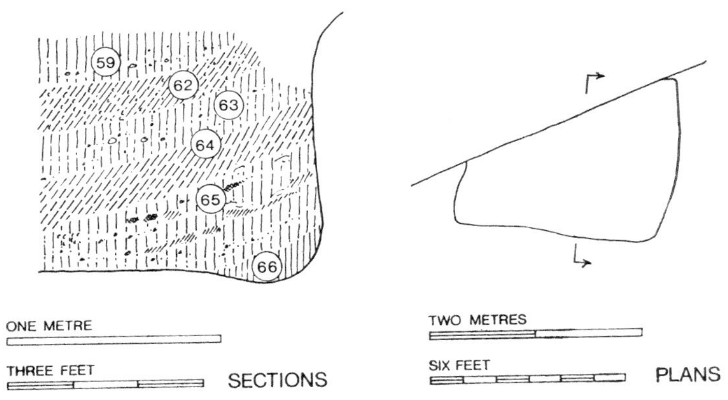

Fig. 76. Pit 167b

Pottery. Late Saxon (fig. 126)

From layer 65:

Portchester ware and associated types, no. 479.

Not illustrated: 6 body sherds in Portchester ware fabrics.

From layer 59:

Portchester ware and associated types, nos. 476–478, 480.

Not illustrated: 4 body sherds: 1 rilled Portchester ware, the others in coarse cooking pot fabrics.

Animal Bones

68 fragments identified (including 10 ribs and 1 skull fragment).

Species represented: cattle, 53; pig, 12; bird, 7; horse, 4; sheep, 2; roe deer, 2.

Pit 175 (PC 68, trench 73, layer 35; PC 70, trench 99, layer 60)

Irregular hollow 6 ft. by 4 ft. 9 in. (1·83 × 1·45 m.) cut to a maximum depth of 7 in. (0·18 m.) below the surface of the natural clay.

The filling was uniform, consisting of black soil mixed with occupation debris.

Pottery. Late Saxon (fig. 126)

Portchester ware and associated types, nos. 481, 482.

Not illustrated: 4 body sherds in coarse cooking pot fabrics.

Animal Bones

16 fragments identified (including 2 ribs and 1 skull fragment).

Species represented: cattle, sheep, pig.

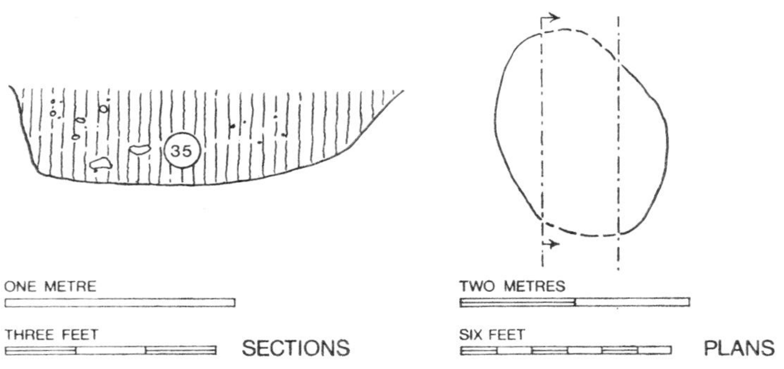

FIG. 77. Pit 175

Pit 180 (PC 70, trench 99, layers 78, 97)

Pit of uncertain size but approximately 8 ft. (2·44 m.) in diameter. Only partly excavated and substantially destroyed by a sixteenth-century footing. Originally cut to a depth of about 1 ft. 3 in. (0·38 m.) from the surface of the natural brickearth.

The filling comprised a layer of grey soil mixed with flints, roof tile and occupation debris (layer 97) sealed by a mass of burnt clay and charcoal (layer 78).

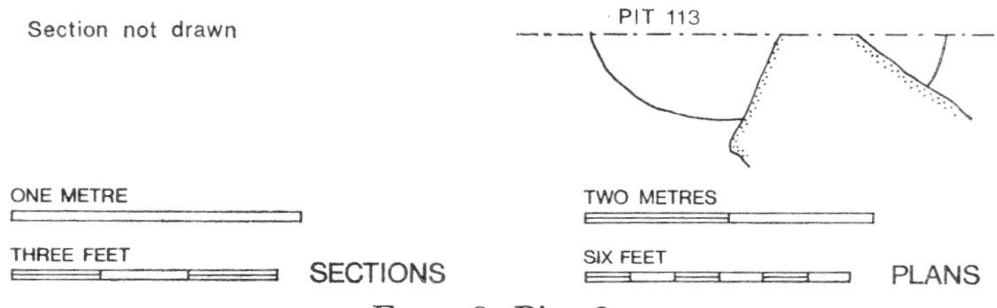

FIG. 78. Pit 180

Pottery. Late Saxon

Not illustrated: 2 body sherds of Portchester ware.

Pit 188 (PC 70, trench 99, layer 94; PC 72, trench 109, layer 79)

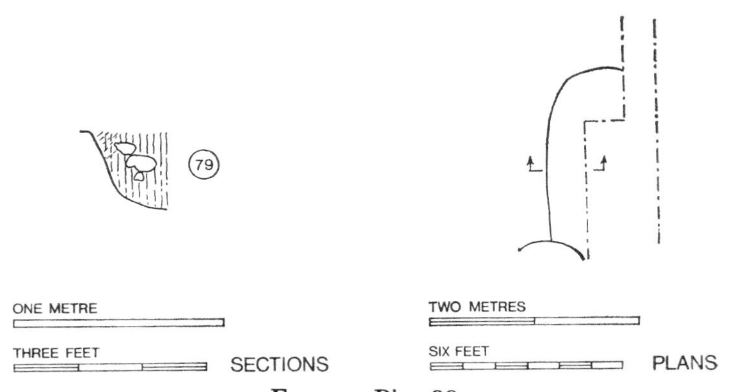

FIG. 79. Pit 188

Oval-shaped pit of undefined size only partly examined, cut to a depth of 1 ft. 2 in. (0·36 m.) below the surface of the natural clay.

The filling was uniform, consisting of brown soil, large flints and some occupation debris.

Pottery. Late Saxon

Not illustrated: 1 body sherd in Portchester ware.

Pit 191 (PC 71, trench 102, layers 43, 47, 54, 55, 67, 72, 84, 89, 90, 91, 92; trench 103, layers 29, 32, 33)

Large rectangular pit dug against the face of the Roman south wall: 15 by 6 ft. (4·57 × 1·83 m.) at the top but undercutting the foundations of the wall so that the bottom width of the pit measured approximately 8 ft. (2·44 m.). Dug to a depth of 10 ft. (3·05 m.) below the contemporary ground surface (pl. XII*b*).

The lowest layer, 89, represented a rotted down cesspit filling of crumbly brown soil which merged into layer 91, the difference between the two being that the upper layer contained some flints and mortar eroded from the overhanging Roman wall footings. The lowest filling was sealed by a mass of loose flints and mortar (layer 90) which presumably represented the erosion of the Roman wall face above. Above this was a lens of clay (layer 92) sealed by a lens of mortary soil (layer 84), both derived from the erosion and weathering of the pit sides. Then came a thick tip of black occupation rubbish (layer 67), which contained oyster shells and charcoal. It merged upwards into a mass of loose flints which would appear to have been tipped in from the north side. After a while a layer of brown clayey soil formed (layer 54), followed by further tips of flints (layer 43) and some wedges of eroded mortar, particularly against the wall face (layer 55). How much of the flint layer was deliberate fill, how much the result of the weathering of the wall, is impossible to say. Finally, after the pit had almost silted up, a layer of soil (layer 47) began to accumulate in the hollow.

Small Finds

From 103, layer 32:

Iron bar (2253): fig. 131, no. 13.

Pottery. Mid–late Saxon (fig. 109)

From layer 43:

108. S311. Rim sherd in fine black sandy ware burnished on both surfaces.

Not illustrated: 9 body sherds belonging to coarse jars. The fabrics are smooth and tempered with crushed flint grits. The surfaces are irregular but roughly burnished.

From layer 47:

Not illustrated: 3 body sherds belonging to coarse jars in smooth paste tempered with crushed flint grits. The surfaces are irregular.

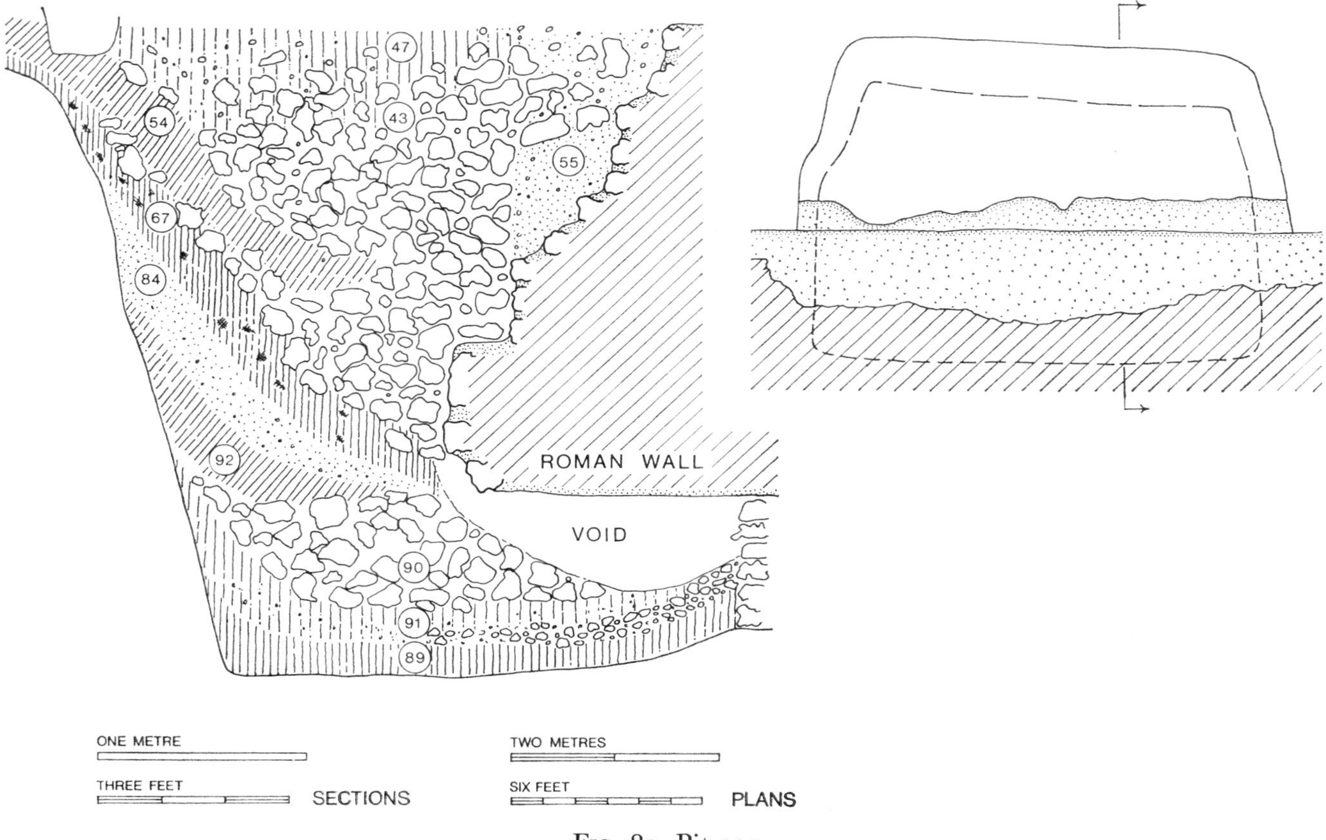

FIG. 80. Pit 191

From layer 54:

110. S324. Sherd decorated with shallow grooving. Fine sandy grey ware fired to black on the surfaces and highly burnished.

Not illustrated: 4 body sherds of one large coarse jar in a grey sandy ware containing some flint grits and chaff tempering. The surface is smoothed.

From layer 67:

Not illustrated: body sherd in smooth black ware tempered with crushed flint and chalk. The surface is smoothed and fired to a reddish-brown.

From layer 89:

109. S325 Jar with out-bent rim in black sandy ware burnished on the outside surface.

Animal Bones

512 fragments identified (including 36 ribs and 35 skull fragments).

Species represented: cattle, 49; sheep, 28; pig, 16; bird, 5; dog, 1; horse, 1; red deer, cat.

Many of the sheep bones in this pit were complete and unbutchered. Their 'fresh' condition suggested that they might have been deposited in the pit with flesh still attached to the bone.

Pit 192 (PC 71, trench 100, layers 40, 45, 50, 59, 68)

Rectangular pit measuring 5 ft. 3 in. by 4 ft. (1·60 × 1·22 m.) at the bottom but eroded to larger proportions at the top. Cut to a depth of 4 ft. (1·22 m.) below the contemporary surface.

The pit had originally been lined with horizontal planks kept in position by circular stakes driven into the bottom of the pit at the corners (pl. XII*a*). After abandonment a layer of soil, clay and gravel washed in (layer 59), following the accumulation of which the timber lining was burnt. Some fragments of charred timber remained in position, the rest, together with burnt clay from the sides of the pit, eroded in (layers 50 and 68). The resulting hollow was then filled with a mass of grey soil mixed with occupation debris, including flint, tile, bone, and oyster shells (layer 45) above which was a thick packing of redeposited brickearth (layer 40).

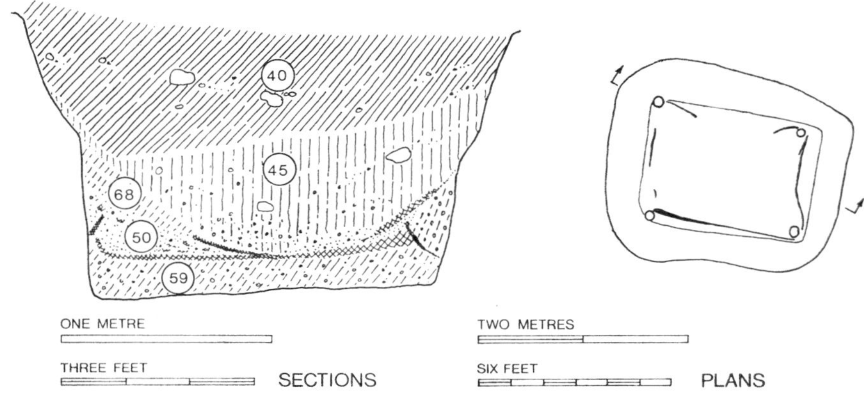

Fig. 81. Pit 192

Small Finds

From layer 40:

Shale spindle whorl	(2078):	fig. 141, no. 80.

From layer 50:

Bronze spoon	(2094):	Roman, residual: not illustrated.
Iron strip binding	(2125):	heavily corroded: not illustrated.

Pottery. Mid–late Saxon (fig. 109)

From layer 40:

111. S313. Rim, black sandy ware tempered with coarsely crushed flint grits. Rough surface.
112. S314. Rim, grey sandy ware, smoothed but irregular surface.

Not illustrated: body sherd from coarse jar in smooth grey-brown ware tempered with flint grits.

From layer 45:

Not illustrated: 4 body sherds, 3 in black sandy wares with some chaff tempering and with smoothed surfaces, and 1 in light grey sandy ware with a burnished surface.

From layer 50:

Not illustrated: 1 body sherd in grey ware with flint grit tempering.

Animal Bones

40 fragments identified (including 6 ribs and 2 skull fragments).
Species represented: cattle, pig, cat, sheep, bird.

Pit 193 (PC 71, trench 100, layer 52)

Sub-rectangular pit measuring 8 ft. (2·44 m.) in length but of unknown width since part of the pit had been destroyed by the sixteenth-century footings. The pit filling was excavated to a depth of 3 ft. 2 in. (0·97 m.) but extended further.

The filling consisted of a fairly uniform deposit of black stony soil with lenses of stone, some large flints and oyster shells.

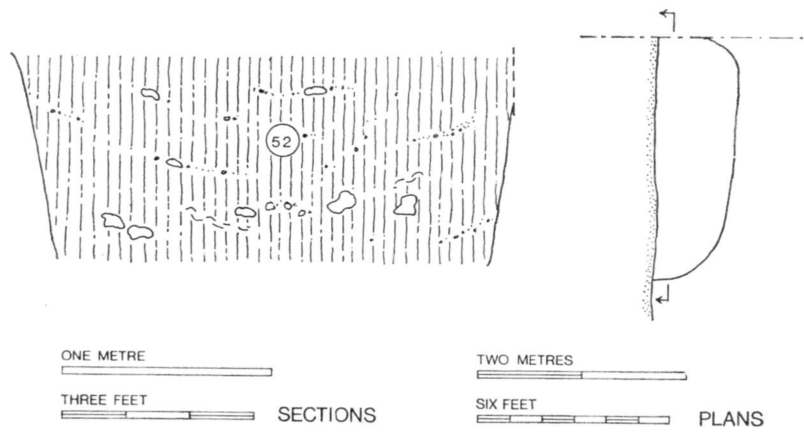

FIG. 82. Pit 193

Pottery. Late Saxon

Not illustrated: 9 body sherds: Portchester ware, 2 rilled and 2 plain; coarse cooking pot fabrics, 5 body sherds.

Animal Bones

56 fragments identified (including 2 ribs and 18 skull fragments).
Species represented: cattle, pig, sheep, horse.

Pit 194 (PC 71, trench 102, layers 56, 70, 73, 81, 82, 83)

Irregularly shaped pit of maximum extent 10 ft. by 6 ft. 6 in. (3·05 × 1·98 m.) shelving to a bottom 4 ft. 6 in. (1·37 m.) below the contemporary ground surface.

The lowest layer (layer 83) was derived from the erosion of the sides of the pit. Above this the lower filling (layer 81) consisted of occupation material, large flints and washed-in clay mixed with grey-brown soil and sealed by a more clayey layer (layer 73), again derived by erosion. At this stage charcoal, bones and oyster shells were tipped into the partially silted hollow to be followed by an accumulation of brown soil containing occupation debris (layer 70). The upper part of the pit was levelled with tips of clay, clayey soil and some flints (layer 56), the slight hollow caused by subsidence finally being filled with gravel (layer 82).

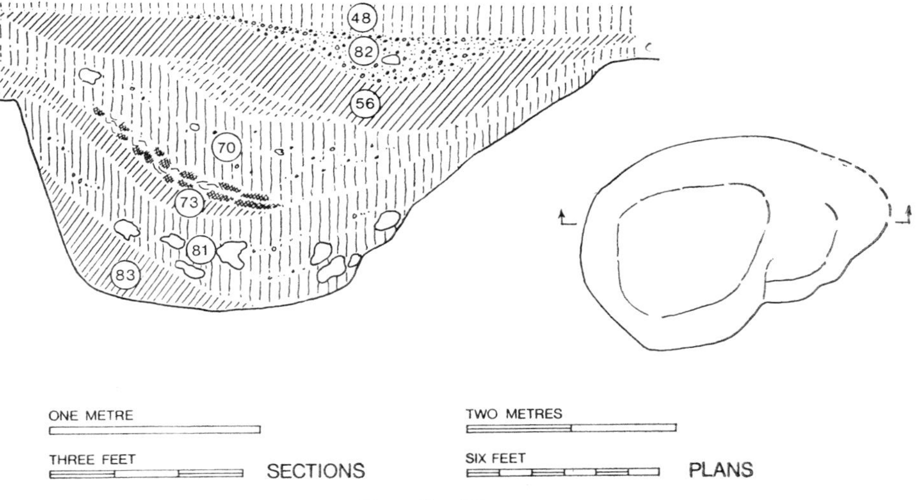

Fig. 83. Pit 194

Small Finds

From layer 56:
- Bronze pin (2099): fig. 139, no. 56.
- Crucible (2208): fig. 141, no. 78.

From layer 70:
- Roman bronze coin (2221): Urbs Roma (A.D. 330–45).

From layer 73:
- Iron spoon (2126): Probably Roman: not illustrated.

Pottery. Early–mid Saxon (fig. 109)

From layer 70:

113. S316. Dish in black sandy ware with sparse large flint grits and some chaff tempering: burnished on the surface.

114. S315. Dish, smooth grey ware with grog tempering: burnished on the surface (possibly late Roman).

Not illustrated: 5 body sherds, 3 in hard grey sandy ware, 1 in a finer light grey sandy ware with smoothed surface and 1 in a black sandy ware with finely crushed flint grits.

From layer 73:

Not illustrated: body sherd in black sandy ware tempered with chaff: smoothed surface.

Animal Bones

169 fragments identified (including 32 ribs and 16 skull fragments).
Species represented: cattle, 75; sheep, 8; pig, 6; red deer, 4; dog, 3; bird, 3; horse, 1.

Pit 196 (PC 71, trench 100, layer 38)

Rectangular pit 4 ft. by 4 ft. 9 in. (1·22 × 1·45 m.) cut to a depth of 2 ft. (0·61 m.) below the contemporary surface. The pit was only partially excavated.

The filling was uniform, consisting of black soil and occupation debris with a number of large flints and occasional wads of redeposited brickearth.

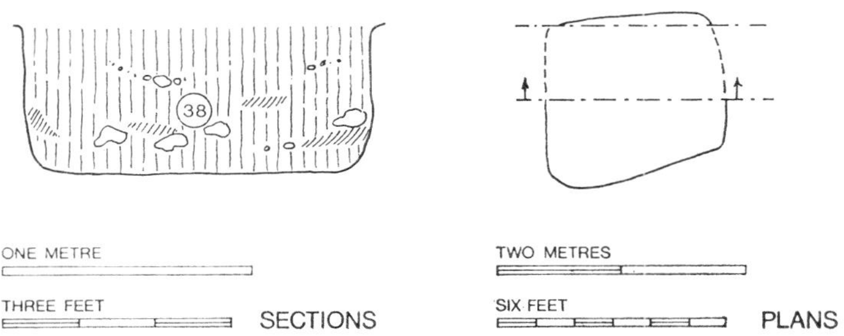

FIG. 84. Pit 196

Pottery. Late Saxon (fig. 127)

Portchester ware and associated types, nos. 483–6.
Not illustrated: 9 body sherds; Porchester ware, 2 rilled and 1 plain; coarse cooking pots, 6 sherds.

Animal Bones

28 fragments identified (including 8 ribs).
Species represented: cattle, sheep, pig.

Pit 198 (PC 71, trench 101, layers 47, 63, 68, 82, 83)

Rectangular pit 6 ft. by 5 ft. 3 in. (1·83 × 1·60 m.) cut to a depth of 3½ ft. (1·07 m.) below the contemporary ground surface.

The lowest filling (layer 83) consisted of brown-black soil, having the appearance of decomposed cesspit fill, mixed with some washed-in brickearth and occasional large flints. Above this was a lens of fine chalk fragments (layer 82) followed by a layer of chalky soil containing flints and oyster shells (layer 68). The upper part of the pit was filled with black soil mixed with charcoal, some flints, oyster shells and other occupation debris including some fragments of chalky daub (layer 63). The upper part of this layer was recorded as a separate layer (layer 47) but it was indistinguishable from layer 63.

Cut by pit 199.

Small Finds

From layer 47:

Iron rod fragment	(2161):	fig. 134, no. 30.
Roman bronze coin	(2168):	Gratian (A.D. 378–83).

From layer 83:

Bronze pin fragment?	(2210):	not illustrated.

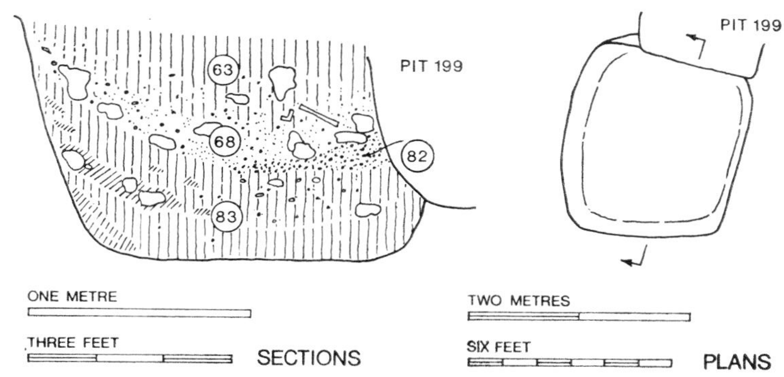

Fig. 85. Pit 198

Pottery. Mid–late Saxon (fig. 109)

From layer 47:

Not illustrated: 3 body sherds, 1 in smooth grey ware tempered with crushed flint grits, 2 in black sandy fabrics.

From layer 63:

115. S317. Large jar with everted rim, represented by 1 sherd of the rim and 9 body sherds decorated with all-over stamping (four of the sherds come from layer 68). The fabric is smooth red ware copiously tempered with finely crushed flint and chalk; the surface is smoothed and fired to a grey-brown.

116. S318. Jar with slightly everted rim in smooth grey ware tempered with chaff. The outer surface is burnished and fired black.

Not illustrated: a body sherd belonging to no. 116 and a body sherd in black ware with crushed flint grit tempering.

From layer 68:

117. S326. Rim sherd, fine grey sandy ware with some chaff tempering, fired to a pinkish surface, burnished.

118. S328. Rim, fine grey sandy ware.

119. S329. Rim, fine grey sandy ware tempered with chaff. The surfaces are well smoothed.

120. S330. Rim, everted. Black sandy ware fired red on the surface.

121. S327. Everted rim jar in grey ware tempered with crushed flint grit. The surface is smoothed and fired to a black colour.

122. S331. Body sherd, grey sandy ware.

Not illustrated: body sherd of S318 and 2 body sherds in grey ware with fine flint grit tempering.

Animal Bones

187 fragments identified (including 59 ribs and 13 skull fragments).

Species represented: cattle, 49; sheep, 25; pig, 18; red deer, 3; bird, 3; roe deer, 2; horse, 1.

Pit 202 (PC 71, trench 101, layer 56)

Small rectangular pit approximately 3 ft. (0·91 m.) square, cut to a depth of 7 in. (0·18 m.) below the contemporary surface.

The filling was uniform consisting of grey-black soil containing flecks of charcoal with ash lenses towards the bottom.

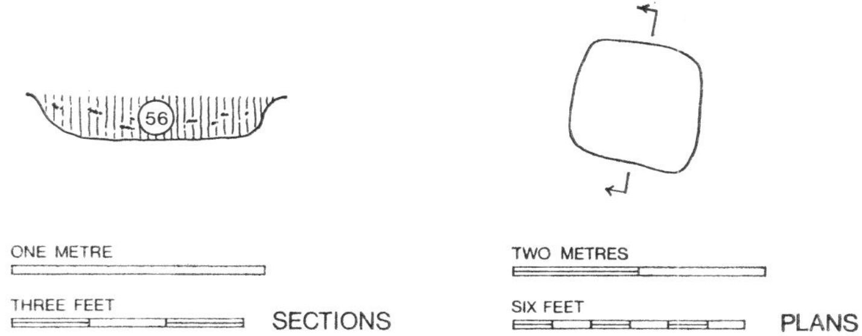

Fig. 86. Pit 202

Small Finds

Iron pruning hook (2195): fig. 131, no. 11.

Pottery. Mid–late Saxon

Not illustrated: 2 body sherds in black sandy ware with coarse flint grits.

Animal Bones

27 fragments identified (including 4 ribs and 4 skull fragments).
Species represented: cattle, sheep, roe deer, pig, dog.

Pit 203 (PC 71, trench 101, layers 48, 72, 95)

Approximately circular pit 4 ft. (1·22 m.) in diameter, cut to a depth of 2 ft. 4 in. (0·71 m.) below the contemporary ground surface.

The lowest level of the fill (layer 95) consisted of black soil containing some small flints. The upper layers (layers 72 and 48) were of similar material arbitrarily dug. For both there is the possibility of contamination since they were not adequately distinguished from the surrounding layers.

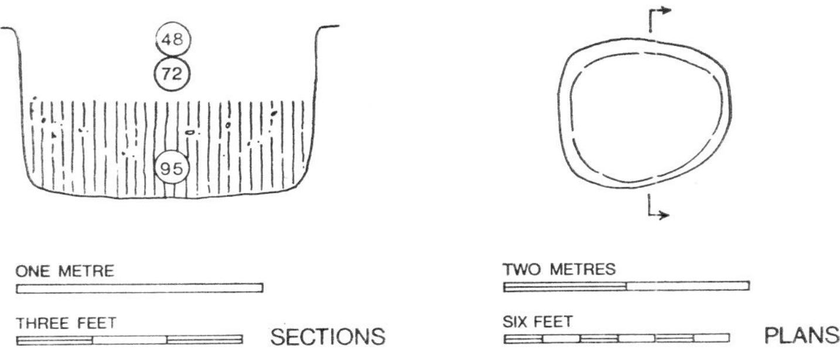

Fig. 87. Pit 203

Small Finds

From layer 72:

Roman bronze coin	(2201): third/fourth century, illegible.
Iron knife blade	(2200): fig. 132, no. 20.
Bone knife handle	(2199): fig. 140, no. 71.

Pottery. Mid–late Saxon

From layer 48:

Not illustrated: fragment of a strap lug in grey ware with finely crushed flint grits: burnished surface; 2 body sherds, 1 in grey sandy ware tempered with chaff, and 1 in coarse black sandy ware with some flint grits.

Animal Bones

31 fragments identified (including 7 ribs and 2 skull fragments).
Species represented: cattle, sheep, pig, horse, dog.

Pit 204 (PC 71, trench 101, layers 80, 91, 96, 97, 98, 100, 101, 102)

Rectangular pit 7 ft. 3 in. by 6 ft. (2·21 × 1·83 m.) cut to a depth of 4 ft. (1·22 m.) below the contemporary surface.

The pit was originally lined with horizontal planks kept in place by five stakes rammed into the floor.

Most of the pit had been filled with deliberate tips of redeposited brickearth interleaved with black soil and occupation debris thrown in in alternate layers (layers 102, 101). Above this were mixed layers of soil, mortar and clay in five lenses (layers 100, 98, 97, 96 and 91) sealed by a lens of burnt chalky daub fragments bearing the impressions of 1 in. wattle marks (layer 80).

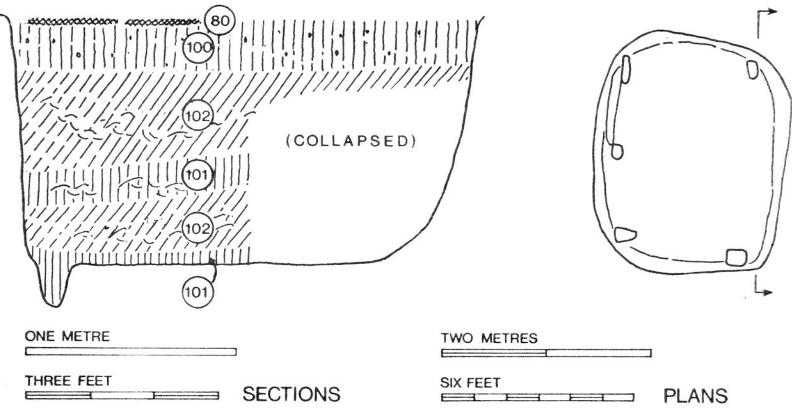

Fig. 88. Pit 204

Small Finds

From layer 101:
- Bone with knife cuts (2213): not illustrated.
- Quernstone (2215): fig. 144, no. 5.

From layer 102:
- Roman bronze coin (2237): Constantine I (A.D. 310–17).

Pottery. Mid–late Saxon (fig. 110)

From layer 98:

Not illustrated: 2 body sherds from large jars, 1 in brown fabric tempered with crushed flint and shell, the other in smooth grey ware with copious chaff tempering.

From layer 101:

Not illustrated: large jar in grey-brown ware tempered with finely crushed flint. The surface is smoothed and stamped overall. 3 sherds from layer 101 and 20 from layer 102 (N.B. this is the same vessel as no. 115 from pit 198). 11 body sherds from coarse jars in smooth fabrics tempered with crushed flint and chalk: 4 body sherds from coarse grey sandy wares: 1 body sherd in smooth black ware with chaff tempering.

From layer 102:

123. S312. Rim in coarse grey sandy ware fired grey-brown on the surface.

Not illustrated: 11 body sherds from coarse jars in smooth fabrics tempered by crushed flint and chalk grits; 2 body sherds in fine sandy fabrics with chaff tempering.

Animal Bones

590 fragments identified (including 139 ribs and 39 skull fragments).

Species represented: cattle, 42; sheep, 33; pig, 15; roe deer, 4; bird, 3; red deer, 1; horse, 1; dog, 1; hare.

The nature of many of the sheep and roe deer bone fragments suggests that bone tool waste may have been thrown into this pit with the domestic refuse.

Pit 207 (PC 71, trench 103, layers 39, 40, 41, 42, 43, 44, 48; PC 72, trench 104, layers 6, 8, 9, 10, 11, 12)

Rectangular pit dug against the face of the Roman wall, measuring 12 by 5 ft. (3·66 × 1·52 m.) at the surface but undercutting the Roman wall footings so that the bottom width reached 6 ft. (1·83 m.). Dug to a depth of 10 ft. (3·05 m.) from the contemporary ground surface.

The lowest filling (layer 73) consisted of yellowish-brown soil, containing some charcoal and winkle shells, representing decomposed cesspit filling mixed with occupation material. This was sealed by a layer of black occupation material (layer 48) above which was a thickness of grey soil containing much occupation debris, in particular oyster and winkle shells (layers 44, 43, and 42). The soil became blacker towards the top and eventually merged with a tip of winkle and oyster shells (layer 41). Above this the hollow against the wall face was filled with accumulations of grey soil interleaved with flints and mortar, derived from the erosion of the wall face (layer 40). Grey soil containing some occupation debris sealed the pit (layer 39).

Trench 104, layers 9–12 are equivalent to trench 103, layers 41–44. Trench 104, layer 8 equates with trench 103, layer 40, and layer 6 with layer 39.

Small Finds

From 104 layer 6:

Bone comb	(2286):	fig. 140, no. 72.

From 104 layer 8:

Iron hinge pivot	(2289):	fig. 131, no. 10.
Iron knife	(2291):	fig. 133, no. 22.
Whetstone	(2290):	fig. 142, no. 86.

From 103 layer 39:

Iron strip	(2273):	fig. 134, no. 28.

From 103 layer 40:

Bronze belt fittings	(2268):	fig. 136, no. 55.

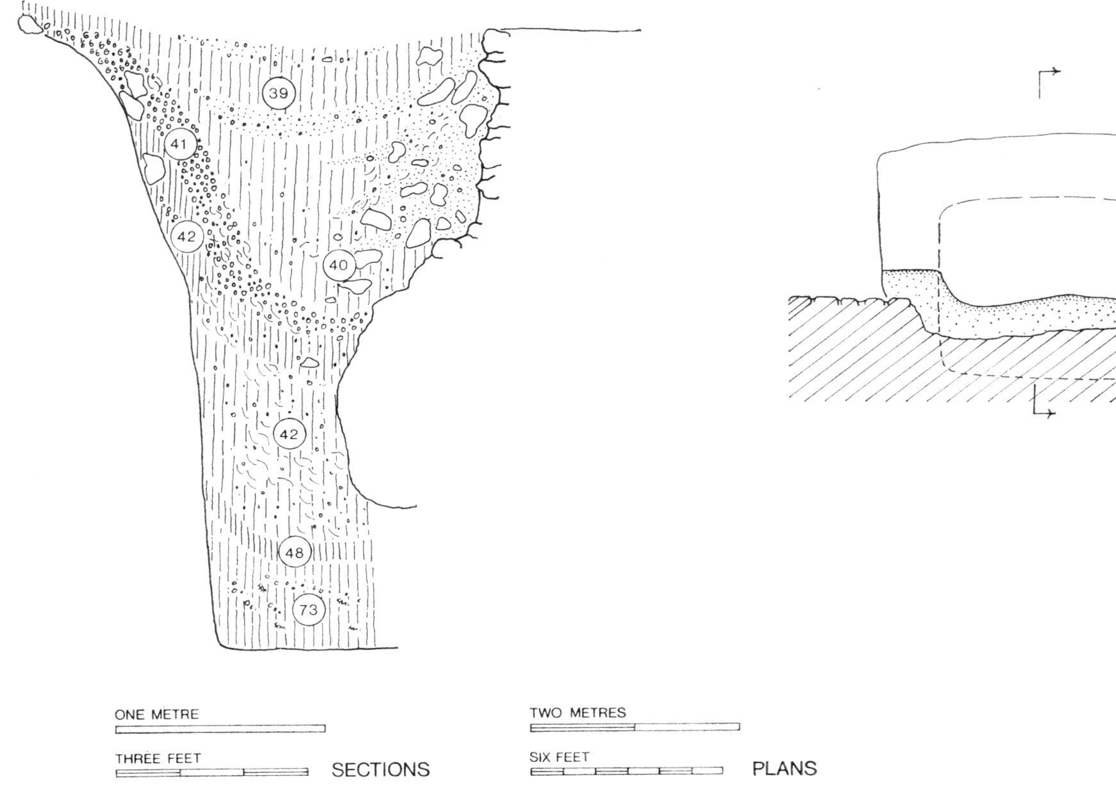

Fig. 89. Pit 207

Pottery. Mid–late Saxon (fig. 110)

From 103 layer 40:

128. S319. Rim from a coarse vessel in black sandy ware with sporadic large flint grits.

Not illustrated: 2 body sherds from cooking pots in coarse sandy ware, and 1 from a large vessel in laminated fabric tempered with copious chaff.

From 103 layer 41:

Not illustrated: 2 body sherds from coarse jars in grey fabric tempered with flint grit. See 125.

From 104 layer 8:

124. S320 Cooking pot with everted rim in coarse black ware tempered with crushed flint grits.
125. S321. Spouted pitcher in fine hard grey-brown ware, wheel-turned. The surface is fired to an even dark grey and is smoothed and burnished. Import (also sherds from trench 103 layer 41).
127. S322. Rim, grey sandy ware with chaff tempering and a burnished surface.

Not illustrated: 9 sherds from coarse cooking pots in grey wares with crushed flint and chalk grits; 4 body sherds in grey sandy wares and 3 body sherds in fine sandy or smooth fabrics tempered with chopped chaff; the surfaces are burnished.

From 104 layer 10:

305. S333. Rim in black sandy ware with burnished surface.
307. S332. Rim in coarse grey sandy ware with smoothed surface.

Not illustrated: 16 sherds, 1 rim fragment in very coarse gritty fabric with chaff tempering, 3 sherds in similar wares, 1 in finer chaff-tempered ware; 8 in sandy wares and 2 in hard wheel-turned grey sandy wares with a highly burnished black surface (?imports).

From 104 layer 11:

Not illustrated: 2 body sherds in fine hard light grey ware with slightly darker grey surface, wheel-turned (? imports).

From 104 layer 12:

126. S334. Rim, grey-brown sandy ware with coarse flint grits.

Not illustrated: Rim sherd similar to no. 124 but broken at the lip. 15 body sherds, 11 in coarse chaff-tempered wares, 2 in flint-gritted fabrics, and 2 in sandy wares. 5 sherds of the imported vessel no. 125.

Animal Bones

1730 fragments identified (including 374 ribs and 85 skull fragments).

Species represented: bird, 44; cattle, 23; sheep, 19; pig, 12; fish, 2; red deer, horse, hare, dog, cat.

A large number of bird bones were found in this pit, together with a greater than usual number of fish bones.

Pit 211 (PC 72, trench 104, layer 7)

Shallow elongated pit dug parallel to the back face of the Roman fort wall, 2 ft. (0·61 m.) wide and cut to a depth of up to 9 in. (0·23 m.) below the contemporary surface.

Filled with stone-free grey-brown silt.

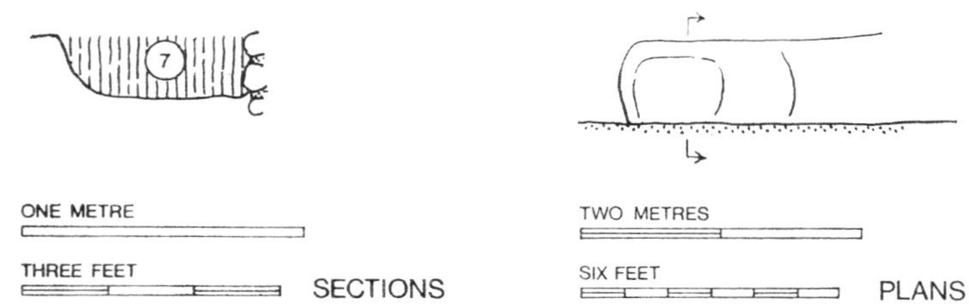

FIG. 90. Pit 211

Pottery. Early–mid Saxon (fig. 110)

129. S323. Jar in coarse black sandy ware with chaff tempering. The surface is burnished.

Pit 216 (PC 72, trench 108, layer 38)

Sub-rectangular pit 5 by 7 ft. (1·52 × 2·13 m.) dug to a maximum depth of 1 ft. 3 in. (0·38 m.) below the contemporary surface.

Filled with mixed occupation rubbish including charcoal, oyster shells, flints and wads of redeposited brickearth.

Cut by pit 214.

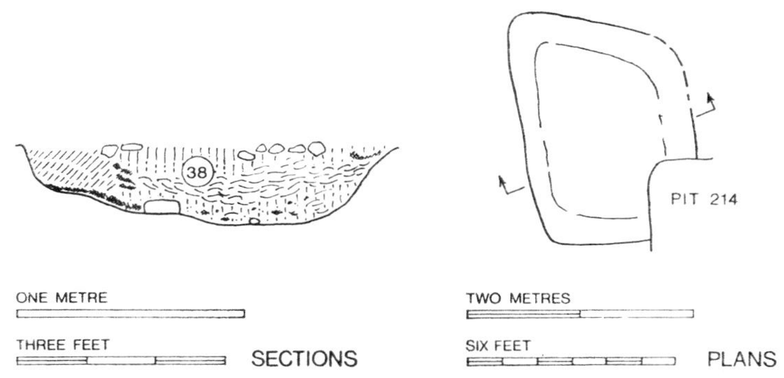

Fig. 91. Pit 216

Small Finds

Iron rod (2436): fig. 135, no. 43.

Pottery. Mid–late Saxon (fig. 110)

130. S356. Substantial part of a large jar with outcurved rim. The fabric consists of a smooth red paste tempered with coarsely crushed flint grit. The base is rounded. The surface is uneven and unburnished. 12 body sherds and 2 rim sherds.

Not illustrated: 9 body sherds in grey wares tempered with varying amounts of flint grit. 1 body sherd in smooth grey ware with chaff tempering.

Animal Bones

57 fragments identified (including 15 ribs and 1 skull fragment).
Species represented: cattle, sheep, pig, roe deer, bird.

Pit 217 (PC 72, trench 108, layers 43, 54, 69)

Oval pit 3 ft. 6 in. by 5 ft. (1·07 × 1·52 m.) cut to a depth of 4 ft. (1·22 m.) below the contemporary surface.

The lowest filling (layer 69) consisted of a crumbly grey-brown soil derived from decomposed cesspit filling, interleaved with a lens of brickearth presumably eroded in from the sides. Above this was a thickness of black soil with flints, stones and oyster shells (layer 54). The pit was sealed with a layer of clayey soil (layer 43) which extended south and east of the pit.

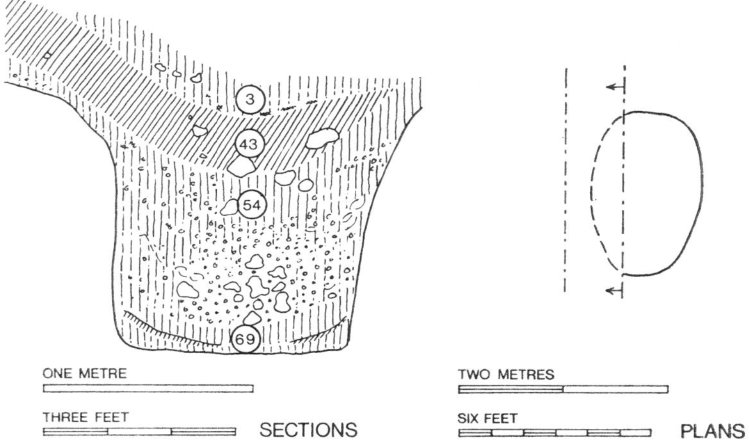

FIG. 92. Pit 217

Pottery. Mid–late Saxon

From layer 54:

Not illustrated: 4 body sherds in coarse flint-gritted ware.

Animal Bones

63 fragments identified (including 17 ribs and 10 skull fragments).
Species represented: cattle, sheep, bird, pig, roe deer.

Pit 218 (PC 72, trench 107, layers 51 and 62)

Small irregular pit measuring 5 ft. by 1 ft. 6 in. (1·52 × 0·46 m.) cut against the back face of the Roman wall to a depth of 2 ft. 3 in. (0·69 m.) below the contemporary surface.

The lowest level (layer 62) consisted of fine dark grey soil mixed with flints, shells and charcoal. This was sealed by more mortary soil derived from the erosion of the Roman wall face, mixed with oysters, winkle and cockle shells.

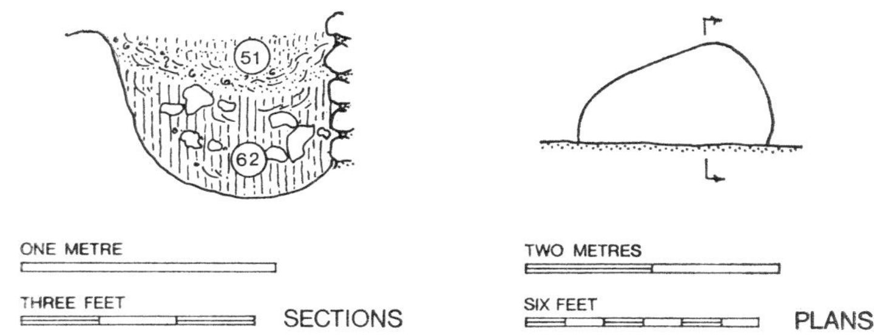

FIG. 93. Pit 218

Pottery. Mid–late Saxon

From layer 51:

Not illustrated: coarse sandy sherd.

Animal Bones

84 fragments identified (including 14 ribs and 14 skull fragments).
Species represented: hare, cattle, sheep, bird, pig, dog.

Human

Part of an infant burial.

Pit 219 (PC 72, trench 108, layers 56, 57, 68)

Rectangular pit 3 ft. 6 in. by 7 ft. (1·07 × 2·13 m.) at the top, dug to a depth of 5 ft. (1·52 m.) below the contemporary surface.

The lowest level of filling (layer 68) consisted of fine green-brown crumbly soil resulting from decomposed cesspit filling. The rest of the pit was filled with loose packed flints in black soil intermixed with some occupation rubbish (layer 57; layer 56 was the top few inches which were dug and recorded separately from 57, but otherwise indistinguishable).

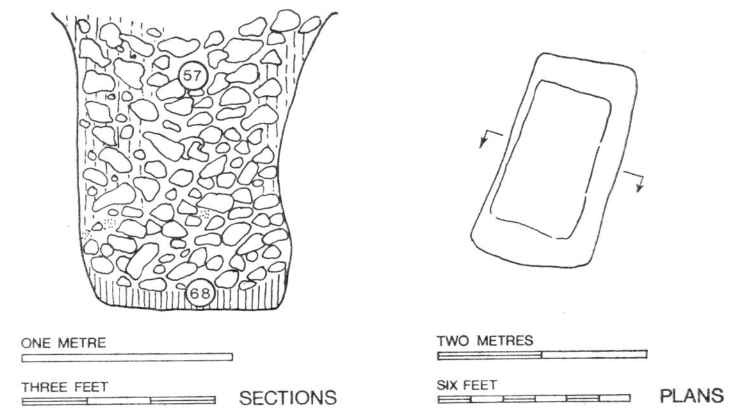

Fig. 94. Pit 219

Small Finds

From layer 57:

Iron knife (2435): fig. 132, no. 18.

Pottery. Late Saxon (fig. 126)

From layer 57:

Portchester ware and associated types, nos. 487–491.
Not illustrated: 21 body sherds; Portchester ware, 11 rilled and 4 plain; coarse cooking pot fabrics, 6 sherds.

From layer 68:

Not illustrated: 3 body sherds in coarse cooking pot fabrics.

Animal Bones

298 fragments identified (including 67 ribs and 21 skull fragments).
Species represented: cattle, 50; sheep, 26; pig, 10; roe deer, 5; red deer, 5; bird, 2; horse, dog, cat.

Pit 220 (PC 72, trench 108, layers 79, 80, 84)

Large pit of oval plan measuring 10 ft. by 7 ft. 6 in. (3·05 × 2·29 m.) at the top but with steeply sloping sides, dug to a depth of 4 ft. (1·22 m.) below the contemporary surface.

The main filling (layer 84) consisted of fine ashy soil containing a high clay constituent and some charcoal. The layer was uniform but showed signs of fine lamination. Above was a mass of black occupation rubbish containing large numbers of oyster shells (layer 80). This was sealed by a layer of yellow clay burnt in patches (layer 79) which represented the floor of building S11. It had slumped into the pit, the hollow being filled with tips of ash and occupation material contemporary with the use of the house.

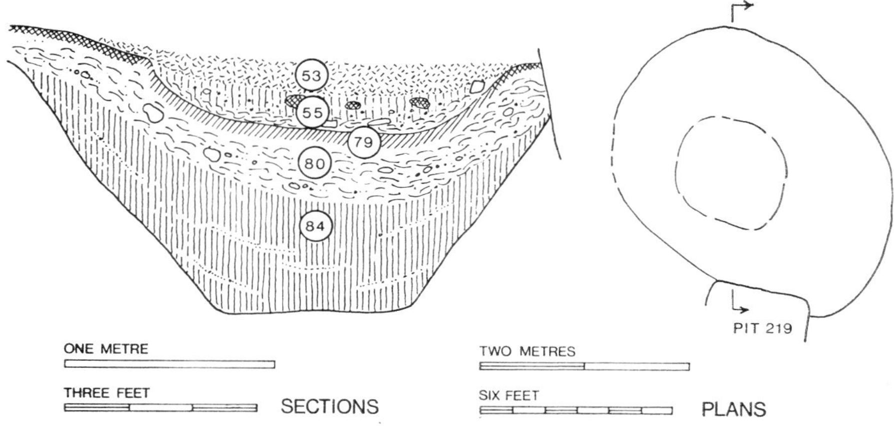

FIG. 95. Pit 220

Small Finds

From layer 84:
Bronze pin (2462): fig. 139, no. 54.
From layer 80:
Iron pronged object (2522): fig. 130, no. 2.
Bone comb (2523): fig. 140, no. 74.

Pottery. Mid–late Saxon (fig. 110)

From layer 79:
131. S335. Rim in black sandy ware with flint grit tempering.

Not illustrated: body sherd in grey sandy ware.

From layer 80:
132. S336. Decorated sherd from the shoulder of a vessel in fine light grey sandy ware with a smoothed surface fired to an even black colour. The two horizontal zones of stamps are separated by 3 deeply tooled horizontal lines.

133. S338. Rim sherd in black ware tempered with large quartz grits.
135. S337. Two rim sherds in fine reddish sandy ware. The surface is smoothed and fired black. At the base of the neck is an area of impressed decoration.

Not illustrated: 39 body sherds; 13 sherds of one vessel in a smooth grey sandy paste with much chaff tempering; 1 sherd from a different vessel but in a similar paste; 2 sherds of one vessel in a hard grey sandy fabric with large quartz grains and flakes of mica: 6 sherds from one vessel in smooth black paste with large flint grits: 6 sherds in grey fabrics with crushed flint grits: 10 sherds in grey sandy wares: 1 sherd in a fine light grey sandy ware with a burnished black surface, wheel-turned and ? an import.

From layer 84:

134. S357. Rim of coarse jar in black sandy ware with some flint grits.

Not illustrated: 4 body sherds in grey wares tempered with crushed flint grits; 1 body sherd in dark grey sandy ware.

Animal Bones

555 fragments identified (including 142 ribs and 19 skull fragments).

Species represented: cattle, 28; bird, 27; sheep, 24; pig, 16; roe deer, 2; horse, 1; red deer, 1; fish, 1; fallow deer, 1.

This pit has a high percentage of bird bones in it. The nature of many of the bone fragments suggests that bone tool waste may have been thrown into this pit with normal domestic refuse.

Pit 227A (PC 72, trench 109, layers 18, 37)

Oval pit measuring 3 ft. 6 in. by 3 ft. (1·07 × 0·91 m.) but widely eroded at the top, dug to a depth of 2 ft. 8 in. (0·81 m.) below the contemporary surface.

The lower filling (layer 37) consisted of grey-black earth containing charcoal and a lens of clayey soil. Above this the pit was filled with brown clayey soil containing flints and fragments of tile (layer 18).

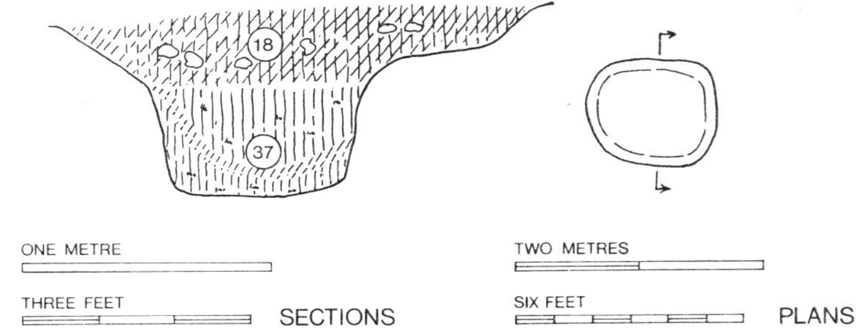

Fig. 96. Pit 227A

Small Finds

From layer 18:

Roman coin	(2527):	unidentified.
Bronze fragment	(2542):	not illustrated.

Pit 240 (PC 72, trench 109, layers 89, 101, 104)

Rectangular pit measuring 4 by 6 ft. (1·22 × 1·83 m.) cut to a depth of 2 ft. 6 in. (0·76 m.) below the surface of the natural clay.

The lowest layer (layer 104) consisted of a decomposed cesspit filling of green-grey crumbly soil. Above this was a mixed layer (layer 101) containing much ash, some clay, flints and oyster shells. This was sealed by a brown soil and occupation debris, more clayey towards the north side where erosion of the pit side occurred (layer 89). The pit was cut by an eighteenth-century fence trench.

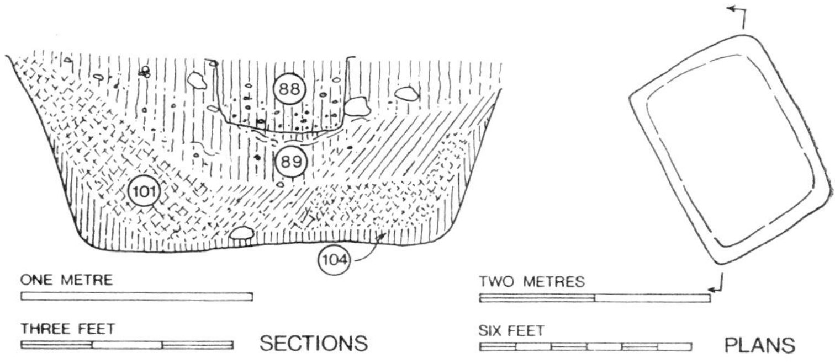

Fig. 97. Pit 240

Pottery. Late Saxon (fig. 127)

Portchester ware and associated types, nos. 492–499.
Not illustrated: 24 body sherds in Portchester ware fabrics.

Animal Bones

11 fragments identified.
Species represented: cattle, bird, sheep.

THE ESTABLISHMENT OF A SEQUENCE (figs. 98 and 99)

There are three kinds of evidence which enable a sequence to be established at Portchester in the Saxon period: (a) the direct stratigraphical relationship of one building or structure with another; (b) the assignment of relative dates, derived from the pottery sequence, to individual structures; (c) the interpretation of the overall ground plan in terms of likely usage. Clearly the permutations possible with the 18 buildings and 61 pits and wells are many and any interpretation must be open to a considerable margin of error. At best we can offer only a simplified development history within each phase of which there will be several alternative interpretations. With these provisos in mind, eight phases can be defined.

Phase 1. Fifth–seventh century

The structures assigned to this phase are the four *Grubenhäuser* and the two irregular post-built huts, together with the well (pit 135) and the period of ploughing. Hut S1 and the well are dated on the basis of associated pottery and metal work to this phase: huts S2 and S4 by virtue of their stratigraphical positions are also early. Hut S3 and the two post-built structures S5 and S6, are regarded as early on the basis of their form, and their spatial relationship to later buildings, while the ploughing can be shown to pre-date eighth–ninth-century occupation.

Within this period of 300 years or so there must have been change. The evidence from the well (pit) 135, suggests active use, followed by possible abandonment before it was refitted with a new timber lining. Similarly, the ploughing activity cannot have been contemporary with the occupation of building S6, since plough marks came too close to its wall.

Any detailed interpretation of the relationships of the component elements is open to such a margin of error as to render it almost worthless. Nevertheless, one *possible* sequence would be to suppose three sub-phases, the first represented by the *Grubenhäuser* and the water-hole, dating to the second part of the fifth century; the second being a period of ploughing while occupation centred elsewhere in the fort, while in the third the fields were re-colonized by post-built houses, and the well was refitted some time in the sixth century. It must, however, be stressed that this is only one of the explanations possible on the available evidence. That the use of the site was virtually continuous throughout this time is suggested, but not proved, by the range of datable material recovered from the excavation.

Phase 2. Seventh–late eighth century

In terms of the ceramic development, phase 2 spans the changeover from chaff-tempered to gritty fabrics (p. 182). To this phase are assigned posthole building S9, which can be shown to pre-date S10, but is otherwise undated; building S7 (pre-dating S8), building S12 and its fenced yard, and the possible building represented by 'posthole complex A'. Well (pit) 135 remained in use and two new wells were dug, well (pit) 143 close to the corner of building S7 and well (pit) 56 close to 'posthole complex A'. Three pits, nos. 34, 35 and 38, clustered around building S12, the first two serving as cesspits. Pit 141 may have been contemporary with building S7, while pits 194, 198, 203, 204 and 220 would appear to have belonged to building S9, pits 194 and 220 once serving as cesspits. It was probably by the end of this phase that well (pit) 135 finally went out of use.

All the features listed here seem to have pre-dated the common occurrence of the characteristic ninth- to mid tenth-century gritty pottery; some levels, such as pits 38, 220, the lowest material in well (pit) 143 and the latest occupation contemporary with the use of well (pit) 135 are closely related in time by the occurrence of the mica-gritted pottery (p. 182). Pit 34 produced a fragment of datable glass; the rest have less definite associations, but pits 198 and 204 contained fragments of the same decorated pot.

If these buildings and features can be regarded as belonging to the same broad phase, a certain apparent order will be seen to emerge, with the structures falling into two separate groups divided by an open area. Each group comprised at least two buildings, a well and a number of pits, some for storage and some for use as cesspits: in other words the groups were self-contained units, each perhaps representing a single household.

A more elaborate explanation could be constructed in which each house is seen as a separate social entity. Since buildings S9 and S12 were without their own water supply but were close to the old well, they could be considered to be the earliest structures, augmented at a later stage by buildings S7 and 'posthole complex A', each with their own wells immediately adjacent. If this view of the sequence is accepted, one of three alternative explanations follows: (a) that the 'new' buildings replaced the old; (b) that they represented an increase in the size of the two existing establishments; (c) that the two households were now increased to four. Each is equally plausible: clearly the situation was a complex one for which no single definitive explanation is possible.

Phase 3. Eighth–mid ninth century

This phase is difficult to distinguish in detail, but building S10 can be shown to replace building S9 and is clearly contemporary with building S11. The two large cesspits, pits 191 and 207, belong to this phase, together with storage pits 192 and possibly 202. Well (pit) 135 now served buildings S10 and S11, at least during the first part of this period. Well (pit) 143 remained the source of fresh water for building S7 while it continued in use. What happened elsewhere is less clear, but buildings S12 and 'posthole complex A' may well have continued to be inhabited.

In other words phase 3 was simply a continuation of the phase 2 occupation in which the only significant change was the replacement of building S9 by buildings S10 and S11.

Phase 4. Ninth–tenth century

Phase 4 is represented by a thick deposit of occupation rubbish containing large quantities of animal bones and many thousands of oyster shells and other shell fish. The layer was at its thickest over the hollow which represented the now-silted up well (pit) 135, but spread south to the wall of the fort and west to seal the destroyed remains of buildings S10 and S11. It slumped down into the two cesspits, pits 191 and 207, thus demonstrating that they were still partially open at that time. The deposit thinned out to the north, and disappeared altogether by the northern limit of Area A.

The general homogeneity of the layer leaves little doubt that it was created by a process of organized rubbish tipping over an area which had ceased to be occupied. No trace of any contemporary structure was found in Area A, nor is any likely to have existed for the stench of the decaying muck would have been unbearable. Area B was largely clear of rubbish, but wells (pits) 56 and 143 were both in disuse and were rapidly eroding. Presumably occupation had ceased here too. The surviving remains in Area C are more difficult to interpret: it is possible that some of the postholes found here relate to buildings lining the main central road, although no pits, wells or contemporary occupation layers survive.

Phase 4 must then mark a significant break in the traditional occupation of the fort when much of the excavated site was converted into a refuse dump, the habitations now being sited elsewhere. The possible significance of this change will be returned to again below (p. 303).

Phase 5. Tenth century

After the rubbish tip had rotted down, soil began to accumulate above it, containing sherds of characteristic Portchester ware (pp. 187–9) — a type of pottery found both in association with buildings S8, and S13–18, which occupied Area B, and in the broadly contemporary pits which lay to the west and north of them. The interrelationships of the

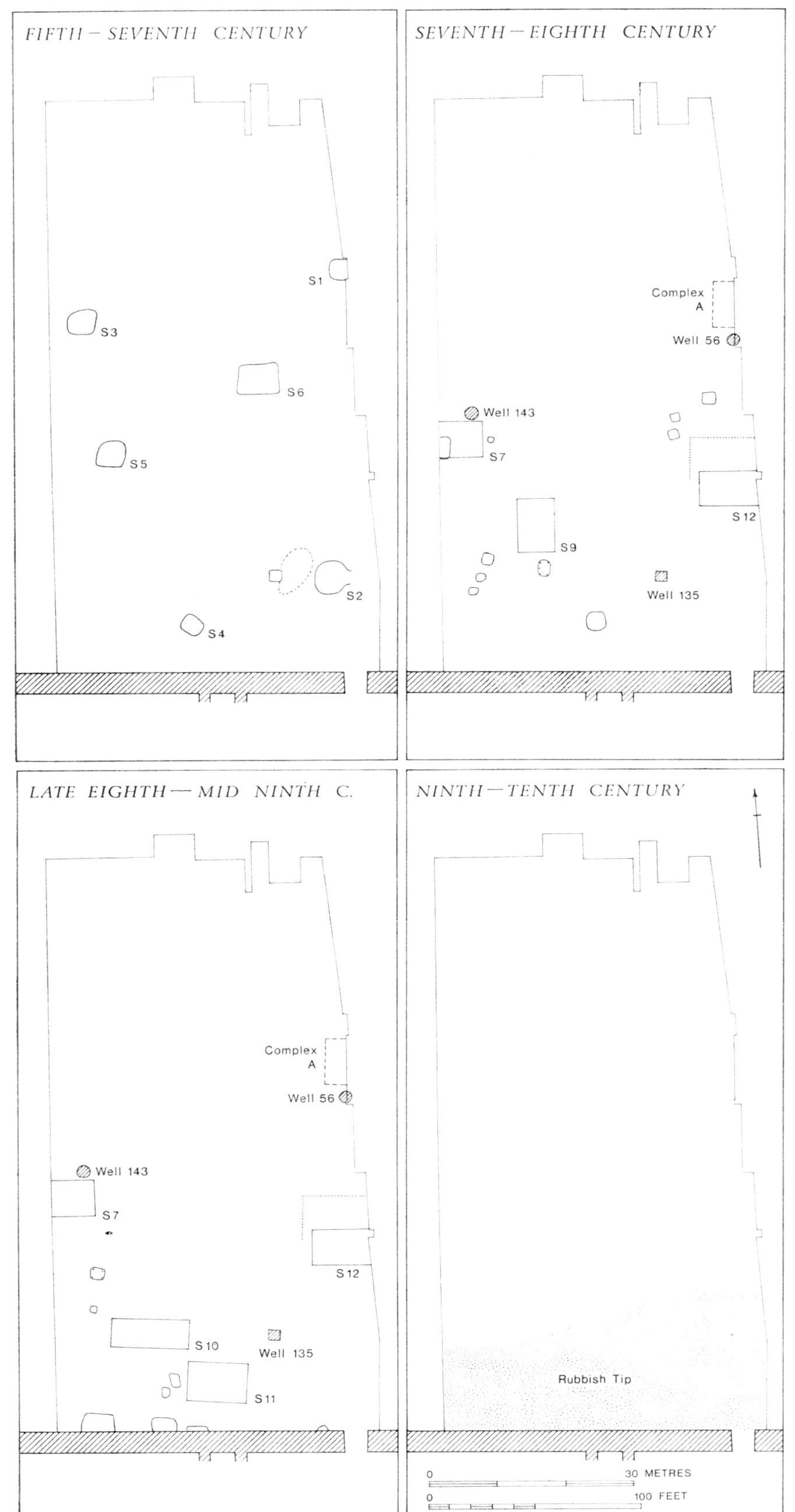

FIG. 98. Diagrammatic plans to illustrate the structural development of the site

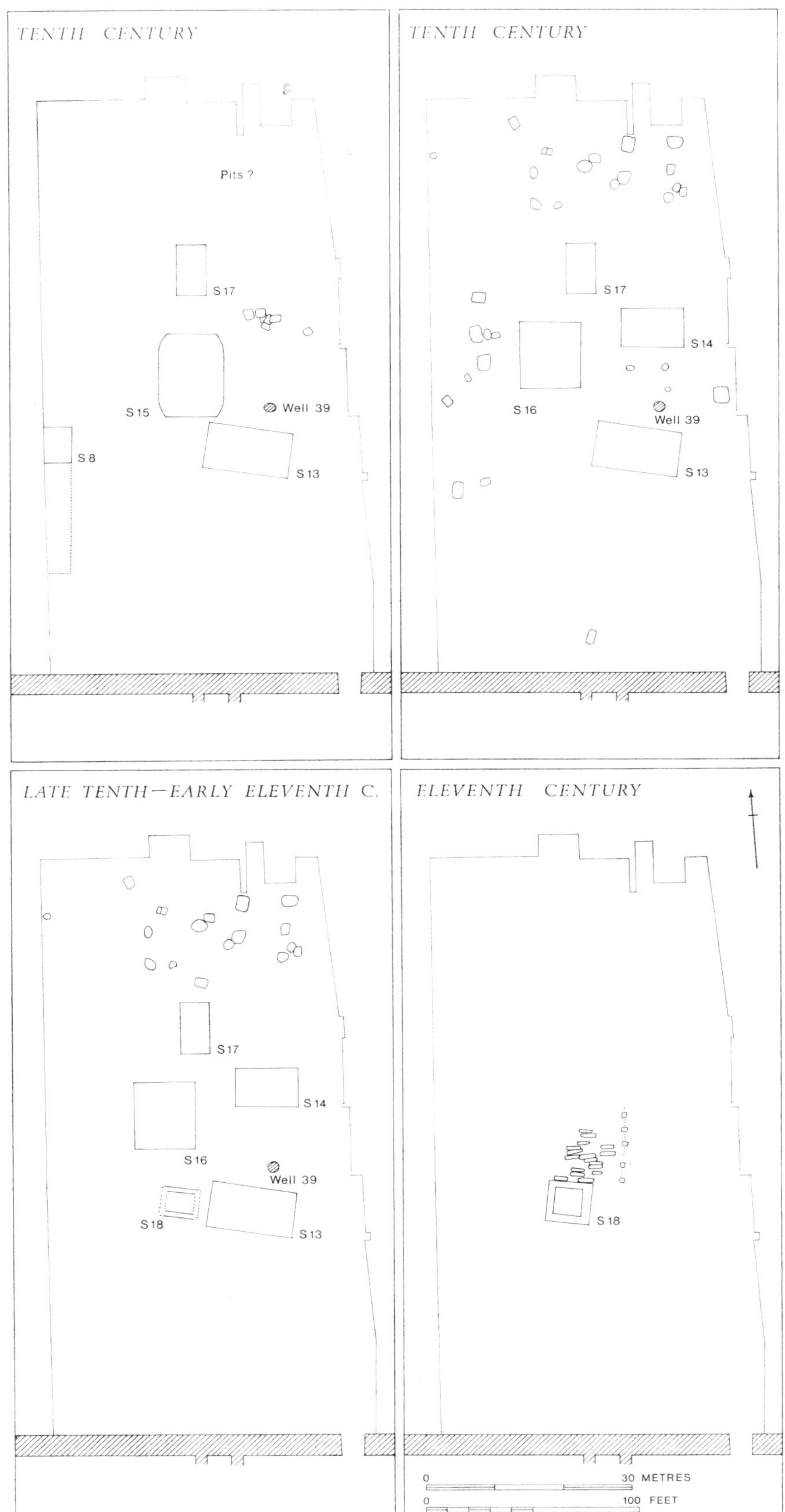

FIG. 99. Diagrammatic plans to illustrate the structural development of the site

buildings make it clear that several changes took place which can be tentatively arranged in four phases, phases 5–8.

To phase 5 belongs the earliest stage of building S13, building S15 and probably the original construction of building S17. Building S8 and its fenced enclosure may also belong to this phase, but proof is lacking. The first three form a coherent complex, S15 clearly representing a hall of some pretensions. S17 was a smaller structure possibly a store building, while the buttressed hall S13, with its internal subdivision, might reasonably be interpreted as a domestic structure of some kind, perhaps in part a solar range or a kitchen. The buildings flanked a courtyard, within which lay the well, and a latrine building represented by the group of cesspits, 59, 67, 68, 71, 72, 73. Other pits, probably spanning phases 5–8, were dug to the north.

Phase 6. Tenth century

This phase was represented by the demolition of the aisled hall S15 and its replacement by an almost identical structure S16, sited a little to the west but overlapping the site of the original hall. It was probably at about this time that a new latrine area was designated to the west of the hall, while the site of the old latrine was replaced by a timber building, S14, possibly a store house. Building S17 may now also have been rebuilt. The mass of postholes which constitute 'posthole complex B' could, in theory, have constituted a building, one phase of which was standing at this time, but proof is lacking: the state of building S8 is unknown.

The general impression given is that the size of the social group represented in phase 6 was much the same as that already established in the preceding phase.

Phase 7. Late tenth to early eleventh century

To phase 7 belongs the first phase of the masonry 'tower' (building S18) which was erected on the plot of land between buildings S13 and S16, possibly as a replacement for an earlier timber structure represented by the group of postholes referred to as 'posthole complex B'. A rebuilding of this magnitude would provide a context for the reconstruction of the corner of building S13. The second rebuilding of S17 may have taken place at about this time.

The reason for suggesting that the early 'tower' belonged to a later phase than phase 6 is to allow time for the existence of whatever structure posthole complex B represented. A separate phase 7 also neatly accommodates the alterations to buildings S13, S17 and possibly S14.

Phase 8. Mid eleventh century

Some time after the erection of the early 'tower' a cemetery began to develop close to its north wall. Since the graves soon impinged upon the site of the hall (building S16) the structure cannot have remained in use, and once the hall had been abandoned it is highly unlikely that the subsidiary buildings survived.

A little later the 'tower' was rebuilt in a more massive manner, an event demonstrably later than the removal of building S13. At least one body was added to the cemetery after

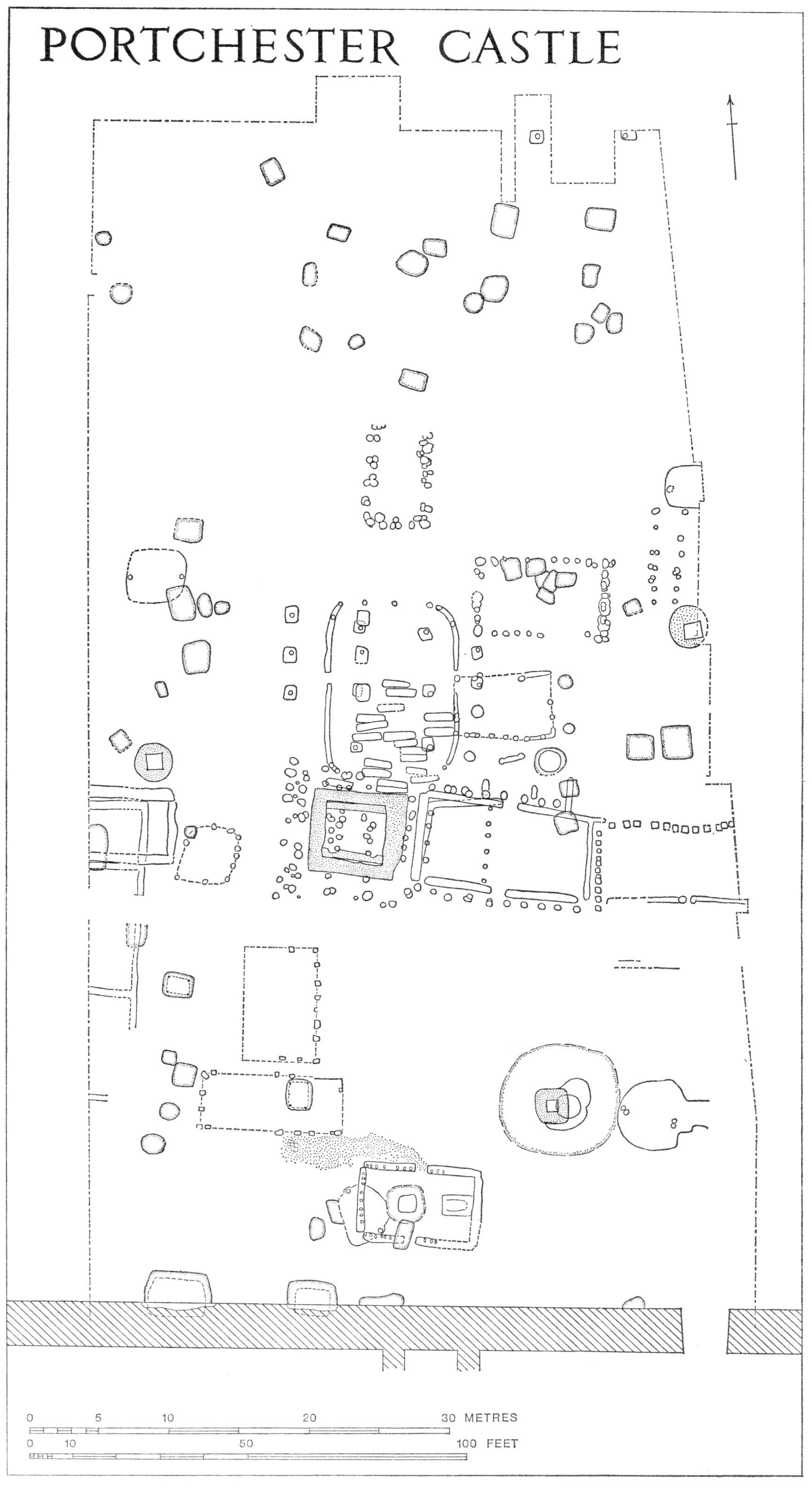

FIG. 100. General plan of all Saxon features (for numbering of individual features see figs. 101–3)

facing p. 126

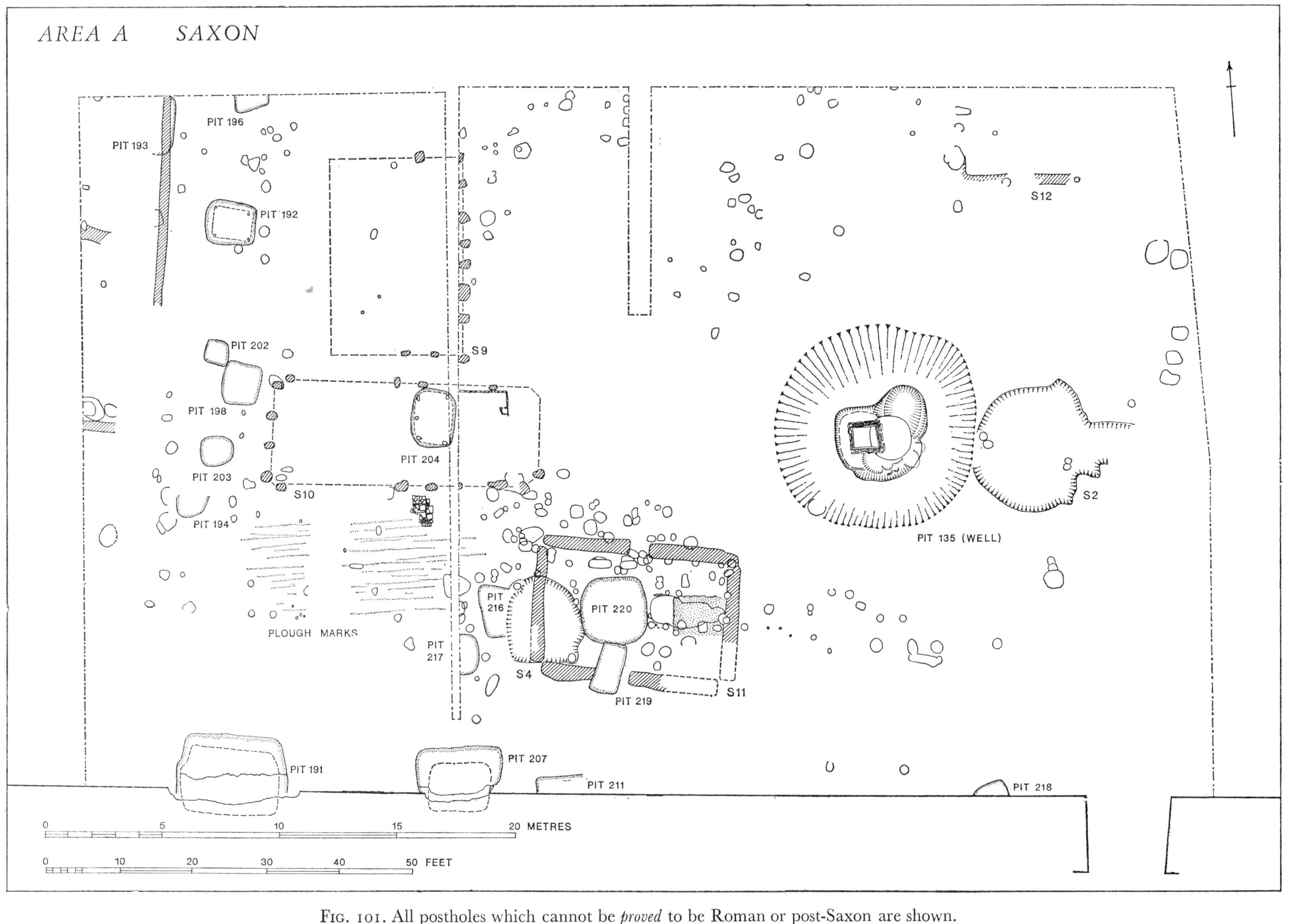

Fig. 101. All postholes which cannot be *proved* to be Roman or post-Saxon are shown.

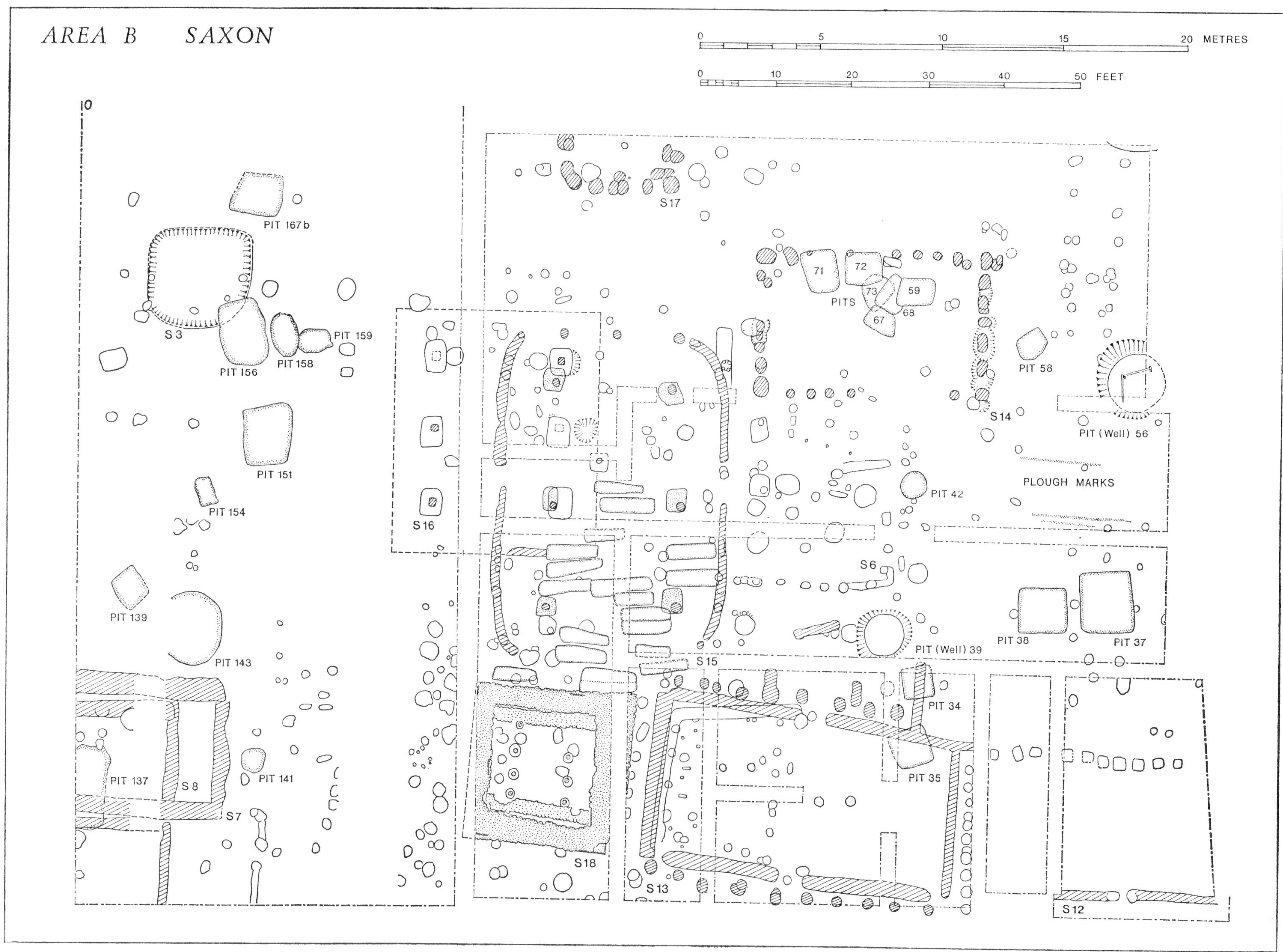

Fig. 102. All postholes which cannot be *proved* to be Roman or post-Saxon are shown.

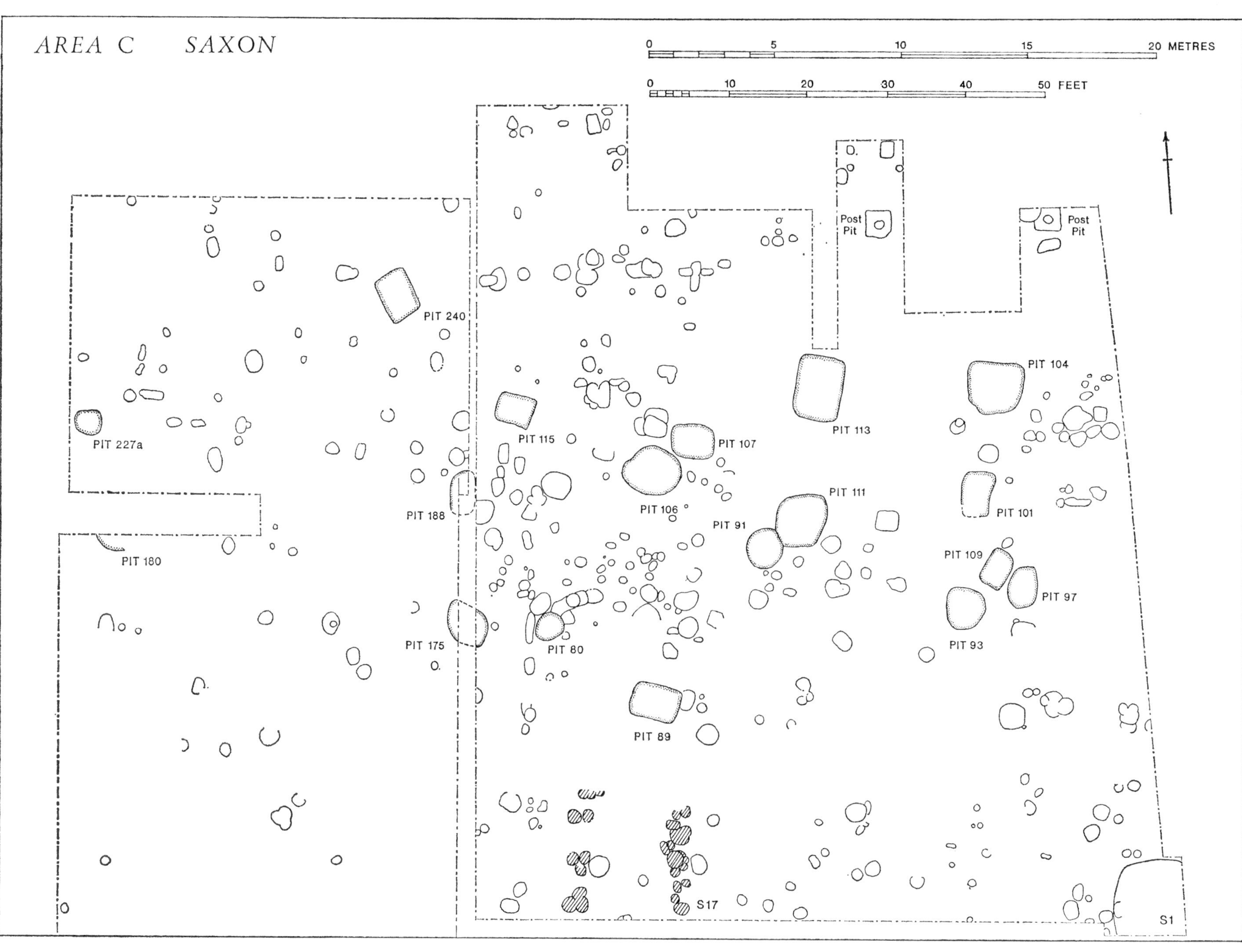

FIG. 103. All postholes which cannot be *proved* to be Roman or post-Saxon are shown

this, and it is possible that the graveyard was now partially enclosed. The tower may well have remained standing into the early decades of the post-Conquest period, before its eventual demolition about 1100.

BIBLIOGRAPHY

ADDYMAN, P. V. 1972. 'The Anglo-Saxon house: a new review.' *Anglo-Saxon England* i, 273–308.

ADDYMAN, P. V., LEIGH, D. and HUGHES, M. J. 1973. 'Anglo-Saxon houses at Chalton, Hampshire.' *Med. Arch.* xvi, 13–32.

ALCOCK, L. 1971. 'Excavations at South Cadbury Castle, 1970.' *Antiq. J.* li, 1–7.

BELL, M. 1971. 'Note on Bishopstone.' *Britannia* ii, 284–5.

BUTLER, R. M. 1955. 'A Roman gateway at Portchester Castle?' *Antiq. J.* xxxv, 219–22.

DAVISON, B. 1969. 'Sulgrave.' *Current Arch.* 12, 19–22.

JOPE, E. M. 1958. 'Titchfield Church and the Roman gateways of Portchester.' *Antiq. J.* xxxvii, 246–7.

RAHTZ, P. 1964. 'The Saxon and medieval palaces at Cheddar, Somerset — an interim report of excavations 1960–62.' *Med. Arch.* vi–vii, 53–66.

SMITH, J. T. 1964. 'Romano-British aisled houses.' *Arch. J.* cxx, 1–30.

WADE-MARTINS, P. 1969. 'Excavations at North Elmham 1967–8. An interim report.' *Norfolk Arch.* xxxiv, 352–97.

WADE-MARTINS, P. 1970. 'Excavations at North Elmham 1969. An interim report.' *Norfolk Arch.* xxxv, 25–78.

III. THE POTTERY

INTRODUCTION

THE pottery can be divided into two broad groups; finds from sealed deposits, in particular from pits, and sherds from general layers disturbed by ploughing. The policy adopted here is to illustrate the closely stratified material together in its groups, but to arrange the less well associated sherds in a rough typological order. Each illustrated sherd is given a unique publication number, allowing each to be described consecutively, together with its sherd record number (prefixed S or M) and its location. Anyone wishing to trace the associated material has only to look under the pit description (pp. 62–121) in the case of closed pit groups, or the layer description (pp. 171–81) in the case of sherds from general layers. For the sake of convenience the descriptions of the illustrated sherds are repeated in the section dealing with the pits, where the associated material is also described. The summaries of the layer contents list only the publication number of the vessels together with descriptions of the unpublished sherds.

The pottery has been divided chronologically into two groups, the hand-made vessels in use from the fifth to the tenth centuries and the wheel-turned 'Portchester wares' and associated types current in the late tenth to eleventh centuries. In the case of the former group practically every rim and decorated sherd is drawn and all sherds are listed. With the later material, while almost all the rims and decorated sherds from the closed groups are illustrated, only a selection of the less securely stratified sherds is drawn. All rims and decorated sherds are however listed, but no attempt is made to record the location of every body sherd.

DESCRIPTION OF THE PUBLISHED SHERDS

Early and middle Saxon Pottery (figs. 104–117)

1. S12. Rim sherd belonging to an open bowl. Rough surface burnishing on upper part of body with vertical wiping below.
Dark grey-brown sandy ware with iron-stained sand grains: fired black.
Pit 24.

2. S29. Jar with an everted rim of which substantial parts survive. Soft grey ware tempered with copious chopped chaff. The surface is burnished and fired to a red-brown colour.
Pit 34, layer 7.

3. S20. Jar with smoothed surface in black sandy ware.
Pit 35, layer 14.

4. S51. Jar with everted rim slightly hollowed inside. Coarse black sandy ware with chaff tempering. The surface is unsmoothed.
Pit 38, layer 9b.

5. S52. Upright rim in fine black sandy ware, smoothed surface.
Pit 38, layer 9b.

6. S56. Sherd near rim in fine black sandy ware, burnished surface.
Pit 38, layer 9b.

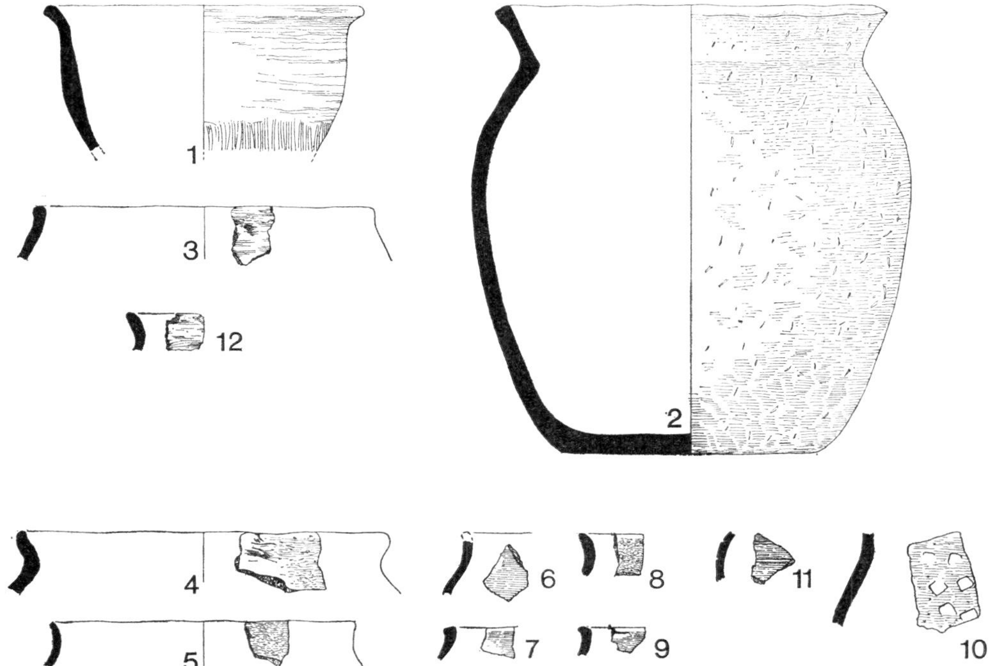

FIG. 104. Early–mid Saxon pottery from pits 24, 34, 35, 38 and 56 (pp. 128–9). Scale $\frac{1}{4}$

7. S55. Jar rim in dark grey sandy ware fired red-brown on the surface. Burnished.
Pit 38, layer 9b.

8. S54. Rim in black sandy ware with flakes of mica. Smoothed surface.
Pit 38, layer 9b.

9. S53. Rim in black sandy ware. Smoothed surface.
Pit 38, layer 9b.

10. S50. Body sherd in a light grey sandy ware containing large flakes of mica. The surface has been decorated using a plain square stamp shallowly impressed.
Pit 38, layer 9b.

11. S57. Body sherd in smooth black sandy ware tempered with chaff. The surface has been burnished and decorated with horizontal grooves.
Pit 38, layer 9b.

12. S354 Rim in hard black, sandy ware containing some flecks of mica. Burnished surface.
Pit 56, layers 38–41.

13. S250. Base in fine grey sandy ware with smoothed surface (? Roman).
Pit (well) 135, layer 103.

14. S249. Decorated sherds in dark grey sandy ware with large quartz grits: the surface is smoothed, fired black and decorated with circular stamps in horizontal rows divided by horizontal shallow tooled lines (4 sherds).
Pit (well) 135, layer 33.

15. S248. Rim in dark grey sandy ware with some chaff tempering, burnished surface with impressed decoration.
Pit (well) 135, layer 33.

16. S129. Rim in fine sandy ware with chaff tempering, burnished surface fired black.
Pit (well) 135, layer 33.

17. S244. Rim in grey sandy ware, burnished exterior.
Pit (well) 135, layer 33.

18. S260. Rim in coarse black sandy ware.
Pit (well) 135, layer 33.

19. S246. Rim in grey sandy ware.
Pit (well) 135, layer 33.

20. S245. Rim in grey sandy ware with chaff tempering, smoothed surface.
Pit (well) 135, layer 33.

21. S263. Body sherd in coarse grey sandy ware with crushed flint grits.
Pit (well) 135, layer 33.

22. S261. Body sherd in fine light brown sandy ware, surface fired grey and burnished (?Roman).
Pit (well) 135, layer 33.

23. S247. Decorated sherd in coarse grey sandy ware.
Pit (well) 135, layer 33.

24. S236. Rim in coarse grey sandy ware with quartz and mica grits, roughly smoothed surface.
Pit (well) 135, layer 31.

25. S252. Decorated body sherd, part of vessel 171.
Pit (well) 135, layer 31.

26. S251. Decorated body sherd in fine red-brown sandy ware fired dark grey on the surface, stamped.
Pit (well) 135, layer 31.

27. S235. Rim in coarse black sandy ware, roughly smoothed surface.
Pit (well) 135, layer 31.

28. S208. Rim in coarse grey sandy ware, roughly burnished surface.
Pit (well) 135, layer 31.

29. S210 & S211. Rim in grey sandy ware with chaff tempering (2 sherds).
Pit (well) 135, layer 31.

30. S209. Rim in grey ware with copious chaff tempering.
Pit (well) 135, layer 31.

31. S253. Rim in coarse grey sandy ware tempered with crushed flint grits.
Pit (well) 135, layer 31.

32. S234. Rim in coarse grey sandy ware with sporadic large flint grits (2 sherds).
Pit (well) 135, layer 31.

33. S212. Rim in grey sandy ware with chaff tempering.
Pit (well) 135, layer 31.

34. S262. Rim in coarse grey ware tempered with crushed flint grits.
Pit (well) 135, layer 31.

35. S111. Jar in coarse grey sandy ware with crushed flint grit tempering.
Pit (well) 135, layer 52.

36. S115. Jar in coarse grey sandy ware with crushed flint and chalk tempering.
Pit (well) 135, layer 52.

37. S113. Jar in coarse grey sandy ware with crushed flint grit tempering.
Pit (well) 135 (trench 89), layer 22.

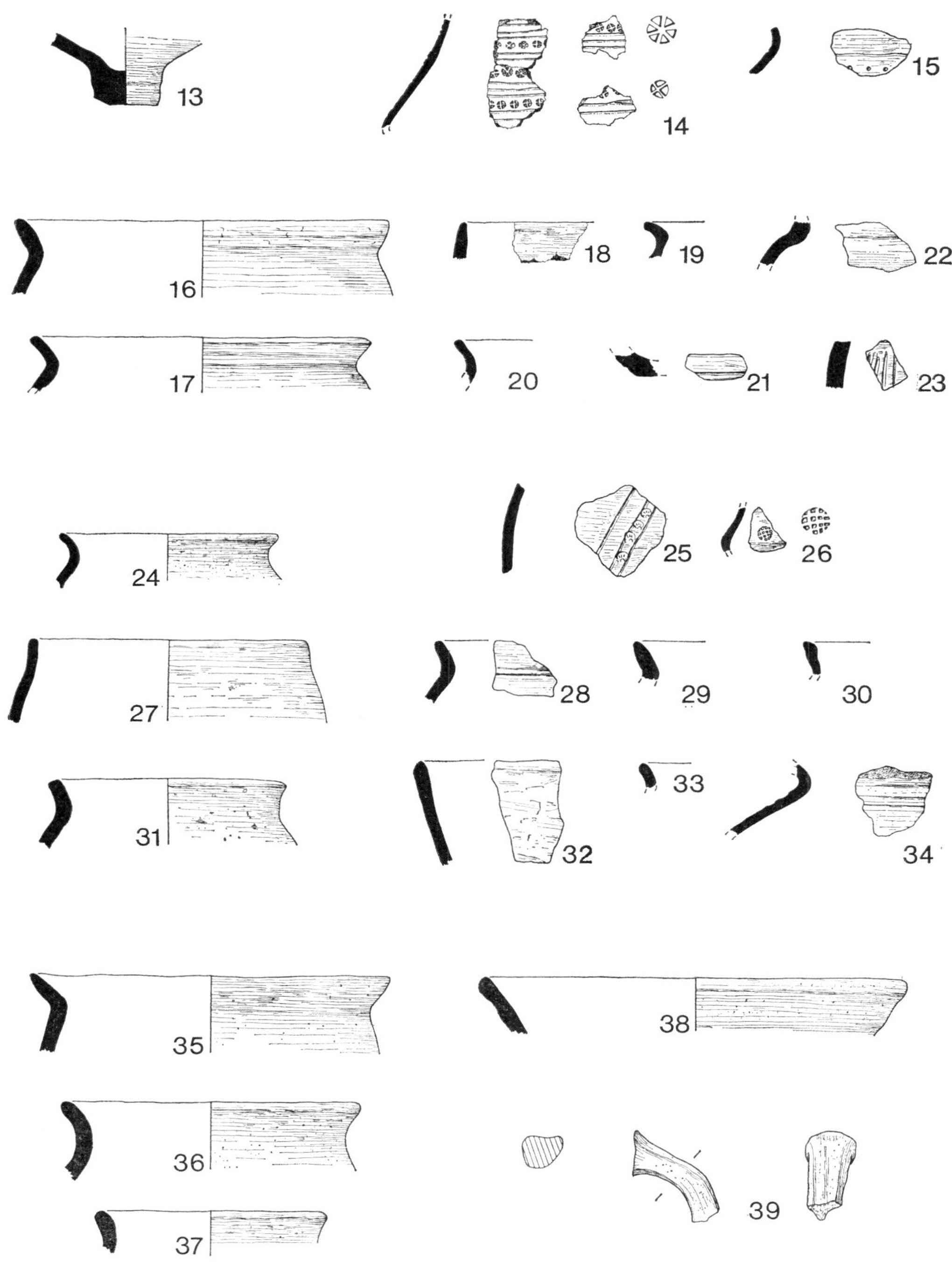

FIG. 105. Early-mid Saxon pottery from pit (well) 135 (pp. 129–32). Scale $\frac{1}{4}$ (stamps $\frac{1}{2}$)

38. S116. Jar in coarse grey sandy ware with some finely crushed flint and chalk tempering.
Pit (well) 135 (trench 89), layer 22.

39. S114. Handle in grey sandy ware with crushed flint tempering.
Pit (well) 135 (trench 89), layer 22.

40. S110. Jar in red-grey ware tempered with crushed flint grits.
Pit (well) 135 (trench 89), layer 28.

41. S117. Jar in coarse grey sandy ware with some crushed flint tempering.
Pit (well) 135 (trench 89), layer 28.

42. S125. Jar in grey sandy ware with finely crushed chalk and shell tempering.
Pit (well) 135, layer 12.

43. S104. Jar in grey sandy ware with finely crushed flint tempering.
Pit (well) 135, layer 12.

44. S112. Jar in grey ware tempered with chaff, burnished surface.
Pit (well) 135, layer 50.

45. S126. Jar in coarse grey sandy ware, some flint grits.
Pit (well) 135, layer 12.

46. S127. Jar in grey sandy ware with crushed flint grit tempering.
Pit (well) 135, layer 12.

47. S128. Rilled Portchester ware sherd.
Pit (well) 135, layer 12.

48–84. S95–107, 213–233, 237. Coarse jars with everted rims. The fabrics are all grey and sandy and all contain tempering of crushed flint, sometimes mixed with crushed chalk. The degree of fineness of the crushing varies. The surfaces are smoothed and occasionally roughly burnished. All vessels show irregularities, demonstrating their hand-made origins—total of 49 sherds.

The exceptions to the general description are:

64. S241. Hard grey sandy ware, smoothed surface.

79. S243. Black sandy ware with chaff tempering, smoothed surface.

80. S242. Hard grey sandy ware, burnished surface.
Pit (well) 135, layer 11.

85. S109. Handle in hard light grey sandy ware. Imported vessel. See also no. 192.
Pit (well) 135, layer 11.

86. S108. Decorated jar in grey sandy ware tempered with flint and chalk grits. The chalk has leached out inside giving the fabric a vesicular appearance. The surface is smooth and decorated with panels of stamping and incision.
Pit (well) 135, layer 11.

87. S240. Rim in grey ware heavily tempered with crushed flint and chalk grits.
Pit (well) 135, layer 9.

88. S239. Rim in coarse sandy grey ware, smoothed surface.
Pit (well) 135, layer 9.

89. S238. Rim in grey ware tempered with crushed flint and chalk grits, smoothed surface.
Pit (well) 135, layer 9.

90–96. S118–124. Wheel-made Portchester ware fabrics, hard grey sandy ware with finely crushed flint and chalk tempering. S124 is a dish, the others are from cooking pots with rilled and rouletted surfaces.
Pit (well) 135, layer 9.

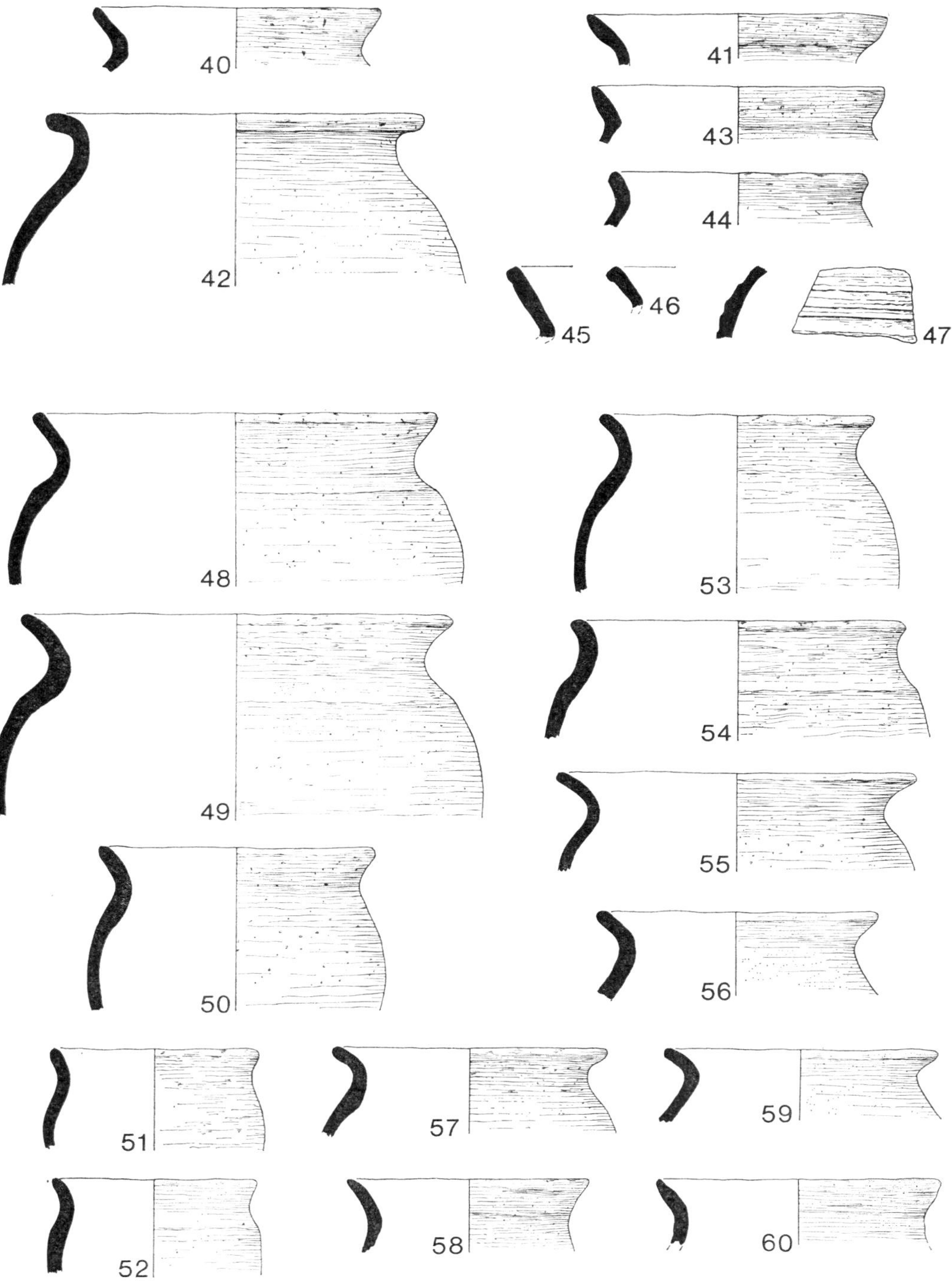

Fig. 106. Late Saxon pottery from well (pit) 135 (p. 132). Scale $\frac{1}{4}$

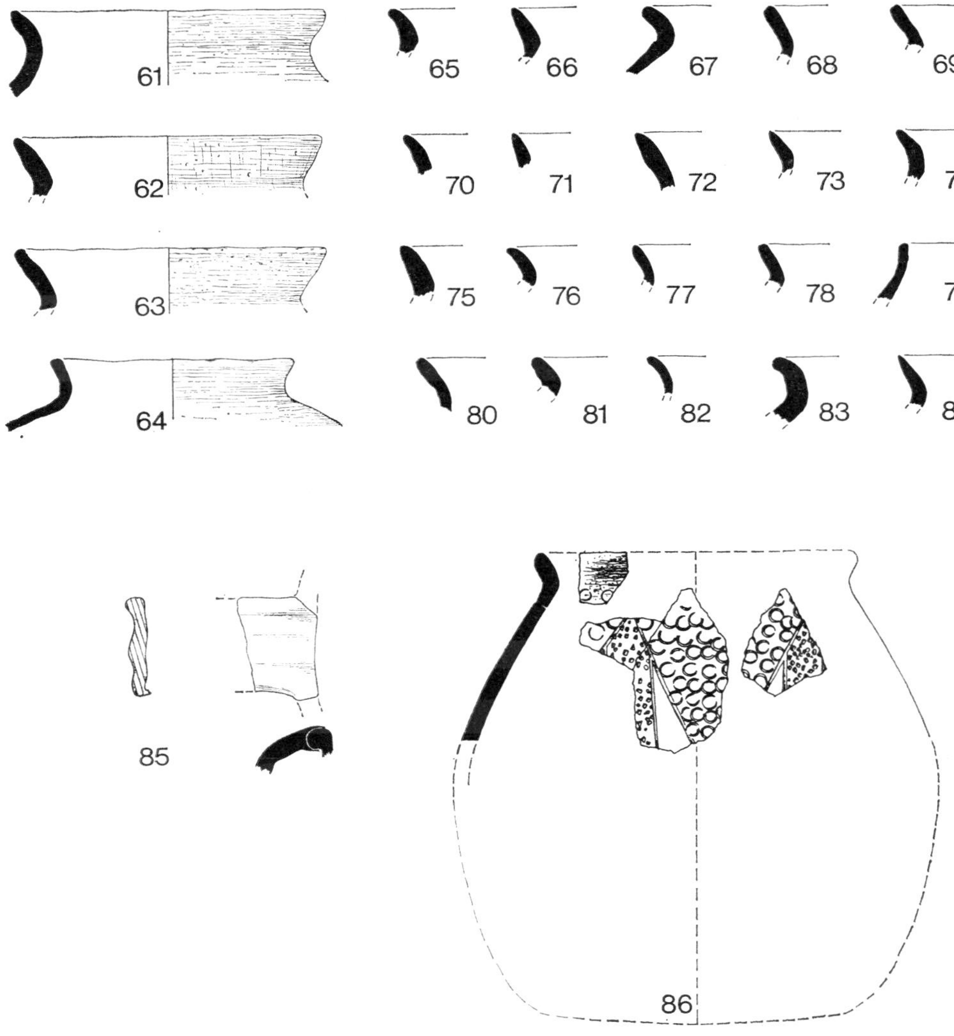

FIG. 107. Late Saxon pottery from well (pit) 135 (p. 132). Scale ¼

97–100.	S256–259.	Jars in Portchester ware, hard sandy fabric with finely crushed flint grits, wheel-turned. Pit (well) 135, layer 5.
101.	S254.	Jar in grey ware with copious crushed flint grits. Pit (well) 135, layer 5.
102.	S255.	Jar in grey ware with crushed flint grits. Pit (well) 135, layer 5.
103.	S355.	Body sherd in fine black sandy ware. The surface is burnished and decorated with vertical grooves. Pit 137, layer 111.
104.	M401.	Rim in coarse black ware tempered with crushed flint grits. Pit 143, layer 131.

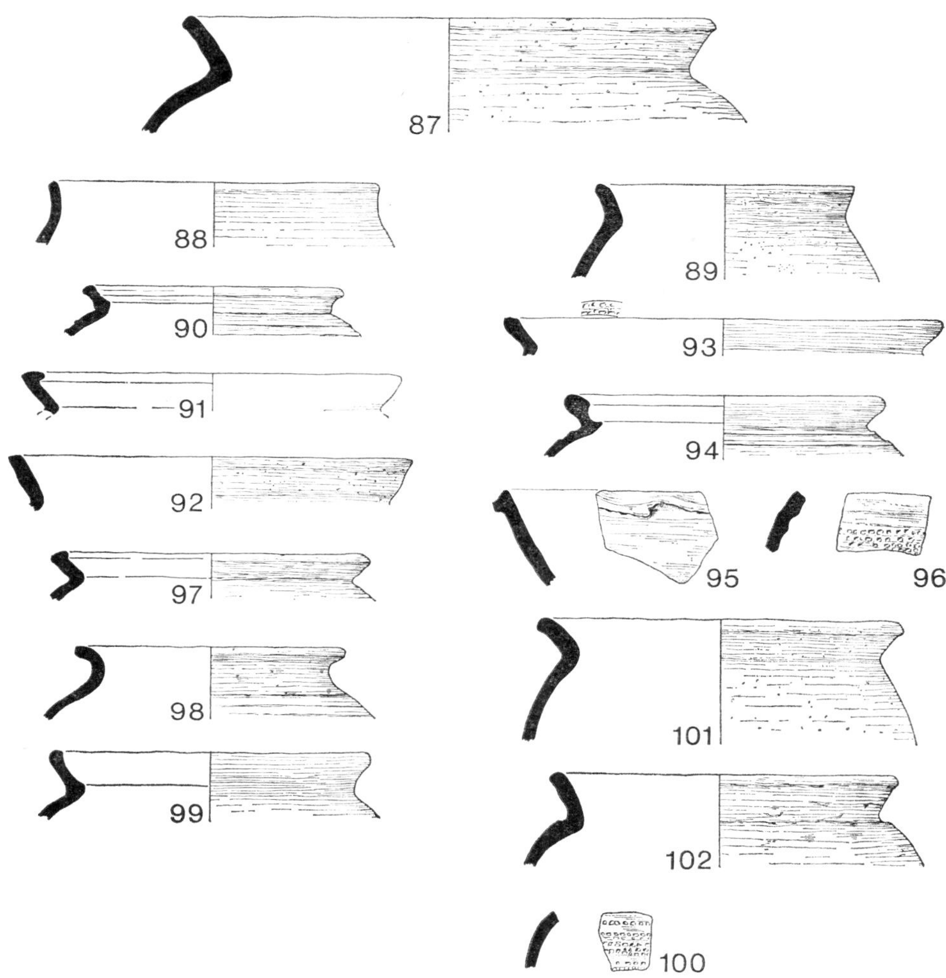

Fig. 108. Late Saxon pottery from well (pit) 135 (pp. 132–134). Scale ¼

105. M402. Rim in coarse grey-brown ware tempered with coarse grits of quartz and mica. Pit 143, layer 131.

106. M403. Rim in dark grey sandy ware. Pit 143, layer 131.

107. S339. Rim in grey-brown sandy fabric tempered with chaff. The surface is smoothed. Pit 141, layer 106.

108. S311. Rim sherd in fine black sandy ware burnished on both surfaces. Pit 191, layer 43.

109. S325. Jar with out-bent rim in black sandy ware burnished on the outside surface. Pit 191, layer 89.

110. S324. Sherd decorated with shallow grooving. Fine sandy grey ware fired to black on the surfaces and highly burnished. Pit 191, layer 54.

111. S313. Rim in black sandy ware tempered with coarsely crushed flint grits. Rough surface.
Pit 192, layer 40.

112. S314. Rim in grey sandy ware with smoothed but irregular surface.
Pit 192, layer 40.

113. S316. Dish in black sandy ware with sparse large flint grits and some chaff tempering: burnished on the surface.
Pit 194, layer 70.

114. S315. Dish in smooth grey ware with grog tempering: burnished on the surface (possibly late Roman).
Pit 194, layer 70.

115. S317. Large jar with everted rim, represented by one sherd of the rim and 9 body sherds, decorated with all-over stamping (four of the sherds come from layer 68). The fabric is smooth red ware copiously tempered with finely crushed flint and chalk; the surface is smoothed and fired to a grey-brown.
Pit 198, layer 63 (sherds also from pit 204, layers 101 and 102).

116. S318. Jar with slightly everted rim in smooth grey ware tempered with chaff. The outer surface is burnished and fired black.
Pit 198, layer 63.

117. S326. Rim sherd in fine grey sandy ware with some chaff tempering, fired to a pinkish surface; burnished.
Pit 198, layer 68.

118. S328. Rim in fine grey sandy ware.
Pit 198, layer 68.

119. S329. Rim in fine grey sandy ware tempered with chaff. The surfaces are well smoothed.
Pit 198, layer 68.

120. S330. Everted rim in black sandy ware fired red on the surface.
Pit 198, layer 68.

121. S327. Everted rimmed jar in grey ware tempered with crushed flint grit. The surface is smoothed and fired to a black colour.
Pit 198, layer 68.

122. S331. Body sherd in grey sandy ware.
Pit 198, layer 68.

123. S312. Rim in coarse grey sandy ware fired grey-brown on the surface.
Pit 204, layer 102.

124. S320. Cooking pot with everted rim in coarse black ware tempered with crushed flint grits.
Pit 207 (trench 104) layer 8.

125. S321. Spouted pitcher in fine hard grey-brown ware, wheel-turned. The surface is fired to an even dark grey and is smoothed and burnished. Import.
Pit 207, 104, layer 8 and 103, layer 41.

126. S334. Rim, grey-brown sandy ware, with coarse flint grits.
Pit 207, 104, layer 12.

127. S322. Rim in grey sandy ware with chaff tempering and a burnished surface.
Pit 207, 104, layer 8.

128. S319. Rim from a coarse vessel in black sandy ware with sporadic large flint grits.
Pit 207, 103, layer 40.

129. S323. Jar in coarse black sandy ware with chaff tempering. The surface is burnished.
Pit 211, layer 7.

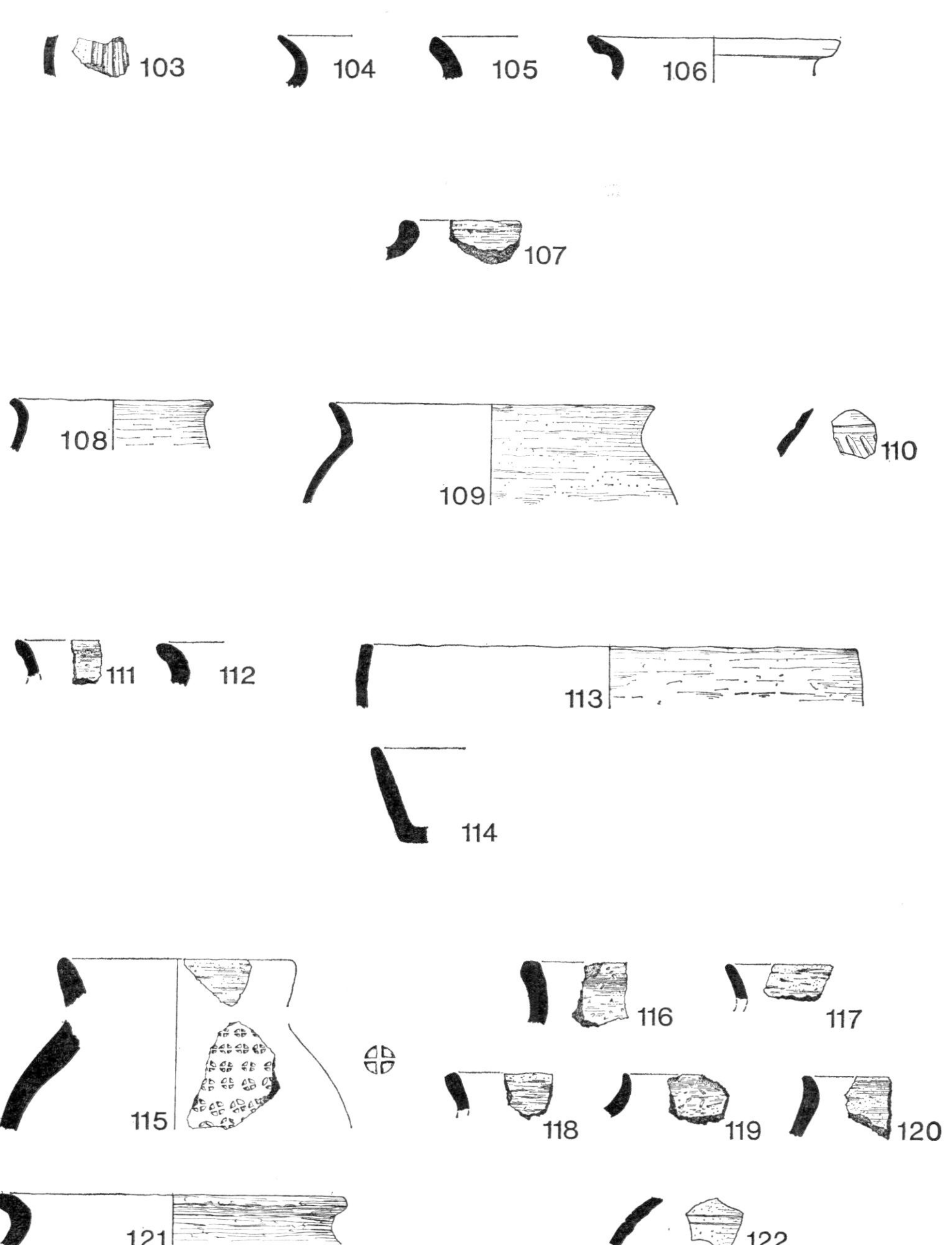

FIG. 109. Mid–late Saxon pottery from pits 137, 141, 143, 191, 192, 194 and 198 (pp. 134–6). Scale $\frac{1}{4}$ (stamps $\frac{1}{2}$)

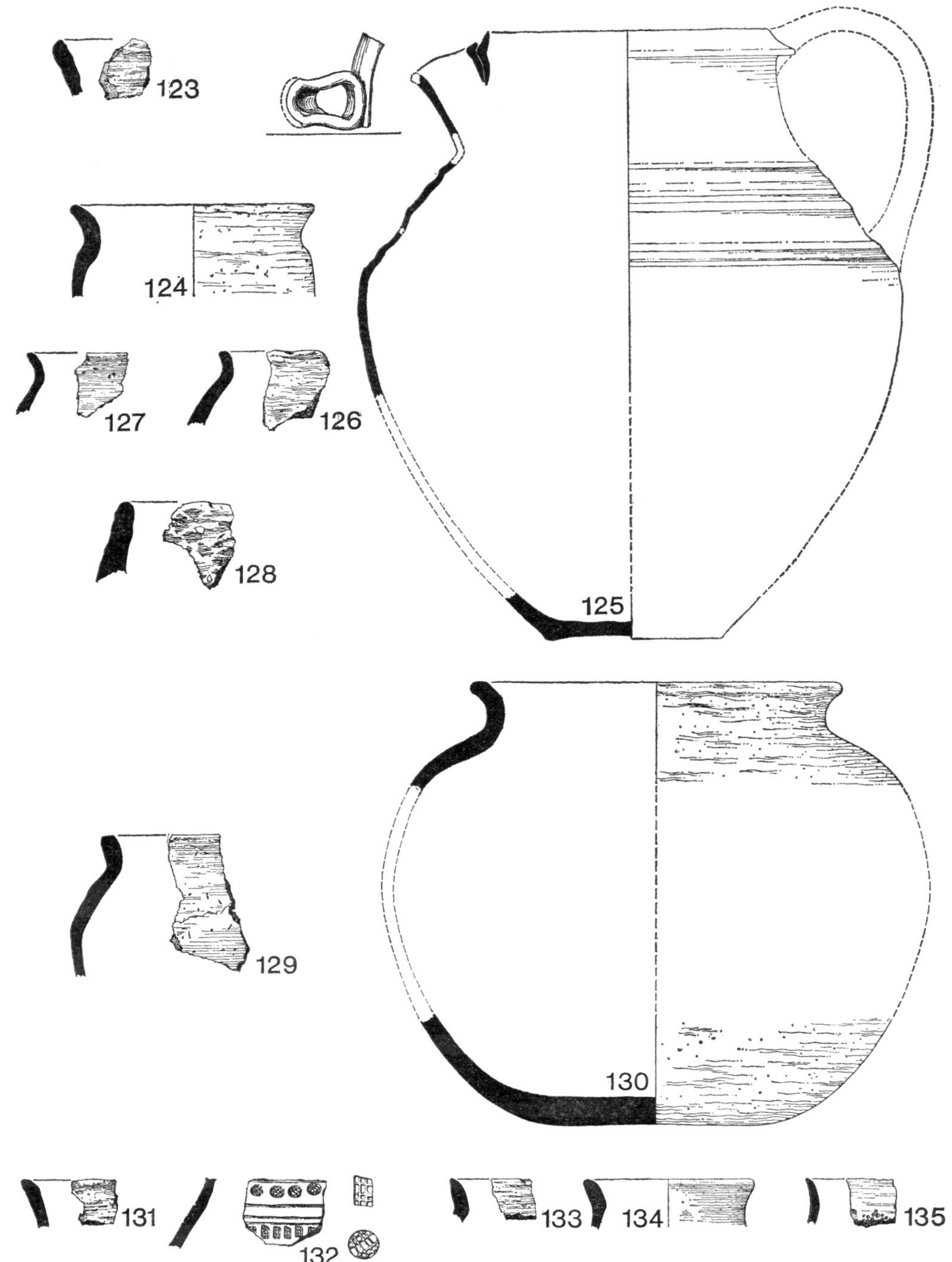

FIG. 110. Mid–late Saxon pottery from pits 204, 207, 211, 216 and 220 (pp. 136, 139). Scale $\frac{1}{4}$ (stamps $\frac{1}{2}$)

130. S356. Substantial part of a large jar with outcurved rim. The fabric consists of a smooth red paste tempered with coarsely crushed flint grit. The base is rounded. The surface is uneven and unburnished. 12 body sherds and 2 rim sherds.
Pit 216, layer 38.

131. S335. Rim in black sandy ware with flint grit tempering.
Pit 220, layer 79.

132. S336. Decorated sherd from the shoulder of a vessel in fine light grey sandy ware with a smoothed surface fired to an even black colour. The two horizontal zones of stamps are separated by 3 deeply tooled horizontal lines.
Pit 220, layer 80.

133. S338. Rim sherd in black ware tempered with large quartz grits.
Pit 220, layer 80.

134. S357. Rim of coarse jar in black sandy ware with some flint grits.
Pit 220, layer 84.

135. S337. Two rim sherds in fine reddish sandy ware. The surface is smoothed and fired black. At the base of the neck is an area of impressed decoration.
Pit 220, layer 80.

136. S76. Jar represented by 1 rim and 7 body sherds in a black sandy ware with occasional large grits and pieces of chaff. The surface is well burnished and fired red.
Grubenhaus S1, layer 30.

137. S82. Jar represented by 2 rims and 3 large body sherds in dark grey sandy ware with occasional large flint grits and some chaff. The surface is smoothed.
Grubenhaus S1, layer 30.

138. S78. Bowl in hard black sandy ware burnished inside and out.
Grubenhaus S1, layer 30.

139. S77. Shoulder of a bowl in hard black sandy ware with well smoothed surface.
Grubenhaus S1, layer 29.

140. S81. Rim of bowl in a black sandy ware tempered with some flint grits and fragments of chaff. The surface is well burnished.
Grubenhaus S1, layer 30.

141. S79. Rim of bowl in fine hard black sandy ware with a well sealed black-burnished surface.
Grubenhaus S1, layer 30.

142. S23. Rim in grey-brown sandy ware with smoothed outer surface.
56, layer 8.

143. S24. Rim in dark grey sandy ware.
56, layer 8.

144. S22. Rim in grey sandy ware tempered with crushed chalk.
56, layer 8.

145. S25. Rim in smooth dark grey sandy ware.
56, layer 8.

146. S27. Rim in dark grey sandy ware with smoothed surface.
58, layer 7.

147. S154. Rim in coarse black sandy ware tempered with crushed chalk and shell: roughly smoothed surface.
87, layer 16.

148. S342. Rim in grey sandy ware with crushed flint grits.
108, layer 93 (building S4).

149. S344. Rim in smooth grey-red ware with chaff tempering. Surface is black and burnished (same vessel as S318 from pit 198).
108, layer 66 (building S11).

150. S345. Decorated sherd in red sandy ware with flint grit tempering, decorated with impressed circles.
108, layer 67 (building S11).

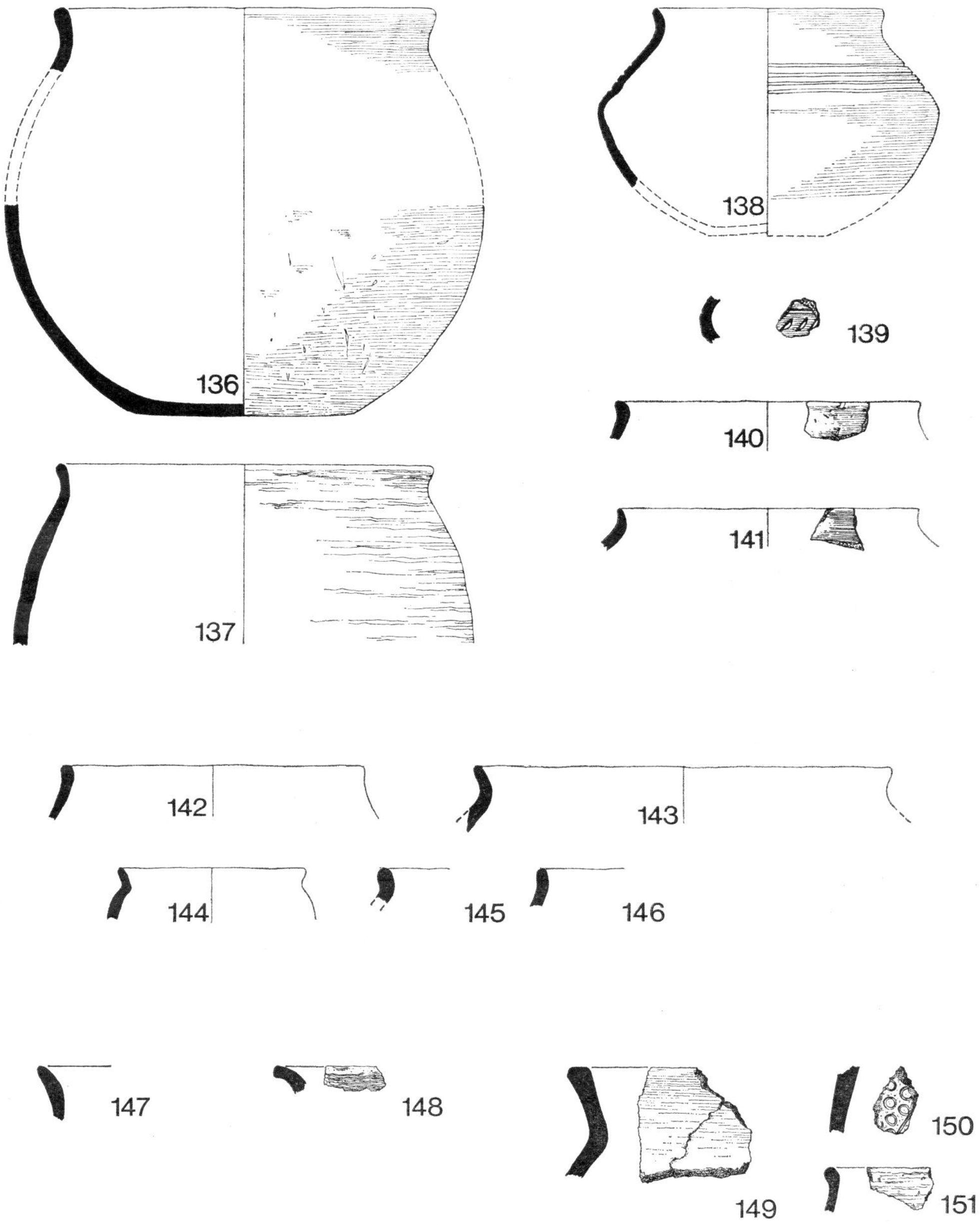

FIG. 111. Saxon pottery associated with buildings (pp. 139–41). Scale $\frac{1}{4}$

151. S347. Rim in hard black sandy ware, smoothed surface.
108, layer 78 (building S11).

152. S5. Decorated sherd in dark grey-brown ware lightly tempered with sand, smoothed surface, deeply impressed with rosette stamps and points.
5, layer 3.

153. S6. Decorated sherd in dark grey-brown ware with lightly sand-tempered paste, burnished outer surface, impressed decoration.
5, layer 3.

154. S7. Decorated sherd in dark grey ware slightly sandy with some chaff tempering, burnished surface stamped and shallow tooled.
5, layer 3.

155. S17. Decorated body sherd: same as no. 156.
45, layer 3.

156. S77a. Decorated body sherd in smooth dark grey slightly sandy ware with chaff tempering. Impressed decoration. Same as no. 155.
69, layer 32.

157. S19. Decorated body sherd in grey sandy ware with chaff tempering, fired to a reddish brown on the surface.
45, layer 2.

158. S35. Decorated sherd in hard grey sandy ware with some chaff tempering, stamped and shallow tooled decoration.
63, layer 10.

159. S185. Decorated body sherd in hard black sandy ware with some chaff tempering: smoothed surface fired black and decorated with stamps and horizontal shallow grooved lines.
89, layer 31.

160. S155. Decorated body sherd in coarse dark grey sandy ware with inclusion of rounded quartz grains. Fired black with the surface smoothed. Stamped.
87, layer 5.

161. S183. Decorated body sherd in fine grey sandy ware with a smooth black surface. Stamped.
87, layer 14.

162. S41. Body sherd in smooth grey sandy ware with some chaff tempering. Deeply stamped decoration.
60, layer 5.

163. S30. Bowl in greyish sandy ware tempered with chaff and fired to a red colour on the surface (3 sherds).
59, layer 7; 61, layers 19 and 21.

164. S36. Decorated sherd in coarse grey sandy ware with well smoothed surface; stamped decoration. Same as S38 and S39.
63, layer 4.

165. S38. Decorated sherd, same as S36 and S39.
63, layer 20.

166. S39. Decorated sherd same as S36 and S38 in coarse grey sandy ware, well finished surface.
63, layer 10.

167. S37. Decorated sherd in smooth grey sandy ware with some chaff tempering: stamped and shallow tooled decoration.
65, layer 4.

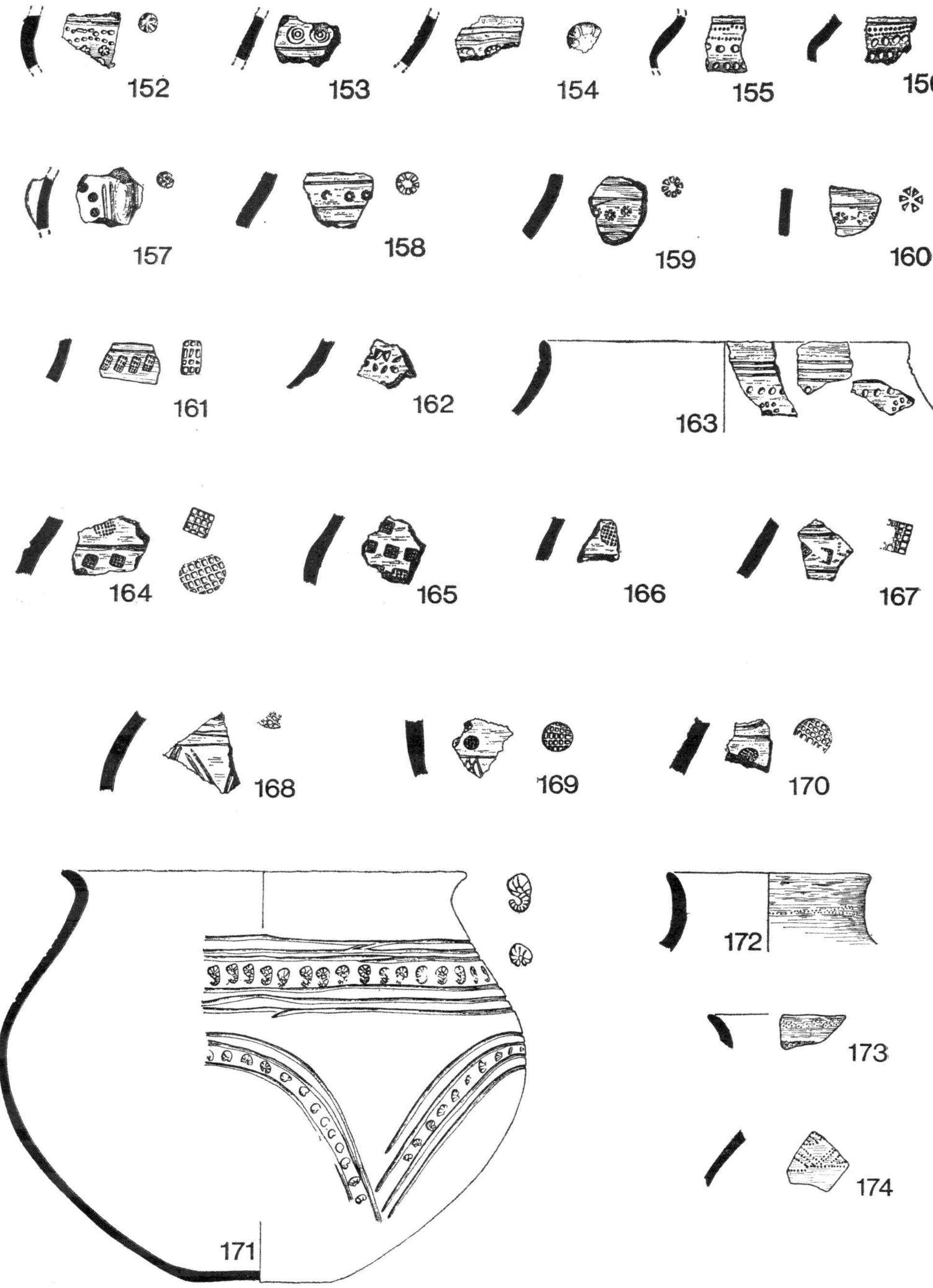

FIG. 112. Early Saxon decorated pottery from various locations (pp. 141, 143). Scale $\frac{1}{4}$ (stamps $\frac{1}{2}$)

168. S181. Decorated body sherd in hard grey sandy ware with burnished surface fired red. Decorated with stamps and deeply incised lines.
89, layer 4.

169. S90. Decorated sherd in hard light grey sandy ware, smoothed surface, stamped and incised.
85, layer 8.

170. S69. Decorated sherd as nos. S36, 38, 39.
67, layer 4.

171. S94. Much of one vessel in hard black sandy ware with chaff tempering: stamped decoration same as no. 25.
Sherds from 89, layer 26 and 108, layer 60.

172. S141. Rim in coarse grey sandy ware, fired red on the surface and burnished. Decorated with comb impressions.
87, layer 9.

173. S189. Rim in black sandy ware, burnished on the surface. Decorated with comb impressions.
87, layer 9.

174. S180. Decorated body sherd in fine hard grey sandy ware; smoothed surface decorated with comb impression.
87, layer 7.

175. S300. Decorated sherd in' fine black sandy ware with a well burnished black surface. The decoration is in the form of wide grooves.
102, layer 44.

176. S276. Body sherd in dark grey sandy ware with burnished surface and grooved decoration.
55, layer 6.

177. S89. Decorated body sherd in dark grey sandy ware; smoothed surface decorated with grooves.
77, layer 5.

178. S309. Body sherd in fine black sandy ware with burnished surface, decorated with grooves; cf. nos. S300 and S303 of which it might be a part.
103, layer 23.

179. S153. Decorated body sherd in fine black sandy ware with a burnished surface decorated by grooving.
88, layer 5.

180. S72. Decorated sherd in grey sandy ware fired red-brown on the surface. Decorated with grooving on the shoulder.
67, layer 4.

181. S143. Rim in grey sandy ware with some chaff tempering; smoothed surface decorated with shallow tooled horizontal lines.
87, layer 9.

182. S197. Body sherd decorated with shallow tooling in reddish-brown sandy ware, the smoothed surface fired black.
94, layer 87.

183. S15. Rim in black sandy ware with burnished surfaces.
45, layer 3.

184. S267. Bowl in fine light grey sandy ware: surface is smooth and decorated with shallow tooling.
100, layer 24.

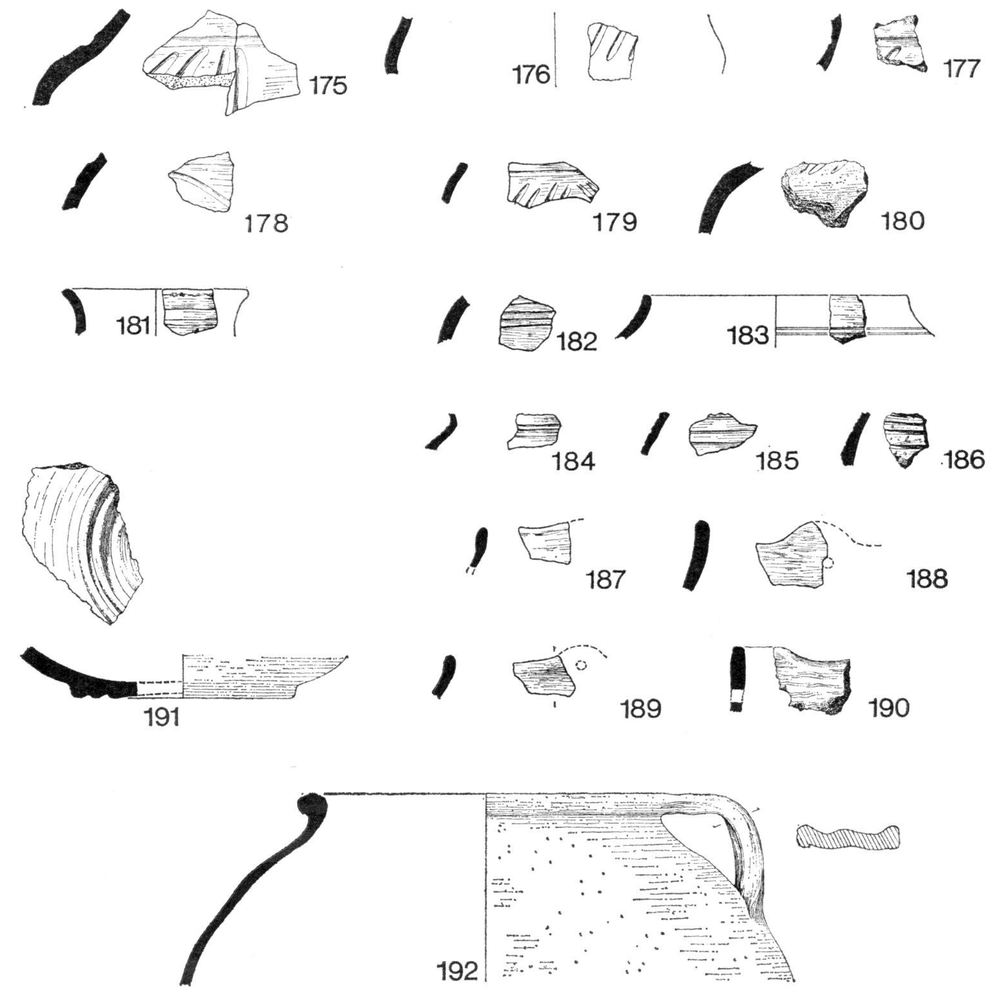

FIG. 113. Saxon pottery from various locations (pp. 143–5). Scale $\frac{1}{4}$

185. S291. Decorated sherd in grey sandy ware with chaff tempering. The decorated lines were shallow tooled.
102, layer 44.

186. S73. Decorated body sherd in fine black sandy ware with chaff tempering.
69, layer 12.

187. S307. Rim in grey sandy ware with smoothed surface.
102, layer 33.

188. S144. Rim in coarse black sandy ware.
87, layer 9.

189. S175. Rim in coarse grey sandy ware.
87, layer 9.

190. S86. Rim in hard grey sandy ware.
75, layer 5.

191. S148. Base in coarse grey sandy ware with chaff tempering, smoothed surface. Possibly Roman.
91, layer 43.

192. S305. Handled pitcher (in 8 sherds) in fine light grey fabric. Import (sherds also from 108, layer 48 and no. 85).
102, layer 33.

193. S3. Rim in black sandy ware with burnished surfaces.
1930 excavation.

194. S11. Rim in smooth dark laminated ware with occasional flint grits and chaff tempering, burnished exterior.
5, layer 3.

195. S33. Rim in grey sandy ware with some larger inclusions, smoothed surface.
62, layer 5.

196. S34. Rim in black sandy ware.
63, layer 20.

197. S26. Rim in dark grey sandy ware with smoothed outer surface.
56, layer 8.

198. S203. Rim in coarse grey sandy ware.
96, layer 18.

199. S204. Rim in dark grey sandy ware fired black on the surface and smoothed.
99, layer 50.

200. S191. Rim in even grey sandy ware, fired red-brown.
95, layer 20.

201. S284. Rim in coarse sandy ware with smoothed surface.
102, layer 44.

202. S198. Rim in hard black sandy ware with some large quartz grits. Well burnished surface.
94, layer 93.

203. S190. Rim in 2 sherds, fine black sandy ware with a burnished surface.
96, layer 20.

204. S188. Rim in fine grey sandy ware with some chaff tempering, smoothed surface.
90, layer 15.

205. S186. Rim in fine black sandy ware with chaff tempering, burnished surface.
87, layer 33.

206. S201. Rim in fine black sandy ware, burnished surfaces.
95, layer 61.

207. S18. Rim in black sandy ware fired red outside.
46, layer 7.

208. S40. Rim in light grey sandy ware with occasional flint grits.
63, layer 4.

209. S48. Rim in smooth grey brown ware with chaff tempering.
65, layer 5.

210. S283. Rim in fine grey sandy ware with burnished surfaces.
102, layer 44.

211. S293. Rim in fine grey sandy ware with black burnished surface.
102, layer 44.

212. S43. Rim in smooth grey slightly sandy ware.
63, layer 4.

213. S296. Rim in grey sandy ware with roughly finished surface showing some burnishing.
102, layer 44.

214. S269. Rim in coarse grey sandy ware with roughly smoothed surface.
100, layer 24.

215. S13. Rim in grey sandy ware with roughly burnished exterior.
5, layer 3.

216. S294. Rim in fine black sandy ware with smoothed surface.
102, layer 44.

217. S281. Rim in fine grey sandy ware with a smoothed surface.
101, layer 31.

218. S297. Rim in coarse black sandy ware with smoothed surface.
102, layer 44.

219. S295. Rim in fine black sandy ware with smoothed surface.
102, layer 44.

220. S147. Rim in black sandy ware with burnished surface.
91, layer 43.

221. S202. Rim of bowl in even black sandy ware with black burnished surface.
99, layer 8.

222. S88. Rim in black sandy ware with smoothed surface.
85, layer 4.

223. S87. Rim in grey sandy ware.
80, layer 44.

224. S66. Rim in coarse sandy ware with smoothed surface.
67, layer 5.

225. S92. Rim in hard grey sandy ware with smoothed surface.
76, layer 6.

226. S91. Rim in fine sandy ware with smoothed surface.
78, layer 5.

227. S64. Rim in black sandy ware with rough external surface.
72, layer 7.

228. S84. Rim in hard grey sandy ware.
75, layer 4.

229. S149. Rim in black sandy ware with a smoothed surface.
88, layer 26.

230. S59. Rim in black sandy ware with quartz and mica grits.
69, layer 3.

231. S351. Jar in grey-brown sandy ware with chaff tempering.
108, layer 48.

232. S352. Rim in black sandy ware with smoothed surface.
108, layer 62.

233. S49. Rim in smooth grey sandy ware with chaff tempering.
60, layer 10.

234. S289. Rim in fine black sandy ware with burnished surface.
102, layer 44.

235. S288. Rim in fine black sandy ware with smoothed surface.
102, layer 44.

236. S156. Rim in grey sandy ware with copious chaff tempering, smoothed surface.
91, layer 53.

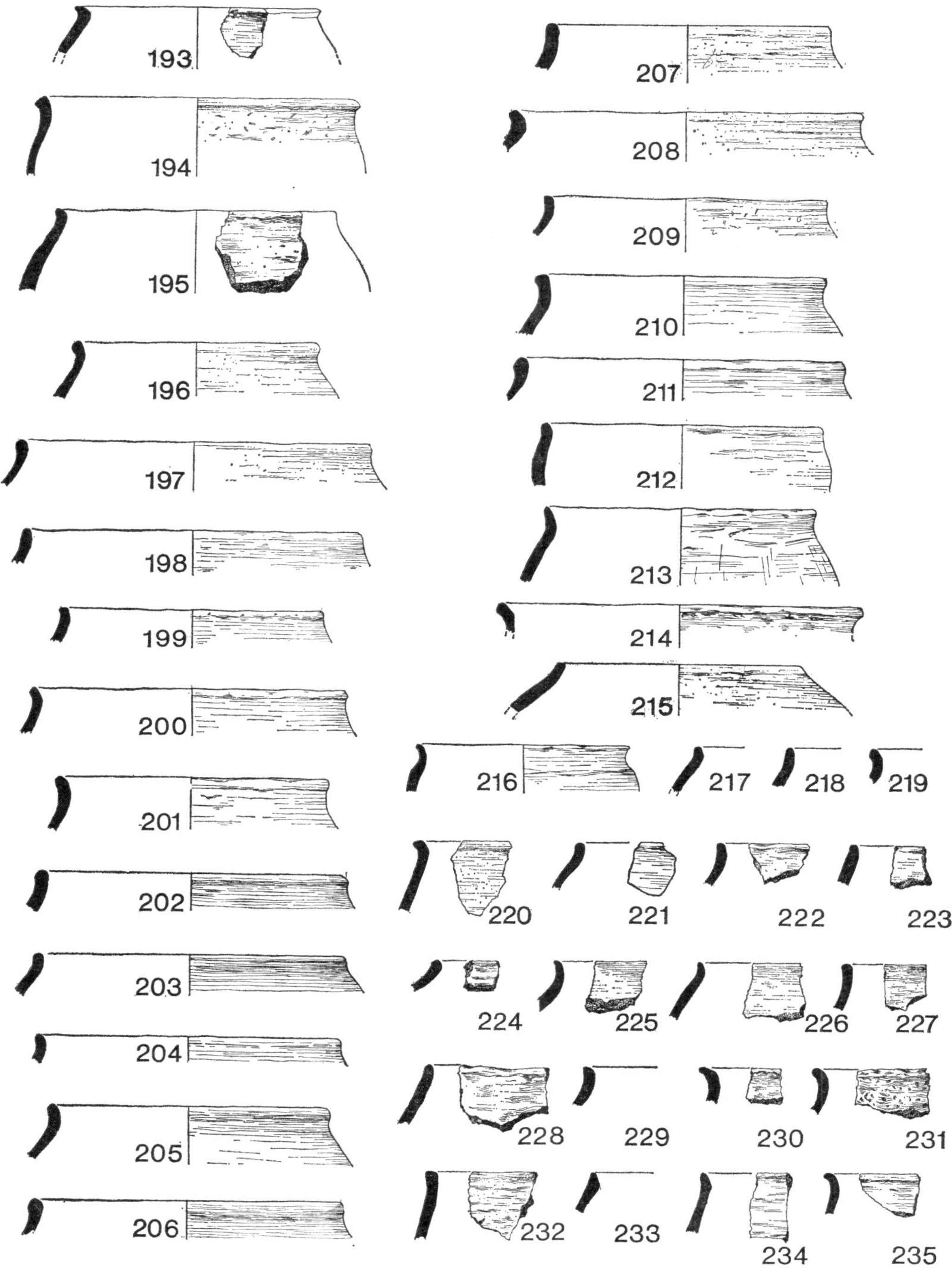

FIG. 114. Plain early–middle Saxon pottery from various locations (pp. 145–6). Scale $\frac{1}{4}$

237. S158, S159. Two rim sherds and two body sherds of one vessel in grey sandy ware fired red-brown on the surface, which is smoothed. The inner surface is heavily burnished.
91, layer 46.

238. S21. Rim in black sandy ware with smoothed surface.
54, layer 6.

239. S266. Jar in black sandy ware with large quartz grits.
100, layer 24.

240. S162. Rim in black sandy ware, tempered with chaff, burnished surface.
91, layer 30.

241. S176. Rim in grey sandy ware with some chaff tempering, burnished surface.
91, layer 53.

242. S145. Rim in coarse black sandy ware, tempered with chaff, well-burnished surface.
91, layer 43.

243. S85. Rim in fine sandy ware with some chaff, smoothed surface.
77, layer 6.

244. S14. Rim in dark grey sandy ware, well burnished inside and out.
5, layer 3.

245. S9. Rim in grey sandy ware with burnished surface.
5, layer 3.

246. S31. Rim in hard black sandy ware with some chaff, burnished black surface.
63, layer 5.

247. S199. Rim in grey sandy ware with occasional large water-worn grits and some chaff. The surface is burnished.
99, layer 64.

248. S184. Rim in coarse grey sandy ware.
87, layer 14.

249. S157. Rim in grey sandy ware with burnished external surface.
89, layer 38.

250. S340. Rim in black ware with crushed flint grits, some external burnishing.
87, layer 24.

251. S193. Rim in fine black sandy ware with smoothed surface.
94, layer 37.

252. S152. Rim in grey ware tempered with crushed flint and some chaff, surface highly burnished and fired red-brown.
91, layer 37.

253. S187. Rim in reddish sandy ware with burnished surface.
87, layer 33.

254. S177. Rim in coarse grey sandy ware with burnished surface fired black.
89, layer 27.

255. S161. Rim in fine grey sandy ware with burnished surface.
91, layer 30.

256. S353. Rim in black sandy ware with chaff tempering.
108, layer 74.

257. S67. Rim in fine grey sandy ware with smoothed surface.
68, layer 3.

258. S268. Bowl in coarse black sandy ware with roughly smoothed irregular surface.
100, layer 24.

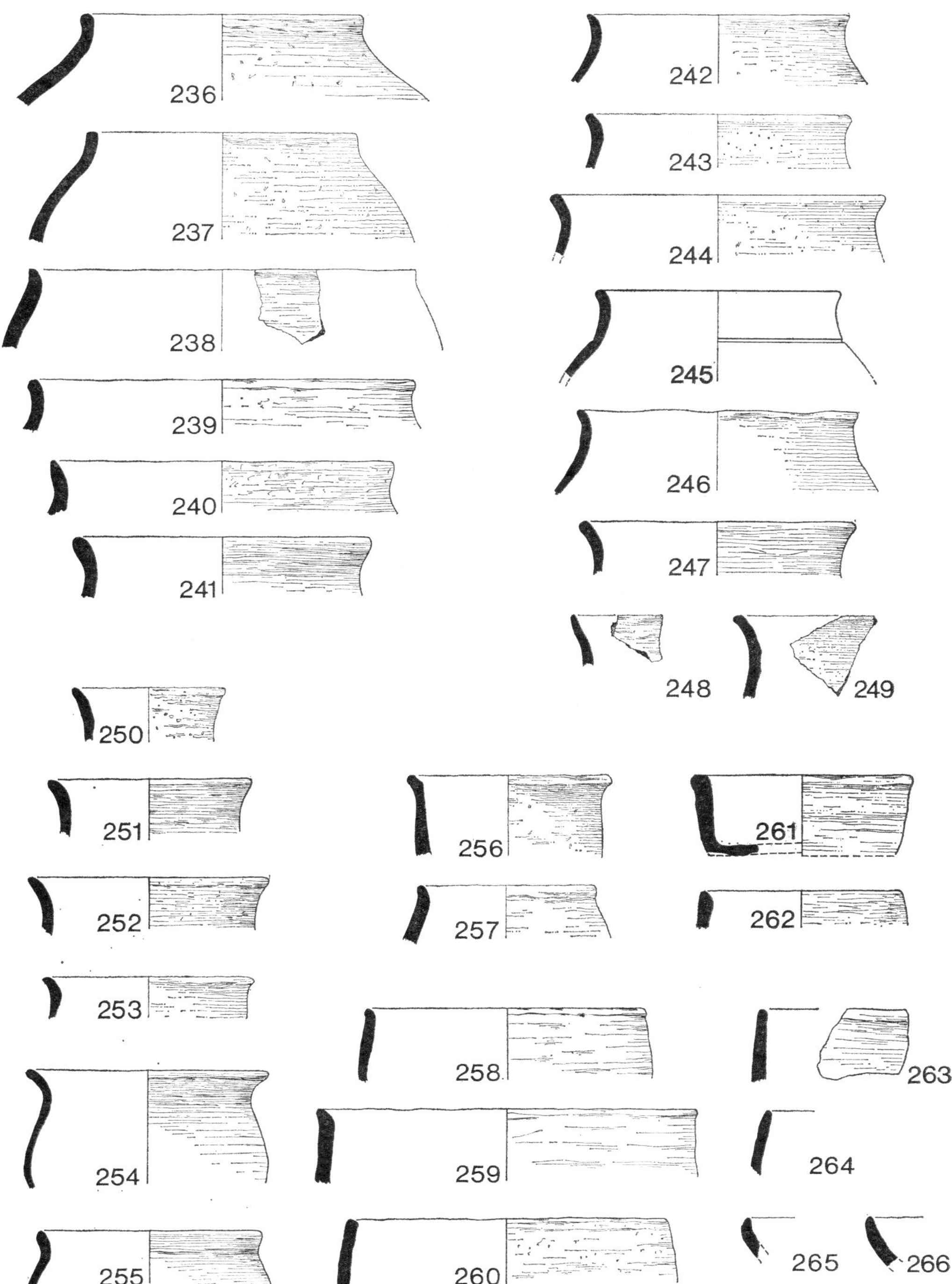

FIG. 115. Plain early–middle Saxon pottery from various locations (pp. 146–50). Scale $\frac{1}{4}$

259. S286. Rim in fine black sandy ware with smoothed surface.
102, layer 44.

260. S303. Joining with S300 from layer 44.
102, layer 46.

261. S2. Dish in smooth dark grey-brown ware with burnished surface inside and out.
5, layer 3.

262. S179. Rim in coarse grey sandy ware with chaff tempering.
87, layer 7.

263. S178. Rim in coarse grey sandy ware.
87, layer 7.

264. S285. Bowl in coarse sandy ware with smoothed surface.
102, layer 44.

265. S279. Rim of bowl in coarse black sandy ware.
101, layer 81.

266. S280. Bowl in grey sandy ware with some large quartz inclusions.
101, layer 31.

267. S151. Rim in even red sandy ware fired black on the surface and burnished (2 rim sherds and 1 body sherd).
88, layer 5.

268. S32. Rim in fine black sandy ware with well-smoothed surface.
63, layer 5.

269. S42. Rim in grey sandy ware fired black on the surface; some chaff tempering and flecks of mica.
63, layer 4.

270. S46. Rim in grey sandy ware with crushed flint grits.
60, layer 5.

271. S44. Rim in black sandy ware.
60, layer 12.

272. S192. Rim in coarse grey sandy ware with occasional flint grits.
95, layer 20.

273. S205. Rim of coarse jar in dark grey sandy ware with copious chaff tempering.
98, layer 37.

274. S1. Rim in hard grey brown sandy ware with burnished surface inside and out.
5, layer 3.

275. S146. Rim in coarse black sandy ware with smoothed surface.
91, layer 43.

276. S265. Rim in black sandy ware with chaff tempering. Residue from post-Saxon layers.

277. S290. Rim in coarse grey sandy ware with burnished surface.
102, layer 44.

278. S292. Rim in coarse grey sandy ware with smoothed surface.
102, layer 44.

279. S16. Rim in dark grey sandy ware, burnished outside.
46, layer 3.

280. S182. Rim in black sandy ware with large flint grits.
87, layer 13.

281. S45. Rim in black sandy ware with chaff and mica tempering.
60, layer 6.

282. S278. Rim in coarse black sandy ware.
101, layer 81.

283. S282. Rim in even grey brown sandy ware with burnished surface.
102, layer 44.

284. S68. Rim in fine black sandy ware with smoothed surface.
71, layer 7.

285. S194. Rim in grey sandy ware.
97, layer 65.

286. S62. Rim in black sandy ware with well smoothed surface.
72, layer 5.

287. S160. Rim in coarse black sandy ware tempered with crushed flint and chalk.
91, layer 30.

288. S195. Coarse jar in grey brown sandy ware.
94, layer 93.

289. S140. Rim in smooth grey sandy ware with chaff tempering.
87, layer 9.

290. S196. Coarse jar in black sandy ware with crushed flint tempering.
94, layer 93.

291. S200. Rim in grey sandy ware with some chaff tempering.
95, layer 61.

292. S264. Rim in coarse grey sandy ware with smoothed surface. Residue from post-Saxon layers.

293. S172. Rim in grey sandy ware.
87, layer 9.

294. S298. Rim in coarse grey sandy ware with smoothed surface.
102, layer 44.

295. S61. Rim in black sandy ware with smoothed surface.
67, layer 4.

296. S306. Rim in coarse grey sandy ware.
102, layer 33.

297. S304. Rim in black sandy ware with chaff tempering, smoothed surface.
102, layer 46.

298. S47. Rim in black sandy ware with chaff tempering.
60, layer 14.

299. S93. Rim in dark grey sandy ware.
76, layer 6.

300. S150. Rim in grey ware tempered with crushed chalk and shell.
88, layer 5.

301. S272. 2 rim sherds in coarse grey ware tempered with crushed flint grits.
100, layer 81.

302. S310. Rim in coarse black sandy ware.
103, layer 15.

303. S308. Jar in coarse grey sandy ware tempered with finely crushed flint grits (5 rim sherds and 25 body sherds).
103, layer 45.

304. S301. Jar in coarse grey sandy fabric with crushed flint grits.
102, layer 46.

305. S333. Rim in black sandy ware with a burnished surface.
Pit 207, 104, layer 10.

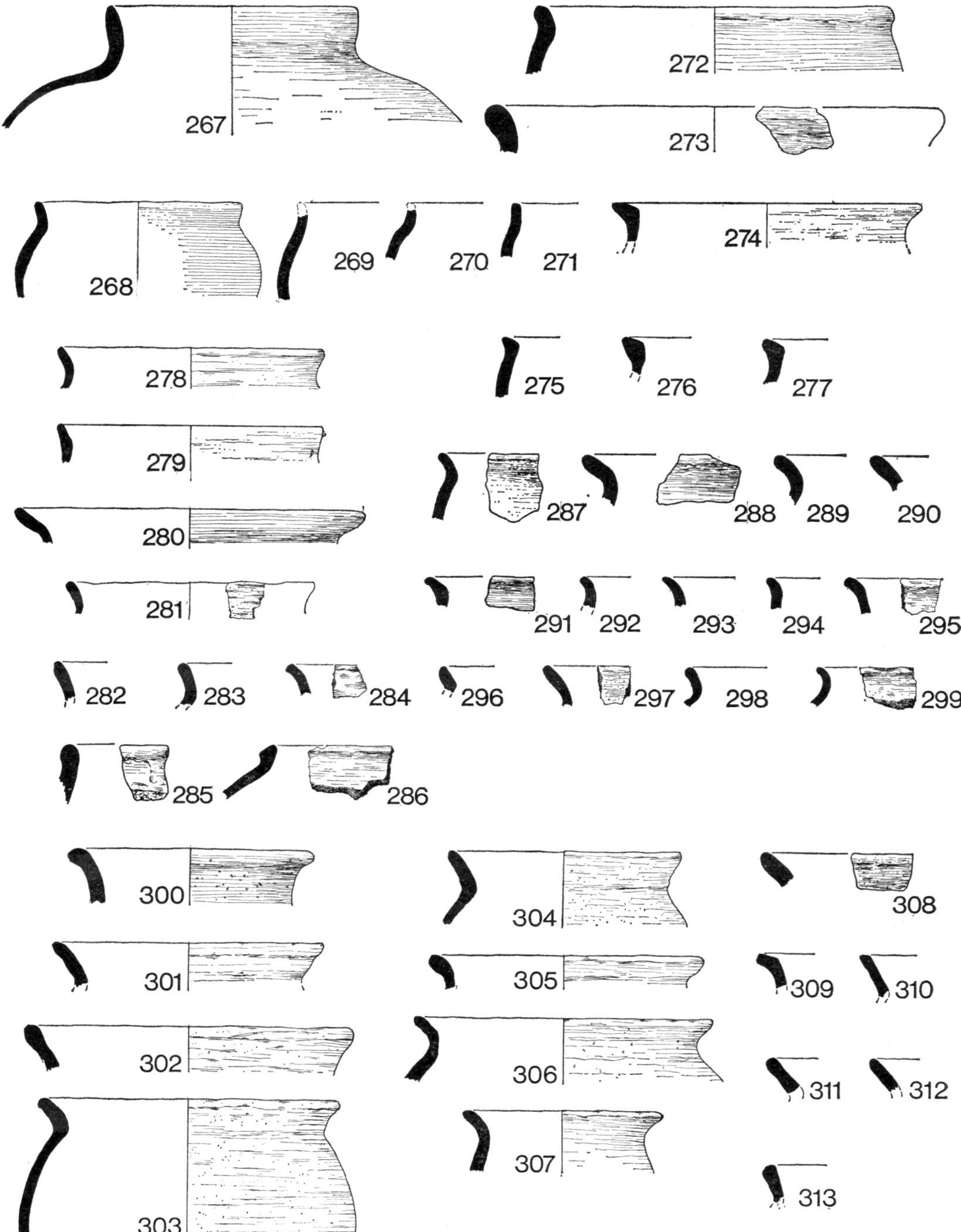

FIG. 116. Plain early–late Saxon pottery from various locations (pp. 150–3). Scale $\frac{1}{4}$

306. S270. Jar in smooth black ware with ?limestone grits. The surface is black and burnished.
100, layer 66.

307. S332. Rim in coarse grey sandy ware with a smoothed surface.
Pit 207, 104, layer 10.

308. S163. Rim in dark grey sandy ware tempered with finely crushed flint grits.
89 layer 23.

309. S275. Rim in grey sandy ware tempered with some finely crushed shell.
101, layer 22.

310. S271. Jar in grey sandy ware with crushed flint grits.
100, layer 66.

311, 312. S273, S274. 2 rim sherds of same vessel in hard grey sandy ware with crushed chalk and flint tempering.
100, layer 38.

313. S302. Rim in grey sandy ware, burnished surface.
102, layer 46.

314. S341. Decorated body sherd in soft grey ware tempered with crushed flint grits. The surface is smoothed and decorated with impressed circles and groups of dots.
88, layer 5.

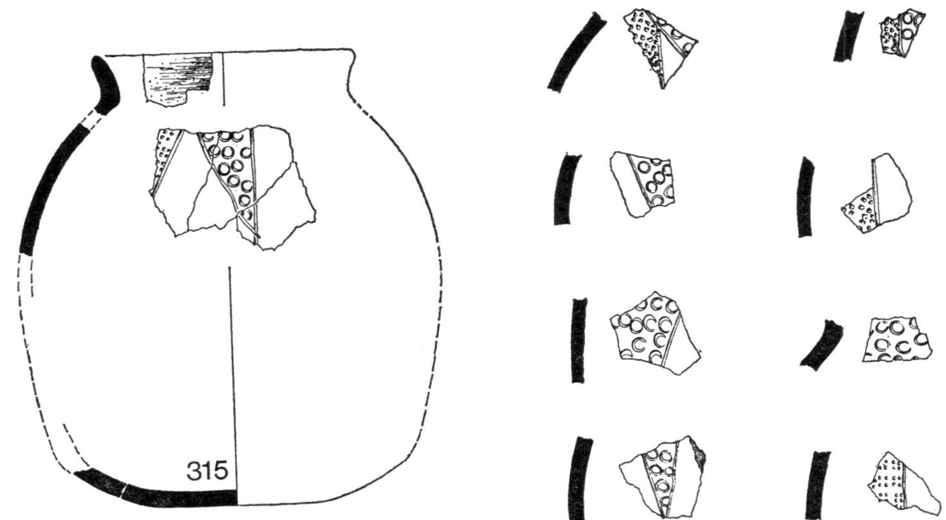

FIG. 117. Panel-decorated late Saxon pottery (p. 153). Scale $\frac{1}{4}$

315. S348. Decorated jar in grey-brown ware with crushed flint grits, decorated in panels with impressed dots and circles. The surface is smoothed (1 rim and 12 sherds).
108, layer 40.

Late Saxon Pottery

316. M112. Cooking pot: grey ware fired red-brown with coarsely crushed flint grit tempering.
Pit 37, layer 10.

317. M111. Cooking pot in red-grey ware with crushed flint and chalk tempering.
Pit 37, layer 12.

318. M115. Cooking pot in grey with crushed flint and chalk tempering.
Pit 37, layer 10.

319. M126. Cooking pot with hollowed rim in grey sandy ware, some crushed flint grit tempering.
Pit 37; layer 10.

320. M127. Cooking pot with hollowed rim in grey-brown sandy ware, some crushed flint grit tempering.
Pit 37, layer 10.

321. M116. Cooking pot with hollowed rim in fine grey sandy ware with some crushed flint tempering.
Pit 37, layer 10.

322. M121. Cooking pot, undercut rim, in fine grey sandy ware with some flint grit tempering.
Pit 37, layer 10.

323. M113. Cooking pot, undercut rim, in fine grey-brown sandy ware with some crushed flint tempering.
Pit 37, layer 10.

324. M123. Cooking pot, hollowed rim, in grey sandy ware with some crushed flint grit tempering.
Pit 37, layer 10.

325. M109. Cooking pot in grey sandy ware with crushed chalk and some crushed flint tempering; the chalk has largely leached out.
Pit 37, layer 12.

326. M107. Three joining body sherds in hard white sandy ware. The surface is decorated with applied strips which have been stamped; coated with a thick yellow-green glaze.
Pit 37, layer 10.

327. M106. Body sherd in fine pinkish-buff sandy ware: surface irregular but wiped to a smooth finish. Traces of red paint.
Pit 37, layer 10.

328. M125. Cooking pot, hollowed rim, in grey-brown sandy ware with some crushed flint grit tempering.
Pit 37, layer 10.

329. M124. Cooking pot, hollowed rim, in grey sandy ware with some crushed flint grit tempering.
Pit 37, layer 10.

330. M128. Cooking pot, base angle, in grey sandy ware with some crushed flint grit tempering.
Pit 37, layer 10.

331. M129. Cooking pot, hollowed rim, in grey sandy ware with some crushed flint grit tempering.
Pit 37, layer 10.

332. M120. Sherd, rouletted, in grey sandy ware with some fine flint tempering.
Pit 37, layer 10.

333. M119. Sherd, rouletted, in grey sandy ware with some fine flint tempering.
Pit 37, layer 10.

334. M118. Sherd, rouletted, in red sandy ware with some fine flint tempering.
Pit 37, layer 10.

335. M108. Spouted jug in light buff-brown sandy ware with a grey core: wheel-turned. Smooth surface decorated with applied stripes which have been stamped.
Pit 37, layer 12.

336. M130. Cooking pot, hollowed rim, in grey sandy ware with some crushed flint grit tempering.
Pit 37, layer 12.

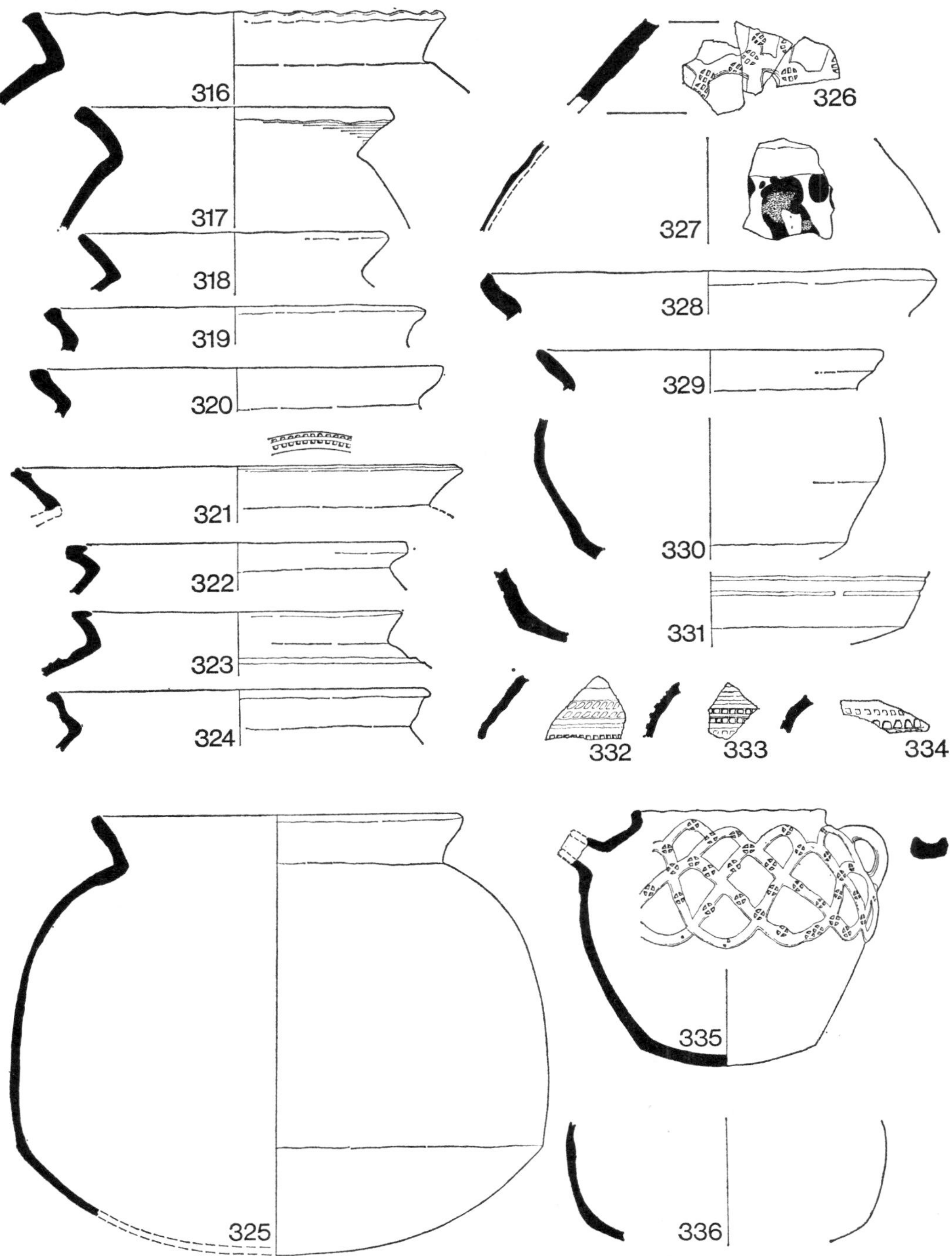

FIG. 118. Late Saxon pottery from pit 37 (pp. 153–4). Scale $\frac{1}{4}$

337. M122. Cooking pot in grey ware tempered with crushed flint and chalk grits.
Pit 37, layer 12.

338. M117. Cooking pot in grey sandy ware with crushed flint tempering.
Pit 37, layer 12.

339. M110. Cooking pot in grey-brown ware tempered with crushed flint and chalk grits.
Pit 37, layer 12.

340. M114. Cooking pot, hollowed rim, in fine grey-brown sandy ware with some crushed flint tempering.
Pit 37, layer 12.

341. M157. Cooking pot in grey sandy ware with fine flint grits, fired reddish-brown.
Pit 39, layer 10b.

342. M131. Cooking pot in reddish-brown sandy ware with flint grits.
Pit 39, layer 10.

343. M153. Cooking pot in grey sandy ware with flint grits, fired reddish-brown.
Pit 39, layer 10b.

344. M158. Cooking pot in grey sandy ware with flint grits, fired reddish-brown.
Pit 39, layer 10.

345. M147. Cooking pot in grey sandy ware with flint grits, fired reddish-brown.
Pit 39, layer 10b.

346. M170. Cooking pot in grey sandy ware with fine flint grits.
Pit 39, layer 10b.

347. M168. Cooking pot in grey sandy ware with fine flint grits.
Pit 39, layer 10b.

348. M161. Cooking pot in grey sandy ware with fine flint grits.
Pit 39, layer 10.

349. M149. Cooking pot in grey sandy ware with fine flint grits.
Pit 39, layer 10.

350. M159. Cooking pot in grey sandy ware with fine flint grits.
Pit 39, layer 10.

351. M156. Cooking pot in grey sandy ware with fine flint grits, fired reddish.
Pit 39, layer 10.

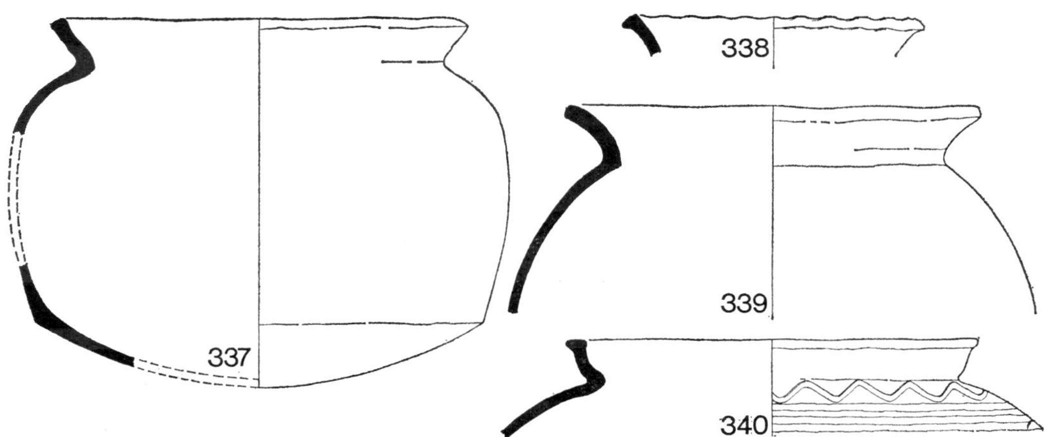

FIG. 119. Late Saxon pottery from pit 37 (p. 156). Scale $\frac{1}{4}$

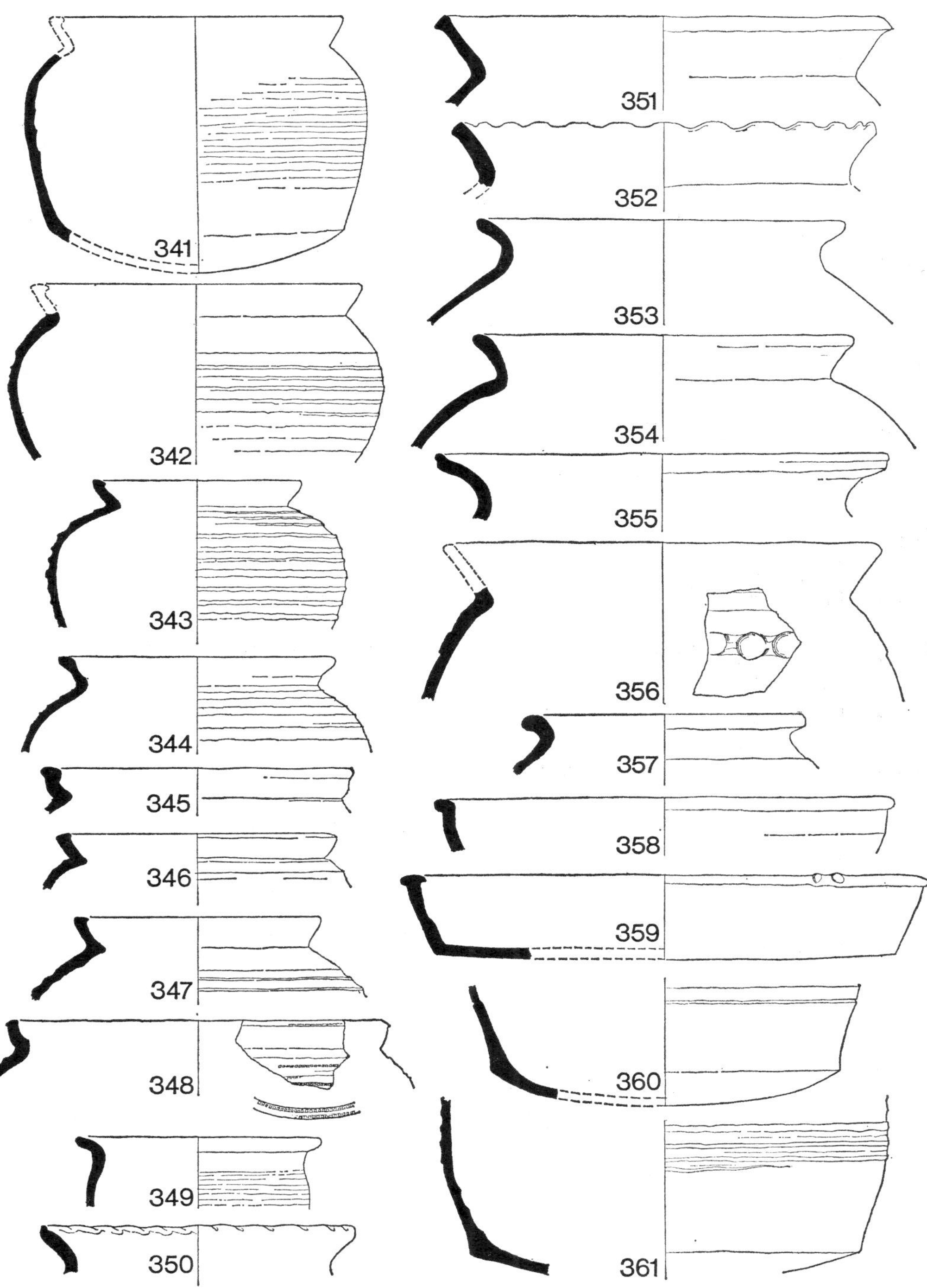

FIG. 120. Late Saxon pottery from pit 39 (pp. 156, 158). Scale $\frac{1}{4}$

352. M171. Cooking pot in grey ware with flint and chalk grits, fired reddish.
Pit 39, layer 10b.
353. M148. Cooking pot in grey sandy ware with flint grits, fired reddish.
Pit 39, layer 10.
354. M154. Cooking pot in grey ware with flint grit tempering, fired reddish.
Pit 39, layer 10.
355. M155. Cooking pot in grey sandy ware.
Pit 39, layer 10.
356. M151. Cooking pot in hard grey ware with flint grit tempering, fired even red.
Pit 39, layer 10.
357. M169. Cooking pot in hard red sandy ware with fine flint grits.
Pit 39, layer 10b.
358. M160. Dish in reddish brown sandy ware.
Pit 39, layer 10.
359. M152. Dish in hard grey sandy ware with fine flint grits, fired reddish.
Pit 39, layer 10b.
360. M132. Cooking pot base in hard grey sandy ware with fine flint grits.
Pit 39, layer 10b.
361. M133. Cooking pot base in greyish-brown sandy ware with fine flint grits.
Pit 39, layer 10b.
362. M180. Cooking pot in grey sandy ware with flint grit tempering.
Pit 58, layer 10.
363. M182. Cooking pot in grey-brown sandy ware with flint grit tempering.
Pit 59, layer 23.
364. M181. Cooking pot in grey sandy ware with flint grit tempering.
Pit 59, layer 23.
365. M191. Cooking pot, undercut rim, in grey sandy ware with some flint grit tempering.
Pit 68, layer 31.
366. M193. Cooking pot in grey sandy ware with flint tempering.
Pit 67, layer 30.
367. M192. Rim in grey sandy ware with coarse wiped surface.
Pit 67, layer 30.
368. M183. Cooking pot in grey sandy ware with some flint grit tempering.
Pit 71, layer 42.
369. M188. Cooking pot in coarse grey ware with much flint tempering (2 sherds).
Pit 71, layer 32.
370. M187. Cooking pot, hollowed rim, in grey sandy ware with flint grit tempering.
Pit 71, layer 32.
371. M185. Cooking pot, undercut rim, in grey-brown sandy ware with some flint grit tempering.
Pit 71, layer 32.
372. M186. Cooking pot, undercut rim, in grey-brown sandy ware with some flint grit tempering.
Pit 71, layer 32.
373. M184. Cooking pot in grey sandy ware with flint and chalk tempering.
Pit 71, layer 42.
374. M189. Cooking pot, undercut rim, rilled on body, rouletted on rim, in grey sandy ware with some flint grits, fired red.
Pit 73, layer 34.

375. M190. Body sherd, rouletted, in grey sandy ware with some flint grits, fired red on the surface. Pit 73, layer 34.

376. M323. Cooking pot in grey-brown sandy ware with flint grit tempering, rilled body (4 rim and 6 body sherds).
Pit 89, layer 30.

377. M326. Cooking pot in grey sandy ware, tempered with some flint, fired red, rilled body.
Pit 89, layer 30.

378. M324. Cooking pot in grey sandy ware fired red, tempered with some flint grits, rilled body.
Pit 89, layer 50.

379. M325. Cooking pot in coarse black sandy ware with flint grit tempering.
Pit 89, layer 50.

380. M328. Cooking pot in grey sandy ware with fine flint grit, rilled.
Pit 89, layer 30.

381. M330. Cooking pot in grey-brown sandy ware with some flint grit, rouletted.
Pit 89, layer 50.

382. M329. Cooking pot in grey sandy ware with fine flint grits, rouletted.
Pit 89, layer 30.

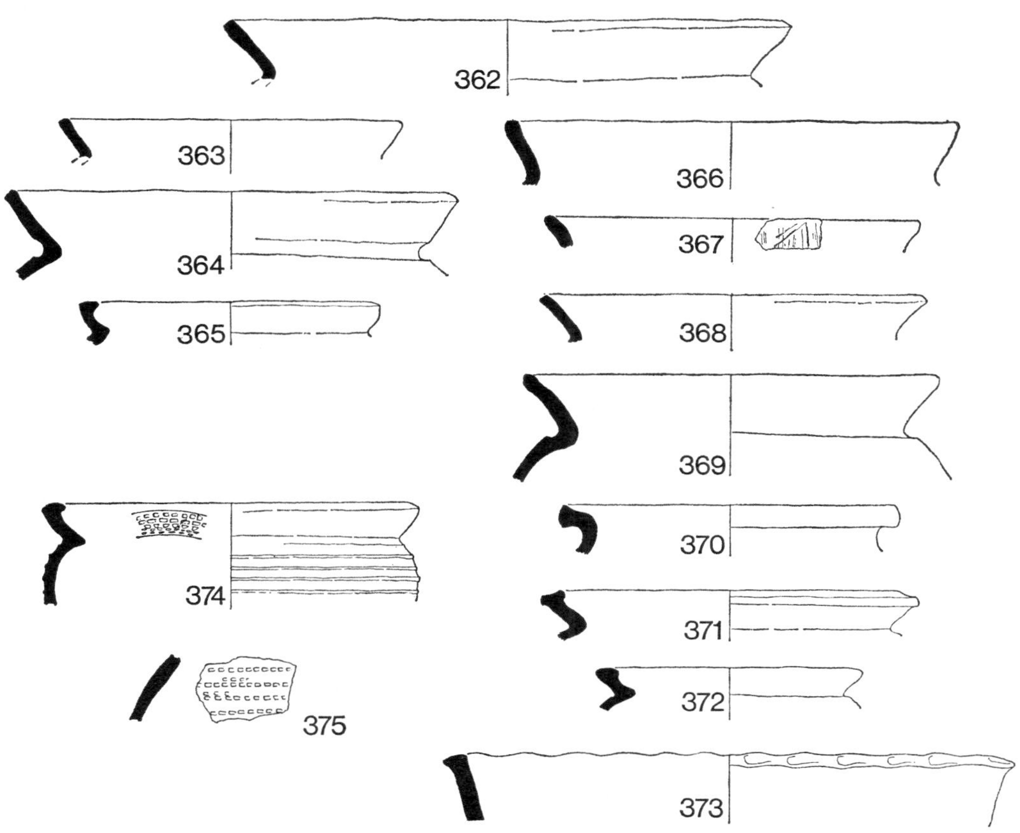

Fig. 121. Late Saxon pottery from pits 58, 59, 67, 68, 71 and 73 (p. 158).
Scale $\frac{1}{4}$

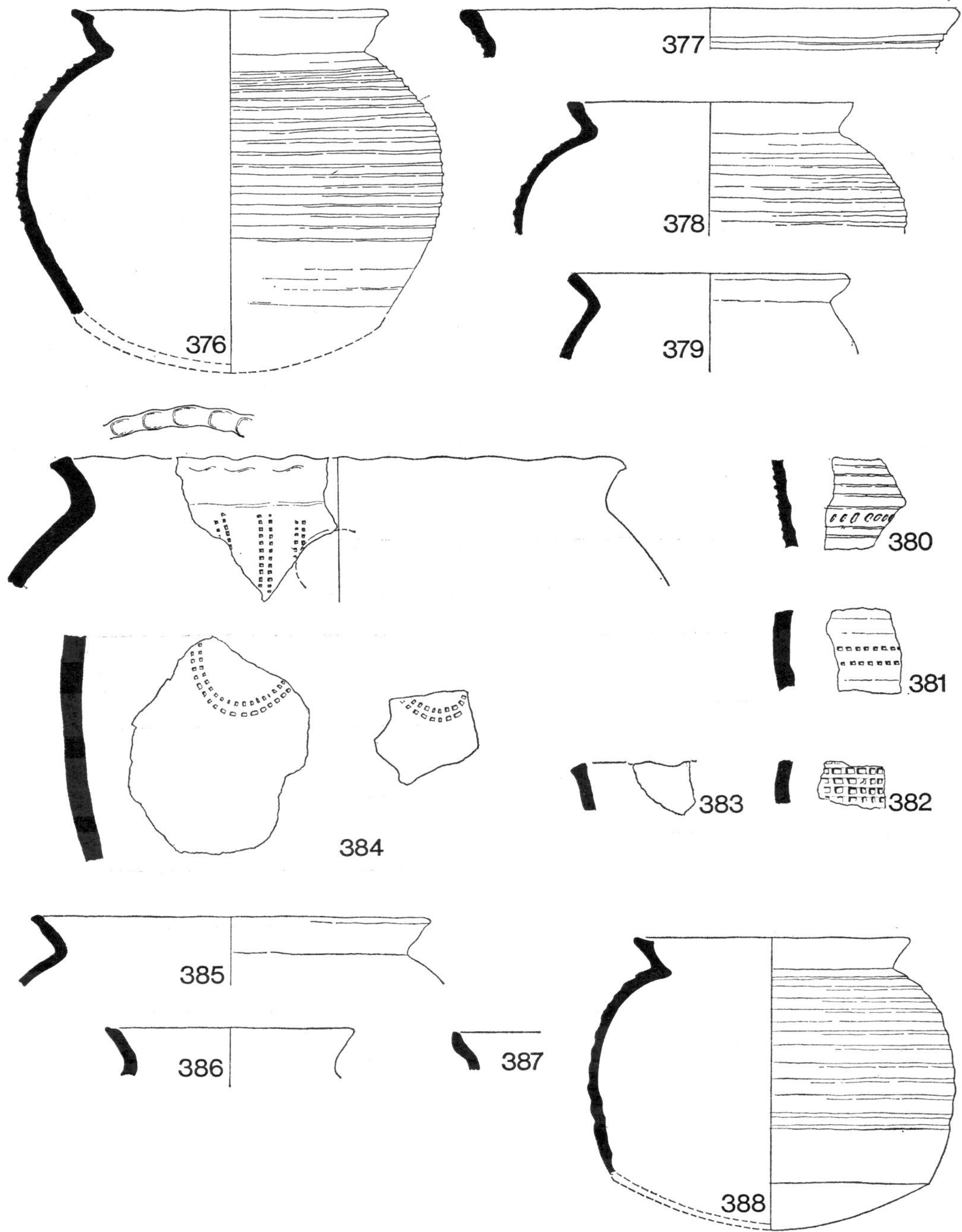

Fig. 122. Late Saxon pottery from pits 89, 91 and 97 (pp. 159, 161). Scale $\frac{1}{4}$

383. M327. Dish in grey-brown ware tempered with flint and chalk.
Pit 89, layer 30.

384. M331. Large jar, once with a spout for which the attachment scar now remains, in grey sandy ware with flint grit tempering, fired red on the surface, decorated with rouletting.
Pit 89, layer 50.

385. M200. Cooking pot in coarse grey-brown ware with flint grit tempering.
Pit 91, layer 29.

386. M199. Cooking pot in coarse grey ware with flint grit tempering.
Pit 91, layer 29.

387. M265. Cooking pot in grey-black ware with fine flint grits.
Pit 97, layer 36.

388. M264. Cooking pot in grey-brown sandy ware with finely crushed flint grits, rilled (1 rim and 8 large body sherds).
Pit 97, layer 9.

389. M271. Cooking pot in grey sandy ware with crushed flint grits (2 rim and 29 body sherds).
Pit 101, layer 11.

390. M270. Rim in grey-brown sandy ware with some flint grits.
Pit 101, layer 6.

391. M281. Cooking pot in grey ware with copious flint and chalk tempering. Distorted and over-fired, possibly a waster.
Pit 104, layer 41.

392. M273. Cooking pot in grey-brown sandy ware with finely crushed flint grits.
Pit 104, layer 38.

393. M278. Cooking pot in grey-brown sandy ware with some fine flint grit tempering.
Pit 104, layer 41.

394. M274. Cooking pot in grey sandy ware with finely crushed flint grits.
Pit 104, layer 38.

395. M276. Cooking pot in grey-brown sandy ware with some fine flint grit tempering.
Pit 104, layer 41.

396. M277. Cooking pot in grey-brown sandy ware with some fine flint grit tempering.
Pit 104, layer 41.

397. M275. Cooking pot in coarse grey ware tempered with flint grits.
Pit 104, layer 38.

398. M279. Cooking pot in grey-brown ware with flint and chalk tempering.
Pit 104, layer 41.

399. M280. Dish in grey-brown sandy ware with some flint grit tempering, rouletted.
Pit 104, layer 41.

400. M283. Cooking pot in grey-brown sandy ware with flint grit tempering, rouletted decoration.
Pit 106, layer 26.

401. M282. Cooking pot in grey sandy ware with finely crushed flint grits.
Pit 106, layer 26.

402. M284. Cooking pot in black sandy ware with flint grit tempering, rilled decoration.
Pit 107, layer 23.

403. M289. Dish in dark grey ware with flint and chalk tempering (5 large rim and 1 base sherds).
Pit 107, layer 23.

404. M287. Cooking pot in coarse grey ware with flint and chalk grit tempering.
Pit 107, layer 23.

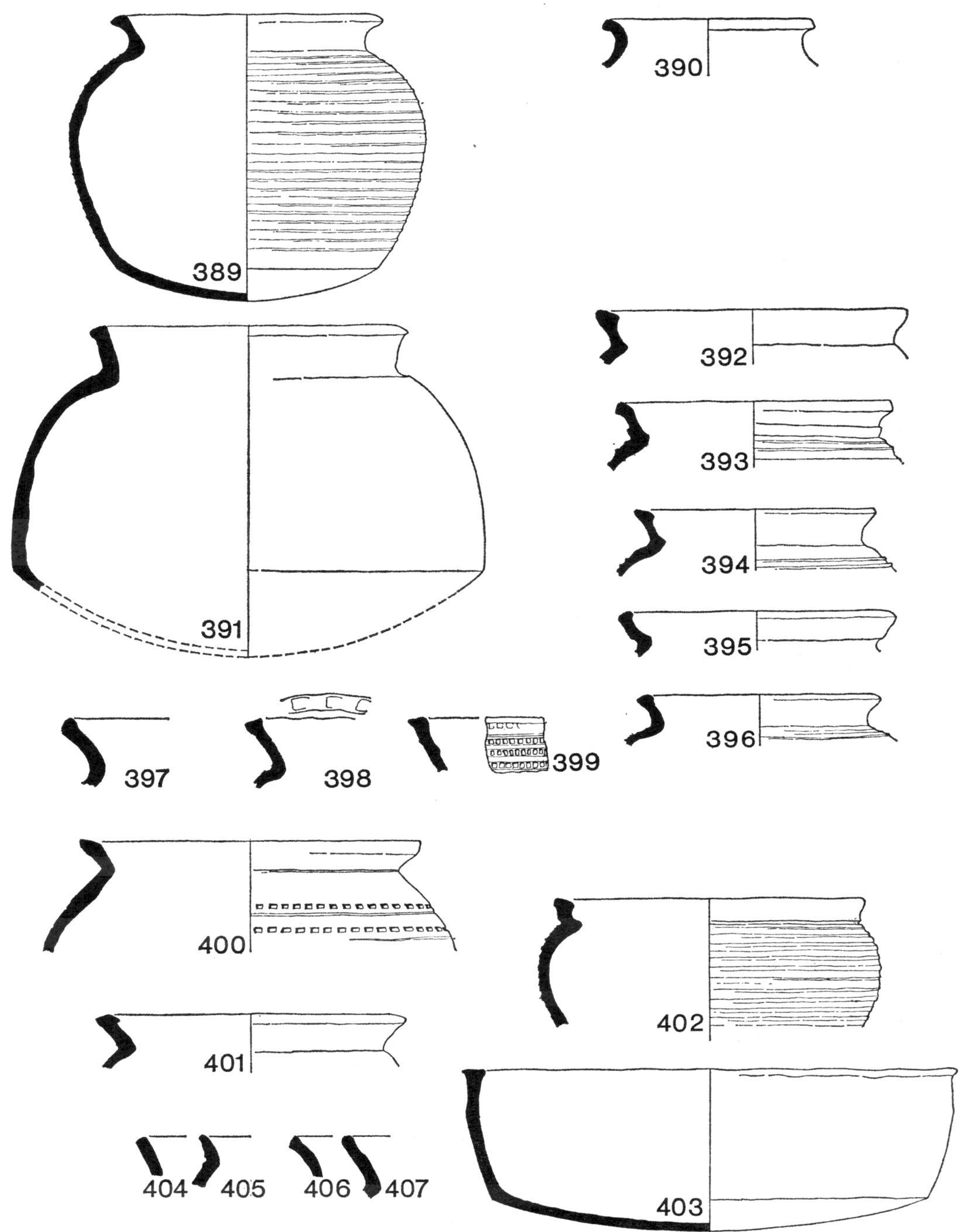

Fig. 123. Late Saxon pottery from pits 101, 104, 106 and 107 (pp. 161, 163). Scale $\frac{1}{4}$

405. M288. Cooking pot in black sandy ware with some fine flint tempering.
Pit 107, layer 23.

406. M285. Cooking pot in coarse grey ware with flint grit tempering.
Pit 107, layer 23.

407. M286. Cooking pot in coarse grey-brown ware with flint grit tempering.
Pit 107, layer 23.

408. M209. Pitcher in ochre sandy ware with some very fine flint grits. Glassy orange glaze spotted light green, dribbles inside.
Pit 111, layer 32.

409. M212. Body sherd in ochre sandy ware with fine flint grits. Orange-green glassy glaze outside.
Pit 111, layer 32.

410. M211. Dish with socketed handle in coarse grey sandy ware tempered with flint and chalk.
Pit 111, layer 32.

411–422. M213–M224. Rim fragments of cooking pots, all in typical Portchester ware, sandy fabrics with some crushed flint tempering.
Pit 111, layer 32.

423. M210. Body sherd in fine grey sandy ware with some crushed flint grits, fired red on the surface and stamped.
Pit 111, layer 32.

424. M226. Body sherd in typical Portchester ware with rouletted decoration.
Pit 111, layer 32.

425. M225. Body sherd in typical Portchester ware with rouletted decoration.
Pit 111, layer 32.

426–432. M234–6, 238–9, 242–3. Cooking pots in typical Portchester ware, grey sandy fabrics with some crushed flint grits. The surfaces are often rilled or rouletted.
Pit 113, layer 47.

433. M237. Cooking pot in grey flint and chalk-tempered fabric.
Pit 113, layer 47.

434–435. M233, M240. Cooking pots in typical Portchester ware, grey sandy fabric with some crushed flint grits. The surfaces are often rilled or rouletted.
Pit 113, layer 51.

436. M241. Rim in grey sandy ware with some chaff tempering.
Pit 113, layer 47.

437. M249. Cooking pot in grey-brown sandy ware with flint grits.
Pit 115, layer 28.

438. M252. Dish in grey sandy ware with flint grits (3 sherds).
Pit 115, layer 28.

439. M253. Dish in grey-brown ware tempered with flint grits.
Pit 115, layer 53.

440. M251. Cooking pot in grey sandy ware with finely crushed flint grits.
Pit 115, layer 28.

441. M250. Cooking pot in grey sandy ware with finely crushed flint grits.
Pit 115, layer 28.

442. M254. Cooking pot in dark grey ware with flint grits.
Pit 115, layer 28.

443. M255. Cooking pot in grey sandy ware with fine flint grits.
Pit 115, layer 28.

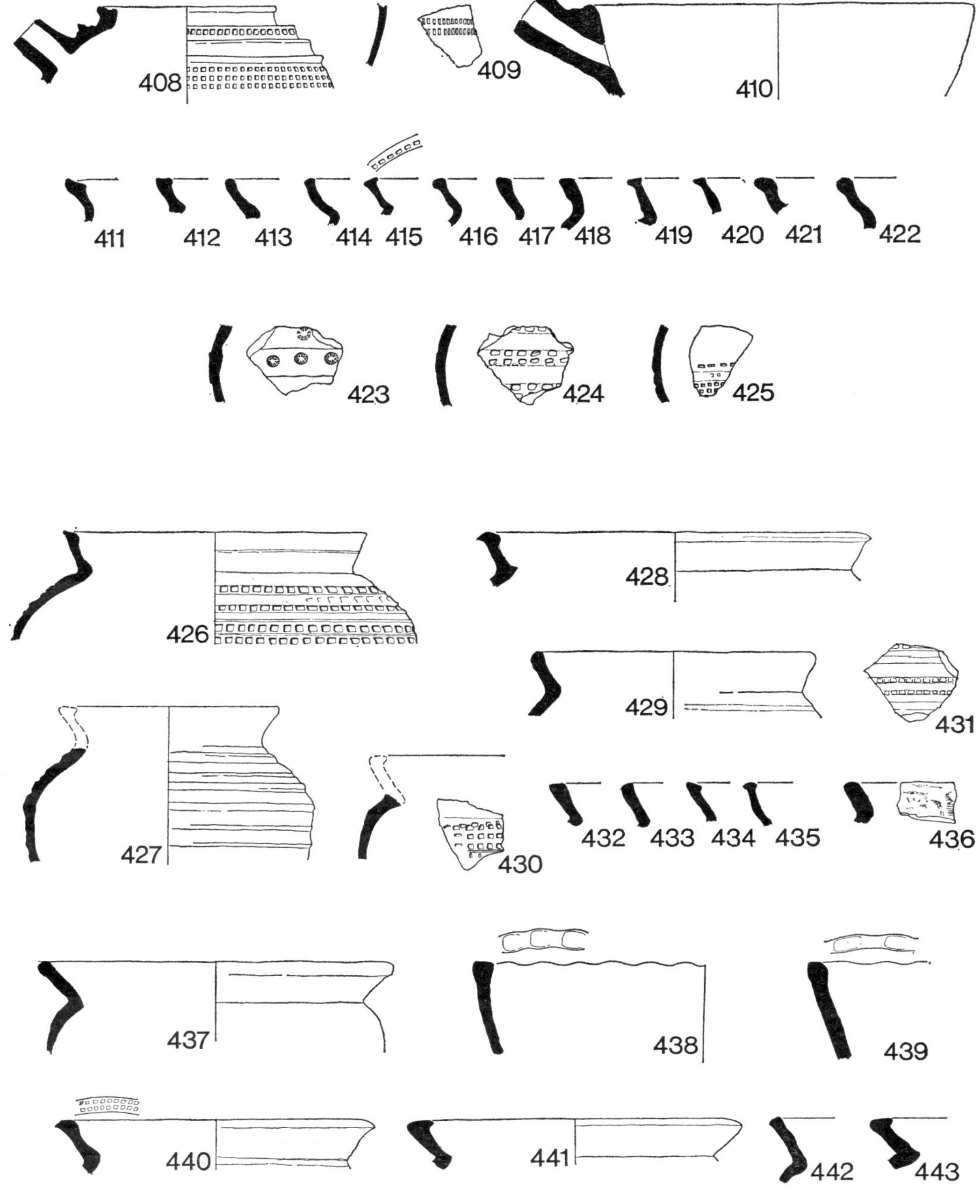

FIG. 124. Late Saxon pottery from pits 111, 113 and 115 (p. 163). Scale $\frac{1}{4}$

444. M400. Cooking pot in grey sandy ware with flint and chalk grits. Overfired.
Pit (well) 143, layer 111.

445. M386. Cooking pot in grey-brown sandy ware with flint grits.
Pit (well) 143, layer 82.

446. M398. Dish in grey-brown ware with flint and chalk grit tempering.
Pit (well) 143, layer 110.

447. M397. Dish in grey sandy ware with flint and chalk grit tempering.
Pit (well) 143, layer 110.

448. M396. Rim in grey sandy ware with fine flint grits.
Pit (well) 143, layer 110.

449. M395. Rim in grey sandy ware with large flint grits.
Pit (well) 143, layer 110.

450. M399. Rim in grey sandy ware with fine flint grits.
Pit (well) 143, layer 110.

451. M393. Rim in grey ware with flint grits.
Pit (well) 143, layer 82.

452. M391. Rim of cooking pot in grey sandy ware with fine flint grits.
Pit (well) 143, layer 82.

453. M390. Rim of cooking pot in grey sandy ware with fine flint grits.
Pit (well) 143, layer 82.

454. M392. Rim of cooking pot in grey sandy ware with fine flint grits.
Pit (well) 143, layer 82.

455. M394. Rim of cooking pot in grey sandy ware with fine flint grits.
Pit (well) 143, layer 82.

456. M389. Dish in grey-brown ware with large flint grits.
Pit (well) 143, layer 82.

457. M388. Body sherd in grey ware with flint grits: stamped.
Pit (well) 143, layer 82.

458. M387. Rim in grey sandy ware with flint grits: stamped.
Pit (well) 143, layer 82.

459. M374. Cooking pot in grey sandy ware with fine flint grits.
Pit 151, layer 49.

460. M375. Cooking pot in grey sandy ware with fine flint grits.
Pit 151, layer 49.

461. M377. Rim in dark grey sandy ware with some flint grits.
Pit 151, layer 51.

462. M376. Dish in grey-brown ware with flint grit tempering.
Pit 151, layer 49.

463. M523. Rim in hard grey ware with flint and chalk tempering.
Pit 154, layer 35.

464. M524. Rim in hard grey sandy ware with some flint tempering.
Pit 154, layer 35.

465. M525. Rim in hard grey sandy ware with flint tempering.
Pit 154, layer 35.

466. M526. Rim in hard grey sandy ware with flint tempering.
Pit 154, layer 35.

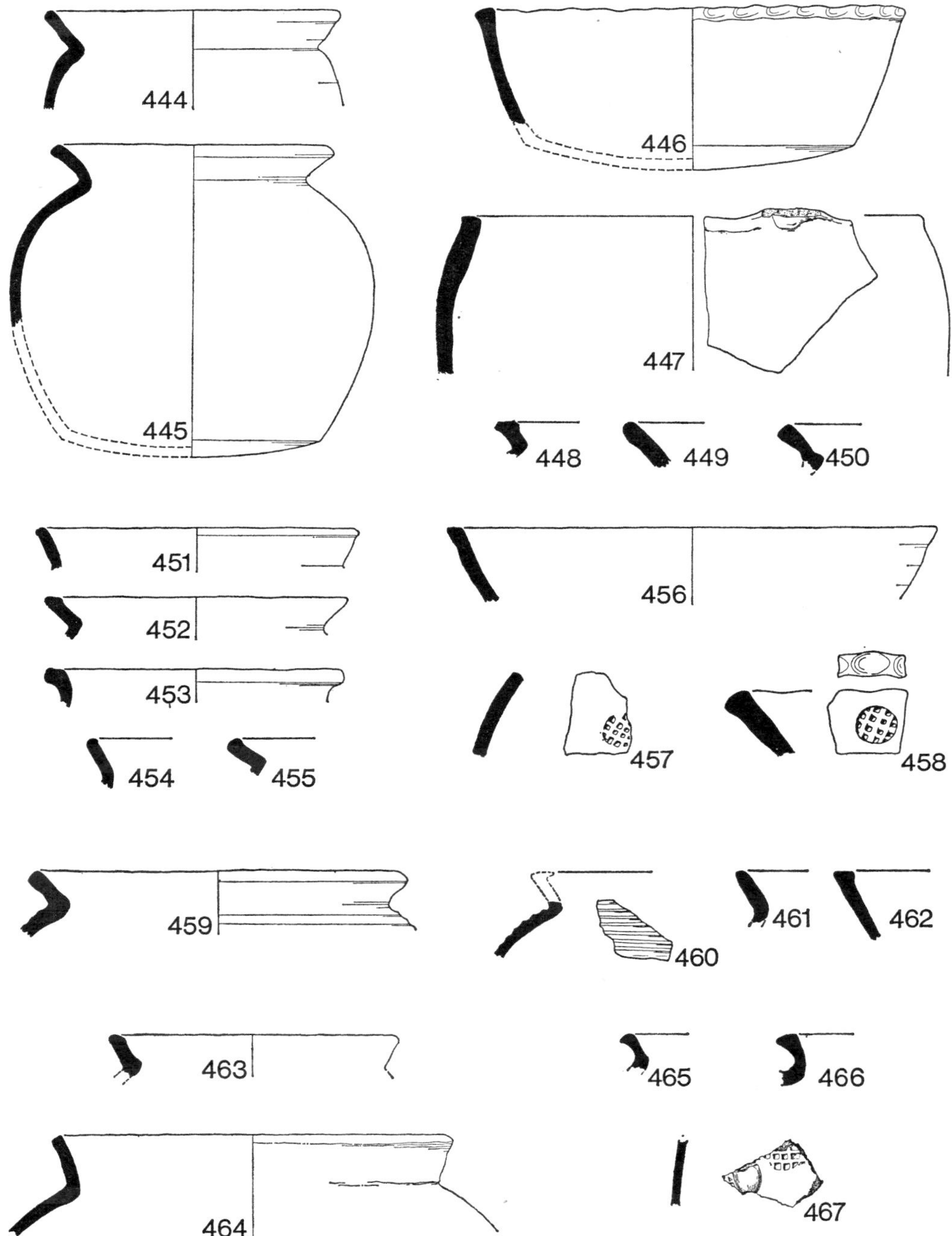

Fig. 125. Late Saxon pottery from pits 143, 151 and 154 (pp. 156, 158). Scale ¼

467. M527. Body sherd in hard grey sandy ware with some flint tempering; decorated with stamping and an applied strip.
Pit 154, layer 35.

468. M380. Rim in grey sandy ware with fine flint grits.
Pit 156, layer 58.

469. M379. Rim in grey sandy ware with fine flint grits.
Pit 156, layer 58.

470. M378. Rim in grey sandy ware with fine flint grits.
Pit 156, layer 58.

471. M381. Rim in grey ware with large flint grit tempering (2 sherds).
Pit 156, layer 58.

472. M382. Rim in grey-brown ware with flint grits.
Pit 156, layer 58.

473. M384. Dish in dark grey ware with flint grit tempering.
Pit 158, layer 59.

474. M383. Rim in grey sandy ware with flint grit tempering.
Pit 158, layer 59.

475. M385. Dish in grey ware with crushed flint and chalk tempering.
Pit 159, layer 66.

476. M361. Rim in grey sandy ware with fine flint grits.
Pit 167b, layer 59.

477. M358. Rim in grey sandy ware with fine flint grits.
Pit 167b, layer 59.

478. M360. Rim in dark grey ware with flint grits.
Pit 167b, layer 59.

479. M351. Rim in grey ware with flint grits.
Pit 167b, layer 65.

480. M359. Rim in grey ware with flint grits.
Pit 167b, layer 59.

481. M350. Rim in grey ware with flint grits.
Pit 175, layer 60.

482. M349. Rim in grey ware with fine flint grits.
Pit 175, layer 60.

483. M506. Rim in red sandy ware with fine flint grits.
Pit 196, layer 38.

484. M507. Rim in grey sandy ware with flint grits.
Pit 196, layer 38.

485. M508. Rim in grey sandy ware with flint grits.
Pit 196, layer 38.

486. M509. Rim in grey sandy ware with coarse flint grits.
Pit 196, layer 38.

487. M510. Cooking pot in red-grey sandy with some fine flint grits, rouletted (2 sherds).
Pit 219, layer 57.

488. M514. Dish in red-grey sandy ware with flint grits.
Pit 219, layer 57.

489. M513. Rim in grey sandy ware with fine flint grits.
Pit 219, layer 57.

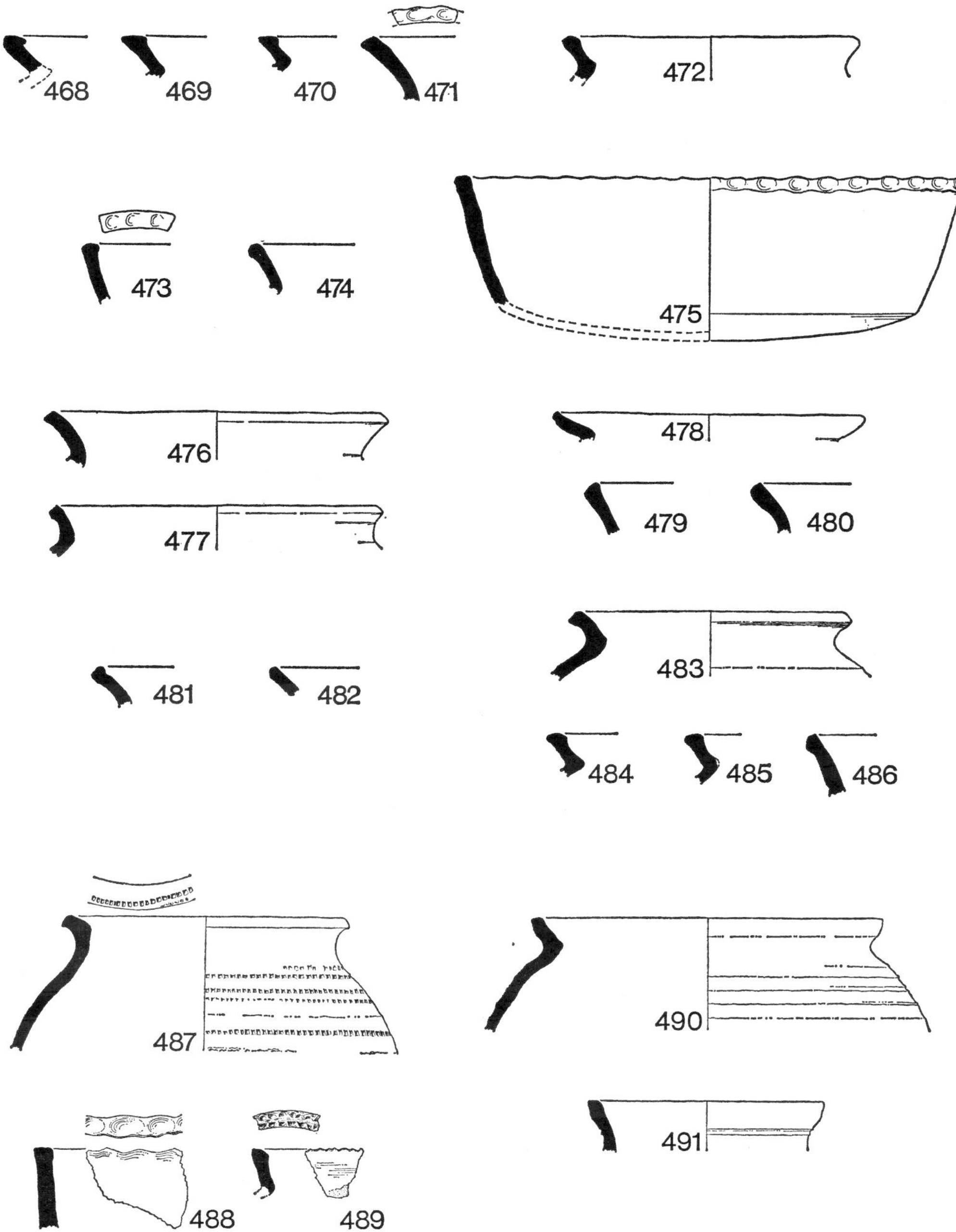

FIG. 126. Late Saxon pottery from pits 156, 158, 159, 167, 175, 196 and 219 (pp. 167, 170). Scale $\frac{1}{4}$

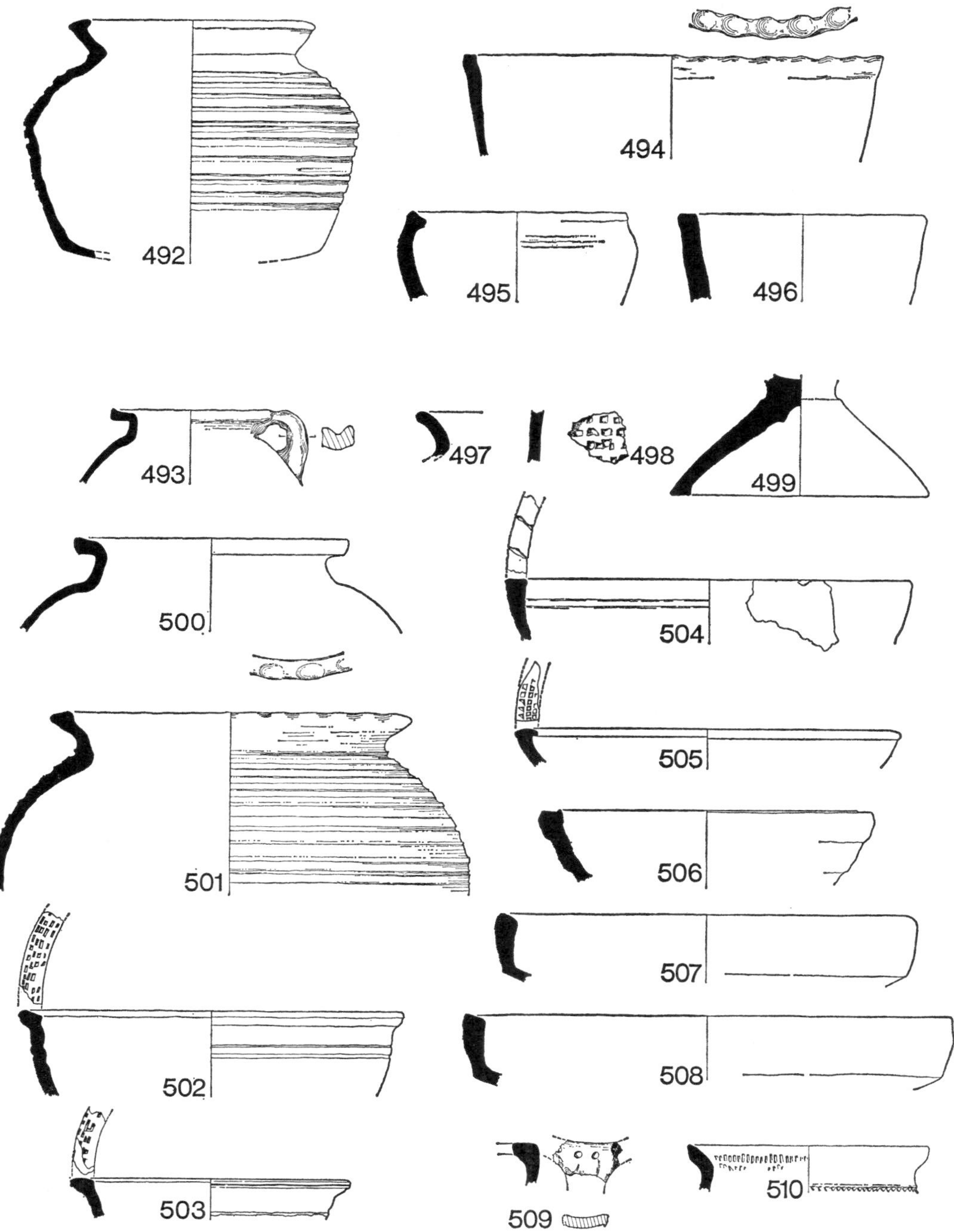

FIG. 127. Late Saxon pottery from pit 240 and other locations (p. 169). Scale ¼

490. M511. Cooking pot in grey sandy ware with flint grits.
Pit 219, layer 57.

491. M512. Rim in red-grey sandy ware with fine flint grits.
Pit 219, layer 57.

492. M515. Cooking pot in hard black sandy ware.
Pit 240, layer 101.

493. M516. Handled vessel in hard black sandy ware with flint grit tempering.
Pit 240, layer 101.

494. M518. Dish in grey sandy ware with flint grits.
Pit 240, layer 101.

495. M519. Dish in grey sandy ware with fine flint grits.
Pit 240, layer 101.

496. M520. Dish in grey sandy ware with fine flint grits.
Pit 240, layer 101.

497. M517. Rim in grey sandy ware with flint grit tempering.
Pit 240, layer 101.

498. M522. Body sherd in grey ware with fine flint grits.
Pit 240, layer 101.

499. M521. Lid in grey ware with flint grit tempering, fired red on the surface.
Pit 240, layer 101.

500. M528. Cooking pot in grey ware, with flint grits.
87, layer 9.

501. M529. Cooking pot in fine grey sandy ware with some flint grits, fired reddish.
69, layer 8.

502. M92. Dish in grey sandy ware, fired reddish.
40, pit A.

503. M58. Dish in grey ware with flint grits, fired red-brown.
57, layer 10.

504. M49. Dish in grey sandy ware with flint grits, fired red-brown.
54, layer 6.

505. M21. Dish in grey sandy ware with occasional flint grits, fired reddish.
45, layer 3.

506. M48. Dish in grey sandy ware, fired red.
54, layer 6.

507. M145. Dish in coarse grey sandy ware with flint grits.
60, layer 17.

508. M144. Dish in coarse grey ware with large flint grits.
60, layer 17.

509. M57. Handle in hard white sandy ware with pale green glassy glaze.
54, layer 5.

510. M530. Rim in pinkish sandy ware with orange glassy glaze.
109, layer 13.

SAXON POTTERY FROM GENERAL LAYERS

The detailed listing of the Saxon pottery from closed contexts such as pits or occupation layers associated with buildings will be found in the descriptive text of the individual features above. Here all the Saxon pottery from the general layers is listed and quantified.

The first list covers the early–middle Saxon material, arranged in trench and layer order. Pottery which has been illustrated and described above (pp. 141–53) is recorded only by its publication number, but sherds not illustrated are described. No attempt has been made to note residual Roman material nor, in the case of layers disturbed by ploughing, to record the presence of late Saxon and medieval sherds.

The second list, Table I, dealing with the late Saxon material, is also arranged in trench and layer order, but because of the standardization of types the listing has been simplified. Where later material has been found in the layers it is noted in the first column. The numbers in the subsequent columns refer to the numbers of recognizable sherds of the individual types: plain body sherds are not included. Most of the illustrated sherds, nos. 316–499, are from closed contexts; only nos. 500–510 are from general layers. Their publication numbers are not recorded in the list but the locations are discoverable by reference to the sherd descriptions.

Early–middle Saxon pottery

1930 excavations	193.
Trench 5, layer 3	152, 153, 154, 194, 215, 244, 245, 261, 274.
Trench 45, layer 2	157.
Trench 45, layer 3	155, 183. Not illustrated: 2 body sherds in grey sandy ware.
Trench 46, layer 3	279.
Trench 46, layer 7	207. Not illustrated: 2 body sherds in sandy ware with chaff tempering.
Trench 54, layer 6	238.
Trench 55, layer 6	176.
Trench 56, layer 8	142, 143, 144, 145, 197. Not illustrated: chaff-tempered sherd.
Trench 58, layer 7	146.
Trench 59, layer 7	163.
Trench 60, layer 5	162, 270. Not illustrated: 4 body sherds in black sandy ware with chaff tempering. One glazed sherd.
Trench 60, layer 6	281.
Trench 60, layer 7	Not illustrated: body sherd in black sandy ware with chaff tempering.
Trench 60, layer 10	233. Not illustrated: 2 body sherds in black sandy ware with chaff tempering.
Trench 60, layer 12	271. Not illustrated: body sherd in coarse sandy ware with chaff tempering.
Trench 60, layer 14	298.
Trench 61, layer 4	Not illustrated: body sherd in black sandy ware with chaff tempering.
Trench 61, layer 19	163.
Trench 61, layer 21	163.
Trench 62, layer 4	Not illustrated: 4 body sherds in sandy ware with chaff tempering.
Trench 62, layer 5	195.
Trench 63, layer 4	164, 208, 212, 269. Not illustrated: 2 body sherds, one in grey ware tempered with crushed flint grit, the other in black ware tempered with chaff and some mica.

Trench 63, layer 5	246, 268.
Trench 63, layer 10	158, 166.
Trench 63, layer 20	165, 196.
Trench 65, layer 4	167.
Trench 65, layer 5	209. Not illustrated: 5 body sherds in grey wares with chaff tempering.
Trench 66, layer 5	Not illustrated: body sherd in black chaff-tempered ware including some fine grits.
Trench 67, layer 4	170, 180, 295. Not illustrated: 4 body sherds in grey ware with chaff tempering.
Trench 67, layer 5	224. Not illustrated: 1 body sherd in black sandy ware with chaff tempering.
Trench 67, layer 11	Not illustrated: 1 body sherd in sandy ware with chaff tempering.
Trench 67, layer 20	Not illustrated: chaff-tempered sherd.
Trench 68, layer 3	257.
Trench 68, layer 4	Not illustrated: 4 body sherds tempered with chaff and flint grits.
Trench 69, layer 3	230.
Trench 69, layer 5	Not illustrated: body sherd in black sandy ware with quartz and mica grits.
Trench 69, layer 6	Not illustrated: body sherd in grey sandy ware with chaff tempering.
Trench 69, layer 8	Not illustrated: body sherd in black sandy ware with chaff tempering.
Trench 69, layer 12	186. Not illustrated: body sherd in grey sandy ware with chaff tempering.
Trench 69, layer 32	156.
Trench 70, layer 3	Not illustrated: body sherd in sandy ware tempered with chaff and some crushed flint.
Trench 71, layer 7	284. Not illustrated: body sherd in black sandy ware tempered with chaff.
Trench 71, layer 11	Not illustrated: chaff-tempered sherd.
Trench 71, layer 48	Not illustrated: body sherd in black sandy ware tempered with chaff and flint grits.
Trench 72, layer 5	286.
Trench 72, layer 7	227.
Trench 73, layer 10	Not illustrated: body sherd in smooth grey ware with chaff tempering.
Trench 74, layer 4	Not illustrated: body sherd in grey sandy ware with chaff tempering.
Trench 74, layer 12	Not illustrated: body sherd in grey sandy ware with chaff tempering.
Trench 75, layer 4	228. Not illustrated: body sherd in coarse grey sandy ware with chaff tempering.
Trench 75, layer 5	190. Not illustrated: body sherd in sandy ware with chaff tempering.
Trench 75, layer 10	Not illustrated: body sherd in sandy ware with chaff tempering.
Trench 76, layer 4	Not illustrated: body sherd in sandy ware with chaff tempering.
Trench 76, layer 6	225, 299.
Trench 77, layer 5	177.
Trench 77, layer 6	243.
Trench 78, layer 5	226. Not illustrated: body sherd grey in sandy ware with chaff tempering.
Trench 78, layer 10	Not illustrated: body sherd in grey gritty ware with chaff tempering.
Trench 78, layer 13	Not illustrated: body sherd in coarse grey sandy ware with chaff tempering.

Trench 78, layer 45	Not illustrated: body sherd in grey sandy ware with flint and chaff tempering.
Trench 79, layer 51	Not illustrated: body sherd in grey sandy ware with chaff tempering.
Trench 80, layer 5	Not illustrated: body sherd in grey sandy ware with chaff tempering.
Trench 80, layer 27	Not illustrated: body sherd in grey sandy ware with chaff tempering.
Trench 80, layer 30	Not illustrated: body sherd in grey sandy ware with chaff tempering.
Trench 80, layer 44	223.
Trench 80, layer 45	Not illustrated: body sherd in grey sandy ware with some chaff.
Trench 80, layer 48	Not illustrated: body sherd in buff sandy ware with chaff tempering.
Trench 80, layer 55	Not illustrated: body sherd in grey sandy ware with flint and chaff tempering.
Trench 80, layer 57	Not illustrated: body sherd in grey sandy ware with chaff tempering.
Trench 85, layer 4	222. Not illustrated: body sherd in grey sandy ware, chaff tempering.
Trench 85, layer 7	Not illustrated: 2 body sherds in grey sandy ware with chaff tempering.
Trench 85, layer 8	169. Not illustrated: 2 body sherds in grey-brown sandy ware with chaff tempering.
Trench 87, layer 2	Not illustrated: body sherd in coarse grey sandy ware.
Trench 87, layer 5	160. Not illustrated: 2 body sherds in sandy ware with chaff tempering.
Trench 87, layer 7	174, 262, 263. Not illustrated: 2 body sherds in coarse sandy ware with some chaff tempering.
Trench 87, layer 9	172, 173, 181, 188, 189, 289, 293. Not illustrated: 25 body sherds, 14 in coarse grass-tempered fabrics, 3 in coarse grey sandy wares and 8 in grey fabrics tempered with crushed flint grits.
Trench 87, layer 10	Not illustrated: 9 body sherds in coarse sandy wares, 1 with chaff tempering and 3 in coarse fabrics, sandy, with crushed flint grit tempering.
Trench 87, layer 13	280. Not illustrated: 7 body sherds, 4 in coarse fabrics tempered with chaff, 3 in coarse sandy fabrics.
Trench 87, layer 14	161, 248. Not illustrated: 6 body sherds, 2 in grey chaff-tempered fabrics and 4 in coarse grey ware with a tempering of crushed flint.
Trench 87, layer 16	147. Not illustrated: 2 body sherds, 1 coarse black sandy ware, the other in grey sandy ware tempered with crushed flint and chalk.
Trench 87, layer 24	250. Not illustrated: body sherd in coarse grey sandy ware with crushed flint grits.
Trench 87, layer 33	205, 253.
Trench 88, layer 5	179, 267, 300, 314. Not illustrated: 14 body sherds, 8 sandy sherds, 4 in chaff-tempered fabrics and 2 in grey sandy fabrics with crushed flint grit. See also late Saxon list.
Trench 88, layer 26	229. Not illustrated: body sherd in coarse grey sandy ware with some chaff tempering.

Trench 89, layer 4 — 168.

Trench 89, layer 23 — 308.
Not illustrated: 5 body sherds; 1 in coarse grey sandy ware and 4 in dark grey chaff-tempered fabrics.

Trench 89, layer 26 — 171.

Trench 89, layer 27 — 254.

Trench 89, layer 31 — 159.

Trench 89, layer 32 — Not illustrated: body sherd in dark grey sandy ware tempered with chaff, smoothed surface.

Trench 89, layer 38 — 249.

Trench 90, layer 15 — 204.

Trench 90, layer 28 — Not illustrated: body sherd in grey sandy ware with chaff tempering, burnished surface.

Trench 91, layer 30 — 240, 255, 287.
Not illustrated: 7 body sherds, 4 in grey sandy ware with chaff tempering, 1 in grey sandy ware with flecks of mica, 2 in grey fabric tempered with crushed flint grits.

Trench 91, layer 37 — 252.
Not illustrated: 4 body sherds, 1 in grey sandy ware with mica flecks, 1 in grey sandy ware tempered with chaff, 2 in grey sandy ware tempered with crushed flint.

Trench 91, layer 43 — 191, 220, 242, 275.
Not illustrated: 6 body sherds, 3 in grey chaff-tempered fabrics, 3 in coarse sandy ware.

Trench 91, layer 41 — Not illustrated: body sherd in coarse grey sandy ware with chaff tempering.

Trench 91, layer 46 — 237.
Not illustrated: body sherd in coarse grey ware tempered with flint grits.

Trench 91, layer 53 — 236, 241.
Not illustrated: 3 body sherds, 1 in very thick coarse black ware with chaff tempering, 1 in grey sandy ware with chaff tempering, 1 in fine grey sandy ware.

Trench 94, layer 37 — 251.
Not illustrated: 3 body sherds in grey sandy ware, 1 with occasional flint grits; all surfaces well smoothed.

Trench 94, layer 87 — 182.
Not illustrated: 2 body sherds in grey sandy fabric.

Trench 94, layer 93 — 202, 288, 290.
Not illustrated: 29 body sherds, 1 in grey sandy ware with chaff tempering, 1 in fine black sandy ware with some chaff, 13 in a range of coarse sandy fabrics and 14 in coarse grey wares tempered with flint grits.

Trench 95, layer 20 — 200, 272.
Not illustrated: 2 body sherds, in grey sandy wares with chaff tempering.

Trench 95, layer 61 — 206, 291.
Not illustrated: 10 body sherds, 2 in grass-tempered grey ware, 7 in coarse sandy fabrics, 1 in grey ware with some crushed flint grits.

Trench 95, layer 62 — Not illustrated: body sherd in coarse black sandy ware.

Trench 95, layer 64 — Not illustrated: 3 body sherds in fine grey sandy wares with sporadic chaff tempering.

Trench 95, layer 86	Not illustrated: 2 chaff-tempered body sherds.
Trench 96, layer 18	198.
Trench 96, layer 20	203.
Trench 96, layer 21	Not illustrated: coarse grey sandy sherd.
Trench 96, layer 22	Not illustrated: 3 body sherds in grey sandy fabrics.
Trench 96, layer 38	Not illustrated: 1 chaff-tempered body sherd.
Trench 96, layer 63	Not illustrated: 1 chaff-tempered body sherd.
Trench 97, layer 10	Not illustrated: body sherd of large vessel in light grey sandy ware with copious chaff tempering.
Trench 97, layer 41	Not illustrated: body sherd in grey sandy ware.
Trench 97, layer 60	Not illustrated: body sherd in black sandy ware with chaff tempering.
Trench 97, layer 65	285.
Trench 98, layer 18	Not illustrated: 2 body sherds in black sandy fabrics.
Trench 98, layer 19	Not illustrated: 2 body sherds in grey sandy ware with chaff tempering.
Trench 98, layer 30	Not illustrated: body sherd in grey sandy ware with chaff tempering.
Trench 98, layer 32	Not illustrated: body sherd in coarse grey sandy ware with some chaff tempering.
Trench 98, layer 37	273.
Trench 99, layer 8	221.
Trench 99, layer 38	Not illustrated: 3 body sherds in dark grey-black sandy wares containing some chaff.
Trench 99, layer 50	199. Not illustrated: 3 body sherds, 2 in fine sandy fabrics with some chaff tempering; 1 in coarse sandy ware.
Trench 99, layer 63.	Not illustrated: body sherd in black sandy ware with chaff tempering and occasional large grits.
Trench 99, layer 64.	247. Not illustrated: 5 body sherds in coarse sandy fabrics with chaff tempering.
Trench 100, layer 24	184, 214, 239, 258. Not illustrated: body sherd in even black sandy ware.
Trench 100, layer 38	311, 312. Not illustrated: 12 body sherds, 1 in fine grey ware with grass tempering, 6 in coarse grey sandy wares with some flint gritting and 5 in Portchester ware fabric, 3 of which are rilled.
Trench 100, layer 66	306, 310. Not illustrated: 4 body sherds, 1 in grey sandy ware, 3 in grey ware tempered with crushed chalk and flint.
Trench 100, layer 62	Not illustrated: 1 chaff-tempered sherd.
Trench 100, layer 80	Not illustrated: 2 joining sherds of an everted rimmed jar in grey ware with crushed flint grits.
Trench 100, layer 81	301. Not illustrated: 5 body sherds belonging to the above.
Trench 101, layer 22	309. Not illustrated: 3 body sherds, 1 in sandy ware with chaff tempering and 2 in sandy wares with some crushed flint tempering.
Trench 101, layer 31	217, 266. Not illustrated: 4 body sherds in even grey sandy wares; 2 of them are tempered with chaff.

Trench 101, layer 32	Not illustrated: 1 chaff-tempered sherd.
Trench 101, layer 46	Not illustrated: body sherd of large vessel in red-brown fabric tempered with finely crushed flint.
Trench 101, layer 81	265, 282. Not illustrated: body sherd in fine grey sandy ware with well burnished surface.
Trench 101, layer 85	Not illustrated: 7 body sherds, 3 in grey sandy ware with chaff tempering, 2 in coarse grey sandy ware and 2 in fabrics with crushed flint tempering.
Trench 101, layer 86	Not illustrated: 3 body sherds, 2 in coarse sandy wares, 1 with grass tempering.
Trench 101, layer 110	Not illustrated: body sherd in grey sandy ware with some chaff tempering.
Trench 102, layer 33	187, 192, 296. Not illustrated: 10 body sherds, 5 in coarse sandy wares, 5 in sandy wares with crushed flint tempering.
Trench 102, layer 44	175, 185, 201, 210, 211, 213, 216, 218, 219, 234, 235, 259, 264, 277, 278, 283, 294. Not illustrated: 24 body sherds, 7 in coarse fabrics tempered with chaff, 16 in coarse grey sandy fabrics and 1 in laminated grey ware with much flint gritting.
Trench 102, layer 46	260, 297, 304, 313. Not illustrated: 2 body sherds, 1 in black chaff-tempered ware, the other in a coarse black sandy ware.
Trench 102, layer 91	Not illustrated: 2 chaff-tempered sherds.
Trench 103, layer 15	302. Not illustrated: 4 body sherds from vessel in coarse sandy ware, the fabrics containing large water-worn quartz grains.
Trench 103, layer 21	Not illustrated: body sherd in coarse grey sandy ware.
Trench 103, layer 23	178. Not illustrated: 5 body sherds from coarse sandy vessels with some chaff tempering.
Trench 103, layer 24	Not illustrated: 3 body sherds, 1 in smooth black ware with chaff tempering, 2 in coarse grey ware with some crushed flint grits.
Trench 103, layer 45	303.
Trench 103, layer 48	Not illustrated: 1 body sherd in thick black sandy ware with occasional flint grits.
Trench 103, layer 55	Not illustrated: 3 body sherds, 2 in very thick black sandy ware with occasional grits, 1 in grey sandy ware with some chaff tempering.
Residue from post-Saxon layers.	276, 292. Not illustrated: 8 body sherds, all in coarse sandy wares, 5 of them with grass tempering.
Trench 107, layer 9	Not illustrated: 56 sherds, 3 body sherds in grey sandy wares with chaff tempering, 1 in grey sandy ware with inclusions of quartz and mica, 52 sherds of coarse ware jars with everted rims all in grey or grey-brown fabrics, tempered with crushed grit and sometimes chalk; of these 12 are rim sherds within the range illustrated, fig. 106.
Trench 107, layer 30	Not illustrated: 2 body sherds in coarse grey ware tempered with flint grits.
Trench 107, layer 34	Not illustrated: 12 body sherds, 11 in grey fabrics tempered with chaff, 1 in grey flint-tempered ware.

Trench 108, layer 3	Not illustrated: 5 chaff-tempered sherds.
Trench 108, layer 22	Not illustrated: 34 sherds, 4 in coarse chaff-tempered ware, 2 in grey sandy ware and 28 in grey or grey-brown ware, tempered with crushed flint and chalk; of these 3 are small fragments of rims.
Trench 108, layer 26	Not illustrated: 5 sherds, 1 in coarse sandy ware, and 4 including a rim in grey ware tempered with crushed flint and chalk.
Trench 108, layer 40	315. Not illustrated: 13 body sherds, 2 in grey chaff-tempered ware, 11 in coarse grey flint-gritted wares.
Trench 108, layer 41	Not illustrated: 7 body sherds, 6 in flint-gritted fabrics, 1 in black sandy ware.
Trench 108, layer 42	Not illustrated: 13 body sherds, 1 in chaff-tempered ware, and 12 in flint- and chalk-tempered fabrics.
Trench 108, layer 48	192, 231. Not illustrated: 52 body sherds, 5 belonging to S348, 11 in chaff-tempered sandy fabrics, 3 in grey sandy ware, 33 in grey wares tempered with crushed flint and chalk.
Trench 108, layer 51	Not illustrated: body sherd, coarse flint-gritted ware.
Trench 108, layer 61	Not illustrated: sherds, 5 in coarse sandy wares, 17 in coarse flint-gritted ware; 3 are rim fragments.
Trench 108, layer 62	232. Not illustrated: 8 body sherds, 3 in grey sandy chaff-tempered ware, the rest in grey wares with crushed flint grits.
Trench 108, layer 72	Not illustrated: body sherd, black sandy ware with chaff tempering.
Trench 108, layer 74	256.
Trench 108, layer 77	Not illustrated: 3 body sherds, 2 in grey-brown flint-gritted ware, 1 in grey sandy ware.
Trench 108, layer 81	Not illustrated: 2 body sherds, 1 in red-brown flint-gritted ware, 1 in black sandy ware with chaff tempering.
Trench 108, layer 96	Not illustrated: 2 body sherds in grey-brown chaff-tempered ware.
Trench 108, layer 98	Not illustrated: 2 body sherds in grey sandy ware with chaff tempering.
Trench 108, layer 103	Not illustrated: 2 body sherds in grey sandy ware with crushed flint grits.
Trench 108, layer 216	Not illustrated: body sherd, grey chaff-tempered ware.
Trench 109, layer 61	Not illustrated: 1 chaff-tempered sherd.

DISCUSSION OF THE SAXON POTTERY

The Early Saxon Fabrics and Forms

The pottery which, on the basis of form or association, can be assigned to the fifth to eighth centuries is hand-made, almost invariably fired to black or grey, and manufactured in fabrics ranging from fine sandy wares to sand-free clays, tempered with organic matter having the appearance of grass or straw (referred to here simply as chaff). As a generalization it may be said that sandy fabrics were more common in the early period, with chaff tempering increasing in popularity with time.

The two extremes are demonstrated by two groups of sherds, one from hut S1, which can reasonably be dated to the mid-fifth century or slightly earlier (fig. 111, nos. 136–41), the

TABLE I

Distribution of Late Saxon Wares

Layer	Date	Portchester and associated wares						Glazed sherds	Ninth- to tenth-century gritty ware	Miscellaneous
		Undercut rims	Hollowed rims	Plain rims	Rilled	Rouletted	Dishes			
54, layer 4	Medieval	1	1		5				1	
54, layer 5	Medieval							1		
54, layer 6	Medieval	9	5	9	4	1				
55, layer 4	Medieval	3	1	2	5					
55, layer 5	Medieval	4	3		4	2	3			
55, layer 7		1		2	1					
56, layer 4	Medieval	2							1	
56, layer 5	Medieval	3								
56, layer 6		2			4					
57, layer 9	Medieval		1		1					
57, layer 10	Medieval									1 rouletted bowl
57, layer 13	Medieval		1							
57, layer 14	Medieval	1								
58, layer 3	Post-medieval		2			3				
58, layer 5		2			4					
60, layer 3	Post-medieval			3						
60, layer 4	Medieval		1	2	1					
60, layer 5	Medieval	7	5	14	16	7	1	1	1	
60, layer 17							2			
60, layer 3	Medieval	6	9	13	3	2	1			
62, layer 4	Medieval	2	1	1						
62, layer 5	Medieval	3	1	4	1					
62, layer 10	Medieval		1	1	1	1				
62, layer 13			1	2	1	1				
62, layer 15	Medieval		1	1						
63, layer 3	Medieval		1		1					
63, layer 4	Medieval	4	3	1	1	1				
63, layer 11				1	2					
63, layer 12				2	1	1				
63, layer 16										
63, layer 17				1						
63, layer 19										
65, layer 4	Medieval	3	2		3					
65, layer 7					1					
65, layer 19										Body sherds
65, layer 20										Body sherds
66, layer 11										
67, layer 3	Medieval	1	1	1		1				
67, layer 4	Medieval	2	4		8					

TABLE I—*continued*

Layer	Date	*Portchester and associated wares*						*Glazed sherds*	*Ninth- to tenth-century gritty ware*	*Miscellaneous*
		Undercut rims	*Hollowed rims*	*Plain rims*	*Rilled*	*Rouletted*	*Dishes*			
68, layer 3	Medieval		1	2	4		1			
69, layer 3	Medieval				1		1			
69, layer 7	Medieval	1	1		2					
69, layer 8										
70, layer 3		2	3	4	2	1				
71, layer 5	Medieval	2				1				
71, layer 6	Medieval	5	3				1			
72, layer 5	Medieval				1					
72, layer 8		1		1						Handle
74, layer 4	Medieval	4	1	2		2	1		1	
76, layer 10					1					
79, layer 4	Medieval	3		1						
79, layer 5	Medieval		2			2				
80, layer 5	Medieval	2			6		2		2	
80, layer 7	Medieval	2			1	1				
82, layer 19		1			1					
85, layer 3	Medieval				2					
85, layer 4	Medieval	1	3	1	3	1	1			
87, layer 5	Medieval	4	11	6	20	3	3		4	
87, layer 7	Medieval		1		3					
87, layer 9		6	2	11	7					
87, layer 23			2	1	2					
87, layer 28				1						
87, layer 45				1	1					
88, layer 5	Medieval	21	17	7	35	7	2	9	5	
88, layer 9								2		
89, layer 4	Medieval			2				1		
89, layer 8	Medieval	2	3	3	3					
89, layer 20	Medieval				1					
89, layer 90	Medieval					1				
90, layer 6	Medieval									
90, layer 22	Medieval		2	2	2	1				
90, layer 38			1		1					
91, layer 23	Medieval	1	1							
91, layer 28			1	5	1	1				
91, layer 30	Medieval			8						
94, layer 37	Medieval		1		1					
94, layer 45	Medieval				1					
94, layer 51	Medieval	3	6	4	7		2			
94, layer 87	Medieval		7	3	7					
94, layer 92	Medieval	1			1					

TABLE I—*continued*

Layer	Date	*Portchester and associated wares*						Glazed sherds	Ninth- to tenth-century gritty ware	Miscellaneous
		Undercut rims	*Hollowed rims*	*Plain rims*	*Rilled*	*Rouletted*	*Dishes*			
95, layer 19			2							
95, layer 20	Medieval	1	1	1	4					
95, layer 30	Medieval		1		2					
95, layer 33					2					
95, layer 61	Medieval		4	4	6	2				1 grid stamped
96, layer 16	Medieval				1					
96, layer 18	Medieval	2			1					
96, layer 20	Medieval				1					
96, layer 22	Medieval	3	2	1	10	1				
96, layer 25		1	2	1	3	1				
96, layer 64			1		11					
97, layer 8			1		1	1				
97, layer 10	Medieval		2							
97, layer 11	Medieval	2	2		5					
97, layer 13			1							
98, layer 14	Medieval				1	1				
98, layer 19	Medieval		2	4	5					
98, layer 30		1	2		5	1				
98, layer 32	Medieval				4					
99, layer 7	Medieval			1	2					
99, layer 8					1					
99, layer 11	Post-medieval			1	1					
99, layer 18	Medieval		1							
99, layer 24					1				1	
99, layer 50	Medieval		1	3		1				
99, layer 57	Medieval					1				
100, layer 12	Medieval		1				1			1 grid stamped
100, layer 24	Medieval			4	1					
100, layer 25	Medieval		1	2	1					
100, layer 26	Medieval				1					1 grid stamped
100, layer 28	Medieval	1	2	1						
100, layer 44			1							
100, layer 47	Medieval		1	4						
100, layer 65	Medieval			3						
100, layer 67			2		3					
100, layer 75	Medieval			1	2					
100, layer 79			1	1	1					
100, layer 87			1	3	2					
101, layer 25	Medieval					1			1	
101, layer 29	Medieval	1			2					?import
101, layer 31	Medieval		2	2	4					

TABLE I—*continued*

Layer	*Date*	*Portchester and associated wares*						*Glazed sherds*	*Ninth- to tenth-century gritty ware*	*Miscellaneous*
		Undercut rims	*Hollowed rims*	*Plain rims*	*Rilled*	*Rouletted*	*Dishes*			
101, layer 32		1		4	4					
101, layer 33	Medieval		1							
101, layer 57	Medieval	1		3	3					
101, layer 71			1	1	2					
102, layer 19	Medieval		1		1					
102, layer 35	Medieval	1	2		1	1				
103, layer 9	Medieval				1				3	
103, layer 13	Medieval								1	
108, layer 3	Medieval				1	1				
108, layer 30			1							
108, layer 32	Medieval							1		
108, layer 48										import
108, layer 37		1	1	4	7	2			2	
108, layer 248									1	
109, layer 9	Medieval	2		1	2	3				
109, layer 10	Medieval	4	4	4	9	4	3			
109, layer 13	Post-medieval		1	1	2			1		
109, layer 14			1		3		1			
109, layer 22		1								
109, layer 52					1					
109, layer 66			1	1						
109, layer 78	Medieval				1					
109, layer 88				1	3					
109, layer 92		1		1	1					
109, layer 93	Medieval			1	1					
109, layer 103					1					

other from pit 34, which contained a fragment of glass identified as an East Mediterranean import dated not earlier than the eighth century (p. 232). In the early group the finer bowls are in hard black sandy wares without chaff, while the larger jars, although basically sandy, do contain a little chaff tempering. The almost complete jar from pit 34 (no. 2), on the other hand, is copiously chaff-tempered, its fabric being essentially sand-free. In between these two extremes must belong the group of stamped vessels which Dr Myres assigns to the sixth century. Reference to their sherd descriptions will show that a high percentage of them contain appreciable amounts of chaff, although almost invariably as an additive to sandy fabrics.

In the absence of large stratified groups of early Saxon pottery it would be unwise to attempt any quantitative assessment of the fabrics, but table II serves to summarize the evidence from the early and mid-Saxon pits, the most informative sequence being that from pit (well) 135, where chaff tempering can be seen to remain dominant until the technique begins to die out with the introduction of grit-tempered fabrics by the end of the eighth century. At best, such figures should be regarded as approximations since rubbish survival from earlier periods tends to distort them.

Towards the end of the currency of chaff-tempered wares, tentatively dated to the late eighth century (p. 191), a distinctive fabric appears tempered with a filler containing large plates of mica and rounded quartz grits, presumably representing sands derived from the decay of granite. Four groups contain sherds of this fabric, pits 38 and 220 and wells (pits) 135, phase 3b, and 143. In each case the combination of fabrics is the same, sandy and chaff-tempered occurring with the characteristic mica-gritted and with sherds of flint-gritted types which were to become common in the late eighth to tenth centuries. It would seem reasonable to suggest that the mica-gritted sherds represent a distinct chronological horizon at the moment when the highly characteristic local gritty wares were beginning to replace traditional fabrics. Added support for this view comes not only from the nature of the

TABLE II

Early–Mid Saxon Pits: Quantities of Fabric Types (total number of sherds)

Pit	*Sandy*	*Chaff-tempered*	*Mica*	*Gritty*	*Stamped*	*Imports*	*Portchester ware*
24	1	—	—	—	—	—	—
34	—	1	—	—	—	—	—
35	1	—	—	—	—	—	—
38	10	6	2	3	1	—	—
56	1	1	1	—	—	—	=
135.2a	1	—	—	—	—	—	—
2b	24	24	—	8	5	—	—
3a	18	38	1	20	2	—	—
3b	—	4	—	—	—	—	—
4a	9	11	—	10	1	1	—
4c	2	—	—	16	—	—	—
4d	12	15	—	408	1	1	12
4e	—	—	—	28	—	—	126
137	2	1	—	—	—	—	—
141	—	2	—	4	—	—	—
143	1	—	1	10	—	—	—
191	3	4	—	13	—	—	—
192	2	3	—	3	—	—	—
194	4	2	—	1	—	—	—
198	3	5	—	15	1	—	—
202	—	—	—	2	—	—	—
203	1	1	—	1	—	—	—
204	5	4	—	46	1	—	—
207	5	5	—	14	—	3	—
211	—	1	—	—	—	—	—
216	—	1	—	23	—	—	—
220	15	14	2	18	1	1	—

associations, but from the stratigraphical positions of the mica-gritted sherds. In well (pit) 135 the layer followed one containing high percentages of chaff-tempered and sandy wares but preceded the rubbish tips filled with gritty types; in well (pit) 143 the mica-gritted sherd was found in the lower layers with gritty fabrics before the accumulation of the upper filling containing gritty and later wheel-turned wares. Similarly the mica-gritted sherds from pit 220 can be shown to precede building S11, the occupation of which was associated with the common use of gritty wares. The micaceous wares then constitute a useful indicator for the period of transition.

There is little that can reasonably be said of the forms of the fifth- to eighth-century ceramics. For the most part the sherds are small, representing bowls, jars and dishes of generalized types commonly in use elsewhere in this period. Extensive parallel quoting, while possible, is hardly likely to be of much value with such fragmented material. The only typological observation of general relevance is that the later contexts appear to contain rather more vessels with distinctive everted rims.

Comments on the Early Anglo-Saxon Pottery by J. N. L. Myres

The most significant pieces for establishing the date of this small collection are the three best preserved, namely 138, 171 and 136. Unfortunately only the first of these is sufficiently distinctive to provide satisfactory evidence.

138 comprises enough of the profile, though the base is missing, to show that it belongs to the group of *Schalenurnen* characteristic of the north German coastlands from the lower Elbe to the Weser and the Ems and spreading thence into Frisia and so to England. The type begins in the fourth century in Holstein and continues until about the middle of the fifth. The earlier examples are comparatively hollow-necked and round-shouldered, but as time goes on the contour becomes more definitely biconical. It is to this later phase that the Portchester vessel belonged. Its profile is not unlike that of the rather wider bowl that was with the warrior buried in Helle Gr. 1 near Oldenburg, accompanied by military belt-fittings of late Roman type that indicate former service in the Roman army (Werner, 1958, 385, fig. 11.2). This grave was dated by Werner in the first decades of the fifth century. The type appears also in the last main occupation phase at Feddersen Wierde that ended about 450, and at Wijster it is Type VIII in the classification of Van Es, where pieces almost identical with Portchester 138 appear (Van Es, 1967, 267–72, 315–7, and fig. 160.11 and 12). They too are dated by Van Es in the first half of the fifth century.

A few other scraps from Portchester also belong to fifth-century vessels, though most are too fragmentary for a date as early as 138 to be claimed. These include sherds with strong vertical or diagonal grooving such as 175, 176, 177, 179. It is possible that 181 is the rim of another small fifth century *Schalenurne*,[1] and that 178 carries a curving groove that formed part of an arch or *stehende Bogen*, a definitely fifth century feature in this simple form (Myres 1968, 36–8 and fig. 7).

Much more difficult to date with confidence is the large wide-mouthed vessel 171 which is also decorated with *stehende Bogen*, but in this case emphasized by a row of very blurred

[1] Cf. e.g. *op. cit.* fig. 160.6. Portchester 139 is part of the slashed carination of another Type VIII *Schalenurne*: cf. fig. 160, 8 and 10.

stamps, which are also repeated in two indistinct forms between the necklines above. It is difficult to find an exact parallel to this arrangement. The form of the vessel is not distinctively early and its fabric is unusually thin; though the design could well be fifth-century, it would be unusual at that time to use stamps, especially in such careless fashion, to emphasize it. The nearest parallels to this treatment seem to be Elkington 48, a wide-mouthed shouldered bowl of more elegant form (Webster, 1952, 37 and fig. 12), Abingdon C67 (Myres, 1968, 36–8, and fig. 7), and Castle Acre 45.58c,[1] both of which are biconical or sub-biconical in shape. All three show rather indistinct stamps used in much the same way as on Portchester 171, to emphasize the necklines and the *stehende Bogen,* but there is no clear dating evidence for any of them. All that can be said is that such a piece is unlikely to be later than about 500.

136 is a large sub-globular cookpot with wide mouth and without decoration. Vessels of this kind are not readily datable since their simple forms arise in response to continuing domestic needs and do not normally reflect changing ceramic fashions. That they can be quite early is shown by Illington 101, a somewhat smaller and rather less spreading example of the type, which contained a late Group I cruciform brooch.[2]

The rest of the illustrated pieces, 152–170, consist of small sherds showing stamped decoration, none of which is large enough to indicate either a complete profile or a complete scheme of decoration. It is thus only possible to say that they provide evidence for some degree of occupation during the sixth century, for this is the sort of ceramic debris that one would expect to result from hut-fills of that period.

The whole collection would thus indicate that there was some degree of Anglo-Saxon occupation within this part of the Roman enceinte at Portchester from quite early in the fifth century, when the place may still have been controlled by some sub-Roman regime, until the middle or later part of the sixth century. Bossed pottery of the later fifth and early sixth century is almost absent (157 seems the only decorated piece), but the collection as a whole is too small for this to be treated as significant evidence for a gap in occupation at that time. On the other hand, it is possibly significant that the best preserved pieces, 138, 171, 136, should be among the earliest. This suggests that they may have been buried, accidentally or otherwise, during initial operations on the site, and thus escaped being reduced to the kind of residual detritus indicated by the sixth-century sherds. It is in any event remarkable that so much of a large decorated vessel like 171 should be found in this domestic context at all, for an urn of this sort would be far more in place in a cremation cemetery than on an occupation site. If the cemetery used by these early Anglo-Saxon folk at Portchester could be found, it might do much to answer the questions raised by the present scanty evidence for their presence.

Coarse Gritty Wares, Eighth to Tenth Century

Although fabrics containing flint grits occurred sporadically among the early forms, it was not until the late eighth century that regular, evenly gritted wares became widespread. As we have seen, this point in time is conveniently marked by the brief appearance of mica-

[1] Castle Museum, Norwich, unpublished.

[2] Castle Museum, Norwich, unpublished.

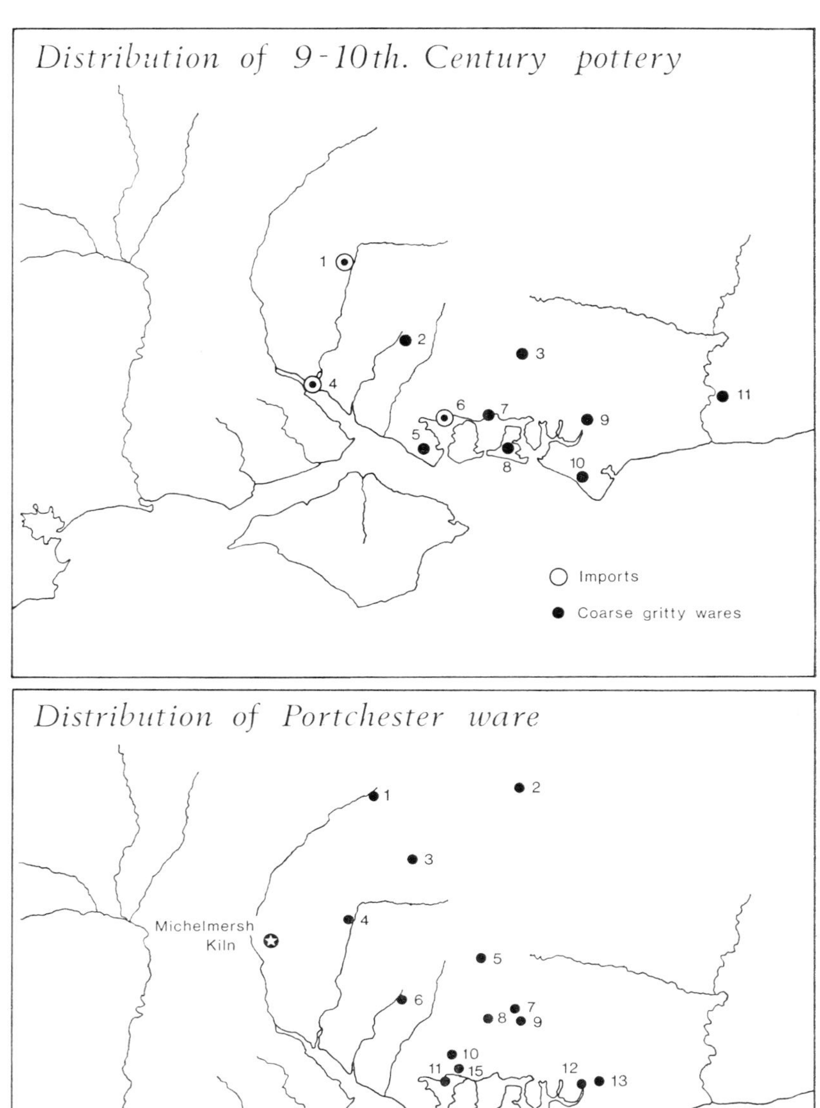

FIG. 128

Upper map: 1 Winchester; 2 Bishops Waltham; 3 Chalton; 4 Hamwih; 5 Rowner, Gosport; 6 Portchester; 7 Emsworth; 8 Hayling; 9 Chichester; 10 Medmerry; 11 Burpham.

Lower map: 1 Overton; 2 Odiham; 3 Brown Candover; 4 Winchester; 5 Westbury; 6 Bishops Waltham; 7 Chalton; 8 Catherington; 9 Idsworth; 10 Southwick; 11 Portchester; 12 Fishbourne; 13 Chichester; 14 Bembridge.

N.B. The Michelmersh kiln does not produce Portchester ware but a contemporary fabric.

gritted types occurring in contexts in which gritty sherds were already present in some quantity. The term gritty ware is here used to include fabrics of fine, slightly sandy paste, heavily tempered with crushed flint, chalk or shell. In the majority of the cases the tempering was produced from crushed flint pebbles, sometimes stained with iron salts, implying that they were derived from river gravels or from the sea shore. Chalk and shell tempering was much less frequently used, but is identifiable particularly when it leaches out, giving rise to a somewhat corky appearance. Many of the vessels were unsealed, but surface wiping and even rough burnishing were practised. For the most part the pots were fired to grey or black but some sherds showed areas of oxidization.

The forms were all of jar type and were hand-made. No complete profile is known, but sherds suggest that bases were flat or nearly so, with no pronounced base angle. Shoulders tended to be narrow with rims everted. The illustrations, particularly figs. 106–7, give an impression of the variations in form. No particularly distinctive types can be isolated except, perhaps, those with rims thinned at the lip with sharp internal angles at the junction of rim and body (e.g. nos. 43, 62, 124, 134, etc.) and jars with rims evenly curved out of the body (e.g. nos. 40 and 53). There is, however, little value in imposing a detailed typology on such material.

Jars in closely similar fabrics and forms have been found in quantity at the port of Hamwih (Addyman and Hill, 1970, fig. 35): a smaller assemblage is known from Rowner, near Gosport, Hants (Lewis and Martin, 1973, fig. 20), sherds of similar type have been recorded from Emsworth, Chalton and Hayling, all in Hampshire, and from Chichester, Medmerry and Burpham, in Sussex (summarized in Cunliffe, 1974). There can thus be little doubt that mid–late Saxon gritty wares were once common in the Solent region (fig. 128).

So far it is only at Hamwih and Portchester that this distinctive type of local pottery has been found in stratified groups in relation to vessels imported from the Continent. Some of the Hamwih groups were also associated with closely datable coins. Although only a small selection of the Hamwih material has been published, and then only in summary form, there is little doubt that much of the gritty ware dates to the ninth century with the possibility of some of it beginning in the late eighth (Addyman and Hill, 1970). When the material has been published in full it will provide the standard sequence against which Portchester groups can be compared. Until then, the Portchester material must stand in its own right, dated broadly to the ninth to tenth century, and possibly a little earlier, by its associated imports and by the stratigraphical relationships of some of the groups.

Late Stamped Wares

A small number of everted-rimmed jars in gritty fabrics were ornamented with stamped and incised decoration. Four distinct vessels can be distinguished, nos. 86, 115, 314 and 315. All were associated with coarse gritty wares, while no. 86 was also found with an imported vessel. The fabrics of all four, while tempered with flint grit and in the case of nos. 86 and 115 chalk as well, were finer and more evenly mixed than was usual for the coarse ware jars. They are sufficiently distinctive to suggest a different origin.

Stamped decorated jars of identical type have been found at Hamwih and at Hayling (summarized in Cunliffe, 1974). Thus it would appear that they form a regular component in the ceramic assemblage of the region in the ninth to early tenth centuries.

Imported Wares

With the exception of two red painted sherds from tenth- to eleventh-century contexts, described below, the small collection of imported sherds from Portchester was all associated with the gritty fabrics and late stamped wares. Two types of vessel in distinctive fabrics can be recognized:

(a) Necked jars with out-beaded rims and wide strap handles, in fine light grey sandy ware, wheel-turned, e.g. nos. 85 and 192: one additional sherd of similar type was recovered from trench 108, layer 48 and one from trench 101, layer 29.

(b) Spouted pitchers with corrugated shoulders, in hard light grey or brown sandy ware with a highly burnished, black-slipped surface, wheel-turned, e.g. no. 125. A sherd of the same vessel was recovered from trench 88, layer 80.

Both fabrics are well known from Hamwih and are evidently imports; since they do not occur at the Dutch port of Dorestad through which much of the trade with the Rhineland passed at this time, it is reasonable to suppose that they must have come from western Europe, possibly from the Frankish area. But until an extensive search of Belgium and Northern France has been made for comparable types, and any apparent similarities confirmed by fabric analysis, further discussion would be inappropriate.

Wheel-turned Portchester Wares

The term *Portchester ware* has been used to describe a highly characteristic range of ceramics which can be shown to succeed the hand-made gritty wares and which represent the last phase of continuous occupation in the south-west quarter of the fort. The fabric is invariably composed of a hard, somewhat sandy clay, tempered with finely crushed flint grit, which has been sorted to an even size and well mixed with the paste. Vessels are wheel-turned and usually fired to a red-brown or buff colour, often with some surface blackening.

The preliminary classification of forms first put forward in 1970 (Cunliffe, 1970, 75–7) may now be restated with modifications:

Cooking pots *Type 1a.* Cooking pots, usually wide bodied, with steep sagging bases and sharply defined base angles. The surface was invariably scored with deep rilling applied whilst the vessel was rotating on the wheel.

Type 1b. Cooking pots, similar to type 1a except that the body is ornamented with the impression of a coarse, square-notched rouletting wheel, applied either within rilled grooves or on the unrilled body of the vessel.

The rims of both types are sharply everted and are treated in a variety of ways, of which the following occur most frequently:

(i) rim hollowed on the inside (e.g. nos. 344, 376, 378);
(ii) rim sharply undercut on the inside (e.g. nos. 343, 345, 366, 792);
(iii) undercut rim, squatter and more upright than (i) and (ii) (e.g. no. 402);
(iv) rim as (i) or (ii), but with finger impressions on the upper edge (e.g. no 501);
(v) rilling around the upper surface of the rim, usually of undercut type (e.g. nos. 348, 374).

Type 2. Small vessel with a simple out-curved rim thickened and rounded at the end. Rarely found but may be rilled (e.g. nos. 349, 390).

Type 3. Small necked jar with the rim out-curved and flattened on the top: may have a handle. No rilling or rouletting has so far been found on vessels of this type (e.g. nos. 493, 500).

Dishes *Type 4.* Dish with flat or slightly sagging base and a short side thickening towards an undifferentiated rim (e.g. nos. 507, 508).

Type 5. Dish with rim top flattened by thumb impressions, giving a 'pie-crust' decoration (e.g. nos. 438, 439).

Type 6. Dish with flat bottom and flattened rim top projecting inside and out (e.g. no. 359).

Type 7. Dish with flattened rim top. Rouletting is usual either around the rim or on the body between rillings (e.g. no. 399, 505).

Although there is some variation within the types as defined, the high degree of standardization implies that the industry was well established and in the hands of specialists.

Distribution of the characteristic Portchester wares has been discussed elsewhere (Cunliffe, 1970, 1974) since when some new evidence has become available. The area of distribution, as it is at present known, spreads from the region of Chichester to the River Test and from the Isle of Wight to the Basingstoke area (fig. 128). Chichester would seem to be on the eastern fringe, for although many groups of the relevant period have been discovered there, Portchester ware is poorly represented compared with more locally produced ceramics. At Portchester, on the other hand, Portchester ware is the dominant type with pottery from the Chichester region occurring only in small quantities. A few examples have recently come to light in Winchester, although the quantity is extremely small compared with the considerable volume of other contemporary types. Excavations in Bishops Waltham have produced some examples in association with Winchester-centred products. No examples have yet been recorded from Hamwih or Southampton.

Its northern extent is more difficult to define. Examples are known from Westbury, near East Meon, from Brown Candover, and from Turrill House, Overton (Moorhouse, 1973). But sherds from Odiham and Well, near Long Sutton, both in northern Hampshire, are considered by Moorhouse to belong to a northern variant and not to be true Portchester ware. A single example from Bembridge in the Isle of Wight shows that some vessels were exported from the mainland.

The evidence at present available therefore suggests that true Portchester ware was probably made somewhere on the Tertiary rocks south of the Downs, possibly in the Wickham area where good potting clay has been worked for a considerable period of time. The industry did not, however, compete with the markets of Winchester and Chichester, but essentially filled in the gap between them.

The antecedents of the Portchester ware pottery can only be fully considered when more is known both of the kiln sites and of their outputs, but the fine quality of the pottery clearly marks a great advance in ceramic technology which must be seen against the general improvement in production evident at various centres in southern Britain during the late Saxon period, giving rise to such well-known products as Stamford ware, St Neots ware and

Winchester ware.[1] The impetus for the improvements must, in part, have resulted from increasing contacts with the continental mainland. It remains a distinct possibility that the output of Portchester ware kilns was more diversified than has been previously realized and might indeed have included the production of glazed wares of the type discussed below. Until the kilns are discovered the problem must be left unresolved.

Glazed Wares

Associated with Portchester ware is found a small but consistent collection of wheel-made glazed sherds: five are illustrated, nos. 326, 408, 409, 509, 510. In addition to these, 9 sherds occurred in 88, layer 5, 2 in 88, layer 9, and one sherd each in 88, layer 12, 108, layer 32, 60, layer 5 and 96, layer 63. Fabrics vary slightly but basically they are hard and sandy, fired white or pinkish in colour. Occasionally a light tempering of finely crushed flint grits has been added. All are covered outside and often inside with a thick glossy green or orange glaze.

Of the recognizable forms, no. 408 is evidently a spouted pitcher decorated with bands of rouletting on the upper part of the body. Nos 409 and 510, possibly from similar but not identical forms, are also rouletted, while 509 is a handle belonging to a pitcher of related type. No. 326 is part of a somewhat coarser vessel decorated with stamped applied strips similar in style to no. 335 made at Michelmersh near Romsey.

Glazed wares are now well known from many sites in south-east England, dating to the late Saxon period. Various names have been given to them, such as Stamford ware (Hurst, 1958) and Winchester ware (Hurst, 1964; Biddle and Barclay, 1974), but the possibility that numerous centres, both in England and the adjacent parts of the Continent, may have been producing their own varieties of glazed fabrics, cannot be ruled out. The group from Portchester is too small to permit detailed typological arguments, but it is perhaps worth remarking that nos. 408, 409, 510 and possibly 509 have stylistic similarities to Portchester wares, while no. 335 is more akin to Michelmersh products. That both centres may have been producing glazed wares, while possible, must, at present, remain unproven.

Red-painted Wares

Red-painted buff wares of French or Low Country origin are not well represented at Portchester. One sherd from pit 37 (no. 327) appears to belong to an amphora of Pingsdorf type, while the only other fragment, from building S13, is smaller and less distinctive. The general lack of red-painted types is noteworthy.

Products from other Southern British Centres

Amid the Portchester ware groups it is possible to distinguish the products from at least three different production centres: one can be located at Michelmersh (Romsey), the others were probably sited in the Chichester area and the Winchester area.

(a) *Michelmersh.* One vessel, no. 335, stands out as unique in the Portchester assemblage. It is a spouted pitcher in pinkish sandy ware, decorated with stamped applied strips.

[1] Wheel-turned rilled pottery of the same general type as Portchester ware has been found at Cheddar in Somerset (Rahtz, 1974, figs. 4 and 5) and at Oxford (Jope, 1954, figs. 33 and 34) in late Saxon contexts. Evidently there were several centres producing similar-looking ware in southern England.

Recently the kiln site manufacturing this type has been identified at Michelmersh in the Test valley, north of Romsey. The products have been briefly discussed (Addyman, Hopkins and Norton, 1972), but full publication is awaited. That only a single example was found at Portchester would suggest that the site lay towards the eastern limit of the kiln's distribution.

(b) *Chichester area?* A few sherds of large everted-rimmed jars have been discovered made in fabrics which differ from the usual range of Portchester ware jars in that they are more sandy and contain some crushed chalk tempering. Decoration consists of rouletted swags (no. 384), grid stamps (nos. 457, 458, 467) and dimple-impressed cordons (nos. 365 and 467). Although vessels of this kind are known at Winchester (Cunliffe, 1964, figs. 15, 16 and 33) and at Southampton (Addyman and Hill, 1970, fig. 34, nos 11–13), by far the largest quantity has been recorded at Chichester. Until the groups from these three town sites have been published in full further discussion is difficult. It should, however, be stressed that more than one production centre for this type may eventually be discovered.

(c) *Winchester area?* A number of simple wheel-made, sagging-based cooking pots with sharply everted rims have been found in direct association with Portchester wares (e.g. 325, 337, 391, 444, 445, etc.). The fabrics usually contain flint grits, often combined with crushed chalk tempering. To the same fabric category belongs the socketed dish (no. 410) and several other sherds of similar dishes. Although the types are simple and could have been manufactured at a number of different localities, they bear a close resemblance to late Saxon and Saxo-Norman wares from Winchester (Cunliffe, 1964, 94–111), whence it is possible that many of the Portchester vessels may have been derived.

THE CERAMIC SEQUENCE AND ITS CALIBRATION

The broad outlines of the ceramic sequence are self-evident from the foregoing descriptions: here it is necessary to restate the more significant relationships and to offer some comment on absolute dating.

The earliest definable group of pottery comes from hut S1. Typologically it has been argued to belong to the first half of the fifth century (p. 183), an assessment which is supported by the proposed dating of the repoussé decorated disc brooch (pp. 208–11) stratified above it. Other mid to late fifth-century pots can be identified among the sherds from general layers (p. 183) while additional evidence for fifth-century occupation is provided by the disc brooch and purse mount/strike-a-light found in well (pit) 135 (pp. 195–7). How much of the general sandy and chaff-tempered coarse ware belongs to this period it is impossible to say.

A selection of sixth-century stamped ware has been recovered and is discussed by Dr Myres above (p. 183). Dating must be based entirely on external considerations. Stamped pottery has however been found in two significant locations: an almost complete vessel (no. 171) was incorporated in spoil thrown out at the time when the timber well frame was inserted into well (pit) 135, not long after a turf line containing the stamped vessels (nos. 14 and 15) had formed. All these sherds are stratigraphically later than the fifth-century metalwork and typologically should belong to the sixth century. Other stamped sherds are without close association.

The general run of early sandy and chaff-tempered pottery presumably belongs to the fifth–seventh century, but distinct seventh-century types are lacking. A spiral-headed pin (no. 46) which is almost certain to be of seventh-century date, does, however, suggest that occupation continued during this period. It is tempting to suggest that the small group of vessels with comb decoration (nos. 172–4) may belong to the seventh century since the type is extremely rare among cremation cemetery material. The single sherd in pit 220 may be a survival from an earlier rubbish layer, but it could be contemporary with the group, for which an early eighth-century date is suggested.

The eighth century was a period of change. An early group is provided by the contents of pit 34, in which an everted-rimmed chaff-tempered jar was found with part of a glass vessel thought to be not earlier than the eighth century. Since both the pot and the glass vessel survived in substantial pieces, neither is likely to be rubbish survival. How late the group should be placed in the eighth century depends upon when the changeover to gritty fabrics occurred. A mixed horizon represented by associations of early gritty wares, sandy and chaff-tempered fabrics together with characteristic mica-gritted ware, can be defined. As we have seen (above, p. 182) three groups of this kind immediately precede the common appearance of the gritty wares.

The dating of the mixed horizon must depend on the Hamwih evidence which has not yet been published in detail. It is already clear, however, that gritty wares were in common use before the beginning of the ninth century and might well date back to the middle of the eighth. The chaff-tempered and mica-gritted wares of the mixed horizon are also found at Hamwih, presumably at the beginning of the occupation, which on coin evidence must lie somewhere in the first half of the eighth century. It is therefore advisable to place pit 34 at the beginning of the eighth century with the mixed horizon groups following not long after.

Little need be said of the gritty wares. Stratigraphically they follow mixed horizon groups at Portchester and are associated with imports of possible Frankish origin. An identical range of pottery has been found at Hamwih, some of it in closed groups dated by coins to the late eighth and ninth centuries. Hamwih appears to have declined after the beginning of the tenth century and was probably largely abandoned by 970. On this evidence the maximum date range for the gritty ware at Hamwih is mid eighth to mid tenth century. The Portchester sequence is in broad agreement with this assessment, but can add no more precision to it.

At what point in time the gritty wares were superseded by wheel-turned Portchester wares it is impossible to say. The stratigraphy sealing the silted-up well (pit 135) and the occupation layers against the south wall of the fort suggests that soil accumulation was continuous and an horizon can be defined in which gritty wares and wheel-turned fabrics occur side by side. However, by the time that rubbish was disposed of in pits in the northern half of the excavated area, gritty fabrics had disappeared from use. The total lack of Portchester ware at Hamwih might suggest that the fabric was not in use by the time the port had declined in the middle of the tenth century. This does not, however, preclude its development before 1000.

The contemporaneity of Portchester wares, red-painted pitchers, glazed wares and other local southern British products, will be apparent from the descriptions of the individual groups (pp. 153–70). The wider associations of the Michelmersh products and the glazed Winchester wares, with which the Portchester wares are contemporary, are now sufficiently well established to leave little doubt that this range of wheel-made forms constitutes an important element in the late Saxon and Saxo-Norman ceramic tradition. In terms of absolute date, it clearly centres upon the first half of the eleventh century but may have begun earlier.

That Portchester wares were no longer produced by 1100 is suggested by the relationship of a pit containing Portchester ware to layers preceding the construction of the inner bailey wall of the Norman castle. The pit had completely silted up by the time that the general sealing layers had formed, and these were in turn cut by the foundation trench for the wall. Since the wall is likely to date to the opening years of the twelfth century, a relative sequence is established which would support (but not prove) the contention that Portchester ware is unlikely to have outlived the Conquest by many years.

A PRELIMINARY PETROLOGICAL EXAMINATION OF A SELECTION OF THE EARLY SAXON POTTERY

By Richard Hodges

A preliminary petrological study was undertaken on selected sherds from Portchester by means of thin section.[1] Further work, particularly heavy mineral analysis and comparisons with other petrologically examined Saxon sherds from Hampshire, might prove very worthwhile. However, these present investigations are sufficient to demonstrate that a variety of fabrics were in existence representing material of differing origins. This has importance when considering contacts and movements of pottery in the early Saxon period. Table III summarizes the results.

Inspection of the data demonstrates a number of different fabric types which can be conveniently considered in three groups. The first, and largest group, is distinguished by clay with quartz grains alone, or with quartz and flint inclusions. The second group, sherds 15, 16, 18 and 33, has inclusions of granitic origin. The third group, represented by a single sherd, P 10, contained a few inclusions of fine-grained limestone in addition to the quartz.

The variety of quartz inclusions within the first group suggests that it is heterogeneous, composed of materials from a number of different sources. However, there is no reason to doubt that all these clays could have been found in the vicinity of Portchester. Study of the table suggests sub-groups: for example the presence of flint is restricted to certain sherds, P 3, 19, 22, 23, 25 and 26. Sherds 4 and 14 represent another sub-group on the basis of a similar distinctive texture with quartz grains set in a relatively clean matrix. A programme of heavy mineral analysis might permit more detailed discrimination than is at present possible, and it could enable sources to be distinguished, providing suitable comparanda are collected. The sherds of the second group are more revealing in thin section. They are characterized by a predominance of quartz, potash and some plagioclase felspars, and mica, the typical constituents of a granitic zone. The Cornish and the west Devon granite outcrops would seem a possible source except that sherd 33 has a series of blank stamps which are

[1] I am deeply indebted to Dr D. P. S. Peacock for helping and advising me in the preparation of this report.

TABLE III

Analysis of Selected Saxon Sherds

Sample ref.	*Publication no.*	*Sherd no.*	*Trench and layer*	*Quartz*	*Quartz grain size*				*Flint*	*Mica*	*Potash felspor*	*Plagioclase felspar*	*Limestone*
					c. 0·6 mm.	*c. 0·3 mm.*	*c. 0·1 mm.*	*c. 0·03 mm.*					
1	—	—	5, layer 3	×	×	×	×	×					
2	195	S33	62, layer 5	×			×	×		×			
3	4	S51	60, layer 9	×		×	×		×				
4	152	S5	5, layer 3	×	×	×		×					
5	261	S2	5, layer 3	×			×	×					
6	154	S7	5, layer 3	×	×	×	×	×					
7	158	S35	63, layer 10	×		×	×	×		×			
8	167	S37	65, layer 4	×			×	×		×			
9	—	S63	71, layer 5	×	×		×	×					
10	164	S36	63, layer 4	×	×	×	×						×
11	186	S73	69, layer 12	×		×	×	×		×			
12	268	S32	63, layer 5	×	×	×		×		×			
13	—	S28	54, layer 3	×				×					
14	180	S72	67, layer 9	×	×	×		×		×			
15	—	—	63, layer 4	×	×		×	×		×	×		
16	—	—	63, layer 4	×		×	×	×		×	×		
17	—	S74	72, layer 40	×	×		×	×		×		×	
18	143	S24	56, layer 8	×	×		×	×		×	×		
19	215	S13	5, layer 3	×	×		×	×	×	×			
20	238	S21	54, layer 6	×		×	×	×		×			
21	157	S19	45, layer 2	×			×	×		×			
22	244	S14	5, layer 3	×	×		×	×	×	×			
23	162	S41	60, layer 5	×			×	×	×	×			
24	—	S10	5, layer 3	×		×	×	×					
25	194	S11	5, layer 3	×		×	×	×	×	×			
26	286	S62	72, layer 5	×		×	×	×	×	×			
27	—	S58	68, layer 3	×		×	×		×				
28	270	S46	63, layer 4	×		×	×	×		×			
29	—	—	108, layer 52	×		×	×	×		×			
30	—	S75	72, layer 5	×		×	×	×					
31	146	S27	58, layer 7	×	×	×	×	×					
32	—	—	108, layer 80	×			×	×		×			
33	10	S50	60, layer 9	×		×	×	×		×	×		
34	274	S1	5, layer 3	×		×	×	×					

alien to the Cornish potting traditions in the eighth century, the date Professor Cunliffe has assigned to these sherds (Thomas, 1968). The nearest alternative source would be in Northern France, in the Breton peninsula, particularly. However, other granitic outcrops in Western Europe must not be ruled out in view of the great variety of European contacts demonstrated by the imported eighth-century pottery in nearby Hamwih. Areas such as the Massif Central, the Rhineland and the Harz Mountains are petrologically possible.

The limestone inclusions in the third group could imply clays found near the limestone outcrops on the Isle of Wight. This might be established if Saxon pottery from the island was to be petrologically examined. Alternative limestone outcrops occur in the Cotswolds and the Purbeck Hills. The Cassington kiln is a good illustration of an 'early Saxon' production centre which was making pottery with limestone inclusions near the Cotswolds (Arthur and Jope, 1963). The grille stamp on sherd 10 suggests the Purbeck Hills to be an unlikely source since Saxon pottery from Dorset is scarce. Finally, a Northern French origin is not impossible, particularly if it is accepted that the second group might be imported from that area.

BIBLIOGRAPHY

ADDYMAN, P. V. and HILL, D. H. 1970. 'Saxon Southampton: a review of the evidence. Part II. Industry and everyday life.' *Proc. Hants F.C.* xxvi, 61–96.

ADDYMAN, P. V., HOPKINS, B. G. and NORTON, G. T. 1972. 'A Saxo-Norman pottery-kiln producing stamped wares at Michelmersh, Hants.' *Med. Arch.* xvi, 127–30.

ARTHUR, B. V. and JOPE, E. M. 1963. 'Early Saxon pottery kilns at Purwell Farm, Cassington, Oxfordshire.' *Med. Arch.* 6–7, 1–12.

BIDDLE, M. and BARCLAY, K. 1974. 'Winchester ware'. In *Medieval Pottery from Excavations*, edited by Evison, V. I., Hodges, H. and Hurst, J. G., pp. 137–65.

CUNLIFFE, B. W. 1964. *Winchester Excavations 1949–1960*, Volume 1.

CUNLIFFE, B. W. 1970. 'The Saxon culture-sequence of Portchester Castle.' *Antiq. J.* l, 67–85.

CUNLIFFE, B. W. 1974. 'Some late Saxon stamped pottery from Southern England.' In *Medieval Pottery from Excavations*, edited by Evison, V. I., Hodges, H. and Hurst, J. G., pp. 127–35.

HURST, J. G. 1958. 'Saxo-Norman pottery in East Anglia. Part III. Stamford ware.' *Proc. Camb. Ant. Soc.* li, 37–65.

HURST, J. G. 1964. 'Winchester ware: a new type of Saxo-Norman glazed pottery.' In Biddle, M. and Quirk, R. N. 'Excavations near Winchester Cathedral, 1961.' *Arch. J.* cxix, 187–90.

JOPE, E. M. 1954. 'Late Saxon pits under Oxford Castle mound.' *Oxoniensia* xvii/xviii, 77–111.

LEWIS, E. and MARTIN, J. 1973. 'Rescue excavations on a Saxon settlement site at Rowner, 1971.' *Rescue Arch. in Hants* i, 38–51.

MOORHOUSE, S. 1973. 'Early medieval pottery from Westbury, East Meon, Hampshire.' *Proc. Hants F.C.* xxviii, 41–8.

MYRES, J. N. L. 1968. 'The Anglo-Saxon cemetery.' In Biddle, Lambrick and Myres, 'The early history of Abingdon and its abbey.' *Med. Arch.* xii, 35–41.

RAHTZ, P. 1974. 'Pottery in Somerset, A.D. 400–1066', in *Medieval Pottery from Excavations*, edited by Evison, V. I., Hodges, H. and Hurst, J. G., pp. 95–126.

THOMAS, C. 1968. 'Grass marked pottery in Cornwall.' In *Studies in Ancient Europe*, edited by Coles, J. M. and Simpson, D. D. A., pp. 311–31.

VAN ES, W. A. 1967. *Wijster, a Native Village Beyond the Imperial Frontier, A.D. 150–425.*

WEBSTER, G. 1952. 'An Anglo-Saxon urnfield at South Elkington, Louth, Lincolnshire.' *Arch. J.* cviii, 25–59.

WERNER, J. 1958. 'Kriegergräber aus der ersten Hälfte des 5. Jahrhunderts.' *Bonner Jahrbücher* clviii, 372–413.

IV. THE FINDS

IN the following pages a description is given of the objects illustrated in figs. 129–144. All objects found in sealed Saxon contexts are illustrated, except for fragmentary scraps. A complete list, including the unillustrated scraps and residual Roman objects, will be found under the description of each individual structure. In the case of the mixed occupation layers, all objects of definite or probable Saxon origin are illustrated. The number given in brackets after the location of each object is the small find number.

The descriptions and identifications given below are largely the work of Mr Martin Welch and Mr David A. Hinton, with the advice of Mr David Brown. Mr Welch was responsible for the discussion of nos. 1, 44, 45, 46 and 47; Mr Hinton for most of the others. Some of the iron objects had not been conserved and X-rayed when the discussion was written.

Objects of Iron and Bronze

1. Purse mount/strike-a-light, iron, length 94 mm., width including the buckle 37 mm. (pl. XVIII*a* and fig. 129).

It consists of a triangular plate, which shows signs of wear in the centre of its flat base, probably caused by the regular striking of a flint against the basal edge to produce a spark.[1] The basal edge is thicker (nearly 3 mm.) than the upper edges (1·5 mm.). The triangular shape is repeated by three broad and deep grooves (width 1 mm.) parallel to the outer edges, creating narrow plain borders (width 2 mm. on the upper part, and 2·75 mm. on the lower part at its widest). The grooves are cross-nicked, possibly to take inlay, or more probably to catch the light and emphasize the grooves.[2] The upper border was beaten out by the smith into a loop extension at either end, each formed from a bird's neck, head and beak, facing inwards. An eye is indicated by a single incised ringlet on each head. Some grooves on the beak of the right-hand bird near its head, not present on the other, are probably the result of wear or damage. The only other decoration on the plate is a frieze of triangles with circular apices immediately above and parallel to the lower grooved line. The base for all the triangles is a single incised line. The majority of the triangles have double incised lines for the upper two sides, usually with a third double line linking the circular apex to the base line, giving an arrow-like appearance. At the narrow ends of the plate, where space is restricted, the triangles diminish in size and lose some details. The back of the plate is flat and undecorated. The buckle loop and plate were separately made. The buckle plate is rectangular, bent backwards on itself with the ends fixed over the triangular plate at its apex by a single iron rivet. The bottom two corners of the buckle plate on the front side are emphasized, and there is decoration of short parallel vertical grooves on either side of the hole cut for the tongue. The buckle loop is a plain oval ring.

[1] It seems probable that this piece was used as a strike-a-light. The tinder and flint were probably carried in a bag or pouch, attached to the strike-a-light by means of the buckle and/or the loops on either side formed by the birds' head terminals. Mr P. D. C. Brown will discuss the evidence for the use of these pieces as strike-a-lights in a forthcoming article.

[2] Prior to cleaning this piece, Mr D. Leigh had it X-rayed and carried out a test for silver, but was unable to discover any trace of metal inlay.

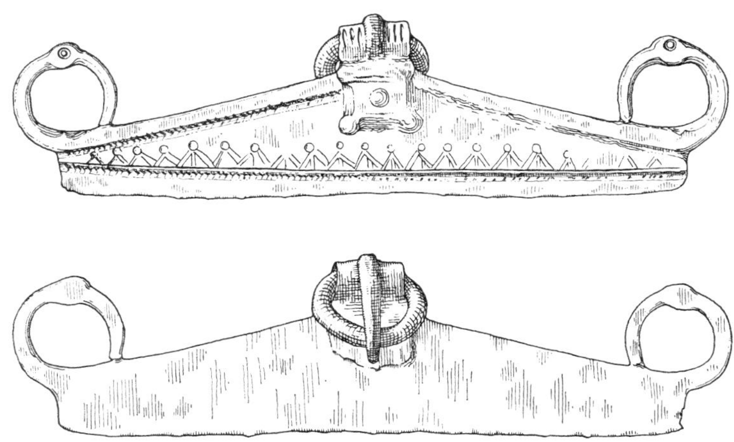

FIG. 129. Iron purse mount/strike-a-light (pp. 195–7). Scale $\frac{2}{3}$

The purse mount/strike-a-light is related to a group of pieces with birds' head terminals and inlaid decoration. Many of these consist of a rectangular iron plate with birds' heads protruding upwards at either end, the heads facing inwards with the beaks touching the upper edge of the plate, and with a buckle at the centre of the upper edge. The inlaid decoration is geometric, often of circle and dot motifs, and the birds' eyes are often indicated by a circle.

The dating of these purse mounts/strike-a-lights is firmly established in the fifth century by the associations of the strike-a-light in Krefeld-Gellep II (Rhineland) Grave 43 (Pirling, 1966, p. 209, pl. 10). The glass claw beaker, the sword, and the zoomorphic decorated buckle (Pirling, 1966, pp. 149–50, 185, 192–4), all agree with a date for the grave in the middle of the fifth century. Two related pieces from Sussex belong to the late fifth and early sixth centuries. High Down, Ferring, Grave 14 contains a glass bowl of the Westbere type (Read, 1895, pp. 374–5, fig. 4, pl. XXVII, 3, 4; Harden, 1956, p. 165, pl. XVIh) and Alfriston Grave 91 possesses a decorated tubular bronze belt fitting and an axe-head of the francisca type (Evison, 1965, fig. 23b).

The sloping shoulders of the Portchester example and the unique delicacy of its birds' head terminals differentiate it from the rectangular group, however. Perhaps a piece from High Down, which has had both its terminals broken off, but retains traces of a bronze wire inlaid triangular frame, originally resembled the Portchester purse mount/strike-a-light fairly closely (Evison, 1955, p. 39, no. 24, pl. VIf). A bronze mount from the Bonn Museum with a similar outline unfortunately lacks any context (Roes, 1967, p. 296, fig. 13).

The typically Germanic border motif of triangle with circular apex (Salin, 1904, pp. 158–60) occurs on a repoussé decorated silver buckle plate from Broadstairs (Kent) associated with an early form of glass claw beaker, two small pairs of tweezers, two small ring brooches and a black and white glass bead (Evison, 1958, pp. 240–1). Thus the incised decoration of the Portchester piece also suggests a date in the second half of the fifth century.

Pit 135, layer 104 (1864).

2. Pronged object, one prong possibly complete. Long point perhaps for driving into a wooden haft. Possibly for use as a hay fork.

Pit 220 (2522)

3. Iron point with wood attached to the end. Possibly an awl. Cf. a chisel with a similar tang, *Southampton*, fig. 24, 12.

Pit 135 (1399)

4. Hook.

Pit 135 (1869)

5. Tapered flat iron strip, one end broken, the other thickened into a knob. No rivets, but perhaps a door fitting.

Trench 107, layer 27 (2401)

6. Iron disc, the centre domed and pierced by a rectangular hole. A round hole would be necessary for an axle-hub. If the disc rotated, it was fixed, not a free wheel.

Pit 72 (330)

7. Hook. Cf. *Maxey*, fig. 16, 14.

Pit 39 (218)

8. A latch-lifter composed of an iron bar with one end a loop, the other a hook. Too delicate to be a pot-hook.

Pit 135 (1546)

9. Horse- (or ox-) shoe fragment, with countersunk nail holes and a wavy edge. Cf. *Eaton Socon*, fig. 11, 18; *LMMC*, 114 and fig. 10, type 1. Probably tenth to eleventh centuries, when shoes cease to be uncommon.

Pit 72 (332)

10. Hinge pivot for hammering through a post or plank. Cf. *Shakenoak*, III, fig. 39, 171.

Pit 207 (2289)

11. Pruning hook, its tang bent. *St Neots*, 1, fig. 3, no. 5; *St Neots*, 2, fig. 5, no. 3. Medieval examples of the same pattern, *Clough Castle*, fig. 11, nos. 13, 14; unpublished from Woodperry D. M. V., in Ashmolean Museum.

Pit 202 (2195)

12. Key with simple wards. Cf. *Southampton*, fig. 24, nos. 14, 15. Since those shown in *LMMC* for the tenth to twelfth centuries are more complex, this should be typologically earlier. It was found in a ninth- to tenth-century layer.

Trench 107, layer 9 (2379)

13. Iron bar with a hook at one end.

Pit 191 (2253)

14. Iron bar with a hook at one end and with rivets projecting from one side.

Pit 68 (356)

15. Hook, broken, with flat attachment plate with a single rivet. Possibly part of a strap end (cf. *Shakenoak*, III, fig. 39, 174) or bucket-handle attachment.

Pit 135 (1610)

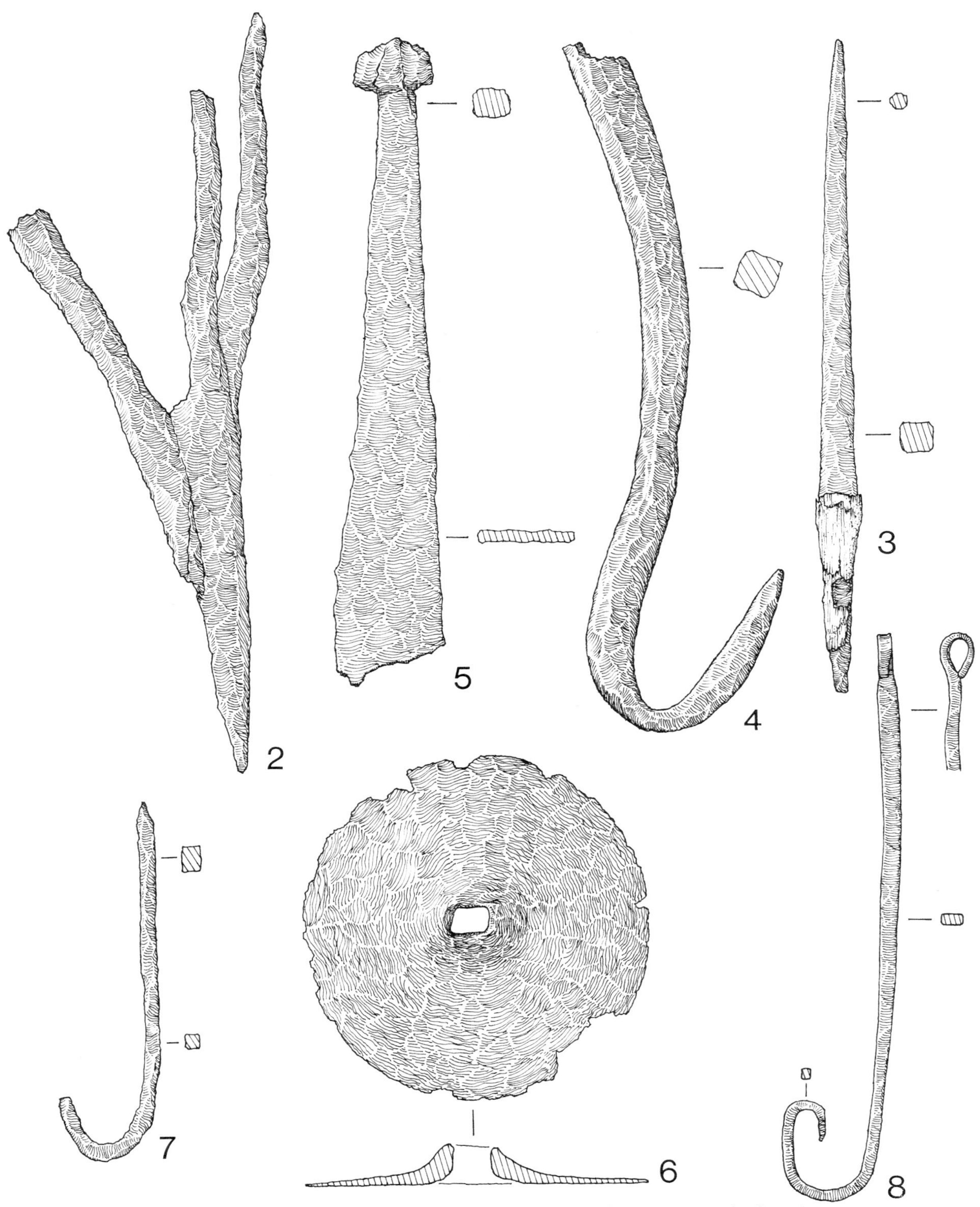

FIG. 130. Objects of iron (p. 197). Scale: 6, 8, $\frac{1}{3}$; remainder, $\frac{2}{3}$

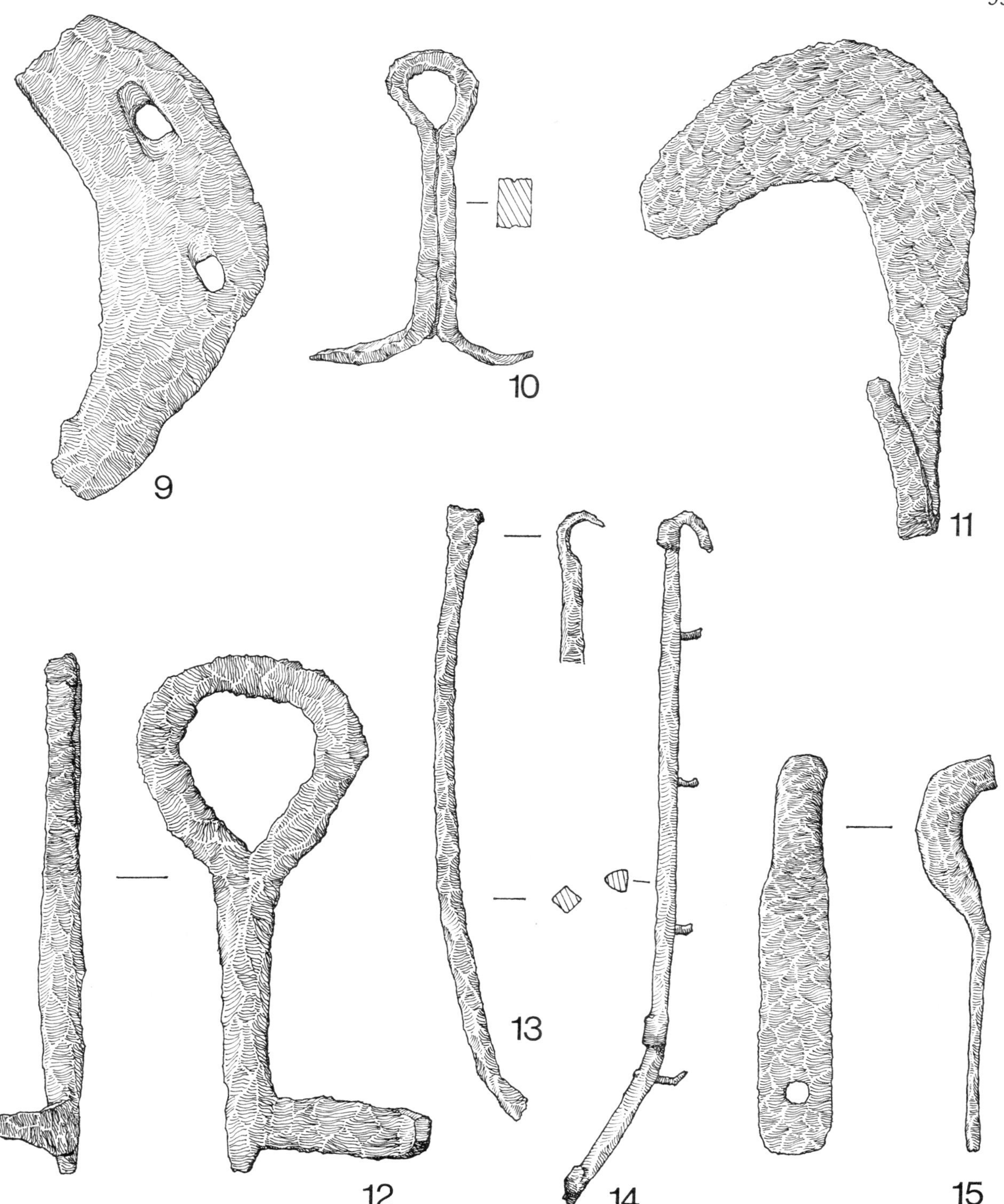

FIG. 131. Objects of iron (p. 197). Scale: 13, 14, ⅓; remainder, ⅔

16. Curved handle with a hook at each end.
Pit 135 (1614)

17. Curved, twisted handle with a hook at each end. The twisting is unusual; cf. *Shakenoak*, III, fig. 40, nos. 178, 184. These are probably bucket or pail fittings. Strips (not illustrated) bound round the wooden staves as hoops were held by the iron bars (nos. 13 and 14), one on each side of the pail. Hooks (e.g. no. 15) projected over the rim to take the handles (nos. 16 and 17).
Pit 135 (1612)

18. Blade with curved back and a ?tang. The blade is shorter, and the tang set closer to the back of the blade than on most Saxon knives. Possibly part of a pair of shears.
Pit 219 (2435)

19–27. Knives. The groove along the edge of the blade of some of the examples is a late Saxon feature; the others have no noteworthy characteristics.
19, pit 135 (1063); 20, pit 203 (2200); 21, pit 37 (113); 22, pit 207 (2291); 23, pit 135 (1567); 24, pit 135 (1611); 25, pit 135 (1587); 26, pit 38 (121); 27, pit 135 (1082)

28. Tapering iron bar.
Pit 207 (2273)

29. Iron strip fragment.
Pit 68 (317)

30. Iron rod fragment.
Pit 198 (2161)

31. Iron fragment.
Pit 72 (333)

32. Iron strip fragment with a rivet hole near one end: fragments of wood adhere to one side. Presumably a binding strip.
Pit 135 (1122)

33. Iron bar fragment.
Pit 135 (1190)

34. Iron rod fragment.
Pit 56 (286)

35. Iron bar fragment.
Pit 35 (97)

36, 37. Iron fragments.
Pit 151 (1823)

38. Iron fragment.
Pit 72 (331)

39. Iron bar of triangular section with rivets.
Pit 71 (328)

40. Curved iron rod, fragment.
Pit 156 (1817)

41. Socketed object, with tip bent over.
Pit 135 (1164)

42. Rod with circular section, flattened at one end, possibly a stylus.
Pit 135 (1788)

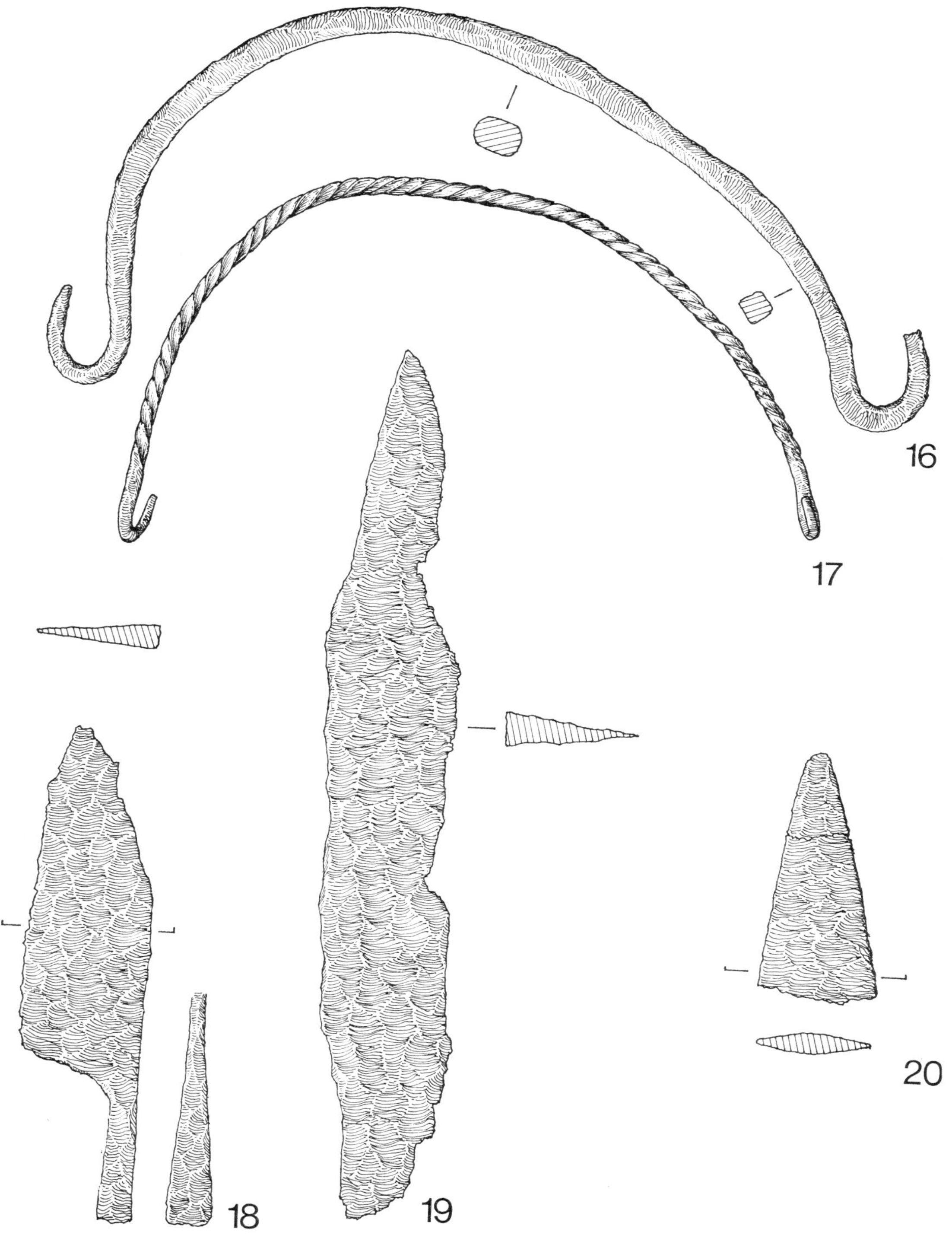

FIG. 132. Objects of iron (p. 200). Scale: 16, 17, $\frac{1}{3}$; remainder, $\frac{2}{3}$

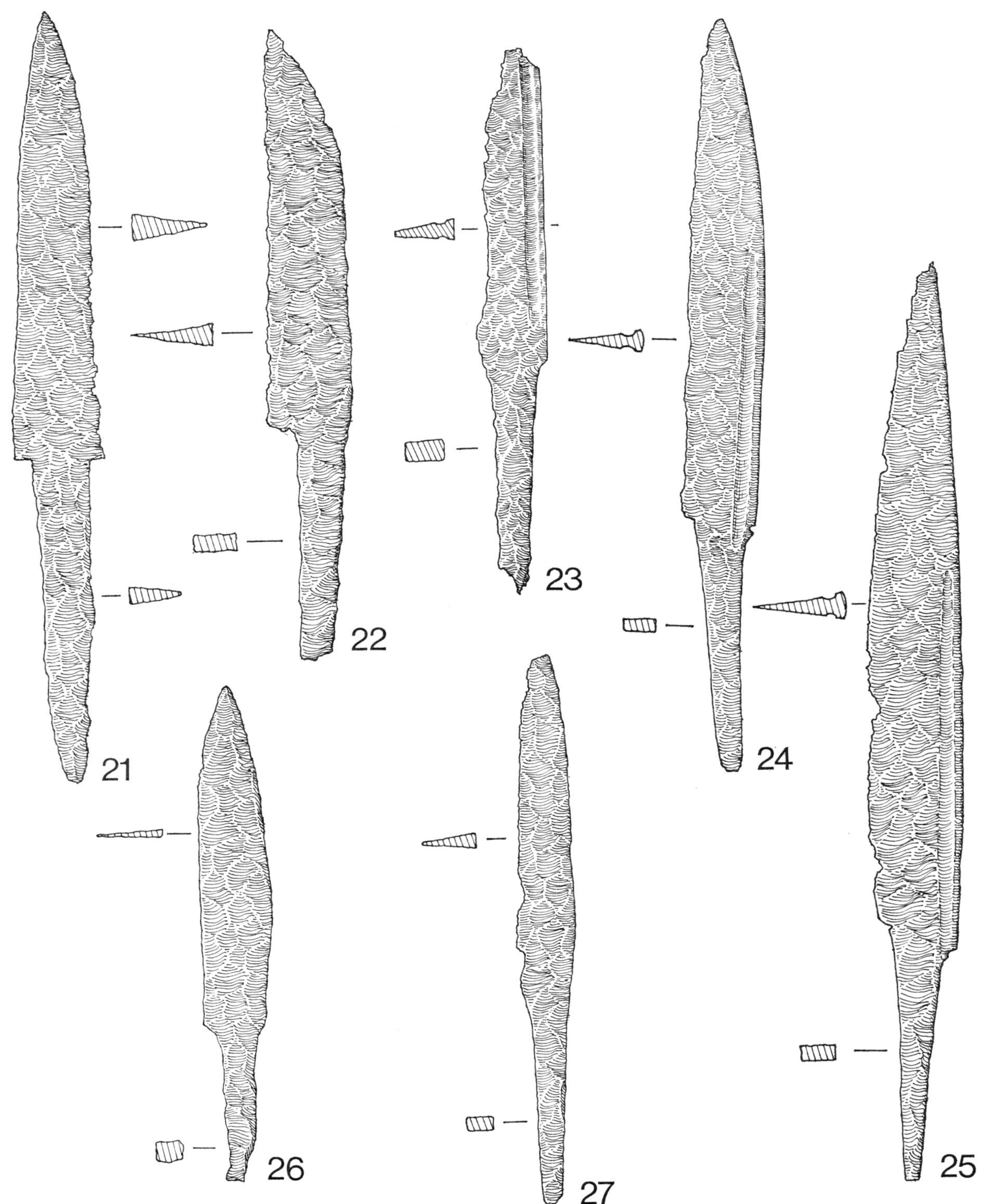

FIG. 133. Objects of iron (p. 200). Scale: 27, $\frac{1}{3}$; remainder, $\frac{2}{3}$

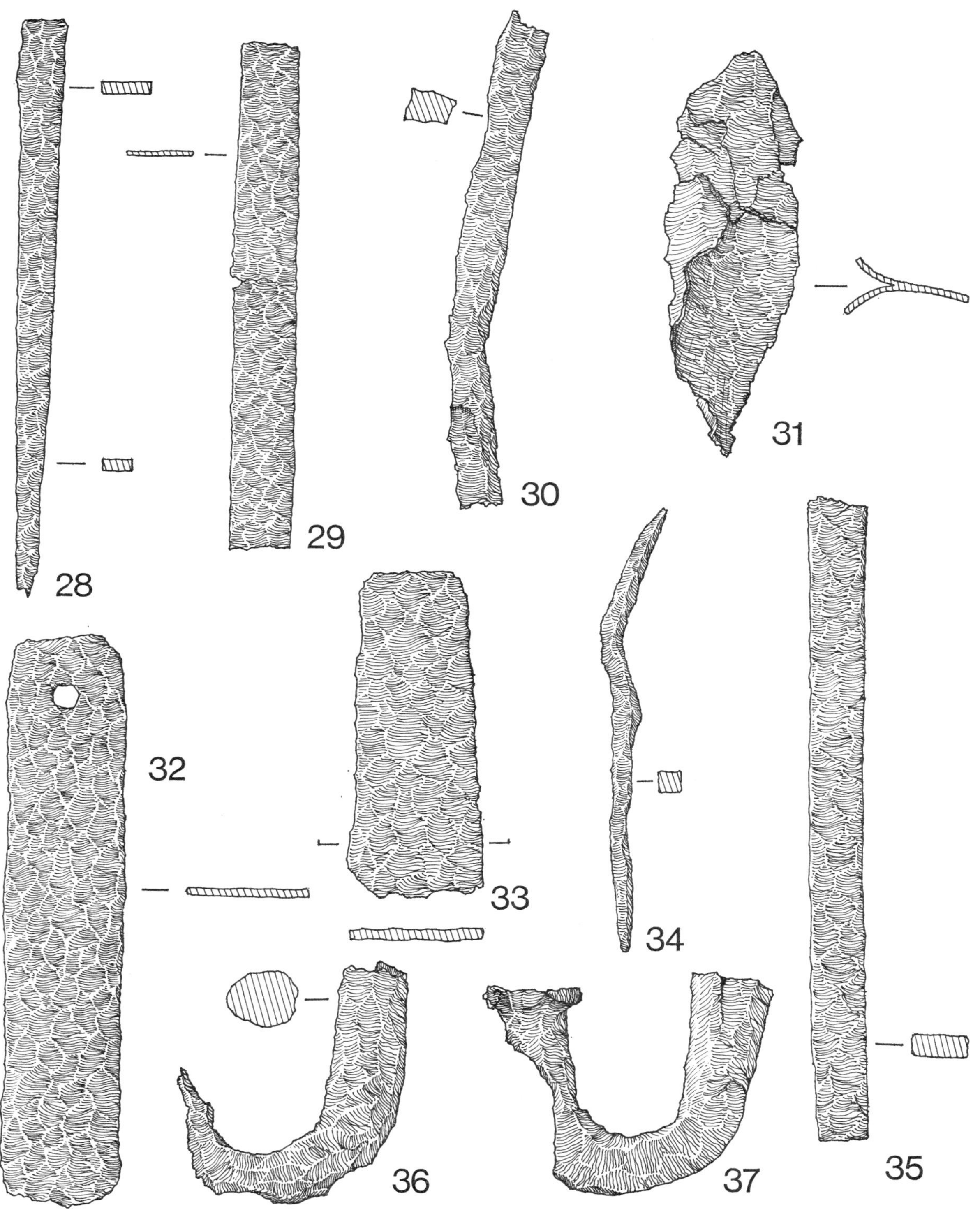

FIG. 134. Objects of iron (p. 200). Scale: 28, 31, 33, $\frac{1}{3}$; remainder, $\frac{2}{3}$

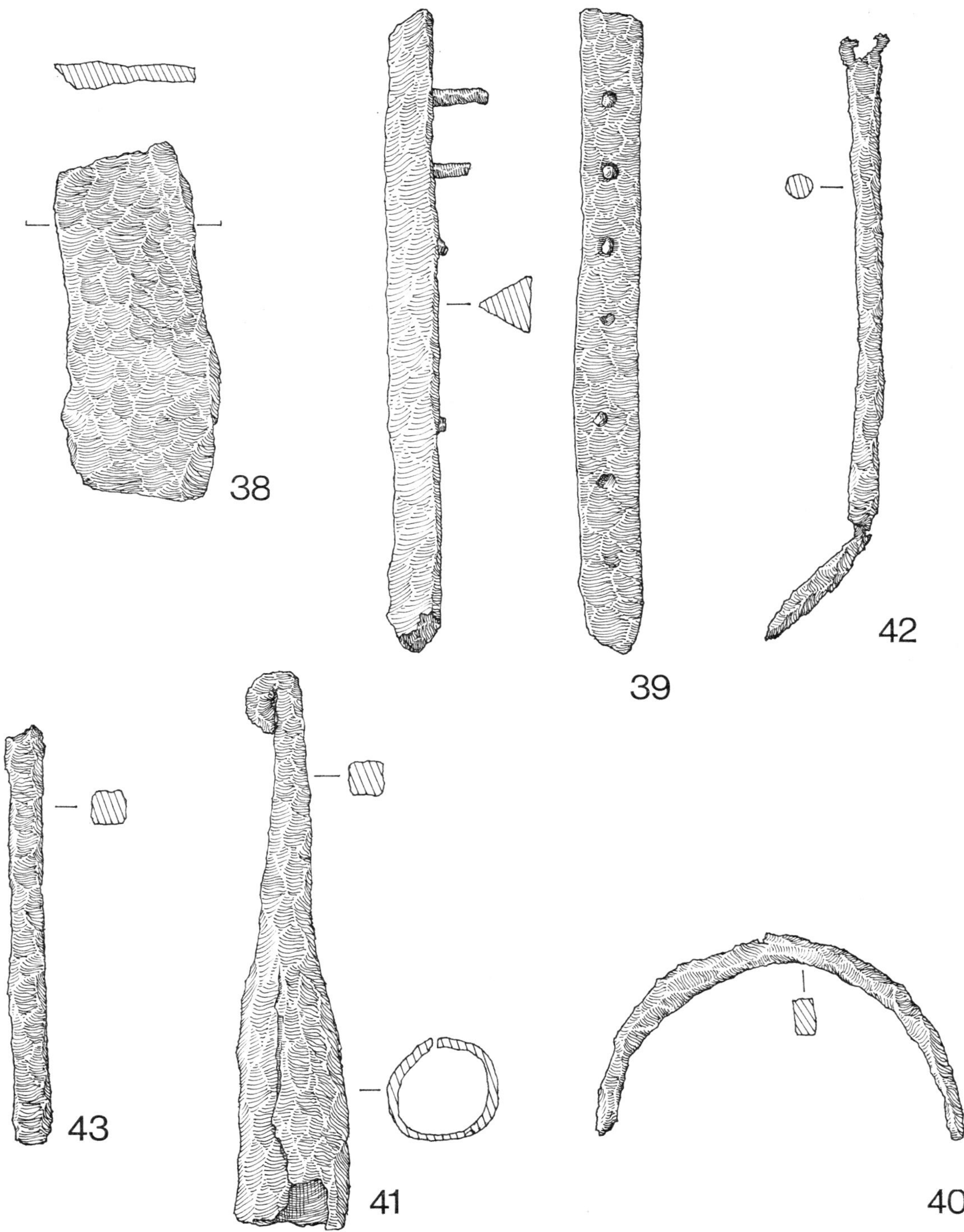

FIG. 135. Objects of iron (p. 200, 205). Scale $\frac{2}{3}$

43. Rod of rectangular section.
Pit 216 (2436)

44. Disc brooch, bronze, diameter 34 mm., thickness 1 mm. (pl. XVIII*c* and fig. 136).

The upper surface is decorated with incised circle and dot motifs, divided from a narrow border by a single concentric circle. The outer edge is decorated with punched triangles with the apex pointing inwards. There is a second border, again separated from the central area by a concentric circle. It consists of a ring of 15 concave hollows, each enclosed by two ringlets. The inner area is decorated with five similar hollows and ringlets, but the central concavity is enclosed by three ringlets. The design is unusually well executed, though the circle and dot motifs are not always evenly spaced. There is no decoration on the back. The iron pin is virtually intact, with three coils to act as a spring.

It is interesting to note that a more crudely executed brooch with 11 circle and dot motifs was discovered unstratified at the Roman site of *Clausentum* (Bitterne, Hampshire) (Cotton and Gathercole, 1958, p. 45, fig. 12, no. 5). This brooch type is commonly found in Anglo-Saxon cemeteries. The type is a cheap version of the round brooch fashionable in southern England in the fifth and sixth centuries, worn by women, one on either shoulder, usually with a string of beads between them. They are generally regarded as dating within the sixth century, and grave groups such as Mitcham (Surrey), Grave 116 (Bidder and Morris, 1959, p. 100, pl. XI) and Girton (Cambridge) Group I (Fox, 1923, pl. XXVII, no. 2) give dates of burial around the middle or second half of the sixth. Such rich grave groups are rare, however, and these brooches are all too often the only datable element.

A number of these graves do suggest that disc brooches may have been manufactured in the later fifth century. Orpington (Kent) Grave 51 (Tester, 1969, pp. 40, 41, fig. 3) contained a brooch with decoration of circle and dot combined with inward pointing triangles on the outer edge. This is associated with a buckle decorated in Quoit Brooch Style, which has had the end of its decorated plate cut off and possesses an iron tongue, suggesting that it was old when buried. A date for the grave in the late fifth or early sixth century seems probable. The pair of tinned bronze brooches with stamped decoration of a 'three dots in a triangle' motif in Orpington Grave 58 (Tester, 1969, pp. 44, 46, figs. 2, 4) are associated with a pottery vessel dated by Dr Myres to the first half of the fifth century. The excavator is convinced that this is a true association in an inhumation grave. This pot can be paralleled at such North German cemeteries as Wehden and Altenwalde (Waller, 1957, pl. 1, no. 6 and pl. 9, no. 66) with its typical *stehende Bogen* (standing arches) decoration. Both on the Continent and in England this type of pot is normally used as a cremation urn. There is no easy explanation for the association of this pot with brooches generally considered to be made at least half a century later. It is possible that this vessel was a treasured heirloom, or that a conservative pottery tradition continued to produce such vessels over a longer period than has been previously considered likely. Alternatively the brooches were being manufactured earlier than the sixth century.

Perhaps a similarly stamped brooch from Beddingham Hill (Sussex) was originally associated in a closed find with a Late Roman buckle of Hawkes type IA (Hawkes and

Dunning, 1961, p. 45), suggesting a date of manufacture in the second half of the fifth century. Unfortunately the associations within this small cemetery are no longer known. A third and rather worn example of this stamp-ornamented type occurs at Bifrons (Kent) Grave 6 (Godfrey-Faussett, 1876, p. 303), which was probably deposited in the early sixth century, with an early form of perforated spoon and two square-headed small-long brooches. A date of manufacture in the late fifth century seems probable for this piece.

Disc brooches also occasionally occur in Continental cemeteries, where they are usually regarded as Anglo-Saxon exports. For example, a pair of brooches with circle and dot decoration occur in Krefeld-Gellep II (Rhineland) Grave 968 (Pirling, 1966, pp. 161–2, pl. 78) associated with a glass beaker of Type 226, a pair of bow brooches of the Bifrons type and a pair of *Armbrustfibeln*, dated by Dr Renate Pirling to early in *Stufe II*, that is in the last quarter of the fifth century.

The Portchester disc brooch does possess one distinctively early feature in the spiral coils of its pin. Its position in the upper part of the well deposit which produced the purse mount/strike-a-light, would agree with a date in the late fifth or early sixth centuries.

Well (pit) 135, layer 103 (1811)

45. Disc, gilt bronze, from an applied brooch, diameter 30 mm. (pl. XVIII*b* and fig. 136).

The repoussé decoration of a six-pointed star was achieved by hammering the sheet bronze disc on to a die. There are two borders, each 2 mm. wide, of miniature sub-rectangular raised bosses, the first on the outer edge and the second surrounding the concave central hollow. Between them are six triangles, each with its apex against the outer edge and its long sides double-lined. Two are noticeably smaller than the others. There was a certain amount of distortion of the pattern from the hammering and the subsequent removal of the disc. Thus the central concavity is not a true circle as intended and the miniature bosses of the inner border show great variety in size and shape. Around the edge of the disc a bronze band was originally fixed as an upright rim.[1] Its height is 4 mm. and there are some traces of gilding still visible on it. The ends of the band overlap and are held by a single rivet.

In Professor Cunliffe's paper on the pottery sequence, a silver applied brooch from the late Roman cemetery of Vermand (Aisne, France) Grave 24 has been cited as a parallel (Cunliffe, 1970, p. 69, n. 1). There is some doubt about the exact composition of this grave group, but the brooch seems to belong with a second silver applied brooch, which has an animal mask design. There are also a pair of Tutulus brooches and a pair of bow brooches, together with a gold *solidus* of Valentinian I (A.D. 364–75), which dates the grave to the late fourth century (Evison, 1965, pp. 12, 101–2, fig. I; Eck, 1891, pp. 25–6, 229–31, pl. XX, no. 36; Pilloy, 1895, pp. 276–7, pl. 19, no. 36). Like the Portchester piece, it has a rim, but of silver, 3 mm. high. It differs from the Portchester brooch in a number of respects, however. In particular, the Vermand star design has 11 points and the central area appears in the published drawing to have a raised boss, while the Portchester disc has six points and the central area is concave.

[1] The disc and rim fragments came from the same fill. Mr D. Leigh found that the remains of corrosion and (?) solder matched up on the rim and the disc, when the rim was placed in an upright position.

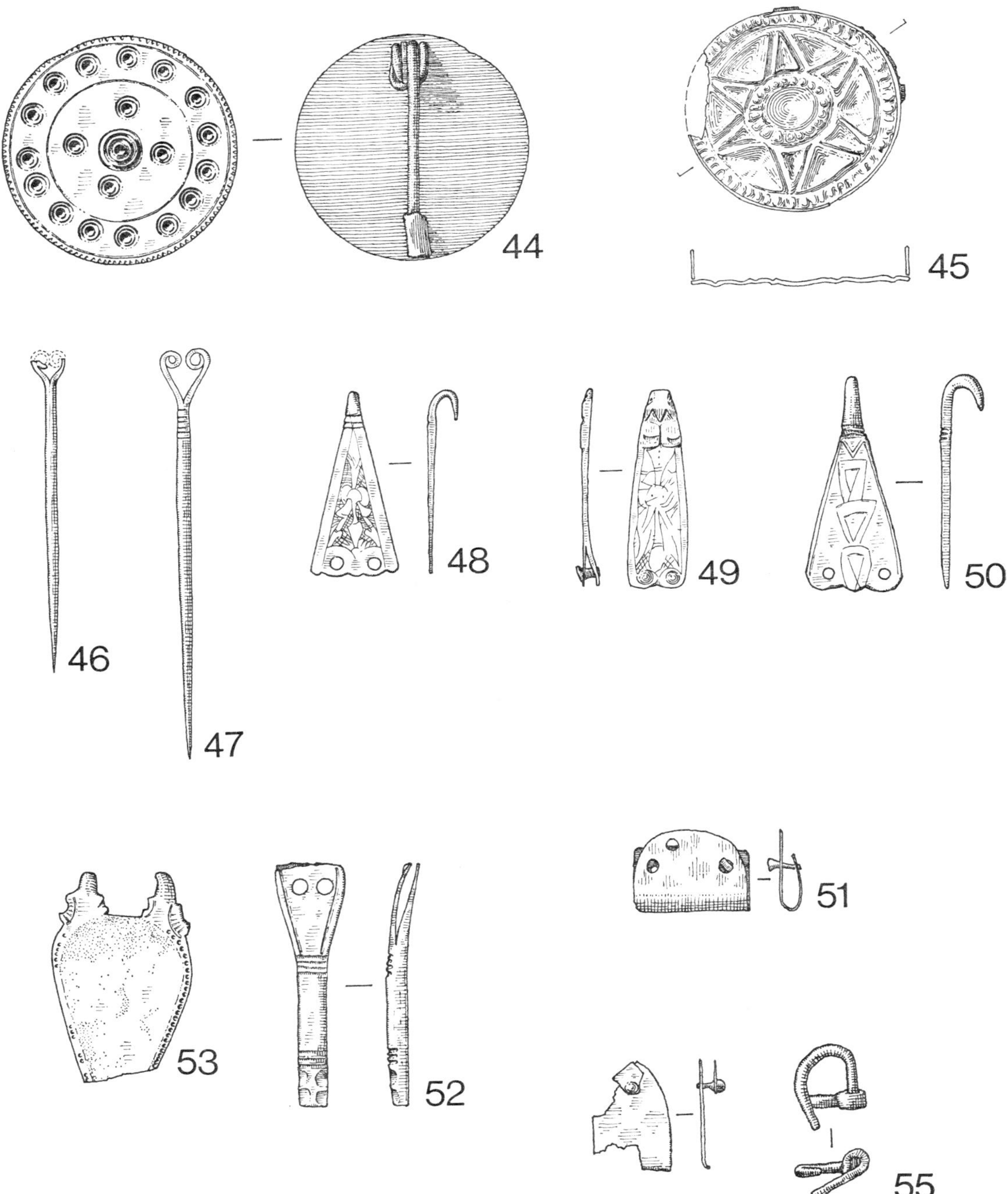

FIG. 136. Objects of copper alloy (pp. 205–17). Scale $\frac{2}{3}$

Thus, although it is probable that the Vermand brooch represents a prototype for the Portchester brooch, it cannot be regarded as a satisfactory parallel.[1]

There is an unfilled gap in the typological development between the Vermand and Portchester brooches, the latter being closely paralleled by applied brooches from Anglo-Saxon graves of the mid-fifth to the mid-sixth centuries. The star design occurs in North Germany on early fifth-century applied brooches only in the form of the David star of interlocked triangles, often with a rosette in the centre.[2] In Rhenen (Netherlands) Grave 356, one of these David star brooches was worn together with an eight-pointed star applied brooch. The star design is double outlined and both the spaces between the points and the central area are elaborately decorated with bosses and dimples. The other associations are a large decorated pin, a subrectangular buckle and an undecorated pottery cup. J. Ypey dates this grave to the mid-fifth century,[3] contemporary with the earliest date probable for the English series of star design applied brooches. The design clearly became popular here and lasted over 100 years: it was also taken up on cast saucer brooches, datable from the late fifth through much of the sixth century. Most of the applied brooch series have five points, though four-, six- and seven-pointed designs also occur, nearly always double outlined. The Portchester disc may well have been intended to have a five-pointed star, until the die-maker discovered that he had left too large a space for the fifth point, and substituted two smaller points instead.

A date in the mid-fifth century is probable for the deposition of two applied brooches in Grave 123 at Guildown (Surrey). One of these has a six-pointed star marked by a single line with separate heart-shaped motifs between each point. It is associated with a floriate cross brooch with four heart-shaped motifs (Lowther, 1931, pl. XII, no. 2).[4] A five-pointed applied brooch from Long Wittenham (Berkshire) Grave 186 was found with a saucer brooch with a compressed form of a heart-shaped motif in each quadrant (Akerman, 1863, p. 142, pl. XI, nos. 4, 5). The star brooch has a small central boss surrounded by a ring of six miniature bosses. Its outer border consists of a ring of sub-rectangular bosses surrounded by a zigzag line. A date in the late fifth or early sixth century is probable. The six-pointed applied brooch from Barrington B (Cambridgeshire) Grave 28 has a similar central design to the Long Wittenham brooch, but its outer border consists of miniature bosses. It was discovered with a bronze disc brooch with circle and dot ornament, a pair of bronze tweezers and beads, which suggest a date in the first half of the sixth century (Foster, 1880–4, pp. 18, 31, pl. V, no. 1).

A five-pointed star with an outer border consisting of a wavy line within a ring of raised bosses comes from Lyminge (Kent) Grave 10. Its associated brooch is a bronze pennanular decorated in Quoit Brooch Style (Warhurst, 1955, pp. 11–12, fig. 6, no. 5). The chronological range of this distinctive animal ornament with its probable origins

[1] Another disc brooch with a star motif decoration in a late fourth century context occurs in Oudenburg Grave 88 (Mertens and van Impe, 1971, pl. XXVIII, no. 6). The decoration is executed in the style used on Tutulus brooches.

[2] This motif is of late Roman origin, for example, a silver fragment from the Coleraine hoard (*British Museum, 1922*, p. 74, fig. 96).

[3] Böhme, 1974, pl. 60, figs. 1–5. I am extremely grateful to Mr J. Ypey for information about this important closed find in advance of the article he has written in collaboration with Miss V. I. Evison on applied brooches.

[4] See the article on the dating of Mitcham (Surrey) Grave 205 and the floriate cross class of applied brooches by the writer (*Antiq. J.* lv (1975), 86–95).

FIG. 137. Distribution of applied brooches with star designs

Four points:
1. Luton, Bedfordshire
2. Fairford, Gloucestershire

Five points:
3. Guildown, Surrey, Grave 75
4. Guildown, Surrey, Grave 116
5. Harnham Hill, Wiltshire, Grave 42
6. Holywell Row, Suffolk, Grave 47
7. Lackford, Suffolk, 50.234
8. Long Wittenham, Berkshire, Grave 186
9. Lyminge, Kent, Grave 10
10. High Down (Ferring), Sussex
11. Islip, Northamptonshire
12. Sancton, Yorkshire

Six points:
13. Barrington B, Cambridgeshire, Grave 28
14. Guildown, Surrey, Grave 123
15. Portchester Castle, Hampshire

Seven points:
16. Blewburton Hill (Blewbury), Berkshire, Grave 2
17. Fairford, Gloucestershire

in insular late Roman art is not known. It is possible that this grave dates within the fifth century, but the similarities between the applied brooch and the pair from Guildown (Surrey) Grave 116 (see below), suggest that we probably have here another case of Quoit Brooch Style metalwork associated with material datable to the first half of the sixth century.[1]

The five-star brooches at Lackford (Suffolk) 50.234 (Lethbridge, 1951, p. 39, fig. 17), and at Guildown Grave 116 (Lowther, 1931, pl. XII, no. 1) are both associated with brooches of the Great Square-headed type. The headplate fragment from Lackford was classified by Leeds as Type A3, but bears little resemblance to the other brooches of this class. It appears to resemble some of the Scandinavian brooches, notably the famous Vedstrup brooch, in the style of the animal ornament, the border of triangles with semi-circular apices and the diagonal cross in a square of the upper corners (Leeds, 1949, pls. 12A, S6). Professor Haseloff has recently dated the introduction of the square-headed brooches decorated in Style I in Kent to the last quarter of the fifth century. If we accept this, a date in the first quarter of the sixth would be appropriate for the Lackford brooch. A trefoil-headed small-long brooch was the only other object associated in the cremation urn, which is decorated with triangular panel style stamped ornament.[2] The square-headed brooch in Guildown Grave 116 is of Leeds Type B2, a class of brooch restricted to Surrey and Sussex (Leeds, 1949, pl. 70). The moulds were made from the same model as a brooch without associations from Alfriston (Sussex). Stylistically a date in the second quarter of the sixth century might be suggested for this piece.

The pair of applied brooches in Grave 116 have inner and outer borders of miniature bosses surrounded by a wavy line. A similar pair of brooches in Grave 75 (Lowther, 1931, pl. XII, no. 3) shares the feature of a wavy line, already seen on the Lyminge brooch. The applied brooch fragment from Lackford is closely resembled by a brooch in Holywell Row (Suffolk) Grave 47 (Lethbridge, 1931, p. 25, fig. IIF, no. 2). Both have inner borders of miniature bosses and the edges of the decorated plates have been cut into scallops. The irregular edges of the upper plate of the Harnham Hill (Wiltshire) Grave 42 brooch indicate that this dish-shaped piece possessed similar scalloped edges (Akerman, 1853, pp. 263, 268, pl. XII, no. 9). Again there is an inner border of bosses, with a blue glass stud set at the centre. A pair of applied brooches from High Down, Ferring (Sussex) are the only other brooches of this design to possess blue glass studs. They closely resemble the Harnham brooch and a published photograph shows that they originally possessed a broad rim (Wilson and Gerard, 1947, p. 7, fig. V). The decorated disc at Holywell Row is much smaller than its back plate and it is possible that this piece also had a similar rim.

The seven-pointed applied brooch from Blewburton (Berkshire) Grave 2 (Collins, 1952–3, p. 52, fig. 19) probably belongs to the second half of the fifth century. It is associated with a late Roman dolphin-headed bronze buckle of Hawkes type IA,

[1] For example Alfriston (Sussex) Grave 43 (Griffith and Salzmann, 1914, pp. 39–41).

[2] Dr Myres has quoted this grave group as supporting his attribution of this type of urn, a product of the Illington–Lackford school, to the second half of the sixth century. A date in the first half of the sixth would suit the metalwork of other grave groups he cites, including Illington 102 and Baginton (Myres, 1969, pp. 57, 134).

which may have been repaired at least once, as it has an iron tongue (Hawkes and Dunning, 1961, p. 45). It is difficult to decide whether this brooch design should be classified with the straight-sided star series. It consists of curved segments meeting at the outer border to form points. The decoration consists of miniature bosses. A pair of brooches of precisely the same size and design as the Blewburton piece are in the Ashmolean Museum from the cemetery at Fairford (Gloucestershire).[1] One of them still retains an upright bronze rim, but their context in the cemetery is no longer known.

The youngest brooch in the series is a fragment in a plain urn from Sancton (E. R. Yorkshire), also in the Ashmolean Museum.[2] There is no trace of the inner border, but the outer border consists of miniature raised bosses. It is associated with the remains of a bronze wrist clasp of a type datable to the middle or even the second half of the sixth century. Similar clasps are associated with three small-long brooches at Girton (Cambridge) Grave 71 (Hollingworth and O'Reilly, 1925, pl. II) and with a Group IV cruciform brooch from Londesborough (E. R. Yorkshire) Grave 10 (Swanton, 1963–6, pp. 279–80, figs. 4, 6).[3]

The majority of the applied brooches of the star series in England then belong to the first half of the sixth century, and it must be admitted that the Portchester disc is stylistically closer to the Sancton than to the Vermand brooch. On the other hand, the Portchester brooch possesses an early feature in its upright rim. It shares this not only with the Vermand and Fairford star-design brooches, but also with the floriate cross applied brooches of Mitcham Graves 201 and 205 (Bidder and Morris, 1959, pl. VII) which are among the earliest applied brooches in England. Its size may be indicative of an early date; a mere 30 mm. in diameter compared to the 35 to 45 mm. of the rest of the series. Thus, while a date in the sixth century cannot be ruled out, the most probable date for the Portchester disc is in the second half of the fifth century.

Grubenhaus S1, layer 29 (588)

46. Spiral-headed pin, bronze, length 50 mm., width across the head 4·5 mm. Pin of plain wire with its head formed by splitting the pin down the middle and curling the two resultant strips inwards in simple spirals. The wire thickens towards the point. Only one of the spirals survives in part, and the pin has been bent halfway along its length.

Mrs S. Hawkes has established that, with one exception, where this type of pin

[1] Nos. 1961.92 and 1961.93.

[2] No. 1886.1316. Mr P. D. C. Brown found this urn to be half full when he recently examined it. He emptied the urn and found that the glass fragments in it matched and even in some cases fitted together with those which had been removed from the urn and separately bagged with the bronze fragments between 1873 and 1886. Thus, despite a caveat in the museum register, it is almost certain that this material represents a closed find (Myres and Southern, 1973, pp. 34–5, fig. 1).

[3] Since writing the above, Mrs T. Dickinson has brought to my notice two further grave groups containing five star applied brooches. In both cases they are decorated with wavy lines in the outer borders and probably belong to the first half of the sixth century. The pair of brooches from Staxton (E. R. Yorkshire) Grave I are associated with a string of 83 amber beads, two blue glass beads and a perforated cowrie shell pendant, a second string of nine amber and three glass beads, a pair of sheet bronze wrist clasps, three bronze strap-ends, a pair of girdle hangers, an ivory ring and other bronze ornaments (Sheppard, 1938, pp. 5–8, pls. I, II, nos. 11, 13). An unpublished grave on the Tickford Park Estate, Newport Pagnell (Buckinghamshire) also contained a pair of brooches associated with 104 glass beads and a bronze bound wooden bucket. Mrs Dickinson informs me that Dr Morris's attribution of a glass claw beaker to this grave is incorrect (Bidder and Morris, 1959, p. 91).

occurs in an Anglo-Saxon datable context, it belongs in the seventh century.[1] The exception is the pin from Girton (Cambridge) Grave 25, which is claimed to be associated with small-long brooches of the sixth century (Hollingworth and O'Reilly, 1925, p. 10, pl. IV, Ib; Fox, 1923, pl. XXXIV, 3, 4), in a cemetery which has produced no other finds for which a seventh-century date could be argued.[2]

The pair of cast silver pins from Eccles (Kent) Grave 12 (Detsicas and Hawkes, 1973, fig. 4) were probably buried very late in the seventh century, as this grave disturbs Grave 23, which Mrs Hawkes dates to the second half of the seventh century. A pair of bronze pins from Worthy Park, Kingsworthy (Hampshire) Grave 62 are dated stratigraphically to some time in the seventh century.[3] Grave 7 at Bourton-on-the-Water (Gloucestershire) also produced a pair of these pins, together with possible traces of a thread which may have linked them (O'Neil, 1960–1, pp. 167–8, fig. I).[4] Mrs Pretty has claimed that a silver spiral-headed pin and a silver union pin with a garnet set head were associated in Bidford-on-Avon (Warwickshire) Grave 96 (Pretty, 1972, p. 84).[5] They are figured together (Humphreys *et al.*, 1923a, p. 104, nos. 35, 36; Humphreys, 1923b, p. 24) without any reference to their grave number. The spiral-headed pin does not appear in the grave inventory as published (Humphreys *et al.*, 1923a, pp. 111–6; Humphreys *et al.*, 1924, pp. 283–8). If they are indeed associated, however, they provide a fourth example of the use of spiral-headed pins as a poor woman's version of wearing linked, or union, pins, characteristic of the later seventh century (Hyslop, 1963, p. 198).

Two pins from Shakenoak (Oxfordshire) were discovered in sections of Ditch F with predominantly seventh-century fills (*Shakenoak III*, p. 73, fig. 31, nos. 156, 157). The pins from Broadwell, Stow on the Wold (Gloucestershire) (Donovan and Dunning, 1936, p. 163, fig. 9) and Bourton-on-the-Water Grave 7 (O'Neil, 1960–1) were found in graves in small burial grounds probably datable to the second half of the seventh century from the humped-backed knives which characterize them. Winklebury Hill (Wiltshire) is again a late cemetery, with its pair of openwork bronze mounts and iron knives (Pitt Rivers, 1888, pp. 259–67).

A previously unpublished bronze spiral-headed pin in the Museum of Kingston upon Hull is illustrated in fig. 136, no. 47.[6] It is 63 mm. long and the width across the head is 7·5 mm. There are six small grooves below the head and the shank tapers slightly towards the point. The records of the museum were entirely destroyed during the last war and the information that this pin was found at the Butts, Driffield (E. R.

[1] In a report on Anglo-Saxon graves excavated at Eccles (Detsicas and Hawkes, 1973, pp. 283–5). I am happy to be able to acknowledge my debt to Mrs Hawkes for allowing me to use her report in preparing the present note and my thanks for her advice in discussing the problems of this pin and those of the applied disc, purse mount/strike-a-light and disc brooch.

[2] It should be noted however that E. T. Leeds, when referring to this pin (Leeds, 1933, p. 249), states that it is associated with a blue head, but mentions no other associations.

[3] Unpublished from an excavation by Mrs Hawkes (Detsicas and Hawkes, 1973, p. 283, n. 7).

[4] O'Neil, 1960–1, pp. 167–8: 'A thin deposit of black dust remained under the left hand side of the lower jaw with the pin, appearing to be the last remnants of some kind of material. Some of the dust was removed and sent for analysis, but without any result. The pin on the right-hand side of the skull had stained the bone black.'

[5] The inventory describes Grave 96 as belonging to a female child, accompanied by an iron knife and 'Fragments of silver ornament, and pin set with garnet under skull' (Humphreys *et al.*, 1923a, p. 115). The spiral-headed silver pin as illustrated cannot be regarded as fragmentary.

[6] I am extremely grateful to Norma Whitcomb, Keeper of Archaeology, Kingston upon Hull, for giving me permission to publish the museum's drawing and description of this piece.

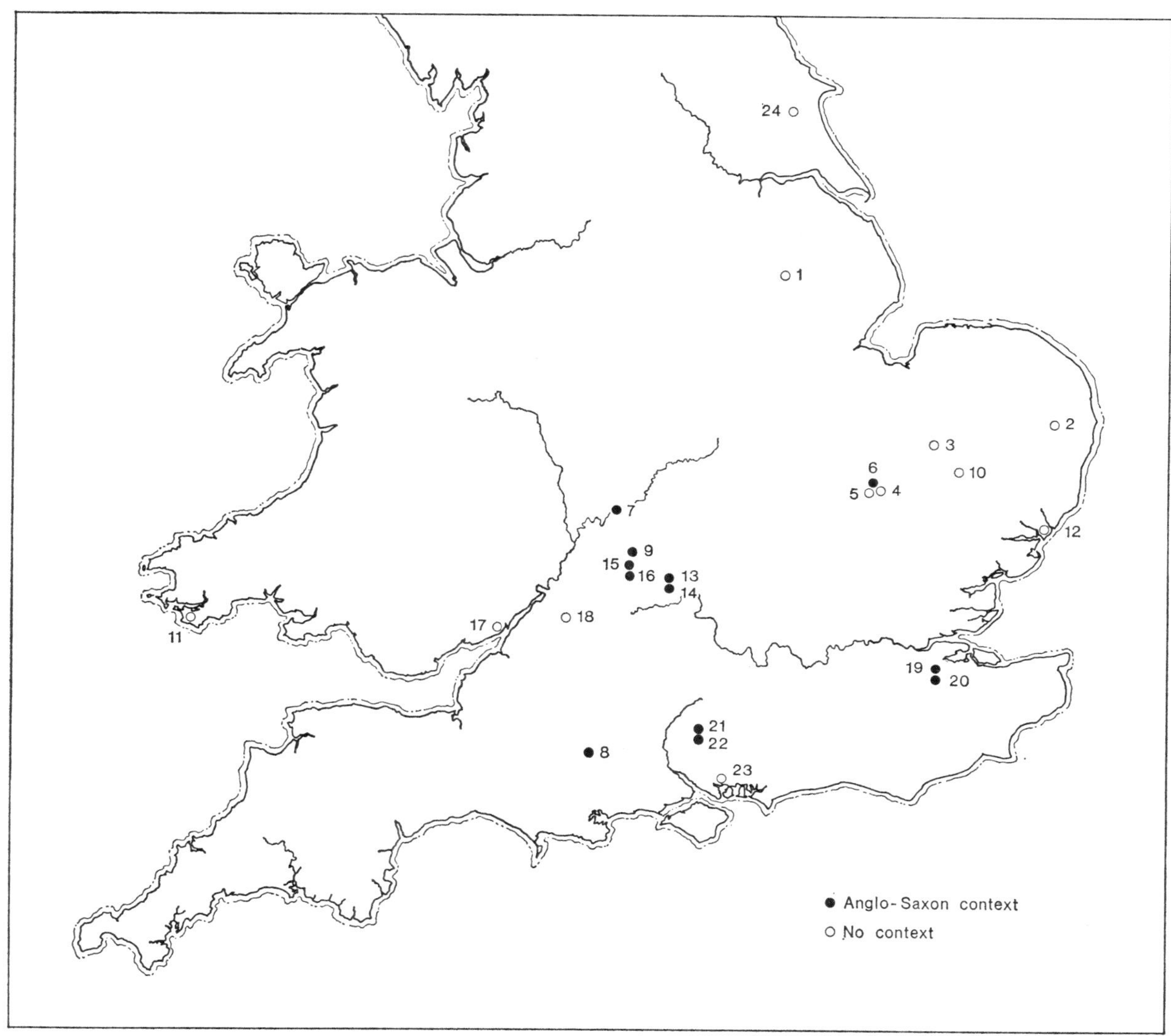

FIG. 138. Distribution of spiral-headed pins in England and Wales

1. Lincoln, Lincolnshire
2. Ellingham, Norfolk
3. Lakenheath, Suffolk
4. Cambridge, Cambridgeshire
5. Comberton, Cambridgeshire
6. Girton, Cambridgeshire, Grave 25
7. Bidford-on-Avon, Warwickshire, Grave 96
8. Winklebury, Wiltshire, Grave 2
9. Broadwell (Stow on the Wold), Gloucestershire
10. West Stow, Suffolk
11. Castlemartin, Pembrokeshire
12. Felixstowe, Suffolk
13. Shakenoak, Oxfordshire, Ditch F
14. Shakenoak, Oxfordshire, Ditch F
15. Bourton-on-the-Water, Gloucestershire, Grave 7
16. Bourton-on-the-Water, Gloucestershire, Grave 7
17. Caerwent, Monmouthshire
18. Kingscote, Gloucestershire
19. Eccles, Kent, Grave 12
20. Eccles, Kent, Grave 12
21. Worthy Park (Kingsworthy), Hampshire, Grave 62
22. Worthy Park (Kingsworthy), Hampshire, Grave 62
23. Portchester Castle, Hampshire
24. Driffield (The Butts), E. R. Yorkshire

Yorkshire) is written on the pin itself. The Butts is a large area to the south of Driffield and no closer location of this pin's findspot is possible. The grooves below the head and its size suggest that it was an Anglo-Saxon piece. It is tempting to think that this pin may have come from a seventh-century burial, perhaps associated with a group of small barrows later used to support archery butts. Mortimer's barrow C38 with its small sixth-century cemetery lies to the west of the Butts (Mortimer, 1905, pp. 271–83).[1]

Mrs Pretty has postulated a native British origin for these pins and cites three pins as coming from possible late or sub-Roman contexts at Comberton (Cambridgeshire), Caerwent (Monmouthshire), and the Chessalls, Kingscote (Gloucestershire) (Pretty, 1972, p. 85). The latter was a surface find from an area which also produced ten third- and fourth-century coins (Eagles and Swan, 1972, pp. 70, 83, fig. 5, no. 22). In the absence of excavation evidence from this site, it remains a very real possibility that this pin came from an Anglo-Saxon burial. None of the remaining pins come from firm contexts, but the only example, apart from the Caerwent pin, from a site outside of the area of Anglo-Saxon seventh-century settlement is an unusual pin from Castlemartin (Pembrokeshire) (Mathias, 1927, pp. 192, 195, fig. 4). This appears to consist of a bronze wire with two inward facing spirals fixed into a separate shaft made from a rolled bronze sheet. It is perhaps closer to the large spiral-headed pins of Early Christian Ireland, with their baluster-moulded shanks, than to the English series (*British Museum, 1923*, p. 137, fig. 183d).[2]

Nearly half the total number of spiral-headed pins in England and Wales have been found in Anglo-Saxon graves of certain or probable seventh-century date. While the possibility of a native British origin cannot be completely ruled out, all the evidence points to a seventh-century date of manufacture for the Portchester pin.

Trench 101, layer 29 (2151)

47. Spiral-headed pin from the Butts, Driffield (E. R. Yorkshire). Illustrated here for comparative purposes.

48. Hooked silver tag, with triangular plate, and two rivet-holes (inverted on figure). It has an incised plant pattern on the plate, sketchily executed (pl. XIX*a* and fig. 136).

A fairly common ninth- to tenth-century object, e.g. *British Museum 1964*, nos. 86, 87, which were found with coins dated to *c.* 970. The type has been very fully discussed by Mrs T. Dickinson (*Shakenoak*, IV, pp. 116–7), who doubts if they can be dated more generally than seventh to tenth centuries by their shape alone (cf. no. 50).

The pattern on the triangular plate is enclosed within a plain border. The plant springs from a diamond-shaped base surrounded by a cup-shaped calix from which grows a short central stem terminating in a lanceolate leaf. The calix also sprouts two side shoots, each a trumpet-like flower out of which grows a short stem with a leaf

[1] Since preparing this note, Mr R. Bradley has informed me of another bronze spiral-headed pin. It was discovered unstratified in the excavation directed by Mr B. Hooper and Mr R. Bradley at Bonhunt Farm, Wicken Bonhunt, Essex (*Essex Journal* ix (1974), 50–1, fig. 8, 2). Subsequent excavations in the area by the D.O.E. have produced a settlement site with associated Middle Saxon pottery and evidence of occupation extending into the twelfth century (Rowley, 1974, pp. 74–7).

[2] The idea of the spiral-headed pin is an extremely common one, occurring in a wide range of cultures and periods, as Mrs Pretty has noted (Pretty, 1972, p. 84). There is no obvious link between the highly ornate Irish pins and the type discussed here. It is quite possible that the Irish series developed independently.

terminal; and on the outside two downward growing curved kite-shaped leaves, that end against the junction of the stem and the calix. The back-ground is cross-hatched. The whole design is very uneven, and poorly worked.

This design is very similar to that on the reverse of the Alfred Jewel (*Ashmolean*, no. 23), which also has a plant with central cup-shaped calix, producing a central stem, two side-shoots and two downward growing leaves, against a hatched background. The tag's design may be a simplified form of the same pattern. The work on the back of the Jewel is of surprisingly poor quality. Nos. 48, 49 and 50 have interesting similarities, in that the crude incising of the patterns is such that a common workshop source must be a possibility, particularly if the design on 49 is indeed the same as on 48. If the comparison of that design to the Alfred Jewel is valid, then a craftsman (to flatter him!) with some association with the shop that produced the Jewel in the late ninth century might be suggested. There is of course no direct evidence about the location of that shop, but the two likeliest places are Glastonbury and Winchester (*Ashmolean*, 47). These three objects, from a site so close to the latter, could perhaps be seen as a very tenuous thread in the argument for Winchester.

Against this, however, is the absence of similar work on any of the strap-ends or other objects from Winchester itself.[1] A leaf design on a strap-end found in 1961 (*Winchester*, 186) has been compared to that on the back of the Alfred Jewel (*Ashmolean*, 38) but the only one with a comparable plant pattern, no. 2857 from the Brook Street excavation of 1968, has a dotted, not a hatched, background. The possibility that the Alfred Jewel, and thus by stylistic association the Portchester objects, can be connected to the Wessex capital is not being substantiated by recent finds there. It has been said in support of a Winchester source (*Ashmolean*, 41) that the lack of a royal title on the St Cuthbert stole and maniple woven for Aelflaed during the episcopacy of Frithestan, 909–31, shows that the Winchester artists did not consider such titles necessary on inscriptions, and that this would explain its absence from the Alfred Jewel, despite the titles on the earlier Aethelswith and Aethelwulf rings (*British Museum 1964*, nos. 1, 31). The title may have been omitted from the embroideries for a more specific reason, however; Asser relates that the West Saxons did not dignify their king's consort with the title of queen, after their disastrous experience of Offa's daughter Eadburh (*Asser*, 11–12). The title was not therefore used on the embroideries, although it was of course used on the Aethelswith ring as Aethelswith was queen of Mercia, not of Wessex.

This may be an interesting example of historical narrative bearing on archaeological survivals, and a further justification of the veracity of Asser, but it does not help the explanation of the title's omission from the Alfred Jewel. I was wrong to say (*Ashmolean*, 40) that the inscription is the only one on metalwork to use the commissioner formula, for the Brussels Cross (*Hand-List*, no. 17) has *het wirican* (=ordered to be made), although it may at least be relevant that the three brothers named in that text have been claimed to be members of the Wessex royal house. The Alfred Jewel cannot be proved conclusively to be from a workshop at Winchester, and so the Portchester objects may not be from there either.

Trench 99, layer 18 (1882)

[1] I am grateful to Mr Martin Biddle for allowing me to examine and refer to the objects from his excavations.

49. Silver strap-end, having stylized animal head terminal, and a very lightly incised and much worn pattern on the plate (pl. XIX*c* and fig. 136).

This appears to be a plant pattern, with a cross-hatched background, sketchily executed. Two dome-headed rivets survive in the split end. Regional variations of the ubiquitous strap-ends of the ninth and tenth centuries have not yet been plotted. The ears on the animal have lunate incisions (e.g. *Ashmolean*, no. 29), a common feature. It is possible to see a kite-shaped leaf growing up the centre of the plate, a form for which there are late ninth- to early tenth-century parallels (*Ashmolean*, nos. 1, 23). This leaf has two curved lines across it to suggest fullness, a typical Trewhiddle style trick. It is flanked by two other leaves, the one on the right perhaps being lanceolate (cf. again *Ashmolean*, no. 1). These are on short stems, possibly rising from a cup-shaped calix, which may grow from a base formed by an inverted V.

If this interpretation is correct, it is a very similar pattern to that on no. 48.

Trench 94, layer 37 (1591)

50. Hooked bronze tag, with triangular plate and two rivet-holes (pl. XIX*b* and fig. 136).

It has an incised design on the plate of a line of three intersecting double-lined triangles and the top of a fourth within the border, very crudely worked. See 48 for a discussion of such tags. The design is probably not very significant, although three interwoven triangles are seen on the River Nene ring (*British Museum 1964*, no. 57), and the triangle can be a symbol of the Trinity.

Unstratified (1098)

51. Bronze strip, one end straight, the other rounded, folded over double. It has three rivet-holes in the round end, and two in the straight end. A tapered bronze rivet survives in one, pushed through from the rounded side, and its point bent back against the straight side.

Buckle plates from Sevington (ninth century: *British Museum 1964*, no. 79), *Eaton Socon* (eleventh to early twelfth centuries, fig. 11, no. 18) and *Seacourt* (medieval, fig. 28, no. 8), are made like this, but are either pierced for the pin, or reduced in width for the loop, at the folded end. This may just be a simple belt- or strap-end.

Pit 37 (112)

52. Bronze tag-end, styliform, flat reverse, rounded top, with two rivet-holes in the split end, incised contour lines on the plate, transverse grooves on stem in bands, the end faceted. The last feature may be a very stylized animal head, as seen on strap-ends of the ninth to tenth centuries (e.g. *Ashmolean*, no. 16). A closer parallel is *Maxey*, fig. 17, no. 2, a round-shafted tag-end found with Middle Saxon pottery (cf. also *Southampton*, 70, figs. 27, nos. 1, 2; *North Elmham*, fig. 19, J; and an example from Winchester, inventory number 1638).

Trench 103, layer 11 (2197)

53. Bronze clasp with kite-shaped plate and two hooks at the wider end. The other end has snapped off. The plate appears to have a silver or tinned panel, but any pattern on this has been rubbed off, and the only remaining decoration is a border of punched dots in the bronze at the edge of the plate. The back is plain, but has a superficial corrosion that may be from whatever the object was attached to. If this is so, it seems to have been metal rather than cloth or leather, as there are no signs of fibres. If it had been a

manuscript cover clasp, it would have required two rivet-holes just behind the hooks.

Shape and beading perhaps derived from Frankish strap-ends, e.g. Baldwin Brown, Vol. IV, pls. CLII, 1, 12; CCIII, 1.

Trench 101, layer 36 (2270)

54. Bronze pin, shaft broken, with six-sided flat head.

For square-headed forms cf. *Maxey*, fig. 17, no. 2, and *Southampton*, fig. 26, no. 11.

Pit 220 (2462)

55. Three bronze fragments including a small broken buckle loop and hook and two plates joined by a rivet as though part of a belt fitting.

Pit 207 (2268)

56. Bronze pin with broken head; there is a slight thickening below the head.

Pit 194 (2099)

57. Bronze tag-end or similar object, composed of a sheet folded into an incomplete tube, one end with grooves and a rivet-hole, the other widened out. Cf. *North Elmham*, fig. 20, B, from a late ninth- to tenth-century deposit.

Pit 135 (1400)

58. Bronze finger ring, plain round hoop with a small bulge for a bezel beside which the hoop is grooved. Probably too small to have held a setting.

Pit 135 (1407)

59. Gold finger ring, plain round hoop with a bulge for a bezel to hold a small stone. Its shape suggests a twelfth-century or later date.

Pit 111 (839)

60. Flat disc with two attachment holes near the edge. One side has incised lines forming a round-armed cross in the centre, the sides produced to the edge, and a further line cut from the centre of each cross arm to the edge. The cross is the round-armed 'Anglian' type suggesting a Saxon date (e.g. *British Museum 1964*, nos. 20, 111, 113). A bronze disc with an identical design and two rivet holes, but with a small hook protruding from the side opposite these, has been recorded from a probable eighth- to tenth-century context at Glastonbury. For this, a function as a book-lid fastening is suggested (*Glastonbury*, fig. 23, no. 14).

Trench 90, layer 13 (1149)

61. Bronze object, possibly a hook from a brooch.

Pit 135 (1408)

62. Gilt bronze decorative binding, a Y-shaped piece, one arm of the Y ending in a broken attachment hole, another in the stem at the junction. Beyond, the stem divides into an open circle, now broken.

Pit 56 (235)

63. Gilt bronze decorative binding strip, a length of semi-circular section, one end now broken, the other opening to an embossed disc with a nail hole for attachment. Presumably to be associated with no. 62.

Bronze binding strips for nailing to a box or casket. Such straps are usually twelfth- to thirteenth-century (Jope, 1959, 267–8), but a late Saxon date is indicated here by the context. A strip from below the rampart at Wareham (Royal Commission, 1959, pp.

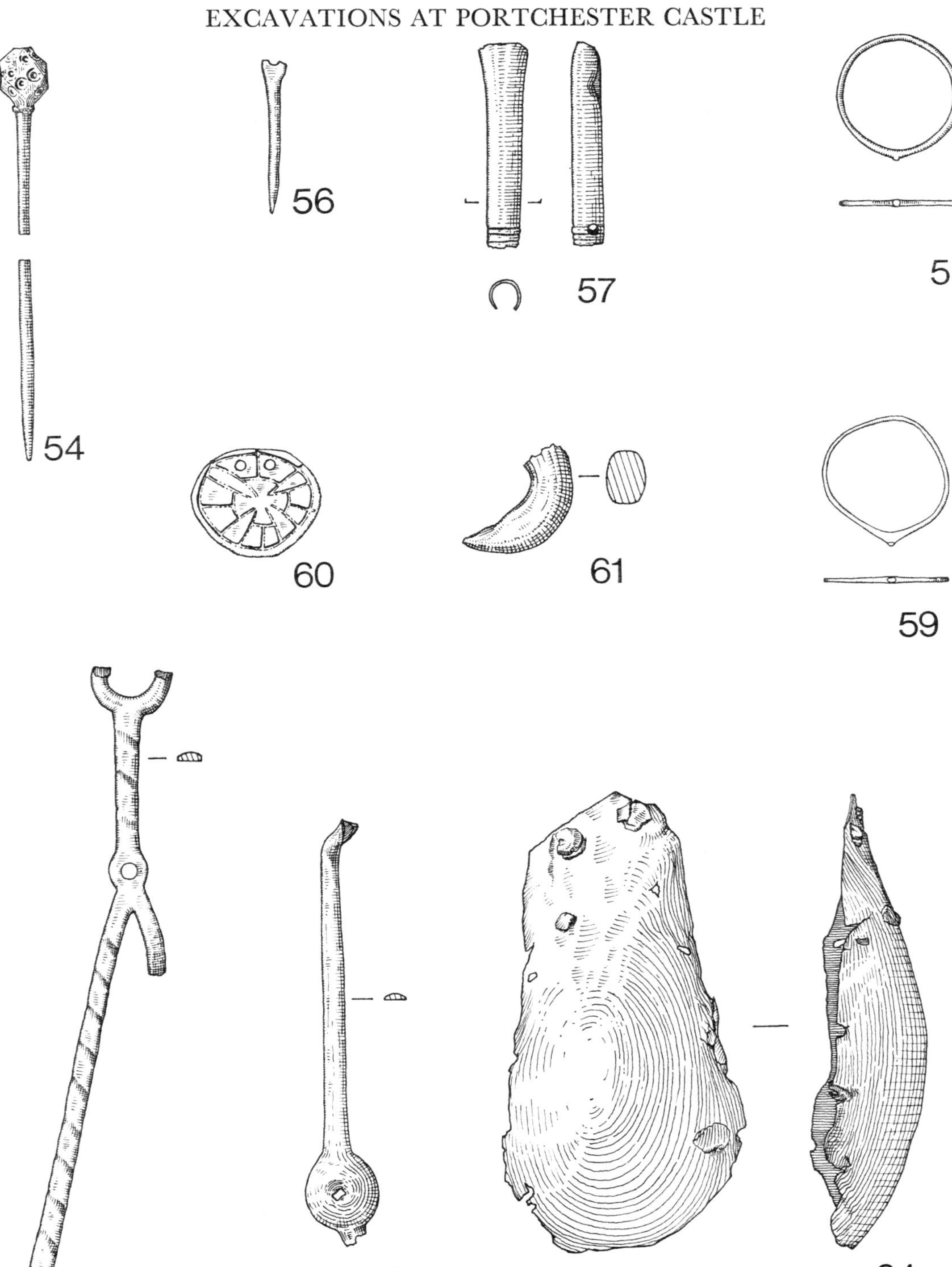

FIG. 139. Objects of copper alloy (pp. 217–9). Scale $\frac{2}{3}$

136–7) was considered intrusive by the excavators but the Portchester example makes a Saxon date for it more probable.

Pit 56 (236)

64. Bronze sheet, convex, with rivets and rivet-holes along the edges. Possibly a repair patch.

Pit 135 (1396)

Objects of Bone

65. Pin-beater. Common in late Saxon/early medieval contexts. Cf. *Southampton*, fig. 29; *Swinbrook*, fig. 1, 13.

Pit 56 (238)

66. Bone pin with triangular head. Cf. *Southampton*, pl. VIB, bottom row.

Pit 135 (1060)

67. Bone strip with diagonal cuts roughly made across it. A rivet-hole at one end. Cf. *Southampton*, pl. VII, nos. 363–69. Possibly part of a comb case.

Pit 39 (220)

68. Bone handle? The centre is hollow, one face is smoothed flat and one end is cut to form two horn-like finials which show signs of considerable wear.

Trench 108, layer 42 (2547)

69. Curved bone strip with a rivet-hole bordered by two transverse grooves on the outer face. Another groove at the broken end. Possibly to be sewn on to a textile as a stiffener.

Pit 135 (1946)

70. Tubular bone handle with incised spiral grooves and two circumferential grooves at each end.

Pit 135 (1830)

71. Roughly cut curved handle with the straight end cut to enclose a blade held in place by a rivet. The inside of the handle end is V-shaped. This would either securely lodge a blade cut to the reverse V at the end (perhaps for a saw) or would allow a bevelled end to swivel so that it could be housed against the inside of the blade when closed.

Pit 203 (2199)

72. Part of a double-sided comb, being a blade with the end parts of the two ribs, held by an iron rivet. A further rivet-hole appears at this broken end. The ribs are both decorated on the face with transverse incised lines forming panels in which are diagonal double lines. The upper edges of the ribs are nicked by saw cuts caused by the cutting of the teeth after the blade had been mounted between the ribs (*Southampton*, 75).

Pit 207 (2286)

73. Iron rivet and bone fragment from another comb.

Pit 38 (207)

74. A piece of the middle section of a double-sided comb, one edge showing part of a rivet-hole, with staining from the iron rivet.

Pit 220 (2523)

75. Double ended thread-picker, with deeply incised double spiral grooves in the centre. (These grooves would necessitate an accurately centred lathe.) For a thread-picker

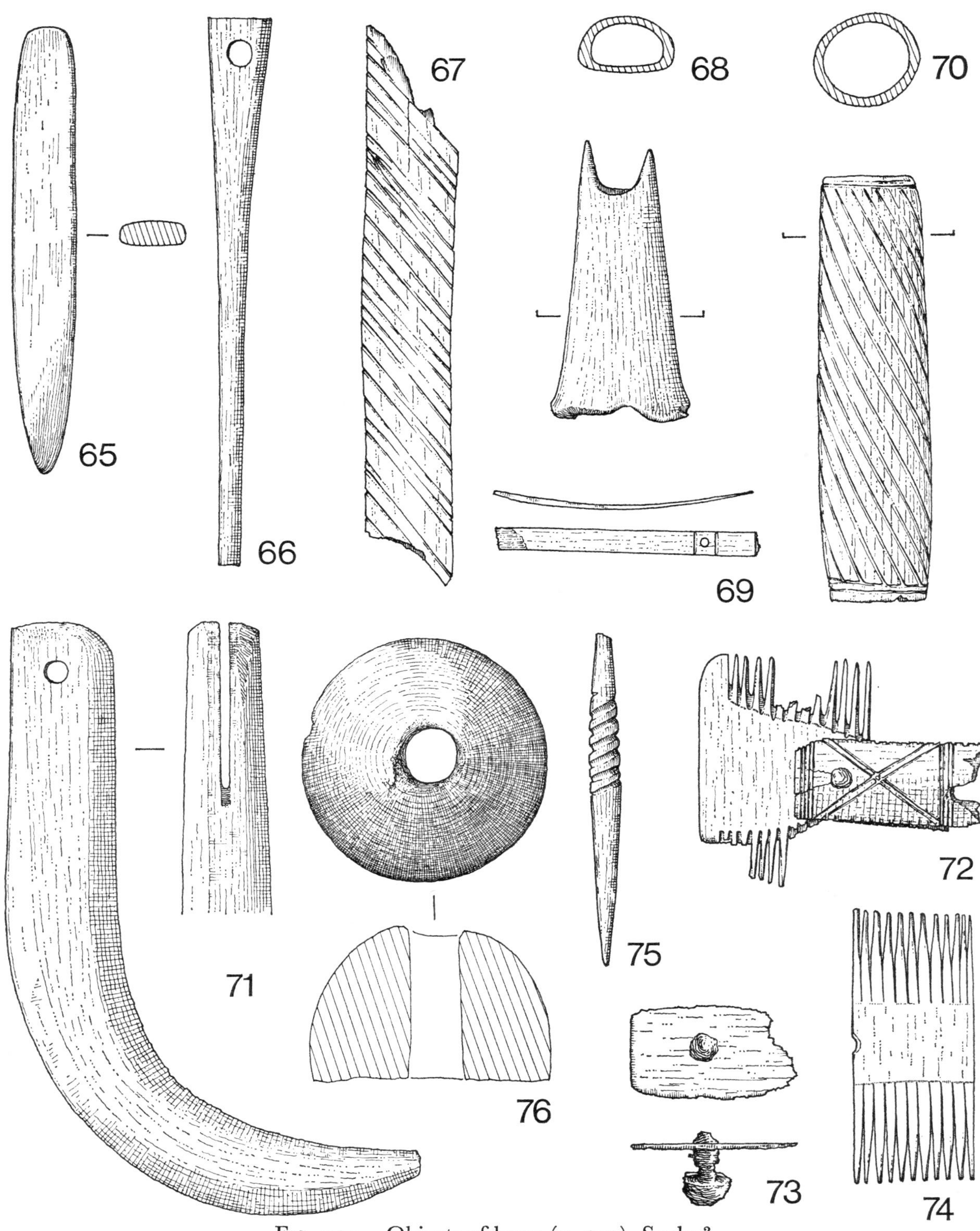

FIG. 140. Objects of bone (p. 219). Scale $\frac{2}{3}$

with central decoration cf. *Southampton*, pl. VIIb, top. Very deep grooving is unusual.
Trench 109, layer 13 (2604)

76. Bone spindle whorl, bun-shaped type. *Southampton*, 72.
Pit 113 (943)

Objects of Lead

77. Piece of flat lead sheet with one edge wrenched off. One side has an incised line forming a rectangle approximately parallel to the edges. The other bears a scratched graffito.
Trench 91, layer 30 (1249)

Objects of Clay

78. Part of the side and base of a small round crucible with a vertically set lug rising above the rim. Crucibles are quite common in late Saxon contexts, e.g. the series from the Angel Inn site, Oxford. Examples with vertical lugs are unusual.
Pit 194 (2208)

79. Annular loom weight made from coarse fabric fired red. Finger mouldings still apparent.
From the floor of sunken hut S1 (no small finds number)

Objects of Stone

80. Bun-shaped shale spindle whorl with grooves and knife cuts on the top. Cf. *Southampton*, fig. 29.
Pit 192 (2078)

81. Annular shale spindle whorl with knife cuts on the top.
Pit 38 (114)

82. Bun-shaped chalk spindle whorl.
Pit 156 (1828)

83. Carved stone fragment, possibly part of the arm of a cross. Undecorated. Green coloured limestone.
From grave 18

Whetstones

By David Peacock

84. (Not illustrated). Whetstone. Fragment of rectangular shaped whetstone in indurated, dark grey, fine sandstone with some mica.
Pit 135 (1393)

85. (Not illustrated). Fragment of whetstone: rock similar to no. 88.
Pit 135 (1691)

86. Complete shaped whetstone in brown, fine-grained silicous rock with fine veining in paler brown silica. ?Chert.
Pit 207 (2290)

87. (Not illustrated). Slab of indurated fine grey sandstone used as whetstone.
Pit 135 (1197)

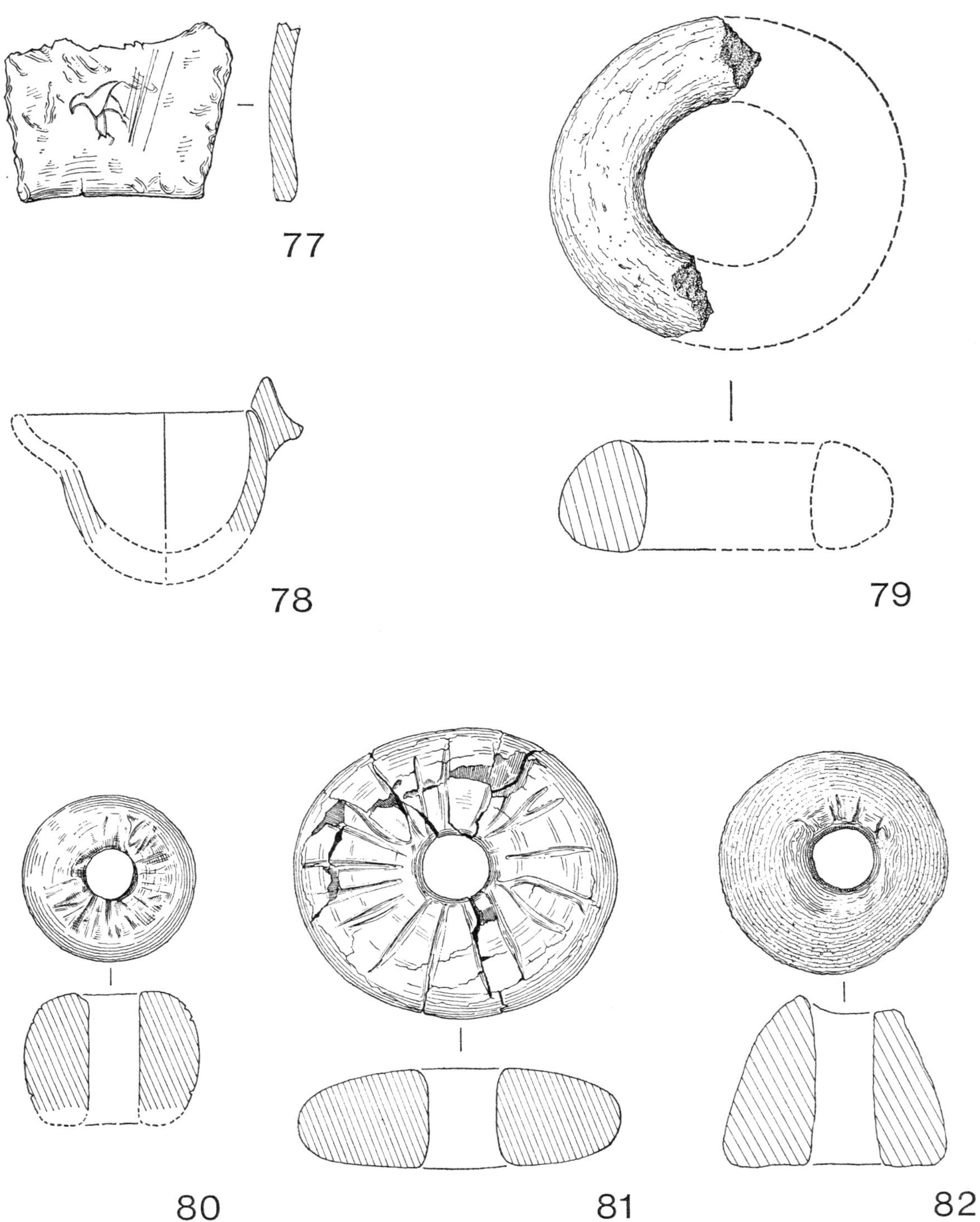

Fig. 141. Objects of lead, clay, shale and chalk (p. 221). Scale: 77–9, $\frac{1}{3}$; remainder, $\frac{2}{3}$

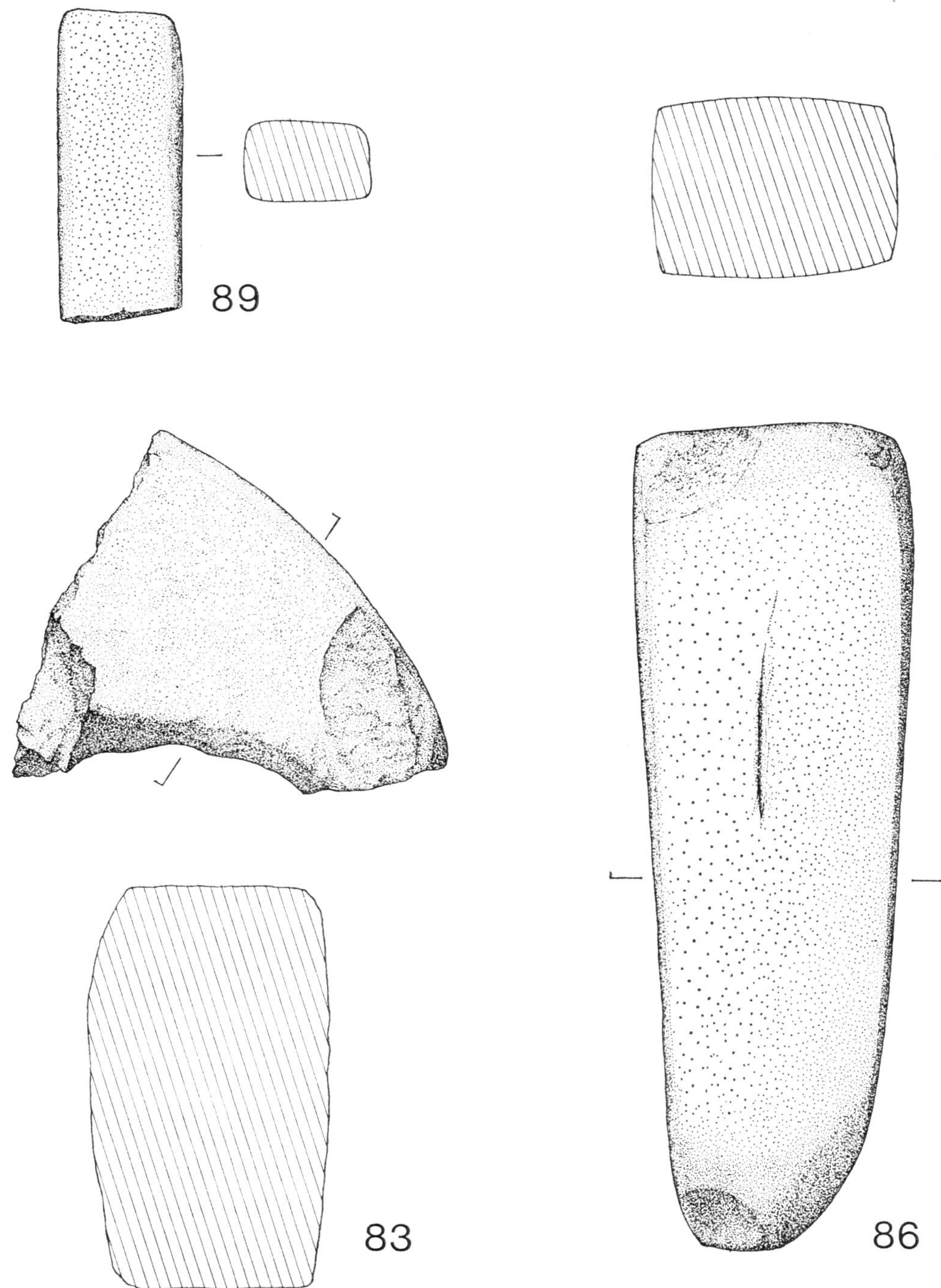

FIG. 142. Objects of stone (pp. 221, 224). Scale: 83, ⅓; remainder, ⅔

88. (Not illustrated). Fragment of rectangular shaped whetstone in grey sandy limestone.
Pit 135 (1411)
89. Whetstone. Fragment only.
Saxon hut S1 (840)

The whetstone fragments were examined in the hand specimen. None of these rocks need be local. Nos. 85 and 88 compare closely with Roman specimens from Portchester believed to originate in the Hythe beds of Kent, and thus their presence in post-Roman levels could be due to survival as rubbish. The remaining specimens would be difficult to match in the Hampshire Basin. Their hard indurated nature suggests a source in the older Palaeozoic rocks, perhaps of Western Britain or Brittany.

Wood (fig. 143)

90. Wooden object, now in three pieces but originally complete. The object is made from a branch whittled down to a thin flat cross-section. One end is slightly expanded and perforated to take a wooden peg which is still in position. At the other end a peg-like projection of similar dimensions was fashioned from a small branch which grew at right angles to the main stem. Both 'pegs' were perforated, presumably to take a string. The function of the object is uncertain, but a string stretched between the pegs would create a bow for which a craft use would be possible.
Well (pit) 135, layer 100 (1563)
91. Fragment from one end of a similar object.
Well (pit) 135, layer 100 (1565)
92–95. (Pl. XX*a*). Four wooden cores resulting from lathe-turning. Three are narrow and elongated with a centring point but no obvious means of attachment to the chuck. The point of one had been roughly whittled after it was detached. The bun-shaped core is evidently from the turning of a different kind of object. It has a square-sectioned chuck hole, 1 cm. across, cut into the base.
All from well (pit) 135, layer 100 (1562, 1566, 1574, 1575)

A number of other wooden fragments from the well show signs of whittling of different kinds, but they do not have a recognizable form and are therefore not illustrated in detail (pl. XX*b*, *c*).

Worked Bone and Antler

By Judi Startin

96. Antler tine. This piece is 5½ in. (14 cm.) long and chopped close to the beam. The tip is smoothed, but this probably occurred naturally.
Pit 135 (1422)
97. Antler beam. This is 5¼ in. (13 cm.) long and worked at both ends. The end nearest the burr of the antler was sawn from one side only.
Pit 135 (1417)
98. Antler ?beam. This is 3¼ in. (8·5 cm.) long and worked at both ends. One end was

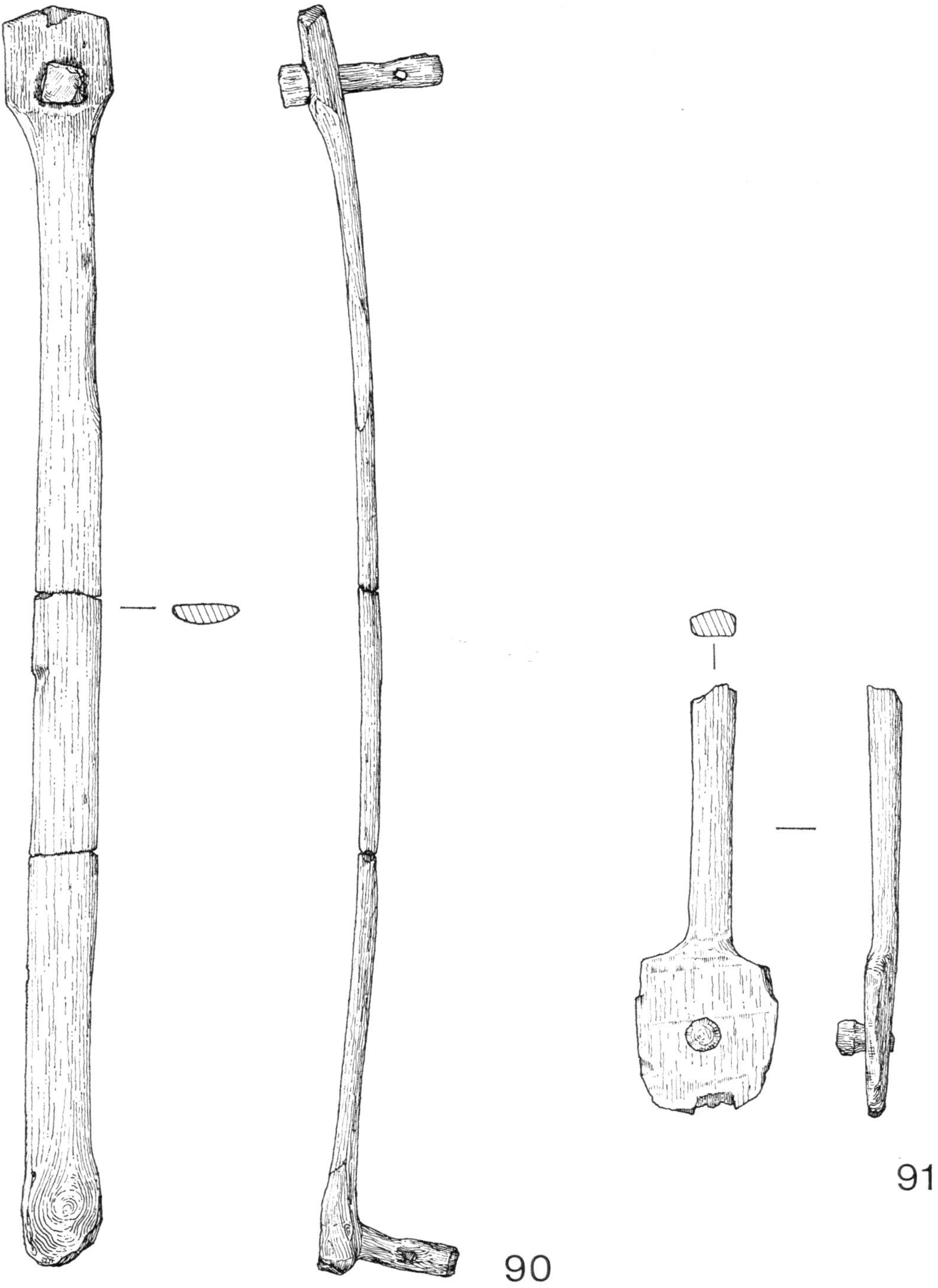

FIG. 143. Objects of wood (p. 224). Scale $\frac{1}{3}$

sawn, and split longitudinally for 1½ in. (4 cm.). The other end was chopped, and slightly smoothed. The surface is partially smoothed.

Pit 135 (1418)

99. Cut bone. This is a 5 in. (12 cm.) long fragment of a long bone, probably of sheep. It was split length-ways, and the remaining surface was shaved and whittled.

100. Worked bone. Complete sheep metacarpal, which has been squared off at the proximal end.

Trench 108, layer 66

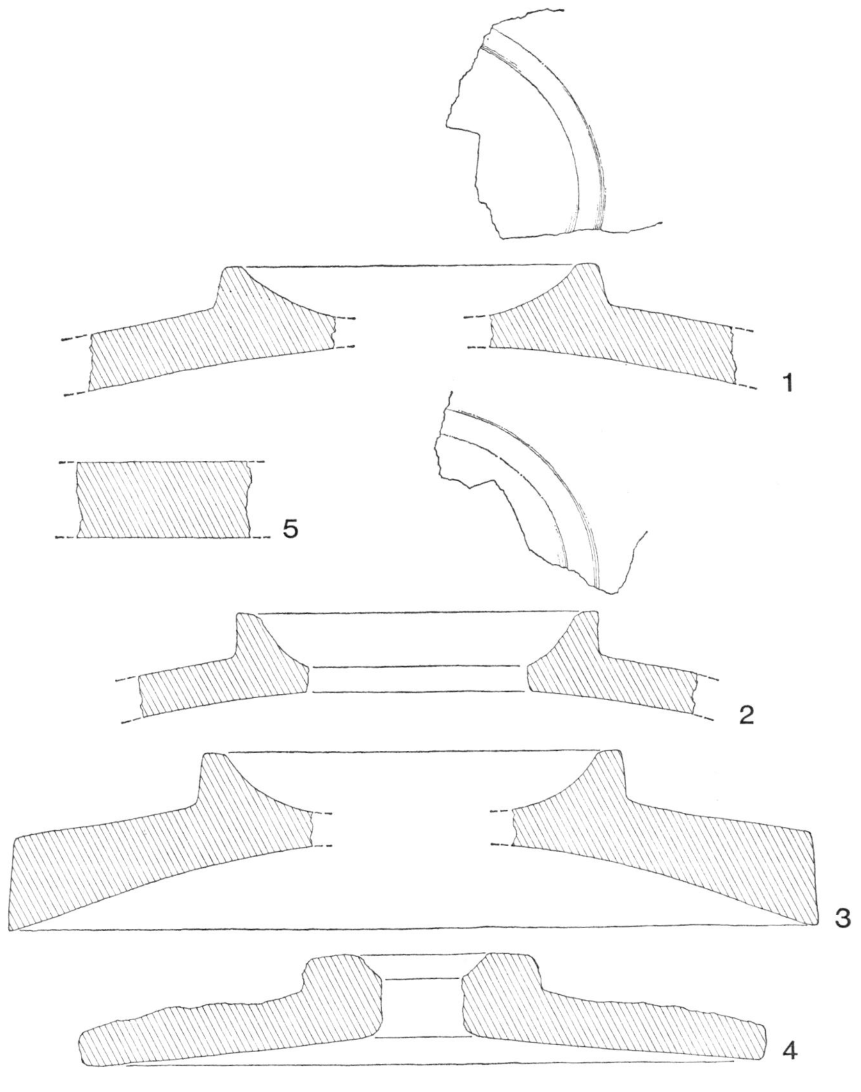

Fig. 144. Quernstones (p. 227). Scale ¼

101. Worked bone. Fragment of a sheep metacarpal, which has been perforated at the proximal end.

Trench 108, layer 22

Other small indeterminate fragments of worked bone and antler have been recorded from trench 54, layer 14; trench 88, layer 85; trench 107, layer 9; and trench 108, layer 48.

Querns (fig. 144)

1. Upper greensand: trench 3, layer 3.
2. Upper greensand: trench 60, layer 5.
3. Upper greensand: trench 18, layer 10.
4. Niedermendig or Mayen Lava: unstratified.
5. Arkosic grit (import?): trench 101, layer 101 (2215), pit 204.
6. (Not illustrated). Millstone grit: the upper surface has roughly chiselled grooves about 1 cm. apart: trench 89, layer 37 (1175).
7. (Not illustrated). Niedermendig or Mayen Lava: trench 82, layer 19.

Of the querns illustrated and described above, only two, nos. 5 and 7, were found in closed Saxon deposits. The remainder are from layers containing both Saxon and medieval material. They are illustrated here because they conform to generalized Saxon types, although an early medieval date cannot be ruled out.

BIBLIOGRAPHY

A. Authors

AKERMAN, J. Y. 1853. 'An account of excavations in an Anglo-Saxon burial ground at Harnham Hill, near Salisbury.' *Archaeologia* xxxv, 259–78.

AKERMAN, J. Y. 1863. 'Report on further researches in an Anglo-Saxon burial ground at Long Wittenham, Berkshire, in the summer of 1860.' *Archaeologia* xxxix, 135–42.

ASSER: W. H. Stevenson, *Asser's Life of King Alfred* (1904).

BALDWIN BROWN, G. 1909–37. *The Arts in Early England.*

BIDDER, H. F. and MORRIS, J. 1959. 'The Anglo-Saxon cemetery at Mitcham.' *Surrey Arch. Coll.* lvi, 51–131.

BÖHME, H. W. 1974. *Germanische Grabfunde des 4. bis 5. Jahrhunderts zwischen unterer Elbe und Loire.*

COLLINS, A. E. P. 1952–3. 'Excavations on Blewburton Hill, 1948 and 1949.' *Berks. Arch. J.* liii, 21–64.

COTTON, M. A. and GATHERCOLE, P. W. 1958. *Excavations at Clausentum, Southampton 1951–1954.*

CUNLIFFE, B. W. 1970. 'The Saxon culture-sequence at Portchester Castle.' *Antiq. J.* l, 67–85.

DONOVAN, H. E. and DUNNING, G. C. 1936. 'Iron Age pottery and Saxon burials at Foxcote Manor, Andoversford, Gloucestershire.' *Trans. Bristol and Gloucs. Arch. Soc.* lviii, 157–70.

DETSICAS, A. P. and HAWKES, S. C. 1973. 'Finds from the Anglo-Saxon cemetery at Eccles.' *Antiq. J.* liii, 281–6.

EAGLES, B. N. and SWAN, V. G. 1972. 'The Chessalls, a Romano-British settlement at Kingscote.' *Trans. Bristol and Gloucs. Arch. Soc.* xci, 60–91.

ECK, T. 1891. *Les deux cimetières gallo-romains de Vermand et de Saint-Quentin.*

EVISON, V. I. 1955. 'Early Anglo-Saxon inlaid metalwork.' *Antiq. J.* xxxv, 20–45.

EVISON, V. I. 1958. 'Further Anglo-Saxon inlay.' *Antiq. J.* xxxviii, 240–4.

EVISON, V. I. 1965. *The Fifth Century Invasions South of the Thames.*

FOSTER, W. K. 1880–4. 'Account of the excavation of an Anglo-Saxon cemetery at Barrington, Cambridgeshire.' *Camb. Antiq. Comm.* v, 5–32.

FOX, C. 1923. *The Archaeology of the Cambridge Region.*

GODFREY-FAUSSETT, T. G. 1876. 'The Saxon cemetery at Bifrons.' *Arch. Cant.* x, 298–315.

GRIFFITH, A. F. and SALZMANN, L. F. 1914. 'An Anglo-Saxon cemetery at Alfriston, Sussex.' *Sussex Arch. Coll.* lvi, 16–51.

HARDEN, D. B. 1956. 'Glass vessels in Britain and Ireland. A.D. 400–1000.' In D. B. Harden (ed.), *Dark Age Britain*, 132–167.

HAWKES, S. C. and DUNNING, G. C. 1961. 'Soldiers and settlers in Britain, fourth to fifth century.' *Med. Arch.* v, 1–70.

HOLLINGWORTH, E. J. and O'REILLY, M. M. 1925. *The Anglo-Saxon Cemetery at Girton College, Cambridge.*

HUMPHREYS, J., RYLAND, J. W., BARNARD, E. A. B., WELLSTOOD, F. C. and BARNETT, T. G. 1923a. 'An Anglo-Saxon cemetery at Bidford-on-Avon, Warwickshire.' *Archaeologia* lxxiii, 89–116.

HUMPHREYS, J. 1923b. 'Excavations of an Anglo-Saxon cemetery at Bidford-on-Avon, Warwickshire, 1922 and 1923.' *Trans. Birmingham Arch. Soc.* xlix, 16–25.

HUMPHREYS, J., RYLAND, J. W., BARNARD, E. A. B., WELLSTOOD, F. C. and BARNETT, T. G. 1924. 'An Anglo-Saxon cemetery at Bidford-on-Avon, Warwickshire: second report on the excavations.' *Archaeologia* lxxiv, 271–88.

HYSLOP, M. 1963. 'Two Anglo-Saxon cemeteries at Chamberlains Barn, Leighton Buzzard, Bedfordshire.' *Arch. J.* cxx, 161–200.

JOPE, E. M. 1959. 'The twelfth century castle of Ascott Doilly, Oxfordshire.' *Antiq. J.* xxxix, 219–73.

LEEDS, E. T. 1933. 'The early Saxon penetration of the Upper Thames area.' *Antiq. J.* xiii, 229–51.

LEEDS, E. T. 1949. *A Corpus of Early Anglo-Saxon Great Square-headed Brooches.*

LETHBRIDGE, T. C. 1931. *The Anglo-Saxon Cemetery at Holywell (or Hollywell) Row, Suffolk.*

LETHBRIDGE, T. C. 1951. *A Cemetery at Lackford, Suffolk.*

LOWTHER, A. W. G. 1931. 'The Saxon cemetery at Guildown, Surrey.' *Surrey Arch. Coll.* xxxix, 1–50.

MATHIAS, A. G. O. 1927. 'South Pembrokeshire early settlements.' *Arch. Camb.* lxxxii, 188–95.

MERTENS, J. and VAN IMPE, L. 1971. 'Het Laat-Romeins Grafveld van Oudenburg.' *Archaeologia Belgica*, cxxxv.

MORTIMER, J. R. 1905. *Forty Years' Researches in British and Saxon Burial Mounds of East Yorkshire.*

MYRES, J. N. L. 1969. *Anglo-Saxon Pottery and the Settlement of England.*

MYRES, J. N. L. and SOUTHERN, W. H. 1973. *The Anglo-Saxon Cremation Cemetery at Sancton, East Yorkshire.*

O'NEIL, H. E. 1960–1. 'Saxon burials in the Fosse Way at Bourton-on-the-Water, Glos.' *Proc. Cotteswold Naturalists Field Club* xxxiii, 166–9.

PILLOY, J. 1895. *Etudes sur d'anciens lieux de sépultures dans l'Aisne*, II.

PIRLING, R. 1966. *Das römisch-fränkische Gräberfeld von Krefeld-Gellep.*

PITT RIVERS, A. 1888. *Excavations in Cranborne Chase*, II, 259–67.

PRETTY, K. 1972. 'Two bronze spiral-headed pins.' In *Shakenoak*, III, 84–5.

READ, C. H. 1895. 'On excavations in a cemetery of South Saxons on High Down, Sussex.' *Archaeologia* liv, 369–82.

ROES, A. 1967. 'Taschenbügel und Feuerstahle.' *Bonner Jahrbücher* clxvii, 285–99.

ROWLEY, T. (ed.) 1974. *Anglo-Saxon Settlement and Landscape.*

ROYAL COMMISSION 1959. 'Wareham West Walls.' *Med. Arch.* iii, 120–38.

SALIN, B. 1904. *Die altgermanische Thierornamentik.*

SHEPPARD, T. 1938. *Anglo-Saxon Cemeteries in East Yorkshire.*

SWANTON, M. 1963–6. 'An Anglian Cemetery at Londesborough in East Yorkshire.' *Yorks. Arch. J.* xli, 262–86.

TESTER, P. J. 1969. 'Excavations at Fordcroft, Orpington.' *Arch. Cant.* lxxxiv, 39–77.

WALLER, K. 1957. *Das Gräberfeld von Altenwalde Kreis Land Hadeln.*
WARHURST, A. 1955. 'The Jutish cemetery at Lyminge.' *Arch. Cant.* lxix, 1–40.
WILSON, A. E. and GERARD, E. 1947. *Guide to the Anglo-Saxon Collection* (Worthing Museum).

B. Sites

Clough Castle: D. M. Waterman, 'Excavations at Clough Castle, Co. Down.' *Ulster J. Arch.* 3rd series, xvii (1954), 103–68.
Eaton Socon: P. V. Addyman, 'Late Saxon settlements in the St. Neots Area.' *Proc. Camb. Antiq. Soc.* lviii (1965), 38–73.
Maxey: P. V. Addyman, 'A Dark-Age settlement at Maxey, Northants.' *Med. Arch.* viii (1964), 20–73.
North Elmham: P. Wade-Martins, 'Excavations at North Elmham, 1969: an interim report.' *Norfolk Arch.* xxxv, part I (1970), 25–78.
St. Neots 1: T. C. Lethbridge and C. F. Tebbutt, 'Huts of the Anglo-Saxon period.' *Proc. Camb. Antiq. Soc.* xxxiii (1933), 133–51.
St. Neots 2: P. V. Addyman, 'Late Saxon settlements in the St. Neots area.' *Proc. Camb. Antiq. Soc.* lxiv (1973), 44–99.
Seacourt: M. Biddle, 'The deserted Medieval village of Seacourt, Berkshire.' *Oxoniensia* xxvi/xxvii (1961–2), 70–201.
Shakenoak: A. C. C. Brodribb, A. R. Hands and D. R. Walker, *Excavations at Shakenoak*, 4 vols. (1968–73).
Southampton: P. V. Addyman and D. H. Hill, 'Saxon Southampton. Part II. *Proc. Hants Field Club* xxvi (1969), 61–96.
Swinbrook: 'Medieval pottery from Swinbrook, Oxon.' *Oxoniensia* xxxvi (1971), 107–10.
Winchester: V. I. Evison, in M. Biddle and R. N. Quirk, 'Excavations near Winchester Cathedral.' *Arch. J.* cxix (1962), 150–94.

C. Catalogues

Ashmolean: David A. Hinton, *A Catalogue of the Anglo-Saxon Ornamental Metalwork, 700–1100, in the Department of Antiquities, Ashmolean Museum* (1974).
British Museum, 1922: A Guide to the Antiquities of Roman Britain.
British Museum, 1923: A Guide to the Anglo-Saxon and Foreign Teutonic Antiquities.
British Museum, 1964: David M. Wilson, *Anglo-Saxon Ornamental Metalwork, 700–1100, in the British Museum.*
Hand-List: E. Okasha, *Hand-List of Anglo-Saxon Non-Runic Inscriptions* (1971).
LMMC: London Museum: Medieval Catalogue (1940).

V. THE COINS

By H. E. Pagan

THE excavations at Portchester produced two Anglo-Saxon coins, both of King Burgred of Mercia (852–74). This raises to four the total of coins of the Anglo-Saxon period known to have been found in the Portchester area. All are of ninth-century date and they may be listed as follows:

Anglo-Saxon

1. Coenwulf of Mercia (796–821). Æ penny.
Obv. +OEИVVLF REXT̄ Bust r., diademed.
Rev. +SIGESTEF TONET Letter Ꭿ in centre.
Die axis: ↑ Weight: 16·8 grains (slightly chipped).

Coin in British Museum (*BMC* 79), purchased Sotheby sale 16–18 July 1850 ('Miscellaneous collection of Greek, Roman and English coins, the property of a gentleman'), lot 355, where it is described as 'dug up in a field near Portchester Castle 1844'.

Sigestef was a moneyer for Kings Coenwulf and Ceolwulf of Mercia, Baldred of Kent and Ecgberht of Wessex and for an issue without a king's name struck intermediate between coins of Ceolwulf and Baldred. His operations may be dated *c.* 820–8 and his coins for Coenwulf *c.* 820–1.[1] He worked at a mint available in turn to all the rulers mentioned and that can be identified as Canterbury; it was not the other ninth-century Kentish mint, Rochester, the coins of which are of a different style.

The letter Ꭿ in the centre of the reverse has been explained as the final *a* of the word *moneta*.[2]

2. Burgred of Mercia (852–74). Æ penny.
Obv. BVRGRED REX- Bust r., diademed, pellets on breast.
Rev. DYDPIHE/MON/ETA ∵ in three lines, MON and ETA ∵ contained in whole lunettes (*BMC* type A).
Die-axis: ↑ Weight: 17·6 grains.
Current excavations: trench 95, layer 61 (1598).

3. Burgred of Mercia (852–74). Æ penny.
Obv. +BVRG[RED RE]+
Rev. Reading not certain, perhaps [DI] ẠṚVLF/MON/[ET] A ∵; inscription divided by beaded horizontal bars (*BMC* type D).
Die-axis: → Weight: 12·3 grains (fragmentary).
Current excavations: trench 96, layer 23 (1726)

Hoard evidence demonstrates that virtually the whole of Burgred's coinage was struck between *c.* 863 and 874.[3] These coins are of similar style to coins known to have been present in the 1838 Gravesend hoard, deposited *c.* 871, which were neither the earliest

[1] C. E. Blunt, C. S. S. Lyon and B. H. I. H. Stewart, 'The coinage of Southern England 796–840.' *BNJ* xxxii (1963), 1–74, especially 13–19.

[2] Op. cit., 13.

[3] H. E. Pagan, 'Coinage in the age of Burgred'. *BNJ* xxxiv (1965), 11–27.

nor the latest of the coins of Burgred in that hoard. The coin of *BMC* type D may provisionally be dated *c.* 867–8 and that of Dudwine of type A to *c.* 869–70. Both coins seem likely to have been struck at London.

Carolingian (1)

4\. Imitation of AV *solidus* of Louis the Pious (811–40).
Obv. 'NIIDOVIINNAV., a rude laureated head to the right'.
Rev. 'A blundered reading, equivalent to *Munus Divinum*, a cross within a wreath'.
Die-axis and weight: not stated, but 'three pieces broken out of the edge'.

Coin forming lot 247 of Sotheby sale 25–26 March 1850 (collection of William Hoare, Southsea), where it is described as above and is stated to have been 'found at Portchester in 1832'; purchased by Curt[1] and not traceable today.

Solidi of regular *Munus Divinum* type, carrying on their obverse a bust of Louis r., with the legend DN HLVDOVVICVS IMP AVG, and on their reverse a cross within a laurel wreath surrounded by the legend MVNVS DIVINVM, were struck for Louis early in his reign, perhaps in 816–8, and have not survived in large numbers.[2] Imitations of them are rather more common and are shown by find evidence to have circulated along the northern and north-western frontiers of the Carolingian empire almost until the end of the ninth century. It appears that there was a local demand for gold coin that lasted into the 880s and that as Louis's *Munus Divinum* coins were the last regular gold issue in circulation they were the coins copied when a further supply was required. The majority of the imitations known are of Frisian or probable Frisian provenance and it is likely that the bulk were struck in that area. Trade along the Frisian coast was brisk enough and cosmopolitan enough to make a gold unit of currency a useful adjunct to the silver *denarius*.

The Portchester coin appears to have affinities with another imitative *Munus Divinum* piece recently discovered at Southampton.[3] Neither is of markedly Frisian style and it may be that they are to be associated with a group of imitative *solidi* with English provenances for which Grierson has been prepared to postulate an English place of manufacture;[4] it could even be that they were the products of a mint on the Hampshire littoral. Another possibility is that they are in fact of Frisian origin and that the divergence in style between them and coins hitherto associated with Frisia has a chronological rather than a geographical cause.

The Portchester imitative *solidus* may be dated to the period *c.* 840–70.

The coins as a group conform to the pattern of discoveries at adjacent Southampton. It is patent that the prosperity of this part of the Wessex coast was at a high point during the ninth century and that the coins in circulation there were those that were used in trade on a national level. The absence of coins of kings of Wessex calls for no particular comment — the total number of coins being so small — while the presence of coins of King Burgred of the London mint is wholly in line with find evidence from Southampton and other sites that coins of Mercia circulated readily in Southern England in the second half of this century.

[1] Joseph Lewis Etherington Curt, a London coin dealer with a special interest in coins of the European continent.

[2] A corpus of the *solidi* and their imitations is given by P. Grierson, *Jaarboek voor Munt-en-Penningkunde* xxxviii (1951), 1–41. The dating of the regular series is discussed on pp. 2–7.

[3] Publication forthcoming.

[4] Op. cit., 11.

VI. THE GLASS

By D. B. Harden

SAXON glass is far rarer than Roman at Portchester. Of the material submitted to me only ten fragments are indisputably Saxon. Six of these (nos. 4*a–c*, 6, 7 and 8) belong to the early (pagan) Saxon period, while the other four (nos. 2, 3, 5 and 9) are late Saxon in date. Beside these ten I list one other (no. 1) bearing unmarvered trails, which may be either late Roman or early Saxon (later fourth or fifth centuries). All eleven fragments are blown.

Of three of the early Saxon examples (nos. 4*a*, 7 and 8) enough remains to enable them to be equated with known Saxon types in my classification.[1] The other three (nos. 4*b–c* and 6) are too fragmentary to be 'typed' in this way, although I have no doubt they belong to this period (unlike no. 1, which could — see above — equally well be fourth-century and late Roman).

Three of the late Saxon pieces (nos. 2, 3 and 5) are trailed in a manner reminiscent of that period (ninth to tenth centuries) as exemplified by Scandinavian finds at Birka and elsewhere.[2] No. 5, of dark blue glass with opaque yellow horizontal trails, seems to come from the neck of a squat jar like those from Hopperstad, Norway,[3] and Birka, grave 649.[4] The other two (nos. 2 and 3), though falling into this general group, are, in detail, quite unusual and would be remarkable in any assemblage of glass. They are closely akin to each other in technique and decoration, but are of different colours and therefore from different vessels. Their polychrome trailing superficially resembles the late Saxon Scandinavian pieces I have cited and also some varieties of trailing on Roman 'snake-thread' ware. Yet I do not know of any direct parallel among Roman 'snake-thread' vessels or late Saxon Scandinavian glasses for the method of 'strapping down' a trail on a vessel by applying cross-binders.[5] We may hope that, in time, parallels will be recognized.

The fourth example of glass of late Saxon date (no. 9) is of a totally different style, being a fragment of a vessel of a well-known eastern (Islamic) fabric, representatives of which have not infrequently been found on western sites. Mostly these vessels are wine-coloured or dark blue with opaque white horizontal trailing, but dark green and brown examples are also known.[6] Many shapes exist in this ware. One of the most typical is a large, ribbed, hole-mouthed bowl with incurved sides, on which the white trailing begins at the centre of the base and runs spirally up the body across the ribs, until, towards the top it is replaced by a series of pale green dashes in interrupted lines lying horizontally across the ribs.[7] The same kind of decoration occurs on our piece (no. 9), but in opaque white instead of green (since the ground colour is green), and the piece also differs in shape, being more beaker-like, with

[1] Harden, in D. B. Harden (ed.), *Dark-Age Britain: Studies presented to E. T. Leeds* (1956), 137ff.

[2] Cf. e.g. H. Arbman, *Schweden und das karolingische Reich* (1937), 52, pl. 8, 1–4; G. Arwidsson, *Vendelstile* (1942), 97, fig. 100.

[3] Arbman, op. cit. in note 2, pl. 8, 1.

[4] Arwidsson, op. cit. in note 2, fig. 100.

[5] I use the term 'strapping down', of course, merely to describe the decorative result, since in glass-making there is no need to hold down a fused-in trail in this way.

[6] For the type in general see C. J. Lamm, *Mittelalterliche Gläser und Steinschnittarbeiten aus dem nahen Osten* (1930), 96ff., pls. 19–32. His inclusive date for the type is eighth to eleventh centuries. For examples from western sites see Harden, op. cit. in note 1, 155f., and id. in *Arch. J.* cxxviii (1972), 93.

[7] For such bowls see, e.g., Harden, op. cit. in note 1, 155f., no. 4, pl. xix *a* (from London; B.M. 56.7–1.604, C. Roach Smith collection), and A. Moschetti, *Il Museo Civico di Padova* (1938), 308–10, fig. 196 (from Via Zattere, Padova; Padova Mus. no. 635, wrongly believed by Moschetti, loc. cit., to be Roman).

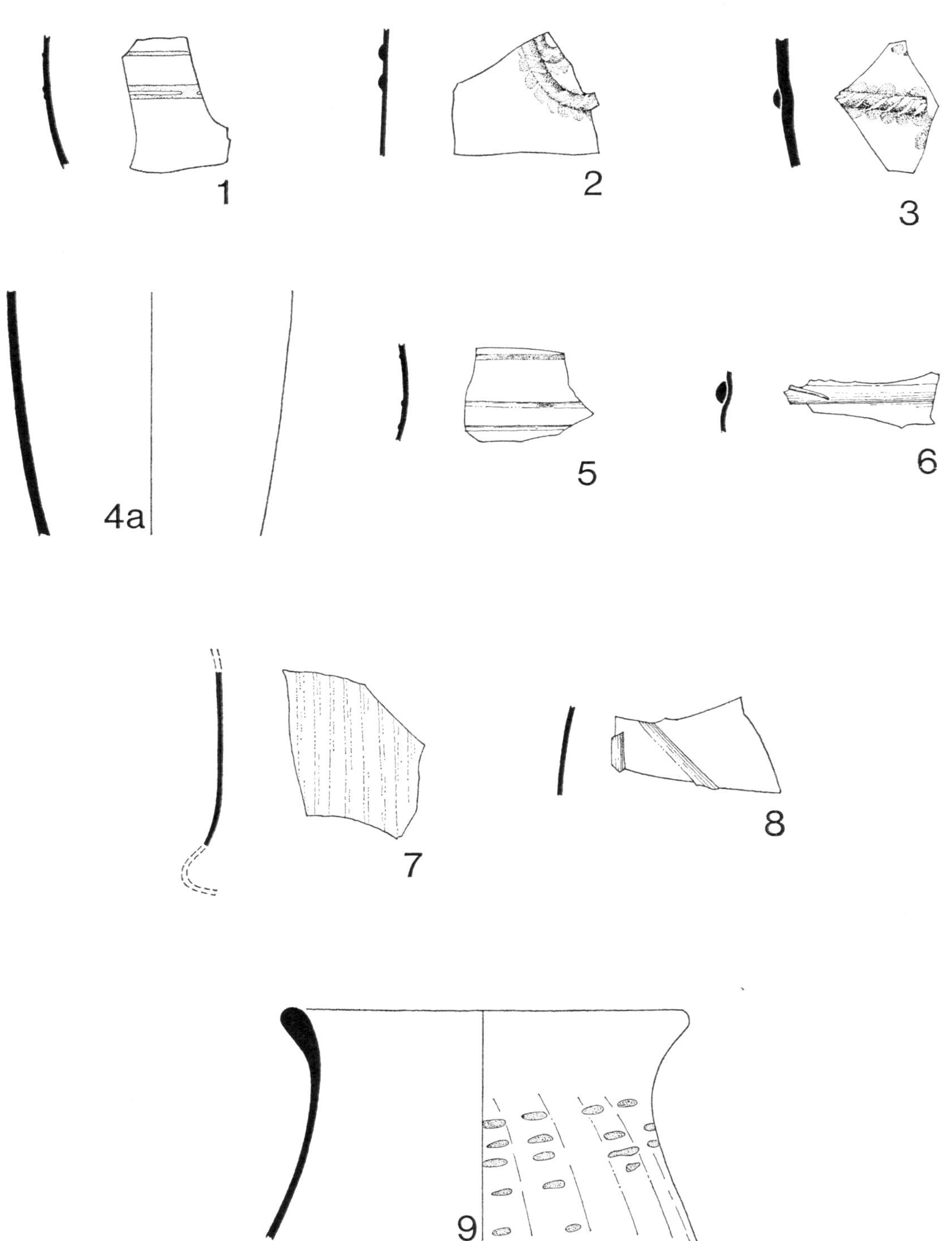

FI . 145. Glass vessels (p. 234). Scale $\frac{1}{2}$

everted rim. Despite these differences there is no doubt about the Islamic origin of our example, and its context at Portchester — it was found in a pit with grass-tempered pottery stratified below a group of tenth-century buildings — fits readily within Lamm's inclusive date of eighth to eleventh centuries.[1]

Catalogue (fig. 145)

1. Fragment of side of bowl or flask; green. Convex side. Three horizontal, unmarvered, opaque white trails, two of which are contiguous. Poor glass; streaks and impurities; iridescent. Late Roman or early Saxon (later fourth or fifth century).
   Trench 94, layer 87: general layer.
2. Fragment of side of bowl or cup; green. Vertical side. Body bears bichrome relief-trailing in form of self-coloured raised festoons, over which, but not underneath it, are placed 'straps' of opaque yellow. Bubbly; iridescent. Late Saxon.
   Trench 56, layer 7 (68): general layer.
3. Fragment of side of bowl or cup; dark- (probably wine-) coloured. Convex side. Decoration as on no. 2. Iridescent. Late Saxon.
   Trench 87, layer 9 (1040): general layer.

4*a–c*. Three fragments, all early Saxon:
   a. Fragment of side of cone-beaker; greenish. From a plain cone-beaker of type III. Sub-types *d–f*, of the later fifth or the sixth century (cf. Harden, op. cit. in p. 232, note 1, 140f., fig. 25).
   b, *c* (not illustrated). Two fragments of bodies, complete shape uncertain; one greenish-colourless, the other yellowish-green.
   Trench 70, layer 30: *Grubenhaus* S1.

5. Fragment of body; clear dark blue. Horizontal, unmarvered opaque yellow trails. Late Saxon.
   Trench 88, layer 9: pit 135.
6. Fragment of body; dark iron blue. Thick, horizontal, unmarvered trail. Seventh century.
   Trench 88, layer 11: pit 135.
7. Fragment of body of bell-beaker; light green. Vertical wall, splayed at bottom. Faint vertical mould-blown ribbing. From lower part of domed bell-beaker of type V, *b* (cf. Harden, op. cit. in p. 232, note 1, 140f., pl. xvii, A, *d*). Sixth or early seventh century.
   Trench 88, layer 22: pit 135.
8. Fragment of body; iron blue. Parts of two unmarvered, self-coloured upright loops. Bubbly and many impurities; no weathering. From lower part of pouch-bottle of type VII, *a* (cf. Harden, op. cit. in p. 232, note 1, 141, pl. xviii, *f*). Seventh century.
   Trench 88, layer 5 (1048).
9. Fragment of lip and neck of beaker or jar with everted lip; green. On the shoulder opaque white dashes in interrupted lines lying horizontally across vertical ribs. East Mediterranean Islamic fabric (see above, p. 232 for discussion and parallels). Eighth to eleventh century.
   Trench 54, layer 7: pit 34.

[1] See note 6 on p. 232.

VII. THE SAXON BURIALS

By Bari Hooper

INTRODUCTION

Condition of the material

THE state of preservation of the bones is generally good and it was not considered necessary to treat any of the material with chemical hardening agents. Unfortunately most of the skulls were found to be in a fragmentary condition due to earth pressures and other post-mortem disturbances. Attempts at cranial reconstruction were often frustrated by distortion of the fragments. This has resulted in a scarcity of skull measurements, but has not adversely affected non-metrical observations.

The basic skeletal measurements have been deposited with the bones in the Portsmouth City Museum.

Estimation of age at death

In order to arrive at an estimated age at which each individual died, the following criteria were considered:

Immature individuals

(i) The development of the dentition.
(ii) The degree of union of the epiphyses.

Mature individuals

(iii) The degree of attrition of the molar teeth.
(iv) The condition of the spheno-occipital suture.
(v) Age changes in the pubic symphysis.
(vi) Senile skeletal changes.
(vii) The amount of osteoarthritis present.

(i) and (ii) Assessment of the age of immature specimens by examination of the state of development of the dentition is well known (*v.* standard dental textbooks). Combined with an examination of the degree of union between the cartilaginous epiphyses and the shafts of the long bones, it provides a fairly precise age indicator (Pyle and Hoerr, 1955; Hunt and Gleiser, 1955, *et al.*).

(iii) The attrition of the occlusal surfaces of the teeth is of great value in ageing adult specimens. The gradual physiological wearing away of the grinding surfaces during mastication is facilitated by the presence of an abrasive medium in the food. This abrasive, in the form of grit from lava and sandstone querns, has been inadvertently introduced into food since the advent of mechanical grinding devices. Fibrous foods may also have played a part in the wear process. Brothwell (1963) states that attrition of the molars of earlier British populations has changed little from the Neolithic to the medieval period. On this assumption he has published a valuable chart showing a tentative classification of age in pre-medieval British skulls based upon molar wear.

(iv) The sutures of the skull generally begin to close after the individual has reached maturity and for many years the degree of suture closure was used for age assessment (Parsons and Box, 1905; Todd and Lyons, 1924, 1925, *et al.*). More recent work by Genoves and Messmacher (1959) has shown this method to be unreliable and its use has been abandoned. The only skull suture that is still regarded as a reliable age indicator is the spheno-occipital which is usually firmly united by the twenty-fifth year.

(v) Because of its gradual change with age, the pubic symphysis can also assist in dating. McKern and Stewart (1957), in a study of American males, proposed a method of assessing age in which the symphyseal changes are evaluated in terms of combinations of component parts. They selected three of these component parts and sub-divided them into five developmental stages, which when combined as a formula, yield an age range.

(vi) Senile changes in the skull include the loss of the teeth and resorption of the alveolar margins, followed by a diminution of the maxillae and mandible. These changes are quite distinctive and have a marked effect upon the facial structure.

(vii) On reaching maturity, many individuals in early populations began to develop osteoarthritis in their joints. By middle and old age the disease was often severe and widespread, particularly in the spine. The extent and degree of severity of the disorder when considered with other ageing criteria can be useful corroboratory evidence.

Using these criteria, the mean age at death for the Portchester males is 36·75 years and the females 27·14 years. The disparity between the sexes is probably due to the women being subjected to the hazards of childbirth. The average age at death for the three children is 7·0 years. The average life expectancy for the whole group is 28·92 years if the adult and child population are both included, but this figure is based upon a very small sample and does not allow for undetected infant burials. The actual life expectancy for these people is likely to be lower than the above figure.

Determination of sex

The sexing of skeletal remains is based upon close examination of those bones which most emphasize sexual dimorphism. Some of the sexual characteristics are relatively unambiguous, but the inevitable overlap in the morphological range can cause some problems. In the author's experience the percentage of sexually indeterminate skeletons is about 10%. Incomplete remains are usually the most difficult to sex satisfactorily, but even a few fragments of a skeleton may include most of the classic sexing criteria.

The pelvic girdle, because of its adaptation for child-bearing in the female, is the most reliable means of sexual identification. Brothwell (1963) divided the sexual characteristics of the pelvis into two groups:

(i) Those depending upon visual examination, and
(ii) Those depending upon measurable dimensions.

In the first category the morphological points are as follows: the male pelvis is more robust with well-marked muscular impressions, larger acetabulum and obturator foramen; deeper pubic symphysis and narrow sciatic notch. In the female the pre-auricular sulcus is more constantly present in the ilium.

In the second category the metrical points are as follows: the male pelvis has a lower ischio-pubic index and a smaller angle of the sciatic notch. A sub-pubic angle of 90 degrees or above is usually indicative of a female.

Another important but less reliable sex indicator is the skull, which has nearly a dozen morphological sex differences. Secondary criteria in the skeleton include the vertebral column, clavicle and scapula.

Of the 19 adults at Portchester, ten are males, seven females and two remain unsexed.

Estimation of stature

The stature estimates in this report have been calculated from the regression equation formulae of Trotter and Gleser (1952, 1958). These equations were computed upon the measurements of long bones of North American Whites. The standard error in the formulae varies from bone to bone, some bones having a smaller error than others. The femur, for example, has a smaller error than the ulna. All the estimations have been calculated where possible from the average of several bones from each individual. The results are shown below.

TABLE I

Stature Estimates — Mean and Range

Sex	*Number*	*Mean*	*Range*
Male	9	175·717 cm. (5 ft. 9¼ in.)	162·220 cm. (5 ft. 3¾ in.)– 183·230 cm. (6 ft. ½ in.)
Female	6	165·273 cm. (5 ft. 5 in.)	160·230 cm. (5 ft. 3 in.)– 171·628 cm. (5 ft. 7½ in.)

Morphological traits

A number of common morphological variations were found among the bones. These and other less common anomalies have been listed in the burial descriptions under the general heading of morphological traits. These genetically determined traits appear to be fairly constant in any given race, and Brothwell (1959) employed ten such characteristics of the skull to ascertain their value in differentiating between groups. His findings for 14 different populations showed that these traits separated the groups as clearly as cranial analysis.

Of the uncommon anomalies, the detached neural arch of a lumbar vertebra in burials 11 and 20 is the most important, for it strongly indicates a close genetic relationship between these two individuals.

The following table (Table II) shows the incidence of the traits with a comparison, where applicable, with Brothwell's percentages.

Pathology

Eleven (57·89%) of the adults were found to be affected by osteoarthritis. Considerable confusion exists in the medical literature on the nomenclature of arthritic and similar osseous diseases. So much so, that it is necessary to define the medical terms used in this report.

TABLE II

Incidence of Morphological Traits

Burial	*A*	*B*	*C*	*D*	*E*	*F*	*G*	*H*	*J*	*K*
1	×									
2	×				×	×				
3	×		×	×	×		×			
4		×								
6	×		×		×					
7		×								×
8	×								×	
9		×								
10	×	×			×					
11	×	×	×					×		
13					×					
14			×							
15	×	×								
17										×
19		×								
20								×		
Total	8	7	4	1	5	1	1	2	1	2
Percentage out of 19	42·10	36·84	21·05	5·26	26·31	5·26	5·26	10·52	5·26	10·52
Brothwell's Anglo-Saxon percentage	55·56	—	27·27	—	—	—	11·80	—	—	—

Legend:

A = Wormian bones
B = Patent premaxillary suture
C = Tori mandibulares
D = Tori maxillares
E = Multiple supraorbital foramina
F = Multiple infraorbital foramina
G = Multiple mental foramina
H = Detached neural arch
J = Fused sacral/coccygeal vertebrae
K = Epitrochlear foramen

Osteoarthritis is a disease affecting the large joints of the limbs and the articulations of the vertebrae. Less frequently it attacks the smaller joints of the appendicular skeleton. It is characterized by primary degenerative and erosive changes in the articular cartilage, and destruction and subsequent reactionary bone formation (lipping) at the articular margins. In its later stages the exposed bone-ends are rubbed together causing friction and a reactionary thickening of the bone. With movement of the joint, the opposed surfaces become polished or eburnated. The aetiology of osteoarthritis is still the subject of discussion, but it is now generally agreed that trauma plays a part in its origin. The trauma may be sudden, involving a fracture in the immediate proximity of a joint, or it may be a consequence of continuous occupational strain. It occurs most frequently during the middle and later decades of life and is commonly seen in the spines of pre-mechanized agricultural peoples.

Burial 13 was found to have suffered a severe affliction of tuberculosis of the thoracic vertebrae (Pott's disease). Today this is one of the commonest forms of skeletal tuberculosis. The infection commences at the anterior margin of a vertebral body, causing it to erode. The destructive changes usually involve the intervertebral disc and adjacent vertebrae. The erosion and subsequent collapse of these vertebrae causes an angular kyphosis (pl. XXI*a*). The main complications are tuberculous infection of other organs and compression of the spinal cord (Pott's paraplegia), causing weakness or paralysis (Adams, 1956).

Archaeologically it occurs from the Bronze Age onwards, a famous early example being the mummy of a priest of Ammon of the XXIst Dynasty from Thebes (Moodie, 1923). It has been previously detected in Britain in a Saxon specimen (Brothwell, 1961), but it is still far from common in early skeletal material.

The most interesting bone disease encountered at Portchester is a case of *osteitis deformans* (Paget's disease) in burial 20. The disease was first described in detail by Sir James Paget (1877), although in an additional paper in 1882 he credited Professor Czerny of Freiburg with the first use of the term 'osteitis deformans' to describe an inflamed bone, some nine years before.

The disorder is slow and progressive and commonly affects the skull, pelvis, femur and tibia. It is characterized by gradual enlargement of the skull and deformation of the long bones. These changes are consequences of widespread resorption and apposition of the bones. The ratio of osteoblastic to osteoclastic activity is still uncertain, but a consensus of the available literature suggests that it is in the region of 2 : 1. The bones are subject to pathological fracture, for the newly deposited bone is not normally distributed along lamellar stress lines. Such fractures usually heal badly with poorly distributed callus. A less common complication is the development of osteosarcoma in the diseased bone (Adams, 1956). The supervention of osteoarthritis in the load-bearing joints is frequently a feature of the later stages of the disease (Mercer, 1936).

Published incidences of the disease are low, but many cases probably go undetected. Schmorl (1932), in a survey of 4614 hospital patients over the age of 40, found an incidence of 3%. This is in accordance with the more recent study of Collins and Hunter (1956), who found an incidence of 3·7% among 650 autopsies. Another recent study showed a mild occurrence of 1 : 3000 in patients over the age of 45, with a 2 : 1 ratio of males to females (Gardner, Drescher and Goodreau, 1963).

The disease is seldom seen before the fifth decade of life, although rare exceptions include the case of an 18-year-old (Aegerter and Kirkpatrick, 1963). The course of the disease may run for 20 years or more, with death usually resulting from cardio-vascular failure.

Archaeological examples of Paget's disease are rare. This is probably due to the fact that the average age at death in early populations was lower than the normal time of onset of the disease. One case that is generally accepted is a Neolithic femur from Lozère, France (Pales, 1929, 1930). Other more doubtful examples from Europe and America are occasionally reported. Some of the New World specimens are particularly controversial due to confusion between the lesions of syphilis and Paget's disease (Jaffe, 1966). The European examples include a Gallo-Roman cranium from Laurabuc, France (Astre, 1957) and some cremated skull fragments from an urnfield at Grote Brogel, Limburg (Janssens, 1963), although this last example may well be a case of pre-senile osteoporosis.

The Portchester skeleton is one of the most convincing specimens to be recovered from an archaeological deposit.

Six adults and one child (36·84%) have cribra orbitalia. This orbital anomaly has been discussed at length by Moller-Christensen (1953, 1961). The condition is characterized by bilateral (occasionally unilateral) strainer-like pitting in the roof of the orbits. Its incidence is world-wide, although its frequency is subject to considerable variation, ranging from 2·02% in Eskimos to 35% in Iron Age/Roman Britons (27·64% in Anglo-Saxons) (Brothwell, 1963). Its aetiology is obscure, but the studies of Moller-Christensen and Sandison (1963) indicate a pathological origin. Their examination of over 700 eighteenth century skulls of mainly Scottish origin, gave an incidence of 52% for children, 6·6% for adults and 8% for all groups. They speculate that the only disease common in childhood which is both ancient and global, and also sometimes affects the lacrimal glands, is mumps. Although it was evident in mid nineteenth-century Swedish material, Henschen (1956, 1961) failed to find any trace of the condition in over 2000 modern Scandinavian skulls. He suggests that malnutrition might therefore be the cause.

Periostitis was noted upon some of the bones of burials 3, 8 and 14. Cortical inflammations such as these are common on early bones, although the specific infection causing them can seldom be identified.

A bony ridge upon the right femur of burial 15 may be an ossified blood clot. Haematomata of this kind are sometimes a symptom of scurvy, but in this instance the presence of the disease could not be verified.

Shallow linear impressions were noted upon some of the long bones. These grooves have been recorded on bones from all parts of the world and have been variously interpreted. In America, Wakefield and Dellinger (1936, 1937) suggested that they were the scars of deep cauterization of syphilitic lesions. To support this unusual theory, they produced flint arrowheads which were supposedly heated and used to carry out the operation. In Europe, Gejvall thought the grooves were made by tight leg-bindings, but Wells (1963a) has conclusively shown them to be vascular sulci of non-pathological origin.

Of the dental diseases (caries and periodontal disease) recorded among the material, destructive periodontal disease is the most common. It is present to a greater or lesser degree in nearly all of the adult remains. As oral hygiene was probably non-existent, it was inevitable that the accumulation of dental plaque upon the teeth would lead to alveolar resorption and eventual loss of teeth in older individuals. Dental caries were found in 22 of the 431 teeth present (5·10%), seven individuals (36·84%) out of 19 being caries free. Several abscesses of carious and periodontal origin were also recorded (*v.* dental formulae).

Trauma

Injuries sustained during life are usually only detectable where the effects have been registered upon the bones. Where the bony structure has not been violated, injuries to the soft tissues can only be inferred under exceptional circumstances. The most commonly reported injuries are fractures, but even avulsed tendons and torn ligaments may sometimes be deduced from the condition of their insertion points on the bones. A healed fracture is generally easy to recognize by the deposit of callus about the break. However, a fracture that has not had time to heal spontaneously, i.e. a fracture occurring shortly before or at the time of death, is often indistinguishable from a post-mortem break. Conversely, a slight fracture or crack may heal leaving little or no recognizable evidence of the trauma. It follows, therefore, that in any group of skeletons, the number of injuries recognized may well be lower than the actual number that occurred during life.

A callus upon the left parietal of burial 12 may be evidence of a healed skull fracture, or even an ossified blood-clot. Unfortunately most of the left side of the skull has been destroyed in some subsequent disturbance of the grave and the exact nature of the injury can no longer be determined.

An incident causing a severe compression of the thorax of burial 11 resulted in the fracture of the sternum and nine ribs. Presumably no complications arose from the injuries, for all of the breaks healed spontaneously. Uncomplicated rib fractures such as these appear to be are not often severely displaced, as the muscles usually provide adequate support.

Burial 3 also sustained injuries to the rib cage and in this instance at least six ribs were fractured, again presumably without serious complications. The position of the breaks suggests that they were received in falling against a hard object, e.g. a low wall or a table.

The only other fracture found is a well-healed break in the sternum of burial 20. This particular type of injury was common among farriers, from the kick of a horse.

Two examples of damage to the fibrous tissues were found. The female in burial 6 appears to have torn a tendon in the right foot after falling from a height. Another female, burial 10, shows evidence of having torn a ligament in the left foot from stumbling over rough ground or upon steps.

The causes of all of the above injuries are open to speculation, but there is no reason to suppose that any of them could not be a consequence of normal occupational accidents. But there can be no doubt that the final injury to be described below is the result of deliberate violence.

The wound in question occurs upon the mandible of the young adult male in burial 8. A small sliver of bone approximately 25 × 5 mm. has been removed from the left angle of the mandible (pl. XXI*b*). The nature of the cut is consistent with a heavy blow from a sword, which, having cut through the bone, entered the neck. The effects of the stroke would have been to sever parts of the masseter and internal pterygoid muscles at their insertions and to open the external carotid artery and internal jugular vein. The ensuing haemorrhage would have brought about a swift death. The blade may even have penetrated through to the cervical vertebrae, but this is not verifiable, as these bones have not survived.

The circumstances of the assault will never be known, but some conjecture of the relative positions of the victim and the assailant can be made, for the evidence imposes certain limitations on the directions from which the blow could have been struck.

To begin with, the angle of the cut is about 140 degrees to the horizontal plane of the mandible. With the jaws in occlusion, if a line is continued upward from the top of the 25 mm. cut, it touches the skull 40 mm. away at a point midway between the external auditory meatus and the mastoid process. With the jaws open, the nearest point on the skull is the mastoid process 15–20 mm. away (the distance varies according to the width the jaws are open). A close examination of this restricted area of the skull shows no trace of injury. This means that if the sword-stroke was delivered from the front or left side with the victim facing his assailant, less than 65 mm. of the end of the blade struck the target. If it were such a frontal assault, the victim probably leaned his body backward and inclined his head to the right in an unsuccessful attempt to avoid the blow.

The alternative possibility is that the victim was lying upon the ground with face upward or head inclined to the right. In this virtually defenceless position the victim could easily have been struck in the throat and jaw with almost any part of the blade.

It is appropriate to mention here that injuries to the angle of the jaw sometimes occur during executions by decapitation (Gray Hill, 1937; Wells, 1963b). In such cases the damage is sustained from the follow-through of the sword-blade from a blow delivered upon the back of the neck. Another type of jaw injury associated with decapitation occurs where the blade accidentally strikes the jaw from a stroke aimed from the side (Hooper, 1968). All of these cuts are quite distinctive and in no way resemble the Portchester injury.

On balance, therefore, it seems unlikely that the man met his fate in a formal execution by the sword. The wound is more consistent with a battle injury, the victim either facing or lying at the feet of his assailant.

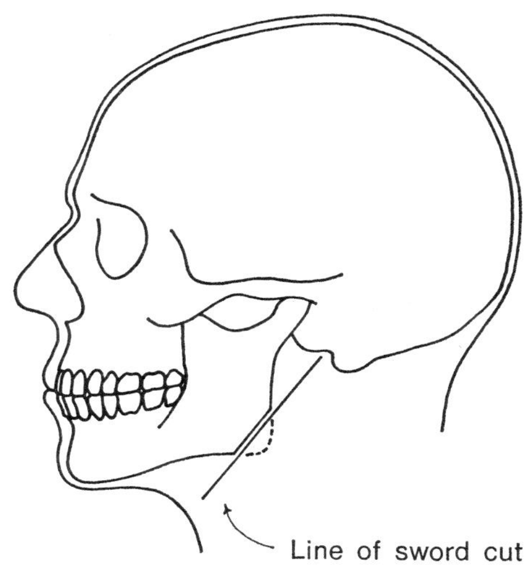

Fig. 146. Diagram to show angle of entry of sword blade across the neck of the body buried in grave 8

Skeletal adaptation

Squatting facets were noted upon the tibiae of eight males and six females. These anterior extensions of the ankle joint suggest habitual squatting upon the ground and lack of household furniture, for they are found in modern primitives who do not use chairs. In contrast, squatting facets are rarely found on the skeletons of urban Roman Britons. In the large Roman cemetery at Trentholme Drive, York, they were only noted in five individuals, all women (Warwick, 1968). They are common in early and middle Saxon populations, although their frequency is seldom constant.

Summary

Twenty-two burials were examined, of which ten were identified as males, seven as females and three as children. The sex of the two remaining adults could not be determined.

The group are tall and of good physique, suggesting that malnutrition during childhood was not a problem. In their prime they must have led active working lives, for the stresses of physical labour upon their joints have left a legacy of osteoarthritis in nearly 58% of the adults. In its later stages the disabling effects of the disease must have seriously impaired their working efficiency and contributed to their physical decline.

The mean age at death for the men was approximately 36 years, although a single example of Paget's disease showed that the occasional individual reached the fifth or even sixth decade of life. The mean age at death for the women was approximately 27 years, the hazards of parturition presumably being the main reason for the disparity between the sexes.

Apart from the two diseases already mentioned, the only other bone disease encountered is a case of a tuberculosis of the spine in a young adult.

The dental health of the group was low, with periodontal disease, caries and abscesses clearly reflecting the abrasive diet and lack of oral hygiene.

Some fractures and lesser injuries were noted, most if not all of which were probably caused by normal occupational accidents. But a sword injury upon the jaw of a young adult male was the fatal sequel to an incident of deliberate violence.

In such a small cemetery as this, it is likely that some of the individuals are related to each other. Evidence for this was found in two skeletons, both of whom share an uncommon vertebral anomaly indicating a close genetic relationship.

DESCRIPTIONS OF THE BURIALS

The symbols used for the dental formulae in the burial descriptions are as follows:

/	Missing post-mortem
X	Missing ante-mortem
C	Caries
A	Abscess
℧	Erupting
○	Unerupted

Burial 1

Inventory: fragmentary skeleton.
Child aged *c.* nine years.

Morphological trait

Wormian bones: four ossicles at lambda.

Pathological observation

Bilateral cribra orbitalia is present.

Dental formula

=	/	6	e	d	/	/	/	/	/	/	d	e	/	7	=
=	/	/	/	d	/	/	/	/	/	/	d	e	6	7	=

Burial 2

Inventory: complete skeleton.
Female aged *c.* 40 years: mesocephalic.
Stature: 164·575 cm. (5 ft. 4¾ in.)

Morphological traits

1. Wormian bones: four right lambdoid ossicles and two at right asterion.
2. Multiple supraorbital foramina.
3. Multiple infraorbital foramina.

Pathological observations

The spine is affected with osteoarthritis with lipping around the margins of the vertebral bodies of L3, L4 and L5. The inferior articulations of ?T12 are severely eburnated and many of the costotransverse articulations are lipped. Osteoarthritic exostoses are also present upon the right patella.

Skeletal adaptation

A squatting facet is present upon the right tibia. (The left tibia is missing.)

Dental observations

All of the teeth are crown-worn with slight deposits of calculus. Periodontal disease has caused considerable alveolar resorption and the loss of the mandibular right 1st molar.

Dental formula

8	7	6	5	4	3	2	1	1	2	3	4	5	6	7	8
8	7	X	5	4	3	2	1	1	/	3	4	5	6	7	8

Burial 3

Inventory: almost complete skeleton.
Male aged *c.* 45 years.
Stature: 180·900 cm. (5 ft. 11¼ in.). Strongly built.

Morphological traits

1. Wormian bones: two right lambdoid ossicles.
2. Multiple supraorbital foramina over right orbit.
3. Multiple mental foramina.
4. Bilateral mandibular tori.
5. Right maxillary torus.

TABLE III

Osteoarthritis in the Spine of Burial 3

Vertebra	*Superior articular facet*		*Inferior articular facet*		*Vertebral body*
	Left	*Right*	*Left*	*Right*	
Cervical					
1					
2			E	+	
3	E	+	+		
4	E	E	E		S+
5	E	X		X	S+
6		X		X	S+
7		X	E	E	S+
Thoracic					
1	E	E			
2					
3					
4					
5		+			
6					
7			X		
8					S+
9			X	X	S+
10					S+
11			E		S+
12	E				S+
Lumbar					
1					
2					
3	+	+	+	+	
4	+	+	+	+	S+
5	+	+			
Sacral					
1	+	+			

Legend:
E = Eburnated   + = Lipped around margin
S+ = Slightly lipped margin   X = Missing post-mortem

Pathological observations

There is severe and widespread osteoarthritis in this skeleton, particularly in the spine (see table *infra*). Further lipping is present at the acromioclavicular, sternoclavicular, sacro-iliac, iliofemoral, humero-ulnar and digital joints.

Periostitis is present upon the shafts of the femora.

Trauma

At least six ribs have well-healed fractures. Most of the ribs are in fragmentary condition making positive identification difficult, but a tentative list of the fractures is as follows: 2, 3, 4, 5, 6 and 7.

Dental observations

All of the teeth are crown-worn with slight deposits of calculus. Caries is present in the maxillary right 1st and 2nd molars. Periodontal abscesses are present at the roots of the maxillary left 2nd and 3rd molars with considerable destruction of bone in this region. Other abscesses are present at the roots of the mandibular right 1st and 2nd and left 1st and 2nd molars. The mandibular left 3rd molar has over-erupted as a consequence of the loss of its opposing tooth.

It is noteworthy that the right gonial region of the mandible is strongly developed, with a marked lateral eversion. The ridges for the insertion of the internal pterygoid muscle are also strongly pronounced.

Dental formula

	C	C													
/	7	6	5	4	3	2	/	1	2	3	4	5	6	X	X
														A	A
8	7	6	/	4	3	2	1	/	2	3	4	/	X	/	8
	A	A											A	A	

Burial 4

Inventory: almost complete skeleton.
Female aged *c.* 17 years.
Stature: 165·250 cm. (5 ft. 5 in.).

Morphological trait

Patent premaxillary suture.

Pathological observation

Bilateral cribra orbitalia is present.

Dental observation

The mandibular left 3rd molar which was still erupting at the time of death, has a small lingual caries cavity.

Dental formula

⑧	7	6	5	4	/	/	/	1	2	/	4	5	6	7	⑧
(8)	7	6	5	4	3	2	1	1	2	3	4	5	6	7	C (8)

Burial 5

Inventory: fragmented skeleton.
Child aged *c.* five years.

Burial 6

Inventory: complete skeleton.
Female aged *c.* 30 years: dolichocephalic.
Stature: 164·956 cm. (5 ft. 5 in.).

Morphological traits

1. Wormian bones: two left lambdoid ossicles.
2. Multiple supraorbital foramina.
3. Unilateral (right) mandibular torus.

Pathological observations

Early signs of osteoarthritis are present in the spine and feet, with incipient lipping at the articulations of L1, L2, L3 and L4, the sacro-iliac joints, the vertebral bodies of T9 and T10, the costotransverse articulations of ten ribs and the metatarsophalangeal joints.

Bilateral cribra orbitalia is present.

Skeletal adaptation

Squatting facets are present upon the tibiae.

Trauma

An osseous irregularity between the plantar process and the tuberosity of the right navicular bone suggests that the tendon of the tibialis posterior has been torn from its lodgement. Such an injury is consistent with falling from a height and taking the force of the fall upon the right foot.

Dental observation

All of the teeth are moderately crown-worn with slight deposits of calculus.

Dental formula

/	7	6	5	/	3	2	/	/	2	3	4	5	6	/	8
8	7	6	5	4	3	2	1	1	2	3	4	5	6	7	8

Burial 7

Inventory: almost complete skeleton.
Female aged 17–25 years.
Stature: 171·628 cm. (5 ft. 7½ in.).

Morphological traits

1. Patent premaxillary suture.
2. Epitrochlear foramina.

Pathological observations

Early osteoarthritis is present in the spine with slight lipping of the vertebral bodies of L2, L3 and L4. The costotransverse articulations of the 3rd and 4th ribs are also slightly lipped.

Skeletal adaptation

Squatting facets are present upon the tibiae.

Dental observation

Most of the teeth have slight deposits of calculus upon them.

Dental formula

8	7	6	5	4	3	2	1	/	/	3	4	5	6	7	8
8	7	6	5	4	3	/	1	1	2	3	4	5	6	7	8

Burial 8

Inventory: almost complete skeleton.
Male aged 20–25 years.
Stature: 183·850 cm. (6 ft. ½ in.). Strongly built.

Morphological traits

1. Wormian bones: two right and two left lambdoid ossicles and a bipartite inca bone.
2. 5th sacral and 1st coccygeal vertebral segments fused together.

Pathological observations

The posterior and medial areas of the shaft of the right femur show evidence of an inflammation of the periosteum.

Bilateral cribra orbitalia is present.

Skeletal adaptation

An incipient squatting facet is present upon the right tibia. (The left tibia is missing.)

Trauma

A portion of bone measuring approximately 25 × 5 mm. has been cut away from the angle of the mandible (pl. XXI*b*). The wound is consistent with a sword cut. The effects of this injury are discussed on pp. 241–2. Two transverse grooves on the anterior of the lower third of the right femur may have been caused by a weapon cutting through the soft tissues and touching the bone (pl. XXI*c*). It is tempting to link these marks with the jaw wound, but they could just as easily have been made in some subsequent post-mortem disturbance of the grave.

Dental formula

8	7	6	5	4	3	2	1	1	2	3	4	/	6	7	8
8	7	6	5	4	3	2	/	1	2	3	4	5	6	7	8

Burial 8a

Inventory: fragmented skeleton.
Child aged *c.* seven years.

Burial 9

Inventory: skull and mandible; clavicles; humeri and ulnae; tibiae and right femur.
Female aged *c.* 17 years.

Morphological trait

Patent premaxillary suture.

Pathological observation

The fibro-cartilaginous pulley or trochlea, which in life is attached by fibrous tissue to the orbital plate, has become ossified within each orbit (pl. XXI*d*). The tendon of the obliquus oculi superior muscle, which serves to depress and turn the eyeball outward, traverses this pulley. The reason for this unusual ossification could not be determined.

Skeletal adaptation

A squatting facet is present upon the right tibia. (The left is too eroded to discern.)

Dental observations

The maxillary left 2nd incisor is hypoplastic. The hypoplasia is limited to the lateral aspect of the tooth with the markings arranged vertically. The occurrence of unilateral hypoplasia is uncommon and probably resulted from a localized causative factor of long standing (Bennett, 1931).

Dental formula

(8)	7	6	5	4	3	2	1	1	2	3	/	/	6	7	(8)
(8)	/	6	5	4	3	2	1	1	2	3	4	5	6	7	(8)

Burial 10

Inventory: almost complete skeleton.
Female aged *c.* 25 years: brachycephalic.
Stature: 160·230 cm. (5 ft. 3 in.).

Morphological traits

1. Wormian bones: two lambdoid ossicles at right and left.
2. Patent premaxillary suture.
3. Multiple supraorbital foramina.

Pathological observations

Osteoarthritis is present in the spine with lipping about the margins of the vertebral bodies of C7, T3, T4, T9 and L1. Further lipping was noted at the costotransverse articulations of the 4th rib, acromioclavicular and sacro-iliac joints.

Bilateral cribra orbitalia is present.

Skeletal adaptation

Squatting facets are present upon the tibiae.

Trauma

A small bony ridge on the dorsal margin of the proximal surface of the left navicular bone is probably a reaction to a straining of the talonavicular ligament. Severely twisting the foot in a fall over rough ground or upon steps could cause this type of injury.

Dental observations

Most of the teeth are crown-worn with slight deposits of calculus. Caries is present in the maxillary right 3rd molar and the mandibular left 3rd molar. A severe abscess surrounds the roots of the maxillary right 2nd and 3rd molars. This abscess has irrupted into the antrum, the medial wall of which has become infected with chronic osteitis.

Dental formula

C 8 A	7 A	6	5	4	3	2	/	/	2	3	4	5	6	7	8
8	7	6	5	4	3	2	1	1	2	3	4	5	6	7	C 8

Burial 11

Inventory: complete skeleton.
Male aged *c.* 40 years: dolichocephalic.
Stature: 182·784 cm. (6 ft.).

Morphological traits

1. Wormian bones: ossicles at lambda.
2. Patent premaxillary suture.
3. Bilateral mandibular tori (pl. XXII*a*).
4. Detached neural arch of 5th lumbar vertebra.

Pathological observations

There is extensive osteoarthritis in the spinal column (see table IV below). Osteoarthritis is also present around the margins of the pelvic actetabula, sternal and acromioclavicular articulations, costotransverse articulations and many of the metatarsals, metacarpals and their phalanges.

Skeletal adaptation

Squatting facets are present upon the tibiae.

Trauma

The sternal body has a line of callus at the union between the 3rd and 4th segments. This union is normally completed shortly after puberty. The callus therefore represents a natural repair of a sternal fracture occurring in adulthood. Nine ribs are also fractured with well-established healing and it is likely that they and the sternum were damaged in the same incident.

Dental observations

All of the teeth are severely crown-worn with thick deposits of calculus (pl. XXII*a*). In three instances, maxillary right 1st and 2nd molars and mandibular right 1st molar, the deposit covers the grossly worn occlusal surfaces (pl. XXII*a*). Caries is present in the maxillary right 2nd molar and the mandibular right and left 3rd molars. Periodontal disease has caused considerable alveolar resorption and abscesses at the roots of the maxillary right 2nd premolar and 3rd molar, left 2nd and 3rd molars, and mandibular right 2nd and 3rd molars. The abscess at the root of the maxillary left 2nd molar has destroyed much bone and tracked into the antrum. The calculus deposits covering the grinding surfaces of the right molars show that the pain from the abscesses effectively prevented the right side of the jaws being used for mastication.

Dental formula

/ A	C 7	6	/ A	4	3	2	1	1	2	3	4	5	6	X A	X A
C 8 A	/ A	6	5	/	/	2	1	1	2	3	4	5	6	7	C 8

TABLE IV

Osteoarthritis in the Spine of Burial 11

Vertebra	*Superior articular facet*		*Inferior articular facet*		*Vertebral body*
	Left	*Right*	*Left*	*Right*	
Cervical					
1					
2			E	+	
3	E	E+	E	E+	
4	E	E+	E+	E+	
5	E+	E+		A+	S+
6		A+	+		S+
7				E+	S+
Thoracic					
1		E+	E+	E+	
2	E+	E+		E+	
3		E+			S+
4	+	+	E+	E+	S+
5	E+	E+	E+	E+	S+
6	X	E+	X	X	S+
7	E+		+	+	S+
8					S+
9					S+
10				+	S+
11		+	+	+	S+
12	+				M+
Lumbar					
1			+		M+
2			+	E+	M+
3	+		+	+	M+
4	+	E+	+	+	S+
5	+	+	E+	+	S+
Sacral					
1	E+	+			

Legend:

E = Eburnated
S+ = Slightly lipped margin
× = Missing post-mortem
A+ = Ankylosing
\+ = Lipped around margin
M+ = Medium lipped margin

Burial 12

Inventory: fragmented skull less mandible; most of the bones from the right side of the body.
Female aged *c.* 40 years.
Stature: 165·003 cm. (5 ft. 5 in.).

Pathological observations

The surviving bones are in poor condition, but osteoarthritis is recognizable upon the vertebral bodies of L3, L4 and L5, and around the head of the right humerus and distal articulation of the right femur.

Trauma

A callus on the left parietal may be an osseous repair of a skull fracture, or an organized haematoma. Unfortunately most of this side of the skull is missing, so that the exact nature of the injury cannot be established.

Burial 13

(?)Male aged 20–25 years.
Stature: 166·902 cm. (5 ft. 5¾ in.).

Morphological trait

Multiple supraorbital foramen above left orbit.

Pathological observations

The spine is severely affected by tuberculosis (Pott's disease). The focus of the infection is in the thoracic region. The vertebral bodies of T11 and T12 have collapsed, allowing the spine to bend forward sharply (pl. XXI*a*). T9 and T10 have fused at their anterior margins and where the inferior surface of T10 has come into contact with the collapsed vertebrae, eburnation has resulted. The inferior articulations of T10 and the corresponding superior articulations of T11 are also eburnated. Slight movement of the trunk has caused a pseudo-arthrosis to form next to the superior right articular facet of T11. The left facet is atrophied, as is the opposing left inferior facet of T10. The articulations between T11 and T12 have fused and the bodies of L4 and L5 are in the process of collapse and merger, fusion having already taken place at the articulations.

Skeletal adaptation

Squatting facets are present upon the tibiae.

Dental formula

8	7	6	5	4	3	2	1	1	2	3	4	5	6	7	8
8	7	6	5	4	/	2	1	1	/	3	/	5	6	7	8

Burial 14

Inventory: complete skeleton.
Male aged 40+ years: dolichocephalic.
Stature: 175·100 cm. (5 ft. 9 in.). Strongly built.

Morphological trait

Slight left mandibular torus.

Pathological observations

Osteoarthritis is present in the spine, pelvic girdle and the feet. The bodies of the thoracic vertebrae are lipped at their anterior margins and the inferior articulations of C6 are eburnated. Further lipping is present at the costotransverse articulations and metatarsal joints.

The surfaces of the right femur, left tibia and the fibulae are periostitic.

Skeletal adaptation

Squatting facets are present upon the tibiae.

Dental observations

All of the teeth are crown-worn with medium deposits of calculus. Caries is present in the maxillary right 2nd premolar and the mandibular right 2nd and 3rd molars. Abscesses are present at the roots of the maxillary right 2nd and the left 1st, 2nd and 3rd molars. The left maxillary abscesses have caused much alveolar destruction and irrupted into the antrum. As a direct consequence of this destruction the three left molars have been lost. Two more abscesses are present at the roots of the mandibular right 2nd and 3rd molars. The mandibular left 3rd molar has a coating of dysfunction calculus upon its occlusal surface due to the loss of its opposing tooth.

Dental formula

8	7 A	X	C 5	4	3	2	1	/	2	3	4	5	X A	X A	X A
C 8 A	C 7 A	6	5	4	3	2	1	1	2	3	4	5	6	7	8

Burial 15

Inventory: almost complete skeleton.
Male aged 35–40 years: dolichocephalic.
Stature: 177·844 cm. (5 ft. 10 in.).

Morphological traits

1. Wormian bones: three ossicles at lambda and three right and left lambdoid ossicles.
2. Patent premaxillary suture.

Pathological observations

There is much evidence of osteoarthritis in this skeleton, with lipping around most of the costotransverse articulations, right sternoclavicular articulation and left proximal tibio-fibular articulation.

A slight swelling on the medial aspect of the shaft of the right femur may be an ossified haematoma. A haemorrhage beneath the periosteal membrane sometimes clots and forms new bone such as this, particularly in the deficiency disease of scurvy. In severe cases of scurvy the haematomata are frequently associated with advanced alveolar disease. In this instance the jaws are in fact severely diseased with several alveolar abscesses in the maxillae. But this in itself is not sufficient proof of scurvy and its presence remains unproven.

Skeletal adaptation

Squatting facets are present upon the tibiae.

Dental observations

All of the teeth are crown-worn with slight deposits of calculus. The lower incisors are slightly overcrowded. Caries is present in all of the maxillary right molars and 2nd premolar, the premolar and 1st molar being reduced to their roots (pl. XXII*b*). Severe abscesses at the roots of the maxillary molars and right premolar have entered the antrum (pl. XXII*c*).

Dental formula

C	C	C	C												
8	7	6	5	4	3	2	1	1	2	3	4	5	6	7	8
	A	A	A										A	A	
8	7	6	5	4	/	2	1	1	2	3	4	5	6	7	8

Burial 16

Inventory: almost complete skeleton.
Male aged *c.* 40 years: brachycephalic.
Stature: 168·709 cm. (5 ft. 6½ in.).

Pathological observations

The spine is affected by osteoarthritis with lipping of the articulations of L4 and L5. Osteophytes is also present around the anterior margins of these two vertebrae. Of the remainder of the spine, two thoracic vertebrae have slight lipping and eburnation of their inferior articulations.

Cribra orbitalia is present in the left orbit.

Skeletal adaptation

Squatting facets are present upon the tibiae.

Dental observations

All of the teeth are crown-worn with slight deposits of calculus. Periodontal disease has caused considerable alveolar resorption. Caries is present in the maxillary right 1st and left 3rd molars and the mandibular left 2nd molar.

Dental formula

		C													C
8	7	6	5	4	3	2	1	1	/	3	4	5	6	7	8
														C	
8	7	6	5	4	3	2	1	1	/	3	4	5	6	7	8

Burial 17

Inventory: complete skeleton.
Male aged 25–30 years.
Stature: 175·103 cm. (5 ft. 9 in.).

Morphological trait

Epitrochlear foramen in left humerus.

Pathological observations

Bilateral cribra orbitalia is present.

Skeletal adaptation

Squatting facets are present upon the tibiae.

Dental observations

Caries is present in the maxillary right 1st and left 1st and 3rd molars.

Dental formula

		C											C		C
/	/	6	5	4	3	2	/	1	2	3	4	5	6	7	8
8	7	6	5	4	3	2	/	/	2	3	4	5	6	7	8

Burial 18

Inventory: fragmented skeleton.
Male aged *c.* 20 years.
Stature: 174·946 cm. (5 ft. 9 in.). Strongly built.

Skeletal adaptation

Squatting facets are present upon the tibiae.

Burial 19

Inventory: very eroded skeleton.
Male aged *c.* 35 years.
Strongly built.

Morphological trait

Patent premaxillary suture.

Dental observation

All of the teeth are crown-worn with slight deposits of calculus.

Dental formula

/	/	6	5	4	3	2	1	1	2	3	4	5	6	/	/
/	/	/	5	4	3	2	1	1	2	3	/	/	/	/	/

Burial 20

Inventory: complete skeleton.
Male aged 50+ years.
Stature: 162·220 cm. (5 ft. 3¾ in.).

Morphological trait

Detached neural arch of 4th lumbar vertebra (pl. XXII*d*).

Pathological observations

The skeleton exhibits most of the classic criteria of *osteitis deformans* (Paget's disease). A brief description of this disease and its incidence has already been given (p. 239).

The skeletal changes noted are as follows:

Skull

Externally the whole of the skull presents a gross swollen appearance, with a marked left facial asymmetry involving the maxillo-malar region (pl. XXIII*a*). Most of the cranial sutures have been obliterated, although faint traces of the lambdoid and squamosal sutures can still be seen. Osteoporosis covers much of the cranium and facial area. The mandible is grossly distended with considerable alveolar resorption (pl. XXIV*a*). The foramen magnum is constricted transversely and internally the vault presents a spongy appearance.

Radiographic examination shows a general thickening of the vault to a maximum of 15 mm., with areas of rarefaction apparent throughout.

Long bones: femora, tibiae and left humerus

The affected bones show increased thickness of the cortex and reduction of the medullary cavities. The right femur is more seriously affected than the left, which is almost normal in appearance. The necks of the femora have yielded beneath the weight of the body during the soft stage of the disease (pl. XXIV*c*). Similarly, the stresses of load-bearing have bowed the tibia in an anterior direction (pl. XXIV*b*).

Of the arm bones, only the left humerus appears to be affected, with thickened cortex and reduced medulla.

TABLE V

Osteoarthritis in the Spine of Burial 20

Vertebra	*Superior articular facet*		*Inferior articular facet*		*Vertebral body*
	Left	*Right*	*Left*	*Right*	
Cervical					
1			E	E	
2	E	E	E	E	
3	E	E	E		
4	E	E	E	E	
5	E	E	E	E	S+
6	E	E	E	E	S+
7	E	E			S+
Thoracic					
1		E			
2				E	
3		E			S+
4					S+
5					S+
6					S+
7					S+
8					S+
9					
10					
11					
12			E		
Lumbar					
1	E				
2					
3					
4			E	E	M+
5	E	E			C+

Legend:

E = Eburnated[1] S+ = Slightly lipped margin

M+ = Medium lipped margin C+ = Considerably lipped margin

[1] Except for cervical vertebrae 4 and 5 the eburnation on the articular facets is slight.

Osteoarthritis

There is widespread osteoarthritis in the spine (see table V opposite), the ribs and the digital joints.

Skeletal adaptation

Squatting facets are present upon the tibiae.

Trauma

The sternum has a well-healed fracture running obliquely from the right 3rd and 4th costal facets to the left 4th costal facet.

Dental observations

All of the remaining teeth are severely crown-worn with slight deposits of calculus. Periodontal disease has caused massive alveolar recession and the loss of nine teeth. Osteitis around the alveolar margins may be a consequence of the periodontal infection or Paget's disease. Periodontal abscesses were probably present at the roots of the maxillary and mandibular molars. The mandibular left 1st and 2nd molars are on a higher occlusal plane than the 3rd molar. This abnormal occlusal pattern appears to be a consequence of the loss of the opposing maxillary teeth and the changes in the mandibular structure wrought by Paget's disease.

Dental formula

8	X	X	X	/	3	/	/	X	/	3	4	X	X	X	X
?A	?A	?A											?A	?A	?A
														C	
8	7	X	5	4	3	2	1	1	2	3	4	5	6	7	8
?A	?A	?A											?A	?A	?A

Burial 21

Inventory: fragments of pelvis, carpals and ribs.
Young adult of 16–20 years.

Acknowledgements

I wish to express my thanks to Dr D. R. Brothwell of the British Museum (Natural History) and Dr C. Wells of Norwich for their valuable comments on the pathology of the skeletons. I would also like to thank Mr D. Silver of Saffron Walden for his advice on the dental pathology.

BIBLIOGRAPHY

Adams, J. C. 1956. *Outline of Orthopaedics* (Edinburgh), pp. 186–91.

Aegerter, E. and Kirkpatrick, J. A. 1963. *Orthopedic Diseases*. London.

Astre, G. 1957. 'Maladie osseuse pagétoïde d'un crâne Gallo-Romain.' *Revue Path. Gén. Physiol. Clin.* lvii, 63–9.

BENNETT, N. 1931. *The Science and Practice of Dental Surgery* (London), Vol. I, pp. 122–4.

BROTHWELL, D. R. 1959. 'The use of non-metrical characters of the skull in differentiating populations.' *Ber. 6 Tag. dtsch. Ges. Anthrop. Kiel*, 103–9.

BROTHWELL, D. R. 1961. 'The palaeopathology of early British man: an essay on the problems of diagnosis and analysis.' *R. Anthrop. Inst. London* 318–44.

BROTHWELL, D. R. 1963. 'Digging up bones.' *The Excavation, Treatment and Study of Human Skeletal Remains* (London), pp. 192 ff.

COLLINS, D. H. and HUNTER, J. 1956. 'Paget's disease of bone: incidence and sub-clinical forms.' *Lancet* ii, 51–7.

DAVIS, D. G. 1968. 'Paget's disease of the temporal bone: a clinical and histopathological survey.' *Acta Otolaryng.* (Supplement), 330–45.

GARDNER, A. F., DRESCHER, J. T. and GOODREAU, G. J. 1963. 'Study of 24 cases of Paget's disease involving the maxilla and mandible with reference to dentistry.' *J. Gal. Dent. Assoc.* xxxix, 2.

GENOVES, S. T. and MESSMACHER, M. 1959. 'Valor de los patrones tradicionales para la determinación del edad por medio de las suturas en craneos mexicanos.' *Cuadernas del Instituto de Historia.* Serie No. 7.

GRAY HILL, N. 1937. 'Excavations on Stockbridge Down, 1935–36.' *Proc. Hants Field Club & Arch. Soc.* xiii, part 3, 254.

HENSCHEN, F. 1956. 'Zur Paläopathologie des Schädels — über die sog. Cribra Cranii.' In *Verh. dtsch. Ges. Path. Stuttgart*, 39 ff.

HENSCHEN, F. 1961. 'Cribra Cranii, a skull condition said to be of racial or geographical nature.' In 7th Conf. Inter. Soc. Geograph. Pathol. 1960. *Path. Microbiol.* xxiv, 724–9.

HOOPER, B. 1968. In BRADLEY, R., 'Excavations at the George Inn, Portsdown.' *Proc. Hants Field Club & Arch. Soc.* xxv, 46–7.

HUNT, E. E. and GLEISER, I. 1955. 'The estimation of age and sex of pre-adolescent children from bones and teeth.' *Amer. J. Phys. Anthrop. Washington* (n.s.), xiii, 479–88.

JAFFE, H. L. 1966. In JARCHO, S. *Human Palaeopathology* (London), pp. 66–7.

JANSSENS, P. 1963. 'De crematieresten uit het urnenveld te Grote-Brogel.' In ROOSENS, H., BEEX, G. and BONENFANT, P. 'Een urnenveld te Grote-Brogel.' *Archaeologia Belgica* lxvii, 261–300.

MCKERN, T. W. and STEWART, T. D. 1957. *Skeletal age changes in young American males* (Technical report. Headquarters Quartermaster Research and Development Command, Natick, Mass.), pp. 179 ff.

MERCER, W. 1936. *Orthopaedic Surgery* (Edinburgh), pp. 138–43.

MØLLER-CHRISTENSEN, V. 1953. *Ten Lepers from Naestved in Denmark* (Copenhagen), pp. 160 ff.

MØLLER-CHRISTENSEN, V. 1961. *Bone Changes in Leprosy* (Copenhagen), pp. 29 ff.

MØLLER-CHRISTENSEN, V. and SANDISON, A. T. 1963. 'Usura Orbitae (Cribra Orbitalia) in the collection of crania in the anatomy department of the University of Glasgow.' *Path. Microbiol.* xxvi, 175–88.

MOODIE, R. L. 1923. *Palaeopathology: an Introduction to the Study of Ancient Evidences of Disease* (Illinois), pp. 567 ff.

PAGET, J. 1877. 'On a form of chronic inflammation of bones (osteitis deformans).' *Trans. Med. Chir. Soc.* x, 37.

PALES, L. 1929. 'Maladie de Paget préhistorique.' *L'Anthropologie* lxxxix, 263–70.

PALES, L. 1930. *Palaéopathologie et pathologie comparative* (Paris), pp. 352 ff.

PARSONS, F. G. and BOX, L. R. 1905. 'The relation of the cranial sutures to age.' *J. R. Anthrop. Inst. London* xxv, 30–8.

PYLE, S. I. and HOERR, N. L. 1955. *Radiographic Atlas of Skeletal Developments of the Knee* (Illinois), pp. 82 ff.

SCHMORL, G. 1932. 'Über Osteitis Deformans Paget.' *Virchows Arch. Path. Anat.* cclxxxiii, 694–751.

TODD, T. W. and LYONS, D. W. 1924. 'Endocranial suture closure. Part I. Adult males of White stock.' *Amer. J. Phys. Anthrop. Washington* vii, 325–84.

TODD, T. W. and LYONS, D. W. 1925. 'Cranial suture closure. Part II. Ectocranial closure in adult males of White stock'. *Amer. J. Phys. Anthrop. Washington* viii, 23–71.

TROTTER, M. and GLESER, G. C. 1952. 'Estimation of stature from long-bones of American Whites and Negroes.' *Amer. J. Phys. Anthrop. Washington* (n.s.), x, 463–514.

TROTTER, M. and GLESER, G. C. 1958. 'A re-evaluation of estimation of stature based on measurements of stature taken during life and long-bones after death.' *Amer. J. Phys. Anthrop. Washington* (n.s.), xvi, 79–123.

WAKEFIELD, E. G. and DELLINGER, S. C. 1936. 'The probable adaptation of utilitarian implements for surgical procedures by the "Mound Builders" of Eastern Arkansas.' *J. Bone Jt. Surg.* xviii, 434–8.

WAKEFIELD, E. G. and DELLINGER, S. C. 1937. 'Artefacts found among the remains of the "Mound Builders".' *Bull. Inst. Hist. Med.* v, 452–60.

WARWICK, R. 1968. In WENHAM, L. P. *The Romano-British cemetery at Trentholme Drive, York* (Ministry of Public Buildings and Works Archaeological Reports No. 5. London), pp. 150 ff.

WELLS, C. 1963a. 'Cortical grooves on the tibia.' *Man* cxxxvii, 112–14.

WELLS, C. 1963b. In KNOCKER, G. M. 'Excavations at Red Castle, Thetford.' *Norfolk Arch.* xxxiv, Part II, 170–1.

VIII. FAUNAL REMAINS

THE ANIMAL BONES

By Annie Grant

In all, some 22,960 animal bones from Saxon contexts were examined by the writer. Of these, 2406 were not positively identified, being in the main small fragments: the remaining 20,554 form the basis of this report.

For the purposes of some analyses the bones were divided into three main groups. These are shown in table I with their archaeological contexts and approximate dates.

TABLE I

Group	*Context*	*Date*
Early–Middle	Pits	*c.* 5th–*c.* 8th century
Middle–Late		
(a)	Pits	*c.* 8th–*c.* 10th century
(b)	Occupation layers	
Late	Pits	*c.* 10th–*c.* 11th century

A small group of bones was recovered from the early Saxon huts 1 and 4. They are included separately in table II, but since the pottery analysis indicated a large amount of residual Roman material in the group they have otherwise been excluded from the analyses.

When examining the bones from a multi-period site the possibility that material from earlier periods may be included with material from later contexts cannot be ruled out. Although it may be possible to distinguish a Roman potsherd from a Saxon one, it is not possible to distinguish visually Roman from Saxon bone. Some have argued that, for this very reason, analysis of bone material from multi-period sites should not be attempted. The writer is not of this opinion. Care was taken to include in the sample only the bone from those contexts where there was least likelihood of contamination. The percentage of Roman bones included by chance in the sample should thus be small, and should not invalidate the general conclusions made from a fairly large sample of bones. It is believed that the enormous interpretative advantages of having bone material from such a long period of occupation at one site far outweigh the disadvantages.

Other potential sources of error and bias have been discussed in the report on the Roman bones from Portchester (Grant, 1975), and apply as much to the Saxon as to the Roman material. The bone sample is again an unsieved one.

THE ANIMALS REPRESENTED

Bones were recovered from cattle, sheep, pigs, red deer, roe deer, horses, birds, fallow deer, hares, cats, dogs, badgers, voles, fish, foxes, frogs and an unidentified small mammal. 'Sheep' is used throughout the report to mean 'sheep and/or goat'. These are the same animals that were found in the Roman period, the only differences being the presence of a few frog bones in the Saxon group and the presence of a few mouse bones in the Roman group. The bone report for the Roman period includes a discussion of the merits of different methods of determining the relative proportions of the various species. The three methods used there are used again in this report. The 'epiphyses only' method counts only those bones with part of an epiphysis or fusion surface present, and mandibles with at least one tooth present. 'Total fragments' counts all bone fragments except ribs and skull fragments that do not include part of the horn core or a tooth. 'Minimum numbers of individuals' are calculated by dividing by two the number of the most commonly represented part of the bone of the animal. This method has only been calculated for the better represented animals.

The results are shown in table II, and are plotted in histogram form in fig. 147 for the better represented animals. Table II also includes the Roman totals for comparative purposes.

The 'epiphyses only' method and the 'total fragments' method give broadly similar results. The main differences are that the second method indicates more cattle and less bird than does the first method. This is as expected and is due to the difference in size between the two animals. The 'epiphyses only' method should therefore give the more accurate results of the two. Using the results of this method, we have, for the Saxon period as a whole, cattle bones as the most common, forming 35% of the total. Sheep bones form 22% of the total, and bird bones are almost as numerous, forming 21%. Pig bones form 14%. The only other species whose bones form any significant part of the total recovered are deer bones, and horse, cat and fish bones. All other species form less than 0·5%. If these results are compared with those of the Roman period, some significant differences are seen. Cattle bones are far more common from the Roman levels, while bird bones are significantly less common. Sheep bones are more common in the Saxon period, as are deer bones, but dog and cat bones were found more frequently in Roman contexts. The implications of these differences are discussed in the final section of this chapter.

Differences too are to be found amongst the various groups of the Saxon period. The importance of cattle appears to decline from 57% in the earliest group to 31% in the latest group. The percentage of sheep bones is highest in the middle–late groups, while pig bones remain a fairly constant 13–16% throughout the Saxon period. Bird bones show a change from 9% in the earliest period to 25% in the latest group. Dog and cat bones only form a significant part of the total in the latest group. Changes in the amounts of the other animals found at the site cannot confidently be considered significant. It is perhaps interesting to note that the largest range of species occurs in the latest group.

The results obtained using the 'minimum numbers of individuals' method (table II*c*) emphasize most of the differences between groups already noted, although they give very different individual figures. The calculations based on this method indicate that cattle represent only 18% of the animals kept, caught or eaten in the Saxon period, while sheep and pig each form over 30% of the total, and bird only 10%. It should be noted that statistically the differences between the results calculated by this method are less likely to be significant than those calculated by the other two methods. The results in the early/middle group especially should be treated with caution.

The reasons for the differences in the results obtained by the 'minimum numbers of individuals' method and the 'epiphyses only' method are easily understood. Deciding which method gives the more accurate results is a more difficult problem, and depends very much

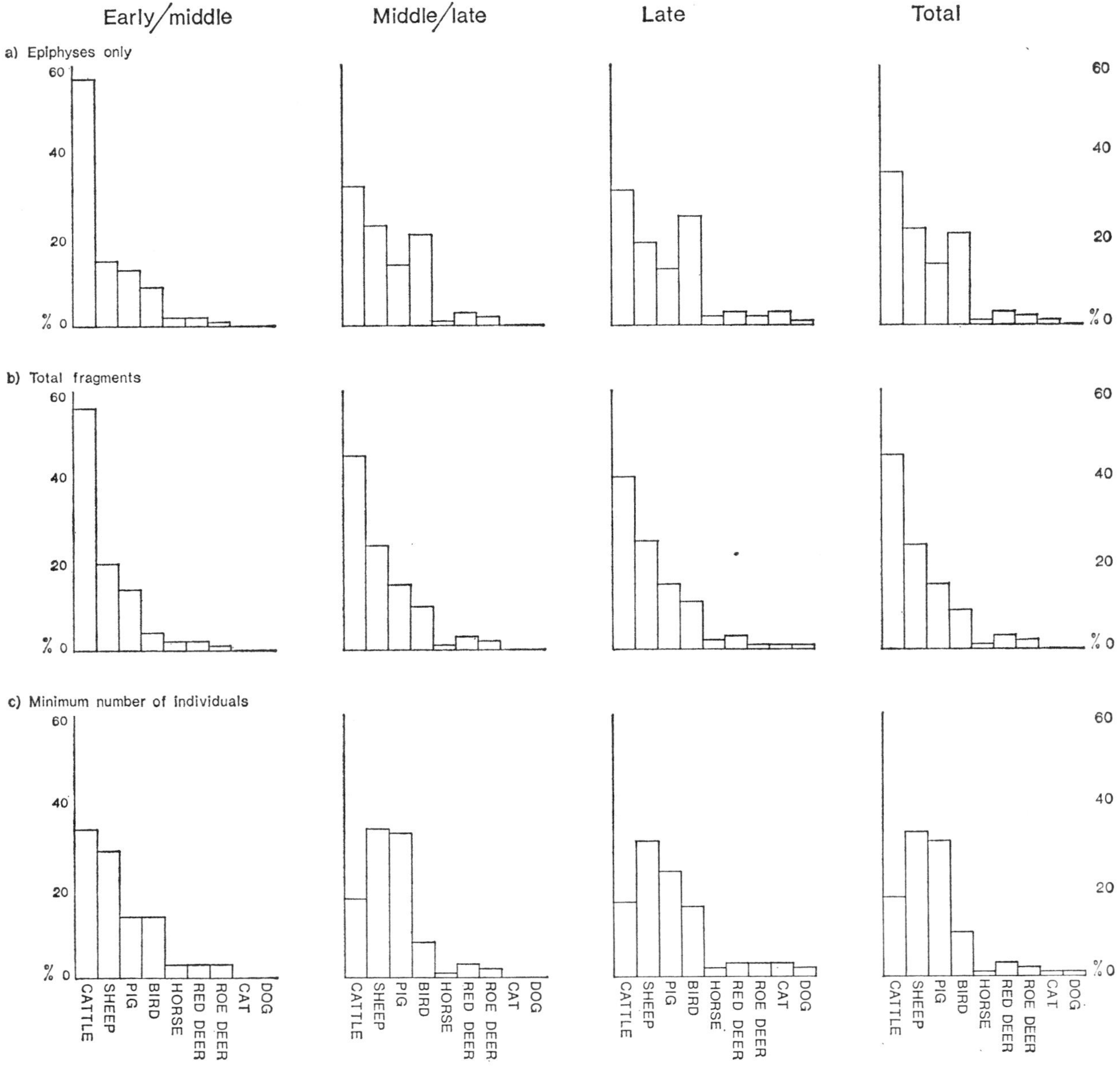

FIG. 147. Animal bones: percentages of species represented

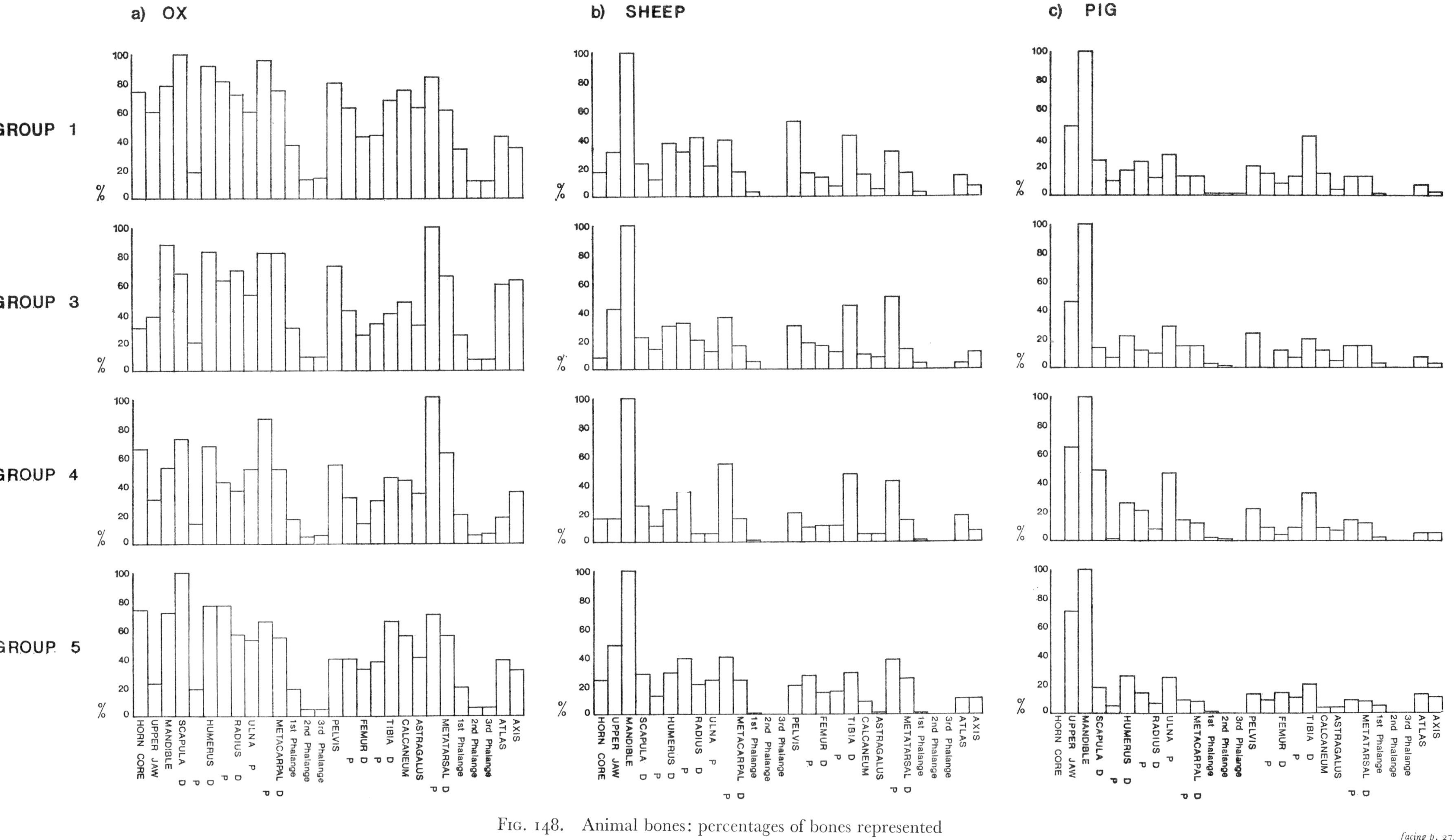

FIG. 148. Animal bones: percentages of bones represented

facing p. 274

TABLE II

	Early–middle		Middle–late (*a*)		Middle–late (*b*)		Middle–late (*a*+*b*)		Late		Huts 1 and 4		Total		Roman total	
	No.	%	*No.*	%	*No.*	%	*No.*	%	*No.*	%	*No.*	%	*No.*	%	*No.*	%
(*a*) *Epiphyses only*																
Cattle	287	57	1507	35	428	32	1935	34	439	31	35	51	2696	35	5332	52
Sheep	74	15	940	22	363	27	1303	23	267	19	9	13	1653	22	1551	15
Pig	64	13	604	14	213	16	817	14	185	13	17	25	1083	14	1361	13
Bird	46	9	954	22	223	17	1177	21	352	25	6	9	1581	21	992	10
Red deer	9	2	124	3	27	2	151	3	43	3			203	3	148	1
Roe deer	5	1	75	2	52	4	127	2	24	2			156	2	20	
Horse	9	2	42	1	8	1	50	1	22	2	1	1	82	1	60	1
Cat			13		6		19		39	3			58	1	281	3
Dog			16		3		19		15	1	1	1	35		418	4
Fallow deer	1		6		4		10		1				12		8	
Hare			24	1	2		26		2				28		17	
Badger			1				1						1		13	
Vole									2				2		6	
Fish	5	1	29	1	3		32	1	5				42	1		
Fox									1				1		22	
Frog									4				4			
Small mammal					1		1						1		8	
Total	500		4335		1333		5668		1401		69		7638		10239	
(*b*) *Total fragments*																
Cattle	553	56	3784	47	1290	40	5074	45	1029	40	90	49	6746	45	10774	57
Sheep	197	20	1750	22	945	29	2695	24	626	25	49	27	3567	24	3212	17
Pig	138	14	1172	15	547	17	1719	15	385	15	35	19	2277	15	2654	14
Bird	42	4	847	10	245	8	1092	10	268	11	5	3	1407	9	798	4
Red deer	23	2	232	3	63	2	295	3	74	3			392	3	262	1
Roe deer	7	1	109	1	90	3	199	2	27	1	1		234	2	38	
Horse	21	2	63	1	9		72	1	46	2	3	2	142	1	119	1
Cat			10		5		15		36	1			51		296	2
Dog			17		5		22		35	1	1	1	58		680	4
Fallow deer	1		18		7		25		2				28		11	
Hare			27		2		29		4				33		22	
Badger			1				1						1		13	
Vole									1				1		3	
Fish	5	1	29		3		32		5				42		11	
Fox									1				1		22	
Frog									3				3			
Small mammal					1		1						1		5	
Total	987		8059		3212		11271		2542		184		14984		18923	

TABLE II—*continued*

	Early–middle		*Middle–late (a)*		*Middle late (b)*		*Middle–late (a+b)*		*Late*		*Total*		*Roman total*	
	No.	%	*No.*	%	*No.*	%	*No.*	%	*No.*	%	*No.*	%	*No.*	%
(*c*) *Minimum numbers of individuals*														
Cattle	12	34	89	18	28	17	117	18	20	17	149	18	216	32
Sheep	10	29	169	34	54	34	223	34	36	31	269	33	151	33
Pig	5	14	166	33	50	31	216	33	28	24	249	31	180	27
Bird	5	14	38	8	16	10	54	8	19	16	78	10	56	8
Red deer	1	3	18	4	4	2	22	3	4	3	27	3	18	3
Roe deer	1	3	8	2	6	4	14	2	3	3	18	2	not calculated	
Horse	1	3	3	1	1	1	4	1	2	2	7	1	7	1
Cat			2		1	1	3		3	3	6	1	15	2
Dog			2		1	1	3		2	2	5	1	25	4
Total	35		495		161		656		117		808		668	

on the interpretation given to the representation of the different bones of the body. This is discussed in the next section.

If the actual numbers of animals indicated by the results of this method are considered, it is clear that for an occupation of some 600 years we have only a very small number of animals, even if we allow for the fact that only an eighth of the fort has been excavated to date. This raises the problem of the nature of the sample of bones with which we are dealing, and underlines the great dangers inherent in any interpretative analysis of bone material from a site which has not been totally excavated and whose immediate surroundings have not been fully investigated. The danger is that the domestic refuse found in one particular area of settlement may not necessarily truly reflect the economy of the settlement as a whole. However, this is a problem with no hope of an immediate practical solution.

In table III, the results calculated by the 'minimum numbers of individuals' method have

TABLE III

	Early/middle			*Middle/late*			*Late*			*Total*			*Roman total*		
	No.	%	*m.y.* %	*No.*	%	*m.y.* %	*No.*	%	*m.y.* %	*No.*	%	*m.y.* %	*No.*	%	*m.y.* %
Cattle	12	44	83	117	21	60	20	24	64	149	22	62	216	39	78
Sheep	10	37	10	223	40	16	36	43	16	269	40	15	151	28	8
Pig	5	19	8	216	39	24	28	33	20	249	37	23	180	33	14
	27			556			84			667			547		

m.y. = meat yield.

been adjusted in order to indicate the relationships of the three main food animals in terms of meat yield. The weights used are those given by Carter *et al.* (1965) as a rough guide. They are: cattle 900 lb., sheep 125 lb., pigs 200 lb. The Roman total is again included for comparative purposes.

The results of this calculation show that in terms of meat yield only, cattle are the most important animals although, especially in the middle and late groups, pork and lamb might be expected to have formed a reasonable part of the diet. They certainly seem to have been more important in the Saxon than in the Roman diet at the site. This of course excludes the contribution that cows', sheep's or goats' milk might have made to the diet.

ANALYSIS OF BONES REPRESENTED AND BUTCHERY

Table IV gives a detailed analysis of the bones recovered for each of the three main food animals. Table V gives the number of ribs and skull fragments found for all species in each group. Ribs were not included in table IV because of the difficulty of positive species identification. Fig. 148 shows the main results of table IV in histogram form. The percentages are percentages of the greatest number, with adjustments made to allow for accurate comparison between bones — for example, the numbers of atlases and axes are multiplied by two before the percentage is calculated. Three figures are given for the skull. The first includes all large and diagnostic fragments. The second, in brackets, includes all small fragments. These are generally broken frontal bone and other thin areas of the skull. The third includes all skull fragments which have part of the lower margin of the orbit present. These fragments are also included in the first figures for the skull. The orbit figures are given to provide a check on the horn core and upper jaw figures.

The analysis of the cattle bones (table IV*a*) gives a picture very similar to that found in the analysis of the Roman bones, with those bones least well represented whose density and age of fusion of epiphyses make them most vulnerable to decay and fragmentation (see Brain, 1969; Isaac, 1967; discussed in Grant, 1975). Those bones best represented, proximal metapodia, pelves with acetabulum and distal tibiae are all formed of dense bone, and fuse fairly early. The bones that carry the most meat — scapulae, humeri, proximal radii, pelves, femora and proximal radii — are neither consistently well represented nor consistently ill represented. It would thus be very unwise to assume that the scarcity of some bones is due to the selling off or buying in of particular parts of the body. The high degree of correlation between the results of the analysis of the Saxon and Roman material, and amongst the individual Saxon groups might argue that survival and recovery were the principal factors affecting the distribution of the various bones.

The same problems arise in a discussion of the representation of the bones of sheep and pig. The sheep bones (table IV*b*) again show a similar pattern to that seen in the analysis of the Roman sheep. There are though some differences that might be meaningful. There is an even greater discrepancy between the numbers of jaws and the numbers of all other bones in the Saxon group. Were this paralleled by a corresponding increase in the numbers of metapodia and phalanges, the presence of butchery waste might be deduced. However, in fact there is the opposite situation, with far fewer metapodia recovered in the Saxon group. The figure for the proximal end of the metacarpal is 41% in the Roman group, but only

TABLE IV

	Early–middle		*Middle–late (a)*		*Middle–late (b)*		*Middle–late total*		*Late*		*Total*		*Roman total*	
	No.	%	*No.*	%	*No.*	%	*No.*	%	*No.*	%	*No.*	%	*No.*	%
(*a*) *Cattle*														
Horncore	18	75	114	64	38	68	152	65	27	69	197	71	271	73
Skull	11		364		113		477		47		535			
	(9)		(317)		(98)		(415)		(117)		(541)			
Orbit	4	17	66	37	24	43	90	38	14	36	108	39		
Maxilla	5	21	130	73	25	45	155	66	16	41	176	64	159	43
Mandible	13	54	178	100	56	100	234	100	30	77	277	100	298	80
Scapula D	17	71	75	42	23	41	98	42	15	38	130	47	355	96
Humerus P	1	4	27	15	1	2	28	12	2	5	31	11	70	19
D	19	79	95	53	18	32	113	48	28	72	160	58	248	69
Radius P	19	79	74	42	25	45	99	42	39	100	154	56	265	71
D	10	42	31	17	16	29	47	20	11	28	68	25	232	63
Ulna P	3	13	62	35	24	43	86	37	21	54	110	40	227	61
Metacarpal P	22	92	113	63	32	57	145	62	35	90	202	73	349	94
D	9	38	46	26	20	36	66	28	11	28	86	31	263	71
1st Phalange	9	21	42	12	16	14	58	12	16	21	83	15	205	28
2nd Phalange	2	4	15	4	10	9	25	6	4	5	31	6	62	8
3rd Phalange	1	4	6	2	4	4	10	2	1	3	12	2	67	9
Pelvis: acetabulum	14	58	111	62	29	52	140	60	38	97	192	69	258	70
Femur P	10	42	68	38	13	23	81	35	18	46	109	39	176	43
D	8	33	50	28	13	23	63	27	10	26	81	29	115	31
Tibia P	5	21	52	29	8	14	60	26	11	28	76	27	149	40
D	13	54	106	60	23	41	129	55	24	62	166	60	230	62
Calcaneum	14	58	73	41	13	23	86	37	16	41	116	42	233	63
Astragalus	19	79	73	41	18	32	91	39	18	46	128	46	177	48
Metatarsal P	24	100	115	65	29	52	144	62	24	62	189	68	371	100
D	18	75	47	26	13	23	60	26	18	46	96	35	259	70
1st Phalange	18	38	43	12	11	11	54	12	27	36	99	18	206	28
2nd Phalange	1	4	16	4	6	5	22	5	7	10	30	5	64	8
3rd Phalange	2	4	7	2	2	2	9	2	3	5	14	3	67	9
Atlas	2	17	18	20	6	21	24	21	8	41	34	25	83	45
Axis	1	8	19	21	9	32	28	24	5	25	34	25	81	44
Cervical vert.	9		63		17		80		16		105			
Thoracic vert.	12		104		10		114		21		147			
Lumbar vert.	7		49		10		59		7		73			
Sacrum	—		8		1		9		3		12			
Caudal vert.	—		3		1		4		1		5			
Vert. frags.	24		162		84		246		59		329			
Loose teeth	94		453		251		704		150		948			

18% in the Saxon group. It seems likely that, since metapodia are formed of dense bone and should have a good survival potential, this implies a shortage of metapodia in the Saxon group, rather than an abundance in the Roman group. One possible explanation for this is the use of the bone for tool manufacture. This aspect is discussed below.

Amongst the Saxon groups, few differences are seen. The figures for the early–middle group are probably not reliable, since the sample is small. The best represented bones,

TABLE IV—*continued*

	Early–middle		*Middle–late (a)*		*Middle–late (b)*		*Middle–late total*		*Late*		*Total*		*Roman total*	
	No.	%	*No.*	%	*No.*	%	*No.*	%	*No.*	%	*No.*	%	*No.*	%
(*b*) *Sheep*														
Horncore	5	26	59	18	18	17	77	17	21	29	103	19	54	18
Skull	1		29		16		45				46			
	(2)		(26)		(36)		(62)		(10)		(74)			
Orbit	2	11	15	4	4	4	19	4	1	1	22	4		
Maxilla	3	16	56	17	17	16	73	16	12	17	88	16	100	34
Mandible	19	100	337	100	108	100	445	100	72	100	536	100	292	100
Scapula D	5	26	58	17	5	5	63	14	15	21	83	15	74	25
Humerus P	2	11	20	6	6	6	26	6	8	11	36	7	38	13
D	8	42	60	18	28	26	88	20	15	21	111	21	88	30
Radius P	4	21	49	15	24	22	73	16	23	32	100	19	102	35
D	1	5	23	7	13	12	36	8	8	11	45	8	44	15
Ulna P	2	11	13	4	11	10	24	5	5	7	31	6	47	16
Metacarpal P	4	21	44	13	20	19	64	14	14	19	82	15	129	66
D	—		30	9	16	15	46	10	5	7	51	10	56	19
1st Phalange	1	5	4	1	4	2	8	1	1	1	10	1	17	3
2nd Phalange	—		1		—		1		—		1		—	
3rd Phalange	—		—		—		—		—		—		1	
Pelvis: acetabulum	3	16	45	13	22	20	67	15	18	25	88	16	137	47
Femur P	5	26	21	6	8	7	29	7	6	8	40	7	56	19
D	2	11	29	9	7	6	36	8	8	11	46	9	43	15
Tibia P	2	11	20	6	3	3	23	5	11	15	36	7	35	12
D	9	47	78	23	35	32	113	25	33	46	155	29	122	42
Calcaneum	3	16	8	2	2	2	10	2	2	3	15	3	29	10
Astragalus	—		6	2	2	2	8	2	1	1	9	2	14	5
Metatarsal P	3	16	44	13	34	31	78	18	15	21	96	18	119	41
D	—		29	9	9	8	38	8	8	11	46	9	54	18
1st Phalange	—		4	1	3	2	7	1	1	1	8	1	15	3
2nd Phalange	—		1		—		1		—		1		—	
3rd Phalange	—		—		—		—		—		—		—	
Atlas	1	11	12	7	3	6	15	7	3	8	19	7	18	12
Axis	—		13	8	2	4	15	7	2	6	17	6	13	9
Cervical vert.	1		18		6		24		7		32			
Thoracic vert.	2		27		3		30		12		44			
Lumbar vert.	—		27		15		42		8		50			
Sacrum	—		1		1		2		1		3			
Caudal vert.	1		1		—		1		—		2			
Vert. frags.	4		34		19		53		12		69			
Loose teeth	33		169		169		338		70		441			

apart from the mandibles, are, as among the cattle bones, the pelves, distal ends of tibiae, and the distal ends of the humeri and proximal ends of the radii.

In the analysis of the pig bones (table IV*c*) there is a very large discrepancy between the numbers of pig mandibles and all other bones recovered. (Again the results of the analysis of the early–middle group are not likely to be very reliable.) The proportions of the other

TABLE IV—*continued*

	Early–middle		*Middle–late (a)*		*Middle–late (b)*		*Middle–late total*		*Late*		*Total*		*Roman total*	
	No.	%	*No.*	%	*No.*	%	*No.*	%	*No.*	%	*No.*	%	*No.*	%
(*c*) *Pig*														
Skull	3 (3)		99 (40)		60 (11)		159 (51)		14 (30)		176 (84)			
Orbit	—		40	12	14	14	54	13	5	9	59	12		
Maxilla	7	70	123	37	65	66	188	44	15	27	210	42	199	56
Mandible	10	100	331	100	99	100	430	100	55	100	495	100	355	100
Scapula D	8	80	47	14	13	13	60	14	12	22	60	12	96	27
Humerus P	—		7	2	4	4	11	3	3	5	14	3	22	6
D	4	40	35	11	6	6	41	10	9	16	54	11	77	22
Radius P	3	30	18	5	11	11	29	7	9	16	41	8	64	18
D	2	20	5	2	3	3	8	2	2	4	12	2	32	9
Ulna P	8	80	17	5	15	15	32	7	16	29	56	11	113	32
Metacarpal P	2	10	23	4	15	8	38	9	8	7	48	5	90	13
D	3	20	19	3	12	6	31	7	6	5	40	4	80	11
1st Phalange	1	10	1		6	3	7	1	2	2	10	1	11	2
2nd Phalange	1	10	1		1	1	2		—		3		3	1
3rd Phalange	—		—		1	1	1		—		1		1	
Pelvis: acetabulum	3	30	48	15	4	4	52	12	31	56	66	13	119	34
Femur P	4	40	3	1	2	2	5	1	2	4	11	2	33	9
D	3	30	9	3	1	1	10	2	3	5	16	3	32	9
Tibia P	2	20	10	3	—		10	2	6	11	18	4	35	10
D	4	40	24	7	10	10	34	8	8	15	46	9	104	29
Calcaneum	2	20	—		1	1	1		2	4	5	1	37	10
Astragulus	—		4	1	5	5	9	2	2	4	11	2	17	5
Metatarsal P	3	20	21	3	9	5	30	7	11	11	44	4	89	13
D	2	10	17	3	7	4	24	6	8	7	34	3	79	11
1st Phalange	1	10	1		3	2	4		2	2	7	1	10	1
2nd Phalange	—		—		1	1	1		—		1		2	
3rd Phalange	—		—		—		—		—		—		1	
Atlas	—		5	3	7	14	12	6	2	7	12	5	13	7
Axis	—		1	1	1	2	2	1	1	3	3	1	8	2
Cervical vert.	2		6		2		8				10			
Thoracic vert.	1		10		6		16		9		26			
Lumbar vert.	1		—		4		4		2		7			
Sacrum	—		—		—		—		—		—			
Caudal vert.	—		—		—		—		—		—			
Vert. frags.	5		34		9		43		5		53			
Loose teeth	32		204		154		358		92		482			

P = proximal
D = distal

bones are similar to those found in the Roman period, with scapulae, distal humeri, ulnae, pelves and distal tibiae best represented. The large numbers of pelves in the late group is the most obvious difference between the Saxon groups. The reason for this is not immediately apparent.

The writer believes that the indications are that the main factors influencing the repre-

TABLE V

	Early–middle		Middle–late		Late		Huts 1 and 2		Total		Roman total	
	No.	%	No.	%	No.	%	No.	%	No.	%	No.	%
Ribs	198	16	3067	20	717	21	88	31	4070	20	8090	28
Skull frags.	37	3	1228	8	224	6	11	4	1500	7	1895	7
Other frags.	987	81	11271	72	2542	73	184	65	14984	73	18923	65
Total	1222		15566		3483		283		20554		28908	

sentation of individual bones are those of survival and recovery, and that originally all parts of the body might have been fairly evenly represented. The very large percentages of sheep and pig jaws compared to the jaws of cattle are probably due to the smaller size and generally younger age at death of these animals (see the next section). The differences between the Saxon and Roman representation of jaws may possibly be due to differences in butchery technique. Other explanations are of course possible.

Much of the discussion in the previous section revolved around an evaluation of the merits of the three different methods of calculating the percentages of animal represented. The reason for the very large difference between the results of the first two methods and the 'minimum numbers of individuals' method is the very large number of mandibles recovered compared to other parts of the body. The understanding of the reason for this is thus crucial in an evaluation of the potential accuracy of the three methods. If better recovery and survival is the cause of large numbers of jaws being recovered, then the 'minimum numbers of individuals' method should give the most reliable results. If, however, the cause is the buying or selling of some parts of the carcass in preference to others, then the 'epiphyses only' method should show a far more accurate picture of the actual meat consumption of the inhabitants of the site. This should not be confused with the structure of the livestock group as a whole, which may be quite different.

Large numbers of the Saxon bones had been gnawed. The size of the tooth marks indicated that the animals responsible were dogs, or possibly foxes. Some examples of gnawed bones are given in pl. XXVI*a*, *b*, *c*. The frequency of these marks, which were found on the bones of cattle, sheep and pigs, and occasionally on deer and horse bones too, is especially interesting in relation to the small numbers of dog bones recovered from Saxon levels. This may be an indication that dogs were not necessarily scarce at the site, but that they were not buried amongst the normal domestic refuse, at least not in this part of the site. Cats and horses might also have been dealt with in a special way.

An analysis of the Saxon butchery techniques as revealed by the chop marks on the bones was also undertaken. The very clear pattern of butchery that emerged from the analysis of the Roman bones was not found in the Saxon group. One of the differences is the greater fragmentation of the Saxon cattle bones, demonstrated in table VI. The many whole skulls found especially in the wells of the Roman period allowed a discussion even of the method of slaughter used. Whole skulls were not found in the Saxon period. However, some sort of butchery pattern has been deduced.

As in the Roman period, there is evidence of the use of three different types of tools. The most commonly used tool seems to have been a fairly heavy chopping tool, but the use of a sharp knife is also indicated. Saws seem to have been used mainly in bone tool manufacture, but may also have been used for the purposes of butchery. Pl. XXVI*d*, *e*, *f* gives examples of the use of these three tools.

Cattle horn cores have quite frequently cuts on them that indicate their deliberate removal from the skull. The position of some of these cuts indicates that the horn itself would have been damaged by the blow, so the precise purpose of the removal of the horn is not clear. Marks on the skull itself, just below the orbit, may result from the removal of the cheek meat. Horizontal chops across the vertical part of the ramus may indicate a method of removal of the mandible from the skull.

The spine of the scapula is frequently cut off, but the consistency of cuts on the distal end of the bone noticed in the Roman material is not repeated in the Saxon bones. A much more haphazard technique is indicated.

Cuts are found on the bones of the elbow joint, and are of two main types. One results in the splitting of the bones longitudinally. Pl. XXVI*h* shows a humerus that has been split by a blow to the front of the distal facet. Radii and ulnae are found with corresponding cuts (pl. XXVI*j*). The other type of cut is one across the distal facet of the humerus at right angles to the bone; this would have separated the humerus from the radius.

As one might expect, the metacarpals are not generally seen with butchery marks associated with meat removal. They are, however, fairly frequently split longitudinally in an anterior–posterior direction.

Pelves are found with cuts across or near the acetabulum, and the ilium and ischium may be chopped into small pieces (pl. XXVI*d*). The femur seems to have been removed from the pelvis by cutting off the head. Cuts have occasionally been found across the distal end of the femur, as if to separate this bone from the tibia. Both femora and tibiae are found split longitudinally, but in some cases bones were found with holes bored through the interior spongy bone into the marrow cavity.

Cuts on the calcanea and astragali indicate the separation of the bones of the upper and lower part of the leg at this point, and cuts on the metatarsals may indicate that the toes were sometimes cut off. One metatarsal had been sawn through, but this is more likely to have been for tool manufacturing than for butchery purposes (pl. XXVI*e*).

The wings of lumbar vertebrae are frequently cut off, sometimes with a chop that also removes part of the side of the body. The meat of the lower part of the body at least seems generally to have been removed from either side of the vertebrae, as they are not found split. Cervical vertebrae are occasionally found split, and the axes and atlases often have several cuts on them, perhaps resulting from the removal of the head from the body. Cervical, lumbar and thoracic vertebrae all are found with cuts across them at right angles to the line of the spine.

Knife marks are found on the shafts of bones, and above and below the epiphyses. Knives seem to have been used to remove the meat from the bone.

Perhaps the most conspicuous characteristic of the Saxon butchery technique is the frequency with which the limb bones are split longitudinally, presumably to facilitate the removal of the bone marrow. There is also an impression of greater fragmentation in the Saxon material — the bones may have been cut into smaller pieces than in the Roman period. Certainly there are few whole bones found — this is seen in table VI, which gives the percentages of complete bones found. The figures for the broken bones are the number of either the proximal or distal ends, depending on which is greater for each individual bone. It is interesting to contrast the butchery techniques used in the Saxon period with modern butchery techniques. The Saxon use of the chopping tool would be considered heavy-handed in a modern butcher's shop. The essence of good modern butchery is the accurate and careful separation of the 'good' meat from the cheap. The chopper and saw are used with discretion, and a sharp knife is the most used tool. The Saxon technique would indicate little regard for the modern cook's distinctions between expensive and cheap cuts of meat. In fact the assessment of the chop marks on the cattle bones and on the bones of the other animals leads to a very tentative suggestion that stews may have been a popular form of meat consumption in the Saxon period.

The sheep bones also reveal evidence of butchery. The horn cores of both sheep and goats are found cut from the skull, but judging by the position of the cuts on many of the cores, the purpose cannot have been to remove the horn intact from the skull. Pl. XXVI*k* shows a skull fragment cut in a fairly typical way. Small chop marks can be seen on the skull that indicate the direction of the blows that severed the horn core. The skulls themselves are sometimes split along the frontal suture (pl. XXVI*l*).

Knife marks around the joint surfaces of the bones are the most common type of butchery marks on sheep bones. They are found around the distal end of the humerus and proximal end of the radius, and are more or less identical to those found on these bones when the radius and humerus are separated by knife in modern butchery practice. Similar marks are also found on the hind limb (pl. XXVI*f*, *g*).

There is also evidence for the use of a heavier tool on the bones of sheep. Bones are split longitudinally for the removal of the marrow, and are separated from one another by chopping through the bone rather than with a knife. Pl. XXVI*m* shows a radius that appears to have been chopped away from the humerus.

Vertebrae are found that have been chopped across at right angles to the line of the vertebral column.

Table VI indicates that as might be expected the bones of sheep are more frequently found whole than are the bones of cattle.

Pig skull fragments are found split along the line of the frontal suture, apparently with a chopping tool. The left and right mandibles too have frequently been split apart, generally between the two central incisors.

Because smaller numbers of limb bones have been recovered from pigs than from the other animals, it would be unwise to assume a consistent butchery practice from the relatively small number of examples of cuts on the bones of this animal. Bones are, however, found split longitudinally with reasonable frequency, and cuts indicate the use of both chopping tools (pl. XXVI*a*) and knives. Table VI indicates that the metapodia were infrequently butchered. The figures given in this table are not only an indication of the frequency with which bones were cut up while the carcass was being butchered, but also reflect the accidental fragmenta-

TABLE VI

Percentages of Complete Bones

	Early–middle			*Middle–late (a)*			*Middle–late (b)*			*Late*			*Total*			*Roman total*		
	Br	*C*	*%C*	*Br*	*C*	*%C*	*Br*	*C*	*%C*	*Br*	*C*	*%C*	*Br*	*C*	*%C*	*Br*	*C*	*%C*
(a) Cattle																		
Humerus	19	0	0	89	6	6	18	0	0	27	1	4	153	7	4	321	7	2
Radius	18	2	10	65	9	12	24	1	4	36	3	8	143	15	9	232	38	14
Metacarpal	20	2	9	92	21	19	23	9	28	29	6	17	164	38	19	213	136	39
Femur	10	0	0	64	4	6	12	1	7	15	3	16	101	8	7	169	10	6
Tibia	12	1	8	102	4	4	22	1	4	22	2	8	158	8	5	193	17	8
Metatarsal	18	6	25	102	13	11	29	0	0	20	4	17	169	23	12	246	128	34
Total	97	11	10	514	57	10	128	12	8	149	19	11	888	99	10	1374	336	20
(b) Sheep																		
Humerus	8	1	11	46	14	23	25	3	11	12	3	20	91	21	19	67	22	25
Radius	4	1	20	29	20	41	19	5	21	18	5	22	70	31	31	79	23	23
Metacarpal	4	0	0	20	24	55	15	5	25	10	4	29	49	33	40	86	43	33
Femur	5	0	0	24	5	17	7	1	13	6	2	25	42	8	16	39	18	32
Tibia	9	1	10	68	10	13	34	1	3	28	5	15	139	17	11	102	20	16
Metatarsal	3	0	0	21	23	52	29	5	15	12	3	20	65	31	32	72	47	39
Total	33	3	8	208	96	32	129	20	13	86	22	20	456	141	23	445	173	28
(c) Pig																		
Humerus	4	0	0	31	4	11	6	0	0	9	0	0	50	4	7	64	13	17
Radius	3	0	0	16	2	11	11	2	15	7	2	22	37	6	14	51	13	20
Metacarpal	3	2	40	5	18	78	15	12	44	3	5	63	26	37	59	18	71	80
Femur	3	1	25	7	2	22	2	0	0	3	0	0	15	3	17	34	11	24
Tibia	4	0	0	16	8	33	10	0	0	5	3	38	35	11	24	89	15	14
Metatarsal	3	2	40	4	17	81	9	6	40	3	8	73	19	33	63	19	71	79
Total	20	5	20	79	51	39	53	20	27	30	18	38	182	94	34	275	194	41

B = broken
C = complete

tion of the bone, both in antiquity and during excavation. Higher percentages of complete bones, especially those of pig and sheep, are found in the pits of the middle–late group. The bones thrown into pits will have been better protected from accidental breakage than those left lying in occupation areas.

The other factor that affects the fragmentation of the bones is the use of some bones in tool manufacture. It was very noticeable in some pits and in some of the occupation layers that the nature of many of the bone fragments was not such as would have resulted from normal butchery techniques and accidental breakage. Pl. XXVI*o*, *p* show fragments of bone of the distinctive shape and form that would appear to result from the techniques of bone tool manufacture. Pits with large amounts of this bone tool waste in them are Pits 220 and 204.

Some of the middle–late occupation layers also included tool waste. The presence of a bone industry at a site or in an area of a site will not only affect the nature of the fragmentation of the bone but might also affect the percentages of species found. The occupation layers with bone waste in them contained a higher than usual percentage of sheep and roe deer bone. In the analysis of the animal bones from the thirteenth-century industrial complex at the deserted medieval settlement at Lyveden (Grant, 1971) a large amount of bone tool waste was found and was related to the high percentage of deer bones found at the site. The percentage of roe deer is highest in the middle–late occupation layers at Portchester. Large numbers of bone tools were not recovered at Portchester, but those that were found indicate a skilled and practised craft. The fact that many tools were not recovered could be explained if they were traded away from the site or if they were particularly prized and not often lost. Excavations at Southampton on the Saxon settlement at Hamwih (Addyman and Hill, 1969) revealed evidence of an extensive bone and antler industry, with waste, partly completed and completed bone tools. Unfortunately, analysis of the animal bones from this site has not yet been undertaken.

THE AGE OF THE ANIMALS

Analysis of the age structure of the bones of cattle, sheep and pigs was attempted by reference to the state of fusion of the long bones and by analysis of the eruption and wear of the teeth using the methods outlined in Grant (1975, Appendix B).

Table VII shows the analysis of the fusion of the long bones using the method of grouping bones together according to their approximate age of fusion (see Silver, 1969). Figs. 149–51 give the analyses of tooth wear and eruption for the three animals.

The analysis of the state of fusion of the cattle bones is seen in table VII. This indicates an age structure very similar to that seen in the cattle bones of the Roman period. Approximately 30% of the animals were killed in their third or fourth year, while almost 60% of the bones recovered were from mature animals. Few bones were recovered from animals that were less than two years old when they were killed, but since survival and recovery factors adversely affect the proportions of young bones, the figures may well underestimate the numbers of young animals. Between the three Saxon groups there are few differences that can be confidently assumed to be significant, although in the middle–late period, compared to the other two periods, a slightly larger proportion of animals were killed between two and four years and correspondingly fewer were kept beyond four years.

This method gives only a rough age grouping; the ages of fusion used are not necessarily correct for medieval cattle, and are used as a general guide and to facilitate discussion. Fig. 149 shows the results of the analysis of the tooth wear for the cattle jaws recovered from the occupation layers and pits of the middle–late period. Unfortunately there were not enough suitable jaws recovered from the pits of the other two periods to allow meaningful analysis of the mandibles of these periods. In an attempt to allow some correlation between the two methods of ageing, the results of the epiphyseal fusion analysis have been plotted on the graph.

The tooth wear analysis shows a small number of young animals. There is a small group around stage 25, which occurs just after the eruption of the third molar. Silver's (1969) data give 2–2½ years as the age of eruption of this tooth. The next peak appears at stage 36, and then 55% of the cattle mandibles fall between stages 40 and 54. Relating this somewhat tentatively to the results of the epiphyseal fusion analysis, the 30% of animals falling within the 2–4-year group seem to be subdivided into two groups, the first of these occurring at the beginning of the period, at stage 25, and the second group at the end of the period, at stage 36. This would suggest that animals were either killed at around two years old, or,

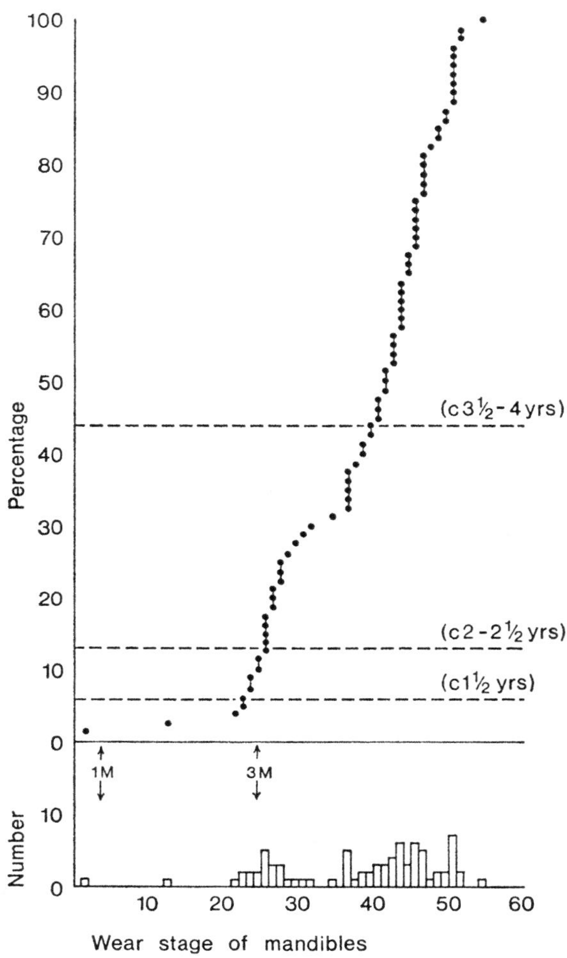

FIG. 149. Cattle tooth wear: middle–late period.

if they were not killed then they would be kept at least two more years. Few would seem to have been killed at three years.

Mature animals appear to have been killed throughout the period of time represented by stages 40 to 46, with almost all the oldest animals being killed at stage 50. The actual age that the tooth wear stages represent, especially in the later stages, is difficult to assess, but the time between stages is much greater in the late stages than in the early stages.

Comparisons between the analysis of the Saxon and Roman cattle jaws indicate some differences in mortality or management patterns in the two periods. In the Roman period there was no evidence of the peak at stage 25 seen in the Saxon period, and a more gradual killing of the older animals was indicated. In both periods the majority of the animals were killed when fully mature.

Table VII gives the results of the analysis of the epiphyseal fusion of the sheep bones. There is evidence of changes in the management practices for sheep during the Saxon period,

TABLE VII

	Saxon				*Roman*		*Saxon*				*Roman*
	E/M %	*M/L* %	*L* %	*Total* %	*Total* %		*E/M* %	*M/L* %	*L* %	*Total* %	*Total* %
(*a*) *Cattle*											
Over 10 months	89	92	96	93	91	Under 10 months	(11)	(8)	(4)	(7)	(9)
Over 1½ years	95	94	98	95	97	10 months to 1½ years	5	6	2	5	3
Over 2–2½ years	94	87	91	89	89	1½–2½ years	1	7	7	6	8
Over 3½–4 years	68	56	64	58	65	2–4 years	26	31	27	31	24
						Over 3½–4 years	68	56	64	58	65
(*b*) *Sheep*											
Over 10 months	66	92	85	89	71	Under 10 months	(34)	8	15	11	29
Over 1½–2 years	89	74	52	71	60	10 months to 2 years	11	18	33	18	11
Over 2½–3 years	30	47	45	45	30	1½–3 years	59	27	7	26	30
Over 3–3½ years	17	25	39	36	23	2½–3½ years	13	22	6	9	7
						Over 3–3½ years	17	25	39	36	23
(*c*) *Pig*											
Over 1 year	90	84	81	84	78	Under 1 year	10	16	19	16	22
Over 2–2½ years	67	34	48	39	32	1–2½ years	23	50	33	45	46
Over 3½ years	17	14	19	15	10	2–3½ years	50	20	29	24	22
						Over 3½ years	17	14	19	15	10

E/M = early/middle; M/L = middle/late; L = late.

notably an increase in the numbers of animals kept beyond maturity. In the early–middle period only 17% of the bones were from animals older than three years, while in the late period 36% of the bones were from fully mature animals. In the early–middle period and to a lesser extent in the middle–late period a large proportion of the animals were killed when they were between 18 months and 3½ years, whereas in the late period the majority were killed in their second year. Inevitably, because of the overlap between some of the age groups, the figures can only give a rough guide, but the changes would seem to be significant. The reason for the change could be a change in emphasis during the Saxon period from meat to wool production. The early–middle group especially, with its relatively high numbers being killed in the third and fourth years, might indicate meat production was the prime purpose of sheep rearing. The change, beginning in the middle–late period but seen most clearly in the late period, to increased numbers of mature animals, might indicate an increase in the importance of wool production. This could also be related to the increase in the proportion of sheep being kept in the later periods. The Roman pattern was most like the middle–late Saxon pattern, but there were far larger numbers of young animals in the Roman period as a whole. This could be a result of a management policy where milk

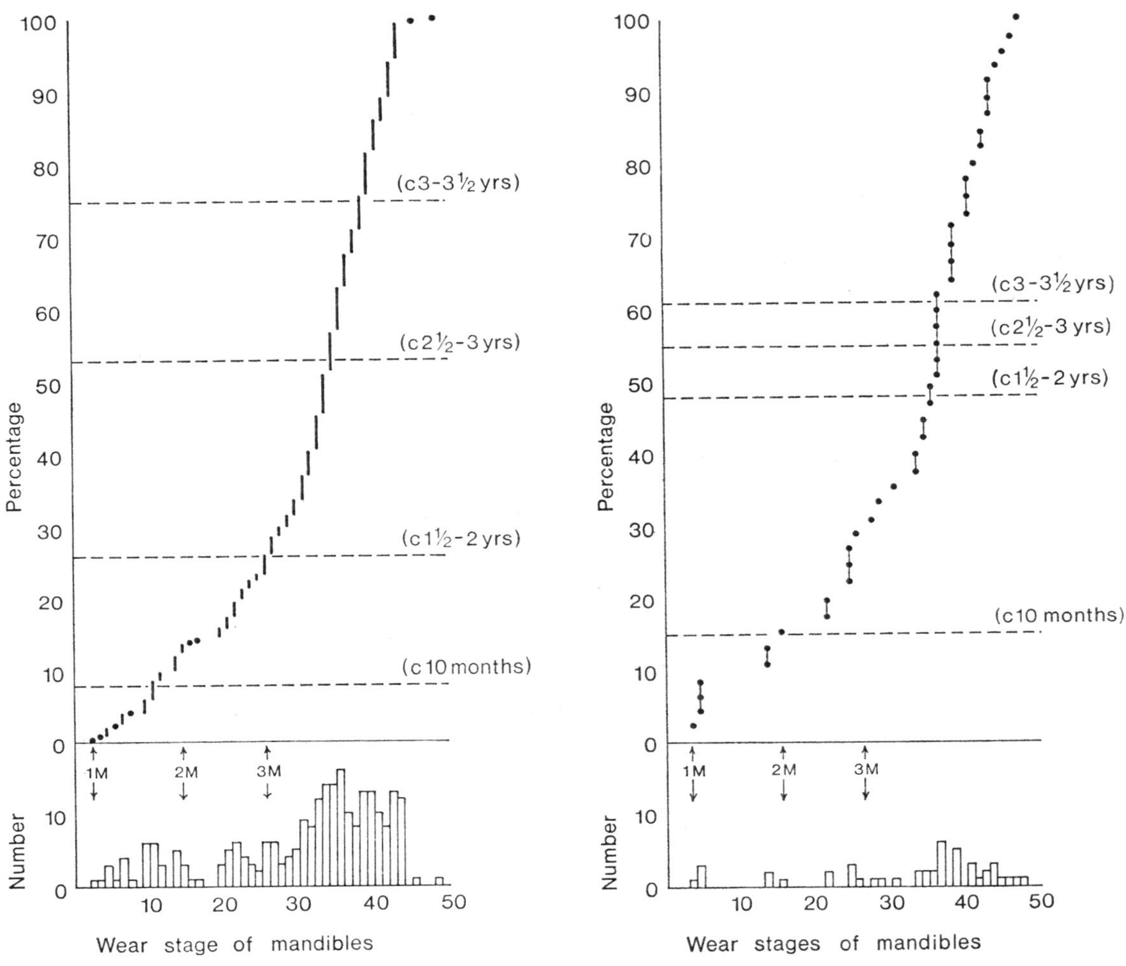

FIG. 150. Sheep tooth wear: middle–late and late periods.

production was very important, but could also be due to better management in the Saxon period, with lower infant mortality, or equally differences in recovery, survival or rubbish disposal practices.

Fig. 150 shows the results of the sheep tooth wear analysis for the middle–late and late periods. The sample from the early–middle group was not large enough to allow a full analysis. The results show a pattern similar to that deduced from the epiphyseal fusion analysis with, in the middle–late group, low infant mortality, a small group between stages 9 and 14 probably representing animals of 1 year to approximately 18 months, another small group between stages 19 and 27, representing animals from about 18 months to $2\frac{1}{2}$ years, and the majority of the mandibles between stages 30 and 43, which probably represents animals from 2 or $2\frac{1}{2}$ to 6 or 7 years old. Although large numbers of animals appear to have been killed

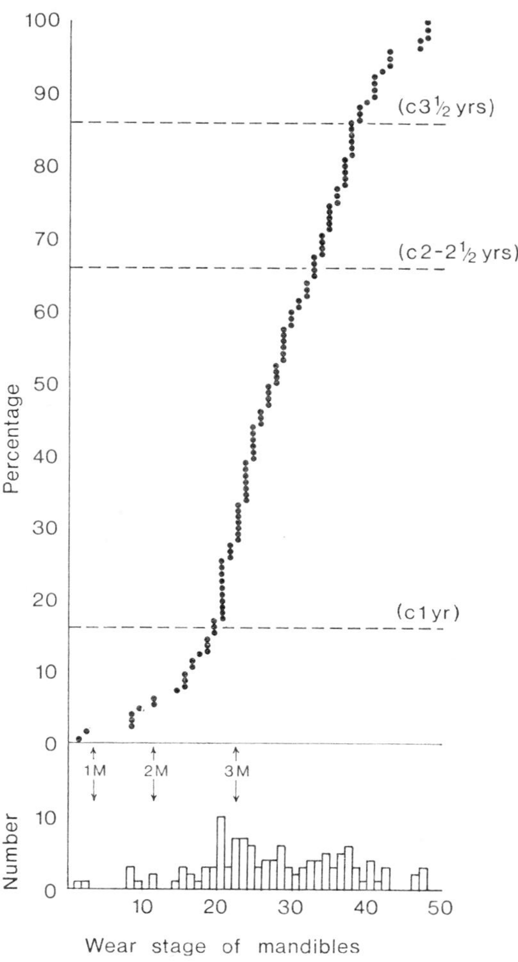

FIG. 151. Pig tooth wear: middle–late period

at all stages from 30 to 43, there are some stages where peaks occur, notably at stages 35, 38 and 39, and 41 and 42. This might suggest some seasonal or annual killing.

The analysis of the mandibles from the late period, although based on rather a small sample, reflects the picture given by the fusion analysis, with slightly higher numbers of young animals, and 1–2-year-old animals, and larger numbers of mature animals than in the middle–late group. Twenty-seven per cent of the mandibles were at stage 40 or later stages in the late group compared to 18% in the middle–late group.

19

Table VII gives the results of the epiphyseal fusion analysis for the pig bones. These show that as in the Roman period, relatively few animals were kept longer than $3\frac{1}{2}$ years. The largest percentage of old animals was in the later period, and in fact in all three Saxon periods slightly more old animals were kept than in the Roman period. Between the Saxon groups changes can be seen in the ages at which the animals were killed. In the early–middle group approximately 25% were killed between 1 and $1\frac{1}{2}$ years, while 50% were killed between 2 and $3\frac{1}{2}$ years. In the middle–late period the pattern is reversed, with 50% being killed at $1–1\frac{1}{2}$ years, while 25% were killed between 2 and $3\frac{1}{2}$ years. In the late period fairly equal numbers of animals seem to have been killed at these ages.

The tooth wear analysis of the mandibles from the middle–late period seen in fig. 151 shows small numbers of young animals — fewer in fact than were indicated by the fusion analysis — and then a peak occurring at stage 20. Animals were then killed at all ages represented by stages 21 to 42, although some peaks occur too. The pattern would suggest that pigs were killed as and when they were required for meat although there may have been some ages at which pigs were most commonly killed.

There are obvious limitations to reconstruction of the age structure of the live herd using either of the two methods used here, and these have already been discussed (Grant, 1975). As a general comment on the use of the tooth wear method, a detailed comparison of the tooth wear of the Saxon and Roman mandibles for all animals indicated that there had been no marked changes in either the rate of wear or the age of eruption of the teeth over the eight centuries covered by the two reports.

METRICAL ANALYSIS

Bones were measured whenever their condition made it possible, but fewer complete bones were recovered from the Saxon layers than from the Roman layers. It is planned to include a full discussion of the metrical analysis of the bones in the final volume of the Portchester reports, when all periods can be compared.

The method of determining the sex of cattle proposed by Howard (1963) was applied to the complete metacarpals recovered from the Saxon layers. The metacarpal indices

$$\frac{\text{distal breadth}}{\text{length}} \times 100$$

and

$$\frac{\text{minimum transverse shaft breadth}}{\text{length}} \times 100$$

were calculated: the results are given in table VIII, and are shown in histogram form in fig. 152 with the approximate sexual divisions indicated. The sample of metacarpals which were complete enough to be fully measured was very small, and so no division into periods was attempted. In fact, no complete metacarpals were recovered from the early–middle group, and thus only bones from the middle–late and late groups are included in this analysis. The results suggest that the castrate group is the largest group in the Saxon herds. The distal index indicates that the female : castrate : male ratio was 7 : 14 : 1. This ratio applies only to animals of approximately two years and over. The metacarpal fuses at 2–2½ years, and no measurements of unfused metacarpals were taken. If these results have any validity, they have important implications for the agricultural practices of the Saxon period, and show a significant change from the situation in Roman times, when females seem to have formed the largest group. This is discussed further in the final section.

Measurements of the distal ends of tibiae, and the length and distal breadth of the metatarsals of cattle were compared to those given by Jewell (1962) in his study of the size changes in cattle. The range and number of these measurements are given in table IX, together with the measurements of these bones from the Roman layers at Portchester.

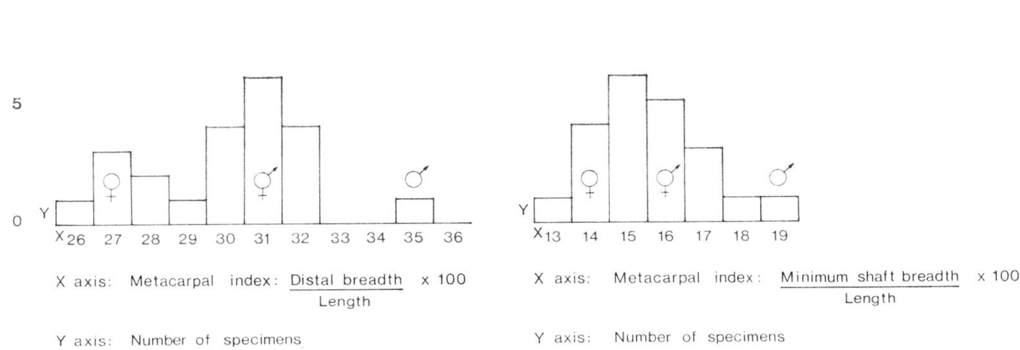

FIG. 152. Metrical analysis of cattle metacarpals

The measurements of the metatarsals indicate a smaller range of sizes in the Saxon than in the Roman period. The very small sample from the Saxon site of Sedgeford falls within the Portchester Saxon range. The measurements of the distal width of the tibia show a wider range in the Saxon period. However, it is in this area of analysis that the dangers of interpreting bone material from multi-period sites becomes most acute. Further interpretation must wait until the bones of the later periods have been studied.

DISEASE AND INJURY

The bones of the animals were examined for evidence of disease. The incidence of diseased bones was quite low, possibly lower than in the Roman period. Most evidence of disease and abnormality was found in the jaws of the animals.

Evidence of periodontal diseases of the jaws of sheep was not infrequently seen amongst the Saxon material, but the incidence of diseased jaws was not as high as in the Roman period. Pl. XXV*a* shows a sheep mandible with an abscess below the 4th premolar; this tooth is impacted against the 1st molar. The overcrowding of the jaws, seen with great frequency in the sheep mandibles from every site the author has studied, is also common in the jaws of this site.

Periodontal diseases of the jaws of pigs are rarely encountered; however, an example of a mandible that had been severely diseased was found and is shown in pl. XXV*b*. At least two examples of the congenital absence of one central incisor in the jaws of pigs were seen. One of these is shown in pl. XXV*c*. The congenital absence of the 2nd premolar and the absence of the third pillar of the third molar of cattle mandibles, fairly frequently encountered in prehistoric material, were also found in the Saxon material.

Arthritis in the bones of Roman cattle was not uncommon, but evidence of this disease was much less frequently seen in the Saxon cattle bones. A severely arthritic spine fragment was found, and is illustrated in pl. XXV*d*.

Some rehealed fractures were found, especially in the ribs of both large and small animals. One of these is illustrated in pl. XXV*e*. Very few fractured limb bones were found. A rehealed

TABLE VIII

Distal index	*Possible sex*	*Shaft index*	*Possible sex*	*Distal index*	*Possible sex*	*Shaft index*	*Possible sex*
30·5	C	16·3	C	—	—	15	F/C
—	—	14·4	F	32·9	C	16·6	C
28·4	F	—	—	28·8	F	13·9	F
31·2	C	16·4	C	27·1	F	15·2	F
35	M	19·1	M	31	C	15·7	C
30	C	15·4	F/C	32	C	17·1	C
30	C	14·7	F	29	F/C	14·9	F
31·5	C	18	C/M	—	—	15·6	C
31·7	C	17	C	26·6	F	—	—
27·7	F	—	—	27	F	14	F
32·3	C	17·4	C	31	C	16	C
32·6	C	—	—	31·8	C	15·3	C
30·1	C	16·4	C				

F = female; C = castrate; M = male.

TABLE IX

(*a*) *Distal width of tibia* (mm.)

Portchester (Saxon)	44–70	No.: 81
Sedgeford	53–67	No.: 8
Portchester (Roman)	50–69	No.: 143

(*b*) *Length and distal width of metatarsal* (mm.)

	Length		*Distal width*	
Portchester (Saxon)	198–232	No.: 16	46–63	No.: 25
Sedgeford	214–220	No.: 2	51–57	No.: 3
Portchester (Roman)	183–240	No.: 108	43–70	No.: 172

bird femur, and the sheep metatarsal and radius shown in pl. XXV*f*, *g* are the only examples. The fractured metatarsal has healed at an angle and would probably have made the animal slightly lame.

Pl. XXV*h* illustrates a fragment of sheep skull with two left horn cores, one in the normal position and the other slightly below the first and projecting sideways from the skull. This might be an example of a chance mutation, or it might indicate the presence of a four-horned breed of sheep at the site.

CONCLUSIONS AND DISCUSSION

Cattle

Since complete or even fairly complete skulls were not recovered from the Saxon layers, any discussion of breeds of cattle is not really possible, although there was some variation seen in the horn core forms that might be suggestive of breed differences. The metrical analysis undertaken was not conclusive, and further discussion of this aspect of the animals must wait until a full metrical analysis is completed.

There is evidence for the decline in relative importance of cattle from the Roman period to the late Saxon period although this does not necessarily mean that fewer cattle were kept. Beef appeared to provide the bulk of the meat protein at the site both in Roman and Saxon times.

Analysis of the age structure of the cattle bones has shown that at least 50% of the animals killed and eaten at the site were fully mature, with 30% being killed in their third or fourth year. This is very similar to the pattern found in the analysis of the Roman bones. The analysis of the sexual distribution of the Saxon bones indicated that approximately one-third of the animals were female and that the other two-thirds were castrates. This is the reverse of the situation in the Roman period, where approximately two-thirds of the animals were female. A possible explanation of this is an increase in agricultural activity which required the use of oxen for ploughing and other heavy traction. Until the development of improved harnesses late in the Saxon period, horses could not be used to pull heavy weights, and teams of four or even eight oxen at the end of the period would have been used to pull the plough (Slicher van Bath, 1963). In many areas oxen continued to be used for all heavy traction until modern times.

The low incidence of disease, especially arthritis, could imply generally healthy animals, but this could also mean that as soon as any animal showed the first signs of disease or inability to work, it would have been killed and eaten.

Sheep and goats

The horn cores indicated that both sheep and goats were present at the site, but in what proportions it is impossible to say at the present time. There is evidence of at least four types of sheep at the site — one with a small horn core, one with a much larger horn core, a hornless sheep and one with four horns (pl. XXV*j*, *h*). It is possible that this last type might be only an isolated example caused by a chance mutation, as only one example was found, and only one side of the skull was present.

There is a steady increase in the relative importance of sheep from Roman until late Saxon times, and mutton, especially in the middle and late periods, forms a not insignificant part of the diet. Using the 'minimum numbers of individuals' calculations, more sheep were kept than cattle in the two latest periods of Saxon occupation. This fact, together with the indications that there is a significant increase in the numbers of sheep kept over three years old during the Saxon occupation, may indicate an increase in the importance of wool to the economy of the inhabitants. The larger numbers of mature animals, the smaller numbers of very young animals and the lower incidence of periodontal disease might imply that much better feeding conditions existed for sheep by the end of the Saxon occupation. Sheep kept for meat would seem to have been killed in their third year, or in the late period, their second year. Those kept longer would also have been eaten ultimately.

Sheep bones particularly may have been used in the manufacture of tools.

Pigs

Pigs are fairly consistently represented throughout the Saxon period and are more numerous than cattle and almost as numerous as sheep in all periods with the possible exception of the earliest period. In the Roman period more pigs were found than sheep.

Pork appears to have provided approximately 20% of the meat diet.

There is evidence that fewer young animals and larger numbers of old animals were eaten than in the Roman period, although the number of animals kept beyond maturity is still fairly small and most pigs were killed in their second or third years, as in the Roman period.

Pigs are among the easiest of animals to feed, as they can be driven into the forests to forage for themselves.

Deer

Roe, red and fallow deer were all found at the site, although only very few fallow deer bones were found. The percentage of deer bones recovered is higher in the Saxon than in the Roman period. Antler is an obvious source of raw material for tool or ornament manufacture, and antler offcuts and fragments associated with such an industry were found. The limb bones of deer are also very suitable for tool manufacture, being long, straight and slender. The higher numbers of roe deer bones recovered from the middle–late period may be related to the possible presence of the waste from a bone tool industry in the layers of this period. The nature of the fragmentation of some of the roe deer bones would add weight to this suggestion, but the presence of more typical butchery cuts on the bones of all three species of deer indicates that venison formed an occasional part of the diet.

Horses

Horse bones were not frequently found at the site, although they form 2% of the bones of the early and late Saxon groups. It is possible that since horses are not normally eaten, they may have been buried elsewhere than among the domestic refuse; however their presence in only small numbers is by no means surprising. Horses would have been used only for riding and possibly light traction since, although swifter than oxen, they were not so suitable for heavy work at this period and were more expensive to feed than oxen.

Cats and dogs

Cat and dog bones which were perhaps surprisingly numerous in the Roman period were very rare in the Saxon period. However, the large numbers of cattle, sheep and pig bones that had been gnawed, almost certainly by dogs, suggest that the numbers of bones recovered from dogs belie their true importance at the site. It is possible that the real difference between the Saxon and Roman periods in respect of these two species is one of the method of disposal of their dead bodies. In the Roman period, cat and dog bones, and complete or nearly complete skeletons, were thrown in with the domestic refuse. In the Saxon period they may have been buried specially or separately away from the particular area of the fort that has so far been excavated. Although there is circumstantial evidence for the presence of dogs at the site, there is in fact no such evidence for the presence of cats and they may simply have only been kept in very small numbers. Dog bones are most frequent in the latest period of Saxon occupation.

Birds

Birds are the subject of a separate report (see pp. 287–94). The relatively large numbers of bird bones found at the site is interesting. They are more common in the Saxon than in the Roman period and there is an increase in their numbers from early Saxon to late Saxon times.

Hares, foxes, fish, badgers, voles and frogs

The bones of these animals were found in very small quantities. This may be partly related to their small size and small chance of recovery.

The number of fish bones recovered was far greater than in the Roman period, although this might be due to better survival and recovery. Certainly one would expect a fairly considerable exploitation of the resources of the sea at a site in the position that Portchester occupies.

There is much to suggest that by the end of the Saxon period quite considerable changes had taken place in the agricultural practices of the inhabitants of the site since the first occupation of the fort in Roman times. Many of these changes may have taken place within the Saxon period itself, and in some respects there is more continuity from the Roman to the early Saxon period than from the early to late Saxon periods. The percentages of species represented in the early–middle group are very like those of the Roman period, the only major difference being the smaller numbers of cats and dogs in the Saxon period. However, other analyses indicate that the changes began at the beginning of the Saxon period. One of the significant differences appears to be in the nature of the filling of the pits and the rubbish disposal generally. In some of the pits, especially wells, of the Roman occupation, the presence of whole skeletons of young animals and cats and dogs, and complete cattle skulls together with human baby bones indicated that some of the bones found in the pit may have been deliberately, if not 'ritually' placed there, and had not just been thrown in with normal domestic refuse. No such inferences can be made from the pit fill of the Saxon period, the only possible exception being Pit 207 which contained a very high percentage of bird bones. There is also the possibility that dogs, if not cats, may have been buried separately.

Another significant cultural change from the Roman to Saxon period is seen in the evidence of different butchery techniques. There may be a general change in cooking methods, with perhaps a liking for stews cooked in the 'gritty cooking pots' that were so common amongst the pottery at the site. The method of marrow extraction, if not the importance in the diet of marrow itself, is certainly very different in the Saxon period; the split bones that are so frequently found in the Saxon material are not seen at all in the Roman period.

The lower incidence of disease, especially arthritis and periodontal diseases of sheep, is apparent in the Saxon period. This may be due to a more rigorous culling of sickly animals or a generally healthier animal population, perhaps related to better feeding conditions generally, and better supplies of fodder in the winter months especially.

Within the Saxon period, the increase in the numbers of sheep may imply a change to or an increase in wool production. It is possible to argue that the relatively higher numbers of sheep and pigs and lower numbers of cattle indicate a decline in the wealth or agricultural efficiency and productivity of the site, since the feeding of sheep and pigs is generally easier than that of cattle. Surrounding forested areas could have provided much of the food for these animals. However, the fact that in general the animals were kept to an older age than in the Roman period, the increase in the numbers of oxen kept, and the low incidence of disease amongst the animals, give more credence to the view that agricultural prosperity and efficiency had increased by middle and late Saxon times. This in fact agrees with the other evidence from the site.

If we do have an increase in prosperity, an increase in agricultural efficiency is implied. For a settlement to survive on the same site for any length of time, especially when as at Portchester, the site is at the end of a peninsula, where access to, and availability of land is more restricted than if it were in open country, implies a knowledge at least of the importance of manuring, and possibly even of crop rotation. If the land were not being regenerated, one would expect to find far more disease, especially periodontal disease, increased mortality in young animals, and finally abandonment of the site.

The analysis of the bones from the medieval occupation of the site should clarify many of the points discussed, and it will be interesting to see if some of the changes noted in the late Saxon period continue into the medieval period.

BIBLIOGRAPHY

Addyman, P. V. and Hill, D. H. 1969. 'Saxon Southampton: a review of the evidence.' *Proc. Hants Field Club* xxvi, 61–96.

Brain, C. 1969. 'The contribution of Namib Desert Hottentots to an understanding of Australopithecine bone accumulation.' *Scientific Papers of the Namib Desert Research Station* xxxix, 13–22.

Carter, P. L. and Phillipson, D. with Higgs, E. S. 1965. 'The animal bones.' In Hastings, Cunliffe *et al.*, 'The excavation of an Iron Age farmstead at Hawks Hill, Leatherhead.' *Surrey Arch. Coll.* lxii.

Grant, A. 1971. 'The animal bones.' In Bryant, G. F. and Steane, J. M., 'Excavations at the deserted medieval settlement at Lyveden.' *Northants. Mus. J.* ix, 90–3.

GRANT, A. 1975. 'The animal bones.' In CUNLIFFE, B. W., *Excavations at Portchester Castle*. Volume I: *Roman*, pp. 378–408.

HOWARD, M. 1963. 'The metrical determination of the metapodials and skulls of cattle.' *R. Anth. Inst. Occ. Papers*.

ISSAAC, G. L. 1967. 'Towards the interpretation of occupation debris: some experiments and observations.' *Kroeber Anth. Soc. Papers* xxxvii, 31–57.

JEWELL, P. A. 1962. 'Changes in size and type of cattle from prehistoric to medieval times in Britain.' *Z. Tierzüchtung u. Züchtungsbiol.* lxxviii, 159–67.

SILVER, L. A. 1969. 'The ageing of domestic animals.' In BROTHWELL, D. and HIGGS, E. S., *Science in Archaeology*. London.

SLICHER VAN BATH, B. H. 1963. *The Agrarian History of Western Europe A.D. 500–1850*. London.

THE BIRD BONES

By ANNE EASTHAM

Early to Mid Saxon

The following species were represented:[1]

Gallus gallus	Chicken
Anser anser	Goose
Botaurus stellaris	Bittern
Anas platyrrhyncos	Mallard
Numenius arquata	Curlew
Perdix perdix	Partridge
Columba palumbus	Woodpigeon

Table I shows that the early to mid Saxon levels at Portchester contained very few bird bones, a total of 69 in all. Pits 34, 35, 135, 204 and 217 produced mainly goose and chicken bones. Pit 35 also contained a pigeon and pit 204 a mallard. Only in pit 220 was any quantity of bird bone recovered. Of the 30 bones found there, 21 belonged to geese, two were bittern, five belonged to chicken and one each to partridge and curlew.

Such a limited collection allows very little comment. Of the domesticated species, the chickens were all very similar in size and type and, since the single tarsus bone recovered had no attached spur, there is no evidence of any cock birds. The goose bones were slightly more varied, as they are throughout the Saxon levels at Portchester. Their sizes ranged between that of the wild Greylag and the Bean goose, but they overlap so completely that no distinction or grouping was possible in any assemblage on the site, and it seems reasonable to take this as a feature of domestication. It is interesting to see how the proportion of geese is increased, even in the restricted sample from the early Saxon occupation, as compared with the Roman levels, in which a total of only three bones was found. There was no indication that the Romans ever reared geese at Portchester, though they probably did so at Fishbourne (Eastham, 1971) but not on the same scale as during the Saxon period here.

[1] For a general account of the modern habitat and behaviour of the birds mentioned in the following report, see Fisher, 1966; Peterson, Mountford and Hollom, 1954; Witherby, Jourdain, Ticehurst and Tucker, 1938–41; and Vaurie, 1965.

Two other birds, the bittern and the curlew, are worth noting. The bones represent only one bird of each species but in the late Saxon period many more species of wader were brought on to the site. Although the Roman levels contained quite large numbers of water-fowl, there is only one mallard from the early to mid Saxon period and over the period as a whole they are few in number. Marsh birds appear to be preferred in their place.

TABLE I

Bird Bones from the Early to Mid Saxon Layers

		Gallus gallus		Anser anser		Botauras stellaris		Anas platyrrhyncos		Numenius arquata		Perdix perdix		Columba palumbus	
		L	R	L	R	L	R	L	R	L	R	L	R	L	R
Skull															
Mandible -upper															
-lower				1											
Coracoid		2		2	1			1							
Sternum		2		6											
Furcula		1		2											
Scapula			2	1	2										
Vertebrae															
Ribs		2		5											
Pelvis		1													
Humerus	P	3	4	4	4										
	D														
Radius	P		2					1							
	D														
Ulna	P													1	1
	D														
Carpo-Metacarpus	P														
	D														
Digits															
Femur	P	1	2												
	D														
Tibio-Tarsus	P	5	3	2											
	D														
Fibula															
Tarsus-Metatarsus	P	1		1		1	1			1			1		
	D														
Phalanges				1											
Total		31		32		2		2		1			1	2	

Table II attempts to analyse the number of individual birds on the site at this period. It is based on the assessment of comparable bones from each side of the body and the count therefore represents the very minimum number which have been recovered.

TABLE II

Number of Individual Birds from Early to Mid Saxon Contexts

Gallus gallus

Pit	*Number of bones*	*Number of individuals*
35	3	1
220	5	1
34	7	3
204	6	1–2
217	4	1–2
135	6	2
Total	31	9–11

Anser anser

Pit	*Number of bones*	*Number of individuals*
34	2	1
35	4	2
135	3	1–2
204	2	1
217	1	1
220	21	2
Total	33	8–9

Pit	*Species*	*Number of bones*	*Number of individuals*
220	*Botaurus stellaris*	2	1
	Anas platyrrhyncos	2	1
	Numenius arquata	1	1
	Perdix perdix	1	1
35	*Columba palumbus*	2	1

Late Saxon

The following species were represented:

Gallus gallus Chicken
Anser anser Goose

Gavia immer	Great northern diver
Tadorna tadorna	Shelduck
Anas platyrrhyncos	Mallard
Anas crecca	Teal
Anas penelope	Wigeon
Anas acuta	Pintail
Milvus milvus	Red kite
Pluvialis apricaria	Golden plover
Calidris alpina	Dunlin
Tringa totanus	Redshank
Limosa ?lapponica	?Bar-tailed godwit
Numenius arquata	Curlew
Numenius phaeopus	Whimbrel
Scolopax rusticola	Woodcock
Larus argentatus	Herring gull
Sterna hirundo	Common tern
Columba palumbus	Woodpigeon
Columba livia	Rock dove
Corvus corone	Carrion crow
Corvus monedula	Jackdaw

Out of a total of 949 bones from these levels, some 511 were *Gallus*, 147 were *Anser*, 65 bones were not readily determinable, or too fragmentary, but among the remaining 226 bones there was a considerable variety of species, as will be seen from the above check list for the period.

In table III an analysis of all the bones for this period is given. The numerical data have also been presented in terms of stratified groups, from which it will be clear that most of the bird bones and the widest range of species were concentrated in pit 207 and the adjacent occupation layers in trench 108. Other pits and occupation layers may be said to have been dominated largely by chickens, with a limited range of other species.

The supplementary tables (tables IV–VII) for each layer, pit or group of pits give estimates of the minimum numbers of the important species for comparison with the data derived from the early and mid Saxon occupation.

We can assume both chicken and geese to be domesticated species. The geese like those of the early to mid Saxon period showed considerable size variation, though conforming osteologically with *Anser anser*. From the bones it would appear that the remains of a minimum of 33–35 individuals were recovered but too few of them were complete for measurements to have any significance. The tables show the distribution of bones on the site with detailed estimates of the numbers of birds.

The chickens, of which there were the remains of at least 80–83 found in all the late Saxon levels, also suggest quite a considerable interest in poultry farming. From the tarsi there was firm evidence of only four cock birds amongst the hens and these were not particularly large specimens, so that it would appear that the poultry were kept largely for their eggs and subsequently eaten and that there was no specialized breeding of cocks, either for sport, as

TABLE III

Bird Bones from the Late Saxon Levels

	Gallus gallus L	Gallus gallus R	Anser anser L	Anser anser R	Gavia immer L	Gavia immer R	Tadorna tadorna L	Tadorna tadorna R	Anas platyrhyncos L	Anas platyrhyncos R	Anas crecca L	Anas crecca R	Anas penelope L	Anas penelope R	Anas acuta L	Anas acuta R
Skull	3		2						1							
Mandible–upper		1														
–lower		2	3	5												
Coracoid	18	16	5	3					4							
Sternum	19		6						2							
Furcula	16		7						3							
Scapula	3	4		1					1	2						
Vertebrae	11		1						1							
Ribs	46		6						1							
Pelvis	16		6						4							
Humerus P/D	39	30	21	25					3	5	4	1				
Radius P/D	16	23	2	2					4	8						
Ulna P/D	29	27	10	1					3	5	4					
Carpo-Metacarpus P/D	6	1		1					4	2			1			1
Digits			1													
Femur P/D	46	29	6	4				1		3						
Tibio-Tarsus P/D	37	36	16	7					2	1	1		2	1		
Fibula																
Tarsus-Metatarsus P/D	11	9	7	3	2				2							
Phalanges	1		7							1						
Total	511*		147		2		1		62		10		4		1	

	Milvus milvus L	Milvus milvus R	Pluvialis apricaria L	Pluvialis apricaria R	Calidris alpina L	Calidris alpina R	Tringa totanus L	Tringa totanus R	Limosa? lapponica L	Limosa? lapponica R	Numenius arquata L	Numenius arquata R	Numenius phaeopus L	Numenius phaeopus R	Scolopax rusticola L	Scolopax rusticola R
Skull																
Mandible–upper											1					
–lower											2					
Coracoid												1				
Sternum																
Furcula																
Scapula																
Vertebrae																
Ribs																
Pelvis																
Humerus P/D	1							1			6	7				
Radius P/D	1	1									8	3		1		
Ulna P/D	1	1					1	2	1	1	10	5		2	1	
Carpo-Metacarpus P/D		1	1							1	3	7	1			
Digits																
Femur P/D											6	2				
Tibio-Tarsus P/D	1						1				5	13		2		
Fibula																
Tarsus-Metatarsus P/D	1		2		1		1				9	6		1		
Phalanges																
Total	8		3		1		6		3		94		7		1	

	Larus argentatus L	Larus argentatus R	Sterna hirundo L	Sterna hirundo R	Columba palumbus L	Columba palumbus R	Columba livia L	Columba livia R	Corvus corone L	Corvus corone R	Corvus monedula L	Corvus monedula R	Unidentified bird bones L	Unidentified bird bones R
Skull														
Mandible–upper														
–lower														
Coracoid					1	1		1			1			
Sternum					1		1							
Furcula														
Scapula														
Vertebrae														
Ribs														
Pelvis														
Humerus P/D					1									
Radius P/D				1	1	1	2							
Ulna P/D	2	2	6	5	2	1			1					
Carpo-Metacarpus P/D														
Digits														
Femur P/D	1					1						1		
Tibio-Tarsus P/D	1				1						1	1		
Fibula														
Tarsus-Metatarsus P/D														
Phalanges														
Total	6		12		11		4		1		4		59	

[1] This total includes ten bones of a very young chick which was so immature that it was not worth including its bones in the assessment for each section of the body.

may have been the case in Roman times at Fishbourne (Eastham, 1971) or as luxury birds for the table.

As suggested in the section on the birds of the early Saxon occupation, the number and variety of ducks in this late period appears much less than during Roman times. It is true that the waterfowl include great northern diver, shelduck, mallard, teal, wigeon and pintail but, apart from the mallard, some of which may possibly have been at least partially

TABLE IV

Estimate of the Numbers of Gallus gallus *from Late Saxon Pits and Layers*

Pit	*Trench*	*Layer*	*Number of bones*	*Minimum number of individuals*
	102	49	44	1
		56	15	2
		89	2	1
	103	18	4	2
		21	8	2
		45	7	2
	107	9	8	1
		34	2	1
		57	3	1
	108	22	15	2
		30	5	1
		42	7	2
		44	1	1
		48	36	5 or 6 (2 male)
		53	3	2
		60	1	1
		66	1	1
		67	2	1
		93	1	1 male
		94	9	2
		160	2	1
68		31	48	3
71		42	27 (10 immature)	3 (1 immature)
91		29	3	2
104		43	18	4
107		23	32	3
111		32	2	1
115		28	2	1
124		6	5	2
167b		59	3	2
191		72	5	2
		90	3	1
207		10	97	10
		40, 8, 11	36	4
		12	91	10–12
218		62	2	1
219		68	3	2
Totals			511	84–87

TABLE V

Estimate of the Numbers of Anser anser *from Late Saxon Pits and Layers*

Pit	*Trench*	*Layer*	*Number of bones*	*Number of individuals*
	102	49	8	3
		89	1	1
	103	18	1	1
		21	3	1
		45	3	2
	107	9	6	3
		34	2	1
		57	3	1
	108	22	3	1
		30	1	1
		42	1	1
		44	2	1
		48	14	3
		66	1	1
		67	1	1
104		43	4	1
115		28	1	1
191	102	72	2	2
	103	32	1	1
207	103	40, 38	33	7
	104	8, 11		
	104	10	52	3
	104	12	16	2
Totals			147	39

domesticated, there are very few bones. Waterfowl form a relatively small proportion of the avifauna.

The waders, on the other hand, are quite numerous. From the late Saxon pits and occupation levels golden plover, dunlin, redshank, godwit, curlew, whimbrel and woodcock were all recovered, though only curlew, redshank and whimbrel in a quantity which suggests more than isolated specimens. All of these species may be found in marsh lands and estuarine areas of southern England at the present day. The plover tends to feed on arable fields in winter (in this context it should be noted that there were plough marks and evidence of wheat cultivation at Portchester). But most of its food is animal: insects, Lepidoptera, Coleoptera, etc., Mollusca, Annelidae, Crustacea and Arachnidae. The dunlin is a seashore feeder, eating mainly larvae, small Crustacea, Annelidae and Mollusca. Redshank, whimbrel, curlew and woodcock have a similar diet, though the latter shows a marked preference for earthworms over other food items. The environmental evidence about the site does not show any great change in the shoreline habitat between the Roman and Saxon periods. During the Roman occupation there was a deep channel within a quarter of a mile of the fort. In Saxon times there is some suggestion of an encroachment by the sea, gradually increasing

TABLE VI

Estimate of the Numbers of Anas platyrrhyncos *from Late Saxon Pits and Layers*

Pit	*Trench*	*Layer*	*Number of bones*	*Minimum number of individuals*
	103	18	1	1
		45	2	1
	107	9	3	1
	108	22	2	1
		46	1	1
		48	8	3
		53	1	1
		60	1	1
		66	1	1
71		42	2	1
191	102/3	90	1	1
207	103/4	40, 38, 8 and 11	12	2
		10	11	2
		12	17	3
Totals			62	20

TABLE VII

Estimate of the Numbers of Numenius arquata *from Late Saxon Pits and Layers*

Pit	*Trench*	*Layer*	*Number of bones*	*Minimum number of individuals*
	108	22	2	1
		30	1	1
	115	28	1	1
	124	6	1	1
191	102	72	2	1
207	103/4	8, 11, 38 and 40	27	7 or 8
	104	10	31	4 or 5
		12	29	5
Totals			94	21 or 23

the area of mudflats which were then contiguous with the fort. But the habitat of the flats must have remained very much the same, so that it is possible that the increase in waders might be the result of the social rather than the physical changes in the settlement. Since the archaeological record suggests that a residence of some status existed at this period, rich enough to afford exotic goods, it seems not unlikely that there was a demand also for varied and interesting game to eat. Many of the birds found here, including the bittern in the early levels, were recorded on the markets of medieval England, and nearly all are quoted in

Larousse Gastronomique (1961) as edible game, some as esteemed as the woodcock and plover, the rest less highly recommended. All species, because of their feeding habits, were considered better when roasted undrawn, or accompanied by a dish of the intestines. Within the last ten years curlew has been sold in the markets in the north of England as game and one retailer pronounced it 'very tasty'.

In Saxon poetry, too, the curlew, or perhaps the whimbrel, has a special place. Although the surviving poem in which it was used, as a symbol, *The Seafarer*, is of Northumbrian rather than West Saxon origin, it had by the year A.D. 1000 appeared in a version in West Saxon dialect and script known as the *Exeter Book* (Sweet, 1948).

> There I heard nothing but the resounding sea,
> The ice-cold wave, sometimes the wild swan's song;
> Did give me pleasure the call of the Gannets
> And Curlew's cries instead of the laughter of men,
> The singing of the Kittiwake instead of the drinking of mead.
> There storms batter the rocky cliff, there called back to them the
> icy feathered Tern; most often around him screams the Sea eagle
> with spray-covered wings.

The late James Fisher identified the location of this description as fitting the Bass Rock, but the simplest interpretation of the poem is as a comparison between the hardships of the life of a sailor and the luxuries to be enjoyed on land. Here the spiritual aspirations of the seafarer, drawn in spite of himself to the ocean, are symbolized in the cries of the birds, gannet, whimbrel or curlew, kittiwake and tern and are to him beyond compare better than life among the laughter and mead drinking of a man living on land with his kinsmen. In this symbolism the soul of the sailor becomes identified with Christian ideals and the love of God.

Of curlew and whimbrel bones together there was a total of 86 from Portchester. Most of them, representing at least 11 curlew and two whimbrel, were from pit 207: one was from pit 191 and one or two from other late Saxon pits. To suppose any connection between their use as game birds and the poetic symbolism of *The Seafarer* would be fanciful. In European tradition, however, specific foods have come to be associated with certain festivals, and ceremonies, for example fish and turkey at Christmas, peacock and swan for ecclesiastical and royal feasts, and traditional foods for fast days and wedding traditions. It would be interesting to know whether these birds from Portchester recur in similar proportions on other sites of the period.

Among the remaining species, the tern would have been common fishing in the channel; the herring gulls belong with the waders on the shoreline and as scavengers filching food scraps and rubbish from the tips on the site. Similarly the kite, a common scavenger in towns of the Middle Ages, appears here cleaning up animal matter from the tips, or even being killed and thrown there by shepherds, perhaps, defending lambs from its attacks. The single crow may have died in the same way. Lastly, the Stock doves and pigeons could have been killed for food or just as easily be accidental casualties cast into pits or dumps.

Most of the bird remains from the Saxon layers at Portchester come from edible species. Very much the greater proportion of them were the geese and chickens raised on the premises but the rest demonstrate a variety in the hunted species which was apparently greater in Saxon times than in the preceding period of Roman occupation. The possibility that this is a reflection of the change in the social status of the settlement over this period of time cannot be ignored. The birds upon which the straggling garrison of the late Roman period fed largely were chickens supplemented by a few waterfowl and the odd game bird. The early to mid Saxon levels contained very few birds, but included chicken, increased numbers of geese, with a bittern among the game. The late Saxon period shows that during the eleventh century there was a considerable expansion of poultry production and of the variety and luxury of the game birds hunted for the delectation of the thane and his household. Comparison with other settlements of the same date might prove to be of interest and value in a study of Saxon society.

BIBLIOGRAPHY

EASTHAM, A. 1971. 'The bird bones.' In CUNLIFFE, B. W., *Excavations at Fishbourne* (Leeds), Vol. II, pp. 338–92,

FISHER, J. 1966. *The Shell Bird Book*. London.

PETERSON, R., MOUNTFORD, G. and HOLLOM, P. A. D. 1954. *A Field Guide to the Birds of Britain and Europe*. London.

SWEET, H. 1948. *An Anglo-Saxon Reader*. Oxford.

VAURIE, C. 1965. *Birds of the Palaearctic Fauna*. London.

WITHERBY, JOURDAIN, TICEHURST and TUCKER. 1938–41. *The Handbook of British Birds*. London.

IX. BOTANICAL REMAINS

TWO POLLEN ANALYSES ON SEDIMENTS FROM WELL (PIT) 135

By K. E. Barber

DURING the 1970 season of excavations at Portchester Castle a monolith of organic silt with chalk and wood fragments was taken from the bottom of well (pit) 135, layer 100 (see p. 86). The stratigraphy of the monolith is given below; the figures are given in centimetres from the top of the sample. The absolute depth of it was not ascertained, and part of the well deposits had been excavated before the author visited the site, but the monolith, 24 cm. deep, included the chalk at the bottom of the well.

0–3 cm.: crumbly black silt; disturbed sediment of excavated surface.
3–19 cm.: black compressed silt-mud, no obvious laminations. Small fragments of chalk present, and occasional pieces of shell. Oyster shell at side of tin from 9–15 cm.
19–22·5 cm.: black compressed silt with twigs and small flints.
22·5–24 cm.: almost pure consolidated chalk.

Because of the strong probability of disturbance in such a sample from the bottom of a well, an orthodox pollen diagram was not attempted. Two samples, each about 1 cc., were taken from the cleaned surface at 15 and 20 cm. from the top.

They were prepared in the normal way, as set out by Faegri and Iversen.[1] The material was mounted in silicone fluid and the pollen grains counted using a Leitz Laborlux microscope, mainly at ×320.

The results are tabulated below.

All the above figures are percentages of the total pollen counted, 152 and 151, rounded off to one decimal place.

As might be expected from samples such as this the pollen spectra are heavily influenced by local conditions and cannot be taken to be representative of any wide area. The well was quite near one of the castle walls and this, together with the narrow opening of the well itself, must mean that the pollen represented is mainly from the immediate vicinity, perhaps even from plants growing on the sides of the well-shaft itself.

The difference in the stratigraphy between 15 cm. and 20 cm. may mean that the spectra are from two different periods in the life of the well, the lower one being earlier, but even this simple assumption may be questioned.

There is a further difficulty in that most of the grains found belong to families which include a great diversity of species, having different ecological requirements, the Cruciferae and the Rosaceae. Within these two families it is not possible to identify many species on their pollen grains alone and so the conclusions that can be drawn are necessarily very generalized.

However, it seems fairly certain from the very low frequency of tree and shrub pollen,

[1] Faegri, K. and Iversen, J. *Textbook of Pollen Analysis* (1964). Munksgaard, Copenhagen.

TABLE I

Depth	15 cm.	20 cm.
Sum total pollen	152	151
Sum unidentifiable corroded grains (not included in pollen sum)	32	25
% tree and shrub pollen	7·9	6·6
Betula (birch)	1·3	0·7
Quercus (oak)	2·0	2·6
Alnus (alder)	1·3	—
Corylus (hazel)	0·7	1·3
Salix (willow)	1·3	1·3
Hedera (ivy)	1·3	0·7
Gramineae (grasses)	6·5	15·2
Cereals	—	0·7
Calluna (heather)	2·6	3·3
Ericales (other heather)	2·0	0·7
Compositae (Tub.) (daisies)	1·3	5·3
Artemisia (mugwort)	—	0·7
Centaurea cyanus (cornflower)	—	0·7
Cirsium type (thistles)	—	2·0
Compositae (Lig.) (dandelions)	2·6	2·0
Chenopodiaceae (goosefoots)	2·0	0·7
Cruciferae (grasses, mustards)	33·6	4·0
Filipendula (meadowsweet)	0·7	1·3
Helianthemum (rock-rose)	0·7	1·3
Labiatae (mints, dead nettles)	—	1·3
Malva (mallows)	—	2·0
Plantago lanceolata (ribwort plantain)	1·3	2·0
Ranunculaceae (buttercups)	6·0	4·6
Rosaceae (roses, brambles)	25·7	32·4
Jasione montana (sheep's bit)	0·7	—
Rubiaceae (bedstraws)	0·7	2·0
Rumex (docks)	—	0·7
Saxifragaceae (saxifrages)	—	0·7
Scrophulariaceae (speedwells)	—	0·7
Succisa pratensis (devil's bit scabious)	1·3	0·7
Umbelliferae (wild carrot, etc.)	1·3	2·6
Urtica (nettles)	3·3	5·3
Pteridium aquilinum (bracken)	0·7	2·0
Filicales (ferns)	—	0·7

that the interior of the castle and possibly its immediate vicinity, were more or less open ground. The few grains found can be looked upon as regional pollen fall-out and could have come from some kilometres distance.

The grass pollen percentage is also low, and together with the high percentages of low-growing herbs, is indicative of patchy bare ground surrounding the well area. Best represented of these herbs are those of the families Cruciferae and Rosaceae and one may envisage plants such as rock-cress and wallflowers (Cruciferae), brambles and wild roses (Rosaceae), growing on and around the walls of well and castle. Many of the Cruciferae are also plants of coastal areas, though their increase in representation between 20 and 15 cm. cannot be said definitely to have any connection with this factor. It could easily be due to more wallflowers, say, becoming established as the walls of both castle and well aged, or even to the growing of plants such as cabbages, turnips or radishes within the castle.

The presence of pollen of Urtica is to be expected. *Urtica dioica*, the stinging nettle, quickly colonizes piles of stones and rubble and would have been constantly present throughout the life of the castle. The buttercups, Ranunculaceae, occupy similar habitats.

It is noticeable that there is a greater variety of herb species present in the lower sample. The absence of some of these species — docks, dead nettles, thistles, etc. — from the higher sample could be due to more intensive use of the castle's interior, or simply a policy of weeding. Overall, these pollen analyses are not at variance with what one might expect to find from material in such a restricted, specialized location. Though they give evidence of some of the plants growing within the castle and its immediate vicinity, they cannot be used to draw conclusions about the regional vegetation, for which a much more open site with undisturbed sedimentation is needed.

DENDROCHRONOLOGY

By John Fletcher

Timbers from Well (Pit) 135

The numerous oak planks from the sixth century well (pit) 135 (layer 100) are potentially useful both for dating the well to within a few years and for extending the oak chronology for southern England from A.D. 850 back to Roman times.

For English oaks of slow growth, tree-ring sequences match one another well over a large area, as is the case in many parts of the continent of Europe. For the post-medieval period our computer comparisons at Oxford show firstly good agreement between different parts of southern England,[1] and secondly that the mean curve (based on several trees) for this region has similarities to one for the Yorkshire–Derbyshire region[2] and with a tree, dating from the time of Henry VIII, felled recently at Thorpe Market near Cromer.

For the period 900–1500, the evidence comes from oak panels used as supports for English and Flemish paintings of the fifteenth and sixteenth centuries, together with medieval chests and cupboards at Westminster and Oxford.[3] The good agreement between south-eastern England and Flanders extends for some trees to the Netherlands and to western Germany.

Measurements have been made on 24 of the 39 planks that survive from the well. They fall into two groups:

(a) The lowest ones, normally always wet, are thick planks derived from half-trunks of young fast-grown trees. They have only some 40–50 annual rings.

[1] Fletcher, J. M. 1974. 'Annual rings in modern and medieval times'. In *The British Oak* (ed. M. G. Morris and F. H. Perring), pp. 80–96. Clarendon Press, Faringdon.

[2] I am grateful to Miss Ruth Jones for allowing me to have and use this curve prior to publication.

[3] Fletcher, J. M., Tapper M. C. and Walker, F. S. *Archaeometry*, xvi (1974), 31–40.,

(b) All the planks from higher in the well, however, are of different form. They are tapered pieces derived by radial splitting of slow-grown trees, 250–300 years old, and so are capable of periodic drying without undergoing undue warping or splitting.

Technically, therefore, construction of the well was advanced.

The tree-ring measurements indicate that two planks in the lowest tier were replaced some 10–20 years after the well was made. A detailed account is being published elsewhere.[1]

[1] Fletcher, J. M. and Dabrowska, A., submitted for publication in *Archaeometry*, xviii (1976).

X. SUMMARY AND SYNTHESIS

BEFORE attempting to offer a brief summary of the information presented in the preceding pages it is necessary to remind ourselves that only one-eighth of the defended area of the site has so far been excavated. While there is no reason to suppose that the sample is atypical, the possibility remains that the density of buildings and range of occupation so far recovered may not be reflected in other parts of the site. Until further work is undertaken the uncertainty will remain.

In Volume I it has been shown that occupation within the walls was very probably continuous throughout the fourth and into the first decades of the fifth century. Entire families were present and a wide range of domestic activities was practised. Since the garrison, if such it was, does not appear to have been a regular army unit, but in all probability a community of *laeti*, there is no need to conclude that the site was abandoned by 410. Indeed, it is more reasonable to suppose that occupation of some kind continued well into the fifth century.

In assessing the nature of the fifth-century occupation, two structures are of considerable significance: *Grubenhaus* S1 and the earliest phase of well (pit) 135. The lowest layer in hut S1 produced a group of pottery among which was part of a small bowl belonging to a group of *Schalenurnen* which, Dr Myres points out, are characteristic of the pottery of the North German coastlands in the first half of the fifth century. The upper filling of the same feature yielded the disc of an applied brooch dated by Mr Welch to the second half of the century. If it is accepted that the observed stratigraphy represents a time span in the filling of the sunken hut, then the structure is likely to have been in use in the first half of the fifth century but was probably abandoned by or soon after 450, the upper layer of soil accumulating in the next 50 years or so, while occupation continued nearby.

The earliest phases of well (pit) 135 tell much the same story. The shaft in use during the first period had silted to a depth of some 3 ft. (1 m.) before a purse mount/strike-a-light was dropped in. Mr Welch argues that the type was likely to have been manufactured in the period 450–500. Higher in the silt, after the top of the shaft had eroded out into an irregular water hole, a disc brooch of the late fifth or early sixth century was lost in the mud. Thus, continued use is suggested for the second half of the fifth century with the strong possibility that the well had started life much earlier. Further evidence for fifth-century occupation within the fort is provided by a small but consistent group of distinctive potsherds from various parts of the site (pp. 183–4).

The nature and intensity of the fifth-century occupation is more difficult to assess. The simplest explanation would be to suppose that the original 'Roman' population survived to be augmented by further Germanic settlers whose buildings and pottery types serve to distinguish them from the sub-Roman population. Such an interpretation would be wholly consistent with the available historical evidence and with the situation now beginning to be demonstrated for other parts of England. The occurrence of metal-types dated to the second half of the century suggests that contacts were maintained with the continent throughout the century, but there is no necessity to postulate constant infiltrations of new people.

Apart from the well and the *Grubenhaus* already mentioned, the only other structures to survive, for which an early Saxon date may be proposed, are the three remaining *Grubenhäuser* and the two post-built huts. It was during this time, probably towards the beginning of the sixth century, that the new timber-lined well was inserted into the existing well pit. The construction post-dates a few sherds of stamped pottery of the late fifth to early sixth century and from a nearby heap of spoil, probably thrown out at the time of construction, came a substantial part of a wide-mouthed vessel (no. 171), which Dr Myres thinks is unlikely to be later than about 500. The well evidently continued in use for some time into the latter half of the eighth century, during which adjacent areas were subject to ploughing.

A wide scatter of potsherds of stamped type suggests the continued use of the site throughout the sixth century, while a double spiral-headed pin and a few sherds of comb-stamped pottery are probably assignable to the seventh century. Throughout this period, fifth–seventh century, simple coarse ware pot types continued to be manufactured, usually in chaff-tempered fabrics. A sufficient range of domestic debris was discovered to suggest that occupation could have been continuous throughout the period 400–700, although it must be admitted that finds distinctive of the seventh century are rare, and the number of structures is small. Some degree of continuity is however implied by the maintenance of the well.

The reference to Portsmouth in the *Anglo-Saxon Chronicle* is of comparatively little value. If it does indeed refer to Portchester (p. 2), it is at best a further reminder of the sub-Roman use of the old defences into the late fifth or early sixth century. The explicit statement that the young Briton who was killed was 'of very high rank' would, however, be consistent with the surprising number of valuable objects dating to the latter half of the fifth century found during the excavation.

The paucity of finds of the sixth and seventh centuries, with the notable exception of abraded potsherds, taken together with the evidence for agricultural activity and the relative lack of structures, might be thought to imply that the actual habitation area moved about the fort: when one location was abandoned it was turned over to cultivation and perhaps manured with household refuse. Clearly, to test such an hypothesis would require excavation on a much larger scale.

In the late seventh or early eighth century several substantial post-built houses were established on the site. S9 and S12 may have been the earliest, using the old well, with perhaps buildings S7 and 'posthole complex A', each with a new well, added later. The detailed arguments of sequence are tenuous and open to various interpretations (pp. 121–7). Occupation of this kind, once firmly established in the area, continued. Later, in the late eighth or in the ninth century, the pair of buildings S10 and S11 replaced S9 on the southern part of the site.

The Saxon coins from Portchester (pp. 130–1) imply that the site was comparatively rich in the ninth century, particularly the second half of the century. The two coins of Burgred of Mercia found in the excavations both came from the vicinity of building S7, while of the five pieces of decorated metalwork (nos. 48–53) dated to the ninth or tenth centuries, at least three were found on the part of the site occupied by buildings S7, S9 and S10, unfortunately all from levels disturbed in the medieval period. A further indication of wealth from a slightly earlier date is provided by the glass vessel of East Mediterranean origin found in pit 34. The general impression given by this evidence is of a community well above peasant level. The documentary sources provide no indication of the nature or status of the occupants, except that the site was at this time owned by the Bishops of Winchester.

The acquisition of Portchester by the King in 904 provides the first firm date in the history of the fort. The old fortifications were now required to serve as one of the strong points in the defence of Wessex against the Danes: such a change of use would inevitably have involved a change in the nature of the occupation. This may well be the context for the abandonment of the eighth- to ninth-century building complex and the contemporary wells, and the deposition of a thick layer of occupation debris over much of the southern part of the site. While it remains a possibility that contemporary buildings lined the main east–west road at this time, well clear of the rubbish heap, convincing plans are impossible to distinguish from the great mass of predominantly post-Conquest postholes. The occupation refuse itself is of particular interest for although it contains prodigious amounts of food waste, particularly marine molluscs, pottery is relatively uncommon, a mere 160 or so vessels compared with over 700 in the ultimate Saxon phase, and small objects are practically unknown. The contents are not such as would be expected from normal domestic occupation. If these observations are significant, they may suggest that in the phase during which Portchester served as a burh there was no permanent domestic occupation, but instead use of a more transient nature associated with the garrisoning of the defences or the use of the enceinte as a temporary place of refuge. Once more, the final solution to this problem must await the results of more extensive excavation.

Portchester was listed as a defence in the Burghal Hidage of about 920. By the early eleventh century it was still owned by the King, but was divided into three separately held manors, one of which no doubt included the fort itself.

It was probably during the latter part of the tenth century that the final phase of Saxon building began (fig. 99, phases 5–8) typified by a predominance of wheel-made pottery called here 'Portchester ware'. From the beginning it is possible to recognize a single complex in which a large aisled hall occupied a prominent position in relation to three subsidiary structures (phases 5 and 6). Here surely is the establishment belonging to the freedmen who held this part of the Portchester manor of King Edward.

At about the beginning of the eleventh century the owner erected a masonry tower of light construction (building S18, phase 1), possibly replacing an earlier timber structure, on a plot of land between the hall and a subsidiary domestic building. While the function of the 'tower' remains uncertain, it is tempting to remember the early eleventh century compilation which records 'and if a churl prospered so that he owned fully five hides of land of his own, a bell and a castle-gate, a seat and special office in the King's hall, then he was henceforth entitled to the rights of a thane'. Building S18 could well have been a bell tower serving as a symbol of the increased status of the freedman, perhaps no longer a churl but a thane. The fact that the watergate was rebuilt in masonry at about this time lends support to the idea of the increasing status of the site.

The final change came about towards the middle of the eleventh century, when the aisled building appears to have fallen into disuse and a small cemetery was established on the north side of the tower. Not long afterwards the tower was rebuilt on a more massive scale, by which time the surrounding buildings had disappeared. The occasion for these far-reaching changes cannot be precisely defined, but the conquest of 1066 and the redistribution of land consequent upon it, would have provided a reasonable context. The three manors of Portchester were brought together by William and assigned to William Mauduit in whose family the ownership of the site was to remain for more than 50 years. Under the new regime a strongly fortified residence was created in the north-west corner of the old Roman enclosure. It was probably at this time that the late Saxon hall complex was allowed to disintegrate, with the exception of the tower which, in its rebuilt form, served as a religious focus until the Augustinian canons began to erect their Priory close by some time soon after 1130.

APPENDIX A

Commentary on the Sections

Sections 1–25 illustrated here as figs. 154–61 have already been published in Volume I, where a brief commentary on the Roman levels will be found (Vol. I, pp. 432–6). Here layers relevant to the Saxon occupation will be selected for comment.

Section 1: Landgate

Trench 8, layer 3 represents the weathering and partial collapse of the upper part of the Roman gatehouse. The Saxon robbing of the Roman superstructure took place later (trench 8, layers 6 and 7; trench 110, layer 26). The Saxon posthole, ph 1, is shown in section as trench 110, layer 27: the surface from which the post was cut had been obscured by the projecting footings of the Norman gatehouse, not shown on the section.

Section 2: Landgate

The robbing of the Roman masonry, layers 9 and 10, was followed by a period of soil accumulation, layer 8, which must be of late Saxon or early medieval date, since it precedes the construction of the Norman landgate.

Section 3: Landgate

The accumulation of soil and rubble from the end of the Roman period until the late Saxon period is represented by layers 4, 16, 25.

Section 4: Watergate

The robber trenches for the Roman gatehouse were filled with accumulations of soil, rubble and mortar (layers 9, 13) above which a turf line formed (layer 12). It would appear that the robber trench for the south guard-chamber was left open at this stage, possibly because the wall was robbed last, the debris being tipped out over the northern part of the site. Eventually it was filled with soil and rubble (layer 29). The construction of the (?) late Saxon gatehouse was marked by layer 11, a spread of hard pinkish gritty mortar which could be shown to belong to the building period. This was sealed by a stony soil accumulation, layer 10.

Section 5: Watergate

The rubble layers, trench 38, layer 7, and trench 34, layer 37, were deposited at the time when layer 11 on Section 4 was laid down and therefore represent the building period of the (?) late Saxon gatehouse. The immediately preceding levels represent late Roman to Saxon soil accumulations.

Section 6: Watergate

The robber trench for the Roman guardhouse wall is represented by layers 37 and 38. Layer 11 is a discontinuous building spread contemporary with the construction of the (?) late Saxon gatehouse.

Section 7

The soil accumulation above the Roman road surface represents successive Saxon levels, partially disturbed by ploughing. Trench 91, layer 46 contained mainly Roman material, but 37 and 41 have produced some Saxon sherds: lenses of occupation material are apparent within them. In trench 87, layer 48 is a disturbed Roman level. Layer 47 represents a late Saxon ground surface.

Section 8

The filling of Saxon *Grubenhaus* S2 is represented by trench 87, layers 26, 30, 47 and trench 91, layer 65. It was sealed by trench 87, layer 9. Trench 87, layer 5a is a late Saxon ground surface with occupation material contemporary with the rubbish heap filling well (pit) 135. This is of the same date as trench 91, layer 37a and trench 107, layer 9, where the occupation is at its thickest. The pre-tenth-century levels in trench 107 are layers 34 and 41, but 41, like 21 and 31, is essentially a disturbed Roman soil accumulation. Pit 218 is Saxon.

Section 9

The level of stony soil with some large flints (trench 101, layer 115) could be shown to represent the ground surface before building S9 was constructed. It was cut by the post-holes of building S9 and by pit 204. The pit was deliberately filled with interleaved tips of occupation rubbish and clay, before the construction of building S10. The burnt layer associated with its hearth appears as trench 101, layer 80, while the gravel which formed the path between it and building S11 appears as trench 103, layer 24 which can be shown to overlie layer 115. The relationship was clearly defined in trench 103 west of the section. The relationship between this gravel metalling and the wall of building S10 is best appreciated on the plan (fig. 19). The equivalent surface to layers 80 and 24 cannot everywhere be traced. Trench 103, layers 20 and 22 represent a tip of mortary rubbish and redeposited brickearth which was derived from the digging of the large cesspit, pit 207. These layers correlate with trench 101, layer 115 and therefore suggest that pit 207 was broadly contemporary with building S9.

Before the construction period in the ninth century the soil accumulation in trench 103 was disturbed by Saxon ploughing, the plough marks scoring the surface of the primary clay bank. Thus layer 23, whilst basically Roman in origin, was churned up in early–mid-Saxon times. The same is probably true of trench 101, layers 103, 117 and trench 100, layer 66, but no underlying plough marks could be traced. The southern limit of ploughing probably lay in the vicinity of the much later feature numbered as trench 103, layer 7a, to the south of which flint rubble from the erosion of the Roman wall (trench 103, layer 72) would appear to have been undisturbed by agricultural activities.

Later in the tenth century a mass of occupation rubbish was tipped against the Roman wall (trench 103, layers 18 and 8) and into the half-filled cesspit (trench 103, layers 41 and 42). The upper layers (trench 100, layer 65; trench 101, layer 85 and the lower part of trench 103, layer 11) all contained Portchester ware mixed with early medieval sherds.

Section 10

The sequence is equivalent to that shown in Section 9. Layers 44, 46, 47 and 48 were Roman, disturbed by Saxon ploughing. Layer 38 above and to the north of feature layer

68, represents the ninth-century building level from which pit 191 was dug, while layer 49, a thick deposit of occupation rubbish, was deposited in the tenth century and spread into the partially silted pit (pit 191). Subsequent layers produced early medieval pottery. (The layer number 38, slightly south of feature layer 19, is an error: it should read 38a).

Section 11

No Saxon levels were definitely represented, although layer 32 by virtue of its stratigraphical position should be of Saxon date.

Section 12

The Saxon oven belongs to building S11, the wall of which was cut away by pit 212. Further south all Saxon levels were removed by medieval levelling.

Section 13

The Saxon plough soil is represented by trench 102, layer 33a, trench 101, layer 49 and trench 100, layers 24 and 29. In all cases the material contained was largely Roman derived from Roman occupation layers churned up by the plough.

Features, trench 101, layer 24 and 100, layer 44, are of Saxon date.

Section 14

Layer 10 represents the early to mid-Saxon plough soil. Most of the layers in the south end of the trench belong to the complex sequence described in detail under the discussion of pit 135. In summary, layers 52, 49, 11, 11a, and 9, are tips of late occupation rubbish belonging to the tenth and eleventh centuries, the flints below representing the construction phase of the timber well. Layers 33 and 84 were soil accumulations forming in the original waterhole of fifth-century date.

Section 15

The disturbed Roman occupation layer, which probably represents a phase of Saxon ploughing, can be traced across the site as trench 72, layers 6 and 7; trench 71, layer 6; trench 73, layer 10; trench 80, layers 7 and 9. The disturbance of these layers, in the post-Saxon period, particularly over the northern part of the site, can be demonstrated by the finding of sherds of medieval pottery mixed in with the earlier material.

In trench 72 the foundations of the masonry tower of late Saxon date can be seen: layer 8 represents its construction phase, layer 33 the final robbing. An early medieval gully, layer 40, cut through the robbed material.

Pit 175 (trench 73, layer 35) is late Saxon, as is the feature, trench 73, layer 52.

Section 16

The ploughed-up Roman soil accumulation appears as trench 94, layer 37b; trench 95, layer 61 and 113; trench 96, layer 25; trench 97, layer 12; trench 98, layers 30 and 30a; trench 99, layer 56 and trench 109, layer 13. The slots for the Saxon buildings S7 and S8 can be seen as trench 94, layers 94 and 95; trench 95, layer 80 and the unnumbered slot on the section between trenches 94 and 95. They cut through the filling of pit 137 which is of early/mid-Saxon date. Posthole (trench 98, layer 64) is probably early/mid-Saxon by virtue of its stratigraphical position.

Section 17

The ploughed-up Roman soil accumulation is represented by layer 65, the lower part of layers 26, 36, 24. Layer 35 was a gravel spread stratigraphically of the mid-Saxon period. It dipped over the filling of pit 201. Layer 26a represents a slot possibly for a late Saxon fence associated with building S8. Layer 47, the upper part of 26 and 23 contained late Saxon and early medieval sherds.

Section 18

The ploughed-up Roman soil accumulation is represented by layers 85 and 86 and probably layer 36. Pit 203 was cut through this. Layers 29 and 81 contained late Saxon material mixed with early medieval.

Section 19

The ploughed-up Roman soil accumulation survived as trench 70, layer 4 and trench 69, layer 7. Trench 69, layer 4 was a localized patch of cobbles through which the late Saxon pit 68 was cut. The exact stratigraphical position of gully 41 is not clear.

Section 20

Layer 8 represents the disturbed Roman soil accumulation.

Section 21

Layers 24, 8, 18 and 64 represent disturbed Roman soil accumulations. No distinctive Saxon layers were recognized. The position from which the posthole (layer 42) was cut cannot be defined.

Section 22

Layers 19 and 30a represent disturbed Roman soil accumulations.

Section 23

Layers 48 and 29 are part of the filling of the *Grubenhaus* S3. Layer 8 and part of layers 11 and 12 represent soil accumulations, in origin largely Roman, disturbed and mixed in the Saxon period and later.

Section 24

Layers 37, 21 and 25 represent soil accumulations disturbed in the early to mid-Saxon period. Layer 63 (pit 153) was the packing of a post-pit belonging to the late Saxon aisled hall, building S16. Its contemporary ground surface was destroyed in the medieval period.

Section 25

Layers 31 and 80 represent soil accumulations disturbed in the Saxon period. The layer of flint rubble, layer 62, was deposited in the Saxon period contemporary with the construction of hut S5. The layer of clay, stratigraphically later (layer 75), was laid outside the end wall of building S7, the wall slot for which was destroyed at this point by the eighteenth-century posthole, layer 11a. Posthole, layer 38, is of Saxon date.

APPENDIX B

Details of Postholes

Altogether nearly 1200 postholes were discovered in the area excavations of 1964–72. Postholes considered to belong to the individual Saxon buildings are described in the relevant sections above. The details of the remainder are listed here with the exception of those which can be shown to be Roman or post-Saxon. The listing of a post here does not preclude a Roman or post-Saxon date. All measurements are in inches, the depths being taken from the surface of the natural brickearth.

Ph. no.	Trench: layer	Depth	Diameter
2	109:75	11½	21
3	109:73	9½	19
4	109:74	5½	11
6	109:78	16	25
7	109:72	6	24/12
8	109:50	11	16/21
10	109:102	8	18
12	109:55	7	18/18
13	109:66	13½	41/19
14	109:77	10	32/25
15	109:71	6	15
16	109:60	1	10/8
17	109:63	5	14/8
18	109:61	3	13/10
20	109:100	8	24
22	109:35	5	24
23	109:36	1½	12
24a	109:43	9	24/20
24b	109:43	9	12
26	109:34	2	19/9
28	109:32	7	22/13
29	109:21	8	19
32	109:40	½	10
33	109:24	5	11
34	109:95	22	33/25
35	109:30	4	20
36	109:97	17	30/23
37	109:89	6	22/12
38	109:86	5	14
39	109:91	11	26/18
40	109:85	6	14
41	109:103	6	15/9
42	82:10	4	18/14
43	82:11	14	9
44	82:12	4	21/12
45	82:13	3	13/8
46	82:14	4	15
47	82:15	8	17/10
48	82:16	6	10/14
50	80:18	11	19
51	80:32	10	19
52	80:34	11	22
53	80:56	3	10/18
54	80:57	5	14
55	79:63	7	27
56	79:64	8	10/8
58	84:14	8	19/24
59	84:15	13	12/10
60	84:16	5	8 square
61	84:18	4	8
62	84:17	19	22
63	77:26	18	39
64	77:34	51	20
65	77:37	4	30/16
66	77:20	2	9
67	77:21	2	3
68	77:19	4	12/14
69	77:16	3	19 square
70	77:12	10	26/24
71	77:11	5	18/21
72	77:10	2	22/24
73	77:9	3	14
74	77:14	1	15
75	77:17	4	24
76	77:18	2	10
77	77:8	3	12

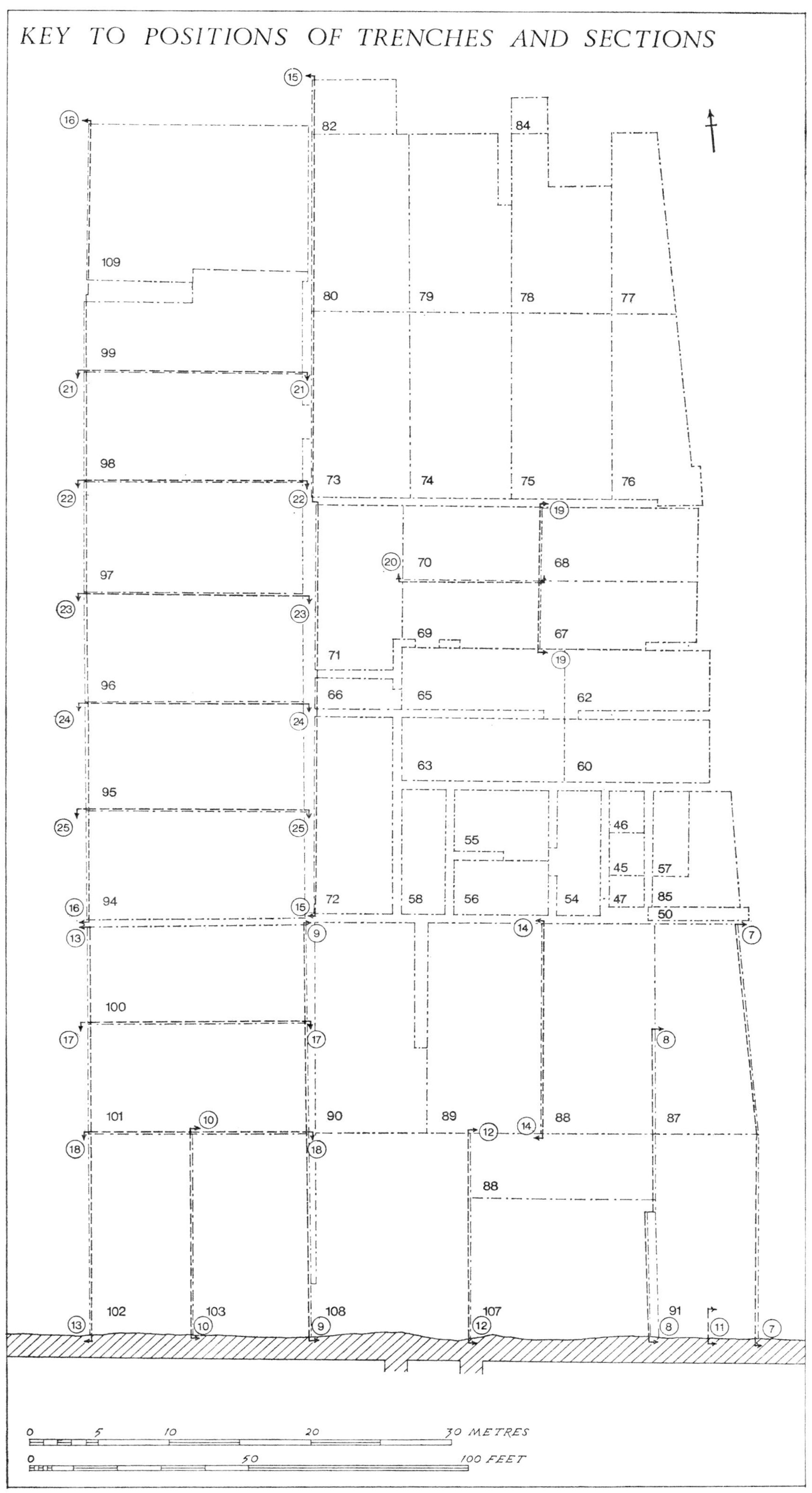

FIG. 153

facing p. 306

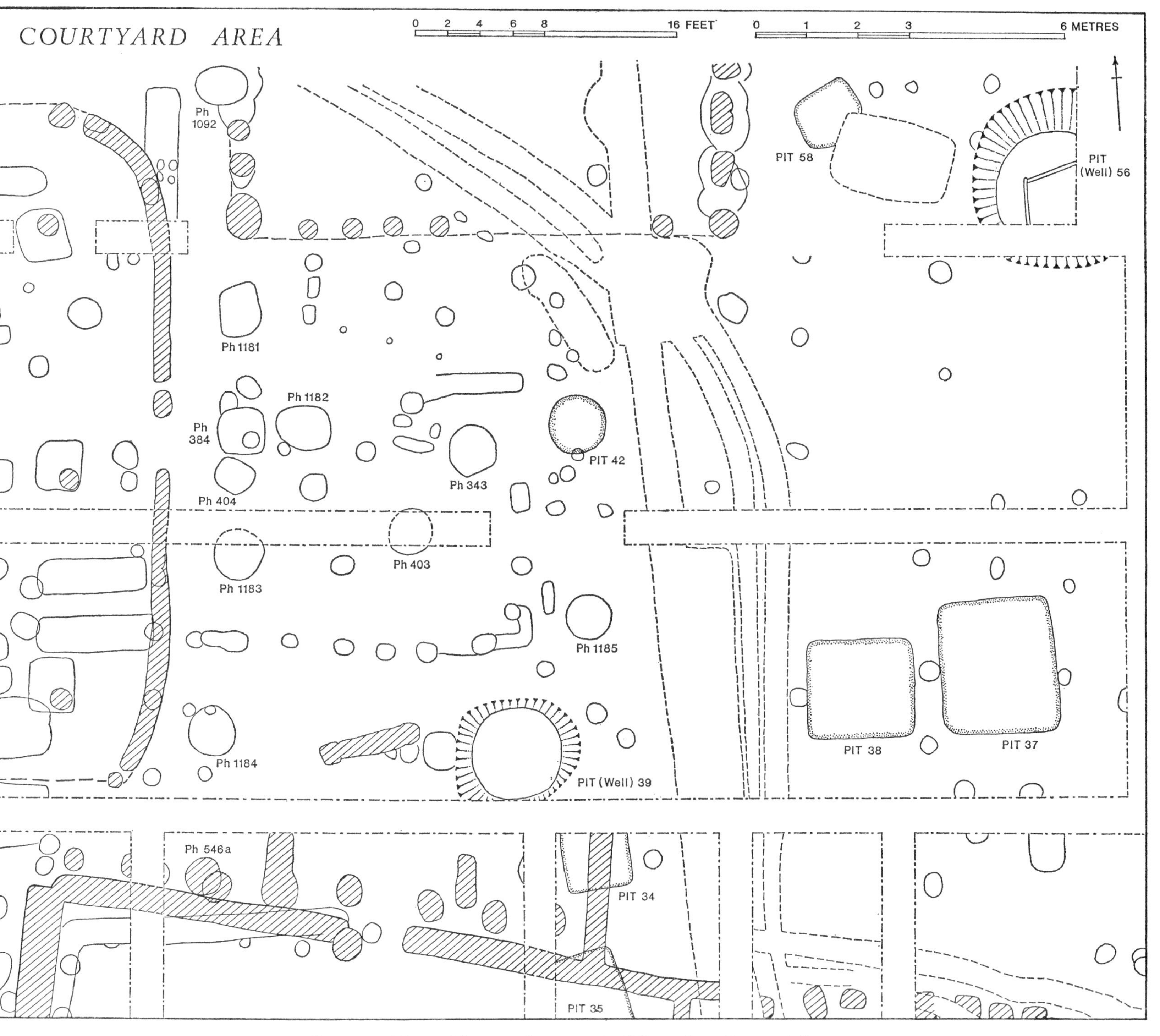

Fig. 33. Plan of features between buildings S13, S14 and S15

facing p. 56

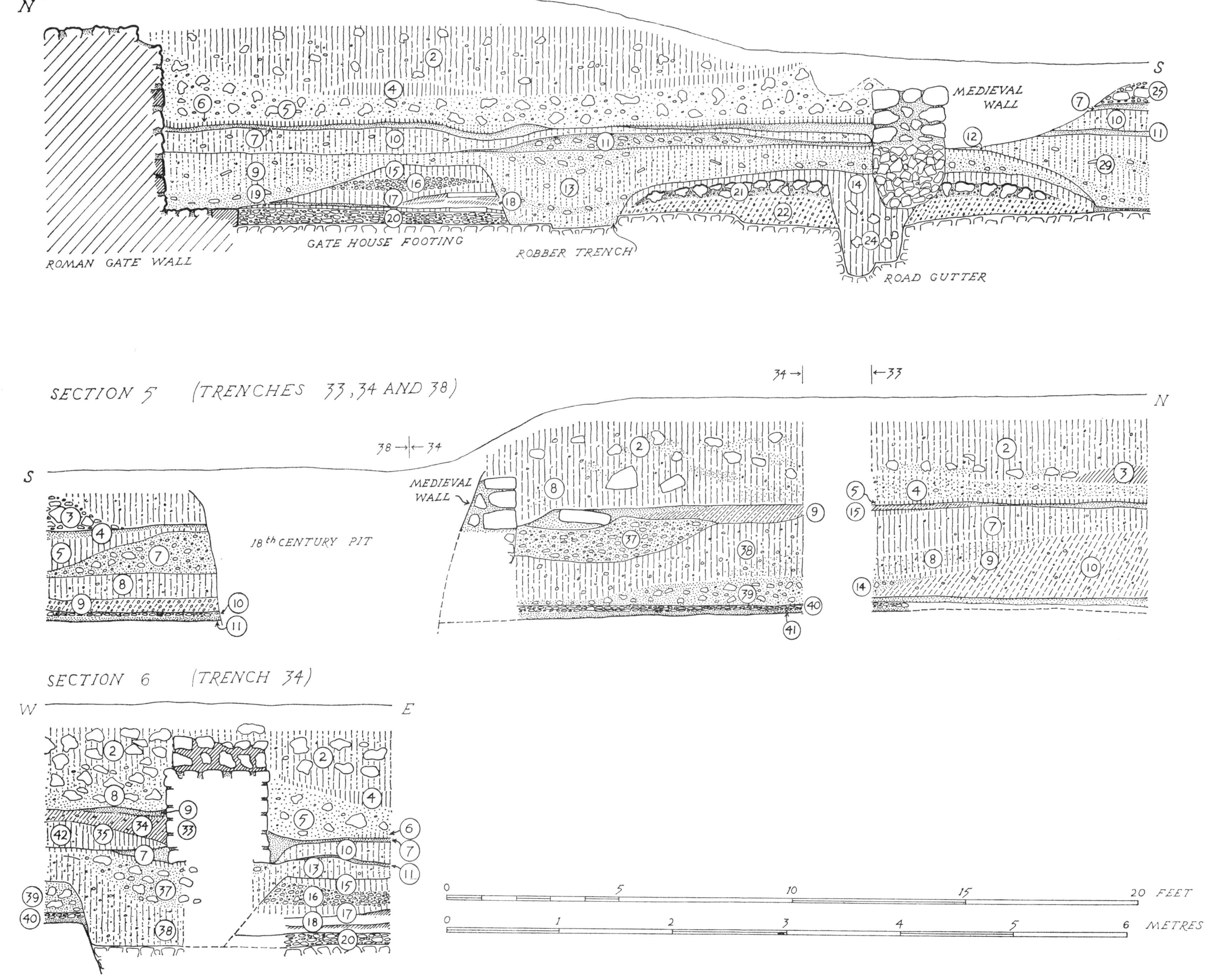

Fig. 155. Sections of the watergate

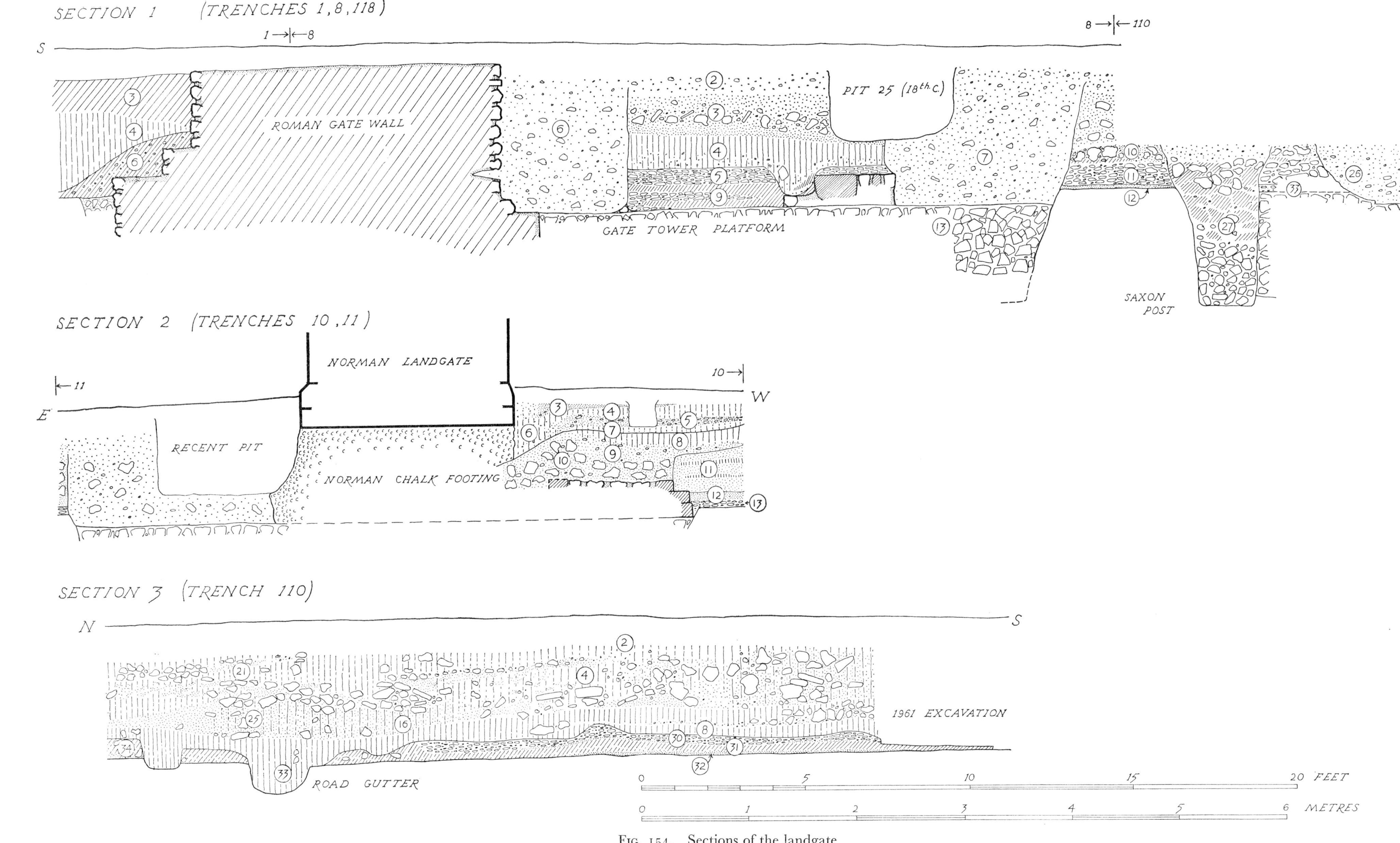

Fig. 154. Sections of the landgate

Ph. no.	Trench: layer	Depth	Diameter
78	77:7	3	18/15
79	77:13	3	12/9
80	78:12	16	12
81	78:10	18–25 void	49–22 void
82	79:15	13	12/18
83	79:22	4	15/10
84	79:19	9	21/12
85	80:64	9	33/22
86	80:32	9	24
87	80:14	6	15/12
89	80:12	6	18
90a	80:72	6	32
90b	80:72	9	33/15
91	80:29	10	33–50
92	80:15	21	12
93	80:16	10	23
94	80:65	5	16/13
95	80:71	3	6/8
96	79:17	3	24–27
98	80:70	11	22
99a	80:46	4	24/11
99b	80:46	5	17/15
100	80:45	9	36
101a	79:57	11	36/30
101b	79:57	7	36
101c	79:57	4	27
102	79:56	2	14/12
103	80:43	8	30
104	80:69	7	15
105	80:40	6	15
106	80:47	5	18
107	80:48	8	9
108	80:38	11	21
109	80:37	21	45/36
110a	80:20	9	27/18
110b	80:20	6	18/12
111	80:41	8	30/30
112	80:22	9	24 square
113	80:23	17	24
114a	80:25	9	16
114b	80:25	6	19
114c	80:25	9	16
115	80:26	14	10½
116	79:54	5	15
117	79:7	5	6
118	79:8	6	10½
119	79:9	3	12
120	79:10	5	15/11
121	79:55	10	22/18
123	73:16	5	14
124	80:21	6	16/12
125	80:24	6	26/12
126	80:57	8	33/24
127	80:39	18	34
128	73:26	3	9
129	73:17	4	11/8
130	73:18	4	11/8
131	73:46	Not given	16/8
132	73:43	6	17
133	73:44	10	17/11
134	73:45	6	13/8
135	73:34	2	6
136	73:19	5	18/15
137	73:20	3	4
138	73:21	9	9
139	73:24	6	12
140	73:25	3	14/8
141	73:22	6	11
142	73:23	4	11
143	73:30	6	11/8
144	74:75	8	12/10
145	74:38	6	14
146	74:76	6	18/10
147	74:77	4	12/10
148	74:78	8	26/24
149	74:34	7	16/8
150	74:25	6	36/24
151	74:36	4	8
152	74:26	12	15
153	74:16	5	16
154	74:17	6	18
155	74:57	6	30
157	75:29	12	13/12
158	75:20	12	24/26
159	75:18	6	36/26
160	75:19	5	16/14
161	75:54	14	24/18
162	77:32	2	10
163	77:24	3	20
164	77:25	6	20/18
165	77:35	4	21/12

Ph. no.	Trench: layer	Depth	Diameter	Ph. no.	Trench: layer	Depth	Diameter
166a	76:14	12	24	206	74:38	3–5	29/24
166b	76:14	6	16/12	218	73:13	13	30
166c	76:14	7	39	220	73:38	5	22/18
167a	76:15	4	14	221	73:29	10	29/21
167b	76:15	3	9	222	73:42	6	12
168	75:44	12	22	224	73:48	10	15/12
169a	76:37	7	6	225	73:47	11	18/21
169b	76:37	7	6	226	73:52	12	23
170	76:16	10	42	227	73:53	9	24/14
171	76:23	4	20	228	73:36	3	11
172	75:26	4	8	229	73:33	6	19/17
173	75:27	5	8	230	73:31	8	18/14
174	75:28	2	6	231	73:50	6	22
175	75:30	4	14/5	232	99:71	14	6
176	75:31	4	7	233	99:70	10	7
177	75:12	4	12/10	234	99:59	10	12/11
178	75:57	5	8	235	99:73	5	25/20
179	76:24	9	24/15	236	99:74	7/8	18 square
180	76:25	8	24/28	237	99:103	4	24
181	76:40	4	14	238	99:104	7	10
182	76:19	5	24	239	99:105	5½	8
183	75:8	4	29/26	240	99:53	5	24/19
184	75:9	11	17	243	99:91	?	21/16
185	75:14	21	30/28	244	99:41	21	32/24
186	75:51	9	12	245	99:96	?	18
187	75:55	4	12/10	246	99:68	5	10
188	75:56	10	20/12	250	99:93	17	20/16
189	75:11	7	23/19	251	98:67	16	29
190	75:45	7	19	252	98:42	6	18
191	75:13	10	22 square	253	98:59	5/6	12
192	75:10	7	29/24	254	98:46	8	32/28
193	74:13	9	21/17	256	98:62	5	16/11
194a	74:41	5	22/16	258	97:61	4	14/10
194b	74:41	6	10	259	97:56	14	21/16
194c	74:41	3	14/10	265	97:68	9	24
195	74:40	5	12	266	97:74	12	14
196	74:23	10	33/30	267	97:55	9	34
197	74:25	15	15	269	71:41	5	18
198	74:55	12	31	272	71:14	10	13
199	74:56	12	30	273a	71:37	8	18
200	74:80	20	30	273b	71:37	4	9
201	74:73	7	21/17	273c	71:37	5	12
202	74:39	6	14/11	278	71:36	10	15/9
203	74:72	6	14	279	71:35	7	22/14
204	74:74	6	15	280	71:34	8	16
205	74:37	6	18/15	286a	70:9	7	27

Ph. no.	Trench: layer	Depth	Diameter
286b	70:9	5	17
287	70:7	2	14
288	70:6	9	20/18
289	70:47	5	31/22
290	70:26	3	12
291	70:25	2	14
292	70:21	6	6
293	70:12	10	18/12
294	70:27	8	11
298	69:24	3	12
300	69:13	6	46/22
302a	69:22	?	14/16
302b	69:22	12	7
302c	69:22	8	6/4
308	69:36	6	13
313	69:49	2	12/10
315	70:40	7	24/10
316	69:17	6	12
317	68:15	3	24/16
318	68:11	4	15/13
319	68:10	4	19/13
320	68:9	5	14
321	68:39	5	13
322a	68:16	3	12/18
323a	68:20	2	14/13
330a	68:32	9	17/15
330b	68:32	5	10
331	68:33	8	13
332a	68:34	3	14
332b	68:34	3	13
340	67:24	9	15
341	67:42	6	17
342	67:43	3	20
344a	67:13	10	14
344b	67:13	6	13
345	67:14	6	13
346	67:11	3	12
347	67:8	8	57/26
348a	67:15	4	10
348b	67:15	3	11
349	62:24	?	24/20
350	62 ph 1	7	7
351	62 ph 2	4	10
352	62 ph 3	?	11
353	62 ph 4	12	17
354	62 ph 5	5	9
355	62 ph 6	5	13
356	62 ph 7	3	12
357	62 ph 8	4	11/9
358	62 ph 9	3	15/9 (irreg.)
359	62 ph 10	6	11
360	62 ph 11	5	9 (irreg.)
361	62 ph 12	12	8
362	62 ph 13	4	9
363	62 ph 14	7	12
364	62 ph 15	7	10
365	62 ph 16	6	17
366	62 ph 17	7	13/10
367	62 ph 18	?	6
368	62 ph 19	?	11
369	62 ph 20	5	10
370	62 ph 21	?	12
371	62 ph 22	?	16/10
372	65 ph 10	9	14
373	67:17	10	34
374	65 ph 7	4	10/7
376	65 ph 9	7	14/8½
377	65 ph 16	5	14
378	65 ph 15	9	20
379	65 ph 17	8	9
380	65 ph 29	?	6
383	65 ph 6	5	30/9
389	65 ph 18	9	25/23
390	65 ph 24	4	14/11
391	65 ph 25	6	14
392	65 ph 22	9	15/14
393	65 ph 26	?	10
394	65 ph 27	?	8
395	65 ph 11	10	13
396	65 ph 12	5	12
397	65 ph 13	6	14/8
398	65 ph 14	8	13/8
399	65 ph 31	?	4
400	65 ph 32	?	4
401	65 ph 33	?	4
402	65 ph 34	5	8
405	66:8		
406	66:7	6	29
407a	96:29	10	24/18
407b	96:29	1	17/11
408	96:24	10	18/14
409	96:33	13	21/14

Ph. no.	Trench: layer	Depth	Diameter	Ph. no.	Trench: layer	Depth	Diameter
412	96:60	8	32 square	472	94:56	3½	4
413	96:79	2½	24/19	473	94:68	4½	4
414	96:75	7½	20/15	474	94:58	3	20
415	96:71	7	24/19	475	94:52	9	25/17
416	96:67	5	181/12	476	94:60	5	12 square
417	96:52	9	26	477	94:59	8	7
418	96:76	3	20/17	478	94:64	3	5
419	96:77	3	11	479	94:65	5	8
420	96:78	4	6	480	94:62	4	6
421	96:48	16	10	481	94:63	2½	4
422	96:62	10	20	482	94:66	3½	6/4
423	95:94	Shallow	24	483	94:67	3	5
424	95:95	3½	26/14	484	94:54	11	22/20
425	95:96	3½	27/21	485	94:55	8	27/23
426	95:97	3	18/16	486	94:72	10½	18
427	95:98	3	11/9	487	94:83	5½	22/18
428	95:99	1½	11	488	94:84	5½	15/12
429	95:100	2	8	489	94:77	3	12/10
431	95:66	2½	10/7	490	94:61	9	16/15
432	95:67	4	10/9	491	94:86	7½	19/14
433	95:70	4	8	492	94:70	5½	12
434	95:71	3	10/7	493	94:71	2½	14 (irreg.)
435	95:73	4	14	494	94:69	10	24/20
436	95:74	5	18/10	495	94:78	3	9/7
437	95:79	6	9/7	496	94:85	6	16
438	95:88	2	10/7	500	72:10	5	16/14
439	95:89	2	8	501	72:23	3	16/8
440	95:90	5	11/8	502	72:25	3	15
441	95:91	3	6	505	72:31	3	32/31
442	95:35	11	25/21	507a	72:29	3	7
443	95:36	14–12	31/24	507b	72:29	3	18
444	95:37	8	19	509a	72:16	6	24
445	95:38	12–	26/24	509b	72:16	8	18
447	95:40	4	5	509c	72:16	4	11
448	95:42	10	12	510	72:18	3	24
449	95:43	5	18	511	72:26	6	13
450	95:44	6	12	513	72:63	?	18
452	94:88	?	17	514	72 ph 11	4	22/14
453	94:82	?	10	515	72:60	?	12
454	94:81	?	8	520	72:64	12	14
455	94:101	4	15	521	72:65	14	15
456	94:102	6	14	522	72:62	9	26/14
457	94:105	4½	14	526	72:56	?	14
458	94:103	5	12	527	72:37	4	19
459	94:108	3½	13	528	72:53	7	18
464	94:116	3½	19/13	529	72:48	9	30

Ph. no.	Trench: layer	Depth	Diameter	Ph. no.	Trench: layer	Depth	Diameter
530	72:66	?	13	603	58 ph 25	5	16
531	72:47	4	14	604	58 ph 26	7	12
532	60 ph 1	7	10/7	605	58 ph 27	7	13/4 rect.
533	60 ph 2	6	12/10	606	58 ph 28	2	14
534	60 ph 3	8	16	607	58 ph 29	6	5
535	60 ph 4	10	16	608	58 ph 30	4	6
536	60 ph 5	6	14	609	58 ph 31	6	5
537	60 ph 6	4	12 square	610	58 ph 32	?	12
538	60 ph 7	2	16/14	611	58 ph 33	?	22
539	60 ph 8	?	15/10	612	58 ph 34	?	18
540	60 ph 9	3	12	613	58 ph 35	8	20/12
541	60 ph 10	3	13 square	614	58 ph 36	7	7
542	60 ph 11	9	12½	615	54 ph 1	6	22
543	60 ph 12	7	14	616	54 ph 2	6	14
544	60 ph 13	6	12	628	54 ph 14	?	16
548	55:18	6	14	629	54 ph 15	?	
549	55:15	8	23/22	630	85:28	12	18/17
552	55:28	?	18	631a	85:30	8	18
554	55:26	4	8/6	631b	85:30	10	16/12
555	55:27	3	5	632	85:31	7	25
558	55:22	5	17/10	633a	85:29	8	18/16
559	55:21	6	11/10	633b	85:29	7	15
560	55:20	9	12	634	85:18	7	10/8
561	55:19	8	10	635	85:23	8	13/10
567	56 ph 6	7	13	636	87:32	?	28/17
568	56 ph 7	2	14/12	637	87:45	5	26/22
573	56 ph 12	3	14/12	638	87:46	6	26/19
574	56 ph 13	5	21/14	639	87:15	7	44/36
569b	56 ph 8	3	9	640	87:16	2	32/28
586	58 ph 8	9	11	643a	87:42	2	35/29
587	58 ph 9	7	14	643b	87:42	9	19/18
588	58 ph 10	12	15	644	87:44	3	39/27
589	58 ph 11	11	14	645	88:70	4	14/12
590	58 ph 12	12	15	646	88:71	7	15/13
593a	58 ph 15	6	18	647	88:78	?	18/14
594a	58 ph 16	2	14	648	88:88	9	12/9
595	58 ph 17	2	4	650	88:18	8	30
596	58 ph 18	5	6	651	88:59	3	22
593b	58 ph 15	6	19½	652	88:24	?	8/6
597	58 ph 19	1	6	653	88:25	4	15
598	58 ph 20	5	16	654	89:43	6	23/21
599	58 ph 21	5	18	655	89:78	?	12
600	58 ph 22	4	12	656	89:53	3	20/13
601	58 ph 23	4	13	657	89:51	?	24/16
594b	58 ph 16	5	14/9	658	89:72	?	18/10
602	58 ph 24	?	5	659	89:73	4	20/13

Ph. no.	Trench:layer	Depth	Diameter	Ph. no.	Trench:layer	Depth	Diameter
660	89:74	2	12 square	711	100:112	5	8
661	89:77	?	16/5	712	100:113	4	11/7
662	89:79	3	12/11	713	100:95	14	20/15
663	89:65	2	14	714	100:64	3	9
664	89:80	?	6/4	715	100:111	8	12/7
665	89:83	?	7/5 (irreg.)	716a	100:44	7	15/9
666	89:84	?	9/7 (irreg.)	716b	100:44	2	7
667	89:52	2	21/17	717	100:58	11	12 square
668	89:87	?	7/5	718	100:56	1	9/7
669	88:79	?	4	719a	100:57	7	22 triangular
670	88:76	10	18 (irreg.)	719b	100:57	4	12 (irreg.)
671a	88:65	3	17	720	100:85	7	8
672	88:66	9	27/17	721	100:104	6	12
671b	88:65	3	17	722	100:105	5	18/16
673	88:50	6	33/26	723	100:96	5	13
674	89:40	2	14/11	724	100:63	3	25
675	89:67	8	15	726	100:107	5	15/9
676	89:68	9	17/14	727	100:108	5	9
677	89:86	4	10/7	728	101:107	5	13/11 (rect.)
678	89:88	5	11/8	731	101:75	2	7/5
679	89:69	?	16/11 (irreg.)	732	101:76	2	8/5
680	89:64	6	36/28	733	101:77	5	17/11
681a	88:57	8	17/14	734	101:78	7	20
681b	88:57	2	24	735	101:79	2	9/6 (rect.)
681c	88:57	4	12	736	101:105	1	14/11
682	90:43	6	17	737	101:106	3	12/7
688	90:53	3	14	738	101:113	3	21/16 (irreg.)
689	90:50	4	24	742	101:128	2	20/10
690	90:63	?	8	743	101:140	2–5	*c.* 3
691	90:42	2	28/24	744	101:133	?	3
692	90:58	2	20/17	745	101:134	?	3
693	90:41	4	16/14	748	101:132	?	$2\frac{1}{2}$
694	90:66	4	14	749	103:52	8	21/21
695	90:64	2	14	752	102:42	10	34
696	90:61	4	16/11	753a	102:57	?	29
697	90:62	?	9/6	753b	102:57	?	22
700	91:54	?8–9	30	754	103:75	4	10/5
701	91:19	16	36	755	102:50	7	8
702	91:59	6–8	42	756	103:60	3	2
704	91:62	?	14	757	103:62	2	4/3
705	100:110	4	12	758	103:83	3	5
706	100:41	6	10	759	103:84	3	5
707	100:42	$7\frac{1}{2}$	10/6 (irreg.)	760	103:60	9	13
708	100:54	4	14/11	761	103:57	3	4
709	100:53	1	12/10 (irreg.)	762	102:58	10	12/10
710	100:53	1	12/10 (irreg.)	763	102:64	3	9

Ph. no.	Trench: layer	Depth	Diameter	Ph. no.	Trench: layer	Depth	Diameter
764	102:69	10	14/10	810	108:161	5	14
765	103:67	6	14/9	812	108:149	6	10
766	103:88	4	5/3	814	108:61	18	36
767	103:56	4	23/8	815	108:70	?	18/17
768	103:79	4	13/9	816	108:172	6	7/5
769	103:80	6	12	817	108:170	7	8
770	103:81	7	15/18 (irreg.)	818	108:169	8	17/15
772	108:108	7	22/19	819	108:182	4	17/14
775a	108:153	3	6	820a	108:130	2	12
775c	108:153	9	8	820b	108:130	10	12/8
776	108:105	5	13	820c	108:130	2	8
778	108:126	4½	8	821	108:112	4	13/10
779	108:127	3	17/10	822	108:117	4	12/10
780	108:107	5	8/7	823	108:129	8	11/8
781	108:106	6	9	824	108:119	5	22
782	108:175	6	20/15	825	108:234	6	12/8½
783	108:128	5	14/9	826	108:196	11	12
784	108:131	8	18/12	827	108:87	3	18/10
785a	108:171	8	8	828	108:203	7	11
785b	108:171	6	8	829a	108:195	7	28/13
786	108:150	13	20 square	829b	108:195	6	20
787	108:132	8	12/10	830a	108:198	10	12
788	108:143	6	8	830b	108:198	3	12
789	108:82	6	21/16	831	108:200	5	22/12
790	108:151	3	10	832	108:241	2	13
791	108:83	8	12	833	108:242	3	8
792	108:144	10	16/13	834	108:240	4	15/10
793	108:85	7½	13	835	108:243	8	14/10
794	108:138	8	9	836	108:248	7	13/8
795	108:77	9	23/18	837	108:239	7	11/10
797	108:142	9	18/19	838	108:238	3	11
798a	108:154	6	9/8	839	108:237	10	11
798b	108:154	4	8	840	108:247	3	9/6 (irreg.)
799	108:156	6	10	841	108:246	7	8
800	108:162	7	11/8	842	108:244	9	12
801	108:164	3	9/7	843	108:245	6	9
802	108:165	4	11/8	844	108:65	9	13/10
803a	108:102	2	12	845	108:64	11	16/17 (rect.)
803b	108:102	2	12	846	108:63	12	14
804	108:177	3	12/9 (rect.)	847	108:97	11	23/20
805	108:140	5	10/7 (irreg.)	848	108:96	8	19
806	108:141	13	17/11 (irreg.)	849	108:146	12	23
807a	108:158	8	12/10	850	108:133	5	15/13
807b	108:158	6	8	851	108:136	6	17/13
808	108:157	6	14	855a	108:216	6	21/17
809	108:112	12	14/13	855b	108:216	2	8

Ph. no.	Trench: layer	Depth	Diameter
855c	108:216	2	7
856	108:218	6	17
858	108:219	7	37/15
859	108:197	15	33/20
860	108:45	1	24
861	108:41	24	26
862	108:110	14	24/22
863a	108:109	10	17
863b	108:109	13	10/6
864	108:115	10	12/8
865	108:36	14	22
866	108:121	24	27/22
868	108:39	7	14
869	108:51	16	32
872	108:122	15	12
873	108:123	17	26
874	107:55	4	16/12
875	107:54	7	15
876	107:48	7	14/11
877	107:46	3	11/10
878	107:47	2	7
879	107:45	5	16/14
880	107:57	12	20
881	107:49	6	5
882	107:63	6	26/16
883a	107:59	18	12
883b	107:59	?	12
884	107:69	12	14
885	107:70	6	16/14
886	107:71	8	11
887	107:78	Not bottomed	6
888	107:64	8	20/19
889	107:80	Not bottomed	10
890	107:68	8	14
891	107:67	26	11
892	107:66	10	18/13
894	57 ph 1	10	18
895	57 ph 2	13	17
896	57 ph 3	4	18/13
906	47 ph 1	14	21/16
908	63 ph 2	6	20/17
909	63 ph 3	5	14
910	63 ph 4	11	15
911	63 ph 5	3	10
912	63 ph 6	3	12
913	63 ph 7	2	10
914	63 ph 8	2	9
915	63 ph 9	7	8
925	63 ph 19	?	18/14
933	63 ph 27	3	22/8
934	63 ph 28	5	26/24
935	63 ph 29	3	12
936	63 ph 30	13	8
937	63 ph 31	10	14
938	63 ph 32	10	13
939	109 ph 1	14	21
940	109 ph 2	6	12
941	109 ph 3	17	12
942	109 ph 4	9	12
943	109 ph 5	14	12/10
944	109:103	6	14
947	82:17	?	28/18
948	83 ph 1	1	17
949	82 ph 2	1	26
950	82 ph 3	?	14/8
951	82 ph 4	1	9
952	80 ph 1	2	15/8 (irreg.)
953	79 ph 1	?	7
954	79 ph 2	?	14/11
955	79 ph 3	?	9
956	79 ph 4	?	17/15
957	79 ph 5	?	13/10
958	79 ph 6	4	33/25
959	78 ph 1	12	42/31
960	78 ph 2	3	30/27
961	77 ph 1	7	47/34
962	77 ph 2	?	7
963	77 ph 3	2	10/7
964	77 ph 4	2	6
965	75 ph 1	12	38/34
966	75 ph 2	3	19
967	75 ph 3	6	9
968	75 ph 4	21	4
969	76:21	14	15/14
970	76 ph 1	20	3
971	76 ph 2	?	9
972	76 ph 3	7	39
973	76 ph 4	13	28/24
974	76 ph 5	12	10/5
975	76 ph 6	5	13

Ph. no.	Trench: layer	Depth	Diameter	Ph. no.	Trench: layer	Depth	Diameter
976	76 ph 7	5	14	1024	74 ph 3	4	6
977	76 ph 8	7	27	1025	74 ph 4	4	22 (irreg.)
978	76 ph 9	6	22	1026	74 ph 5	?	12½/9
979	76 ph 10	5	Against section	1027	74 ph 6	10	9½/8
				1028	74 ph 7	3	10
980	76 ph 11	8	15/8	1029	74:51	7	21/19 (rect.)
981	76 ph 12	6	15	1030	72 ph 1	?	8
982	76 ph 13	?	19/16	1031	72 ph 2	?	5
983	76 ph 14	14	13	1032	72 ph 3	2	10
984	76 ph 15	3	26/22	1033	72 ph 4	2	10
985	76 ph 16	3	10	1034	72 ph 5	2	18/15 (rect.)
986	76 ph 17	5	10	1035	72 ph 6	11	17
987	76 ph 18	5	13/5	1036	72 ph 7	2	13
988	76 ph 19	4	11	1037	72 ph 8	4	10
989	76 ph 20	3	19/18	1038	72 ph 9	6	14
991	76:38	6		1039	72 ph 10	3	16
992	80 ph 1	?	8	1040	99 ph 1	11	24
993	80 ph 2	1	18/11 (irreg.)	1041	99 ph 2	9	26/18
994	80 ph 3	3	9/6	1042	99 ph 3	11	22
995	80 ph 4	4	15/6 (irreg.)	1043	98:42	9	19/16
996	80 ph 5	5	4½	1044	98:43	?	18
997	80 ph 6	5	25/15	1045	97 ph 1	?	7
998	80 ph 7	9	22/18	1046	96 ph 1	3	8/6
999	80 ph 8	4	14/8	1047	96 ph 2	4	12
1000	80 ph 9	13	6/4	1048	94:143	3½	12
1002	80:58	14	14	1049	94:141	3	8/6
1003	80:59	10	21	1050	94:136	11	22 (irreg.)
1004	79 ph 1	6	11/8½	1051	94:138	4½	22/18
1005	79 ph 2	?	17/14	1052	94:139	4	17/7
1006	79 ph 3	11	18	1053	94:140	4	22/8
1007	79 ph 4	3	15/11	1054	95 ph 1	13	23
1008	73 ph 1	?	5	1055	95 ph 2	3	4
1009	73 ph 2	?	14/10	1056	95 ph 3	4	5
1010	73 ph 3	12	20	1057	95 ph 4	3	7
1011	73 ph 4	2	8	1058	95 ph 5	3	8/5
1012	73 ph 5	7	10	1059	95 ph 6	2½	6/4
1014	73 ph 7	4	18/13 (irreg.)	1060	95 ph 7	3	7/5
1015	73 ph 8	?	4	1063	102 ph 1	?	18/11
1016	73 ph 9	4	10 (irreg.)	1064	102 ph 2	?	17/15
1017	73 ph 10	5	10/7	1065	102 ph 3	?	12/8
1018	73 ph 11	9	10/8	1066	102 ph 4	6	10
1019	73 ph 12	9	33/28 (irreg.)	1067	102 ph 6	8	23/20
1020	73 ph 13	4	8	1068	102 ph 5	4	19/14
1021	73 ph 14	1	6	1069	102 ph 7	12	8/6
1022	74 ph 1	15	17/14	1070	102 ph 8	12	5
1023	74 ph 2	8	11/9	1071	102 ph 9	?	22/11½

Ph. no.	Trench: layer	Depth	Diameter
1072	91 ph 1	?	11
1073	91 ph 2	?	10
1074	91 ph 3	?	14
1075	90 ph 1	3	6
1076	90 ph 2	4	8
1077	90 ph 3	5	9
1078	90 ph 4	?	9/4
1079	90 ph 5	?	6
1080	90 ph 6	?	7
1081	90 ph 7	2	12
1082	87 ph 1	?	36/29
1083	87 ph 2	?	10
1084	88 ph 1	?	7
1085	80 ph 2	4	6½/5
1086	89 ph 1	4	17/16
1087	89 ph 2	7	13
1088	89 ph 3	7	12/11
1089	89 ph 4	8	11
1090	89 ph 5	2	11
1091	89 ph 6	8	16/14
1093	69 ph 2	9	15
1094	69 ph 3	15	22
1097	69 ph 6	?	9/6
1099	67 ph 1	3	14
1100	67 ph 2	3	13 square
1101	67 ph 3	?	10
1102	67 ph 4	?	9
1103	67 ph 5	?	13/12
1104	67 ph 6	?	13
1105	67 ph 7	?	5
1106	68:21	?	15
1107	68 ph 1	?	11
1108	68 ph 2	?	11
1109	108 ph 1	4	7
1110	108 ph 2	2	12/9
1111	108 ph 3	7	6
1112	108 ph 4	4	11/8
1113	108 ph 5	6	9
1114	108 ph 6	?	10
1115	108 ph 7	?	12
1117	107 ph 1	?	12
1118	107 ph 2	?	10
1120	107:56	15	6
1122	72 ph 12	11	14
1123	72 ph 13	11	19
1124	72 ph 14	1	11
1126	71 ph 2	5	10
1128	71 ph 4	12	25/20
1129	71 ph 5	6	11
1130	71 ph 6	10	30 (irreg.)
1135	71 ph 11	3	3
1136	71 ph 12	4	8
1137	71 ph 13	8	18
1138	71 ph 14	2	5
1139	71 ph 15	6	13½
1140	71 ph 16	3	11
1141	71 ph 17	3	11½
1142	71 ph 18	3	27/9
1143	71 ph 19	5	14
1144	71 ph 20	5	10
1145	71 ph 21	2	16
1146	71 ph 22	5	8½
1147	71 ph 23	4	9
1148	71 ph 24	6	10
1149	71 ph 25	2	12/8
1150	71 ph 26	10	9 (irreg.)
1151	71 ph 27	2	9 (rect.)
1152	71 ph 28	2	14 (rect.)
1153	71 ph 29	6	18/8 (irreg.)
1154a	85:9	6	17/13
1154b	85:9	4	14
1155	85:10	7	17/13½
1159	85:24	12	14

INDEX

piled against them. Since building S14 appears to have been part of a complex incorporating more spacious halls it may well have served as a store shed. A similar argument could apply to building S17, the walls of which had evidently been strengthened on at least two occasions.

The dating evidence supplied by the associated pottery shows that buildings S9 and 10 belonged to the period when coarse gritty ware was in use, broadly the mid-eighth to mid-tenth centuries, building S10 replacing S9 during this time. Buildings S14 and S17 belong to the last phase of the Saxon occupation.

(c) *Foundation-trench structures*

Of the five buildings constructed of timbers set in foundation trenches, one, S12, was poorly preserved, while two of the others (S7 and S8) lay only partly within the area available for excavation. The remaining two (S11 and S13) were totally excavated, their plans preserving many structural details. It is clear that the lengths of foundation trench were used to bed close-spaced vertical timbers: in no case was there evidence for horizontal timber sole-plates, indeed the wall structures of buildings S11 and S13 showed that horizontals could not have existed. The use of horizontal ties just above ground level is also unlikely in view of the daub infill found in position in the top of the trench for the south wall of building S13. The main tie was therefore presumably at eaves level. The walling between the vertical timbers was in each case composed of wattle and daub: some of the holes for the vertical wattle laths survived in the east wall trench of building S7. No evidence was recovered to indicate the nature of the roof covering which may have been of thatch or shingles.

The similar form of construction of these buildings does not necessarily imply a similar function. Building S11, with its large oven, was probably a domestic structure, serving as an out-building for the hall S10, with which it was contemporary. S13 on the other hand was more substantially constructed with buttress posts along the two main walls, a porch and with an internal partition dividing off a small heated room. It gives the impression of having been a hall of potential social significance.

At Portchester the trench-built structures belonged to the mid to late Saxon period. Buildings S7 and S11 should be dated to the period of use of the gritty pottery, i.e. mid-eighth to mid-tenth century, while buildings S8 and S13 produced sherds of Portchester ware from primary positions and are therefore likely to belong to the mid-tenth to mid-eleventh centuries. S12 cannot be dated.

The general style of construction is well known in south-eastern Britain. Examples have been recorded at Cheddar (Rahtz, 1964), North Elmham (Wade-Martins, 1970) and Chalton (Addyman, Leigh and Hughes, 1973). The style is remarkably similar to a building found at Bishopstone in Sussex (Bell, 1971) which is claimed to be of late Roman date.[1] If this is so, a broad sequence can be offered, starting with Bishopstone in the third–fourth centuries, followed by Chalton in the sixth–seventh, North Elmham, mid-seventh to mid-ninth, Portchester, mid-eighth to mid-eleventh, and Cheddar, tenth to eleventh. The conclusion would seem to be that the style of building was long lived in Britain and may have originated in the late Roman period.

[1] The excavator, Martin Bell, reports (*pers. comm.*) that although only late Roman material was found in association with the building, a Saxon date cannot be ruled out, bearing in mind the general paucity of Saxon pottery even from occupation sites.

(a) *Sunken-floor huts*

The huts conform to the general characteristics of the well-known category, of which over 150 examples are at present recorded in Britain. All four from Portchester were of two-post type, the vertical timbers supporting a ridge post, though building S3 does have additional side posts. In building S2 the vertical timbers were once replaced, the later pair being more deeply bedded. Only in the case of building S2 was evidence of an entrance ramp discovered, leading down from the surface of the adjacent Roman street.

In each case, the filling seems to have been totally or partially deliberate, consisting of black soil mixed with wads of natural brickearth suggestive of separate shovelfuls. *In situ* occupation levels were notably absent in all but hut S1, where a layer of occupation debris was found on the floor. Little survives to throw light on the problem of flooring. In theory the ledges within hut S3 could have supported a planked floor, but there is no positive evidence in favour of this. The replacement of the posts in hut S2 might have been necessitated, in part, by the wearing away of the clay floor around them. Under wet conditions brickearth becomes a tenacious material which will stick to the feet. Without a covering the floor surface would have been rapidly eroded in such circumstances. As to the rest of the superstructure, all that can be said is that the absence of daub from within and around the huts might suggest that the walls and floors were constructed entirely of organic materials.

Huts S2 and S3 cannot be dated except to before the eleventh century, but hut S1 contained material of mid to late fifth-century date while hut S4 can be shown to precede the construction of a pit filled in the mid-eighth century. It is reasonable therefore to assign the sunken-floor huts to the early part of the Saxon occupation.

(b) *Post-built structures*

Broadly speaking two types of post-built structures can be defined, small irregular huts and larger, more regularly constructed, halls. The technique of construction is so basic that little need be said of it. Addyman (1972) has shown that it was widespread in Saxon contexts in Britain and that considerable variety existed both in plan and constructional detail. Buildings S5 and S6 seem both to have been constructed by digging a continuous trench with deeper holes for posts at intervals. When the verticals were in position, together possibly with the wall cladding, the trenches were filled back; in the case of building S5 flints were used. The setting of the posts suggests that hut S6 may have been provided with a door in the east wall: no comparable evidence survives for hut S5.

Of the four larger post-built halls, two, S9 and S10, were of regular plan. In building S10 the pairing of the timbers of the long wall implies a framed structure which could have been of cruck form. The opposed doorways, here evident, are a recurring feature in Saxon timber architecture both at Portchester and elsewhere (Addyman, 1972). Other structural evidence is sparse, but the actual timbers were cut to a rectangular cross-section and quantities of daub show that the spaces between the frames were infilled with plastered wattle.

Building S14, though post-built, differs from the others in that its two short walls were the more massively built, rather similar in style to buildings L and K at North Elmham (Wade-Martins, 1969). What exactly this implies about the form of the roof it is difficult to say. It seems unlikely that the longer (slighter) sides were the gable walls, but the added strength of the end walls could be explained if it is supposed that heavy stores, such as grain, were

PLATE I

West elevation of the watergate showing eleventh-century arch with fourteenth-century rebuilding above

(*Photograph: David Baker*)

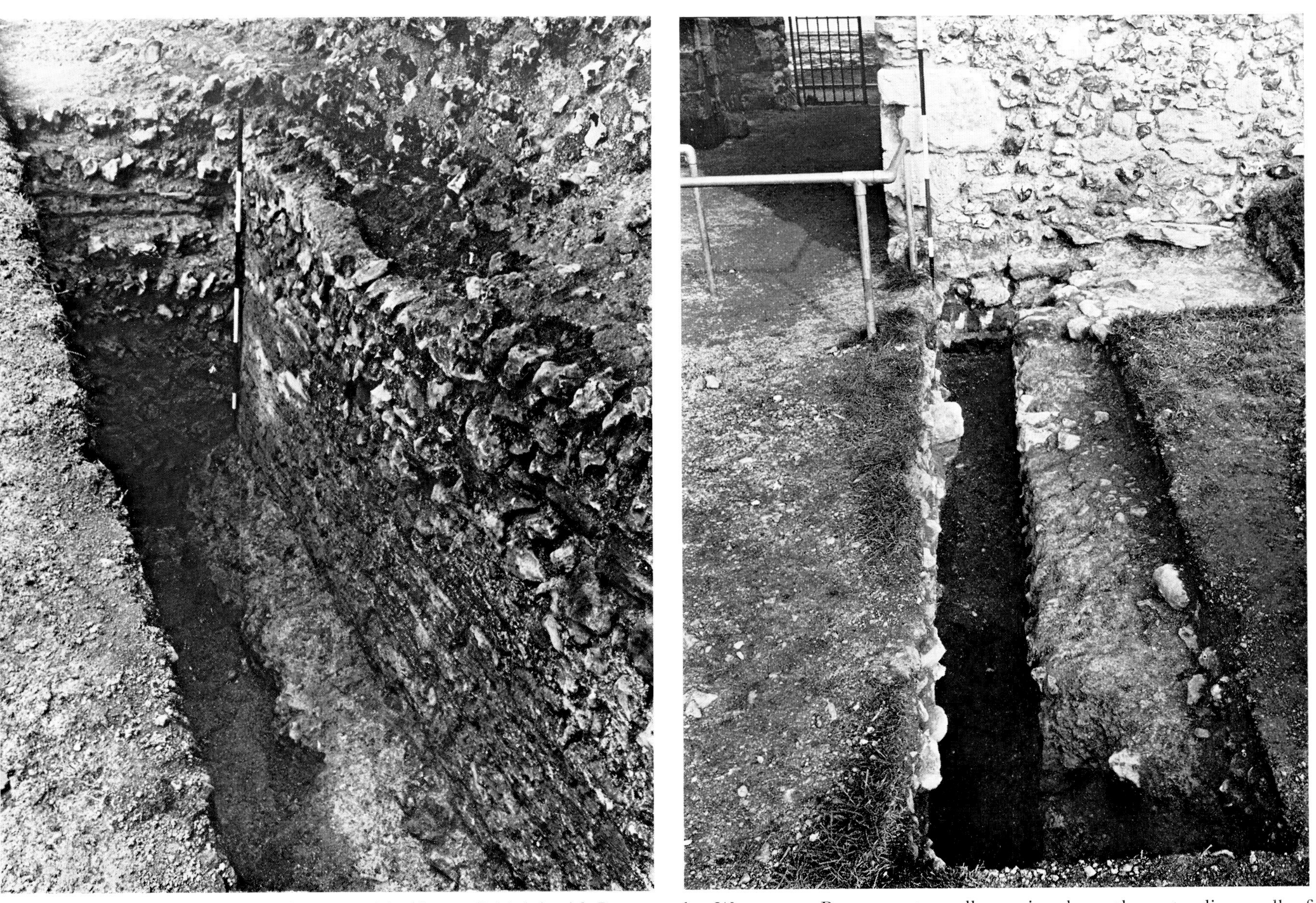

a. Watergate: junction of eleventh-century blocking wall (right) with Roman wall (top).

b. Watergate: Roman gate wall running beneath upstanding wall of eleventh-century gatehouse

(*Photographs: David Baker*)

a. Landgate: postholes of the Saxon gate in front of the west wall of the Roman gatehouse

b. Landgate: rebuilt corner of the Roman gatehouse showing greensand blocks set in clay

(*Photographs: David Leigh*)

a. Grubenhaus S1

b. Building S14 with earlier group of cesspits (top centre). The gullies are medieval

(*Photographs: David Baker*)

PLATE V

General view of area excavated in 1967, showing building S14 and the position of well (pit) 56, with shoring in the top right corner. The gullies are Roman and medieval

(*Photograph: David Baker*)

a. General view of area excavated in 1968 looking across area occupied by late Saxon cesspits

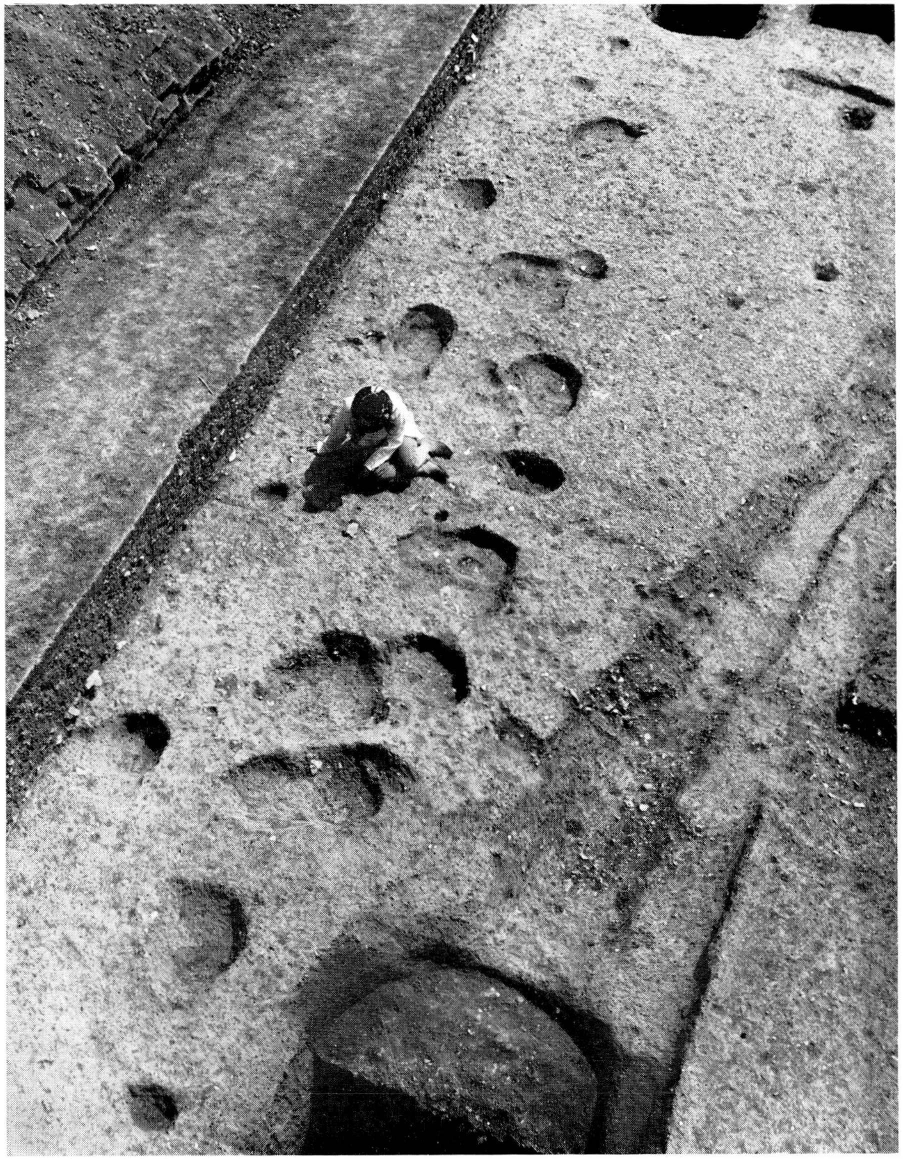

b. The posts constituting the south end of building S17

(*Photographs: David Baker*)

a. Tile feature in the corner of building S10
(*Photograph: David Baker*)

b. Roman tiles laid as door threshold for building S10
(*Photograph: David Leigh*)

Plate VIII

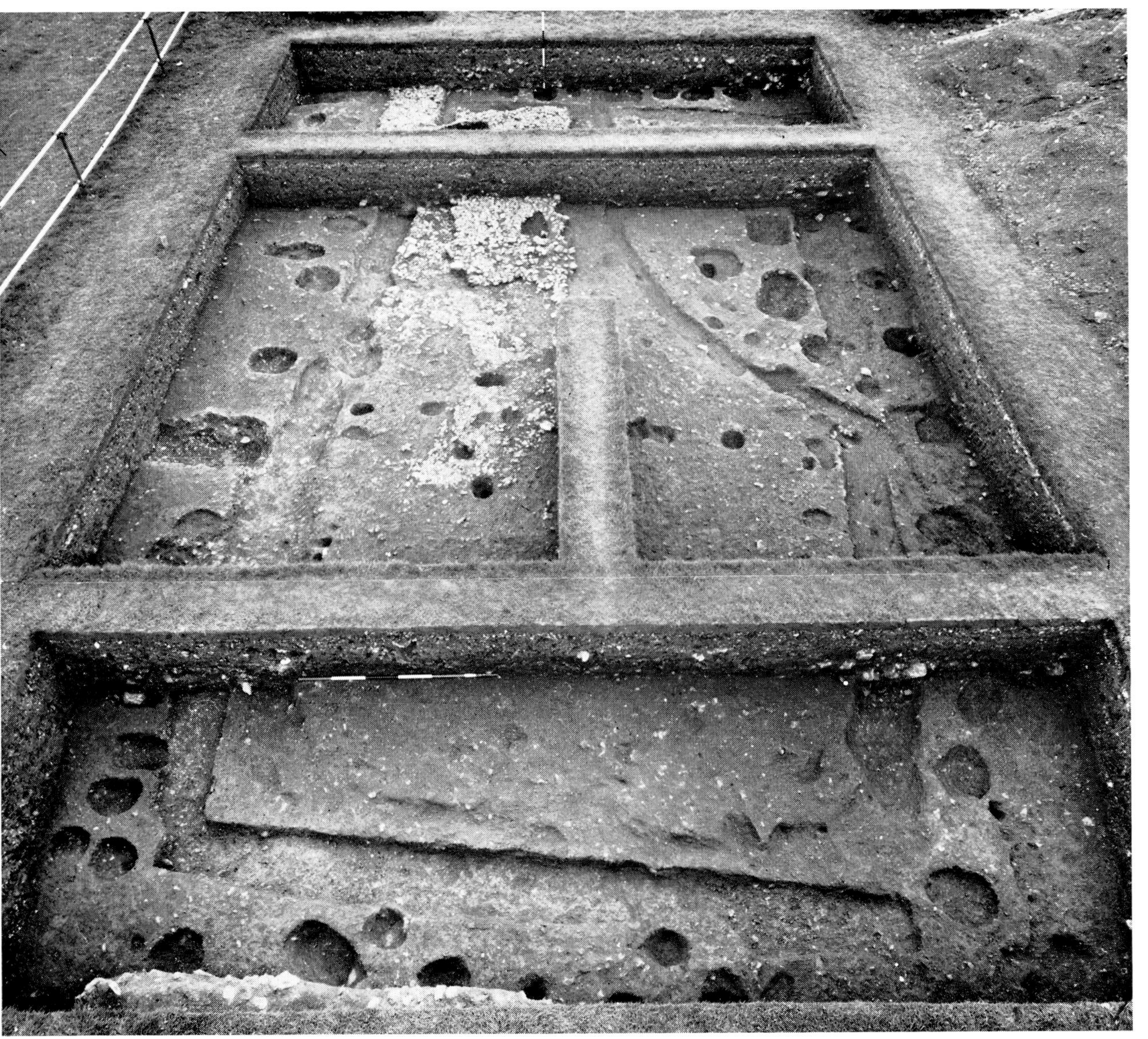

Building S13
(*Photograph: David Baker*)

a. Wall trenches defining floor of building S11

b. Oven in building S11

(*Photographs: Mike Rouillard*)

PLATE X

Masonry tower, building S18
(*Photograph: David Baker*)

a. Late Saxon cemetery: graves 5–9, 18–19

b. Late Saxon cemetery: graves 3–4, 12–17

(*Photographs: David Baker*)

a. Pit 192 showing postholes for timber lining in the bottom

b. Pit 191 cut against the back face of the Roman wall

(*Photographs: David Leigh*)

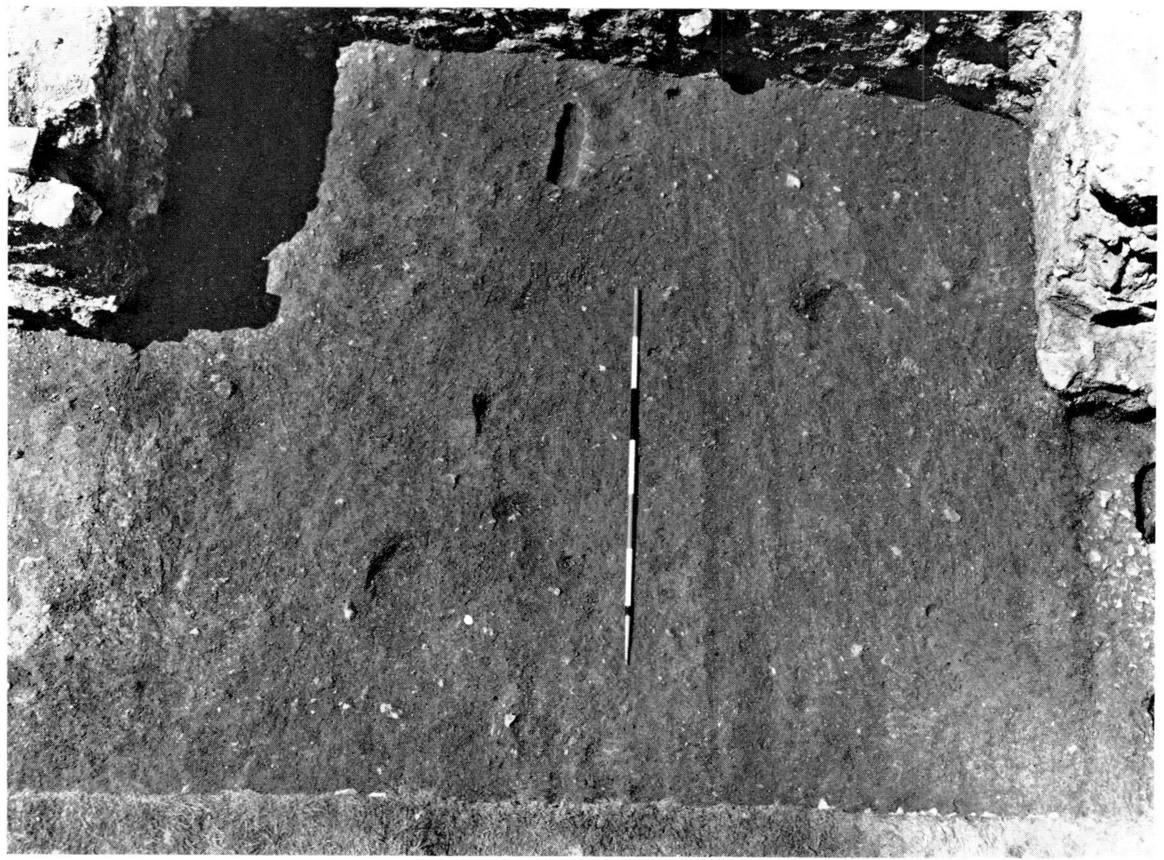

a. Ploughmarks scoring the Roman clay bank

b. General view of the pits west of buildings S9 and S10

(*Photographs: David Leigh*)

a. Well (pit) 56, showing the original timber frame in position in the bottom of the shaft
(*Photograph: David Baker*)

b. Well (pit) 135 after total excavation. The figure in the centre stands on the bottom of the pit for the Saxon timber lined well. Below him is the earlier, unlined waterhole and shaft
(*Photograph: David Leigh*)

a

b

a and *b*. Two views of the Saxon well (pit) 135 with timber in position as excavated

(*Photographs: David Leigh*)

PLATE XVI

a

b

a and *b*. Well (pit) 135: details of the timber joints of the basal frame

(*Photographs: David Leigh*)

a. Well (pit) 135: detail of joint of the upper frame

b. Well (pit) 135: basal frame and side boards

(*Photographs: David Leigh*)

a. Purse mount/strike-a-light (no. 1): 1/1

b. Repoussé decorated disc from applied brooch (no. 45): 1/1

c. Disc brooch (no. 44): 1/1

(*Photographs: R. L. Wilkins, F.S.A.*)

a. Strap hook (no. 48): 2/1

b. Strap hook (no. 50): 2/1

c. Strap-end (no. 49): 2/1. Three views taken with different lighting to show incised decoration

(*Photographs: R. L. Wilkins, F.S.A.*)

a. Wooden cores from lathe turning (p. 224): from well (pit) 135: ½

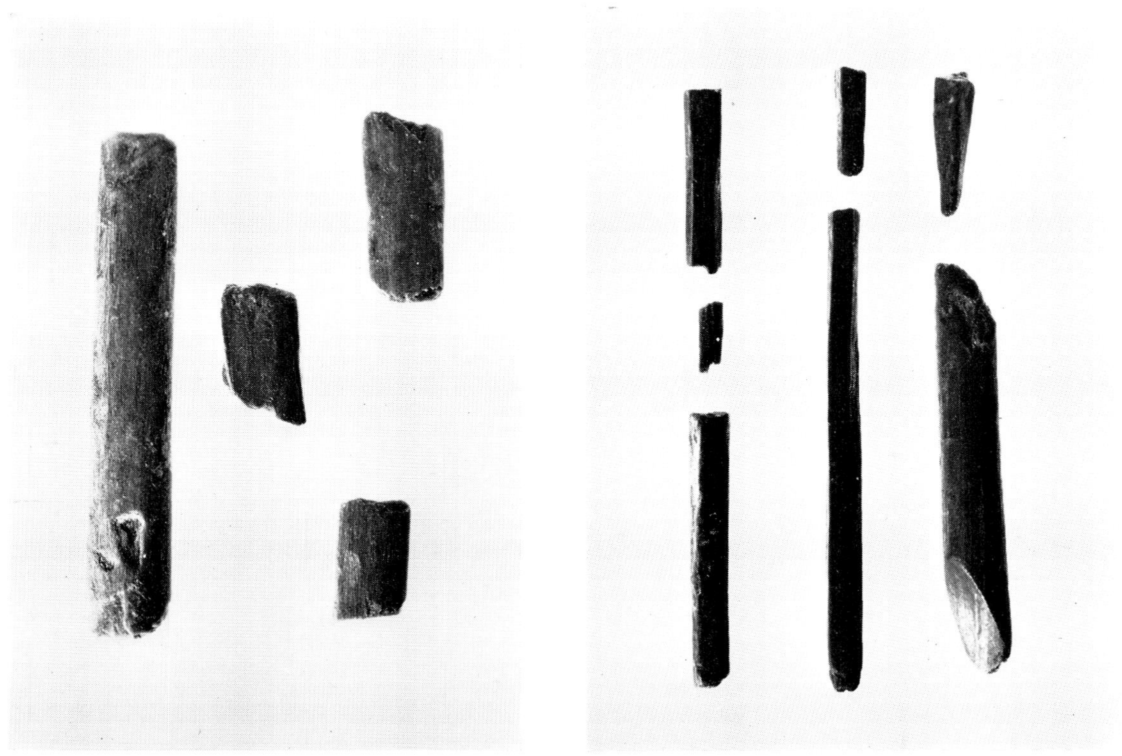

b *c*

b and *c.* Shaped wood from well (pit) 135 (p. 224): ½
(*Photographs: R. L. Wilkins, F.S.A.*)

Plate XXI

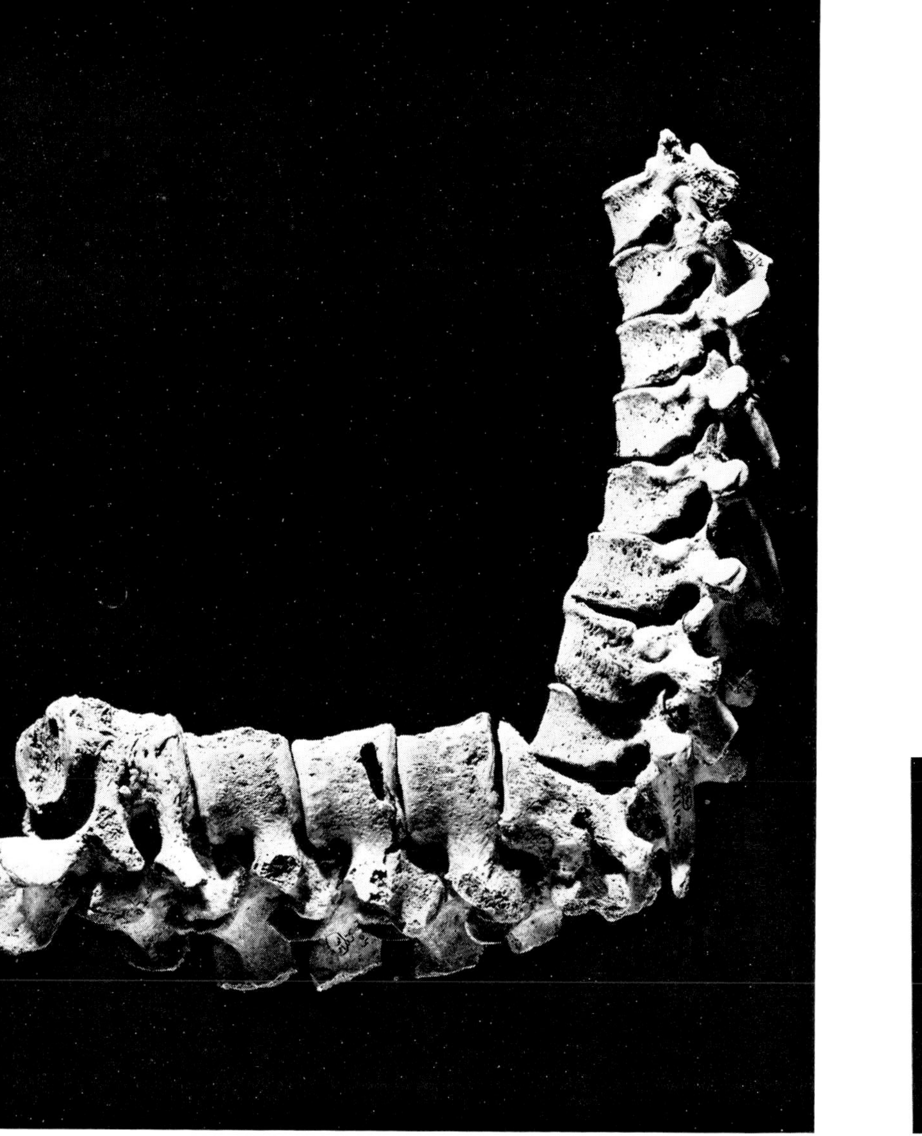

a

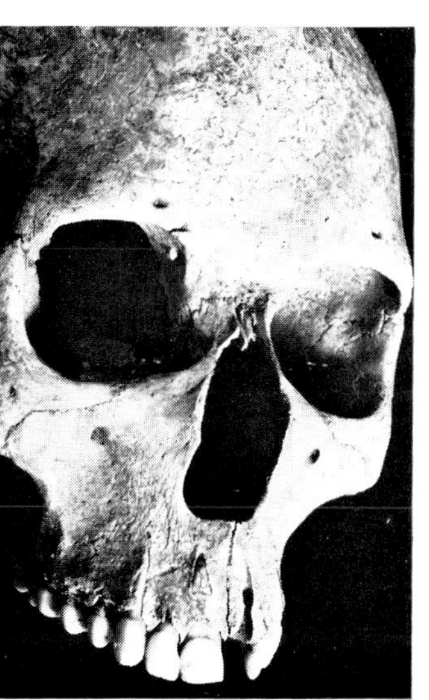
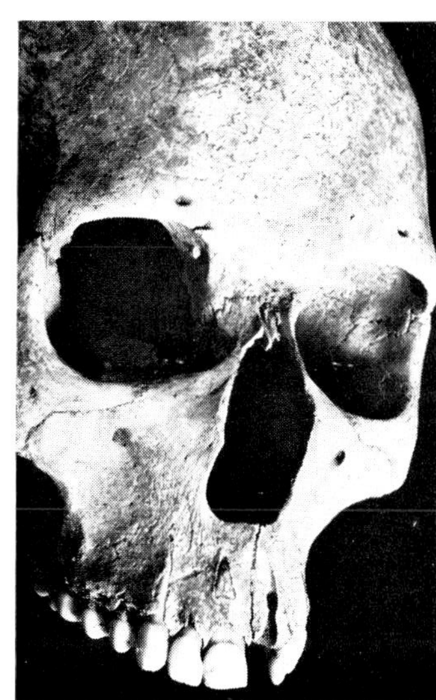

b

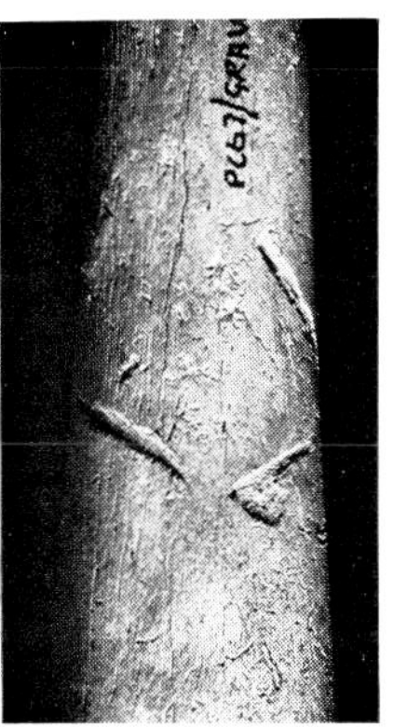
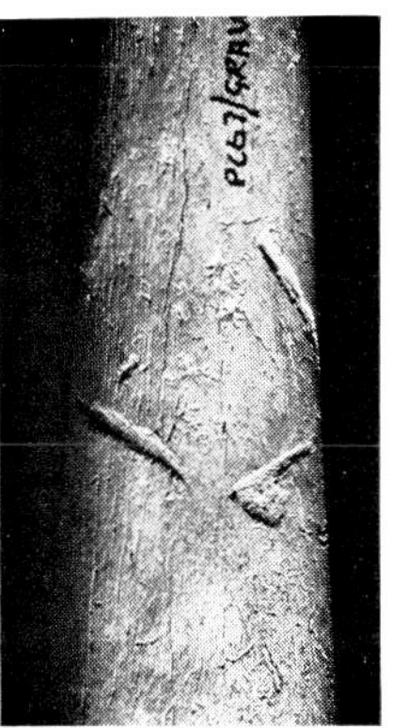

c

d

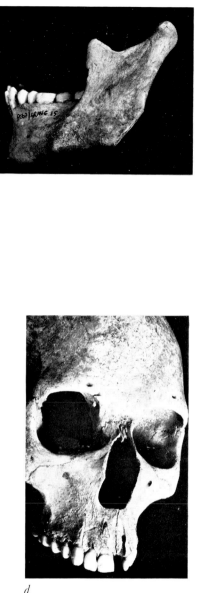

a. Burial 13. Angular kyphosis and vertebral destruction caused by tuberculosis of the thoracic vertebrae
b. Burial 8. Sword cut upon the left angle of the mandible
c. Burial 8. Transverse grooves on the anterior of the right femur. These incisions may have been caused by a sword, or even by post-mortem damage
d. Burial 9. Ossified trochlea within the right orbit. The left trochlea is similarly affected

(*Photographs: R. L. Wilkins, F.S.A.*)

Plate XXII

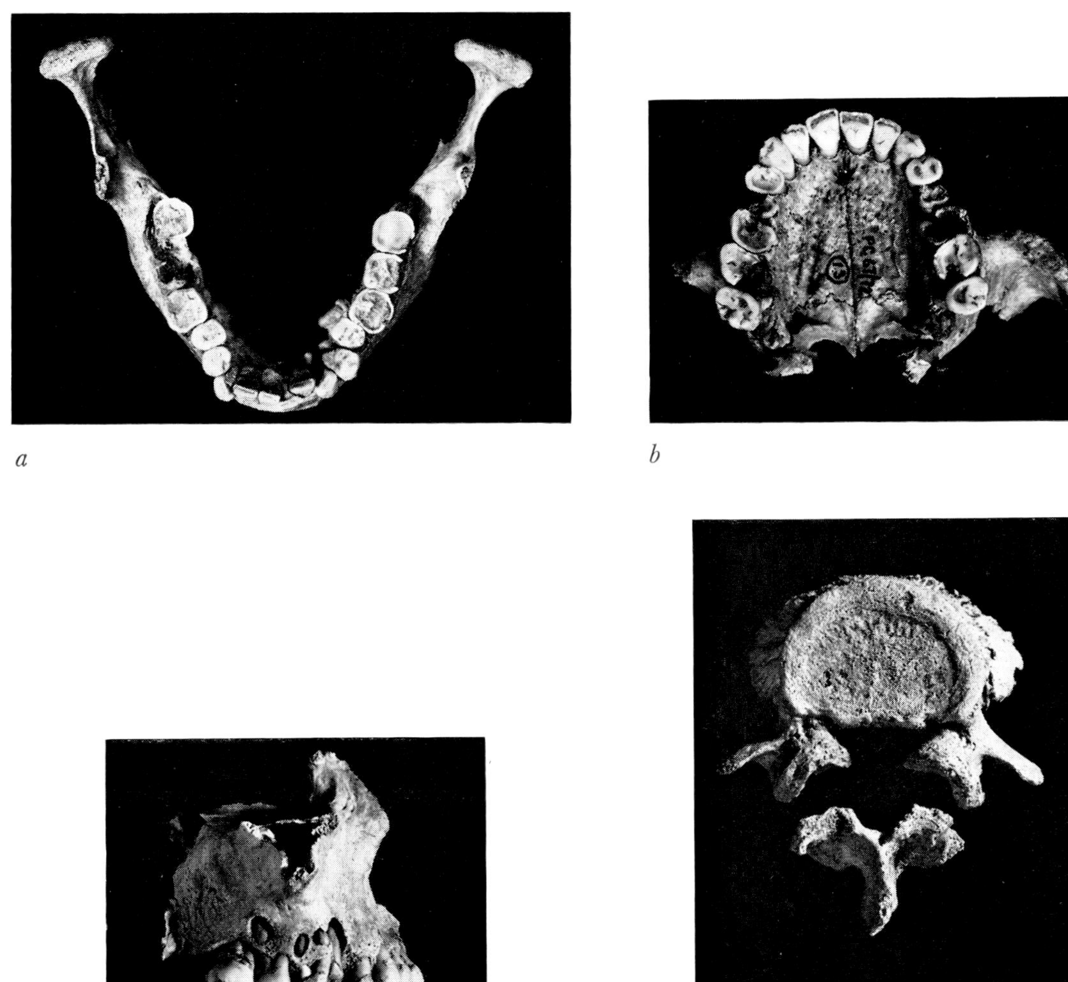

a. Burial 11. Severe attrition of the occlusal surfaces of the molars with dysfunction calculus upon the right second premolar and first molar. Prominent mandibular tori are also present

b. Burial 15. Severe caries with some premolars and molars reduced to their roots

c. Burial 15. Severe alveolar abscesses in the right maxilla

d. Burial 20. Detached neural arch of 4th lumbar vertebra

(*Photographs: R. L. Wilkins, F.S.A.*)

PLATE XXIII

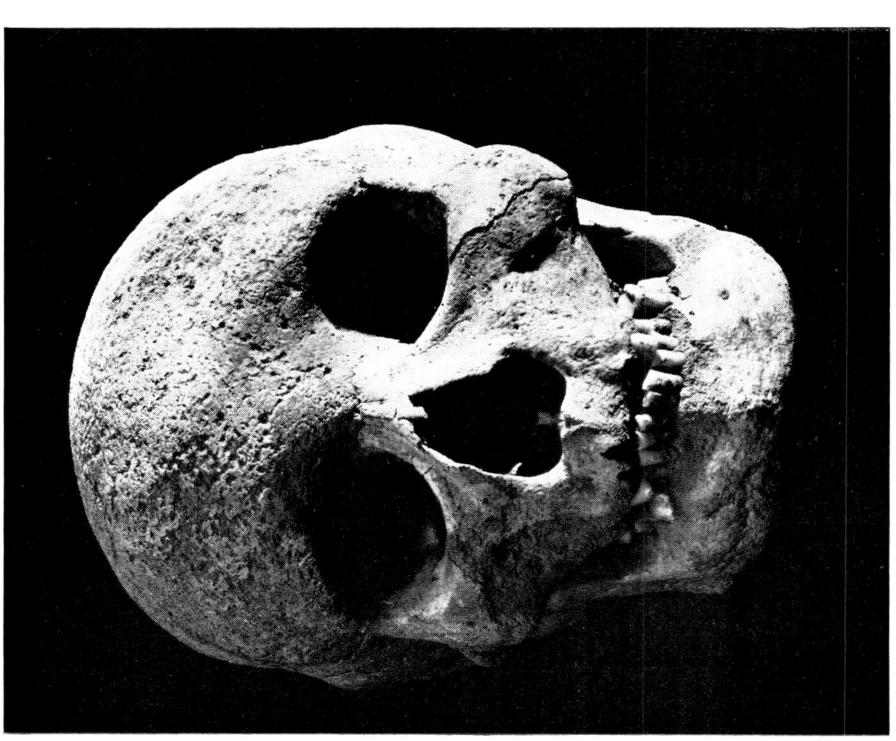

a. Burial 20. Paget's disease. Frontal view of the skull showing marked left facial asymmetry involving the maxillo-malar region

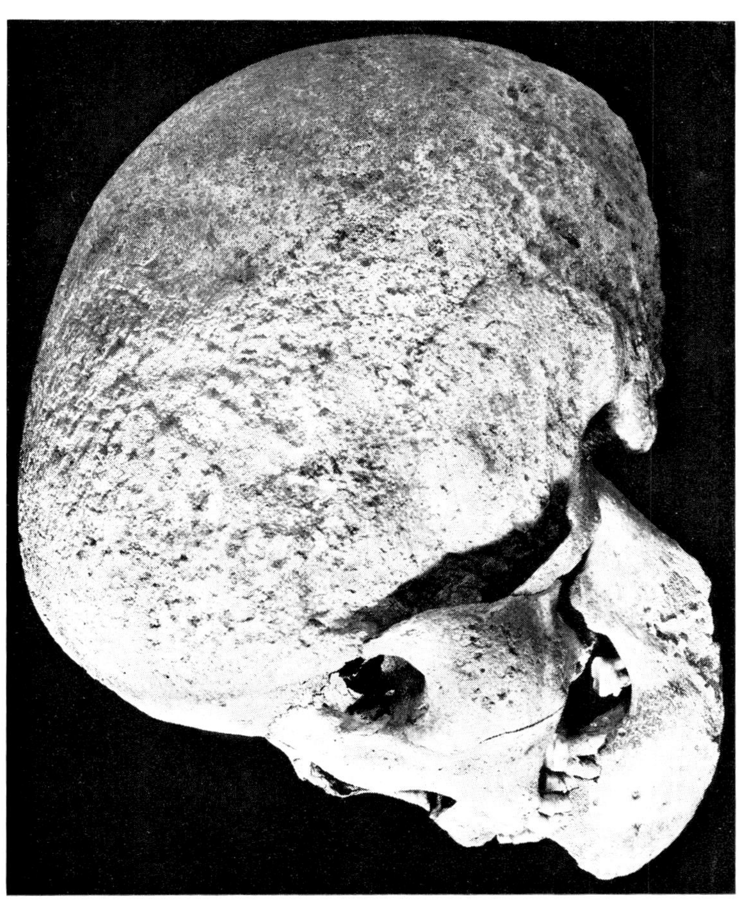

b. Burial 20. Paget's disease. Lateral view of the skull showing the gross swollen appearance

(*Photographs: R. L. Wilkins, F.S.A.*)

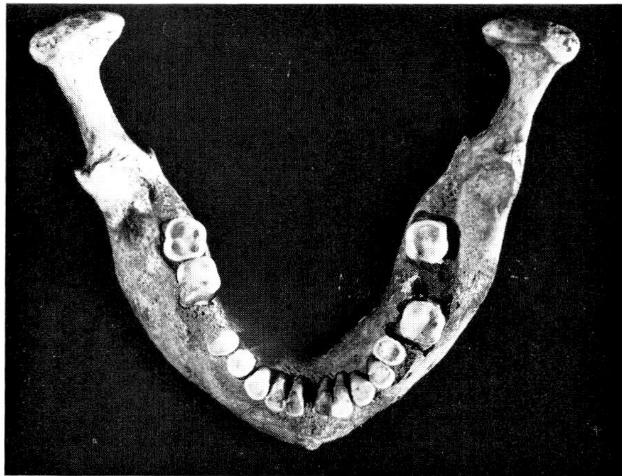

a. Burial 20. Paget's disease. Occlusal view of the mandible showing the distended rami

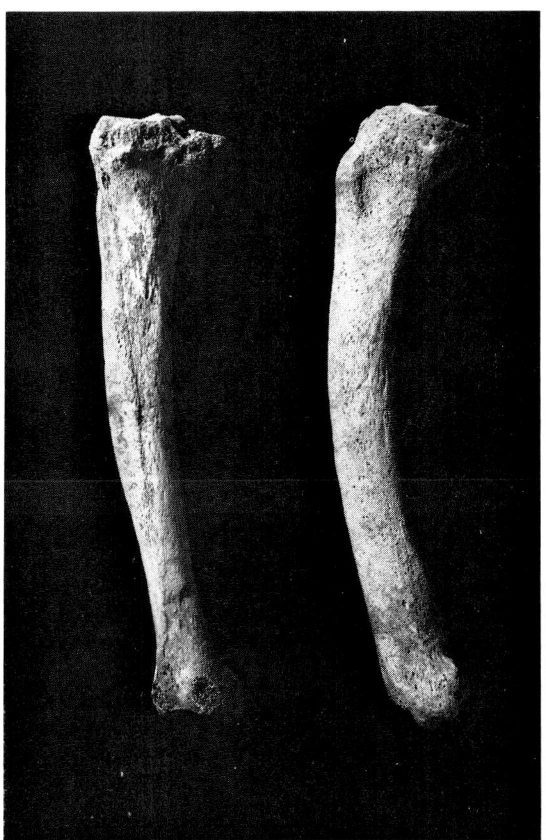

b. Burial 20. Paget's disease. Tibiae showing anterior bowing

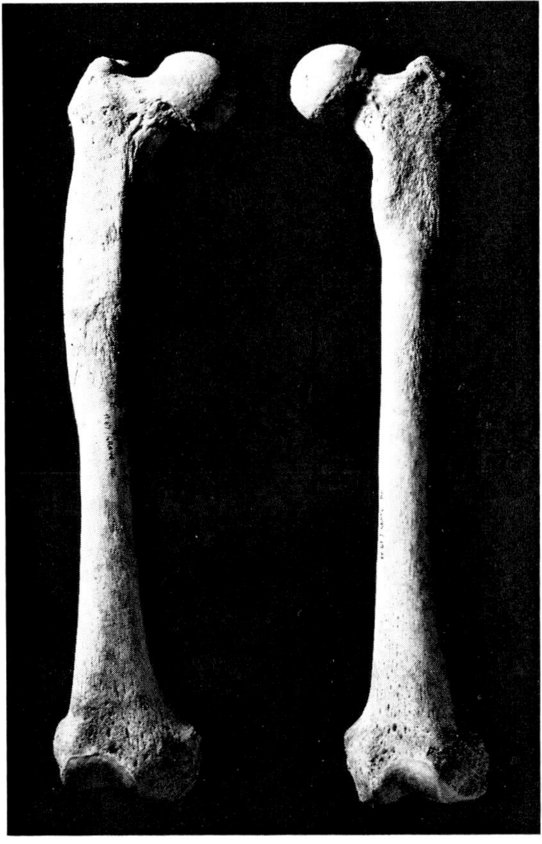

c. Burial 20. Paget's disease. Femora showing depression of the necks and increased thickness of right shaft

(*Photographs: R. L. Wilkins, F.S.A.*)

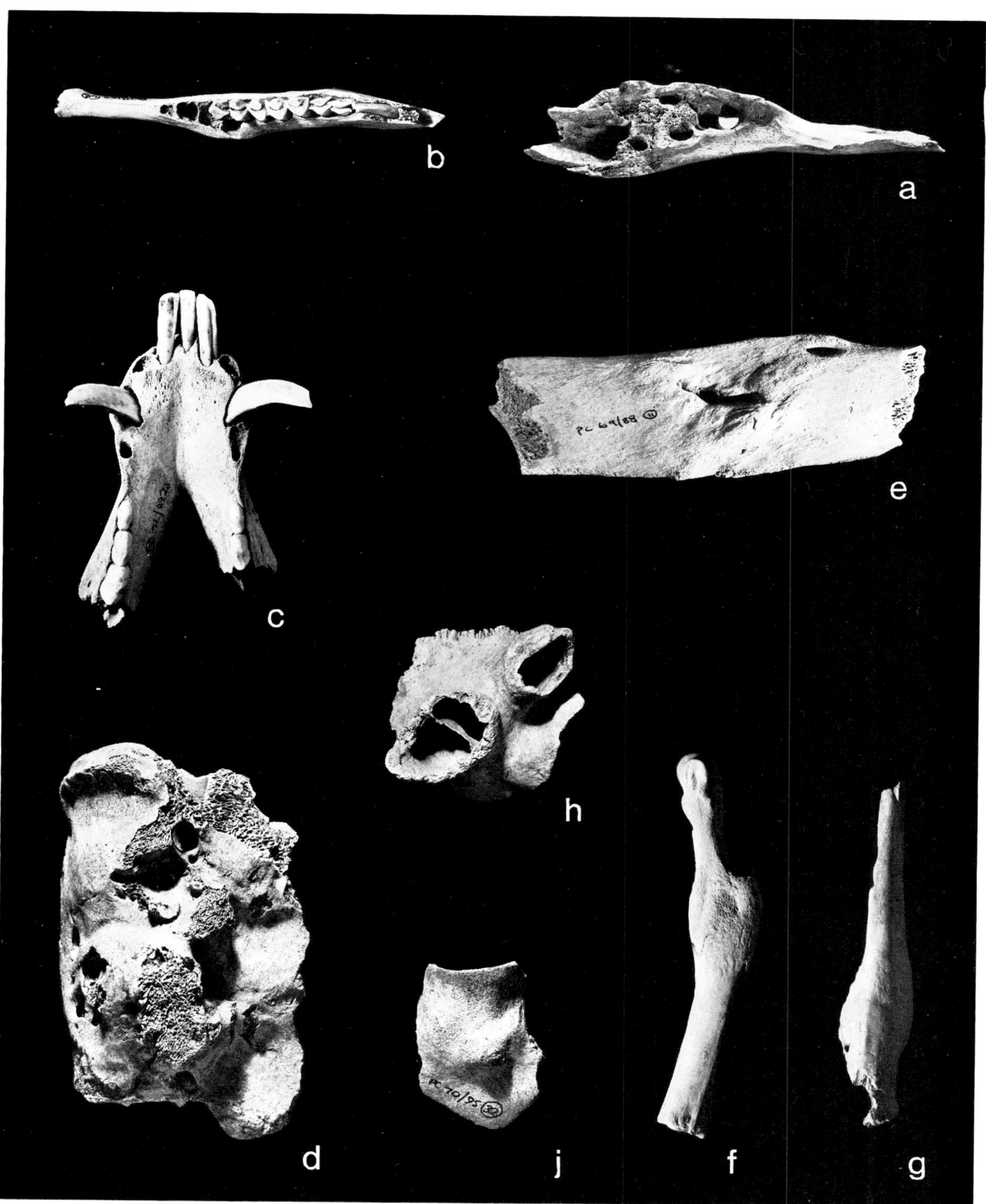

Animal bones showing disease, injury and anomalies

a. Sheep mandible: severe periodontal disease and impacted 4th premolar. *b.* Pig mandible: evidence of disease affecting the jaw around the 3rd molar. *c.* Pig mandible: congenital absence of one central incisor. *d.* Cattle spine: three thoracic vertebrae completely fused together with arthritic or some similar condition. *e.* Cattle rib: healed fracture. *f.* Sheep metatarsal: healed fracture. *g.* Sheep radius: healed fracture. *h.* Sheep skull fragment with two left horn cores. *j.* Skull fragment from a hornless sheep.

(*Photographs: R. L. Wilkins, F.S.A.*)

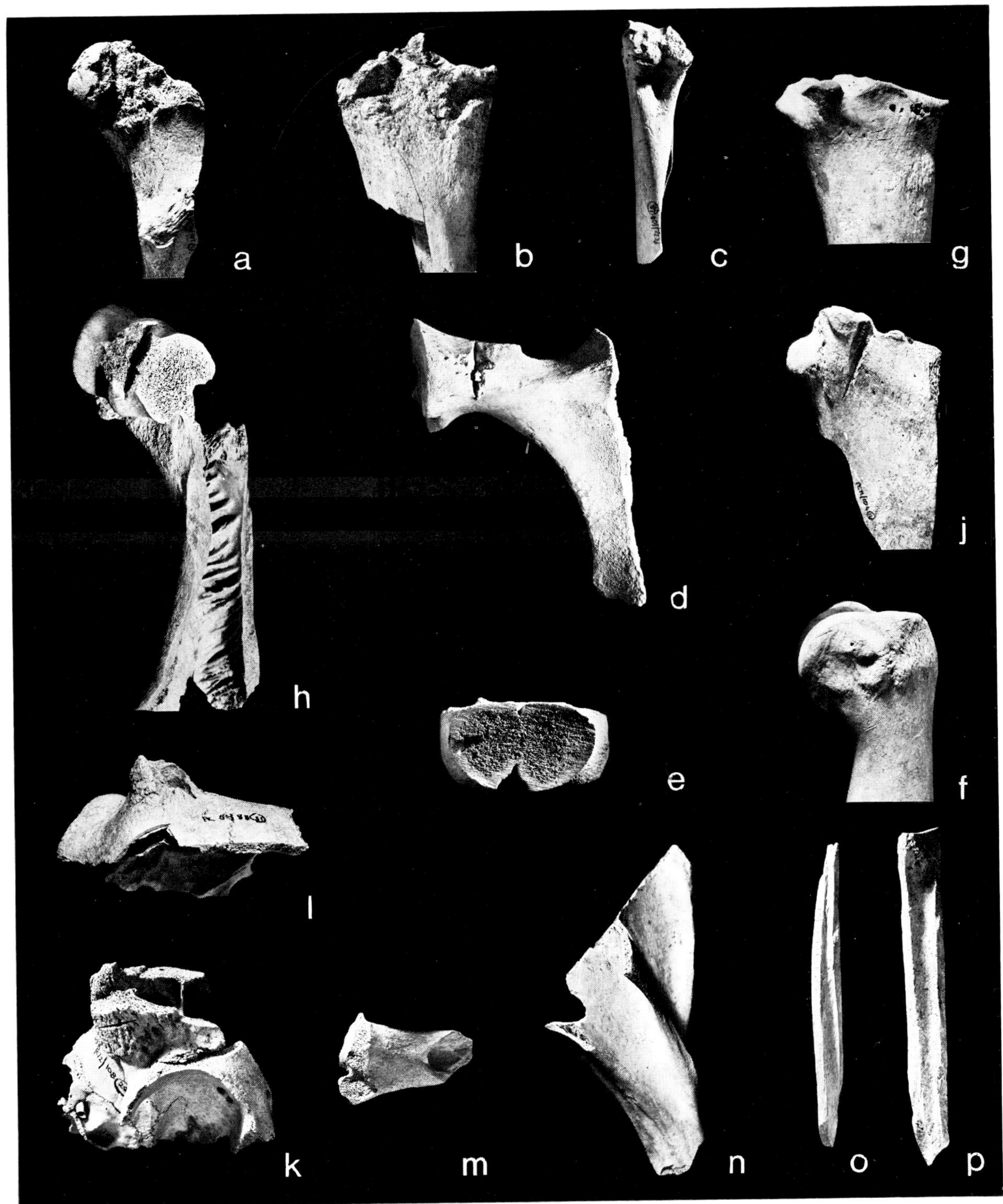

Animal bones showing butchery

a. Cattle femur, severely gnawed. *b.* Cattle tibia, severely gnawed. *c.* Sheep humerus, severely gnawed. *d.* Cattle pelvis, chopped through the acetabulum and into the pubis with a heavy chopping tool. *e.* Cattle metatarsal: the distal end has been sawn from the rest of the bone. *f.* Sheep humerus, with fine knife marks on the distal epiphysis. *g.* Sheep radius with fine knife marks below the proximal epiphysis. *h.* Cattle humerus split longitudinally by a blow to the front of the distal epiphysis. *j.* Cattle radius, with a chop mark into the proximal end. *k.* Sheep skull fragments, with the horn core chopped from the skull. *l.* Sheep skull fragment, split in half. *m.* Sheep radius, which has been chopped from the humerus. *n.* Pig scapula, chopped across the blade and the neck. *o* and *p.* Two splinters of bone, possibly waste from tool manufacture

(*Photographs: R. L. Wilkins, F.S.A.*)